ZOROASTER AND HIS WORLD

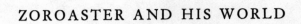

ZOROASTER AND HIS WORLD

BY ERNST HERZFELD

VOLUME I

OCTAGON BOOKS

A DIVISION OF FARRAR, STRAUS AND GIROUX

New York 1974

Reprinted 1974
by special arrangement with Princeton University Press

OCTAGON BOOKS
A Division of Farrar, Straus & Giroux, Inc.
19 Union Square West
New York, N. Y. 10003

Library of Congress Cataloging in Publication Data

Herzfeld, Ernst Emil, 1879-1948.
Zoroaster and his world.

Reprint of the ed. published by Princeton University Press, Princeton.

Includes bibliographical references.
1. Zoroaster. 2. Zoroastrianism. I. Title.
BL1555.H4 1974 295′.63 [B] 74-6219
ISBN 0-374-93877-6

Manufactured by Braun-Brumfield, Inc.
Ann Arbor, Michigan

Printed in the United States of America

PREFACE

It will soon be two hundred years since Anquetil Duperron brought the first manuscript of the Awesta from Bombay and attempted a translation. Sir William Jones, in his famous letter of 1771, rejected this translation in the most sweeping way: "Si Zoroastre n'avait pas le sens commun, il fallait le laisser dans l'obscurité," and "l'Europe éclairée n'avait nul besoin de votre Zende Vasta, vous l'avez traduit a pure perte!" This short-sighted judgment retarded serious study for a long while. Today we judge l'Europe éclairée differently and likewise the great pioneer work of Anquetil Duperron.

In 1924, A. Meillet, in his *Trois conférences sur les Gâthâ de l'Avesta*, delivered in Upsala and published by the Musée Guimet, characterized our present attitude toward the Awesta thus: "Si l'on essaie de lire l'Avesta, on s'aperçoit immédiatement que la lecture en est impossible, pas un chapitre ne forme une unité, pas un morceau ne se suit d'un boût à l'autre. C'est une suite de fragments, à vrai dire, un champ de ruines . . . des ruines informes où ne se reconnait aucun ordre." These words are entirely true and imply that interpreting the Awesta is an eminently archeological task. He further said: "On ne peut traduire les gatha d'une manière sûre et complète," all one can do is "apporter des précisions." This remark refers to the gatha translation by Bartholomae, that of the Awesta by Wolff after Bartholomae; to the gatha translation, at that time incomplete, by Andreas and Wackernagel, later continued by Lommel. Lommel later gave also a translation of the yasht, and in 1929 Maria Wilkins Smith's *Studies in the Syntax of the Gathas, together with text, translation and notes* were published in Language Dissertations, Linguistic Society of America.

Bartholomae still believed in the high antiquity and authenticity of the Awestic text with its confusing orthography, and it was Andreas who first saw that the Awestic script was late and that an archetype written in Aramaic script had existed before the invention of that script. He failed to perfect his discovery to its full import only because, impressed by the then newly found Turfan documents, he adopted the axiom that the "vollste Schreibung" among the countless variants of Awestic spellings was the decisive one. The Iranian inscriptional material shows on the contrary that the orthography was almost as short and simple as the oldest known Aramaic. The schools of Heidelberg and Göttingen were very much opposed to each other, but their results resemble each other so much that Meillet could say: "Ce qui montre que la traduction de M. Bartholomae est en général correcte, c'est que la traduction . . . que MM. Andreas et Wackernagel ont donnée . . . s'en écarte seulement dans le détail. S'il reste beaucoup de passages obscurs, on peut dire que le sens général des gâthâ est connu et qu'il y a maintenant accord entre les savants qui les étudient." Yet the main reason for this conformity is that the translations of the school of Göttingen but rarely depart from the significations attributed to the roots and vocables in Bartholomae's Wörterbuch.

Shortly after Meillet had formed his optimistic judgment, J. Hertel in his various writings advanced a totally different interpretation of the entire Awesta, which, though unacceptable in its entirety, was a great stimulus to further research. And again another, equally different interpretation was given in 1935 by S. Nyberg in his lectures *Die Religionen des Alten Iran*, delivered like Meillet's *conférences* in Upsala, and published 1937 in Swedish, 1938 in German translation by H. H. Schaeder. In the introduction the author says: "1935 hatte ich bereits alle Fäden zur Lösung des Gatha-Problems in der Hand, aber der springende Punkt . . . trat erst ins Blickfeld" during the printing of the book. "Die Lösung des Gatha-Problems bedeutet nicht weniger als eine vollständige Neuinterpretation der Texte," a flattery difficult to surpass and challenge and one which I beg the reader to have in mind when reading the chapters here following.

When studying this latest Neuinterpretation and comparing it with previous ones, one sees soon that it is throughout based upon Bartholomae's great *Iranisches Wörterbuch*, the indispensable instrument of all our studies. But this Wörterbuch, an amazing work, was a first attempt made when only a small part of the now available linguistic material was at the author's hand, and semantics is its weakest side. In the preface to his *Infinitives avestiques* Benveniste says something to the effect that future Iranistic studies are bound to be in controversy with the Wörterbuch. Research has reached a phase where this only instrument has become insufficient and where a corrected form of Andreas' theory of the Awestic archetype must be applied to it.

Behind this linguistic side of the problem arises that of the criticism of the text. Meillet said "Qui vient tirer parti d'un détail du texte ne le peut qu'à condition d'examiner en quelle mesure la traduction du passage considéré repose sur des données positives et certaines." In fact, text criticism of the Awesta is still as undeveloped as Biblical criticism was in 1753 at the time of Dr. Astruc. Though nobody can any longer maintain the unity of the text or deny that it is "un ensemble de fragments que le hasard a conservés et que des rédacteurs dénués d'art et de pensée ont mis côté à côté sans système," one goes on translating the whole as it stands, applying text-critical schemes, developed in editing classical authors, but unfit for this material. The results only prove the bad condition of the transmitted text, and still justify Sir William Jones' sweeping judgment. Thomas Huxley once said: "Scientific method is common sense." Our task today is first to isolate "dans ce champ de ruines informes les fragments authentiques dont l'intérêt est grand," and then to try to put the right fragments together.

Only after overcoming these linguistic and text-critical obstacles can historical criticism set in. With the exception of Meillet and Hertel, most scholars share or cannot free themselves entirely from the old belief that the gatha and the so-called older Awesta belong to a remote antiquity and to an undefined or undeterminable eastern region, the "home of the Awesta." For that reason they do not define the dialect of the Awesta, but stick to the vague term "Awestic" which implies nothing. Only Meillet accepted Tedesco's proof that Awestic is a Median dialect. As to the period, nobody gives an exact date. Nyberg goes to the extreme in "stating" that "in einem Volke dem die Geschichte fehlt . . . die ganze Frage nach der Zeit Zarathustras eigentlich ohne Belang—without interest—ist," a most heedless pronouncement. He himself does not doubt a stratification of the Awesta, that is a relative chronology, and all that is needed to convert a relative into an absolute chronology is some synchronism. The gatha, though being songs, odes, speak of real events and of acting personalities, a few of them bearing names known also in historical sources. The legends preserved in the yasht, too, reflect—though in legendary form—events; they are full of names of persons, tribes, nations, places, of titles, political and social terms etc. It does not require more than defining these things to make history out of this until then prehistoric material.

The historical criticism of the Awesta therefore must consist mainly in the study of personal names, sociology, ethnography and topography. I began such studies long ago, under the title *Zarathustra* in Archeologische Mitteilungen I-II. The years that passed since have brought an unexpected addition to our knowledge of the periods and regions in question. And looking back, I feel that in spite of a great many errors and mistakes I was on the right road. In the following chapters I show to what ends those earlier studies have led me.

Seven years ago, Dr. Paul Tedesco read the first draft of this book—which since underwent considerable changes—introducing a uniform and readable transcription of the Gathic and Awestic words and texts. I shall not, as first intended, explain the mode of transliteration which to an Iranist will be transparent, to others of no use. In a few points I went beyond Tedesco's advice and so I do not want to burden him with any responsibility, but only express my indebtedness for his help which in many places went far beyond this trivial task, and also for his severe criticism which made me consider and reconsider the complex problems many times.

ERNST HERZFELD

Cairo, October 1946

CONTENTS

Hāugavī, at the court of Vištāspa; Fraša.aspa, Gr. Prēxáspes, at
the court of Cambyses, his son Aspačina at the court of Darius.
The Hāugava give the exiled Zoroaster financial help and travel
to the court of appeal of the great-king to obtain the revocation
of Zoroaster's banishment. Damaspia, fem. of the family name,
"zāmāspī," descendant in the fifth generation of Zāmāspa, marries
Artaxerxes I. The family existed still under Shāhpuhr I.

CONTENTS OF VOLUME II

shall be strengthened, Druχš, Evil, shall be destroyed! I desire
the union with Vahumano, Good-Will, I renounce every com-
munion with the drugvant, evildoer." Definition of terms, "dēvayasna, zāraθuštri, mazdayasna."

by irrigation, division of products between owner and cultivator in five parts: for land, water, oxen, seed and labour. On wheat, barley, rice and medic.

ZOROASTER AND HIS WORLD

I. CHRONOLOGY

"Es wird die Spur von Deinen Erdentagen,
nicht in Aeonen untergehn!"

THE traditional date of Zoroaster is "258 years before Alexander." During the last decade new material has come to light which confirms the historicity of that number and elucidates the possibility of its tradition.[1]

The oldest coherent notice of the theory of aeons in Iran is found in Plutarch, *de Iside* 47, on the authority of Theopomp, time of Alexander. The passage, often discussed,[2] runs: "According to the teaching of the magi, each of the two gods (Oramasdes and Areimanios), in turn, rules 3,000 years and is ruled 3,000 years; then they wage war another 3,000 years and destroy each the works of the other; finally Hades succumbs, and men shall be blissful (εὐδαίμονες), neither needing food nor casting shadow. And the god who achieved all this will rest a while and relax."

Although this contradicts the Iranian concept of the omnipotence of AhuraMazdāh and the restricted power of Ahramanyuš—the designation "god" of the Evil Spirit alone contradicts—we are not allowed to interpret the passage differently: this was how Theopomp understood it; it must not be right.

The theory of aeons must have suffered in its long history many changes. The *Mēnōk̦ Xrat, Artavīrāz Nāmak̦* and the Armenian Eznik speak equally of an aeon of 9,000 years, the *Gr. Bundahishn* of a "pact" of 9,000 years granted by Hormizd to Ahriman. Ed. Meyer's words (*Christent.* II,70): "das Abkommen zwischen AhuraMazdāh und Ahriman kennt schon Zoroaster selbst, *Y.*30,4" rest upon an insufficient translation of the passage (see under 'Yamā'). The theory contradicts the one which the *Gr.Bdh.* carries through, of an aeon of 12,000 years,

[1] Cf. AMI II, 1930, and Orient. Studies Pavry, 1934. In BSOS 3, 747-755, 1933, Jarl Charpentier gave a combination of old opinions, directed against Hertel's *Zeit Zarathustraś* in IIQF I. Important contributions are those of S. H. Taqizadeh in BSOS 9,1 1937, *Some chronol. Data rel. to the Sasanian Period,* and ib. 9, 1939, *Various Eras and Calendars of Islam.*—H. S. Nyberg dealt with the subject in his *Religionen des Alten Iran,* 1938, under headline "Die Ansicht Herzfeld's, Kritik an ihr."—Hildegard Lewy's *Calendrier Perse* in Orientalia 10, 1941, appeared after the present chapter was written; where the two overlap, the results agree. Therefore, I have shortened some parts and inserted references to that treatise.—Quotation "Nyberg" with page number in this book refer to the *Religionen.*

[2] e.g. Eduard Meyer, *Anfänge des Christentums* II, 70.—Theopomp's Acmé was in 338 B.C.

6,000 of which lie before the gumēčišn, the struggle of the world's history, and one must not try to reconcile the two.

The Gathas always speak of the course of the world under the poetical figure "apamam rvēsam, the last round of the race-course," the last turn round the meta; yā-ahī!, the shout of victory at the passing of the goal, serves for the victory of the religion. This metaphor is one of the poetical conventions from Aryan antiquity, hence appears also in the Veda.

But it is more than a mere metaphor, it is the same concept. Already the tablets of Kikkuli of Mitanni, about 1380 B.C., describe the chariots driving nine times round the course, and at the races of Gümüš Tepe near Astarābād the horses race nine rounds to the present day. Every round is one rvēsa, períodos. Hence the Aryan term in the Kikkuli tablets: "navartanē važ'anasai̯a, in nine rounds of the race-course," also the name of the race-course in the Husravah legend, *Yt.*5,50: "nava.fraθwrsā razurā, nine-rounds-forest." The fragment of the Yama myth in *Pahl.Vid.*2,19: "prvyahača pasčēta hazahra.zimahya θwarso ās, and therewith the first millennium was a θwarsah," a finished section of the races, is taken into the Awesta from a pre-Zoroastrian stratum of the epics. In an old passage of *Yt.*13,57, the metaphor is applied to the motion of the stars, whom the fravarti show their course: fravazanti aδwano rvēsam nāšamnā.

The nine rounds of the races are the origin of the nine millennia of the world. This notion, not only pre-Zoroastrian but pre-Iranian, is pure myth, not mixed with mystics, astronomy or theology. The number 9 can be observed in the myths of all peoples of IE. language; there is no contact with Babylonian ideas. The 9,000 years are a juvenile thought: unimaginably far off.

Against Nyberg, 23, the chiliadic doctrine is not lacking in the Gathas and in the Awesta, and the fact that the Academy heard of it through a Chaldean pupil of Plato does not make the theory "West Iranian" as opposed to an "East Iranian" Awesta. A. v.Gutschmid had already recognized that the enigmatical statement of Eudoxus (407-357 B.C.),[3] "Zoroaster lived 6,000 years before the death of Plato" (347

[3] Pliny NH. 30,1, from Eudoxus and Aristotle. Also Diogenes Laertius, *prooem.* 2, after Xanthus Lydus, in a report on Plato's pupil Hermodorus. Diogenes, there, ascribes a gloss of Hermodorus to Xanthus himself.—Further in a scholion to the First Alcibiades. Cf. W.

B.C.), reflected somehow this Iranian doctrine. Although no tradition can ever have put Zoroaster and Plato into chronological relation, the words contain something genuine; they combine two thoughts: "Zoroaster shall reappear after 6,000 years" and "Plato is an incarnation of Zoroaster." Eudoxus may have heard this from his Chaldean fellow-student in the following form: "The Persians say, 6,000 years after Zoroaster a new Zoroaster shall appear, he has already appeared in Plato." The rationalistic Greek students calculated therefrom: Zoroaster lived 6,000 years before Plato. It was the time when the Greeks first heard of the high oriental antiquity and believed in astronomical figures. This explanation which implies the Zoroastrian doctrine of the messianic return is the only acceptable explanation of the number.

Zoroaster fitted the metaphor of the race-course and therewith the Aryan concept of an aeon of 9,000 years into his own picture of the world, and, in *Y*.43,5-6, makes AhuraMazdāh stipulate at the creation the returns men receive for their actions after the last round. He sees the history of the world as the contest of good and evil, culminating in the last judgment. Thereby he introduces an apocalyptic thought into a conception that was merely mythical. Certainly he used existing mythical elements as ethical symbols. Every thought is only a new interpretation of an older one. The well-considered dualism and the equation of light and good, darkness and evil, is his own, the struggle between light and darkness itself is a mythical thought.

But neither the date of the last judgment nor the beginning of the aeon is known. Therefore Zoroaster asks in *Y*.48,2: "Announce to me, AhuraMazdāh, thou who knowest what will come, will the pious conquer the impious yet before the atonement which is in Thy plan?" The notions of the end of the world and of the victory of the religion are connected as in early Christianity. Only when these thoughts become separated, after the death of the prophet, when the end of the world recedes into increasingly indifferent remoteness, the idea of messianic return can originate. Then, certain sayings find an eschatologic interpretation. In the "song to the sōšyant, the saviours"[4]—to be dated in the middle of the 5th century B.C., placed in *Yt*.19,88f.—they

Jaeger, *Aristoteles,* 1923, 134ff., who admits a strong influence of Zoroastrian thoughts also on Aristotle.

[4] Cf. text under 'Last Judgment.'

are "the sōšyant and his companions," and in a not much younger passage inserted into *Yt.*13,128, their number is three: astvat.rta, uχšyat.rta, and uχšyat.namah. These names are philosophical abstractions. The first, derived from Gath. astvat rtam hiyāt!, signifies "rtam personified." Thoughts including all the ethics of Zoroaster cannot be pre-Zoroastrian. On the other hand, they are the origin of the attributes describing the essence of the Shiite Mahdī.

G. Messina, in Orientalia 1,173ff., tried to explain the "idea di aumentare il numero dei succorritori" by the "divisione dell' evo" and a "bisogno di parallelismo," with the effect that the "missione finale e definitiva" was reserved for astvat.rta, while a role without "effetto definitivo, ma solo temporario" devolved upon the others. A not-lasting success would be a palliative word for failure, and in *Yt.*19,89 the three come together, not in intervals of a thousand years, and that seems to me the original concept.

In the story of Prēxáspes, Herodotus mentions only the name of the main sōšyant, +'Ἀστυάρτης,[5] but the name 'Ὀξυάρτης, OP. *uχšya.rta, of a son of Darius II and brother of Artaxerxes II[6] shows that the triplication of Zoroaster as sōšyant was known to the Achaemenids about 420 B.C. This does not imply that the term of their appearance was fixed.

Already at Zoroaster's time, the old epic tales were considered as historical past, the length of which was likewise undetermined. In *Y.*32,8, he assails the myth of Yama. This figure characterizes the first millennium still in the latest shapes of the legend, with 762½ regnal years. But *Vid.*II says (st.8): "Of the reign of Yama 300 winters [IE. expression for year] passed . . . . (12-14:) 600 winters, (16:) 900 winters passed," and every time the earth widens, to hold the increasing immortal humanity. And the fragment quoted above says: "herewith the first millennium was a θwarsah," periodos of the race-course. As in *Y.*9,10, "a thousand years," a full millennium belonged originally to

[5] Text: 'Ἀστυάγης; Herodotus writes about 440, but projects the words into the time of Cambyses. Their character is so Iranian that he misunderstands them; they are genuine. The meaning is: If it is true that the dead shall rise after Astva.rta's appearance, you may expect to see Smerdis again, else not.

[6] In Athenaeus, 13,89, after Phylarchus, 3rd cent. B.C.—Another brother bears the name 'Ἀρτόστης < rtam[yahmai]uštā, derived from the Rtam-vahu prayer.

Yama as first man and king.[7] The beginnings of this mythical chronology go back to the time before Zoroaster.

Eudoxus' number "Zoroaster 6,000 years before Plato" proves that about 400 B.C. Zoroaster had already been fitted into the original aeon of 9,000 years as inaugurator of the fourth millennium. Thereby, beginning and end were fixed, and the mythical history was limited to the first 3,000 years, a feature which the epopee preserved to the very end. By inserting Zoroaster, at the same time, the mythical chiliadic system became a historical chronology. Since it contains the return of the prophet, one can call it apocalyptic, but the mythical foundation is otherwise unchanged. In the reappearance of the saviour, the last judgment, and the predetermination of reward and punishment it contains the germs of all later speculations. The old idea is clearly expressed in as late a text as the *Art.Vīr.Nām.* 18, where the tortured soul of the sinner in hell says, "when three days and nights have elapsed: The 9,000 years are completed, and they will not release me!"

But Eudoxus speaks already of an aeon of 12,000 years, a system in which the place of Zoroaster would not be in 3,000, but in 6,000. The prehistory, there, begins with 3,000, and it is evident that the 3,000 years of creation or uneventful preexistence have been put before the 9,000, in order to reconcile the two systems. The original thought is still strong enough to prevent a reduction of the 9,000 years of history. Every millennium has received one zodiacal sign and symbolizes a month. This is no longer the Aryan race-course with its nine rounds, but the Babylonian "cosmic year," the thought of a civilization that looked back to a long past. The zodiacal signs, registered still as late as in the chronological chapter of the *Gr.Bdh.* 288ff., are an intrinsic quality of the system. The change is the effect of the contact between Iranian thoughts and Babylonian science during the Achaemenian epoch.[8] And the attempt to convert the system, still mythical and unconnected with the present at Zoroaster's time, into a chronological one by assigning a fixed place in it to Zoroaster is evidently another effect of Babylonian science.

[7] The first man Gayamart has no place in this old system. He was introduced only by the redaction of the epics at the Achaemenian period, reflected in *Yt.*5,19 and others, while *Yt.*13 agrees with the Gatha and the Vidēvdād.

[8] Not the first contact, as the study of the myths of Yama, Kanha, etc., reveal.

The system of 12,000 years is found, for instance, in the commentary to *Vid.*2,20 (ed. Hosh.Jamasp 34,6ff.): "Ahuramazdāh kept this world in a spiritual existence, mēnōk-hastišn, for 3,000 years; for 3,000 years he kept it in material existence, gētīh-hastišn, without antagonism, apatiyārak; 3,000 years passed from the coming of the contest to the coming of the religion; 3,000 years will pass from the coming of the religion to the last judgment, as is written:[9] How long did the saint creation stay in spiritual existence?"

This catechetic question cannot have stood in any old part of the Awesta, and the exegetic answer has no authority. By making use of this question, detached from its context, the author tries merely to construe the much younger system into the old myth of *Vidēvdād* 2, to which it is foreign.—This is not at all the system of Theopomp, though both have 12,000 years.

But the same aeon of 12,000 years is explicitly presented in the chapter on the disasters befalling Iran (211,5; 220 ult.) and in the chronological chapter (238ff.) of the *Gr.Bdh.*[10] The 3,000 years of spiritual and 3,000 of material preexistence, put before the 6,000 years of gumēčišn, "mixture," i.e. history of the world, are a mere doubling of the 3,000 years with which the aeons of 9,000 and 12,000 years had been equalized. But this entails the important change that now "history" is shortened from 9,000 to 6,000 years, and that the saviour, Zoroaster, is expected to return after 3,000 instead of 6,000 years.

This belief was dominant already at the time of Ardashīr I. *Dēnk.* b.III: "according to the religious rules more than five months shall never be intercalated at one time," as though this case had been known as a singular and maximal one. And at the regulation of the calendar, attributed to Zoroaster, but actually undertaken under Ardashīr I—by which Zoroaster shifted to the beginning of the tenth millennium—it was necessary, as H. Lewy (p.58s) has shown, to intercalate five months, "in order that the time would come back to the point where it was in the beginning," viz. that the beginning of the year would fall

[9] ač ān ǰāk pētāk sounds like "results from the passage," but means "is revealed by," γέγραπται γάρ. The formula—as similar ones—introduces the text, the exegesis of which is reported, hence is no proof for the exegesis.

[10] It was a mistake of mine when I formerly believed that there were two different ways of counting in the two chapters: the chapter on disasters neglects the transcendent 6,000 years and counts, after the manner of the Sasanian epoch, only the "millennia of history, *hazārak andar gumēčišnīk*" as I to VI, not as VII to XII. Biruni does the same, see below.

again, as at the first day of creation, on the 1st Fravardīn, the spring equinox. As long as there is time, a calendar is assumed to exist, even during the 6,000 years of preexistence of the world. But at the end of the world time ceases, eternity is timeless. Whether the preexistence was extended to 6,000, the return of Zoroaster reduced to 3,000 years at that occasion or earlier, is not clear. The system of Theopomp must not be reconciled with this one.

In *Māh Fravartīn,* we find a different presentation. §§1-26: mythical prehistory from creation to acception of the religion by Vištāsp. §27: Eighteen good things come in 18 years to Xusrōy II Hormizdān, who is the only historical figure in the treatise. §28: appearance of Vahrām ē varžāvand from India, §29: of Pišyōθan ē Vištāspšāh from Kangdiz, §30: of Xvaršētar ē Zartuχštān; the millennium of Zoroaster ends, that of Xvaršētar begins. §31: Sām kills Aždahāk and rules over the seven kišvar until KaiXusrōy appears, to whom he hands over the rulership. §32: KaiXusrōy rules 77 years over the kišvar with the sōšyant as mōbeδān mōbeδ. §33: KaiXusrōy commits the kingdom to Vištāspšāh, and the sōšyant the mōbeδ-ship to his father Zartuχšt. §34: Ahura-Mazdāh resurrects the dead. §§35-38: annihilation of evil. §§39-47: description of paradise.

The words of §27 "18 good things happened to Xusrōy in 18 years" furnish an exact date: the treatise is unaware of the change that came in the 19th year, A.D. 608, the first of the 20 years of war with Heraclius. In 629 the emperor entered Jerusalem in state, with the reconquered cross of Christ; abu Ṣufyān was present and told Muhammad about it; in 630 the Muslims took Mekka.—Xusrau died in prison. Ṭabarī tells of a grandee visiting the king in prison: a quince, which the king had in his hand, fell down, rolled over the three brocade cushions of the seat and over the three rugs interwoven with gold, and came to rest at last, dusty, on the floor. When the grandee picked it up, dusted it off, and handed it back to Xusrau, the king said: "Throw it away! When a thing shall go downward, no planning will make it go up again; if it shall go upward, no planning is able to turn that course. These two things come in turn, in both cases all planning is in vain."

Māh Frav. is composed before these events, in 607/8, that is—anticipating a result to be proved later—the year 904 after Zoroaster.

The treatise does not expect figures of disaster coming from the west, but figures of happiness coming from the east. The description is full of optimism: free from misgivings, it leaps from a happy present to a far and happier future.

The millennium of Zoroaster is followed by that of Uχšyat.rta. As in the Bahman yasht 7,2, this name is written HVRŠYTR, and since he is called "son of Zoroaster," the figure is mixed with hvarčiθra. The two other saviours, uχšyat.namah and astvat.rta, are not mentioned; hvarčiθra is the mōbadān mōbad of the millennium who hands over his office, at the morning of resurrection, to his father Zoroaster. The golden age of the heroes Sām, KayXusrau, Vištāsp comes back; how one or two thousand years were filled with it, remains obscure. This is a picture entirely different from the one given in the *Gr.Bdh.* and the *Dēnk.*, which therefore was not yet generally accepted, perhaps not yet established about A.D. 600.

In the *Gr.Bdh.* (213f. and 239f.) and in the *Dēnk.*, Zoroaster is fitted into his millennium in such a way that it begins not with his birth but with the "matan ē dēn, coming of religion," or the conversion of Vištāsp, when the prophet was 30 years old.

The meaning of the thirty years is: In *Yt.*14,17 Vrthragna appears as "nar pančadasa, man of 15 years," in *Yt.*14,27 as "vīra rēvant, mature man, hoplite," two shapes opposed like his appearances as colt and stallion. The youth of 15 years, occasionally the maiden of 15 years (*Had.N.*2,9), are the well known ideal figures. vīro, Lat. vīr, opposed to it, is the ideal of the man of 30 years. In the eschatologic *Vahman yasht* 3,17, the prince with the armies of China and India comes to Balkh 30 years old. Christ, in *Luke* 3,23 is 30 years old.[11] Natural as this number is, it is not a historical, but a mythic-schematical number.

The time between Zoroaster and Alexander is divided up, in *Gr.Bdh.* 239f., in the following way: "Vištāspšāh, after accepting the religion, ruled 90 years; Vahman son of Spandiyāt 112 years; Humāy ē Vahmanduxt 30 years; Dārāy son of Čihrāzāt 12, Dārāy son of Dārāy 14 years." The sum not mentioned is 258 years. Then follow the 14 years of Alexander. This is the picture of the Achaemenian period of Iranian

[11] Against *John* 8,57: "not yet 50 years old." Cf. Tabari 1,711: "Yaḥyā b. Zakariyya [John the Baptist] met 'Īsā at the Jordan, who at that time was 30 years old."

history as conceived in the epic, which clearly identified the Awestic and the historical Vištāspa. He and the three first figures are the residue of history in the legend; the last Dārāy comes from the Alexander romance. The 258 years between Zoroaster and Alexander, hence, are not the sum of traditional regnal dates, but these are a distribution of the existing number 258 over the known names of kings.

The thesis is: The *Gr.Bdh.* puts Zoroaster 258 years before Alexander; Biruni, *athār,* interprets this rightly as 258 before the aera Alexandri. 258 is not a mythical, but a historical date, fitted into the sytem of aeons. The problem is: how could such a date be transmitted?

S. H. Taqizadeh, in his second article, has introduced a new point into the discussion: in the history of Alexander in the *qānūn al-masʿūdī,* Biruni, after having discovered the difference between Alexander's accession and the Seleucid era, corrected the 258 years in 276 before the era, and in his lost work "On the mistake I made regarding the date of Alexander" he seems to have expressly apologized. Therefore S. H. Taqizadeh follows Biruni and regards the year of the death of Darius III, 331 B.C., as Alexander's accession, the term of the 258 years. But the only error in Biruni's deduction is that he believed the *Gr.Bdh.* equal to his own genius and knowledge. The Iranian tradition has preserved neither the date of Darius' death nor any date of Achaemenian history, and the number 258 cannot have been transmitted as interval between any event of that history and the life of Zoroaster. If the authors of the *Gr.Bdh.* had any knowledge of the era of Alexander, i.e. the Seleucid era at all, it began for them with the accession of Alexander, as all later dynastic eras begin with the accession of the ktístes. Biruni's first interpretation in that point was perfectly right.

But the case is more complicated than it looks. Wherever Biruni converts dates before or after the hidjra into Zoroastrian dates by means of the Seleucid era, he follows the Syriac, real chronology. But he knew—as the synchronism, soon to be discussed, in his *qānūn* proves—that the Sasanian Persians reckoned in an entirely different way. He can only have apologized for having made a mistake of 18 years when converting dates, before having knowledge of the true history, but this difference is not implied by the Zoroastrian reckoning: for the Zoroastrian sources 258 before Alexander means 258 before the Seleucid era.

Nyberg 33, calls "gerade die Zahl 258 in hervorragendem Masse apokalyptisch." It rouses his suspicion that it is related to the Seleucid era instead of the history of Alexander. In mazdayasnian tradition Alexander's name would always be connected with his Iranian campaign, especially the destruction of Persepolis. A date "before Alexander" would relate, in those sources, to the time where he made Persepolis go up in smoke.

That 258 is a date relating to the Seleucid era is the point to be proved; no era is mentioned, and 258 is only the not mentioned sum of the unauthentic single numbers in which the interval between Zoroaster and Alexander is divided. I believe I know all records concerning Persepolis: in Greek tradition it occurs but rarely, mostly hidden under the name Persai, in Iranian tradition not at all. The exact date of its destruction—whether before or after the Indian campaign—is not mentioned even in the surviving Greek literature. And Iranian sources speak of Persepolis only in Muhammedan times when identifying the mythical var of Yama with Takht i Djamshīd. Iranian tradition refers no fact by the preposition "before" to the reign of Alexander; the distinction between accession and era was entirely unknown; the real meaning of the name "aera Alexandri" was scarcely understood by the Greeks themselves.

The Iranians, an eminently historical nation, have never developed any historiography. The historical knowledge the Sasanians had of the Achaemenids came to them through belletristic literature like the romance of Alexander or books like Esther and Daniel. But historical tradition lingers in names like Guštāsp, Vahman, Dārā, Spandiyāt, Ardašīr, Sāsān, Humāy and others. If Mithradates the Great, who, as proved by H. Lewy, introduced the calendar in about 120 B.C., resumed in 111 B.C. the title of the Achaemenids with the program of restoring the empire, and if Ardašhīr I, who introduced the Sasanian calendar, took just the coins of this Arsacid restaurator as model for his coinage, there must have been some historical knowledge outside the literary tradition. This is even more true for the reminiscence of facts of the religious history.

p.34: "Dass man bei dem vollständigen Fehlen aller einheimischer

Geschichtsüberlieferung der Jahreszahl '258 vor Alexander' *auch nur die geringste Bedeutung* beimessen könnte, ist *ganz ausgeschlossen."* Things so emphatically "excluded" are usually right, otherwise, why the pathos, and, in this case, why the long discourse that the number "nachträglich konstruiert und in einem Augenblick rückwärts errechnet sein müsse, als man zu einem bestimmten Augenblick unter Verwendung der im Orient allgemein gängigen [here no longer "suspicious"] seleukidischen Aera ankündigte, Zarathustras Millennium erreiche sein Ende, der Erlöser werde oder sei schon erschienen."

On their coins and the Awramān parchments the Arsacids use the Seleucid era, although they had one of their own which they used in Babylonia beside the Seleucid. But the Sasanians never used the "allgemein gängige" era, because to them Alexander was the incarnation of Ahriman, cursed wherever his name is mentioned, and it would have been impossible to reckon by the "era of the cursed Alexander."

On their coins they employ the traditional counting of regnal years, but under a special form: "Fire of NN, year x," because a new fire was lighted at each new accession. The inscription *Pers.B* has "month Tīr, year 48 of Shāhpuhr II, day Hormizd"; *Pers.A* only "month Spandamat, year 2 of Shāhpuhr II." The triple date of the Bīshāpūr inscription, which had been interpreted by A. Christensen[12] and corrected by H. Lewy, runs "in the month fravartīn of the year 58, year 40 of the Ardashīr fire, year 24 of the Shāhpuhr fire, king of fires,"[13] that is the year A.D. 266.—Only a little older are the signatures on the wall paintings of the synagogue of Dura on the Euphrates, dated in various months of the year 14 and the first of the year 15 of Shāhpuhr I, hence A.D. 256-257.

The Ka'ba inscription of Shāhpuhr I speaks (Pahl. l.17) of the šGY' 'trv vrhr'n, ΠΟΛΛΑ ΠΥΡΕΙΑ ΓΟΥΑΡΑΘΡΑΝ, founded in the whole empire, and then of the special purpose of the inscription, the foundation, after the victory over Valerian, of five fires named after the king, the queen, and three sons: "pty LN 'rv'n v p'šn'm—P'N LNH lvb'n v ptn'm—ΕΙΣ ΗΜΕΤΕΡΑΝ ΜΝΕΙΑΝ ΚΑΙ ΟΝΟΜΑΤΟΣ ΣΥΝΤΗΡΗΣΙΝ, for the memory and the perpetuation of the name [soul] of. . . ." The name "Varhrān fire" for such memorial fires is not strictly

[12] In Ghirshman's article Rev.As. x, 1937, 127.

[13] Not "roi des prêtres" as in the edition.

Zoroastrian, but pre-Zoroastrian, and goes back to the Median period, when the dynastic fires were dedicated to Vrthragna as colt and as stallion (see under 'Dēva' and 'Architecture'). The *Gr. Bdh.* uses the term also for the fires founded by Vištāspa in the neighborhood of Tōs, viz. āδar farnbag and āδar burzēnmihr, and says "There are many Varhrān fires, every single one founded by a sovereign, dēhpat. . . . However great their number and different their names, they are all reckoned as Varhrān fires. Though many were extinguished under the domination of the Arabs, many still exist today, every one of them founded at the accession of a dēhpat." The expression of the Bīshāpūr inscription, "King of Fires" distinguishes the fire of the ruling king from those of his predecessors. Darmesteter translated a similar passage in the *Bahman yasht* "Le feu Bahman est roi, il n'y a qu'un roi par pays," and quoted from a *Rivāyat:* "the fire is called dahyupet, every dahyu, province, shall have one only." The reason for the decline of the fires is the same as of the auqāf in Islam: the ruin of their endowments caused by political vicissitudes.

Such fires founded by Cyrus and Cambyses were the OP. *āyadana,* Gr. *ἰασόνια* (rendering Med.*(ā)yazana), which, according to *Beh.* §14, the magus Gōmāta destroyed and Darius restored. These old fires shall become decisive for our problem.

The date of the Bīshāpūr inscription, confirming Nöldeke's chronology of the Sasanian period, is A.D. 266, 40 after the coronation of Ardashīr in 226, 24 after the coronation of Shāhpuhr in A.D. 242. The date 58 relates to 208, year of the death of Volagases IV, in which, according to the *Chronicle of Arbela,* began "the war of the Medes and Persians against the Parthians." One may call 208 the beginning of the de facto reign of Ardashīr I, but it is not the epochal year of the dynasty, 226 according to the Syriac chronicles,[14] the year in which the last generally recognized Arsacid, Ardavān V, was killed in battle against Ardashīr. In that year Ardashīr founded his fire, and this counted 40 years since its foundation, when the fire of Shāhpuhr counted 24. The years are counted through, the fire of the founder of a dynasty, hence, counts the years of the epoch. If temples counted their years, the preservation of a historical date connected with the

[14] e.g. G. Hoffmann, *Syr.Akt. Pers.Märt.* 78, history of Mār Sābhā: "799 Graec., equal to 261 of the Persians," hence A.D. 226.

religion is entirely possible. Assertions like "die Erhaltung ist unmöglich, weil es keine Aera und dem ähnliches gab" are wrong. The number 258 is "preserved," not "subsequently construed."

The inscriptions of the Caucasus limes at Darband are at variance with all other Sasanian inscriptions: "in the year 700." This date looks enigmatical, for, the Ardashīr era came to an end by the Muhammedan conquest shortly after its year 400.

It is again the great Biruni who solves the riddle. He says—a remark often quoted—that Yazdegird I, whose first regnal year was A.D. 399 or 710 Sel., lived about 970 years after Zoroaster. In connection therewith he says, a fanatic, ibn abi Zakariya, appeared in 319 H., 1242 Sel., 1500 p.Zor. He reached these synchronisms under the assumption—for which he later apologized—that the traditional date of Zoroaster was 258 years before the Seleucid epochal year 311 B.C. If one puts in the corrected date 329 B.C., ibn abī Zakariya is no longer 1500 p.Zor.—This date was not a number transmitted, but calculated as a curiosity by Biruni, and he must have given it up when correcting himself: there is nothing remarkable in 1518. Besides, according to Sasanian reckoning it would be 1229 p.Zor. Nor can one infer from Biruni's calculation that Yazdegird believed to have come to the throne in 970 p.Zor. In Sasanian reckoning the year A.D. 399, 173 after Ardashīr's coronation, was not at all 970 p.Zor. The *Māh Frav.* reveals the belief that in the year 19 of Xusrau II, i.e. A.D. 608, the end of the millennium had not yet come, though it was not far away.

Mas'ūdī says, *tanbīh* 98ff.: "The Persians and other nations are greatly at variance regarding the chronology of Alexander, a fact many people forget." G. Messina has dealt with this subject in Orientalia I. Mas'ūdī starts from a prophecy of Zoroaster, a "religious and political secret: after 300 years the empire shall be shaken, the religion shall remain; at the turn of the millennium empire and religion shall perish!" On the strength of this prophecy, Ardashīr—whom Mas'ūdī, following Syriac chronology, imagines to have lived about 300 + 51x, hence 81x (instead of 522) years after Zoroaster—is said to have shortened the duration of the preceding Arsacid period from 500 and odd to 260 years, as it were, in order to delay the doom. This motive is naïvely wrong: the faked dates could never have given to the people, from whom the prophecy was kept a secret, the illusion that the catastrophe was still far away. Mas'ūdī ends his discourse: "By the way, the prophecy is found at the end of Ardashīr's testament: if it was not destined that the doom will come at the turn of the millennium . . .;[15] Ardashīr's mōbad Tansar, too, mentions it in his letter to Māhgušnasp [quotation]." In the Tansar letter as preserved in ibn Isfandiyār, nothing is said about the shortening of the chronology. One assumes the letter to have been composed under Xusrau I who came to the throne according to real chronology in A.D. 530 + 311 Sel. + 258 Zor. = 1099 p.Zor., but according to Sasanian chronology about 250 years earlier. Neither at the time of Ardashīr nor of Xusrau I was there any cause for a "millennium-mood," and certainly Ardashīr did not turn back the clock of time for fear of the end of the world. Darmesteter went rather far in saying that, from the wording of the letter, Ardashīr seemed to have inaugurated a millennium, though this was in contradiction to the reckoning of the *Gr.Bdh.* What he actually inaugurated was the era, the calendar, and at that occasion the real chronology was fitted into the old interrupted system of aeons.[16]

For all these problems a synchronism brought to light from Biruni's *qānūn* by S. H. Taqizadeh (BSOS IX,1937, 133ff.) is decisive: "the correction of the zīǰ i šahriyārān, the astronomical lists, took place in the year 25 of Xusrau I, equal to 3851 of the Sasanian world era." This date does not at all fall into the time of Xusrau I if one assumes Zoroaster as 258 years before the Seleucid era. By substituting the death of Darius for the Seleucid era and Shāhpuhr I for Xusrau I, Taqizadeh reached approximately the 25th year of Shāhpuhr. In fact, there is nothing to be changed; it is an entirely different, shortened reckoning which Taqizadeh indicated as possibility at the end of his discourse: the 25th year of Xusrau I, A.D. 555, is 329 after Ardashīr's coronation in 226. If it is 851 p.Zor., Zoroaster is placed 522 years before Ardashīr's coro-

[15] The "testament," wasāya i Ardašīr, is quoted as source in a tale in 'Aufī's Jawāmi' al-ḥikāyāt, and is the unmentioned source of a chapter of the 'Uyūn al-akhbār.

[16] Mas'ūdī's "strict religious and political secret" contains a truth: such things belong to the esoteric knowledge of priestly astrologers and calendarmakers, Aw. kēta and ratugūt. The shortened reckoning entailed that for the Arsacid period there are two dating systems, represented by the total 260 in Firdausi, but 523 (or 513) in Tabari I,711. The small numbers are those of the Iranian, the big ones those of the Syriac tradition. The early Muhammedan chroniclers double, for the sake of compensation, the series of the Ashkān by one of Ashghān, a theme discussed already by A. v. Gutschmid, *Kleine Schriften* III,ii, 1861.

nation; 522 is the sum of the Zoroaster date 258 plus 264, the number of the duration of the Arsacid domination according to the shortened system.

The epochal year of the Zoroastrian world era is therefore 296 B.C. or +15 Sel.

From the qānūn synchronism follows that, when converting Sasanian dates from the Christian into Zoroastrian era, one must *not* add the 14 years of Alexander. That is only logical, because the Arsacids, as long as they used the era of Alexander, considered it to be a dynastic era, beginning, as later their own, with the accession of the founder. The synchronism proves definitely that the Iranians did not distinguish between "before Alexander" and "before the Seleucid era," and makes unnecessary a discussion of whether the year 258 really relates to 312/11 B.C.

When converting dates given in Christian era, one must put down Ardashīr's accession in A.D. 226/7 as 258 + 264 = 522 p.Zor., hence add 522 — 226 = 296 to the dates of the Christian era. From dates in the Seleucid era, 15 must be subtracted. As example: Yazdegird I came to the throne in 399 + 296 = 695 after Zoroaster, and not in 970.

This does away with Nyberg's whole discussion of the "apocalyptic date of Zoroaster." But he himself has furnished the documentary confirmation for our result: he has published it, without recognizing the importance and implications in the Darband inscriptions.[17]

The mutawalli of this construction is the amārkar, i.e. Arab. 'āmil, subgovernor of Ādharbaidjān, and the most complete text contains the date "in the year 700." Nyberg dates the inscriptions for "paleographic," that means with unique documents "insufficient" reasons, in the 6th-7th centuries A.D., the period of Xusrau I and II. What then is 700?

Xusrau I, 531-579, built a limes against the Chionites in the east (cf. AMI IX,149f.). *Gr.Bdh.*215: "anōšakravbān χusrav ē kavātān . . . avēšān χiyōnān kē.šān aspatāk ō ērānšahr hamē kirt spōχt vitarg bast ērānšahr apēbīm kirt, Xusrau I repulsed the Chionites who made continuous inroads into Ērānshahr, shut the approach, and made Ērānshahr free of fear." The gold coins of his years 31 and 34 which call him "gēhān

[17] Together with E. A. Pakhonov, *Les inscriptions péhlvies de Derbend,* Bull. Soc. Scient. d'Azerbaidjan, Baku, 1929 (Russ.).

apēbīm kirtār, he who freed the world from fear" commemorate the completion of this limes.—The *Ayātḳ.Zar.* uses the expression "darband (= vitarg bast) of iron."

Baiḍawī, *niẓām,* attributes an eastern limes to Pērōz: "among his monuments is a wall 50 farsakh long on the +Tadjand (text: χuǰand) between Ērān and Tūrān."—The *Shahr.Ēr.* §18, s. v. Kōmiš, connect the name of Yazdegird I with these buildings: "pa χvatāyīh ē yazdkirt ē šāhpuhrān krt andar? tčnd (var.l.tčvl) čōl vērōy[18] pāhr[ak] ān ālak." The paragraph is defective in style and grammar and apparently mutilated: *tčnd* is the name of the lower course of the Harēv rōd, river of Herāt and Sarakhs, cf. *Gr.Bdh.* 86; misspelled χuǰand in the ms. of Baiḍawī. This Hyrcanian limes was situated "ān ālak, on the other side, beyond" scil. of the Caspian Sea, opposite Čol and Vērōy. Čol is Darband, Arab. Bāb al-abwāb, the pass between the Caucasus and the Caspian. Vērōy is Iberia. In the much damaged first lines of his Kaʿba inscription Shāhpuhr I mentions the region among the provinces belonging to him: Pahl. vyrvšn—'r.n—as far aṣ the kpy ṬVR' v 'l'n NTRVN?Y, Gr. ΙΒΕΡΙΑΝ ΑΛΒΑΝΙΑΝ ΕΩΣ ΕΜΠΡΟΣΘΕΝ [ΚΑ]Π ΟΡΟΥΣ . . . . Kap ṬVR' is kaf-kōh, the Caucasus, NTRVN is ideogr., read "ālān pāhrak, watch of Ālān." The three Kartēr inscriptions have Pārs. (*KiZ*) 'lmny štry Armenia, v vlvč'n [also in *S.Mshh.*] v 'l'ny . . . ʿD PʿN [*NiR.*: ʿD pr'č ʿL] 'l'n'n BB' [the last words also in *NiR.* and *S.Mshh.*], i.e. "Armin šahr, virōčān, ārān,[19] as far as the Gate of Ālān."

The Syr. Alexander romance renders vērōy pāhrag by Wīrōparhagh, Ioannes Lydos Βιροπαραχ; Agathangelos (Arm.) Jurojpahak, Priskos frgm.31 Ἰουροειπααχ. The limes was begun after the siege of Amida and the peace of Jovian (A.D. 359, 363) under Shāhpuhr II; it was destroyed by the Albanians in 450 and rebuilt with financial contributions of Marcianus (450-457); Łevond reports that in 716 a foundation stone with inscription of Marcianus was discovered; in 464-466 the

[18] For the reading cf. §9: čōl χākān u vērōy χākān; and ibn Khurdādhbih 40f.: وتمرون probably ويروى. Hübschmann, *Arm.Gram.* 218: pahak Čoray "watch of Čor," Gr. τζουρ πύργος; čor is the old, seemingly indigenous name of Darband, also durn čolay "gate of čol."—The chronicle of Dionysius of TellMahrē uses the older form "gate of the Ṭōrāyē," Gr. Τούρ.—Without the Pahl. material, Markwart wrote the history of the Caucasus limes in *Ērānš.* (cf. index) and in *Karmpalouḳ,* Rev. Orient. 1910, 20, but failed to recognize the names in *Shahr.Ēr.* in his *Cat. Prov. Cap.*

[19] Gr. Albania is Arm. ałvan.kʿ, Syr. 'rn, Iber. rani, Arab. arrān. This, and not Ālān, must be the dastākrta Allānu in *Dar. Sus.e.*

contributions were subject of diplomatic negotiations between Iran and Byzantium.

According to their wording the inscriptions of Darband are not foundation but restoration texts, which do not refer to the first construction under Shāhpuhr II, but to the repairs and raisings made under Yazdegird. He ruled A.D. 399-420, or 695-716 p.Zor.; "in the year 700," hence is a date in Sasanian world era, in agreement with Biruni's qānūn synchronism: 700 p.Zor. is A.D. 404, the fifth year of Yazdegird.

Therefore, there is neither reason nor purpose "irgend ein Ereignis aufzuweisen, das gerade damals die apokalyptische Phantasie in Bewegung gesetzt hätte," as Nyberg attempts, because he believes the year 401 to be the year of the "invention" of the date of Zoroaster. But one must go into one argument produced in this connection, in order to do away with another error (43): the "nahezu selbverständlichen Zusammenhang zwischen Kalenderveränderung und Weltalterspekulationen." "Börsenspekulationen" would be more to the point.

The event is—cf. Nöldeke's note to *Tabari* 78—that under Yazdegird the disorder of the calendar was regulated by intercalation of two months. The year is unknown. Nyberg chooses 401 as "angemessen für das grosse Schaltungsfest, eine Grossthat, die nicht schlecht zu der megalophrosýne passt, die Prokop ihm in seinen jüngeren Jahren nachrühmt."

But the Sasanian calendar had to be regulated every 120 years by intercalating one full month; every 120 years the kings would have had megalophrosyne, and every 120 years the Sasanian "time and milieu" would have been "gesättigt mit astrologischen Spekulationen." The last of these intercalations took place, according to Kušyār b. Labbān, astronomer of the 10th century A.D., under Xusrau I, according to Biruni, *Chronol.* 33, about 70 years before Yazdegird III, which would be not before 562. This problem has been fully stated by H. Lewy. But the exact date is known, for it is the very same controle of the zīǰ—mentioned above—in the year 25 of Xusrau I, A.D. 555 or 3851 of the world era. The years A.D. 228, 348, 468 and 588 would be the regular leap-years. The intercalation to be expected 120 years after that of Xusrau was prevented by the Arab conquest. Biruni remarks that the interval between Xusrau's intercalation and the preceding one under Yazdegird exceeded the normal 120 years. There are cogent reasons to delay or to prevent an intercalation, namely money.

Disorder of the calendar is the chronic disease of oriental chronology. In an edict (A. Ungnad, *Babyl. Briefe* n° 14) Hammurapi says: "The year has a surplus. The new month shall be reckoned as Second Ulūl. And wherever the order has been given that the taxes shall arrive in Babylon on the 25th of Tašrīt, they shall arrive on the 25th of Ulūl II." Ungnad remarks in MAOG XIII,1940, 21: "Die Schaltung hatte im wesentlichen rein praktische Gründe" and adds examples relating to the harvest of grain, dates, fulfilment of delivery contracts etc. It is not aeons and apocalypses that stand behind the "Schaltungsfest," but something that causes joy everywhere: a remission of taxes. For the calendar rules the payment of taxes, paid at the term of the new year, Med. nava sarda, later naurōz.[20] At the Achaemenian period the term was the miθrakāna, OP. bāgayadiš, the subject of the great tribute processions of Persepolis. Strabo 11,14,9: "Aṛmenia . . . sent every year 20,000 colts for the mithrákina." Biruni, the mathematician, was interested only in the consequences for the chronology, but the people of the time only in the consequences for their purses: the intercalary months were free of taxes.

Under the Arsacids, one intercalation took place between A.D. 16 and 46, by which the Macedonian Xanthikos instead of Artemisios became coincident with the Babylonian Nisān.[21] During the Abbasid period I know of two such shiftings, one under al-Mutawakkil, in 245 H. "from 21. III to 21. rabīʿ I.=18. hazīrān=20. ardvihišt," i.e. to 17. VI. 859 A.D., hence three months difference, cf. Tabari III,1448, ibn al-Athīr VII,57. In affairs related to taxes, the Arabs use the Persian term of payment and the Iranian solar year. The other intercalation was under al-Muʿtaḍid, from 21. III to 21. VII, hence four months, cf. Taghriberdi I,93 and A. v. Kremer, *Culturgesch.* I,279f. The calendar can only be corrected when the financial situation is a good one and when people think less than ever of the end of the world. Nyberg: "Mit allem Vorbehalt hinsichtlich der Einzelheiten glaube ich also die

[20] Legends concerning the institution of naurōz are often quoted, e.g. that in the *Māh. Frav.;* only one has attracted but little attention, viz. that in Yāq.I,669, story of the mōbed of Kaskar, calling it naurōz i mihradjān.

[21] Cf. McDowell, *Coins from Seleucia,* p. 190.

Zahl 258 deuten zu können als einen integrierenden Bestandteil der Zarathustra-Apokalypse . . . in Zusammenhang mit Yazdegird's grosser Schaltung entstanden. . . . Die Zahl ist von gewisser Bedeutung für die Geschichte der sasanidischen Theologie. Mit dem geschichtlichen Zarathustra hat sie nichts zu schaffen." This is a verdict, but a "dušrθriš, miscarriage of justice." Under Yazdegird, 699-717, p.Zor., when the finances permitted a great intercalation, this number has not been invented, it has not been computed at all.

In his discourse, Nyberg takes 288 as original number and 258 as arrived at by subtracting 30 years of life. He overlooked that 288 would be 600 B.C., a round mystical number. Theodorus bar Kōni, end of the 8th century A.D., puts the birth of Zoroaster 628 years 7 months before the birth of Christ. That is a number transmitted by prophetic, apocalyptic literature, of the type of the Zoroastrian prophecy about Christ in the *Book of the Bee,* ed. Budge, transl.p.9. Any connection with the birth of Christ cannot be older than the 5th century A.D., and it is not possible that the Zoroastrian tradition had obtained its number 258 from a Christian source by the calculation 600 — 30 — 312 = 258. The number 258 in the Zoroastrian sources is only the not mentioned sum of years between Zoroaster and Alexander, and the idea of separating birth and public appearance by 30 years, following a mythical pattern, is an interpretation of the primary number 258 which did not distinguish between the two points of time. 258 + 30 + 312 = 600 is a coincidence; 258+311 = 569 B.C. is authentic.

There is still a trace of another reckoning. According to Firdausi, Vullers III,1499, Zoroaster had planted in memory of the conversion of Vištāspa, a cypress, in front of the fire-temple of Kishmar, district Turshīz in Khurāsān, inscribing on its stem "Guštāsp has accepted the Good Religion." According to the *Dabistān* (transl. Shea and Troyer I,306-309) al-Mutawakkil had cut down the cypress in 232 H., for use in the Dja'farī palace, at Dja'fariyya, North-Samarra, when the tree was 1,450 years old. The caliph was murdered when the transport had reached the last stage before Samarra.[22] I have seen, in Iran and

[22] Literature in A. V. W. Jackson, *Zoroaster,* 1899, 80, 163f. and 217; A. Houtum-Schindler, *Cypress of Zoroaster* in JRAS, Jan. 1909; E. P. Tate, *Seistan,* 1910, 188f.; Henry Yule, *Marco Polo* I,128-39, on "arbre Sol," i.e. draxt i sarw, esp. p. 131.

Afghanistan, many cypresses 500 years old, and in Northern Europe yews of almost a thousand years. The age is possible. The Muhammedan tradition does not record this act of al-Mutawakkil, but contains reports that make it all but probable. In 235 H. the caliph issued an edict against the ahl al-dhimma, including Zoroastrians, in which the pulling down of all recently built sanctuaries was ordered; in 239 H. the edict was repeated in severer form. In 241 he incorporated e.g. the old cathedral of Ḥimṣ into the Gr. Mosque there. But the order to build the Dja'farī palace was given only in 245 H.; the construction lasted no more than a couple of months, and on the new-year of 246 (8. III.860) the caliph moved into the new town; he was murdered on the 4th of shawwāl 247 (11. XII.861). The order to fell the cypress was not given before 245, and the execution and the transport may well have taken all that time. The date cannot be 232, year of al-Mutawakkil's succession, but only 245 H., i.e. January-March A.D. 860, 1172 Sel.[23] The 1,450 years of the cypress are the sum of 1,172 + 278. This number is between 288 for Zoroaster's birth and 258 for the conversion of Vištāspa, but at the bottom of this reckoning is nothing but the same tradition: Zoroaster 258 years before the Seleucid era. It is inadmissible to reconcile the dates by assuming a reckoning in lunar years, not only because the Iranians never used them, but—a decisive point—because this system is not that of the Sasanian world era, in which the cypress, in the year 232 H. would have been 1,145, in 245 H. 1,158 years old. The small fault is not in 278 for 258, but in 1172: it is a counting of real years which equals 245 H. with 1192 instead of 1172 Sel., under the same presumption: "Zoroaster —258 Sel." The computation cannot have been: 258 years before 331, death of Darius III, plus 20 years (epochal year of the Sel. era), plus 1172=1450, for the interval of 20 years between the death of Darius and the epochal year was as unknown as the two facts themselves. On the contrary, the Seleucid era was used in Khurasan, since the Arsacid calendar, in Seleucid era, introduced by Mithradates II about 120 B.C., remained in use in Khwārizm down to 1270 Sel. The number 258, here, appears in the

[23] Computations under other assumptions are faulty, cf. Shea-Troyer p. 308; E. Roth, *Zoroastr. Glaubenslehre* in *Gesch. unserer abendländ. Philosophie,* p. 350, beginning of the "era of the cypress," 560 B.C.; Floigl, *Cyrus und Herodot* 1885, followed by Roth.

reckoning of the years of a temple, without the reduction peculiar to the Sasanian world era.

The year 1000 of this era is equal to A.D. 704. In 635 (931 p.Zor.) the Muslims conquered Ctesiphon; 642 (938 Z.) or little later was the battle of Nihāwand; 674-676 (970-972 Z.) were the first advances against Bukhārā and Samarkand, regions which were finally conquered in 711 (1007). That is the time in which the Bahman yasht 1,5 and 11,21 puts the end of the millennium, and *Māh Frav.* is still a hundred years away from this end. At this time, hence, Zoroaster's prophecy ex eventu in Mas'ūdī was conceived.[24] The same thoughts lead to the emigration of the Parsis into India, as K. Inostrantzev has shown.[25]

At the very same time the system of aeons, preserved in the *Gr.Bdh.,* received its pessimistic-eschatologic character. The prophecy talked of the downfall of the empire and the religion; here it becomes practically the end of the world, by reserving the following two millennia for its preparation by the two precursors of the third sōšyant. This picture is most unconvincing: why should one need an aeon of 12,000 years, when 6,000 years are wasted on a preexistence, 3,000 on mythical history, and 2,000 on preparing the end, so that human history is actually limited to one thousand years? In this system nothing is alive of Zoroaster's optimism, the final victory of Good over Evil, which can yet be felt in *Māh Frav.* It is a new interpretation of the old doctrine, born out of the time of calamity, the Muhammedan conquest, out of the passionate hope for the end of the world expected to come at once, and out of the equally passionate belief in the old doctrine: "The kingdom of Heaven is near!"

[24] A similar case: R. Hartmann, *Eine islam. Apokalypse der Kreuzzugszeit,* Schriften d. Königsberg. Gelehrt. Gesellschaft 1,3, 1924.

[25] Journ. Cama Orient. Inst. Bombay, 1, 1922, 32-69; J. J. Modi, *A Few Events in the Early Hist. of the Parsis,* Bombay 1903, 1-9. According to the Qiṣṣa i Sanjān, the Iranians who faithfully adhered to Zoroastrism took refuge in Kohistan, between Khurasan and Kirman, after Yazdegird's death in A.D. 651 = 947 p.Zor. A hundred years after, about 751, they moved to Hormuz on the Gulf, where they stayed till 765 = 1061 p.Zor. In the year of the foundation of Baghdad, they emigrated to Dīw, and landed, 19 years later, in 784 = 1081 p.Zor. in Gujerat "guided by astrological prognostics." The waiting sojourn in Kohistan, hence, lasted from — 50 to + 50 of the millennium, to the downfall of the Umayyad dynasty. In this, a second prophecy concurs: a dream of Yazdegird III, after the defeat at Jalūlā in A.D. 637/8 = 933/4 p.Zor., told by Tabari: "The Arabs shall rule 100 + 100 + 100 + ... years." There the dream stops short. The year of the foundation of Baghdad brought the last disillusion.

But Zoroaster's date, "258 before Alexander" is not affected by such thoughts and changes, and survives all of them untouched.

The resolution of these 258 years into regnal years of legendary Achaemenids can scarcely have been undertaken before Ardashīr I. In *Shahr.Ēr.* §1 we read: "Alexander burnt the Dēnkart (= Awesta) written by order of Vištāsp, which had existed under seven kings." A gloss explains the number of seven—recorded nowhere else—as seven mythical kings before Vištāsp, against all logic. The seven is a vague remembrance of the fact that there were seven Hystaspids. The archetype of the *Shahrihā ē Ērān* was composed for Kavāt, at the very end of the 5th century, and must have used an old form of the chiliadic system which contained "3,000 years prehistory, appearance of Zoroaster, seven kings reigning 258 years, Alexander 14 years." The scholars of Ardashīr's time—if this filling of the gap in the *Bdh.* is theirs—could find out for the seven only five kings in the legendary material. Zoroaster himself stands at the beginning of the Achaemenid epoch, the Arsacids do not get more than half of their real domination, only a few years more than the Achaemenids, and only with the Sasanids real chronology begins.

The number 258 predicates when the prophet lived, and such facts are not quickly forgotten by oriental nations, even when illiterate. It appears in a system of aeons and those who were in charge of it must have been the people that preserved the memory. The date known to Plato's Academy, "Zoroaster 6,000 years before Plato," shows that already about 400 B.C. Zoroaster had his place as inaugurator of the 4th millennium in that system, and that his return was expected after 6,000 years.

With this insertion of Zoroaster into the system and the limitation of the prehistory to the first 3,000 years, the chiliadic system had been converted into real chronology. The system requires the counting of years. Quintus Curtius III,3,9 says, speaking of Alexander's time: "The magi had a year of 365 days," viz. beside the civil calendar. As in the Sasanian period, this was certainly connected with the system of aeons.

One instance of priests counting the years of their temple in antiquity, just as in Sasanian times, we have come to know in the "era of the cypress." Another one is the number preserved by Herodotus I,130 in the Median story of Harpagos: "Cyrus dethroned Astyages after 35 years of his reign, after 128 years of the Median rule, *παρὲξ ἢ ὅσον οἱ Σκύθαι ἦρχον*, not counting the years of the Scythian domination." The double date is in the style of the Bīshāpūr inscription: "year 58, year 40 of the Ardashīr-fire, 24 of the Shāhpuhr-fire." The number 128 comes from a Median source (Harpagos is a Mede) and contradicts the artificial calculation followed by Herodotus in I,102-106: "Dēiókes 52 years, Phraórtes 23; Kyaxáres 40, *σὺν τοῖσι Σκύθαι ἦρξαν*, including the 28 years of the Scythians; Astyáges 35 years," sum $2 \times 75 = 150$, which would give 122 without the Scythians. With the words *παρὲξ* Herodotus tries to reconcile the variance of his two sources, but the 128 years were not meant to be interrupted by a span of 28 years. 150 is wrong, 128 is right. The end is the conquest of Agbatana in 550 B.C., Agbatana is the home of the record. In Agbatana stood the memorial fire of the Median ktístes, the āδar kavātạkān, which burned as long as the dynasty lasted. Its priests counted 128 years of their temple, 35 of the Astyages fire, when Cyrus took Agbatana. The Ardashīr fire, too, burned as long as the Sasanian dynasty lasted: Yazdegird III was crowned in this temple in A.D. 632/3 (406 p.Ard., 928 p.Zor.); its priests counted 40 years of their temple when the statue of Shāhpuhr I was made in Bīshāpūr; the priests of Kishmar counted 1,450 years when their cypress was felled.

The disturbed condition in which the chiliadic system is preserved in the *Gr.Bdh.* is explained by the facts that the years were counted before Alexander, that Hellenism led to an interruption, and that under Ardashīr the gap was filled by calendaric-astronomical methods—whereby the strange shortening occurred.

The number 258 appears as interval between Zoroaster's epiphany, the "matan ē dēn," and Alexander's accession, which was not preserved as a date by the Iranian tradition. One did not know that the Seleucid era was something different. The calendar-makers of Ardashīr I, in bringing down the epochal year of the Zoroastrian era from 569 to 296 B.C., bring down with it the year 258 p.Zor. from 311 to 38 B.C. as epochal year of the Seleucid era, without changing its signification.

This first dynastic era[26] has not been introduced as such. Seleucus counted, as usual, the years of his reign, beginning with the year in which Alexander IV was defeated and murdered, and in which Seleucus returned to Babylon. The epochal year is 312/11; the variations of its beginning, 1. X.312 in the west, 1. III.311 in the east, do not affect the problem of its origin. During Seleucus' last years, Antiochus I was co-regent with the full royal title. Seleucus' death, 32 Sel. = 280 B.C., did not entail a change of protocol, and under Antiochus whose first year had never counted as year 1, one simply went on counting the years of Seleucus. In course of time, one must have realized that this was a new practical method, with the effect that Antiochus II in 51 Sel. = 261 B.C. consciously went on doing the same. Thus the first dynastic era originated. As a whole and in its varieties it received various names, like "Seleucid, of the Greeks, of the Babylonian astronomers," but all of them are subsequently given, among them "aera Alexandri" and *ἀπὸ τῆς Ἀλεξάνδρου τελευτῆς*. It seems to me impossible that this last name could mean the era of Alexander IV, just as impossible as an era of the "cursed Alexander" with the Sasanians. The name supposes the belief that the era, the beginning of which was obscure, had been used since the death of Alexander.

"Zoroaster 258 years before Alexander" is an expression that can result only from "258 years before *our* era." The Seleucid era was used by the Arsacids in Iran, where, of course, it passed as era of Alexander the Great. In the year 65 of this era, the Arsacids introduced their own dynastic era, which in Babylon was never used alone, but at the side of the Seleucid. The Sasanians, with their xenophobe tendencies, abandoned it, just as they renounced the title philhéllēn, and the occasion was the reform of the calendar under Ardashīr I, A.D. 227/8, 539/40 Sel.

According to that old reckoning, the year 300 p.Zor. falls in the reign of Antiochus I, when people became aware of having an era. 300 p.Zor. would be 42 Sel., 270 B.C. Fifty years earlier Curtius attests the existence of a religious calendar, and 247 B.C. is the epochal year of the Arsacid era. Only as early as that, in about 300 p.Zor., hence in pre-Arsacid antiquity, the number 258 could be introduced into the chiliadic system. Under the dissolving influences of Hellenism, the

[26] Cf. Eduard Meyer, *G.d.A.* 1,1, and Bouché-Leclerq, II,515ff.

counting of years stopped, but this fundamental number, the interval between Zoroaster and the Seleucid era remained. New materials allow us also to recognize how and where it was preserved.

The great temples counted their years, and one of them was the temple where the foundation-document was kept with the memorial list of *Yasht* 13, a document to be discussed in our next chapter. A headline calls this list "fravartayo of the purvyatkēša and nabānazdišta, souls of the first-faithful and next-of-kin," namely of Zoroaster and Vištāspa, and the fact that Zoroaster and his family precede Vištāspa and his relatives shows that the temple was founded by Vištāspa "for the soul of Zoroaster and for his own soul." The list of names is the last paragraph of the entire document, and was introduced into the yasht at the time of its first redaction, that means about 400 B.C. The priests who kept this document and recited the names by heart when celebrating the prescribed masses, counted the years of their temple and knew, at the time of Antiochus I, that Zoroaster had lived 300 years before.

Only the list of names is preserved, and only the discovery of names historically known among them can furnish means of dating the document. I anticipate here some results to be proved in the following chapters.

Among the sons of Vištāspa appears Spantadāta, who at his accession to the throne assumed the "throne-name" Dārayavahuš. That gives the terminus ante quem: before 522 B.C. A terminus post quem, with rather large margin, is 539, the year in which Cambyses was šar Bābili and not yet lieutenant in Iran. The proscription of Zoroaster from Ragā may have taken place already in 538. In the list he has three wives, one of them the Hāugavī whom he married in exile, and by her he has a daughter, Puručistā, unmarried, hence not yet 16 years old. Some years must have passed between his banishment, the marriage, and the birth of the daughter. He has already a grandson bearing the same name as his son Rvatatnara (probably the second son), hence must have been at least 40 years old.—If 569 is the year of his birth, the terminus post quem would be 529, year of Cambyses' accession. Finally, Brzi.rštiš = Brzya, Smerdis, appears in the list.

According to Herodotus III,65, Cambyses would have ordered Prexaspes to have Smerdis killed in prison, after the Egyptian campaign had started; when he received the news of the proclamation of the Pseudo-Smerdis the king at once returned. Herodotus tells the Prexaspes story during that return, and speaks wrongly of a non-existing "Syrian Agbatana," product of a banal interpretation of the oracle of Buto: Cambyses killed himself in the real Agbatana. Thus it is possible that the date of Smerdis' death was nearer to 523, but the greater probability is that he was killed when Cambyses started for Egypt. A list "for the souls, the memory" may contain names of deceased persons, as does the list in the Ka'ba inscription of Shāhpuhr I, but the first assumption would be that Smerdis was still alive when his name was put into the list. In that case, 525 is the terminus ante quem—a year in which Puručistā was not over 12 years old, and the probable date of the memorial list of *Yt.*13 is limited between 528 and 526 B.C.

If the temple was founded in 527, it counted exactly 258 years in the year 300 p.Zor. (258 before Alexander plus 311=569 B.C. or 42 Sel.), the time when the Seleucid era had become established under Antiochos I. At that time the priests could say: "Remarkable that the year 300 of Zoroaster, who was born 258 years before the era we now use, is exactly the year 258 of our temple." This number is a tradition, not a calculation. It does not affect our problem, but one may infer from the preservation of this date that such temples, at the time of Antiochus I, started to use two eras, as did the Arsacids a few years later.

The number 258 is a historical reminiscence, introduced into the chiliadic system at the Seleucid period and faithfully preserved to the end. No more than the date for the birth of Christ is it a historical date in the strictest sense, for the notion "pētākīh, epiphany" is a too indefinite one.[27] The birth of a prophet—since the child is not born with its work accomplished—can never be exactly retained; the first public appearance, the success of which manifests itself only much later, is remembered only in rare cases. But that does not matter. The

[27] Like Gr. epiphanía and Arab. ẓuhūr, the word is used for appearance of stars, cf. the Syr. n.pr. Īšō'denah "Christ has risen!", and Gr. epiphanḗs in royal protocols. In Hellenism, Ptolemy V, 190 B.C., is the first "epiphanḗs, the god who appears to men in calamity"; then Antiochus IV, 175-164.—In Iran Xusrau I uses the title. In Islam, there are many malik al-ẓāhir; the title has an intense meaning in the case of the Fatimid caliph al-Ẓāhir, who followed, as a child, his father al-Ḥākim after his disappearance, ghaiba.

late Awestic concept, expressed e.g. in *Yt.*13,93f., is, that "all waters, plants and animals of the good creation rejoice at the *birth* and shout: Thank God! the priest is born, he who is the Spitāma Zarathustra!" The Pahl. commentary to *Vid.*1,15 (on Ragā) likewise makes no distinction between birth and appearance: some codd. have "zrtvšt MN ZK y'k YḪVVN.t, Zoroaster was from that place (meaning: born)," another ms. has "pyt'k YḪVVN.t, appeared from there," same meaning. It is not only that the birth is the more naïve and original conception —cf. the legends emanating from the birth of Christ—and that the appearance with 30 years is a legendary, though probable, pattern. The decisive point is that the name "matan ē dēn" or "acceptance of the religion" is a religious term which must of necessity be later than the fixing of the era. The distinction between birth and appearance is secondary. The analogy to "appearance" would be, in Christianity, the Jordan baptism as epochal year. From the historical point of view, there has never been a year, day or hour, in which Vištāspa became converted. This is a religious tint laid on events entirely neutral. What actually happened was that Vištāspa gave refuge to the proscribed Zoroaster. Such an act was not announced with trumpets, but kept as secret as possible. It seems that, at first, Zoroaster lived in concealment as a hermit at the farthest corner of Vištāspa's province, on the mount Ušidam in the ḷake Kansavya. At any rate, the exact date of his reception by Vištāspa has been no more preserved than the date of his birth. The only real date known in later times was the foundation of the temple; this was attested by the document, to which the memorial list belonged. In that temple the number 258 was preserved.

The birth date allows forthwith a margin of ± 10 years. But in agreement with all that can be gathered about the prophet's lifetime from the Gathas and the rest of the Awesta, it puts Zoroaster in the sixth century, about 570-500 B.C., and the time of his activity under the reigns of Cyrus, Cambyses, and Darius.

In UGE II,210ff. (1905) J. Markwart had calculated the years 489-486 B.C. as date of the "introduction of the mazdayasnian calendar"; Nyberg[28] calculated 485 B.C. and calls (45) this date "das einzig sichere Datum der älteren Geschichte des Zoroastrismus." The non-Zoroastrian

[28] *Texte zum mazdayasn. Kalender,* Uppsala, Universitets Årsskrift 1934.

magi would have induced the non-Zoroastrian Xerxes to introduce a calendar of Zoroastrian coloring in order to give the king in the Zoroastrian dēva-notion a weapon against a revolt in Babylon! The Babylonians use, before and after, their own religious calendar without noticing the coloring of the names of the months used in Iran. The revolt is imaginary, and Xerxes never introduced this "mazdayasnian calendar." The last point is proved by the cuneiform tablets from Persepolis which use, throughout, the Old Persian calendar. The reasons adduced by Poebel in his first report on these tablets, for dating them in the time of Artaxerxes I, were unconvincing and have now been revoked in Cameron's notice *Darius' Daughter:*[29] the 30,000 tablets of the wall-archives are all from the time of Darius, years 12-28, the 800 tablets from the "Communs archives" go from the 30th year of Darius to the beginning of Artaxerxes' reign. Down to about 460 the Old Persian calendar was used and the officials were magi. H. Lewy remarks as to the number 485: "Cette erreuṛ s'explique du fait, que M. Nyberg ignorait la réforme d'Ardashīr et la différence fondamentale entre les calendriers sasanide et pré-sasanide." Of the various theories about the date at which the mazdayasnian calendar was introduced, it is only what Taqizadeh calls "the second reform" about 441 B.C. that has a chance to be true. Obviously this reform is mazdayasnian, not Zoroastrian,[30] and we shall see at the same time the mazdayasnian redaction of the Awesta took place.

In "stating" that "in einem Volk dem die Geschichte fehlt," "die ganze Frage nach der Zeit Zarathustras . . . eigentlich ohne Belang ist, dass der rein chronologischen Frage hier die Bedeutsamkeit fehlt," Nyberg confounds "history" and "historiography"; that is what is

[29] J. Near East. Stud. 1,2, April 1942.—The Persepolis tablets are about 30,000, 500 of them in Aramaic, written in ink, the others in Elamite cuneiform. Only preliminary information has been published, on the strength of which Nyberg says p.15: "Merkwürdigerweise scheint das Elamische die eigentliche Sprache der Achaemeniden zu sein"; p.334: "Wir wissen jetzt, dass die Verwaltungssprache der älteren Achaemeniden hauptsächlich elamisch war," und "das Aramaeische war die Kanzleisprache für die westlichen, vielleicht für alle Teile des Reichs." These pronouncements are rash, contradictory and wrong.

[30] This same opposition finds an expression in the twofold names of the calendar feasts, Zoroastrian gāhambār, mazdaistic-syncretistic naurōz and mihragān etc., H. Lewy, p.63f., comes very near the truth in recognizing in this opposition the expression of truly Zoroastrian and Iranian-Mithraic conceptions. One better speaks of mono- and polytheistic, or Zoroastrian and mazdayasnian: it is the unadjusted coexistence of pre-Zoroastrian and Zoroastrian designations in the mazdayasnian syncretism which prevailed since the time of Artaxerxes II. For these terms see under 'Fravarāni.'

lacking, not history. And the definition of the time of Zoroaster remains the central problem of Old Iranian history, history of religion, archeology and philology.

There is a historical criterion for the value of the traditional date, 6th century B.C.—In his *Christentum* II,17, Eduard Meyer argues: "Der zweihundertjährige Bestand des Perserreichs ist ein Wendepunkt für die gesamte Religionsgeschichte überhaupt. Die nationale Gestaltung des staatlichen Lebens ist für westorientalische Welt begraben, damit die Religion von Staat und Politik gelöst. Das schafft den Individualismus und den Universalismus, die fortan den Grundzug aller Religionen bilden. Aufgabe der Gottheit ist jetzt nicht mehr, das einzelne Gemeinwesen, den auf besonderem Volkstum beruhenden Staat zu schirmen, sondern sie ist zu einer universalen, kosmischen Macht geworden, die sich nicht mehr an das Volk als ganzes, sondern an den einzelnen Menschen wendet. In den arischen Religionen treten diese Züge von Anfang an hervor."

What he says about the significance of the Persian Empire for the religious development of mankind is entirely true. He was one of the most passionate champions of the concept of the high antiquity of Zoroaster. I discussed the problem with him more than once, the last time a few days before his death, but I do not know what he meant by "von Anfang an," Zoroaster or still older phases? The gods of the Aryans in India fight for their worshippers, and in the pre-Zoroastrian passages of the yashts, the gods grant to the worshipping Iranians what they refuse to the worshipping enemies of the heroes: naïve and without a trace of ethics, entirely Homeric. The ritualism, too, the sacrificial and magic rites of the Old Iranian religion, against which Zoroaster fights like the prophets of the Old Testament, do not surpass the level of religious thought reached elsewhere.

Only the book of Job (about the end of the 5th century B.C.?) comes near to the universal monotheism of Zoroaster with his ethical dualism —i.e. the answer to the question: whence comes evil, if God is good?— and with his complementary thought of eternal reward and punishment for the individual. There is a contradiction in the assumption that thoughts, which became possible in the rest of the world only under the Persian Empire, were possible 500-700 years earlier in the Aryan world. In Iran too, the universal conception of the deity, the relation of the god to the individual man instead of to the group, and the replacing, connected therewith, of the cult by ethics, is only a consequence of the world-wide empire.

In *Christentum* II,69, Eduard Meyer considers the passage in Plutarch, *de Iside* 47 (frgm.72) on the paradisiac condition after the defeat of Evil, Areimanios, where "all men, as *μακάριοι*, shall be one politeía, and shall all speak one language," to be genuinely Zoroastrian, perhaps made known to the Greeks by Aristotle's pupil Eudemus. But how could, about or before 1000 B.C., in the unhistorical region beyond Iran proper, such a notion be possible which clearly is the ideal all but materialized by the polyglot Persian Empire?, the χšaθram vispazanam, paruzanam, Akk. ša napḫar lišānu gabbi "where all languages are spoken."

The true cognition that the Persian Empire is the turning point in the history of all religions and brings the katharsis of religion itself makes a higher antiquity for Zoroaster from the beginning impossible. Starting on entirely different lines, Meillet came to a similar conclusion, *Trois Conf.* p.22: "La réforme religieuse . . . suppose de grands mouvements historiques et sociaux. L'établissement d'un vaste empire, gouverné par un roi absolu, a été dans le monde indo-iranien un fait d'un type nouveau; il est sans doute résulté de ces mêmes mouvements auxquels est dûe la secte Zoroastrienne. Ce fait capital domine la question."

The decades of the foundation of the Persian Empire in the 6th century B.C. are a terminus ad quem for Zoroaster. The allegedly "only safe term, before 485" is a mistake, inferred from wrong premises, and the traditional date, Zoroaster appeared 258 years before the Seleucid era, which determines his life between 570 and 500 B.C., is an intrinsically probable date.

II. MEMORIAL DOCUMENT OF *YT.*13

"tyām imēšām martiyānām tōhmā hubrtām paribara,
the issue of these men treat well!"

The headline of the Fravardīn Yasht is: "We worship the fravarti of the blessed first-followers of the law, rtāvan purvya.tkēša, next-of-kin, nabā.nazdišta."[1] This headline, unfit for the main part of the yasht,[2] refers only to its smaller second half, §§87-145, the so-called "Community-list."

Already a cursory glance at that list, as it stands, reveals that instead of being a catalogue of the first followers only and the next-of-kin of Zoroaster and Vištāspa, it is rather, as §145 expresses, a list of "the fravarti of the whole world from the first man Gayamart to the last, the saviour, sōšyant." Even the fravarti of many animal species and other beings of the "good creation" are added. The original list of the community, thus, has been expanded to a list of humanity. This was done when introducing the document into the yasht, after the persons mentioned were all deceased "souls," and, since some of them belong to a third generation, at the earliest, three generations after Vištāspa, i.e. after the—strictly speaking—"Zoroastrian" period, at the period of Mazdaïsm.[3]

Various materials were used for this expansion. In §§131-135, the mythical kings are inserted between the personal names of the genuine list; in §§136-138, a series of mythical heroes. The first of the kings and men is Yama, not Gayamart (of §145). The divergence shows that the filling material belongs to different periods. Hōšyanha is not yet one of the kings, as in other yashts, but ranges with the heroes in the next paragraphs. All other yashts present already the system surviving in Firdausi's form of the Shāhnāmah, where Hōšyanha, the Saka, opens the line of kings. Thus, the redactors of *Yt.*13 have preserved an archaic version of the epics, not affected by a redaction that was undertaken probably at the early Achaemenian period.[4]

Nyberg 291: "Die Heroen des Fravardīn *Yt.*13 gruppieren sich fast ausschliesslich um Ranha und Vourukaša, Jaxartes und Aral-See. Es kann nicht zweifelhaft sein, dass dies geschichtliche Milieu die zoro-

[1] For this term see 'Social Structure.'
[2] See under 'Fravarti.'
[3] Definition of this term under 'Fravarāni.'
[4] For §§143-44, "fravarti of Ārya, Tūra, Sārima, Sāina and Dāha" see under 'Anērān-Tūrān.'

astrische Urgemeinde in dem turischen Friyana-Stamm ist." The alleged Aral-Lake is the ocean, but neither this nor any local or geographical name appears in *Yt.*13, which is a "Lied ohne Orte." It contains the names of all kings and heroes, to the last, Vištāspa, the only member of the Urgemeinde among them. But they no longer "group themselves," for they are all dead, "fravarti, manes," and their "historical milieu" is according to §23 "tušnišad, the land of silence, Hades."

The sōšyant Astvat.rta, twice inserted at the end of §§110 and 117, and the three sōšyant in §128, and the whole §129 on Astvat.rta, belong no more to the first-followers and next-of-kin than do those kings and heroes, neither the preceding six names of the kršvar-iudices, two of which appear again in §121. Also the last three names, compounds in -fδrī, of the list of women in §141 must be eliminated.

That means at the same time that everything which goes beyond the list proper is a commentary added when or after the list was inserted into *Yt.*13. Thus §§88-94 about Zoroaster, with exception of the name of his cousin Maδyomåha, but including the glosses referring to him; the remark on the "apostle" Sēna Ahumstut in §97; the verses §§97-100 on kavi Vištāspa; those on the use of the name of the Hāugava for magic purpose at the end of §104; a remark about Manθravāka in §105; a note to Aršya, father of Vanhu; at last §120, on the magic effect of the name of Yavišta Friyāna. At the best, some of these glosses show what the late Achaemenian Mazdaïsm thought about these figures.

After all these eliminations there remains an astonishingly well preserved list of probably exactly 240 names, 24 of them names of women. Of the male names sixteen are characterized, in §§125-126, as foreigners. Upon them three children follow, bearing the same name as their grandfathers with an "aparazāta, junior" added to it, and finally—not separated, as today, by the first kings and heroes—a list of women in §§139-141.

The only possible origin of this list is an authentic document of that high antiquity. Whatever one may think of the time and place of Zoroaster, this list which must go back to his own time is the rest of a document and must have had a purpose. Only when recognizing that purpose can one give it its true historical value. H. H. Schaeder, in a letter, once compared it to the lists in *Ezra* 2 and *Nehemiah* 7, preserved by a fortunate chance. Those—almost contemporary—lists, too, represent documents and had a purpose, namely for administration. The mere existence of the list of *Yt.*13 ought always to have been a warning not to put Zoroaster into a period long before the known Iranian history. But if the list belongs to an early historical period, the original document could be written only in cuneiform, for one cannot assume Aramaic script on clay tablets or leather for Old Persian texts before Darius, on account of *Beh.*§70:

vašnā[. a]u^{89}[ramaz]dā[ha]. i[--]. dipi[š ------
c.o.^{2}mi.n ^{d}o.ra.mas.ta.na ^{p}u ^{r}tip.pi.me ^{3}ta.i̯.e

-]am. akunavam. patišam.
ik.ki hu.t.ta ar.ri.i̯a.wa ^{4}ap.po sa.s.sa in.ne lip.ri ku.t.ta

a[g]ura[vā] ut[a.] $^{+}$pavast^{90}[ā]y[ā]. [č]āχr[iyatā. pat]išam.
^{r}ha.la^{5}t-uk.ku ku.t.ta ^{r}su^{id}-uk.ku

iya. [d]ipi[--]. $^{+}$nāma. āθahavaža .[---]iš[----] adā^{91}[---]ā
ku.t.ta ^{r}hi.s ku.t.ta e.p.pi hu.t.ta

uta [ap]i[θ]i[ya. u]ta [. -]tiya [--]ya. pai[š]ya. mā[m]
ku. ^{7}t.ta tal.li.k ku.t.ta ^{p}u ti.p.pa pe.p.ra.ka

pasāva. i[ya]m d^{92}ipi[m---]i?ma .[--]āvatā. [-----]
me.ni ^{r}tip.pi.me am.min.ni ^{1}ta.i̯.i̯.o.s mar.ri.ta

antar dahyā[va. k]āra hama amaχamatā
ha.ti.ma ^{p}u ten.ge.i̯a ^{p}tas.su.p.pe so.pi.s

"By the grace of Auramazdā, I made (this?) writing in another fashion [only El.: in Aryan, as it had never been before]; as well on clay-tablets as on leather, and the name and the seal? was put (to it), and it was written and the writing was read off to me. Thereafter, this writing was sent everywhere into the provinces as I had ordered. The people. . . ."

R. G. Kent tried a restoration of the OP. text which I cannot accept because it does not take into consideration the more complete Elamite text and its gloss; every restoration must be a retranslation of the Elamite text.

OP. dipi is El. tippi, loanword from Sumerian, and means "script, writing," only accidentally "inscription" on rock, stone or other objects. Xerx.Van: "the *stāna,* El. s.ta.na, i.e. stela was prepared, but no 'writing' written on it"; there, the El. text has ʳDIPⁱᵈ; here tip.pi.me, which makes the meaning collective [cf. cunki "king," cunkime "kingship"], unmistakably so because the El. text says "as it had never existed before." The writing is done "taị̂e.ikki, in a different fashion"; to this apparently OP. patišam corresponds, cf. Aw. patišå in *Nir.*101 "differing, heterogeneous" and in *Yt.*19,58 "contrarius." The king speaks in the whole paragraph of a general innovation, not only of the special case of copying the Behistun inscription. The El. text does not need to repeat "in other fashion," as the OP. text repeats patišam in 90, because it glosses it by ar.ri.ị̂a.wa —not an El. word, but transliteration of OP. "āryavā, in Aryan (language)," just as it glosses in §§62 and 63 Auramazdā by the illuminating "god of the Aryans, ᵈna.p ar.ri.ị̂a.na.m < OP. āryānām," gen.pl.—Thereby the language is determined as the same as the rock-inscription, and the innovation can only be the kind of script, tippime, and since the two materials are clay-tablets and leather, on which latter cuneiform was never used (while Aramaic appears on the tablets of Persepolis), the thing never done before was writing Old Persian in Aramaic script. A specimen of it is the fourth inscription on Darius' tomb, see *Altp.Inschr.* p.12, fig.6; another proof are the OP. words in the inscriptions of the three Artaxerxes in cuneiform, but transcribed from Aramaic spelling.

El. "halat-ukku, on bricks, clay-tablets" assures the restoration of OP. a[g]ura[vā]. The signs corresponding to ʳSUⁱᵈ, -]ᵃ vᵃsᵃtᵃ[-]y[- must hide the OP. word for leather, Mp. and Np. pōst.[5] To El. "his, name" correspond the signs tran-

[5] *Vid.*3,20 and 18,10 Aw. pąsta.(fraθah), *Frhg.Ēv.* (gen.) pąstahe, Pahl.transl. pōst, meaning "scalp."—Aw. ą is the doubled ligature ą<a+n, which went early out of use and which it replaces; whereas Aw. å is a ligature of a+v. At the time of the invention of Aw. script, n and v, especially in ligatures, are no longer clearly distinguished. Thus the difference between Aw. pąsta and OP. ⁺pᵃvᵃsᵃtᵃ is a graphic problem: the Aw. archetype had pvst in Aram.

scribed by King and Thompson by $n^a m^a$, Kent $h^a m^a$; it must be OP. n^a a m^a. El. "tallik, was written" = OP. √piθ-, ni.piθ-, gives [ni- or a- p]i[θ]i[ya].—The last sentence, "thereafter," speaks of the copies of the *Beh.* inscription being sent into all provinces, as an example.[6] The obscure verb a m χ m t a must mean "were able to understand" or "minded it in their hearts."

The introduction of Aramaic script made cuneiform soon go out of use, and the list of *Yt.*13 must have been transmitted by word of mouth only for at least 600 years, until it was first written down in Aramaic script together with the whole Awesta, unless one would assume that, at the time of Darius, an aide-mémoire had been noted in Aramaic. The names as we have them show clear traces of being based on a text in Aramaic script.

On the Ka'ba i Zardušt, a tomb-tower in front of the Royal Tombs and the sculpture of Shāhpuhr I at Naqsh i Rustam, is a trilingual inscription of Shāhpuhr, which solves the riddle of the list of *Yt.*13, and that is the importance, far surpassing its historical contents, of that inscription.

In the style of Assyrian foundation documents, thousand and more years older, in which likewise a long historical introduction occupies most of the space and the proper purpose is confined to the very last lines, the preface of Shāhpuhr's inscription is a detailed account of his victorious campaign against Valerian, which is symbolized in the triumphal sculpture opposite the Ka'ba. Only the middle lines, 21-23, deal with the special purpose, the foundation of five memorial fires. The expression is Pahl. pty LN 'rv'n v p'šn'm, Pārs. P'N LNH lvb'n v ptn'm, Gr. ΕΙΣ ΗΜΕΤΕΡΑΝ ΜΝΕΙΑΝ ΚΑΙ ΟΝΟΜΑΤΟΣ ΣΥΝΤΗΡΗΣΙΝ, "for his own soul (memory), and for the souls of the queen ĀδarAnāhīt, and their three sons Hormizd-Ardašīr (later Hormizd I), Šāhpuhr Mēšānšāh, and 'yly-mzdysn-Narsahe (later Narseh)." To these temples endowments for sacrifices and singing of masses are given, to perpetuate the memory, and the "souls" of those whose names are

script; the first transcription in Aw. characters used å to express the diphthong au; younger codd. used short ą instead (not a unique case); when this went out of use, long ą was noted.

[6] A stone fragment discovered in Babylon and the Pap.El. with a copy of the Behistūn inscription are documentary proof.

enumerated shall have part in it. The list of names of these souls fills the rest, ll.22-34.

Not the religious contents, but form and matter are the same as the dedication of stelae by the Elamite kings, e.g. ŠilhakInšušinak (about 1160 B.C.) "for his life, the life of Nahhunte.Utu, his wife, and the life of their sons HutelutušInšušinak, Šilhina.lamru.Lagamar, etc. etc. and her daughters Išni.karabbat etc. etc."[7] The list of names of *Yt.*13 is a link between the Elamite and the Sasanian lists, and establishes a tradition over more than 2,000 years. Shāhpuhr's list has 135 names, mostly of men, but thirteen ladies of the royal house and a few little girls are among them. The arrangement is (1) some ancestors in straight line, beginning with Sāsān χvatāy, some more living members of the narrowest family, still more younger members, among them children with hypocoristic names, the future. Upon which follow in historical order the great number (2) of "those that were under Pāpak Šāh," (3) "under Artaχšīr šāhānšāh," (4) "under Šāhpuhr šāhānšāh." The provisions are valid for the souls of them all. Inside these sections, the names are arranged according to rank and dignity; where the rank is the same, equal or similar names are often grouped together—for purposes of mnemonics; family names are borne only by the high aristocracy; besides, there are titles, among them e.g. the grand eunuch.

Comparing it with Islamic waqf inscriptions, which like this one are written on the walls of existing sanctuaries, and are excerpts of a document, the waqf-nāmah proper, deposited in archives, one can call the Ka'ba inscription a waqf, with such distinctions as required by the different cult. This is the notion which the Greek version of the inscription tries to express by *ἔγγραφον τοῦ ἀσφαλίσματος τῆς τειμῆς*. The mafātīḥ al-'ulūm rightly translate the Ir. term "rawānagān"—i.e. pa-ravān of the inscription—by auqāf: the Sasanian institution is the origin of the Islamic one. At the Achaemenian epoch, the originals were clay tablets, as for instance some found in Susa, or stone tablets like the fragments of Darius' tomb inscription discovered at Persepolis; also papyri.

The analogy between the Shāhpuhr inscription and the so-called "Community list" of *Yt.*13 is perfect. There, too, the majority of names

[7] P. Scheil, Mém.Dél. Perse XI, 21ss.

are such of men, but ten per cent are names of women; in the Ka'ba inscription they stand between the names of men, in *Yt*.13 they are in a separate paragraph; all the women belong to the highest nobility, with their family names added, most of them are married, but not all. In both documents the names extend over three generations, with a special group of children. The sequence is one of rank and dignity. In *Yt*.13, Zoroaster and his next relatives take precedence even over Vištāspa and his family. Within groups of equal rank one observes the same grouping of identical or similar names. Members of the same noble families, distinguished by their family name which none but a nobleman can have, are grouped together in both inscriptions, etc.

All persons in both lists are without exception high and highest dignitaries and their relatives, in old language "χšayant, kavi and hvētu." The 16 "aryaman, clients," form a kind of codicil in *Yt*.13. But neither here nor there "commoners" are mentioned, "vāstrya.fšuyant or hūti, peasants and laborers." That changes the concept of the "first community" considerably. This was not a community of people converted or of the same religious conviction, but the clan and the clientela of a vispatiš and satrap who had espoused a cause and whose lead all his clansmen, officers and clients were in duty bound to follow.

In spite of an interval of about 800 years, redaction and style of both lists are the same, and it follows that the list of *Yt*.13 is taken from the original of the waqf, the rawān-document, which was "made fast, Arab. waqafa or ḥabasa, OP. han.drang-, handraxta, han.dungā," when Vištāspa founded a memorial fire, with masses for the "souls," or "memory" of all persons named. The fact that Zoroaster and his relatives rank before Vištāspa shows that Vištāspa founded the temple "for the soul of Zoroaster and for his own soul," but also that Zoroaster was a "homótimos, of equal rank" with Vištāspa (see under 'Social Structure').

This was a temple like the one in which the cypress was planted. Kishmar lies close enough to Tōsa, the residence of Vištāspa, for them to be regarded as the same. But the legends of the great "ātaχš ē Varhrān or dynastic fires," viz. the āδar χvarrah or farnabag on the rōδita mountain, or the āδar burzēnmihr of Rēvand, both quite near Tōsa and Nīshāpūr, ascribe their foundation likewise to Vištāspa, and just as

Shāhpuhr founded five, the grand vizier Mihrnarseh three fires—among them a "fire of the cypress, sarwistān"—Vištāspa may have founded more than one fire at the same time. Firdausi identifies the Burzēnmihr fire with that of Kishmar.

The reason for incorporating the memorial list just in *Yt.*13 was not an intrinsic connection of ideas, but a matter of form. The names were recited by the priests at the masses with "We pray for the souls of. . . ." No yasht offered so perfectly fitting an occasion as this hymn to the heroes and manes. Both are "souls," the fravarti and the ruvan;[8] only the Zoroastrian term "ruvan" had to be replaced by the mazdayasnian "fravarti"; even the genitive case is the original form of the list (except for some names written without inflection).

Though preserved in a yasht, the list is a gathicissimum. It has the value of an inscription on a ruin of its period. It is composed by order of Vištāspa for Zoroaster. All its names—and that means all the names appearing in the Gatha and those which passed over into the Awesta—are real and historical. The date of this document, between the years 529 and 522, probably in 527 B.C., has been discussed under 'Chronology.'

The single names, therefore, are worth studying thoroughly. The following is only a beginning.

Among the brothers and cousins of Vištāspa is one ātarhvarnah. On the Persepolis tablet, dated "month ādukaniš, year 16 of Darius," i.e. April 506 B.C., one (El.) par.na.k.ka, i.e. (OP.) hvarnaka, (Gr.) Pharnakes, transmits to the chief of the archives, (El.) ke.so.pat.ti.s, OP. *gēθupatiš (Akk. gitepatu), the order of the king to slaughter a hundred sheep for (the celebration of the birth of) his daughter's daughter, duχθ^r^īš, Artystone (II). Cameron notes that the same Parnakka appears in a similar action on another tablet to which he apposed his seal: "Hvarnaka, son of Ršāma." In 506, the well known Ršāma was the father of Vištāspa and grandfather of Darius, who was still alive in 522 B.C.—It is he who uses, on his gold tablet, for the first time the gentilic "haχāmanišiya." A son of Darius and Artystone (I) was called after him (Her. III,88 and VII,69), evidently as the first great-

8 According to Benveniste's etymology "rvan<*vr̥.van, to √ var-," one should write urvan; the MMed. spelling is 'rv'n, MPers. rvb'n.

grandson, possibly born shortly after Ršāma's death. Artystone (II) is certainly called after her maternal grandmother whom Darius loved so much that he had a golden statue made of her (Her. VII,69). The name Ršāma goes on in the Achaemenid family: Arsames, governor of Egypt about 420, bears the title BR BYT', *vāisapuθra, on a parchment from Elephantine. Hvarnaka, son of Ršāma, is a brother of Vištāspa and uncle of Darius. His name is a hypocoristic of a compound in -hvarnah. The ātar.hvarnah of *Yt.*13 is also a brother of Vištāspa; cf. the case of Pišišyōθna, son of Vištāspa in *Yt.*13, and historic Pissouthnes, son of Hystaspes (II), under 'Nōtarya.' The conclusion is: the full name of Parnakka-Hvarnaka was ātar.hvarnah, and the ātar.-hvarnah of *Yt.*13 is the historical Pharnakes. Combining therewith a remark of Diodorus 31, 19,1 he was the brother-in-law of his cousin Cambyses I, and is the Pharnakes whom the kings of Pontus considered —unhistorically—as their ancestor. Pliny NH.33,151 tells of a silver statue of his.

Vistaroš in *Yt.*13,102 is gen. of the nom. "vis(a)taruš nōtaryāno," metrical formula of *Yt.*5,76. Wb. offers two unsatisfying Awestic etymologies, one of them: vi + √star- "bed-maker." He is placed in the line: Zoroaster-Vištāspa-Vistaroš-several great families, to which correspond in the list of women, §139, Hāugavī-Hutōsā-Vispatarušī-Frānī-Asabānā. The name, hence, is not a personal, but a family name, as are Frānya and Asabāna, and Vispatarušī is a sister or daughter of Vistaroš. One must read +visataruš and +visatarušī, Old Persian against Median "*vispa.tarvan and vispatarvarī, all-vanquisher."[9] Visatarušī does not mean "the all-vanquishing woman," but "lady Visataruš, née Visatarušī"; it is the fem. of the gentil. *visatarušya, derived from the nom. visataruš, like OP. haχāmanišiya from the nom. haχāmaniš, and Zoroaster's patr. vivahuša from the nom. *vivahuš of vivahvah. These neologisms belong all to the very same period of the language, and OP. haχāmanišiya is attested in the gold tablet of Ršāma just a few years before Gath. vivahuša and *Yt.*13 visatarušī. The name visataruš follows in *Yt.*13 that of Vištāspa's brother (called "brother" already by Chares of Mitylene) Zarivariš, and precedes Spantadāta and other sons

[9] With OP. visa against Med. vispa, as in visadahyuš and *visaδana (in El. wissatana) against Med. vispazana. -uši would be regular fem. of a stem in -vah, nom.m. -uš, but the gen.m. would be Aw. -ušo, not -oš. In OP., apparently, the -vah-stems had been transferred, from the nom. in -uš, into the u-class.

of Vištāspa; thus, he belongs to the generation of brothers and cousins of Vištāspa. In the Shāhnāmah the "nōtaryāno" became a "son of Nōδar" under the synonymous, equally OP. name Gustahm, Gr. 'Υσταίχμης < *visatahman "all-powerful." This name does not come from the Awesta, but may well be an immediate tradition of the epics and actually the personal name of the man who was "the visatarušya, vispatiš of that clan."

The second element of the name vaŋhu.δāta in 13,119 can be Med. dāta (Ar. *dhā-, in which τίθημι and δίδωμι coalesce); that would make the name a syn. of vahyazdāta, name of the second Pseudo-Smerdis in Behistūn. But the name of the father is χvaδāta, which does not mean "self-created," but "well-born," hence is OP. hv.āδāta = Med. hvāzātā, epithet of Ardvī in *Yt.*5,127 (Aw. √zan-, OP. √δan-, Gr. γίγνομαι). According to rules of IE. onomastics, names of sons and fathers contain identical elements; therefore vaŋhu.δāta is Old Persian, a synonym of the father's name hvāδāta, and corresponds to Med. *vahu.zāta, cf. VYZT' in Esther 9,9, i.e. vēzāta < *vahyazāta > NP. Behzāδ, a very frequent name: Eugene. In the same §119 the name of this family appears as "vaŋhu.δātayana, the Eugenians"; they were a noble Persian clan.—In *Beh.* §68, Darius does not give the family names of his six companions, but only their fathers' names. One of them, Bagabuχša, had a grandson of the same name who was married to Amytis, daughter of Xerxes and Amēstris, through her mother granddaughter of another companion, Otanes, Hutāna of *Beh.* §68; they had a grandson called Spitāma (see under 'Spitāma'). The father of Bagabuχša I is called OP. [- - - -]hyahya (gen.), El. ta.t.tu.wan.i̯a (nom.), Akk. za.'.tu.'.a. The striking variance of the El. and the Akk. forms assures restoration and etymology of the OP. name: [d a t v] h y,[10] δātavahya. The El. spelling shows the archaic OP. pronunciation δātovaŋhya, Akk. the contemporary Med. zātovēh, which has almost reached Med. zādōē (Syr.), NP.Arab. zādōy, zādveh. Ibn Khurdādhbih knows this to be title (or family name?) of the rulers of Sarakhs in Khurasan. OP. δātovahya is VYZT' (*Esther* 9,9), vahya.zāta > Behzād with elements transposed, and this is the original compound, an appellative "well-born, εὐγενής," while the transposition is only the product of rules governing the onomastics of proper names traditional in

[10] If the gap would allow one more sign: [d a t^{u} v] h y, read dāt^{u}vahya > *dāδvēh.

families. Thus, the name δātovahya reveals that the man belonged to a Persian family in which the OP. names hvāδāta, vahu.δāta, vahya.-δāta were hereditary, that means to the family called vaŋhu.δātayano in *Yt*.13,119.

By analogy one may connect another companion in *Beh.* §68, Ardumaniš ("straight-minded," to Gath. rzva) vahaukahya puθ^{r}a, son of Vahōka (Gr. Ὦχος, short form of a name with Vahu-) with *Yt*.13.108 vaŋhauš aršyahya puθro, Vahu-X, son of Aršya, (right-acting, -minded, to Gath. ršva).

At a prominent place, after Zoroaster's cousin Maδyomåha and Sēna Ahumstut, his so-called "apostles," before the three Frānya, his brothers-in-law, and before his sons, a pərəidiδaya is enumerated in §97. Bartholomae attempted an Awestic etymology also of this name, which is evidently Old Persian: paridēδiya with OP. diδā against Med. dizā.[11] It is equivalent to Firdausī, and in view of its adjectival form, a name of family or provenance rather than a proper name.

Other Persian names are e.g. rta.rvēθa in §116, against Med. -rvēsa, √*vrik-.[12] Arava.uštra, i.e. ⁺arva.uštra, against Med. arvat.aspa. Also the name of the Hāugava avāra.uštri is OP., in the most likely case that avāra- hides a participle stem. Zoroaster as well as Vištāspa have many Persians in their closest surroundings. This observation extends, as we shall see later, to the Hāugava and the Vēhviya. And the study of the names of foreigners in §§125-26 shows people really unexpected in that circle and gives an indication that Vištāspa himself—though his name is purely Median—must have been a Persian.

Not counting Sēna, there are seven names of provenance which must, from the beginning, be understood as ethnics, not as gentilicia.

The first is muža from the mužayå dahyauš, then a rōžd(i)ya and a tan(i)ya from the countries of the same name. In the entire Iranian area nothing resembles the last two names but there are similar names in the Far West. rōždiya is apparently formed from *ružd, *ruzd, as Aw. tōžiya from *tuč. This ruzd must present a foreign local name; r may replace l, zd dd, thus Lydia, Ass. luddi, and Rhodos are to be

[11] Cf. *Art.II.Sus.*: ǰ^{i} i v d^{i} i y p r d y d m, i.e. MPers. pardēδ, in Aram. script prdyd, transposed into cuneiform. Gr. parádeisos < Med. paridēza.

[12] Cf. the OP. orthography of rviθyati, with θ for s, in *Purs*. 56.

considered.[13] Lydia is represented in OP. inscriptions by the name of its capital Sardis: Sparda, cf. *Isa.* 60,9; 66,19: Taršīš Φουδ and Lūd; or *Chron.* 1,7: rōdānīm. Tanis is, in Herodotus, Strabo and Ptolemy, the capital of the nomos of the same name at the "Tanitic" mouth of the Nile, not far from Suez, and must have been known to Iranians since the time of Cambyses.

For mužaya two explanations are possible. The name of Egypt, Arab. Miṣr, in the OP. inscriptions is mudraya, Akk. miṣir (nom. miṣru), El. mucir (c may be palatal). The vowel u in OP. and El. expresses the darkening of i before Semitic emphatic consonants.[14] d is no real rendering of Sem. s; it is the group dr that renders ṣr. In *NiR*.d, the OP. equivalent of Aw. vazra, in *vaδra.bara is spelled v θ^r (b r). OP. cuneiform has no sign for δ^r, but the phonetic development tr > θr > θ^r > ss demands the parallel dr > δr > δ^r > zz. The OP. notation vaθ^ra means vaδ^ra, and mudraya means spoken *muδ^raya, *muzzaya, and Aw. mužaya renders this OP. pronunciation of the name of Egypt in Awestic characters.[15]

But Aw. ž is a sign invented only in the 4th century A.D. on account of oral tradition; the written archetype had no sign for it, but expressed č, ǰ and ž by Aram. š. Therefore, mužaya is mudraya if the oral tradition was right. Otherwise, another way is open. The region on the Indian Ocean, old Magan, is called maka, adj. mačiya in the inscriptions, but Scylax of Caryanda (source of Hecataeus and Herodotus) wrote, in the very years of the memorial list, mykoi, with y = ū, of which the adjective would be *mučiya. The vowel is justified in such aboriginal names, as Kaššu: kuššu, Qardū: Qurṭi, Amman: Umman etc. Thus the equation would be: maka: mačiya = mykoi: *mučiya, and the archet. notation for *mučiya would be the same as for Aw. mužaya: mvšy.

A little farther down in the list follows a Puδa: akayaδa puδānām. Aw. δ renders archet. t: PVT,[16] i.e. OP. pūta, adj. pūtiya, Akk. pūṭa,

[13] Cf. *Shahp. Ka'ba,* Pahl.l.10: rvt?'s = Gr. Λυδια (not Rhodos).

[14] Cf. mod. Arab. måṣr, also ḥömṣ < ḥimṣ, Emesa.

[15] Cf. Aw. sāθra hāmaχšaθra, instead of sāsθra in *Yt.*10,109 and 111, title of the commander in chief of all Iranian armies, which may be OP. θāsθ^ra > θāsa transposed into Awestic with s for OP. θ and θr for OP. sθ^r.

[16] as in būδi: būti; rūδi: rōtah; harδi: harta. Some more examples will soon be given. Archet. t causes the frequent unetymological change between t, θ and δ in Aw. notations, cf. *Grdr.* §268, 50 and 51.

Punt, the frankincense country, see zrayo pūtikam under 'Sea.' The inhabitants were partly Arabs, partly negroes, and the man may have been a black eunuch of Vištāspa. In the Ka'ba inscription, too, the grand eunuch of Shāhpuhr, Pārs. 'ndlyk'n srd'r, Pahl. drykn š'kn?, Gr. ΤΟΥ ΕΠΙ ΤΩΝ ΔΡΙΓΑΝΩΝ is mentioned. His proper name, in that case, ought to belong to the sphere of names of jewels like lu'lu', yāqūt, kāfūr, and akayaδa,[17] i.e. 'KYT resembles indeed Gr. *ἰάκινθος*, Arab. yāqūt.[18]

Between mužaya and rōždiya stand two pairs, fraturå asrutå bēšatasturå and 'vrgvš rzvtv ōiγmatasturahe. With these two exceptions, all of the 16 or 17 foreigners have their indispensable ethnic, two of them only the ethnic, two ethnic and patronym, two ethnic and names of father and grandfather, two ethnic and name of the clan.

The first pair of names is preserved in the archaic form of a gen. dual[19] "of the two bēšatasturå," which can only be a term of profession or an ethnic. The following pair, on the contrary, has singularic form, hence "of the 'v. (son) of rz., of the ōiγmatastur(a)." Here the long word could be a personal name; but since its second element is the same as in the foregoing case where it cannot be a personal name, this is ruled out and one must detach -stura or -tura as the indispensable ethnic. The s may be the initial of the ethnic or a rest of the case-ending of the foregoing word, but probably it is a sandhi s, introduced when the foregoing words, written without inflection, were considered as first elements of a compound.

Bēšata and ōiγmata are clear, and interesting words. bēšata, archet. BYŠT, with t for δ: OP. bēšaδa, Med. bēšaza, OI. bheṣajá "physician." The Achaemenids had several Greek physicians, e.g. Apollonides of Cōs and Ctesias; in the Sasanian period they used to be Syrians, like Gabriel of Singara under Xusrau II; their title was drustpet. Here the foreign physicians apparently bear Iranian names which can only be

17 not "a.kayaδa, nicht mit der (non-existing) kayaδa-Sünde behaftet?". kayaδa is KYT = kēta.

18 or Gr. *ὑάκινθος*; Aram. yqvnt' > yqvnd, whence Pahl. y'knd, NP. yākand; today replaced by Arab. yāqūt. Cf. change of initial in Akk. [aban]ašpu or ịašpu, Arab. yašp, jaspis, jasper; and Akk. [aban]asmur, Eg. j s m r, Arab. sāmūr, Gr. *σμύρις*, Germ. schmirgel, emery.

19 Ending -å of a cons.-stem, hence not simply fratura-, asruta-. The ending of bēšatasturå, contrasting with the thematic inflection of the gen.sg. ōiγmatasturahe, means likewise a gen. dual.—Bartholomae took it as gen.sg. only because he did not doubt that the word was a patronym.

assumed or bestowed, and do not reveal the nationality of the bearers. An example is Daniel with his Babylonian honorific (Nabū)balāṭsu-uṣur, Beltshazar.

ōiγmata is Aw. interpretation of archet. VYGMT. γmata is part.perf. pass. of √gam- "come"; the prev. vi- is not attested and not likely to be used with √gam-. The archaic OP. name vahyazdāta in *Beh.* §68 is rendered in El. by wi.s.ta.t.ta, Akk. wi.iz.da.a.ta, both trisyllabic, Pap.El. 62 and 56 Aram. VYZDT hence pronounced in 520 B.C. vēzdāta.[20] The book Esther writes VYZT' for vahyazāta. Aram. typty < *θahyapati, chief of heralds, shows likewise -ahya-> ē. Ctesias translates Οἴβαρας by ἀγαθάγγελος, hence *vahya.bara, pronounced before 400 vēbara, with deriv. *vāhyabari > MP. vāvarīk "evangelic."[21] Wherever, after 520 B.C. proper names with vahya- are not spelled vēh-, vē-, the spelling is historical.

If the Pap.El. render in the *Beh.* inscription vahyazdāta by VYZDT, and *vēhva.δana by VYVDN (see under 'Vēhviya'), then VYGMT of the memorial list is *vahya.γmata. Gath. vahu āgmata in *Y.*44,8 is the greeting "welcome!" (see under 'Welcome'). Now, γmata, the part. perf. of √gam-, which enters into the name of the town hangmatāna, is a form strictly limited to west Iranian dialects, Median and Old Persian. One needs only to insert vahu.āγmata and vahya.γmata in Tedesco's "Dialectologie" 229-232:

I. Persis:	OP. *γmata in parāgmata, hangmata, MP.NP. ā.maδ name of town han.gmatāna
II. Media:	capital *angmatāna, in Akk. ag(a)matana, El. akmatana, Herodot agbatana, with Med. psilosis
	Aw. γmata; Gath. vahu.āgmata; *Yt.*13 *vahya.γmata > ōiγmata
	Centr. and Casp. dialects all < *γmata, but Kurd. and Bal. dialects all < *āγata.
III. East Iran:	Sak., Soghd., Pāmir, all < *āγata or āχt.
	*γmata is lacking in all East Iranian dialects.

[20] The sandhi z shows that this -dāta is Med. dāta, IE. *dhā-.

[21] Cf. Ptolemy's *οἰχαρδας* < vāikrta. The Elamites, too, transcribe Ir. āi by oi, e.g. θāigrčiš: soikrcis. The darkened pronunciation of OP. āi, hence, is real; it explains the Awestic alternance ē: oi. Cf. also vifra: ōifra. Vice versa: the Arabs render the NP. termination -ōy by -waih.

As name of a foreigner (in an Awestic, i.e. Median text), vēγmata, like the word bēšaδa, can only be Old Persian. The fact that physicians in ordinary have an OP. title, and that foreign clients assume OP. names —or receive them as honorifics—proves the nationality of their employer, not their own: the ethnic tvr- must not be Iranian at all, but *Vištāspa must be a Persian.*

The name "vahya.gmata, welcome" and its type is not attested as n.pr. of an Iranian. MP. Behāmaδ < *vahya.āγmata, it is true, corresponds exactly to vēgmata, but appears only among the many names of the three magi, into which also other names of the memorial list intruded, in the group Behāmaδ, Zūdāmaδ and Drustāmaδ,[22] all three synonyms of the greeting "welcome!" and all three philosophical inventions.—On the contrary, such names are common among all Semitic peoples. The oldest are theophoric, with the name of the god Šulmānu, Šalamānu, Šalāmu, Šalim; but the verb is the general word for greeting. The type of names is most frequent among Jews (cf. Solomon and Jerusalem). Vēgmata may well be the translation of such a Semitic name, and tvr may hide the name of a Semitic country. In the *Shahr.Ēr.* §57, s.v. Nūn-Nineveh, the prophet Daniel, balāṭsuṣur > balāturuš, is called a "tūra," from an original aθūra. This name, Assur of old, had become the name of the satrapy "Syria and Mesopotamia" under Achaemenian administration. Thus, "tura" may be "Syrian" in that meaning, from an original aθūra. It may also designate the town Tyrus, Ṣōr, through an Aramaic intermediary.[23]

22 In Bar Bahlūl, cf. Markwart, UGE II,13, "Names of the Magi."

23 If -tura is "Syrian," since this name includes Palestine, the Vēgmata-Solomon and the physician may have been Jews, and Vištāspa, protector of Zoroaster, would have had a Jewish physician in ordinary like many princes since. It was not even necessary to get him from Jerusalem. Jews lived in Gozan, the Rās al-'ain region, since the time of the Assyrian captivity. TiglathPileser III and Sargon exiled some men of conquered territories: two officials of Gozan, in a letter to an Assyrian king, are possibly Jews, cf. H. G. May, Bibl.Archeologist VI,1943,55-60, *Cuneif. Texts from Kannu in Mesopotamia, about 700 B.C.* The Jewish colony of Ctesiphon, the māqōm Kāspiya, from which Ezra got Levites for Jerusalem, goes back to the foundation of that "castrum" by Cyrus, when he conquered Opis in 539 B.C.

According to Moses of Chorene, Artaxerxes III Ochos, settled Jews in Hyrcania. The source of this note is, with Markwart, *Ērānš.* 137 and 142, *Fundam. Isr. u. Jüd.Geschichte* 30, a passage of the Armenian Eusebius, preserved in Syncellus, which he reconstructed as: *Ὦχος ἀποδαμόν τινα Ἰουδαίων αἰχμάλωτον ἑλὼν Ὑρκανίᾳ κατῴκισε πρὸς τῇ Κασπίᾳ θαλάσσῃ.* This is assured by two signatures on the acts of the Council of 424 A.D.: "Aëtius, bishop of the šebītā of Balāshfarr, and Domitianus, bishop of the šebītā of Gurgān," in Sachau, *Verbreitung d. Christentums.* Balāshfarr, Gr. *Βολογεσίφορα*, was built (Ḥamza,56:) "by Balāsh [i.e. the Arsacid Volagases] at the side of Ḥulwān, called Balāshfarr." The Jewish colony of Ḥulwān, mod. Sarpul, existed down to recent times, and was regarded, at an early period, as Ḥalaḫ in *II.Reg.*17,6, place of the

Another name, which like bēšaδa indicates a special office and like Pūta belongs geographically to the lands at the Indian Ocean, is khrkāna. Aw. khrka, OP. krka means "cock." In the OP. inscriptions it is the name given to the Carians, but not those at the southwest corner of Asia Minor who were subjects of the empire since 545 B.C., but those called Bannēšu in *Xerx.Pers.daiv.,* the crew of the Persian fleet who, along with the Yōna, Ionian sailors, transported the building materials to Susa. This was done by the fleet under the command of their admiral, Scylax of Caryanda, a Carian. Bannēšu is no ethnic, but the name of the "Carian villages" which Alexander visited and where he founded an Alexandria, later Charax Spasinou, on the bank of the Shaṭṭ al-'Arab opposite Baṣra, see under 'Navigation.'

The name of the Khrkāna of *Yt.*13 is hufravāχš, HVPRV'XŠ,[24] which may render a foreign, e.g. a Greek name like Ὑπε(ι)ροχος[25] or a Carian name in -ax; cf. *φύλαξ* "watch-dog." In this document no galley slaves or sailors can appear; the Carian was the chief of the colony, an admiral, nāvapatiš, like the Carian captains of the "Ship-building Papyrus" and Scylax. In the inscriptions, the Carians -Krkā always occupy the last place; so does the khrkāna in the document.

Under Cambyses, at the very time of our document, Scylax was commander of the navy. "skylax" means "dog." He explored for Darius, before 515 B.C., the navigability of the Indus and the Indian Ocean as far as Suez, also the northern coast of the Mediterranean as far as the Pillars of Hercules, and, besides, in a few fragments preserved, he described the Black Sea and the Caspian, and the countries Parthava and Hvārazmiš. He must have been in Tōsa, the capital of Parthava. A remark on shipbuilding material in the Armenian mountains (see under 'Navigation') shows that he was there before

"captivity" of Salmanassar IV, and this entailed the wrong identification, e.g. in the Acts of S. Pethion, of the Diyala with the river Gōzan. Both the šebītā are no unknown Christian, but Jewish "captivitates," used by the bishops as local names. The Eusebius passage, hence, is historical, and its source is, as has been surmised, the book περὶ Ἰουδαίων, wrongly attributed to Hecataeus of Abdera, in reality composed about 100 B.C. Cf. E. Jacoby in Pauly RE VII,2766-68, and E. Meyer, ***Christentum*** II, 24ff.

24 Not a genitive, but a form without inflection. *Wb.* explains "bene mentulatus," which might be an Arab laqab, but is impossible as an Iranian assumed or honorific name. Of course other Ir. etymologies are possible.

25 In view of Gr. Apollonia, MP. 'PLVNY,' Syr. 'BRVMY' (Theodor bar Kōnē), Arab. afrūniyya, Hellenistic name of Sitakene and its capital Sitake, hvprv'xš could also contain Gr. Apollo, with hu- for a-, as vice versa Gr. a- for Ir. hu-.

Darius' accession, at the very time when Vištāspa resided there and gave Zoroaster asylum. Scylax seems to have lived till 480 B.C. Caryanda may have been his or his father's home. Living in the Carian colony at the Gulf would have qualified him specially for his great exploration. Perhaps Scylax "dog" was a popular surname. In the script of the Aw. archetype this name would appear as 'SKVR'xš. There must have been some relation between him and the HVPRV'xš of the document, perhaps that of father and son.

The investigation of the names of foreigners reveals with different degree of probability the occurrence of Rhodos or Lydia (rōždiya), Egyptians (taniya and mužaya), Abyssinians (pūta), Syrians or town Tyros (tura), Carians (khrkāna). A strong confirmation of the single equations is their being grouped together. In the OP. inscriptions correspond the satrapies: *Beh.* 4-5 aθūra-arbāya, 6 mudraya, 7 tyē drayahya (Ionian islands and Cyprus), 8 sparda (Lydia), and in a codicil at the end 23 maka. In *Pers. e:* 5-6 arbāya-aθūra, 7 mudraya, 10 sparda, 12 yōnā tyē drayahya, and 25 maka. In *NiR* 17-18 aθūra-arbāya, 19 mudraya, 22 sparda, 23 yōnā (incl. Cyprus, Rhodos) and at the end 27 pūtiya, 9 mačiya, 30 krka. Finally *Xerx.daiv.* 14 sparda, 15 mudraya, 16 yōna of the islands, 18 mačiya, 19 arbāya, and at the end 28 pūtāyā, 29 krka. The horizon of the document is the same as that of the inscriptions: the Persian empire.

III. HOUSE SPITĀMA

صلى الله عليه وعلى آله الطيّبين الطاهرين

Zoroaster bears the gentilic Spitāma, MP. Spitāmān. This is probably the short-form of a compound name, and the only known one is Spitamenes, *spitamanah. These names are to each other as Arsames, Ršāma to Arsamenes, ršmanah.[1]

The Spitāma must have been a great family, for they bear a second gentilicium hēčataspāna. They were an historical family, because their name occurs in Greek as well as in Babylonian literature. The business documents of Murašū Sons of Nippur, the greatest banking firm of their period, which conducted money affairs for Darius II and Parysatis, mention a ^{lu}iš.pi.ta.am.mu.[2] This is the exact time when Ctesias also speaks of them. He was told at the court, at the end of the 5th century, that Amytis, daughter of the last Median king, Astyígās, whose dowry was the whole of Media, had first married the Spitamas, and later Cyrus.

It must have been a well known fact that Astyages had no male heirs, else the Median pretenders, Fravartiš in *Beh.*24 and Čiθrantaχma in §53, would have claimed descent from him instead of Cyaxares. The daughter was the heiress, and Cyrus married her for legitimating his succession.

Ctesias heard his stories from the ladies of the court and thus got a truly Persian presentation of the facts. The Iranian legend kept the memory of the marriage of Nebuchadnezzar with the Median princess in the reversed, more flattering form: Θrētōna asked three daughters of Nebuchadnezzar in marriage for his three sons; and the fact of the conquest of Niniveh under the form: "Nūn came to KaiKavāt [the founder of the Median dynasty] by marriage." Tu felix Austria nube! Behind these distortions of history is the idea that, who is not an agnate, āzāta, must at least legitimate himself by affinitas, as son-in-law, an idea which comes down from the matriarchal past of the country and survived to the present time.

[1] Lommel: "spita.ama, mit heller Kraft"; Duchesne, §201, against it: nowhere attested as foursyllabic; tentatively "Skr. amáti, à l'éclat brillant." I assume short form of a fuller name.

[2] "The Museum," Publ. of the Bab.Sect. II,1, *Business Documents of Murashū Sons of Nippur, dated in the reign of Darius II,* by A. T. Clay, publ. by the Univ.Mus., Philadelphia, 1912.

The name Amytis may be, but is not of necessity historical. In Berossos' story, the name 'Αμυίτη, of the wife of Nebuchadnezzar, is historical: for her he built the "Hanging Gardens" the substructure of which has been excavated in Babylon. Amyíte-Humāyā (see under 'Nōtarya') was the name of ladies of the Median house, as later of Achaemenids, and the two families were related by marriage.

The name of Zoroaster's parents does not appear in the memorial document, so they died probably before that time. Yet, as Visatahma may be the proper name of "the Visatarus̆," so Spitrasp may have been the proper name of "the Spitāma." The mother's name appears only once in an ungrammatical fragment of the *Hat.Nask*: Dugdōvā, MP. Duγdāv. It sounds archaic and mythical, and, since married ladies were called with their family name only, must not be historical, no more than Amytis. A story in Tabari III,1632 is instructive: "Ibn Shujā' al-Balkhi told: I was with the emir (Muhammad the Tahirid) who quietly talked with me while he was listening to the curses upon every member of his family (shouted by a mob besieging his palace in Baghdad). When they came to the name of his mother, he laughed and said: I wonder how they come to know the name of my mother, even among the slave-girls of my father, abul l-'Abbās 'Abdallāh b. Ṭāhir, there were many that did not know it! I said: O prince, I have never seen a cooler and more forbearing spirit than yours! He replied: And I certainly have never seen anything more efficient than patience with men!"

Ctesias was told that Astyages' daughter had two sons from the Spitamas, Spitakes and Megabarnes. The first name is, like the family name, a short form of Spitamanah; the second is baga.hvarnah,[3] a decidedly non-Zoroastrian name. These two Spitāma would have been Astyages' heirs and successors to the throne. Ctesias regards them as half-brothers of Cambyses and Smerdis, and hence makes them receive satrapies when Cyrus settled the succession. Spitakes would have received the satrapy of the Derbissoi, i.e. the darwīshs,[4] whose country he seems to locate towards India, while it was adjacent to Hyrcania and Parthava. Megabarnes is said to have received the Barkanioi=

[3] Ctesias writes β, where others, in this case Xenophon, have φ.

[4] *Δερβισσοι* or Τερ°; elsewhere *Δερβικες*, *Δερβικκαι*, *Δροπικοι* (Her. I,125), i.e. OP. *drivika, adj. *drivičiya or *drvičiya, from "drigu, poor." When assuming a compound, as Markwart does, *Gāth.Ušt.*14, the second element would be √īs-, "poor in property."

Hyrcanians.[5] On all four, obeisance to their mother is imposed: One all but hears the ladies telling the story.

Like most things Ctesias wrote, this settlement of Cyrus' succession is considered to be unhistorical, and Markwart tried to prove it so in UGE. It is proved to be historical by the strange word *πατιζείθης*, i.e. paθyāzāta "heir presumptive, Germ. Neben-Agnat" (see under 'Magophonia'), which Herodotus quotes erroneously as name of the Pseudo-Smerdis, but which can only be the title of the true Smerdis. Whether the half-brothers received any satrapies, and which ones, cannot be checked, but it would be the most natural thing that their mother insisted on their being indemnified for having lost, by her second marriage, the succession to the throne, and the whole settlement has an analogy in the succession of the caliph al-Mutawakkil, by which the two elder designated sons divided almost the whole empire between them, while the third received a small territory only.

The half-brother relationship is not disproved by the fact that Cambyses and Smerdis were sons of Cassandane, daughter of Pharnaspes, and not of the Astyigas daughter, as Ctesias believed. Cambyses and Gōmāta as Pseudo-Smerdis both marry Atossa, hence were not sons of her mother. They do so, because she was by her mother the heiress, agnate, a granddaughter of Astyages. The Atossa-Hutōsā of the Awesta is called āzātā, and Darius, in order to prove his claim to the succession, says: "of old we were āδāta, agnates." Thus Ctesias shifts the relationship only in an unessential point: the two Spitāma as well as Cambyses and Smerdis were half-brothers of Atossa.

The traditional date of Zoroaster leaves some margin: the second marriage of Astyigas' daughter was contracted in 550 B.C. after the conquest of Agbatana. If born before 569, Zoroaster could be the first husband, Ctesias' Spitamas; if after 569, her son Spitakes. A man designated by the gentilicium alone must be regarded as the vispatiš of the house, hence Spitamas as "the Spitāma," and therefore Zoroaster rather as Spitakes, the "viso puθro, heir of the family Spitāma, the younger Spitāma." On the other hand, the mention of a grandson, Rvatatnara aparazāta, in the document of *Yt.*13, certainly before 522,

[5] *Βαρκάνιοι* < *vārkaniya, vrddhi of vrkāna, as vārθragni: vrθragna. cf. *Στιβοίτης*, Ziboetis < *stuvi.vati, in Diodor and Curtius, from a historian of Alexander. Trogus from Ctesias: Soebares < **Σιαβαρσας*, syāva.ršā. Against Wackernagel's remark, *Stud. Indo-Iran. Geiger* 230, to *Βαρζάνης*: "in the 4th century B.C. Gr. *β* could not serve as rendering of Ir. v."

probably about 527 B.C., prevents us from lowering the date 569 considerably. Cyrus' marriage to the Median heiress was a political one; she was no longer young. If she was born in 585, Zoroaster, born about 569, may be her son of the first husband, and Atossa, born soon after 549, her daughter of the second husband.

Another Spitamas appears in Ctesias, *Pers.* 38-40, under Artaxerxes I. Amytis, daughter of Xerxes and Amēstris, full sister of Artaxerxes I, whom Dinon calls the most beautiful and most unbridled woman of Asia, was married to Bagabuχša II, Megabyzos of Xerxes' campaign against Greece, of the family Vaŋhuδātayana (see under 'Mem.Doc.'). Having subdued Egypt in 455, he became satrap of Syria, but revolted in that vast province, and defeated a first army sent against him under Usiris, and a second under Menostates. The latter was the son of Artar(e)ios, i.e. Akk. Artarēwa, father of Manuštana, "mār bīti šarri, royal prince," in 431-424, a half-brother of Artaxerxes. After the defeat of his son, Artarēwa opened negotiations which Amēstris persuaded her son, the king, to approve. Thus an envoy was sent to Bagabuχša. The poorly preserved text of Ctesias says: *πέμπεται οὖν* Ἀρταρ[ε]ῖος *τε αὐτὸς καὶ* Ἄμῦτις *ἡ γυνὴ καὶ* Ἀρτοξάρης *ἐτῶν ἤδη ὢν εἴκοσι καὶ* Πετήσας *ὁ* Οὐσίριος *καὶ* Σπιτάμα *πατήρ.*

As it stands, this is impossible. That Artarēwa heads the mission is natural, and also Petēsas was welcome, because his father Usiris, though defeated, had been a friend of Bagabuχša. Amytis went with the mission, hence had not been with her husband in Damascus, but with her brother at Susa. But the two remarks regarding Artoxares and Petēsas are utterly senseless. Artoxares was the name of a Paphlagonian eunuch of Darius II, often mentioned by Ctesias (*Pers.* §§49-53) and as Artaḫšāra in the same business documents from Nippur, where the Spitāma, too, is mentioned, between 443 and 420. Eunuchs were sent on diplomatic missions, but not when they were "already 20 years old" and had no experience at all. And there is not the slightest reason to tell that Usiris' son, a rather young man, was father of a child Spitāma. Moreover, the "*καὶ*" is stylistically objectionable. Obviously Ctesias said "already 20 years old and father of a son Spitāma." Somebody who saw the eunuch in the name Artoxares separated therefore the fathership and attributed it to Petēsas. In reality Artoxares—the name is probably corrupt—is not the eunuch, but was a son of Bagabuχša and Amytis, and Ctesias adds this remark thinking that Amytis, whom her father Xerxes, as he tells, had lectured many times, did not change her way of life even as a grandmother. With the two envoys—both friends of Bagabuχša—came the family, the wife with son and grandson, in order to show that one was serious and did not retain the family as hostages. Spitāma was the name of a grandson of Bagabuχša, a Vanhudātayana, whose own paternal grandfather, as the maternal grandfather of his wife, had been companions of Darius. These families were also related by marriage to the Spitamas: Bagabuχša's mother seems to have been a Spitāmī.

In the Gatha and the Awesta the following members of the Spitāma appear:

Purušaspa + Dugdōvā (brother)	Arastiya
|	
Zoroaster (cousin)	Maδyomåha
|	
sons: Isatvastra, Rvatatnara, Hvarčiθra (in *Y*.53,2 "a son of Zoroaster"), daughter: Puručistā (*Y*.53,2: "youngest daughter")	Rtastū
|	
Rvatatnara aparazāta	Maδyomåha aparazāta

In the memorial document there are, besides, a Θrimiθwant "triplet" and "dēvatbiš, hater of the dēva" without degree of relationship.

The old messianic belief in the return of the prophet after 6,000 years was the reason that the religious tradition of the following periods transferred the sons of Zoroaster entirely into eschatologic legend. In this literature many generations of descendants are enumerated, but none of the names is otherwise known. But as the Babylonian documents are a testimony for the early history of the Spitāma, so two Sasanian documents are testimonies for their late period. Those are two bullae of the office of the magus of Nihawand, in my collection, which beside the official seal bear the personal seal of the magus, the judge himself, a small male bust with the legend:

Zartuχšt ē magū ē Spitāmān
Zoroaster, the magus, of the Spitāma.

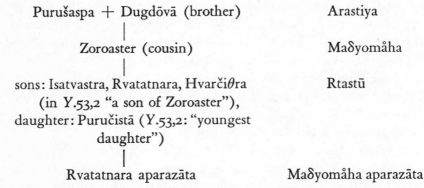

The date is about A.D. 500. After a thousand years, a descendant may have been qāḍī of Nihawand, just as many Ṭālibids have been and are still qāḍī, or as an Umayyad, ibn Abī l-shawārib, was qāḍī al-quḍāt under al-Mu'tazz and al-Musta'īn. But without claim nobody could bear that family name; to prevent it was the duty of the "āyīnpet, or naqīb al-ashrāf."

The name Zoroaster, in antiquity, is known to us only as that of the prophet. It is attested by a graffito on the wall of the Mannaean rock-tomb of Fakhrīka, in Aramaic script of the same character as the script of the Darius tomb and the Elephantine papyri: זרתוש i.e. z r t v š [t r].[6] Whether the graffito means the name of the writer simply or the prophet, at any rate, the name was known in Media in about 500 B.C. Earlier, in the detailed account of Sargon's eighth campaign [Thureau-Dangin], we find a chief ^{P}za.ar.du.uk.ku ša ^{al}Ḫa.ar.-zi.a.nu; in the "broken prism A" [H. Winckler, II,pl.44,29] we read ^{P}ḫa.ar.du.uk.ku ša ^{mat}Ḫa.ar.zi.a.nu, with ḫa as clerical error for za. The notation in the original ephemerids was certainly d/tuk for du.uk. ḫarzianu is mod. Harsīn,[6a] SE of Kirmānshāhān, not far from Bīstūn. The personal name is an archaic hypocoristic in -ukku of a Median, beginning with zarat-; the only known name is zaraθuštra, but one may assume *zarat.aspa.

The unsolved problem of the etymology of the name has shifted by the discovery of MP. z r h v š t.[7] The Aw. archet. was *z r t v š t r, as on the graffito, four-syllabic; in the fourth century A.D., with respect to oral tradition, this was throughout rendered by zaraθuštra. MMed. zrhvšt, confirmed by zarhušt of the Mss. of ibn al-Faqīh, proves the θ to be phonetically genuine. On the other hand, one cannot doubt that zaraθ- is a participle stem. Therefore one must assume -t.v->-θv->-θu-

[6] See J. de Morgan, Mission en Perse IV, *Rech.Archéol.* p.298, fig.176, "tombeau d'Endirkach"; older authors call it Fakhraka. A. Houtum-Schindler gave me the correction Fakhrīqa for Fakhraka; Farmān Farmā, who owned estate in that region, said "andarγāč or andar.aqāč" for Endirkach; his son, Muhammad Husain Mirza said Dilmaqān for Dilmān (near Salmās).

[6a] Usual modern spelling, but as careful an observer as the botanist Haussknecht wrote Herzīn.

[7] In Henning, *Mir.Man.*III.—Excepting Markwart, *Gāth.Ušt.*22f., recent etymologies—cf. Duchesne, *Comp.av.* §§213 and 239—take the second element as Med. "uštra, camel," and the first zarat- as weak grade participle, deriving MP.NP. zartuχšt, zardušt directly from zaraθuštra, without attaching importance to the spelling with θ.

in the joint of composition: zaraθuštra < *zaratvaštra.[8] Markwart recognized this even before knowing the MMed. form.

In the identical case of the names isaṭ.vāstra, frādaṭ.vanhu, χšayaṭ.vaχš the Awesta text notes not *θ*, but ṭ, which differs in function only, not in sound from t. Therefore, zaraθuštra is only a uniform spelling, consistently used in the Gatha and the Awesta for the name of the prophet; otherwise, the spelling should be *zaraṭ.uštra.

Opposed to this form there are two Greek ones: *Ζαθραύστης* and *Ζω/οροάστρης*.[9] Whatever their distribution among the oldest Greek authors may have been—*Ζωροάστρης* was soon generally accepted—they render real forms of the name which were heard independently, at least three times, at the beginning of the fourth century B.C.

Ζαθραύστης appears only in Diodor I,94: *παρὰ μὲν γὰρ Ἀριανοῖς Ζαθραύστην ἱστωροῦσι τὸν ἀγαθὸν δαίμονα προσποιήσασθαι τοὺς νόμους αὐτῷ διδόναι*. Whereas the note on Oxyartes and Ninus in Bactria, in II,6, comes from Ctesias, this passage must have another source. Markwart assigned it to Megasthenes, about 300 B.C.; but the expression *ἀγαθὸς δαίμων* for AhuraMazdāh connects it closely with the remarks made by Eudemus and Eudoxus, pupils of Plato and Aristotle.[10] The r of the last syllable may have been dropped in Greek before it disappeared in Iranian, and *Ζαθραύστης*, either *zarθaušta or *zaraθaušta, belongs to zaraθuštra > z r h v š t.

But *Ζωροάστρης* is too old to reflect the phonetic change *θ* > h. The difference is not one of time but of dialect. In the Achaemenid royal names, dāraya and χšaya are weak grade participles, same as Aw. dārayat, χšayat. OI. kṣayád; the fading away of the final dentals characterizes the OP. dialect.[11]

8 vaštra perhaps thematic for vaštar, as in Med. huvaχštra, n.pr. Cyaxares and epithet of Vrthragna, cf. awyaχštra, *patiyaχštra > bitaχš.

9 Cumont, Messina and Markwart cite *Ζαραθρούστης* and *Ζωροθρύστου* from commentaries to poems of Gregor Nazianzen (about A.D. 360) in Cosmas of Jerusalem (about A.D. 743), and Markwart assumes for them a Makedonian source. A recently discovered TPārs. zrdrvšt confirms the forms, but this is a secondary MP. development, and the source must be the MP. original of the *Χρήσεις Ὑστάσπου*, made known to the West by Lactantius, beginning of 4th century, also known to Ammian Marc.

10 Cf. Plutarch, *de Iside* 47, under 'Chronology' and Eudemus in Damascius under 'Fravarāni.'

11 Cf. Meillet, *Gramm.* §§165, 166.

In 678 B.C., in the Šamaš omina of Esarhaddon, the EN.ER of all Medes bears the name wa.mi.ti.ar.ši, assimilated to Ass. mamītu "oath," from Med. *vahmayat.rša, with the Med. form of the participle, denom. of vahma.[12] But already in 716 B.C., in the Sargon annals, the chief of Šurgadia (between Sihna and Kirmānšāhān, in Ardilān), a "parsua, Persian," is called šēpašarri, assimilated to this Ass. name from OP. χšēpaya.ršti, -.ašθʳa or the like, against Aw. χšvēwayat.aštra.

To these names we can attach:

Med. *dārayat.hvarnah and Ach.Akk. dariparna, with i for ē and p=f for -t.vh-

Aw. vidaṭ.hvarnah and vinda.farnā in OP. inscriptions, but not OP., Gr. Ἰνταφέρνης

Aw. frādaṭ.hvarnah and Gr. Φραταφέρνης, with φ for -t.vh-

Aw. dārayaṭ.raθa against OP. dāraya.vahu, Gr. Δαρειαιος (Ctes.)

Aw. χšayaṭ.vīra against OP. χšaya.rša, El. ¹k.se.r.sa, Gr. Ξέρξης

Aw. uχšyaṭ.rta against OP. *uχšya.rta in Gr. Ὀξυάρτης

Aw. astvaṭ.rta against OP. *astva.rta in Gr. +Ἀστυαρτης (for Ἀστυάγης)

Aw. arvaṭ.aspa against OP. *arva.aspa in Gr. +Ἀρυάσπης (for Ἀριάσπης)

Also arava.uštra, i.e. +arva.uštra of the memorial document, *Yt.*13,124, belongs here as counterpart to Med. arvat.aspa. Markwart, *Cat.Proc.Cap.*45, explained the name as "a.raγvat.uštra, possessing slow camels"; Duchesne, who calls the form "gênante," §30, contradicts: "t aurait subsisté, comme le prouve arvat.aspa." But the case is that of Aw. arǰat.aspa against NP. arǰāsp. Nöldeke's interpretation of arǰāsp as analogy to Jāmāsp, *Pers.Stud.* II,1, is older than the knowledge of the dialectic differences. *arǰa.aspa > arǰāsp is the Persian form. The same with arava.uštra: *α* priv. is unlikely on account of the meaning, and prev. ā does not fit ragu; hence: +arva- for arava-.

To these names with participles without dental Gr. Ζωροάστρης < *zara.uštra attaches itself as Old Persian form

[12] A. V. W. Jackson, *Gramm.* §§695, 696; Duchesne §240; like namahya-, srāvahyati, gōšayat.uχδa.

of the name. Since the vowels are rendered by oa—cf. Φραόρτης < frovartiš—not by the diphthong au[13] as in Μιθραύστης < *miθra.vahišta, Τιθραύστης < *čiθra.vahišta etc., the Greeks must have heard a form of four syllables, without contraction, *zara.oštra < *zara.vaštra, not *zarauštra. Although at the end of the 4th century all these groups of vowels were contracted to ō, the name of the prophet preserved its archaic pronunciation.[14] It follows that the Persians had assimilated the name to their dialect, and hence knew the prophet, during his lifetime.

There are at least two genuine dialectic forms of the name, zaraθuštra < *zarat.vaštra and zara.uštra < *zara.vaštra. The participle stem is beyond doubt. The fact that Med. vaštra was not supplanted by OP. *vašθ^{r}a, *vaša, is no more contradictory than Med. aspa for OP. asa in OP. names. But if the name of the "Gatha-prophet" were Gathic, one would expect važdra.[14a] Gathic is no nationality and no vulgar dialect. Zoroaster was a Mede, and Med. vaštra is right.

Thus, the difficulty lies in the MP. and NP. forms zartuχšt, zardušt. Syr. zarāδušt in Ps.Meliton (Cureton, *Spicileg.Syr.*25) attests already in the middle of the 3rd century A.D. the pronunciation with δ < t; the vocalization is Syriac. Only in the middle of the 4th century A.D., Āturpāt ē Mahraspandān, the inventor of the Awestic script, introduced everywhere the spelling zaraθuštra. Down to the Sasanian period we know the name only as that of the prophet. Therefore, the two pronunciations with θ > h and t > δ must have been used, in contradiction to the uniform spelling. But zardušt would be a genuine development only in case that an old dialect would have had *zarat.uštra.[15]

[13] Markwart started, as a remark in *Südarmenien* shows, from *zarvati-, hence stresses the Gr. vocalization Zoroas-, which actually is the effect of assimilation to *ἀστὴρ* and Greek euphony, cf. *ἀραχώσια* for haravhatī (inst. of *-ωχα-*); *φαρνακῶτις* for vharnauχatī (inst. of *-ωκα-*); *ἀνασώζαδος* for anōšāzāδ (inst. of *-ωσα-*).

[14] The family name Γεόποθρος preserves, in A.D. 50, the θr, while Μειριδάτης (Awramān) and Meherdates (Tacitus) show that the change θr > hr had taken place, and the common word was no longer puθr, but puhr.

[14a] In analogy to Med. bāχtriš (in El. pakt^{u}ris), OP. bāχθ^{r}iš (in El. paksis), and Bactr. Bāχθriš (in Aw. vāχθrīka) > MP. bāχl, the Bactrian form would be Zarat.ušθra.

[15] Presupposing an unattested ablaut, cf. OIr. θwaχš-, but MP. tuχšīdan; and the generalization of θ for t in OP. gāθu, χraθū, prθu, and its counterpart paθi.

Let alone an equally impossible theory of Hertel, *Beitr.*216-221, it is assumed, without reason and contradictorily—I myself did so in 1930, AMI II,17—that Zoroaster had one wife, Hvōgvī, and three daughters, Frānī, Θritī and Puručistā, e.g. Nyberg, 265: "Zarathustra hatte . . . drei Töchter; davon dass er mehrere Frauen gehabt habe, weiss unser Awesta nichts." Polygamy was general, and no excuses are needed. The Awesta leaves no alternative.

Just as Zoroaster opens the list of men on the memorial document, so his wife Hvōgvī[16] opens the list of women in *Yt.*13,139. Hāugava is the gentilicium of the two brothers Frašauštra and Zāmāspa, the benefactors of Zoroaster; hence "née Hāugavī." Her name is followed by Frānī and Θritī. In 13,140 there are four Frānī, all married to men of the highest nobility, two of them Xštavayo; another Xštavi has an Asabānā, "née Asabānā." In 13,97, after the Persian Paridēδiya and Zoroaster's sons, three men appear with the family name frānyehe;[17] frānya and frānī are masc. and fem. of a gentilicium, hence "née Frānī." The three Frānya are her brothers. Then follows Θritī, fem. of Θrita, likewise the name of a man of the nobility in the list, hence "née Θritī." Then comes Puručistā, who is called Zoroaster's "youngest daughter" in *Y.*53,3 and bears the gentilicium of her father: "née Spitāmī Hēčataspānā." Women who bear a different family name cannot be daughters, but only wives of Zoroaster.—In the list of men, Vištāspa and his male relatives follow upon Zoroaster, and likewise in the list of women the ladies of the house of Vištāspa, Hutōsā and Humāyā, also Visatarušī, follow upon the ladies of Zoroaster's family. They are enumerated not according to age, but to rank.

Therefore, Zoroaster had three wives and one daughter. Hāugavī was the last wife he married, but the highest in rank. "The youngest daughter" in *Y.*53,3 seems to mean "youngest child," since no other daughters, but only brothers appear. Immediately before, the gatha speaks of the zāraθuštriš spitāmo. With the exception of Hertel, all consider this as "son, descendant of Zoroaster"; according to him it would refer "in der gewöhnlichen Bedeutung Anhänger Zoroaster's" to Vištāspa. Zoroaster cannot speak, in a gatha, of a "Zoroastrian,"

16 *Gath.* spelling; Aw. hvōvī, fem. to patr. *hāugava, vrddhi deriv. from *hugu.

17 *Wb.*1016: "Eigenname, viell. patron.adj." and 1022f.: "frənya, Eigenname, der ältesten Tochter Z.'s, wohl Kurzname." Likewise 1857: "hvōvī, Eigenname, eigtl. fem. zu hvōvā 'die aus der Hv. Familie.'" Only the last remark is right: none of these names is a personal name.

no more than Christ of a "Christian," and where else zāraθuštriš occurs, thus in *Yt.*13,98 (repeated in *Y.*23,2; 26,5), it must mean "son"; in Ragā zāraθuštrīš it expresses the possession. Zāraθuštriš Spitāmo restricts the general, wider name Spitāma even more than hēčataspāna, and designates, at Zoroaster's lifetime and at the side of the daughter, a son, excluding a grandson.

Of the three sons mentioned in *Yt.*13, the name of the second, Rvatatnara, is assured by the name of a grandson, Rvatatnara aparazāta. The definition of the notion nabā.nazdišta (under 'Social Structure') shows that this child was a grandson, not a great-grandson of Zoroaster. One reason to call a son after his father is his posthumous birth, and it is possible that the list, like the Ka'ba inscription, contains names of deceased persons. Puručistā was still unmarried at the time of the document, hence under 16 years (see under 'Maga'). The "Wedding Gatha," 54,1-7, is composed in honor of her marriage, hence is later than the document. The anonymous son, in this gatha, is certainly the third and youngest, since the second brother was already married before.

The proper name of the Hāugavī is nowhere mentioned, neither are those of other wives. Apparently, for married women, that was against the custom. The later Parsi conception of the family relations is unaware of these main facts which it replaces by erroneous interpretations of *Yt.*13; therefore it is no real tradition. But in *Yt.*16,15,[18] verses dating in the 2nd century B.C., like parts of the *Vidēvdād,* the Hāugavī is with reason considered to be the wife of Zoroaster, against Hertel's attempt to eliminate the words, and at that time one may still have known that she was the daughter of Frašauštra. This is what the later tradition asserts and must not have been inferred from a wrong interpretation of *Y.*51,17 in combination with *Yt.*13, as late as in Sasanian times. Rather *Y.*51 was misinterpreted because this tradition existed, for it is confirmed by the Gatha, 49,7: "O Hāugava Frašauštra, go there, where both our most ardent wishes accompany you!" (see under 'Poetry'), that means "my and your daughter's, the Hāugavī's wishes." Sister is improbable: Zoroaster was about forty years old at that time; his influ-

[18] Where differing interpetations were caused by wrong translations of vahu baga—with Duchesne §82: "souhaitant un sort heureux."

ential benefactors were older; Zāmāspa had a grandson and a great-grandson, his namesake, and Zoroaster did not marry a great-grand-aunt. Under 'Nōtarya' we shall mention cases where children were born as grand-uncles and grand-aunts, and the Hāugavī may have been a grand-aunt when 16. Her daughter was Puručistā.

But the fact, never contested except by Hertel, that the Hāugavī was a daughter of Frašauštra does away with the equally uncontested assumption that, according to *Y.*53,2-3, Zoroaster married Puručistā to Zāmāspa, the elder brother of her grandfather, who was already a great-grandfather while she was about 12 years old. Puručistā Spitāmī Hēčataspānā married, if her father makes it an occasion for a poem, as first main wife a young man, just as her elder, but young brother married his first wife (see under 'Maga').

The misunderstanding of family and proper names caused the misunderstanding of the whole relationship. It was equally thoughtless not to recognize the social significance of the gentilicia. These are derived from ancestors that lived generations ago; only aristocratic families, "gentes," can have eponyms, but no "nicht gerade besitzlose Proletarier" (Nyberg, 194f.). The same type of names is still today used in Persia, Iraq and Turkey: Taqizādeh, Gīlānīzādeh, Mikhāilghāzizādeh etc. One of the four Frānī in *Yt.*13,140, wife of Usinamah, is considered by the Sasanian legend to be the ancestress of the kavi-dynasty; in Firdausi, Frānak is the mother of Frēdōn. Such families are hvētu and kavi, and the Frānya seem to have been like the Spitāma, a Median family.

To these names belongs also Damaspia, wife of Artaxerxes I, i.e. "zāmāspī, née Zāmāspī," a Hāugavī zāmāspānā, as Puručistā is a Spitāmī hēčataspānā (see under 'Hāugava'). This manner of naming women survives in Arsacid and Sasanian times in formations with -duxt, which have been dealt with by Hübschmann and Nöldeke. A number of seals—only ladies of property had seals—and the Ka'ba inscription furnish more examples.[19]

[19] Šāhpuhrduχt, 1. wife of Narseh Sakānšāh, 2. daughter of Šāhpuhr Mēšānšāh; Hormizduχtak, daughter of Narseh Sakānšāh; Narsehduχt, herself a queen: Sakān bānbišn; Varāčduχt, a queen. This -duχt is not "daughter," but title of the ladies of highest rank. The formation corresponds to the gentilics in -puθra which replace at the same time older styles. Cf. Neriosengh: Spitāma: spitāmaputraḥ; Vivāna: Geopothros. Later, the neutral -zādeh enters for puhr and duχt.

Ctesias' remark on the marriage and dowry of Astyages' daughter implies that the Spitāma were a rich Median house, and this gives from the beginning an historical background to the Iranian tradition which, unanimously, locates Zoroaster's birth in the house of his father Purušāspa at Ragā. Ragā is the natural capital of one of the great fifths of Media, today represented by Teheran. OP. Ragā, NP. Ray, is first mentioned in the *Beh.* inscription in 521 B.C.; under Seleucus Nicator it was called, as capital of its province, Eúrōpos, under the Arsacids Arsakía (see under 'Vidēvdād'). In the Awesta, the town appears only twice, in *Vid.*1,15, pre-Christian half of the Arsacid period; and in *Y.*19,18, according to contents, language and unreal forms raγa, rǰoit, not older.

*Vid.*1,15: "As the twelfth best country, I, AhuraMazdāh, created Raγām θrizantum"; Ahriman created there as "patiyāram, antagonism" uparō.vimanō.hīm, i.e. "+upara.vimanahyam, hyperscepsis."[20] At this place the *Pahl.Vid.* comments: "They say, Zartust ač ān ǰāk būt, Zoroaster was from there," one cod. has "pētāk būt, appeared from there," both meaning his birth.

Vidēvdād 1 is a geographical textbook in verses, of the Arsacid period. The epithets of the towns, here θrizantu, are understood as gifts of AhuraMazdāh, by which he made peaceful the "else-unpeaceful, noit kudāt.šāti" countries (see under 'Vidēvdād'). Ahriman's counter-creation is a well known thing.

*Art.Vīr.Nām.*1,1: "For three hundred years, till the time of Alexander, 'apēgumānīh, freedom from doubt'[21] prevailed, after him came sectarianism, false doctrines, 'gumānīh' and heterodoxy. . . ." Also *Māh Frav.* §30: Hvlšytl teaches men the dēn ē māzdēsn and they become "apēgumān." Of Nisaya-Alexandropolis, the oldest capital of the Arsacid kingdom, *Vid.*1 says: "Ahriman created there 'vimanahya, scepsis.'" With these two remarks, the *Vidēvdād* describes the very capitals of its period, Nisaya and Ragā, as the Greek towns Alexandropolis and Europos.

The Pahl.transl. has: "rāk (or: rāγ) ē III-tōχmak, (gloss:) hast kē

[20] Pahl.transl. apar.vimānakīh, cf. Duchesne §154.

[21] al-Mutawakkil says in his edict against the ahl al-dhimma, Tabari III,1389ff.: "Allāh . . . in His immeasurable greatness and the omnipotence of His will, has chosen Islam . . . and has made it victorious over the other religions, *free from doubts.*"

ray gōyēnd"; rāk is transliteration, ray pronunciation. tōχmak, a word of OP. origin, "species, genus," is syn. of Aw. zantu only in its ethnic acceptation; zantu was not used in OP., hence not in MP., and therefore not clearly understood. One commentator says: "III-tōχmak, because good priests, warriors and peasants come from there," taking zantu as "station in life." It is "district," and tōχmak is unfit as translation of "θrizantu, consisting of three districts." This is the official designation of that fifth of Media, itself a unit of three parts, a term of administration like Μηδία καὶ Παραιτακηνή for the whole of the satrapy. The three natural parts of Rhagiane are 1. Qazwīn, 2. Teheran, Ragā itself, 3. Kum, pre- and early Muhammedan Kamindān.

Aw. θrizantu is a word like Gr. τριχάϝικες, with ϝικ = Ir. *vis*. *Od*.19, 117:

Δωριέες τε τριχάϝικες δῖοι τε Πελασγοί

and Hesiod, *Aigimos*: πάντες δὲ τριχάϝικες καλέονται
τρίσσην οὕνεκα γαῖαν ἑκὰς πάτρης ἐδάσαντο

comment: τρία γὰρ Ἑλληνικὰ ἔθνη τῆς Κρήτης ἐποικῆσαι, Πελασγούς, Ἀχαίους, Δωριεῖς οὓς τριχάικας κεκλήκασι. The Greeks, too, did no longer understand their archaic word. O. Schrader compared with it the name of the Thracians: Θρῆξ < *Θρήϝικες, with θρᾶ "four," hence "consisting of four *vis*." One sees how archaic the whole idiom is.

The second place, *Y*.19,18, is a catechism: "Who are the ratu, judges? —The lord of the house, of the clan, of the district, of the province, fifth Zoroaster, in all provinces except Ragā zāraθuštriš; this is čaθru.-ratuš, has only four ratu.—Who are the ratu? (those four?)—The lord of the house, of the clan, of the district, fourth Zoroaster."

This is a perfectly clear statement. Leaving aside the role it attributes to Zoroaster as highest authority everywhere,[22] it makes him the "ratu of the dahyu Ragā," while in other provinces other men were satraps. Therefore the Pahl. translation and Neriosengh's Sanskr. translation (see Jackson, *Zor*. 203f.) add to Ragā "dēh i χvēš, his own province." This is not a documented historical tradition, but some knowledge supported by a right interpretation of zāraθuštriš as "belonging to Z.," combined with an interpretation of θrizantu as "nmāna, vis, zantu"

[22] Connected with the thought that, as epithet of Ragā in *Vidēvdād* 1, *θrizantuš* ought to be a special advantage, a gift of AhuraMazdāh.

instead of "three zantu," vertically instead of horizontally, not so big a mistake, and the result is not far from truth. The gathas teach that Zoroaster was banished from his province by a verdict of the court of his home town, and Ctesias speaks of "satrapies" the two sons of the Spitāma received from Cyrus. The difference between satrapy and hereditary possession is slight. But, building upon this passage the theory of "Ragā as Papal See, or Priesterstaat," as Jackson and Nyberg do, is a colossal inflation of just the slight mistake made by the authors of the catechism.

Y.19,18 disproves also Markwart's words in *Ērānš*. 123,1: "Beinahe selbverständlich, dass aus dem epitheton zāraθuštriš geschlossen wurde, dass Ragā der Geburtsort Zoroaster's sei, so z.B. 'Städteliste' §60, wo ohne Zweifel eine Angabe über die Gründung von Ragā ausgefallen ist." It is right, that the *Šahr.Ēr*. (composed about A.D. 490) ended with a §60 on Ragā, of which only the appended note remains: "zartušt ē spitāmān ač ān šahristān būt, Zoroaster was from that town." But that is the real meaning of the epithet, and all other inferences, drawn by modern interpreters, are wrong.

Another local indication is found in the strange story of Zoroaster's "temptation" in *Vid*.19,4 and 11:

,drəǰya' pati zbarahi   nmānahya purušaspahya

The reading of the first word is doubtful; it is apparently mutilated, for with one syllable more, the passage which is a quotation would be a regular verse. Cf. *Yt*.9,26: "baršnuš pati garīnām drāǰaŋhe (drāǰåho?) . . ."

Gr.Bdh.88 (*Ind.Bdh*.20,38) takes the word for the name of a river: "dāraǰa (in Aw. script) rōt pat ērānvēž kē.š mān ē parušasp pitar e zartušt pa bār būt, D. is a river in Ērānvēž, on the bank of which stood the palace of Purušasp, father of Zoroaster." The relative clause is a mere paraphrase of the *Vidēvdād* passage, and the only base for the assumption of a river is the wrong translation of Aw. zbarah by bār.[23] This river is located "in Ērānvēž" because Zoroaster prays in *Yt*.5,104 "at the mouth of the Vahvī Dātiyā of the Aryans," a pseudo-Awestic name of the Arsacid period for later Ērānvēž (see under 'Ērānvēž'),

[23] Also used in Y.9,29 for "zbaraθa, foot of a creeping animal."

"hizvo danhahā, in the language of erudition," i.e. in Awestic, not in the contemporary Middle Persian:

yaθa azam hāčayāne	puθram yat arvataspahe
taχmam kaviyam vištāspam	anu.mataye dēnayāi
anu.(u)χtaye dēnayāi	anu.varštaye dēnayāi

"That I always may pursue Vištāspa, the son of Arvataspa, for thinking-according to the religion, talking-according to, acting-according to the religion."

These verses are produced wholesale: in the *Druvāsp Yasht,* 9.26, the same words are repeated with Hutōsā as object; one could paint the steatopygic kallipygos "kicking against the pricks." In *Yt.*5,17, Zoroaster himself is driven, the god asks another one, to let him always be the driver: a deus otiosus and a propheta otiosior. Benveniste, *Inf.av.* 53, calls the late passage of *Y.*8,7: "haχšaya ahyå dēnayå anu.matayēča . . . , dois-je inciter à l'observance en pensée de la religion etc." the "énoncé ancien; de là on passe" to the form of *Yt.*5,18, 105; 9,26, verses which therefore are even later. No other passages than this one locate Zoroaster in Ērānvēž.

The abstract nouns formed with the preposition "anu, according to" are malformations; dēnā, always trisyllabic, counts here only for two syllables. In this false language the verses are fashioned after the genuine prayers of the mythical heroes in the old hymns, where they pray for victory over gods and men or personal adversaries. The genuine passages locate those prayers in Ērānvēž, the home of the myth. In the feeling of the diaskeuasts, AhuraMazdāh and Zoroaster cannot remain behind and therefore must likewise pray in the land of the golden age, only "la pire misère intellectuelle (Meillet)" of the period prevents them from achieving a decent prayer. On account of this illusionary location, Zoroaster is no more "born in Ērānvēž" than Ahura-Mazdāh, and one cannot conclude from the added "river in Ērānvēž" of the *Gr.Bdh.* that in the 9th century A.D. the notion of Ērānvēž was somehow connected with Ragā.

*Gr.Bdh.*121 (*Ind.Bdh.*24,5): "dārağa rōt rōtbārān rat čē mān ē pitar ē zartušt pa bār[aš], zartušt ānō zāt, the D. river is the iudex of the rūdbār, for the palace of Zoroaster's father stood on its bank, bār; Zoroaster is born there."

The first part, the raising of the rank of the river to "iudex of the rūdbār" is not possible without the wrong translation of zbarah by bār in *Bdh.*88; its source is that paraphrase of *Vid.*19.—Rūdbār "fluviatile" is a common notion, also a local name: the best known are between Qazwīn and Rasht, later famous by its rūdbārī textiles, and Rūdbār on the Hilmand, called Paraitakene by Isidorus of Charax; a third one near Djīruft in Lār. The second part, "Zoroaster is born there," comes from the commentary to Ragā zāraθuštriš in *Vid.*1,15. Thus, the commentaries to *Vid.*1 (with Ragā) and 19 (without name) come from the same source, from which also the passage in *Šahr.Ēr.* comes, and this tradition—although the *Gr.Bdh.* says "river in Ērānvēž" —had not this "home of the Aryans" in mind, but only Ragā.

zbarah designates a part of the palace. Whether it be the broken entrance, dargāh, or the vaulted main hall, drǰy at any rate is no name and no river. It may be a mere adjective, e.g. drāǰyah, comp. of drga "long," or a term of fortification, see under 'Architecture.' The passage of *Vid.*19,4 and 11 means "in the drǰy at the zbarah" or "in the drǰy zbarah of the palace of Purušaspa," and the palace is imagined to be in Ragā.

To this tradition belongs a tale in the *Dēnkart* VII (ed. Darab XIII, 25ff.), concerning Duγdōvā, Zoroaster's mother. The Aw. form of this name appears only in an ungrammatical fragment of the *Hat. Nask*; the Pahl. form is Duγdāv; it says: Zoroaster's father sent her "ō spitrasp pitar ē dūtak ē andar spitāmān dēh ē apar raγa rōtastāk, to Spitrasp, the paterfamilias, who was in the country of the Spitāma in the district Ragā." District Ragā in the province of the Spitāma is in agreement with dēh ē χvēš of *Y.*19,18 and with Ctesias' remark about the Spitāma in Media. The notion that Zoroaster's father went on to live in his father's house after being married is genuine.

Finally the much revealing proverb which the *Čīt. Zātsp.* 16,12 attribute to Zoroaster's mother: "I shall not do this, even if the two towns would meet here, Ray and Tōs," explained: "irreal, 60 farsakh [in fact good 60 double farsakh] from one another, Zartušt ač Ray, Vištāsp ač Nōtar būt, Z. was from Ray, V. from [Tōs ē]Nōδar." The last town is near modern Mashhad, famous as the birthplace of Firdausī.

That is the Iranian tradition about the home of Zoroaster.

Nyberg, who first allows "einen schwachen Reflex zarathustrischer Lokaltradition" in the personal and geographical names of the Zoroaster biography of *Dēnk̨*. VII—that is not the source and hence indifferent—continues "Alles fällt zusammen, wenn wir zu hören bekommen, Zarathustra sei in Adharbaidjan, genauer in Shēz am Urmiya-See geboren, und dass seine iranische Heimat Ērānvēž sei."

Many Greek towns claimed to be the home of Homer. The similar claim of Šēz is disposed of in a few words. Šēz < čēčista is one of the oldest fire temples of Media, the "āδargušnasp, Fire of the Stallion," shape of appearance of Vrthragna. It is pre-Zoroastrian and one of the dēvadāna destroyed by Xerxes. One could gather much information from the legends of the great fires. They like to usurp events of the religious history. The claim of Šēz has the same tendency, but appears only as late as A.D. 1225 in Yaqut and A.D. 1275 in Qazwini. Before that time, e.g. in ibn Khurdādhbih, about 860, Tabari, end of the 9th century, and ibn Faqīh, about 910, it is Urmiya. This conception is connected with the political attitude, at first wavering, of the Muhammedan government towards Magism, which caused that Zoroaster, in order to make him acceptable to the Muslims, was connected with the Old Testament. This was done by primates like Āturfarnabag son of Farruχzād and his son Zartuχšt, Atropatenians,[24] and the special figures to whom Zoroaster became assimilated were Abraham and the prophet Jeremiah.[25]

The Arab. name of the last is Armiya, in Tabari (1,506) also Urmiya, and the resemblance of these names led to Urmiya as place of Zoroaster's origin. Later Urmiya was replaced by the more important temple of Šēz near the Urmiya Lake. That is no Iranian tradition at all, but an invention made in order to enjoy some advantages of the ahl al-dhimma, like lower taxes, and not to perish entirely.

The other assertion is wrong: we are nowhere told that Zoroaster's West Iranian home was Ērānvēž. *Yt.*5,104 and *Yt.*9,24, to which these words refer, are unauthentic products of the Arsacid period, as discussed above. In Iranian tradition, down to the Muhammedan period, Ērānvēž is never anything but the aboriginal home, the country on

[24] Cf. *Dēnk̨.*, end of book III, and under 'Zoroaster's Death.'

[25] That is why the "lord" of the Kūh i Khwāǰa is called Sarā i Ibrāhīm, viz. Ibrāhīm Zardušt, and why remarks appear like "The prophet Daniel was Cyrus' maternal uncle" or "Bahman's mother was a Jewess of the house of king Saul," influenced by the book of Esther.

the Oxus and Iaxartes, see under 'Ērānvēz.' But not a single ancient passage connects Zoroaster with Ērānvēž.

There is only one consistent tradition from the second century B.C., not more than 250 years after Ctesias, that Ragā was the birthplace and the property of Zoroaster. At that time, the surname zāraθuštrīš was already old. The *Vidēvdād* describes Ragā with its hyperscepsis as the Greek town Europos. That was not the time to claim the glory to be the prophet's birthplace. The surname is older and the tradition must be older. The town that had banished the prophet—see under 'Hospitium'—can only have gloried in being his home just after the public recognition of his doctrine, in order to cleanse itself of the slur, or for fear.

Nyberg, 49: "Im Westen fehlt eine authentische örtliche Überlieferung gänzlich, die Lokalisierungen von Ereignissen des Lebens Zarathustras zeigen durch ihre Unbestimmtheit und ihr Schwanken, dass sie Konstruktionen sind, so muss man sich grundsätzlich darauf einrichten, die Gatha-Gemeinde und Zarathustras Heimat in Ostiran zu suchen." In the East there is not only no authentic tradition, but none at all. Ragā, as birthplace, is definite and unvacillating; it is no "construction," as e.g. the "Gatha-Gemeinde" and the "Hauptmissionsstation Ragā"; and the "systematic orientation" to find a wanted result is what one must never do. 401: "Und so kommen die Mystifikationen auf, die die alten östlichen Orte im Westen verörtlichen. Daraus folgt, dass die ganze westliche Überlieferung über die Örtlichkeiten des östlichen Zoroastrismus geschichtlich gesehen wertlos sind."

That stands at the beginning (p.49) and at the end (p.401) and is "von Anfang bis zu Ende verkehrt" (p.202). There are neither eastern localities and eastern tradition, nor a western localization of eastern localities of the life of Zoroaster. The whole terminology is wrong. There is only an Iranian and no Turkistanian tradition, not only about the life of Zoroaster, but about everything. Some indications in the gathas can be interpreted as referring to Ragā, Kōmiš and Tōsa; in the Awesta some old passages refer equally to Tōsa and besides to Sīstān. And there is, later, the definite tradition, old already in the 2nd century B.C., that Zoroaster was from Ragā which belonged to his family, that the Spitāma, therefore, were, as Ctesias says, a Median house.

IV. HOUSE NŌTARYA

"avahyarādi vayam haχāmanišiyā θahyāmahi,
therefore we are called Achaemenids"

THE real family name of kavi Vištāspa, the protector of Zoroaster, does not appear at all in the Awesta, or in the epics. At the four places in the gatha there is no reason for Zoroaster to mention the name, to him a matter of course. In the memorial document of *Yt.*13, Vištāspa is no more characterized by the family name than are the Sasanian kings in their inscriptions.[1] But in the following group, §102, before the first man of another family, the Hāugava, appears, a man bearing the OPersian name Visataruš, known also from the epical fragment *Yt.*5,76, is designated by the clientela adjective "nōtaryāno," and this confirms a surmise—for other reasons—that the group between Vištāspa and the Hāugava are the Nōtarya.

nōtara < *navatara, is the comparative of "nava, new." The positive occurs only in *Vid.*21,3: "the waters, plants, medicinal herbs become new," i.e. renovate, rejuvenate themselves, "by rain." The comparative occurs in *Yt.*17,55—see below—"the Tūra, swift horsemen and youthful ones." Only because Bartholomae believed the phonetic detail of the Aw. text to be authentic and the interpretations of the *Bdh.* and *Dēnk.* to be based on independent knowledge, could he explain this word as produced "durch Verschiebung des Wortakzents aus *nōtara, n.pr. eines Sohnes des Manuščiθra." Such a Nōtara, unknown to the Awesta, never existed; MP. nōδar is, like Vēžan and others, nothing but the old surname personified.

Being the comparative of an adjective, nōtara—quite independent from its signification—is no heros eponymos and no true family name, and the single member of the house is not "a Nōtara." In the prayer of Hutōsā, *Yt.*5,98, "vis nōtarānām, clan of the nōtara" is the name of the place they owned. Individuals are designated, as in other IE. languages, by the derivative in -iya: nōtarya, thus in *Yt.*15,35, where the "nōtaryåho, nōtarians," appear beside the hāugavåho, whom the gatha, too, connect with Vištāspa. From nōtarya again the IE. adj. of clientela in -āna, nōtaryāna, is formed, just as in Lat. Julus, Julius, Julianus.

[1] The absence of these names is usually not realized; E. G. Browne once said to me: I am glad that just you found for the first time the name Sāsānakān in an inscription.

There is only the adjective "nōtara, the *νεώτεροι*; nōtarya, one of the nōtarya; and nōtaryāna, client of the nōtarya," but there is no man Nōtara and there are no *Nōtarids, **νεωτερίδαι*. The nōtaryāno bears an Old Persian name; there are not a few Persians round Vištāspa in the list; some foreign clients, in §§125-126, even have assumed or received Old Persian names, hence one may expect from the beginning that the nōtarya were Persians.

The comparative signification of nōtara determines one branch of an unnamed great family in opposition to another branch whose determinative must have been an antonym of nōtara. Gr. *νεώτερος* can be antonym of various words. Lommel, in *Idg.Forschg.* 53, 1935, 165ff., tried to prove by reason of metrics that nōtara could not be *νεώτερος*—which is entirely beyond the argumentative power of metrics—and that Ir. nava meant only "new," not "young" as in Greek—which is not provable, since the word occurs only once in the *Vidēvdād* passage quoted above. On the contrary, it is disproved by the true signification of the comparative nōtara in *Yt.*17,55.

Names of branches of great families are found everywhere, in Iran precisely in the two families most closely connected with the nōtarya, viz. the Spitāma, called also hēčataspāna and zāraθuštri, and the Hāugava, also called zāmāspāna, zāmāspī (see under 'Hāugava'). There is no occasion for mentioning the very gentilicium which the surnames qualify, and less so for mentioning the surname of the other branch in the Awesta, a fact which does not rule out the possibility that individuals belonging to that branch appear.

The Achaemenids, too, had two branches; Darius speaks of them as "dvita.parnam, in two lines"; those were *νεώτεροι* and *πρεσβύτεροι*. The family name itself, haχāmanišiya, is derived from Darius' sixth ancestor Haχāmaniš.[2] The separation was effected by his two grandsons, Cyrus I and Āryāramna, and in the inscription of the latter haχāmanišiya is not yet used; it appears for the first time on the gold tablet of his son Ršāma.[3] It takes a few generations to develop such a

[2] The stem of haχāmaniš cannot be determined, because, like Aw. vandarmaniš, OP. ardumaniš, it appears only in the nominative. The gen. haχāmanišahya in the Āryāramna inscription is an early example of analogic inflection, like χšaya.ršahya (time of Artaxerxes I) and dārayav^{a}/$_{o}$šahya (Artaxerxes II). The stem was perhaps -manyah (cf. vanyah) transferred into the i-class in analogy to -vah > -uš, transferred into u-class, cf. under 'Memor. Doc.,' visataruš.

[3] Since the gold tablet of Āryāramna was "gebrandmarkt" as an antique fake, no collection

gentilicium, and just when this was done it became also necessary to distinguish the two branches.

The Greeks have not transmitted the distinguishing surname "Hystaspids" of the younger branch that we give the descendants of Vištāspa. But the Iranian term for the older branch is hidden in the names Μάρδοι and Μαράφιοι of the Greek tradition. Herodotus I,125 says of the *γένεα* of the Persians: "These are the tribes on which all other Persians depend: Pasargadai, Maraphioi and Maspioi; among them the Pasargadai are the noblest, from which the kings of Persis descend."[4] "Depend" in the political sense, is opposed to ethnic "descend." The "kings of Persis" are a clan of the tribe Pasargadai. But opposed to "kings of Media" this expression sounds as if Herodotus' source was older than 550 B.C.—He enumerates further among the nomads of Persis (Fārs) the Mardoi between Da(h)oi and Dropikoi, Sagartioi. Arrian, *Ind.* 40, from Nearch, mentions Mardoi as neighbors of the Persians, and Ctesias calls Cyrus a "Mardos as to his tribe (descent)."

Nomadic Mardoi in Persis are subject to doubt, since the Da(h)oi, Dropikoi and Sagartioi all belong certainly *not* to Persis, and the Mardoi are well known in Māzandarān on the Caspian. Andreas believed that Ctesias' Mardos, as ethnic of Cyrus, referred to those anaryan Amardoi who left their name to the town Āmul, and that these were the Elamite Hapirti. The last name is in reality Ha(l)tamti, and the theory is twice wrong. The fault in Ctesias' words is only the rendering of Ir. "vis, clan" by Gr. génos. The Pasargadai were the "génos," the Mardoi the "vis." The right translation of "vis" by *φρήτρη* occurs only as exception in Greek, in Herodotus I,125. In IV,167 he mentions one Amasis, *ἀνὴρ Πασαργάδης* beside Badres, *ἀνὴρ Μαράφιος*; the latter name is that of a vis, like Mardos. Stephanus says yet more inexact, s.v. Maraphioi: *ἔθνος ἐν Περσίδι* (from Herodotus) and explains: *ἀπὸ*

dared to purchase a similar tablet of Ršāma, and this remained unpublished; known to me from a photograph. Ršāma calls himself āryāramna-χšāyaθyahya-puθ^ra, and moreover haχāmanišiya, whereas Āryāramna says "grandson of Haχāmaniš." The land Pārsa has instead of the usual huvaspa humartiya, the else unknown epithet "hukāra huvaspa," where hukāra is new and rightly precedes huvaspa.

[4] Nyberg, 343: "Maraphioi and Maspioi sind sicher nicht iranisch; sie enthalten das elam. Suffix -pi und sind also wahrscheinlich als elamisch anzusehen." The El. suffix would have more power than to make the names only "probably Elamite"; but if so, it could not make them "certainly non-Iranian." In fact, the names do not contain an Elam. suffix, which is -ip (plur.), but only the phoneme -pi-.

Μαραφίου βασιλέως (from Eusthatius, Comm. to Ilias II,408) "Maraphios, first king of the Persians, son of Menelaos." This is the personified name of a royal family, like the "nōtara > Nōδar" of the Sasanian legend.

Mardos and Maraphios reflect the same Iranian word in two dialects, just as Mardos, Merdis on the one hand, Maraphis, Merphis on the other, render the OP. form Brδya and Med. Brzya of the name of Cyrus' son (see below). Ctesias' remark is legendary, based on a wrong interpretation of the name, and yet it is not wrong that Cyrus was a "Mardos as to his génos." The comp. nōtara requires an antonym, and the comp. barδyah, barzyah is such an antonym, "higher." Derivatives, corresponding to nōtarya and nōtaryāna, may have been the Ir. designation for the "elder branch" of the family. NP. "buland < brzant, high" is also used for age. Other languages render the same opposition by younger and older, νεώτερος and πρεσβύτερος, and that is the meaning of the Iranian words in this case.

Surely the Persians called their Hystaspids nōtarya, surely the Aw. nōtarya expresses the opposition to brzyåho of the same family, whose very name was so obvious that it was not necessary to mention it. Surely the never mentioned name was haχāmanišiya.

Nyberg, 45: "Hertel und Herzfeld . . . setzen Zarathustras Beschützer Vištāspa mit [Vištāspa] dem Vater Darius' I gleich. . . . Diese Hypothese scheitert indessen rettungslos daran, dass die . . . Gleichsetzung undenkbar ist." The aeon-system—a religious doctrine—makes Zoroaster appear under Vištāspa, 258 years before Alexander. A short period only separates the Awestic Vištāspa from Alexander, that means he is considered as the historical Vištāspa. The epic—a popular, not religious tradition—tells the legends that grew round the Awestic Vištāspa and his relatives—cf. *Yt.*13—and joins to them without gap Dārā = Darius and his successors to the time of Alexander; it identifies the two Vištāspa. Religious and epical tradition, that is all tradition there was, are unanimous in this fundamental equation. It is a colossal mistake to believe, "unthinkable" could dispense with a thought ascribed to H. and H., while it was the dominant thought, and the only one, for 2,500 years.—Let alone individual faculties, "thinkable and unthinkable" contain a time factor: what seems unthinkable today, will be a matter of course tomorrow.

Darius, son of VištāSPa says: "aSabāra huvaSabāra ahmi, as horseman I am a good horseman"; OP. asa against Med. aspa. Huvaspa in the protocol formula "the land with the good horses" and nn.ppr. like Vištāspa, Aspačina, all contain the Median aspa.

The meaning of višta results from *Yt.*5,98:

tām yazanta hvōvåho	to her (Ardvī), the Hāugava sacrificed,
tām yazanta nōtaryåho	to her the Nōtarya sacrificed,
ištīm yaδyanta hvōvō	for riches the Hāugava asked,
āsu.aspīm naotaire	for horses'-speed the Nōtarya.
mošu pasčēta hvōvō	At once the Hāugava
ištīm baon səvišta	became powerfully rich,
mošu pasčēta naotaire?	at once the Nōtarya
vištāspo åhām dahyūnām	Vištāspa became, of those countries,
āsu.aspōtəmō bavat	the speediest-as-to-horses.

The language is bad, the composition of the verses not that of the old-mythical ones, and the lack of a locality—never missing in genuine stanzas—is alone sufficient proof that the insignificant fragment is not old. The poet makes the Hāugava ask for money, with respect to the Gath. attribute "ištoiš hvarnå, blessed with riches" of the Hāugava Zāmāspa, and makes the Nōtarya ask for "horses' speed"—a bad abstr. formation—remembering *Yt.*17,55-56, "Flight of Rtiš":

yat mām tūrā pazdayanta āsu.aspā nōtarāsča

"when the Tūra chased me, the swift-horsemen and nōtara, youthful ones." He regards āsu.aspa as an attribute of nōtara, identifies this with the family name, nōtarya, of Vištāspa, and makes Vištāspa win the speediest horses, because that is his interpretation of the name.—višta is past.part.pass. of √vis-, OP. viθ-, OI. viśáti, "with ready (to start) horses."[5]

[5] Cf. Benveniste, *J.As.*1936,2,229: "Sogd. ''wyštk 'tremblement, agitation'<*ā.višta.ka, dans Višta.aspa 'aux chevaux frémissants.' " The same idea is perhaps expressed by Ass. sīsē pitan birki, Thureau-Dangin: "aux genoux ouverts," unless this be something entirely different: "stallions?"

Darius' father and Zoroaster's protector bear the same Median name, which—excepting a few younger Achaemenids—does not occur in history down to the Muhammedan epoch, when it became popular by Firdausi's Shāhnāmah. Median names for Persians are quite unobjectionable. But those who believe in an "eastern Vištāspa" reject with equal emphasis the theory that he had a Median name and that the Medes knew him, because that would break through the barrier erected between the "eastern Awesta" and the Medes and Persians. The Medes—if that concept is right—must have used the name without any contact; Ršāma must have given it to his son unknowingly; and Vištāspa II, grandson of the historical Vištāspa, must have called his son with the unique name Pissouthnes < Pišišyōθna, without knowing that the "eastern Vištāspa" had done the same, see under 'Throne-names.' This triple coincidence is "unthinkable." And the fact that the two persons bear the same Median name proves in this special case that both are one and the same Persian. As a Persian, Vištāspa orders masses to be celebrated for so many Persians in the foundation document of his temple.

Nyberg,249: "Sein Vater hiess aurvataspa." This passage, *Yt.*5,105, is spurious, it is the empty prayer of Zoroaster, in erudite language, always to pursue "the son of Arvataspa, the swift, kāvian Vištāspa" etc., which we have characterized above, a worthless product of the Arsacid period.

Apart from this passage, "arvataspa, with swift horses" appears only as standing epithet of the gods ApāmNapāt and Hvar Xšēta; cf. Neptunus equester. In the OP. version of the legend, to which Hellanicus (430-400 B.C., frgm.163) alludes, long before the date of the Awestic prayer, Atossa-Hutōsā, too, is called "daughter of Ariaspes," i.e. $^+$aryaspes < OP. *arvāspa. In the later versions the divine epithet is replaced by Luhrāsp, name of the god ΛΡΟΟΑΣΠΟ of the Kūshān coins, i.e. "druvāspa, with healthy horses," with EastIr. δ > l. In the Awesta, *Yasht* 9 is dedicated to the goddess Druvāspā. In both cases, the surname has displaced the lost proper name.

The whole legend which the post-Zoroastrian period has woven around Vištāspa is the rejuvenation of an older myth of gods, which made a hero arvataspa, of the god with that surname. This hero melted together with the East Iranian god druvāspa into the figure of king Luhrāsp. Markwart, *Vēhrōt,* was inclined to see ApāmNapāt in him. But we do not have the old myth, but only the heroized legend, into which historical figures intruded, and seeing original deities of water in all the figures of this cycle is going much too far.

The home of the god Druvāspa prevails as locality of this legend. From such an origin, the notion passed into all pseudo-historical stories, that the Iranian kings Luhrāsp and Vištāsp resided in Balkh, as overlords of Assyrian and Babylonian kings, e.g. of Nebuchadnezzar (see under 'Zoroaster's Death'). This notion is so old that it appears already in a branch of Greek tradition which makes Ninus wage war against Hystaspes and Zoroastres in Bactria.

The real hero of the Vištāspa legend is not Vištāspa, but his brother Zarivariš-Zarēr, of the memorial document in *Yt.*13, who, in *Yt.*5,112f., bears the epithet "aspa.yōδa, fighting on horseback," well fitting into the group.[6] The god druvāspa-arvataspa-equester attracts such names. What the Awesta quotes of Vištāspa himself is poor: he immolates a hundred sheep to Ardvī, praying for victory over Tanθryavant (not traceable in the later legend, nor in the old myth) and Arǰataspa; the place is the lake Frazdānu in Zranka-Sīstān.[7]

In *Yt.*5,112, Zarivariš, too, immolates a hundred sheep: satam . . . anumayānām pašnē āpo dātiyayå.[8] The locality, the river Dātiyā, is insignificant, copied from old myths. The prayer runs: "that I may be victorious

prtačingam aštakānam humayakam dēvayasnam
druvatamča arǰataspam ahmi +gēθyāi (text: gēθe) prtanāhu

over Humayaka with-the-spread-out-claws, haunting-in-a-cave, the devayasnian, and over the drugvant Arǰataspa, in the fight for his family."

In the still later form of the same legend in *Yt.*9,31, we find instead of the last words

uta azam fra.rvēsyāni +humāyē +vrδanakēča

[6] With elements reversed *yuδi.aspa in n.pr. Οὐδιάσπης, Ctesias, in history of Parysatis.

[7] *Yt.*9,29-31 is only a corrupt amplification of this stanza.

[8] pašnē, *Wb.* "angesichts?," Lommel "hinter?," only in *Yt.*5, and only referring to water (Čēčista, Pišinah, Frazdānu and Dātiyā) is perhaps Old Persian, cf. OP. āšnē, Aw. āsnē "near," and OP. nipadi, Gr. πεδά.

and that I may bring home the two, Humāyā and ⁺Vrδanakā.[9] The two feminine names were originally in dvandva form. Humāyā is a name of Achaemenian ladies, Amyïtes. Here, two kidnapped women are brought home. In the older Θrētōna myth, *Yt.*5,34, the motif—if "azāni" means only "to carry away, abduct"—was the rape of women:

uta hē vantē azāni	and I may carry away the two beloved
sahavāčī arnavāčī	Sahavāχš and Arnavāχš,
yē krpa srāištē zātaye	who are the most beautiful of body for bearing children,
gēθyāi tē yē abdatamē	the most excellent for the family.[10]

If the names were right, arnavāčī ought to precede. Skr. has savasvan and ṛṇavan; the Shāhnāmah Šahrināz and Arnavāz.

To the same legend belong the verses in *Yt.*5,76, where the nōtaryāno Visataruš prays "upa āpam (yām) vētahvatīm, on the river V." ("rich in willows, or vines?"):

77: āt mē tuvąm ardvīsūra anāhitā	Open, o Ardvī, . . . to me
huškam prtum rēčaya	a dry passage
taro vahvīm vētahvatīm	through the good Vētahvatī!
78: Ardvī grants the prayer	
armēštå anyå āpo krnōt	one part of the waters she made stand still,
fraša anyå fratačayat	the other she made flow off,
huškam prtum rēčayat	a dry passage she opened
taro vahvīm vētahvatīm	through the good Vētahvatī.

The motif resembles that of *Exodus* 14,22; and more so the story in the acts of Mār Pethion, G. Hoffmann, *Syr.Akt.* p.63: Pethion is

[9] Ed. vrdakanāmča, *Wb.* ⁺vāriδkanā, without etymology. It is hypoc. of a comp. with "vrδa>gul, rose," type *vrδa.čiθra>gulčihr, in *Awr.parchm.*II, 21 B.C. Ὀλεννζείρη; hence read ⁺vrdanakā. Cf. vrdk on a seal (Berlin) and on a Sasan. graffito in the tačara, Persepolis.

[10] Benveniste, *Inf.av.*47f.: "les plus belles de corps pour l'enfantement, les plus parfaites pour le menage." Against Lommel: "die von sehr schöner Gestalt sind, um sie zu gewinnen?, die die wunderbarsten der Welt sind!" Cf. *Yt.*10,113: gēθe prtanāhu; in both cases gēθa is "family." From abdatama>aβdum comes the fem. name Αὔτομα, *Awr.parchm.*, where also Ὀλεννζείρη.

thrown into the Alwān near Sarpul, "the waters rose aloft above to a wall, below they flew off to the river Gauzan which is SNNY."[11]

Athenaeus b.13,575, quotes the story from Chares of Mytilene (*Alex.* b.10) as example of a couple that never met, but saw each other in a dream, a motif that lives on in 1001 Nights, for instance in the story of Qamar al-zamān and the daughter of the king of the Djazā'ir with her seven castles. The legend was so popular at Alexander's time, that it was often told and pictured in houses and palaces, and many named their daughters after the heroine. How quickly the legend worked can be measured by Ctesias' attributing the Bīstūn monument to Semiramis only 120 years after its creation. Also by Herodotus' telling of the myth of the seven walls of Kanhā as an historical description of Agbatana, which at that time was only 230 years old.

Hystaspes had a younger brother Zariadres, whom the "epichorians" called a son of Aphrodite and Adonis. Hystaspes was king of Media and the Lower Country (Ērāg, 'Irāq), Zariadres king of the countries above the Caspian Gates as far as the Tanaïs. Beyond the Tanaïs ruled Homartes, king of the Μαραθῶν[12] who had a daughter Odatis. Zarivariš and Zariadres are two different names.[13] As in the case of arvāspa and druvāspa, two figures are blended into one. Aphrodite stands for Ardvī, and Adonis, god of vegetation, evidently for Druvāspa, god of the animal kingdom. Homartes wants to marry his daughter to one of his grandees, but Zariadres, alone with his charioteer, drives through the Tanaïs and arrives just in time to rescue the bride. The anonymous charioteer of Chares of Mytilene, hence, is Visataruš of the yasht. The expression "ahmi gēθyāi prtanāhu" alludes to the abduction. The theme of the original myth was not the rescue of the bride, but the rape of two women; in the later form, with Humāyā and Vrδanakā instead of Sahavāχš and Arnavāχš, it was the bringing home of abducted women.

Tanaïs stands for the Ranhā, because Alexander believed the Iaxartes to be the Tanaïs-Don. The *Gr.Bdh.* 86, 88 and 91, does not equate the

[11] SNNY is Akk. (ugār)sallu, -sillu, Gr. Sillas, a Diyala canal.

[12] Markwart's Iranian interpretation of marathōn as "*mrθwa = morituri" would involve that a highly archaic name of the original myth was preserved in the late legend. The Greek names do not have that much authenticity.

[13] Hübschmann, *Arm.Gramm.* 40 and 506: Zariadres > Arm. Zareh, but zarivariš > MP. zarēr; perhaps *zarivaδra "with golden mace" and zarivari "with golden cuirass."

vētahvatī—written vātaŋvatī—with the Ranhā, but says: "Vātaŋvatī rōt pa sagistān, bunχān.ič kyānsih būt, the V. river is in Sīstān, its source was from the (sea) Kyānsih (old Kansavya)," as though it was the Shaila which connects the Hāmūn with the Zirih = Frazdānu. The following words, "Frasyāp filled it up; when Hvaršētar appears, it shall flow again," show that the river had become a mere mythical concept.

The OP. original of Gr. Ὄδατις[14] is defined by two conditions: it must be a very popular name, and it must conform to one of the names in a shape of the Iranian legend. Therefore it must be disfigured from +ordakis, OP. vrdakā "rose," +vrdanakā of *Yt.*9,31. Cf. Esther, i.e. Med.*āsθra "myrtle." The name of her father Homartes, who plays the role of Arǰataspa, is probably the ethnic hōma.vrga of the Saka tribe dwelling beyond the Iaxartes-Tanaïs. Akk. umarga', umurgu, Gr. amýrgioi are contemporary pronunciations used sind 520 B.C.; hence, foursyllabic OP. hōma.vrga is from the beginning an historic spelling.[15] Athenaeus' ʽΟΜΑΡΤΗΣ stands for ʽΟΜΑΡΓΗΣ. Arǰataspa, later called (h)yōna and Chionite, is still imagined as a Saka in this oldest version. Humayaka is depicted as a dragon in a cave (see under 'Sculpture'). It is significant for the late origin of the legend that both adversaries are called, in the mazdayasnian manner, "drugvant and dēvayasna" (see under 'Dēva').

Nyberg considers the often discussed myth of the "Flight of Rtiš," *Yt.*17, to be part of this cycle, calling it the "dunkle Blatt in der Geschichte der Naotariden."

This myth is preceded, in the manner of an introduction, by an old sacrificial rule which forbids people not yet mature or no longer procreative to take part in the cult of Rtiš. Then, st. 55 and 56 give the situation:

yat mām tūrā pazdayanta	When the Tūra scared me
āsu.aspā nōtarāsča	the swift-horsemen and nōtara.

The goddess flees, hiding once under the hoof of a bull, once under

14 Not too well attested. The Gr. omikron does not correspond to Ir. hu, nor hvā-, hence neither huδātā nor hvāδātā.

15 Markwart's "*hauma.rta, the true Hōma," is neither materially nor linguistically sound. One Umargi appears already at the end of the 8th century B.C. in the annals of Sargon, year 6. Amorges was the name of a son of Pissouthnes II, on the stela of Xanthos Lyk. humrkkā, Mily. umrggazn. The grandfather was satrap of Bactria, Her.9,64 and Ctesias in Diod.11,69,2.

the neck of a ram, evidently not like Odysseus when fleeing from the cave of Polypheme, but like sorceresses in 1001 Nights, transformed into an insect. Both times she is discovered and frustrated by immature boys and girls. Wolfgang Schultz was right in pointing out that at the second occasion it must be the senile people that discover her, and that the third incomplete stanza, with which the story stops short before a gap, must be the third and successful attempt.

The myth might be an etiologic one, motivating the sacrificial rule, or rather a description of the same qualities of the goddess which are the cause of this rule. There is no place and no allusion in it to more than one tribe; on the contrary, the children and the old people are all of one kind, anāryan Tūra. Tūrā and nōtarā are not two names, but one name with an appellative. nōtarā is not the gentilicium nōtaryåho, but the regular comparative of "nava νεός," referring to the contrasted ages, "the comparatively young Tūrā, the youthful (among them)." āsu.aspā describes them as on horseback.[16]

Nyberg connects this story of the immature children with his idea that Zoroaster, in the "Wedding Gatha" (see under 'Maga')—though in vain—had tried to substitute his own daughter Puručistā as "Goddess of Fertility" for Rtiš. The myth would prove the comprehensible "resistance of the Mithra-community against this innovation," and the "dunkle Blatt" thus becomes a "sehr bedeutsamer religionsgeschichtlicher Vorgang." The flight of the goddess is not a tale specific for Rtiš, but a primeval myth widely spread over the world; in Iran, there was a variant in the tale of the flight of the goddess of Earth before the dragon AžiDahāka-Frahrasyā. On no account is it a "Vorgang" based on real actions of historical or half-historical persons. It was aeons old before Vištāspa and Zoroaster were born, and one can cheerfully tear the "dark page" from the family chronicle of the Nōtarya. There were enough skeletons in the closet.

An independent proof for the identity of the two Vištāspa follows from their place of residence: the Vištāspa of the inscriptions was satrap of Parthava, the capital of which was Tōsa, later Tōs ē Nōdarān <*tōsa nōtarānām. And the residence of the Awestic Vištāspa was,

[16] This explains the misunderstanding in *Yt.*5,98, where āsu.-aspa is taken as appellative of nōtara, this as nōtarya. Ved. tura means "quick, wild."

according to *Yt*.5,15 "viso awi nōtarānām, the vis of the Nōtara," in the fragment of the legend dealing with Hutōsā-Atossa. This place can be determined, and for that purpose one needs the figure of Tusa in *Yt*.5,53-57, who is not an old-mythical, but an historical figure of the Vištāspa circle.

In *Yt*.5,53, the "swift raθēštā, chariot-fighter, Tusa" brings offerings "bršēšu pati aspānām" and prays for victory over the "valiant Vēsaki sons, hunavo vēsakaya[17] upa dvaram +caθrusūkam apanatamam kanhayå brzantiyā rtāvniyā." Tusa furthermore desires victory over all Tūra. The Vēsaki are Tūra, but their town, Kanhā, is always called rtāvan, for reasons unknown, but certainly in the oldest, pre-Zoroastrian connotation of the term, approximately to be rendered by "just."

In st. 57, on the contrary, the Vēsaki sons pray "upa dvaram +caθrusūkam etc." for victory over Tusa and over all Aryans. In this legend, created shortly after the time of Zoroaster, the Vēsaki are a vis and bear an historical name. For vēsaka is written on a seal of the Achaemenian epoch with the picture of a horseman, dismounted, hunting a boar, and with the legend VYSK. This fine seal belonged to the vispatiš of the family, about 400 B.C. The name vēsaki, -°kaya, is a gentilic, derivative of vēsaka, this again short-form of a compound with vrddhi of vis- as first element, as in vāisapuθra, cf. bēvarpati, *spāδapati as family names.

Their locality is broadly described: "at the gate, the market, the distant one, in Kanhā," meaning a famous building: in the legend as told already by Herodotus, Kanhā was the prototype of the "town with seven walls" (see under 'Architecture').

In the late Sasanian legend, the name of the Vēsak who gave his daughter to Siyāvuχš is Pīrān, and Biruni records in his *akhbār Khwārizm*[18] that Fīl, i.e. Pīr, was the old name of the capital Gurganj. The Vēsaki are Tūra, and Tūr was a district of Khwārizm according to Moses of Chorene. This gives the Vēsaki as "lords of Pīr in Khwārizm" and their place Kanhā as Gurganj. In the Kartēr inscrip-

[17] It is not permissible to restore +vēsaka for metrical reasons: the verses are weak in language and meter. vysky means vēsakayo. The seal in the Brit.Mus., in CISEM., II, n.89, pl. VI has VYSK. The family name is personified in the romance of Vēs u Rāmin.

[18] In Yāqūt, *mu'djam* II,843, s.v. Khwārizm, and II,54, s.v. Gurganj; cf. Benveniste, BSOS VII,273.—Markwart saw Kanhā in Chin. kang.kü = Soghd, and was inclined to recognize Sogd. *kaχa = kanha in Ptolemy's *καχάγαι* Scythians.

tions a figure called "kangopet, lord of Kang?" seems to play the role of Virgil in Dante. The NP. form is Gang, for a mythical place only. The etymology of the name is obscure. "antara.kanha, between, within K." is enumerated in *Yt.*19,4 among the names of mountains; today, Kang and Miyān-Kang, i.e. antara.kanha, are partial names of the Hilmand delta in Sīstān, and one would expect a signification connected with water. Below Gurganj, the Oxus delta begins.

If the Tūryan Vēsaki have an historical background, the more so the Iranian Tusa. In *Yt.*5,53, he brings his offerings "at the necks of the horses, praying for health of the bodies," both in plural. These verses imitate the original in *Yt.*10,11, where the "raθēštāro bršēšu pati aspānām, the chariot fighters, standing at the necks of their horses" pray for "force of the two-horse teams, integrity of (their) bodies." There, the plural is right, and the author of 5,53 has failed to adapt his model correctly. The kind of faults resembles those in the inscriptions of Artaxerxes II, and the date of the verses agrees therewith: end of the 5th century B.C.

Tusa is not "eine Kollektivbezeichnung für ein Adelsgeschlecht," Nyberg, 259, because that would require an adj. gent. like *tusiya, *tōsiya. Sasanian tradition knows nothing about Tusa, but speaks of Tōs ē nōδarān, where Tōs is an adjective, nōδarān a gen.pl. There was never a Tōs nor a Nōδar, and Tōs was no "heros eponymus eines mit dem kavi-Hause nahe verschwägerten Geschlechts." Nyberg, 357: "Man hat die Genealogien der Alten immer mit der nötigen Kritik zu verwenden." Compared with the Sasanian genealogies of heroes and priests—all epithets transfigured into fathers, sons and brothers—the begat-chapters of Genesis are a reliable source of history. Arab genealogists like ibn al-Kalbī work similarly, arranging all names of old towns, rivers, canals in pedigrees of men. But, so far, nobody has recognized "nahe verschwägerte Geschlechter" in these topic names.

Tusa is an historical figure, for he gave his name to the capital of Parthava, Tōsa > NP. Tūs, famous by the tomb of Firdausi. Tōs ē Nōδarān, first "spāhpet of Tōs," a military title like bēvarpati as title of the Dānavo in *Yt.*13,38, is not the man Tusa, but the town called after him. Firdausi still uses nōδarān correctly as plural: "šahr i nōδarān Tōs, Tōs, city of the Nōδarān."[19] In the *Čīt.Zātsp.* 16,12 the

[19] Shāhnāmah Vullers 1086,49; 1109,770; cf. Nöldeke, *Iran.Nat.Epos.* p.8.

proverb "not if the two cities Ray and Nōδar would meet here" is explained by "Zoroaster was from Ray, Vištāsp from Nōδar." Such a proverb has an historical background. The man Tōs ē nōδarān is the result of a misinterpretation of the name of the town; therefore the legend has nothing to say about this name. Of necessity it becomes a brother of Vistahm e Nōδarān, i.e. the client Visataruš nōtaryāno transformed into a "son of Nōδar." The purpose of this invention is apparent: a genealogy had to be created for the Arsacid family of the Spāhpet of Tōs, the predecessors of the Kanārang, as the *Šahr.Ēr.* expressly state: "The town Tōs is founded by Tōs ē Nōδarān; for 900 years he was spāhpet;[20] after Tōs, the dignity of spāhpet came to Zarēr, after Zarēr to Bastvar, from him to Kurazm." Perhaps the Spāhpet were actually descendants of Tusa, but these names are taken from the memorial list of *Yt.*13: the *family of Vištāspa became a dynasty of Tōs,* the residence of the historical Vištāspa.

In *Yt.*15,35 Hutōsā prays "viso awi nōtarānām"—the obligatory determination of the locality—"that I may be dear, beloved and esteemed, patizantā, in the nmāna of kavi Vištāspa." nmāna is the small family, a number of which constitute the vis, at the same time their residence, house or palace. Here vis is the place, nmāna the familia; for Hutōsā does not want to be loved by buildings. patizantā is the model of NP. tašrīf, and implies as what she wants to be "esteemed, honored,"[21] namely as "nmānapaθnī > bānbišn," title of the Sasanian queens.

Vištāspa is the vispatiš of the Nōtarya, hence nōtarānām as surname of his residence. Vis signifies the men of the clan, their residence and property. In the OP. inscriptions, Persepolis and Agbatana are called viθ, as residence of the Hystaspids. Thus vis becomes "town." Vis nōtarānām is Firdausi's šahr i nōδarān. Vis nōtarānām and *tōsa nōtarānām, the residence of the Nōtara, are identical. The Aw. vis nōtarānām is, like ārya.šayanam for āryānām χšaθram, the poetical expression, intelligible for everyman, for the capital of Parthava, Tōsa, where Hutōsā prayed.

This town, the capital of Parthava, and not the "Steppen des turischen Friyāna-Stammes an der Ranhā, dem Iaxartes," is conceived

[20] Perhaps originally "they were": 900 years, if counted from the date of the oldest form of the *Šahr.Ēr.*, A.D. 490 would lead back into the 5th century B.C.; if 900 p.Zor., the remark would date from A.D. 604.

[21] Cf. patizantā in Y.29,11 under 'Maga,' and +zaznate in Y.30,10, under 'Myastra.'

in the entire Awesta and in the legend as the residence of Zoroaster's protector Vištāspa. The same town was the residence of the historical Vištāspa as satrap of Parthava according to the inscriptions.

The traditional legends of the temples that claim to be founded by Vištāspa agree with the inscriptions, the Awesta and the epics, and the memorial list of *Yt.*13 proves the historical fact that Vištāspa had founded such temples. One of them was the Kishmar temple, see under 'Chronology.'

Gr.Bdh. 124: "Yam put the āδarχvarrah (=farnabag) on mount Hvarnahvant (GDH'vmnd) in Xwārizm on its cultic place. When they cut Yam in two, the āδarχvarrah saved the χvarrah of Yam from the hand of Dahāk. Under the reign of Vištāspšāh, by a revelation of the religion, it was transferred from Xvārizm to the Rōšan kōf in the country, dēh, of the Kanārang, where it exists still today" [date of the *Gr.Bdh.*, 9.scl. A.D. or of its source?].

Procopius deals with the *χαναράγγαι*, *Bell.Pers.* Bonn p.5, 7 and 23, on the authority of Kavāt, son of Jām, an elder brother of Xusrau II. Since the time of Balāsh, A.D. 484-488, they had been margraves of Nīshāpūr, SW. of Tōs; there, the Arabs knew them still during and after the conquest as kanārang or banū Kanāra, cf. *Yāqūt* II,411. According to ibn Khurdādhbih, "kunār" was the "title" of the king of Nīshāpūr. The name of the mountain, which can also be read rōyēn, refers to Aw. "rōδita, copper mountain" in *Yt.*19,2, written RVDšn'vmnd in the *Gr.Bdh.* The legend (cf. Mas'ūdī IV,75) rightly treats the words "pa pētākīh ač dēn" as meaning that the old fire had been forgotten and had to be rediscovered "by order of Zoroaster." In fact, the temple was not older than Vištāspa's time, and its place was in the Nīshāpūr district.

Gr.Bdh. 125: "When Zoroaster brought the religion . . . , Vištāspa put the āδar-burzēnmihr on its cultic place on mount Rēvand, which is also called pušt ē Vištāspān." That is the rēvant of *Yt.*19,6; *Gr.Bdh.*: "u.š rēvand nām ku rāyawmand," and p.80: "mount Vināpet[22] is together with the pušt ē Vištāspān; from there to rēvand, where the

[22] vināpet < gunābiδ, in the Shāhnāmah place of the battle in which the paladins of Kai-Xusrau defeated the Vēsak Pīrān, is probably the transposition of an Arab. broken plur. of gumbaδ into Pahlavi: "the cupolas." Gumbaδ itself is an Ir. loanword from Ass. qubbatu.

āδarburzēnmihr is, are 9 farsakh towards west." This Rēvand—another one lies not far south—is situated northwest of Nīshāpūr not far from Tōs, near the turquoise mines. Yāqūt, *mu'djam* 1,628, still notes a district Pusht in that area.

"pušt, back" designates a mountain formation; pušt e vištāspān would be "Vištāspian back" or "back of the Vištāspas," rather objectionable.[23] In the legend of the foundation of the fire of Shēz in Ādharbāijān, the āδargušnasp sits down, like a corposant, on the mane of Husravah's horse,[24] pa bušn ē asp. That is a Persian etymology of the Median name "gušnasp <*vršn.aspa, stallion," which presupposes Pers. bušnasp <*vušnaspa. This form appears on the reverse of late Sasanian copper coins from Old Shīrāz and Bīshāpūr as legend at the side of the figure of a human-headed bull: bušaspān or bušnašpān.[25] Hence, it is possible that the name of the mountain pušt ē vištaspān is a new interpretation of pušt ē bušnaspān, when the meaning "back of a stallion" became obscured and the name was connected with the fact that Vištāspa had founded the temple.

The *Gr.Bdh.* goes on: "These fires are ātaχš ē varhrān, dynastic fires." One of them must have been the temple in which the original document of the memorial list was preserved. Thus three temples which retrace their foundation to Vištāspa lie around Tōs.

Tōsa became known to the Greeks through Alexander who passed through it on his march from Zadrakarta in Hyrcania to Areia; Arrian III,25 writes *Σουσια,* Ptolemy *Μυσια,* both for *ΤΟΥΣΑ

In the memorial document, Zoroaster with his kinsmen opens the list of men; Vištāspa with his male relatives follows. In the same way, Zoroaster's three wives and one daughter open the list of women, and

[23] Similar terms of terrain: "grīvā, neck," changing with "kamrδa, skull" in arzurahe grīvā, *Vid.*3,7; "forest-neck or -top," cf. "garīwa i Ṭāq i Girra, pass of the arch of the cupper," name of the Zagros Gates. Or "kōhak, hump," e.g. du.kōhak between Khuzistan and Fārs, kauphiaka of Ptolemy; like Turk. deve boyun, Aram. *gab.gamlā > Gaugamela "camel's hump." Also "baršna, neck, mane"—thus to be read against *Wb.* in *Yt.*19,40; and "a.baršnu beside a.sāra, without neck and head"; this word was recognized by Pagliaro in MP. bušn in Zarērnāmak.

[24] This phenomenon occurs in Samarra when, during electric storms, the sword of the Mahdi is dipped into the basin of the Ghaibat al-Mahdī and carried round in procession; also the golden cupola starts sometimes blazing. It is believed to be a token that the Mahdi visits his tomb.

[25] The obverse shows a male bust with flaming nimbus and legend "Dārā."

Hutōsā and Humāyā, the ladies of Vištāspa's family, follow. Both names appear in the Achaemenid family, the second as name of the Median mother of Atossa, which Ctesias connects with the Spitamas.

Berossos, in Syncellus, from Eusebius and Polyhistor, renders Humāyā by Amyïtēs, as name of the Median wife of Nebuchadnezzar, a better form than Amytis.[26] The later legend mixes Amyites with Semiramis, occasionally also with Khuṭōs-Atossa.[27] The name persists in the Achaemenid family: e.g. Amytis, daughter of Xerxes and Amēstris, sister of Artaxerxes I, wife of Bagabuχša, whose grandson was called Spitāma. It is possible, but not necessary, that the Humāyā of the list was Atossa's and Zoroaster's mother. The occurrence of the name in *Yt.*9,28, along with Vrδanakā, has no other historical significance but that Achaemenid names infiltrate into the legend.

Herodotus 1,75 and 107, regards Cyrus as grandson of Astyages by his daughter Mandane, married to Cambyses I. That would be a relationship of the two houses by marriage one generation earlier, but would not rule out the marriage of Cyrus to another daughter of Astyages. But "father-in-law" as Ctesias says is better than "maternal grandfather," because Astyages, dethroned in 550, can scarcely be of the same generation as Cyrus I who had a son, at least half grown, as hostage at the court of Assurbanipal as early as 640 B.C. There are cases, soon to be mentioned, where children were born as grand-uncles, but in the case of Astyages and Cyrus the great-grandfather did not live long enough to make that possible.

The gatha alludes to the two ladies only by calling Cambyses "bandva, affinis, relative-in-law" of Zoroaster.

The name Hutōsā, Gr. Atossa, means *καλλίπυγος*, corresponding to the ideal of beauty as expressed in representations of women in Achaemenian and Sasanian art. Her appearance in *Yt.*9,26, Zoroaster's prayer in Arsacid Awestic, is significant for one reason only: the

[26] Initial a for hu- as in Atossa-Hutōsā and other cases; as to ūi for āy cf. Parmys <*purumāya, NP. purmāyah; on the other hand the Elam. transcription of OP. āi by oi. As to the ending cf. the common Akk. fem. in -ītu, and assimilation to Anaïtis.

[27] Ḥamza Isf. 38: "Humāy Čihrāzādh is Shamīrān, daughter of Bahman." Tabari 1,678: "Khuṭōs, wife of Luhrāsp." Hellanicus, in Phlegon, frgm.163, 430-400 B.C.: "Atossa, daughter of Ariaspes." Eusebius and Barbarus: "Atossa quae et Semiramis." Yaḥyā b. Djarīr al-Takrītī, Christian physician, of the first half of 6th century H., in Yāqūt II,305, from chronicles like Syncellus or Eusebius: "In the year 59 of the dynasty of Salūkūs (or Bēlūkūs) al-Mauṣilī (i.e Assur), Tausā, who is Samīram, became queen, with her father who founded Aleppo."

quotation of gatha 46,7, whereby Hutōsā, instead of the Hāugava brothers, becomes the person through whom Zoroaster hopes to obtain the official "frasastiš, the proclamation" of his recognition. Else, not counting *Yt.*13, Hutōsā appears only in *Yt.*15,35, where she prays to become honored, as queen, in the family of kavi Vištāspa. These verses stand in a yasht, hence are no direct historical notice. The task is to examine how far they depict the situation in a distorted, how far still in the right way.

The adornment alone of the verses shows, in the luxury it describes, the character of the period and therewith the date of their composition: before the end of the 5th century B.C. Hutōsā prays like a queen

zaranēnē pati gātōu	at the golden throne,
zaranēnē pati fraspāti[28]	at the golden dais,
zaranēnē pati upastarnē	at the golden cushion,

on which she is imagined sitting before she rises for her prayer, just as later the Sasanids and the Umayyads and Abbasids squat on "royal brocades, dībāǰ i χusrawānī" as cushions and rugs on their chryselephantine and canopied thrones.

The identification of Hutōsā-Atossa has been rejected as emphatically as that of Vištāspa-Hystaspes. Nyberg, 358: "Wenn Atossa als Beweis dafür dienen kann, dass die genannte Dame einem zoroastrischen Geschlecht angehöre, so ist jede Ingeborg und Ingegerd . . . ein Beweis dafür, dass ihre Vorfahren der uralten . . . Kultgemeinde der Ingvaeoninnen angehörten."—Hertel concluded that the Awestic Vištāspa was the father of Darius and that *Yt.*15 alluded to Darius' marriage to Atossa. Nyberg: "Es giebt nicht den Schimmer eines Beweises . . . und nicht einmal Herzfeld heisst das gut. Vištāspas Gattin heisst Atossa."

A theory of which not even I approve, must be pretty bad. However, in this presentation, Atossa would be contemporary with Zoroaster; in the contested view equally; how, then, could the family have been Zoroastrian before Zoroaster? The prayer of *Yt.*15 does not say that Hutōsā was a sister of Vištāspa, as the "tradition" assumes; nor that she was his wife; but only that she wished to marry into his narrower

[28] On the signification of "fraspāt-ouraniscus," connected with "spayaθra, vault of heaven," see under 'Astronomy.'

family. Instead of marrying the old vispatiš himself, soon to become dowager lady Nōtarī, she would rather have chosen the heir. Ingvaeoninnen would have felt the same.

A man may have more than one main wife (whose children have full claim to inheritance), and not only in the clan, but in the nmāna there are more than one marriageable man. The man marries young, at the age of 16; not of necessity at first the main wife. He remains in the nmāna of his father. But one is not vispatiš when 16 years old; that is the eldest member of the clan, sometimes the one oldest in rank. The vispatiš, always old, may go on marrying to his liking, but the posts of his main wives, the "zātayē gēθyāi abdatamå," are long since occupied. All that was exactly the same to the present day. The married grandson of such a grandee answered, when asked "how is your grandfather?" only: "les noces continuent." Atossa has in *Yt.*15 the two attributes "āzātā and purubrāθrā." Many girls had "many brothers," in royal families as many as there are days in a year. The above mentioned grandee, a septuagenarian, questioned how many sons he had, answered: "faut demander mon chef comptable." Then he called into the garden where far away a dozen boys between 5 and 10 years were playing, and said "permettez que je vous présente quelques-uns de mes plus jeunes enfants." He knew that the eldest was a grandson, but their names were unknown to him. Thus, a difference of fifty years is possible between the ages of brothers.

purubrāθrā indicates that Hutōsā was married to several brothers, as vice versa the saint Ardavīrāz was married to his seven sisters. The tradition, therefore, regards Hutōsā as sister and wife of Vištāspa. Her attributes are a good description of the homonymous daughter of Cyrus whose brothers were, according to Ctesias, on the one hand the sons of Cyrus, on the other those of the Spitāma, and who married some of them. Nyberg, who denies the identity of the namesakes, calls, 357, the historical Atossa—while he makes Hutōsā "Zarathustra den guten Leumund, frasastis, besorgen"—"eine Dame mit bunter Vergangenheit, sowohl mit Cambyses, als mit dem Pseudo-Smerdis verheiratet gewesen," as though this could reflect on Zoroaster's reputation. Perhaps that makes her so interesting; somebody has said: "interesting are only those men with a future and women with a past." But it should be really "colorful": "mit ihrem Bruder Cambyses, ihrem pseudo-Bruder Gōmāta, und ihrem Vetter Darius verheiratet gewesen." As Cyrus' heiress she could have taken every liberty, except remaining a spinster. The kings had their harem, and for Atossa, too, her marriages were no love romances, no more than for the beautiful Musa who, when widowed, married her son Phraates V only 5 years old, on account of the regency.

The mother of Cambyses II and Smerdis was Kassandane; since Atossa married Cambyses and the pseudo-Smerdis, she was no daughter of Kassandane. And since Cyrus appointed both sons to succeed him and the line became extinct with them, he had no son from Astyages' daughter—the one Ctesias calls Amytes—for he would have been the heir. The true and the false brother marry their half-sister Atossa as "āzātā, agnata," as the heiress. She was the heiress of Media by her mother, whose dowry, Ctesias says, was the whole of Media. Amytes must have been Atossa's mother. Through her she was even more august than Cambyses and Smerdis. Probably born in 549/8, she was slightly older than Darius, her third husband, born about 545 B.C., whom, as Herodotus says, she dominated completely: ἡ γὰρ Ἄτοσσα εἶχε τὸ πᾶν κράτος. Therefore it was her son Xerxes who succeeded, although, as he himself says, there were elder brothers.

Hutōsā has left a deep impress on the minds of the people. They do not only remember that she was the āzātā and purubrāθrā, and linked in marriage to the family of Vištāspa. In *Yt.*9,26 the hope is imputed to Zoroaster that she might obtain for him the frasastiš. In the Gatha he hopes to obtain this revocation of his banishment by the ability of the two Hāugava, but nowhere through Vištāspa, his protector. *Yt.*9 is no Gatha, but the thought must have figured in the legend to which *Yt.*15,35 belongs, and there Hutōsā must have been imagined to have a greater influence on the person granting the frasastiš, than even Vištāspa. Whereas the legend everywhere considers him as an absolute sovereign, it has here preserved a memory of the fact that he had only the limited power of a satrap and was subject to a higher power which Hutōsā could better influence: Cyrus or Cambyses. To imagine her as speaking in favor of Zoroaster may even be a last remembrance of their relationship. This special relationship can be discussed only after having determined the word "bandva," and that requires wider researches.

Atossa's half-brother Smerdis (Ionic form) is called Brδya in OP., rendered by Mardos in Aeschylus, Merdias in a scholion, Merdis in Trogus. But the Median form is Brzya, BRZY of the Pap.El., rendered by Maraphis, Merphis in the scholion to Aeschylus' *Pers.* 775, from Hellanicus.[29] Brzya is the shortform of a name with "brzi, high" as first and with suppressed second element. Other shortforms of such a name are Gr. Mardontes < OP. *brδvant, and Barzaëntes < Med. brzvant. Brδya's daughter Parmȳs was married to Darius and had a son Ariomardos,[30] the second element of which is the first of the name of the grandfather. Such variations of names are general in IE. languages, cf. ršti.-vēga: vēži.rstiš under 'Throne-names.' The suppressed component of the name may have been ršti. In the memorial list of *Yt.*13, brzi.rštiš stands beside vēži.rštiš, after the brothers and before the sons of Vištāspa, just as the Frānya brothers-in-law, Medes, stand among the relatives of Zoroaster. Therefore, one is allowed not only to regard brzi.rštiš as the full form of the hyp. Brzya, but to consider the persons, Brδya of the inscriptions, and Brzi.rštiš of the list, as identical.

If his name appears in the document, Smerdis must have joined the circle around Vištāspa and Zoroaster, as did his sister Atossa. He was thrown into prison and secretly killed, more likely before Cambyses' campaign against Egypt, spring 525, than as Herodotus says, during that campaign. The memorial list can contain his name as that of a deceased, but at first one must assume that he was still alive at that date. The connection of Zoroaster with the great events of that period becomes clearer step by step.

Nyberg calls, e.g. on p.357, the equations "Hutōsā = Atossa" and "Vištaspa = Vištāspa" "den Eckstein der ganzen Konstruktion, die so unsinnig ist, wie nur etwas sein kann," a criticism that can result either from supreme assurance or from great ignorance. His reasons are, p.45: "Die Hypothese scheitert rettungslos daran, dass die erwähnte Gleichsetzung—undenkar ist," an anticlimax. The nōtarya Vištāspa of the Awesta is a Persian with a Median name, vispatiš of the clan nōtarānām,

29 Cf. Markwart UGE II,137; also *Altp.Inschr.* 80.—Cf. θrētōna > Farīdūn, and Russ. Feodor, Marfa, with f for θ. Vice versa: tahmo rupi > tahmuraθ.

30 With ario-, i.e. ārya-, the name gives no sense: "Aryan-high." The Gr. ario- enters for less frequent elements, like arvat-, in Ariaspes for arva.aspa, hara- in ariobarzanes for harā-brzatī. Thus it may here supplant *ārštya-, cf. ārštya.brzan, or *ršti.brδa > Gr. *asti(o)mardos > ariomardos.

a name demanding the existence of an elder branch of the same family. His residence is the capital of Parthava, Tōsa, and his time the last decades of the sixth century B.C. Vištāspa, father of Darius, responds to every detail of that description. The Hutōsā of the Awesta is āzātā, agnate, purubrāθrā, married to brothers of her, related by marriage to the family of Vištāspa, closely connected with another lady, Humāyā, and has power over the highest instance which Vištāspa cannot influence. Atossa, daughter of Cyrus, answers the same description. There is quite a solid foundation of such "cornerstones." With Pharnakes = ātarhvarnah, the Vēhviya = Vivāna, the Hāugava Zāmā.aspa, Fraṣ̌a.-uštra and Fraša.aspa (Prēxaspes), the Vaŋhuδātayana Dātuvanhya, father of Bagabuχša, and in the following generation Pissouthnes, Oxyartes, Artaÿktes, Artostes, Artembares, Damaspia etc., the gathas and the Awesta contain about two dozen of names of persons which appear under the same name in analogous roles in history. Against these facts no invocation can help, no Ingeborg and Ingegerd, no William of Orange or Hohenzollern, no Charles of Spain or Sweden.

V. THRONE-NAMES

"That Son of Man was called in presence of the Lord of Spirits, and his name before the Aged Head"

Herodotus calls the founder of the Median empire Deiokes, i.e. Daiaukku of the annals of Sargon II, l.76 (*Display inscr.* 49) mentioned in 715-713 B.C.—This date is before the foundation of the empire, 678 B.C., so he is not the ktístes, but the eponymus of the dynasty; their name would be in Assyrian mārē Daiaukku, their land bīt Daiaukku.[1] From the Šamaš omina one may infer that Wamitiaršu <*vahmayat.rša was the name of the first king, dahyupatiš of the Māda, and that the motive power behind their coalition (hangmatāna?) was a Deiocid Xšaθrita, Ass. kaštariti, zantupatiš of KārKašši—this place being the pre-Median Agbatana.

It was a mistake of W. König, in AOF VII,6, repeated by Nyberg, 334, to doubt the Iranian character of the name Daiaukku. In the memorial document of *Yt.*13 are several names formed with dahyu, ǰara.dahyu, ātar.dahyu and dahyu.frāδah, dahyu.sruta, and -ukku is an Iranian dimin. suffix, especially common in high antiquity, e.g. Assyrian annals.[2] To them belongs Aru.ukku, name of the eldest son of Cyrus I in the Assurbanipal prism. The names of the inscription of Aghačaqale: ΟΡΟΜΑΝΗΙ ΤΕ ΑΡΙΟΥΚΟΥ ΚΑΙ ΑΡΙΟΥΚΗΙ ΦΙΛΩΙ ΥΙΩΙ suggest aru.ukku = ariuk, both as hypoc. of Āryāramna rather than of Arvataspa.[3] Cf. also OP. ma(n)dauka, Gr. mandaukē, *Altp.Inschr.* p.40; OP. vahauka, Gr. Ὦχος < vahuδāta.

Herodotus calls Deiokes' successor Phraortes, a true Deiocid name, as proved by the fact that the Median pretender in Behistun appears under that assumed name: Fravartiš. Bartholomae regarded it as the shortform of a comp. with the fem. fravarti. Fravarti has many connotations, e.g. "compurgator, cojuror" (see under 'Last Judgment'). Nyberg believes the "bemerkenswert arische Name" to mean "kurzum

[1] Thureau-Dangin, R.Ass. XXIV, 1927, p.75,n.3 and A. G. Lie, *Inscr. of Sargon II,* 1,pp.28ff., consider the previous reading of the local name "bīt Daiaukki" in *Annals* l.140, year 9, as erroneous.

[2] Nöldeke, *Pers.Stud.* 35, noted the contrast between the final -k disappearing elsewhere, but preserved in diminutives. Perhaps the dimin. -k was geminated, as in Assyr. spelling, an instance of gemination in infantile and familiar speech.

[3] Situated southwest of Diwrigi, Asia Minor. S. Reinach, Rev.Ét.Gr. XVIII, 1905, 159ff., and Ad. Wilhelm, Jahrb. Oesterr. Archaeol. Inst. VII, 1909, n⁰ 225.

'Bekenntnis,' durch das man in die Gemeinschaft der Mazdah-Verehrer aufgenommen wird. Dieser Mann war also ein nicht-Arier, der in die arische Religionsgemeinschaft und damit in die herrschende Klasse aufgenommen war." A name "confession," however, would not express what the man confessed. And the numberless hosts of Fravarti, ancestors and "manes" of the Aryans would all be non-Aryans admitted into the ruling class.

The name of the third Mede, Gr. Kyaxares, with k for χ < OP. huvaχštra, is an epithet of the god Vrthragna, written huvaχštəm, i.e. +huv.aχštram in *Yt.*14,25; it is syn. of awyaχštar, abstr. awyaχštra, meaning "good guardian." The name reveals the pre-Zoroastrian religion of the bearer.[4]

The name of the last Median king is Astyágēs in Herodotus, better Astyígās in Ctesias, Akk. ištuwēgu, i.e. "Med. ršti.vēga, brandishing the lance," not "vielleicht skythisch." With elements reversed, as vēži.rštiš, the name appears in *Yt.*13,101, at a very prominent place: behind the brothers and before the sons of Vištāspa, and at the side of brzi.rštiš, Brδya, son of Cyrus. The names around Zoroaster are similarly arranged: first the Frānya, brothers-in-law, then the sons. To form the names of grandfather, father and son of parallel-similar or reversed-equal elements is a general IE. custom, cf. brzi.rštiš-Brδya, grandfather of *ršti.brza > +Astimardos-Ariomardos. Vēži.rštiš, hence, may be a grandson of Rštivēga, Astyages.

The eponym of the Achaemenids is Haχāmaniš. His son was Čahišpiš, probably the king who led the Persians from their original habitat in Media into Fārs. The members of the elder line of his descendants bear alternatingly the names Cyrus and Cambyses.

"Weder Čišpi noch Kūruš sind arische Namen"—thus Nyberg—has been said before, e.g. Mas'ūdī,II,127: "Some maintain Cyrus' mother was a Jewess and the prophet Daniel his maternal uncle." The El. and Akk. transliterations of OP. č[a] i š p[a] i š, viz. ci.s.pi.s and ši.iš.pi.iš, prove a bisyllabic pronunciation in 520 B.C., but allow i or ē. The rendering of OP. +δātovahya by El. ta.t.tu.van.ia and Akk. za.'.tu.'.a proves the coexistence of an archaic pronunciation +δātovanhya and a con-

[4] ukšatar in Sargon's 8th Camp., l.42, year 714 B.C., is more likely Med. hvaχštra than Xšaθrita; both Deiocid names.

temporary zātovēh. It is an error to believe that "OP. čišpi had greater authority than Gr. Teïspēs." The Greeks, who had a name Thisbe, had no reason to render bisyllabic Čispiš by a trisyllabic Teïspēs, unless they heard it. As a rule, the Greeks render the Ir. affricata č in old names by θ; t replaces it only under the law of two aspirates; hence, as Markwart recognized, *τεΐσπης* stands for **θεʿίσπης* = čahišpiš > čēšpiš, an archaic name, resembling čāχšniš in Mem.Doc. *Yt.*13,114, and sāiždriš < *sāyuždriš in 13,113. Phonetics and formation are thoroughly Iranian, and the man was certainly an Aryan.[5]

Andreas expressed, at the Hamburger Oriental. Kongress, 1902, the opinion: "Kūruš ist im Ap. ein u-Stamm, im Elam., Akk. und Hebr. nicht. Nie wird ein Ap. u-Stamm sonst von andren Sprachen in einen a-Stamm verwandelt. Also ist das a ursprünglich und im Ap. in u verwandelt, um das charakteristische -š im Nominativ zu erhalten. Kyros ist also ein Elamit." So says the book of Daniel and Tabari, 1,656: Kīrūš al-ʿAilamī. Markwart called the assertion at once "lächerlich."

Berossus, frgm.2, in Alexander Polyhistor, says of Cyrus II: *Πέρσης ὢν ἰθαγενής*. He must have known a Babylonian document with "parsāʾa mār parsāʾa, arri arrišitir." There is no sense in contesting the nationality of Cyrus. Andreas started from his special "vowel-theory" which he wanted to support by the doubly wrong equation: Cyrus a Mardos = Amardos = Hapirti (cf. above). There was no interest to preserve the -š in the nominative (only), and no other foreign a-stems are changed into u-stems. The first Cyrus is mentioned by Assurbanipal in 639 B.C. (*Assur prism,* Berlin). Assyrian has a type fuʿúl, but no fúʿul, and assimilates OP. kúruš to its type fuʿal:kūraš. The a is insignificant. The Babylonians assume the Assyrian form, and Hebr. Kōräš renders the Akk. form. Cyrus I called his son Cambyses, and the next two generations consider these names important enough to repeat them.

Cambyses is OP. k b u ǰ i y, Aram. knbvzy, pronunciation kanbūža.[6] The connection of both names with the Indian Kurú and Kambōja was recognized a hundred years ago by Windischmann; Weber

[5] Possibly čahi for čahra or čahvant, plus √sū- plus i suff., with -šp- < -sp- < -śv-. Other renderings of čahišpiš: te.ušpa, a Cimmerian, with Assyr. dissimilation; two Achaemenids in Herodotus, Tëaspes; also Thespias in Diodor. after Hieronymus of Cardia. One of Markwart's examples is ambiguous: Tissaphernes for the more common čiθrahvarnah, or for the rare Tīšfarn < *tištrya.hvarnah of the Mahrnāmak? One may add Tithraustes, if from *čiθra.vahišta.

[6] nb with labio-dental b. Ar. -ki̯- > Ir. -šy- > š, hence -gi̯- > -žy- > ž. Greek Kambyses, but as ethnic kambyzoi, recognized by Markwart in Ptolemy's Tambyzoi, VI,11.

considered it as evident; Markwart, UGE II,137, calls them "ethnics, kūruš with vrddhi from kurú"; also Charpentier in ZII II(1923),144f.—The Rgveda knows only a n.pr. kuru.śravaṇa, but in later literature the kurú are frequently mentioned, often together with Gandhāra and Bāhlīka. Aśoka's rule extended over Kambōja and Yōna (Graeco-Bactria),[7] and the Buddhist "List of Sixteen Nations" contains the Kuru, and, at the end, Gandhāra and Kambōja.[8] The Jātaka describe the latter as great horsebreeders, one tells of their killing of insects, snakes, frogs and vermin, considered to be a religious merit.[9] The grammarian Yāska (500 B.C.?) quotes the word "śavati, he goes" as proof that their dialect was foreign, and this is indeed OIr. šavati, not OI. cyavate.[10] The Mahābhārata enumerates them with Andra, Śaka (in Arachosia), Yavana (in Gandhāra), and Vāhlīka (in Bactria), and tells of Arjuna's victory over the Darada (Kashmir) and Kambōja. Kuru and Kambōja, hence, clearly belong to the area of the Iranian satrapy Gandāra. One reason to give a proper name of such type—another example is Amorges, hōmavrga—to a child is that it was born in those lands, but this hardly fits the case of the four generations of Persian kings. Their names recall Lat. Germanicus, Britannicus etc., and were honorific names, for participation in wars and conquests. Gandāra must have been added to the Median empire before 639 B.C.

We do not know the names the first three Hystaspids bore before their accession; the personal name of later kings is only mentioned where the succession was contested. But in dārayavahuš, χšaya.rša, rta.χšaθ^ra, we meet with a species of names differing in principle from all older names of the Medes and of the elder line of the Achaemenids. These are no mere personal names, no real compounds, but sentences clothed in the form of a compound. These sentences are devices in the Old Oriental manner, containing a religious-political program, revealing the religion of their bearers as clearly as do the names of the Assyrian and Babylonian kings or of the caliphs. They are "throne-

[7] Edict 14, a° 258/7 B.C., cf. Thomas in *Cambr.Hist.India* I,503.

[8] Rhys Davis in CHI I,172.

[9] Jātaka IV,464: Kambōjaka horses; VI,208: killing of vermin. This must not be construed as indicating their "Zoroastrism," on the contrary, it shows the origin of such customs which intruded into Mazdaïsm at the Arsacid period of the *Vidēvdād*.

[10] In *Nirukta,* cf. *ZAirWb.* 241 and Grierson, JRAS, 1911, 802.

names," chosen at the accession or bestowed at the nomination to the succession. Only these three have been created; all later members of the house choose one of them.

At the accession, such names are ceremoniously announced, proclaimed by heralds, as the book of Enoch says: "At the inexhaustible fountain of justice that Son of Man was called in presence of the Lord of Spirits, and his name before the Aged Head." How this was done, Tabari describes III,1368: "Afterwards they met to choose a throne-name for Dja'far. Ibn al-Zayyāt (the vezier) said: Let us call him al-Muntaṣir billāh! and they discussed it till no difference of opinion remained. But, the next morning, Aḥmad b. abi Du'ād (the qāḍī al-quḍāt) went to him and said: I have reflected on a throne-name which I hope will be acceptable and find favor, inshallāh, namely al-Mutawakkil 'alā'llāh. And the caliph ordered to seal it, and called Muḥammad b. 'Abdalmalik (ibn al-Zayyāt) and ordered him to make it known to the people. The letters were sent out, and ran: Basmala . . . , the Commander of the Faithful has ordered that the official name under which he will be called on the steps of the chairs and in the letters to his judges, secretaries, tax-collectors, chancellors and others, wherever correspondence takes place between him and them, shall be 'From Allāh's slave Dja'far, al-imām al-Mutawakkil 'alā'llāh, the Commander of the Faithful.' Therefore, you are bound to act accordingly, and confirm reception of this letter! With Allāh's favor, inshallāh!" al-Mutawakkil bestowed their throne-names to his three successors while they were still children. Mutatis mutandis the same must have taken place under Darius and Xerxes.

Thus, the problem is, what was Darius' personal name? Nyberg, 346, says, according to old custom he must have borne as eldest son of Vištāspa, the name of his grandfather, hence Aršāma. One glance at any genealogical table of an Iranian dynasty shows that this is a fallacy. A custom is no necessity.[11] The—probably—first born son of Darius and Artystone (Her.III,88, VII,69) is called after his great-grandfather who was either still alive or had just died. The first granddaughter, from a daughter of the same marriage, born in 506, was called Artystone after her grandmother, who at that time was little over thirty-three years

[11] How names of children come about is illustrated by the anecdote of Muẓaffar al-dīn Mūsā b. Nāṣir al-dīn Ibrāhīm, under 'Poetry.'

old. But the certainly first son of Cyrus I was not called Čahišpiš after his grandfather, but Aru.ukku. And that Darius was the first son is a mere assumption. He was not.

In the memorial list, 13,103, we find, in the group following upon Vištāspa, before Spantadāta, a Pišišyōθna, whom the legend considers as Vištāspa's son, later helper of the sōšyant at the end of the world. An historical Pissouthnes,[12] son of Hystaspes (II) son of Darius, was satrap of Lydia and revolted against Darius II between 422 and 414 B.C.

The name is formed with the frequent Zoroastrian term šyōθna, which in the cultural sense can signify "way of life," but as term.techn. "the ethic conduct ruled by vahumanah, vahoš manaho šyōθnāiš," to √šyu- "to go," e.g. *Y*.30,5 "haθyāiš šyōθnāiš, by conduct as it should be," Democritus' *τὸ πράττειν ἃ δεῖ*, or *Dar.Beh.* §63: "upari rāstam upariy[āyam], in the way of right I walked." Sometimes √ši- "to dwell," that means "to live," is used in the same sense, thus *Y*.39,3, "the spantān amrtān, holy-immortals, yoi vahoš ā manaho šyanti, who live in *εὔνοια*, or *ἐκ τοῦ φρονεῖν*."—Bailey, BSOS VI,947, makes use of *Y*.29,3 "yā šyāvate āδrān ršvåho, how the lofty 'behave' towards the lowly," for interpreting MP. šōn <*savana "way of acting" [or < *šōhn < šyōθna?]. This is connected with MP. "šowān, path," model of Syr. š^{e}bīlā, Arab. sabīl in the Islamic notion sabīl Allāh, equivalent to vahoš manaho šyōθna.

Nyberg, 163: "Vohu Manah's Taten in *Y*.50,9, auch 43,2, sind die sakralen Handlungen und Riten, die den Mysteriengesang begleiten. Mehr: 'That, šyaoθna,' bezieht sich in den Gatha ausnahmslos auf rituelle und magische Vorkehrungen auf dem Mysterium oder Ordalplatz. Das gilt auch für das ganze Awesta." *Vid*.3,41ff. says: The sin of burying men is inexpiable; exception admitted: if the culprit embraces the mazdayasnian religion. Reason: because the mazdayasnian religion "spayate narš āstavanahya vispā tā šyōθnā yāčiča vrzyati, wipes out all šyōθna, whatever he has committed, of the man who embraces it, it sweeps away, so it were, every evil thought, like a high

[12] Ctesias, *Pers*.52; Thukydides II,69, III,19,34; VIII,5,5.—Connecting of piši- with "pišman, look" to √pāh- "to see," or with piš-, s-aor. of √pis- "to paint"; or pišant, pištra to √piš-, pinaš- "to grind," give no satisfying meaning. The name recalls NP. "pēškār, manager."

wind blowing from the south sweeps the atmosphere clean." The šyōθna that are wiped out are no "ritual and magical arrangements" but sinful acts, even inexpiable sins.

šyōθna appears regularly in the frequent triad "manah vačah šyōθna, thinking, speaking, acting," and according to that amazing theory thinking and speaking would likewise be, but are not limited to "mystery and ordeal places." The "mystery places of the Gatha-community" correspond in that conception to the "ordeal places of the Mithra-community," whereas the non-Zoroastrian religion of the Achaemenids would have had "little space for ecstatic exercises on ordeal places." This theory would make the elder Pišišyōθna, son of Vištāspa, an "Ordal-genosse" of Zoroaster. Vištāspa II, on the contrary, would have given this Zoroastrian name to his son entirely ignorant of all that and although his religion gave little room for šyōθna.

The genealogy was: Vištāspa

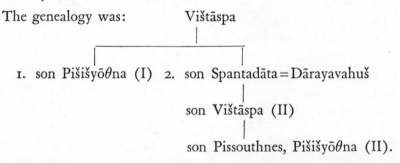

1. son Pišišyōθna (I) 2. son Spantadāta = Dārayavahuš

son Vištāspa (II)

son Pissouthnes, Pišišyōθna (II).

Pišišyōθna I was an elder brother of Darius-Spantadāta.[13] Dārayavahuš is the throne-name, Spantadāta, son of Vištāspa assumed at his accession, and therefore, in the epopee, Spandiyāt-Isfandiyār, son of Guštāsp corresponds to Darius. Ctesias heard this name, Sphendadates, in connection with the murder of the magus Gōmāta, see under 'Magophonia.' The legend which grew around Zoroaster and Vištāspa remembered the son of Vištāspa only as such, with the name of his youth, under which he appears in the memorial list of *Yt.*13,103.—The later epics make Isfandiyār achieve many heroic deeds, but do not make him rule, and add to him two names from other sources, Dārā and Vahman, both in the role of great-kings and successors of Vištāspa. Dārā,

[13] In the eschatologic legend, Pišyōθn becomes immortal "rat, iudex" of Kangdiz and helper of the sōšyant, see under 'Last Judgment.'

i.e. the regular MP. NP. form of Dāreyav(oš), became there a son of Isfandiyār, not at all wrong: the youth is the father of the man, and Spantadāta ruled only as Dāreyavoš.

Vahman, on the contrary, is no personal name, but an aspect of AhuraMazdāh, Aw. vahumano, and has no historical background whatsoever, unless one would believe Mas'ūdī II,127: "They say, the mother of Bahman, son of Isfandiyār, was a Jewess of the house of king Saul."

Dāraya.vahu-, with the part.stem dāraya-, not dārayat-, is an Old Persian formation (see etym. of zaraθuštra under 'Spitāma'). The peculiar meaning of dāraya is illustrated by the Manichaean hymn, *Mir.Man.* II,16,20: " 'vm χvd d'ryd 'vd p'yd, and He himself *holds* and protects me" (before: He accompanies me). That is the relation of χšaθradāra to χšaθrapāvan, both "holder = protector," Germ. "Landpfleger," prefect of a province. Cf. *Mir.Man.* III,43: " 'vmn hvfry'd' 'vmn vχd dstd'r bv'h, help us and hold our hand!"

The second element is vahu, not naiba, the word specific to the OP. dialect. The throne names are devices, with a religious meaning; therefore vahu is used, meaning the same as vahumanah, *εὔνοια, εὐνομία*. In the gathic passages collected in *Wb.* 1395 (below, under n°.3), the subst.neutr. vahu stands likewise for vahu manah. In the Fravarāni *Y.*12,4 the dēva are renounced because they are "a.vahu, an.rta, without vahumano, without rtam." This is the profession of faith, and just there vahumanah is shortened to vahu. Likewise in the name of Darius' general in Armenia, Vahumisa, *Beh.* §§29-30, i.e. "*vahu(mana).misθ^{r}a, cui Vahu(mano) societatem (praebet)," see under 'Myastra.' Nyberg's assertion, 352: "-maniš steht im Westen für das da nie bezeugte manah-" is doubly wrong. First, there is no word maniš, but only a second element of a few nn.ppr., the stem of which may be manyah-, see under 'Nōtarya.' Second, Darius attests the "Gathischen terminus manah" in saying "my own manah, will, volition, I controlled severely."—It does not affect the meaning of the name, whether one is satisfied with vahu, or regards this as a shortening of vahumanah. But it is a shortening, because nothing else explains the double figure

Dārā-Bahman, namely the n.pr. *dāraya.vahumanah dissected into father and son.[14] Nyberg, 361: "Herzfeld's Behauptung, der Thronname dārayavahuš sei eigentlich eine Abkürzung von dārayavahumanah, an sich eine freie Phantasie, fällt damit unrettbar dahin."[15]—The equation Vištāspa = Vištāspa "scheiterte rettungslos," but the anticlimactic "unthinkable" was the rescue. This time, the sheet-anchor is his concession of my term "Thronnamen"; by his accepting it, I win, as in a game of chess, the position "Zoroastrian names."

The throne-name Dārayavahuš was suggested by the gatha *Y*.31,7: "rtam yā dārayat vahištam mano, the rtam through which Ahura-Mazdāh holds the vahu manah," with the superl. vahišta for vahu. We may call the name a gatha quotation. It is a profession of faith. And Dārayavahus—pronounced dāreyavoš and dārēvoš—is itself a short form of the full name *dārayavahumanah. 'Aun, Ghiyāth, Mu'ayyad, Nāṣir al-dīn are all modifications only of the same thought.

The inscription on a silver jug from Hamadan[16] ruled out, by the gen. in -āha of χšaya.ršah, the former notation of the stem of this name as χšayāršan-, and therewith—the point that alone matters—the etymology "stallion among the rulers." Thus the way was opened to find the religious-political meaning of this second throne-name. Benveniste accepted this at once in his *Grammaire,* but Nyberg, 347, still clings to the wrong stem, a straw, though conceding "throne-names." "Wenn das möglich ist," Otto der Faule and Karl der Dicke would be self-chosen throne-names. I had tried χšaya.ršah as formed with *ršah, to rš; Benveniste says something similar. Tedesco wrote to me on this problem:

> "If dāraya.vahu is a shortening of *dāraya^{t}.vahumanah-, χšayāršah- is perhaps shortening of 'χšaya^{t}.ršmanah, who commands the right will,' cf. Aw. 'χšayat.vāχš, who commands speech' and Aw. 'ršmanah- (bahuvrihi only) right-will.' The

[14] Cf. the analogies of Sām and Zāl, Krsāspa and Rustam, AMI VI,7ff.; originally each one person, changed into fathers and sons by the legend.

[15] *dārayavahu(manah) is based on the identity of vahu and vahumanah in the Fravarāni, and on the correspondence between the historical Dārayavahuš with the two legendary figures Dārā-Vahman. The brackets in Nyberg's explanations, 245: "fšənghyō, der sich (von Vohu-Manah) binden lässt," and "ištoiš hvarnå, mit hvarnah versehen hinsichtlich išti, Besitz (von VohuManah)" have no support at all.

[16] *Altp.Inschr.* n°.19.

spelling seems to mean not ār°, but rather 'r̥ in the anlaut of the compound: χšaya.rša, originally foursyllabic.—While, at the shortening of *dāraya.vahumanah- the inflexion was transferred from manah to vahu, in the case of χšaya.ršmana-, where rš does not allow inflexion, only the syllable -man- was ejected, but the original ending of the word remained. χšaya- as participle seems to have first been recognized by Foy, KZ.35,544: 'von RV. kṣayádvīra "Männer beherrschend" im sinn und der Bildung nach wohl nicht zu trennen.' Aw. aršan- however is not equal to OI. vīrá-, but only 'man' in the sexual connotation."

Tedesco's interpretation of the vowel in the joint of the composition is proved by the Elam. transcription ^{i}k.se.^{i}r.sa, i.e. χšē.rša; cuneif. "a" does not mean interior long vowel, but is r̥ son., written with preceding aleph as if in initial position. Greek ε does not result from Ion. ē > Dor. ā, but from OIr. ē < aya, while -ayā- would give ā.

ršmanah alone, Arsamenes, is the name of a son of Darius and Phaidyme, daughter of Otanes, Her.VII,68, and of a satrap of Darius III in the battle on the Granikos, Diodor 17,19,4. Arsamenes is to Arsames, ršāma, as Spitamenes to Spitāma, and Ršāma does certainly not mean (*Wb*). "arša.ama, die (sexuelle) Kraft eines Männchens (Bär, Hengst) besitzend." The thought of the name χšaya.ršah < *χšaya.ršmanah is related to Darius' words in *NiR* B,15: "manaha hvēpašyahya daršam χšayamna ahmi, Akk. ina muḫḫi libbi.i̯a rabāka, I commanded severely my own will." Akk. libbu, lit. heart, is a good translation of manah. By choosing rš.manah instead of manah alone, the name adds a religious quality, "the right will, volition."

The two elements of the third Achaemenid name, rta and χšaθra, are pre-Zoroastrian words, but both notions have become aspects of Ahura-Mazdāh and therewith specifically Zoroastrian. The commentary to the very personal prayer of Zoroaster, the "rtam-vahu" in *Y*.20,3, interprets the last words of this prayer as "rtāi χšaθram, to rtam (belongs, is due) the rulership." That is at the same time the meaning of the throne-name rta.χšaθ^{r}a. Darmesteter called it "l'idéal de la bonne royauté."

Thus, the three throne-names of the Achaemenids are Zoroastrian in the narrowest and strictest sense of the word, just as the throne-names of the caliphs, conceived in the same spirit, are strictly Islamic. As the name of the saviour astvat.rta from Gath. astvat rtam hiyāt, thus dāraya.vahumanah is derived from yā dārayat vahištam mano, rta.-χšaθ^{r}a from rtāi χšaθram. They join the long line of apophthegmatic names which start in the Ancient East with history and go on to the present time, only twice interrupted under the impact of Europe: in Hellenism and today, when one was ashamed of one's own past and religion.

VI. KAVI AND XŠĀYAΘYA

"Quippe ita res humanae se habent:
advorsae res etiam bonos detrectant."
—Sallust, *bell.Jug.* 53,8

Bartholomae, *Wb.* 442, distinguishes three applications of the word kavi: (1) "Princes of tribes hostile to Zoroaster's doctrine, adhering to dēva religion." Therefore Lommel, *Yäšt* 171: "verstockte Fürsten, wegen der abschätzigen Bedeutung." (2) "Title of the dynasty founded by Kavāta, with whom the word had coalesced with the names." His first example, Vištāspa, does not belong to them. (3) "Certain enemies of the people and the faith of the Mazdayasnians." Kavi is a title existing before Zoroaster. Whether the kavi or some kavi sided with or against him, is a mere accident. For understanding kavi, this distinction is not worth more than saying "martiya, mortals, who were enemies of the religion." It is misleading—e.g. "verstockte Fürsten"—because it implants in the word a moral evaluation entirely foreign to it. According to Nyberg, 48f., the kavi would have been "small tribal kings or chiefs," and their title "the only more generally used title of rulers in the Younger Awesta, as unknown in the West as χšāyaθya, the western word for ruler, in the Awesta (i.e. East)." If the words never overlap, and since eastern conditions are an unknown quantity, this synonymity in East and West seems to me not provable.

In the gathas three persons are called kavi: (1) kavi Vištāspa, of the nōtarya. (2) Zoroaster's "bandva" as one of the "kavitāt," see under 'Bandva,' *Y*.49,1: "the bandva, the mazišta, who listened to the miscarried verdict," committed a sin by doing so. Zoroaster's expression is always argumentative, causative, the words mean "he who, being my bandva, yet listened etc.," thereby failing in his duty. (3) The Vēhviya in *Y*.51,12 (see under 'Vēhviya'): "The Vēhviya, the kāvian, denied hospitium to me, the Spitāma!" The sin for which Zoroaster curses him is that he failed in his duty. Being, as a Vēhviya, a kavi, he was bound to give hospitium to a Spitāma. Such duties exist between peers. The families of the bandva, the Vēhviya, the Spitāma, hence are all kavi. Zoroaster himself was a kavi. So was Vištāspa.

The yashts add one more to these applications: kavi as title of the eight kings which the legend arranges as having ruled before Vištāspa; the first of them is Kavāta, the last Husravah. That Husravah-Cyrus is counted as a member of the foregoing dynasty disagrees with real history, and the wrong caesura is caused by the fact that Zoroaster appeared after his reign.

In the memorial list of *Yt.*13, kavi may be a title in the case of puruš-toiš kavoiš in 115; but in 119, kaviš is a n.pr. and g(a)ršta kavoiš in 123 is his son.

kavi never has a local determination. Vištāspa is χšayant, not kavi of his dahyauš; the eight kavi are not kavi, but upamam χšaθram—i.e. n.abstr. sulṭān—of all provinces, vispānām dahyūnām. kavi, therefore, is not an office bound to a place, but a rank. The adj. kavya designates the hvarnah they own as inalienable quality and without which kingdom is not regarded as legitimate. From this adj. or from kavyana comes NP. kāviyāni dirafš, name of the standard of the empire in the late legend.

The kavi are all members of noble houses, to each of which corresponds something in history: the Deiocids to the eight kavis, the Hystaspids to the nōtarya; just as the older kings and Husravah precede Vištāspa, so the Deiocids and Cyrus precede the Hystaspids. The Vēhviya are the Geopothroi, and the Spitāma are Ctesias' Spitamas. Only one of the historical houses would not be represented among them, the older line of the Achaemenids, unless it be by Zoroaster's bandva, and so it is, as we shall still see.

The facts about χšāyaθya are different. It is an adj. of the abstr. noun *χšayaθa; the two possible forms χšāyaθya and χšāyaθiya can both be Median, but the more probable first one cannot be Old Persian. As a historical problem, the word is Median. A special title for a satrap, and in enlarged form for a great king, could only be created in that part of Iran, where the empire was founded. When the Persians succeeded the Medes, they could not do otherwise than take over, with the empire, the style of Median chancery. No geographical question of longitude and latitude enters into the problem. But the fact that the title is Median shows that for the Medes there was nothing to take over, that no empire existed before theirs.

χšāyaθya can be used without objective determination, thus in the introductory formula of the Darius inscriptions, or for Xerxes as prince; but ordinarily it is determined by "of the kings, of the provinces" or "of a special country." Neither the gathas nor the yashts use this official title χšāyaθya. Zoroaster uses either the part. χšayant or the neutr.abstr. χšaθram. √χši-, just as Arab. √mlk, is "to be master, to rule over," and one can be malik, χšāyaθya, χšayant over one's own house or over a kingdom. Every king is a χšayant, but not every χšayant a king. In the gathas χšayant is used without gen.obj. only where the context clearly shows that it means ruling over a province. There is no difference, in content or dialect, between χšāyaθya and χšayant, but the same difference as between šayanam and χšaθram, that between poetry and prose: poetical language prefers to avoid official terms.

Gath. χšayant and χšaθram always refer to a defined territory, evidently so in the "Gatha of the Flight," Y.46, compared with 49 and 51: Zoroaster, proscribed from his home, zam, seeks refuge with the χšayant of another dahyu, viz. Vištāspa (st.14). Each dahyu has a χšayant. Instead of the plur. "rulers of provinces," Zoroaster uses the neutr.pl. χšaθra dahyūnām; the yashts use the sg. "χšaθram vispānām dahyūnām, ruler of all provinces" for χšāyaθya.

Only with this determination, or in "upamam χšaθram vispānām dahyūnām, highest rulership (sulṭān, maiestas) of all provinces" does the title become a sovereign one, equivalent of OP. χšāyaθya χšāyaθyānām χšāyaθya dahyūnām, where equally the territorial determination is decisive, just as even malik al-mulūk without territory is not yet a sovereign title, but that of an heir to the throne or a vezier. No more than χšayant, χšaθra, does χšāyaθya alone signify "king." The only Iranian equivalent to the historical and social content which the words king, basileus, rex imply is ahu or ahura. χšāyaθya > šāh, malkā remains the title of provincial governors and princes of the blood during the whole Sasanian period, just as both classes bear one and the same title under the caliphs: amīr from amara, syn. of χšāyaθya from √χši-, "to rule, to command."

kavi means neither ruler nor king, but designates members of high aristocratic families which rise by power and wealth above the general level of the hvētu, as in Y.46 kavi Vištāspa above the hvētu Hāugava and Friyāna. To the MMed. official formula "kavān u χšatrdārān" corresponds MPārs. "šahrdārān u vāspuhrān"; this equation, in official language, kavān = vāspuhrān, is perfectly right: kavi is *vāisapuθra.

The oldest instance of this notion is *Yt.*5,33 (=17,35): "Θrētōna, viso puθro āθwiyānoiš, heir of the Āθwiya house." In Eg. parchments, contemporary with the Papyri Elephantine, specimens of the correspondence between the satrap and the central government,[1] the satrap Ršāma, an Achaemenid, bears the title BR BYT', previously known only as Pahl. ideogr. for Ir. vāspuhr, and origin of this ideogram. Mittwoch referred to a corresponding mār bīti in an Akk. document.[2] A sentence in Pap. El. Sachau 1,3, Cowley 30, "God may give favor to thee before Darius (II) and the b^{e}nē bētā" means "before the king and his potential successors." MP. vāspuhr is a vrddhi formation, no longer active in MP., hence descends from OIr. *vāisapuθra, translated by bar bētā in the parchment, just as the Arabs, later, translate vāspuhr by ahl al-buyūtāt. In this very meaning kavi functions, in the legend, as predicate of the Median dynasty: they are the vāisapuθra, Ass. EN.ER "vispatiš," the *mārē* Daiaukki of *bīt* Daiaukki: mār bīti. The Ka'ba inscr. of Sapor I translates BR BYT' by ὁ ἐγ βασιλέων, i.e. NP. šāhzādah.

The legend arranges the eight kavi (including Husravah) in four generations with only three ruling kings. That is not a legendary pattern, but a reflex of history. It is, moreover, a striking analogy to Herodotus' four generations of Median kings. Herodotus reconciled what he had heard from Iranians—their legend—with what he had read in Greek logographs, and therefore his presentation has evident similarities with the kavi legend.

None of the localities of the kavi legend is imagined to be in the mythical home Ērānvēž; nor are the places the same as in the Vištāspa cycle. These two cycles originated in different regions and at different times. Vištāspa's place is vis nōtarānām, the city Tōsa nōtarānām in Parthava.

*Gr.Bdh.*127 mentions as one of the dynastic "Varhrān" fires founded by old "dahyupati, sovereigns": "Uzaw ē Tahmaspān [mythical predecessor of the kavi dynasty] founded the āδar k[v]'tk'n in ['h]mt'[n] in memory of the adoption of kavāt." This is an etiologic interpretation of the names: kavāta—so to be read also in *Yt.*14,2 for [ka]vātahya,

[1] Only a preliminary publication by the late Eugen Mittwoch *Neue Aram. Urkunden a.d. Zeit d. Achaemeniden-Herrschaft in Aegypten,* no date, no publisher, no pagination; must have been printed between 1933 and 1936 in Germany.

[2] Probably the same as that referred to by W. König in Reall.Assyr. I, sub "Aršāma," and possibly the tablet Clay, Bab.Exp.U.P. IX,n°.99, of 424 B.C.—Cf. Artarēwa, father of Manuštana, mār bīti šarri, under 'Spitāma.'

which is one syllable short—is not a man's name, but means "colt," and is, like "gušnasp, stallion" a shape Vrthragna assumes when appearing.[3] The dynastic fire of the Medes in Agbatana was dedicated to Vrthragna as colt, kavāta. The legend takes this as name of the founder, a foundling after the pattern of the Sargon and Moses legends, and identifies the founder of the dynastic fire with the ktistes of the dynasty. The date is 678 B.C.; the founder was not Herodotus' Deiokes, Daiaukku, 715-713, the eponym of the dynasty, who was exiled to Ḥamāh in Syria. Cf. the remarks to Ass. Wametiaršu under 'Throne-names.'

*Gr.Bdh.*125: "Husravah founded the temple of Šēz on mount 'ksvnd (read: 'sgvnd) for the āδargušnasp." Šēz, Aw. čēčista, is known as name of the Urmiya Lake; the mountain is Aw. asn(g)vant in *Yt.*19,5, Ass. sangibuti < fem. asngvatī, mod. Sahand, SW of Tawrīz. The fire is called "of the stallion" because it was dedicated to this incarnation of Vrthragna.[4] That it was built in gratitude for the help the fire had given Husravah when destroying the Median uzdēsčār, idol-temples, is a distortion of some historical facts. Wrong is the projection of the Sasanian notion of Buddhist temples into high Iranian antiquity. But Median temples had been destroyed in antiquity, by Xerxes, see under 'Dēva.' In the legend, Husravah is always imagined as fighting in Media, because the conquest of Media by Cyrus, his prototype, was not forgotten: "he who counted (it) to the empire of the Aryan provinces, āryānām dahyūnām χšaθrāi hankrmo" (see under 'Mithra').

In *Yt.*5, mount rzifya (or ārzifya?), "eagle-mountain," MP. ''lvf, NP. ālūh, is the place of kavi Usan. The Assyrian annals mention this widely known mountain several times under the name arzabiia in northwest Media; the Urartaean annals speak of "horses called arṣibini, from arzifya," probably the Baz.qush, east of the Sahand.

Other placenames of the Husravah legend are such of race-courses: "nava.fraθwrsā razurā, nine-rounds-forest," in *Yt.*5,50, "vispē.ārya.-razurā, all-Aryan-forest," in *Yt.*15,32, and "spētitam razuram, spētinī razurā, White Forest," in *Yt.*15,31. The three forests and race-courses are all in Media, the two latter in Lur < rzura and Shahrazur; the former must be sought in Adharbaijan, "pašnē" of the lake Čēčista.

[3] Cf. AMI, VII,102f. and 118ff.

[4] *Gr.Bdh.* gives an etiologic explanation: "because the gušnasp fire set down on the bvvš y 'sp, the mane of the horse of Husravah."

The Awesta ignores the legend of Spantadāta-Isfandiyār, son of Vištāspa. The Vištāspa cycle is represented in the Awesta only by Vištāspa, and his more important brother Zarivariš with his charioteer Visataruš, all figures of the memorial list. At the time when the quotations from their legend were introduced into the yasht, the epic had not yet admitted tales about Spantadāta, and less so of his successors Dārā, Bahman, Humāy etc. down to Alexander. Unless one admits the identity of the legendary and the historical Vištāspa, of Spantadāta and Darius, and of Dārā-Bahman and Dārayavahumanah, these facts are inexplicable. The presentation of the Hystaspid period in the legend is not part and continuation of the Vištāspa cycle, but a separate legend of still younger origin. Nyberg, who regards the "eastern" Vištāspa as founder of a new, otherwise unknown dynasty, remarks 289: "Kein Naotaride nach Vištāspa führt den kavi Titel," and discusses the "Abschaffung des kavi Titels" which he believes to have been "stigmatized" by Zoroaster and replaced by "zoroastrissimus," see under 'Vidēvdạd: Ragā.' It would be equally true to say: no Naotarid after Vištāspa does not bear the title, because there are none. Vištāspa is a one-man dynasty. But at least one would expect that the title had disappeared, yet not even that is true, kavi survives with all honors.

In Pahl. literature kavi Vištāspa remains always kai Vištāsp.šāh; he has assumed beside the "eastern" kavi the "western" title šāh. One sees how near he is to the real Iranian history with their shahs. The heroes of the really old myth, whose places are in Ērānvēž, hence really in the East, become neither šāh, not even after being considered as original kings, nor is one of them, not even Rustam, ever called kavi.—MMed. kavān u χšatrdārān is as good a formula as Sasan. šahrdārān u vāspuhrān. From this MMed. "kav" the Armenians borrowed their "kav." In Mani's religion, the "rōšan-kav, Prince of Light" is the ruler of the realm of light. In the *Kārn. Art.* II,17, Ardašīr I is called "kay ē Pāpakān, kavi, Pāpak's son," because he descends from Sāsān who is imagined to be—without historical support—a Hystaspid, great-grandson, or as son of his own grandfather, grandson of Vištāspa. The kings Yazdegird II, Pērōz and Kavāt call themselves on their coins kay Yazdegird etc., like many Muhammedan kings of the Middle Ages. The seven rulers of the kišvar beyond the horizon, helpers at the resurrection, are called "ān haft kay." The title did not disappear and there is no trace that its value had been impaired by being stigmatized by Zoroaster.

Mani gave it a very peculiar meaning. His "Kavān book" is the "safar al-djabābira" of the *Fihrist,* the "book of the giants." Biruni, *Chron.*102: "the kayāniyya are the djabābira." That the prehistoric heroes were giants is a Semitic conception, first expressed in *Gen.*6,4: "There were giants haggibbōrīm in the earth . . . their children became mighty men which were of old, men of renown (better: to which epics were sung)." Huge ruins, like the dam at the point where the Diyālā breaks through the Ḥamrīn, or the Khosar dam near Nineveh are called Bā Djabbāra, by Syriacs and Arabs, as cairns are called "Hünen and Hünengrab" in German.

One of the titles in the protocol of Xusrau I in Menander, *de Legat.* II,3 is *γίγας γιγάντων,* rendering Ir. kay e kayān through the medium of Syr. g n b r'. This is the title of al-Mundhir of Ḥīra in the *Syr. Chronicle* Nöldeke-Guidi, while Tabari calls him "mahist"; he was one of the "megistanes, Arab. nadīm." A similar thought is expressed by the title "Rustam i Zāl i zamān, the Rustam of his time," and the last echo is found in two inscriptions in Isfahan, of Shāh 'Abbās the Great and of Shāh Ḥusain, where it is said "the djabābirat al-djabābira shall, like the Caesars and Khāqāns, for ever kiss the dust of the threshold of the Šāhinšāh."

Zoroaster has never stigmatized, or used as an invective, his own title and that of his protector Vištāspa. The error rests on a misinterpretation of *Y.*32,15:

anāiš ā vinanāsa	yå karpatāsča kavitāsča
avāiš abi yān danti	noit ǰiyātoiš χšayamnān vaso
toi +abiyābryantē	vahoš ā dmānē manaho

"Because of these (their actions) the priesthood and the kavihood are cursed; but even because of these (their sufferings) shall those, whom they do not let be free masters of their lives, drive to the house of Vahumano!"

Bartholomae: "Deshalb ist die karpan- und kavay-schaft dem Untergang verfallen, durch die (gerade), die sie nicht nach Gefallen über ihr Leben schalten lassen wollen. Die werden von den beiden hinweg in das Haus des Guten-Sinnes getragen werden."

Andreas: "Wegen dieses ihres Thuns ist dem Untergang verfallen die ganze Sippschaft der Opferpriester und der kavi; wegen jenes ihres Tuns werden andrerseits ins Haus des Guten-Sinnes gebracht werden die, von denen man sagt, dass sie nicht frei über ihr Leben verfügen."

Nyberg: "Darum sind die K. und K. dem Untergang verfallen durch die, denen sie nicht erlauben nach ihrem freien Willen über das Leben zu gebieten. Fort von ihnen sollen diese zu Vohu Manah's Wohnung geführt werden." Commentary, 163: "Nach freiem Gutdünken verfügen ist der Ausdruck der gatha für die freie Verfügung über die himmlische Macht, das Befreitsein und Erhöhtsein über die irdischen Schranken, das dem mit der Gottheit vereinten Seher eignet"—the text has nothing but "as they like"—p.229: "bezieht sich, soweit ich sehen kann . . . nur auf die gegenwärtige Situation und sagt einfach aus, dass Vohu Manah's Wohnung in der Ekstase erreicht, Hort und Kraftquelle der aša-Gläubigen im Kampf gegen den neuen Kult werden solle, den die karapan und kavi ausüben." Is that "einfach," simple?

abi—ā are preverbs of bryāntē; √nas-, etym. to "nex, pernicies," semant. to "perire, perditus"; OP. vināsaya "to sin," MP. vināš, NP. gunāh "sin"; the pres.perf. vinanāsa means "they are sinful, sinners," and like the phrase in *Y.*32,12: ēbyo mazdå aka mrōt, one can take it as a curse: they are lost, cursed, "gerichtet," as in the final words of "Faust"—anāiš, by reason of the actions mentioned before. The antithesis of anāiš ā and avāiš is so obvious that not only the first, but also the latter must be taken as adverbs. But there is no talk of actions of the suppressed, only of their sufferings; the pron. ava, hence, does not refer forwards to the following toi—yān, but (*Wb.*164,11,i) back to the preceding anāiš ā. Andreas' "von denen man sagt" for abi—danti is wrong; Bartholomae gave the right translation in *Wb.*718: quos non sinunt vita frui. The signification comes near to Gr. para.dídōmi.

karpatāt and kavitāt are abstr. nouns, but the verses aim at one kavi and at one karpan. The karpan is determined in st.12 as "grahma, favorite" and is the tkēša, mōbed, of Zoroaster's bandva, brother-in-law, the ahura mazišta, in *Y*.49,1-2, see under 'Bandva.' St.11-12 describe how these two persecute the relatives and followers of Zoroaster, confiscate their property, destroy their means of existence. Not because they are a kavi and a karpan, but "anāiš ā, because of these actions" does Zoroaster curse them. He does not think of "stigmatizing" all kavi and karpan. Kavi Vištāspa, and hence all kavi and karpan who join his cause are his friends.

The etymology of karpan is obscure; the only clear fact is they were sacrificers. *Wb*.s.v.: "späterhin, mit dem völligen Siege der zarathustrischen Religion, ist die eigentliche Bedeutung von karapan als Rabbi der daēvischen (=pre-Zoroastrian) Religion verblasst. Zur Etym. vgl. Ai. kálpa 'Ritus.'"[5] For Bartholomae, the "tkēša, judges," are likewise rabbis. He merely chose a word with which he connected the same sentimental value as did the late Mazdayasnians, to whom the meaning was hidden, with karpan: something detestable. That has never been the meaning.

In *Yt*.9 and 13 the kavi and karpan appear among dēva and martiya, sāθra (gen.sg.,=sāsθra "commander"), yātū (sorcerer) and parīkā, as something abominable. In *Yt*.13,104: "vifra, inspired singer, prophet," in parallel with "parīkā, bad fairy" (properly: foreign woman, "gypsy"), is equally misunderstood. Later, vermin like the "she-frog bearing a thousand young ones" is added to this list, clearly revealing its worthlessness. Something similar happened to the "kēta, kayaδa, philosophers" and others. Condemnations of the dēva, the gods that chose evil, are the beginning of such debased values of words.

The Pahl. transl. of kavyām karfnāmča in these formulae is kay(k) u karp, explained by "pa tīs ē yazdān karr u kōr, deaf and blind in things religious," κῶφοι καὶ τύφλοι. Bailey, BSOS VI,591, discussing this

[5] Duchesne's short remark, §184: "karpan 'qui accomplit un rite,' √karp-; MP. kirfak ne garde plus trace de l'acception zoroastrienne," can be misunderstood: kirfak "pious deed" preserves the original signification and is not affected by the deterioration, karpan has suffered in Mazdaïsm. MP. kirfak < *krpaka passed over into Arab. as qurbah, attached to the same root as qurbān, "immolation," and taqarruban "to come near to Allāh." But qurbān is in fact Aram. qorbān (Mark 11,21) and Ass. kurbānu (with k), stem "karābu, offering." The comparison of Aw. karpan with OI. kálpa, therefore, is not enough; the relation to the Sem. vocables should be studied.

phrase in the *Jāmāspnāmak,* remarks "the traditional translation" might be "more than a learned comment," as proved by the letter attributed by Ełiše to Mihrnarseh:[6] "He who holds not the law of the mazdesn faith, is deaf and blind, koir (< Ir. kōr) and deceived by the Dēvs of Ahriman." Yet "karr u kōr" are no more than acrostics of "kay u karp," and have nothing in common with the old words. The misunderstanding of kavi, like that of dēva, sāstar, vifra etc. by the modern interpreters rests on a misinterpretation of Arsacid and Sasanian redactors and commentators who read into the gatha a disjunctive usage of "dēvic" and "ahuric" words, a thing the gatha could not possibly contain. In the case of kavi, the first error is the assumption of a west-east opposition, the second that of the identical signification of kavi and χšāyaθya. Van Berchem wrote: "Des titres sont condamné à descendre un à un les degrés de la hiérarchie sociale et politique." The etymology and function of the Pharisees has nothing to do with the moral verdict later inherent to that title. Dutch "jonkheer" is never an invective, German "junker" is so for millions. The ideal of one period is the abomination of another. History brings about such transvaluation of values. And thus, kavi and karpan, nobles and priests, became the "blind and deaf ones who close eyes and ears to truth."

[6] Meillet, Rev.Ét.Armén. VI,1-2.

VII. SOCIAL STRUCTURE

The political structure of the Iranian people was built up in five steps: nmāno, viš, zantuš, dahyuš and above them χšaθram.[1] The chiefs of these units were the nmānapatiš, vispatiš, zantupatiš and dahyupatiš, all under the χšāyaθya dahyūnām. The military organization runs parallel: groups of ten, dasaθwa or handāma, under a commander, sāstar, whose special title is not preserved. Groups of a hundred are Aram. hīlā, a "power," certain unit of troops, corresponding to Arm. zaur "army," pl. zaurk', troops, hosts; Mir.Man. equally zaur "hosts" (not "power"); zāvar, therefore, was the military term already in OP.—Its chief is a virāǰa, "centurion," clearly expressed in the play upon the word in *Yt.*14,39: "noit satam ǰanti virāzo, the 'chief of a hundred' misses a hundred times." His original title must have been Med. *satapatiš, OP. *θatapatiš, because this is obviously the model for the titles of the higher ranks and is a pre-Iranian word, correspondent to Goth. hundafaþs. Groups of a thousand under a hazahrapatiš, rendered by Gr. *χιλίαρχος*, Ctesias *ἀζαραβίτης*, and of ten thousand under a bēvarpatiš, Xenophon's *μυρίαρχος*, others *μυριόταγος*. Above all stands the *στρατηγὸς καὶ ἡγεμών* (Xenophon and e.g. Curtius 4,12,8, battle of Gaugamela), the sāstā dahyauš hāmaχšaθro of the Awesta, commander in chief of the armies of the whole χšaθram.

The backbone of this organization—as with all people of Indo-European and Semitic language—is the vis, the patriarchal and agnatic clan. The small family, nmāna, is merely part of it, the tribe, zantu, its extension. The difference is: within the vis the degree of relationship, in the tribe only the fact of relationship is known. The vis is the inherited fundamental unit; the units beyond the zantu, first dahyu, then χšaθra, are only the result of common political history.

The vis is the bearer of the political and social, as of all juridical institutions. Military service, duties of blood revenge, law of marriage and inheritance, bail and liability are all based on it. The vis, therefore, is also the original scale for moral concepts, for good and evil.

It consists of the nabā.nazdišta, a notion shared by the Veda, an old

[1] Cf. my report on Andreas' theory in *Iran.Felsreliefs*, 1910, p.16f., Anm.; Selle in review of Morgenstierne's *Etymol. Vocabulary of Pashto*, DLZ 1928, col.225ff.; Benveniste, *Classes sociales dans la trad. avestique*, J.As. XXI, 1932, 117ff.

definition of which is preserved in *Vid.*12, at an insignificant occasion, namely the instructions for the duration of mourning. The center of the nabā.nazdišta are the "nmānapati and nmānapaθnī, master and mistress of the house" as husband and wife, and the circle extends over nine groups, to which belong

father and mother — father's brother, sister

husband-wife — brother, sister — son, daughter of father's brother

son, daughter — brother's son, daughter — son's son, daughter's daughter of the father's brother

grandson, granddaughter

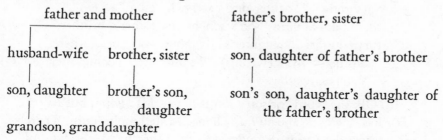

The system is purely patriarchal, it includes neither the kinship of the mother, nor the children of the sister: by their marriage the women enter into the family of their husband. There is only one exception, so striking that one must doubt its authenticity, at any rate its age: "daughter's daughter of the father's brother." It would be less suspicious if it was said of the brother. If true, grandson and granddaughter would likewise stand for children of sons and daughters. That is the relationship, the Arabs designate by sibṭ, of importance for the descendancy of Muhammad by his only daughter Fāṭima. The words in 21: "and anybody else of the tōχma, family," which indicate that not all degrees are enumerated, belong to the redaction only and have no authority for the original condition.[2]

Wb. is inaccurate in interpreting some of the degrees of relationship which appear in this text, without inflection, in middle-Iranian form, or, with wrong inflection added, in pseudo-Awestic form. The original Ir. forms are *trvya, *brātrvya, pronounced already at the end of the 6th century B.C. turya, brāturya, with fem. in -ī, not in -yā. We have:

turya, fem. turī, "father's brother and sister," deriv. of pitar, as OI. pítr̥vya, Lat. patruus.

[2] In order to characterize the intellectual level of the *Vidēvdād,* it must be said, that instead of the expected question "How long shall the mourning be in case of death?" it asks: "How far reaches the infection?" and makes the god answer: "as that of a dried up frog, dead more than a year!"

brāturya, fem. -rī, "brother's son and daughter"; OI. bhrātr̥vya, Lat. fratruus.

turya.puθra "son of the father's brother," cf. Lat. fratruelis.

turya.duγδā "daughter of the father's brother"; *Wb.* (wrong) "Tochter der Vatersschwester."

turya.puθrē.puθra "son's son of the father's brother."

turya.duγδrī "daughter's daughter of the father's brother," *Wb.* (wrong) "Tochter der Tochter der Vatersschwester."

In OP. the word for son's son is napāt, MP. nape; but *Frgm. D.7* has Aw. puθrahe.puθra, whence MMed. puhrēpuhr. There is no -vya derivative of puθra. On the other hand, the fem. of the derivative of duγδar is attested in *Vid.*12,19 by "duγδaire," i.e. duγδrī < *duγδrvī, OP. *duχθ^{r}īš (nom.) in Elam. transcription tu.k.si.s.[3] The masc. would be *duχθ^{r}(v)ya "daughter's son." The fem. duχθ^{r}īš gave MP. duχš, e.g. *Ka'ba,* Pahl. l.21: rvddvχtYH BRBYTH 'nvškYH BRTH, Pārs. l.26: lvdvχty ZY dvχšy ZY'nvšky BRTH, Gr. l.50: ΡΩΔΔΟΥΚΤ. Κ..? ΤΗΣ ΘΥΓΑΤΡΟΣ ΑΝΩΣΑΚ[4]

The fem. to napāt is naftī; *Vid.*12,11: niyako hača nafto (instead of abl.sg.m.) niyakē (for -kā) hača naftī (inst. of abl. sg. f.). The loc.pl. of napāt (m.) is nafšu, fem. would be *naftīšu; in *Y.*46,12, beside nafšu, naftyēšu appears, as plur. of the adj. naftya, which is to napāt as duγδrya to duγδar, hence "greatgrandson."

The notion of nabā.nazdišta, thus, comprises nine groups in four generations; five groups are lateral relatives.

*Vid.*13,3: "Who kills a hedgehog, nava.naftyēšu ho ruvānam para.-mrnčate." Bartholomae translates "schädigt (seine) Seele noch im neunten Geschlecht" (sic), and explains "sodass für sie (die Nachkommen) die Činvatbrücke unüberschreitbar wird." The sentence means: the

[3] In the tablet from Persepolis published by Cameron under the erroneous title "Darius' Daughter" instead of "granddaughter."—Analogy: El. pa.k.si.s for OP. *bāχθ^{r}iš, against Med. bāχtriš.

[4] The mother, Anōšak > Nōšah, was the "Princess with the pea" abducted by Daizan of Hatra. Pārs. duχše is here equated with a fem. to vāspuhr, *vāsduχt? in Pahl., the Greek text omits the title.

killer destroys the life of the nava.naftya, not the life of nine generations of descendants, but of the nine groups of nabă.nazdišta. *Vid.*4,5 says: Breach of a contract concluded by shaking hands is to be repaired with 300 "haδa.čiθa, co-liables" of the nabă.nazdišta—though nobody has that many next-of-kin. Obviously the verses have nothing to do with souls on the Činvat-bridge, promises and hedgehogs, but speak of the liability of the next-of-kin, in crimes and blood-revenge. Their source is a Corpus Iuris, and they have been put in their present context with utter lack of understanding.

The law of other peoples of IE. language offers analogies, and the OT. equally, e.g. *Exod.*20,5 and 34,7: "I the Lord, thy God, am a jealous God who visits the sin of the fathers upon the children unto the third and fourth generation." Similarly II *Kings* 10,30;15,12 and the revocation of the idea in *Ezek.*18.—The "fourth generation, ribē'īm" corresponds to the four generations in direct line of the Iranian schema. Liability, claim to inheritance, etc. do not reach beyond the fourth generation.

In *Yt.*10,18, Mithra, as god of blood revenge, destroys not only the criminal but his whole family and his property, moreover, the fratamaδāta of the community. This term, used there in a threat, in *Yt.*10,18 in a promise, is OPersian "fratamaδāta, primogenitus," first-born, antonym to OP. "pašyaδāta, secundogenitus" cf. (hu)paθyāzāta in Ōgmādēča (see under 'Mithra').

The four steps of social structure find an expression in the way Darius and Xerxes present their genealogies: Xerxes son of Darius = nmāna; haχāmanišiya = vis; pārsa = dahyu; ārya = χšaθra. In OP. the word zantu is not in use, and here this third step is skipped, but it can be inserted from Herodotus: the Pasargadai as tribus, génos (cf. under 'Māda-Pārsa'). zantu, to √zan-, γίγνομαι, is alone a proof that the genetic connection is the base of the system. The various nmāna with the whole retinue of clients, bondsmen and bought slaves form the vis, several vis the zantu. This organization is Indo-European.

The conditions are not rigid. When the master of the house, *danspot, dies, a part of the family dissolves itself into the clan; the clans likewise, in the progress of generations, go over into the zantu. Thus the idea of the nation originates. As a living body, the society is in continuous flow. It is an old custom to call countries after their inhabitants, because the notion of home and its extension "fatherland, patria" is derived from descent. Thus, patriotism originates from love between agnates, expanded to the wider unit of the nation, the χšaθram. To this steady transition from family into clan, clan into tribe, tribe into nation, political history sets limits, and therewith to national spirit. This feeling can overcome limits of dialect, but only with difficulty barriers of language; it takes momentary political conditions as something eternal and thus creates itself frontiers. As in the smallest circle the "anya, alius, other" is opposed to the nabā.nazdišta, thus the "anya, alien, enemy" to the compatriot.

The terms for the vertical structure, nmāna, vis, zantu, have always at least three sides: they may signify the men, their place (immobile) and their (mobile, live) property. As the inscriptions show, the names for tribe, area and main city are identical in regions entirely settled by Iranians. Pārsa may designate Persian, Persis, and Persepolis. Vis, zantu and vrzana may assume analogous significations. But besides there are many specific terms: OIr. šoiθra = OI. kṣétra, a general expression for a settled area, is used in Gath. for Aw. zantu, the OP. equivalent of which, *δantu, is replaced by the higher unit dahyu.—The Pahl. transl. is rōtastāk NP. rustā, cultivated land, MP. āpātīh.—Aw. asah, related to OI. āśā, designates a definite settled spot, Pahl. transl. vyāk > NP. ǰā(y). *Vid.*1 uses šoiθra and asah e.g. for Ragā, Marw, Herāt, hence for provinces and their capitals, at a time when the spoken language was middle-Iranian. In *Purs.*49 "aθā" appears, Pahl. transl. āpātīh, explained by χvāstak: "who does not give hospitality to a fugitive coming to hvāhva aθāhva, to his place." Bartholomae translated "Hof" (or "Grund und Boden"). The Pahl. transl. āpātīh means the soil a man has cultivated, the explanation χvāstak means "which is his property," hence where he exercises his rights and duties of hospitium. aθā, therefore, means "Hof, farmyard" and is an Old Persian word corresponding to Aw. asah.—The nomenclature which extends over a long period and a vast region is rich. The differences are those of dialect or merely of manner of speech, but not of social structure.

*Y.*46,1 puts the political character of the term dahyu in full light: "Into which country, zam, shall I flee?"; as home and habitation it is a zam. It goes on: "the commanders of the province, dahyu . . ."—Lommel translates "des Landes lügnerische Gebieter"—in the political meaning it is a dahyu. This dahyu has a vrzana, an equally political term. In the dahyu to which Zoroaster flees there was (st.5) another χšayans (abs., without gen.object) = χšāyaθya, satrap. The name hvāra.-zmi conveys an idea of the size of a zam: geographically a zam, politically a dahyu, a large province. As early as in *Yt.*10,145, dahyu designates, in the title vispānām dahyūnām dahyupatiš, the provinces of the Median empire, see under 'Mithra.' Later, dahyu > dēh, like other terms and titles, fell from province to village, while dahyupati > dēhbaδ retained its full value as "sovereign."[5]

It is their own lands and their inhabitants that the Iranians call "dahyu." In OP. it has everywhere the political meaning "province of the empire"; in the Awesta especially where it is connected with an ethnic name. The Indians, on the contrary, designate foreign peoples by dásyu. *Wb.*710: "OI. dásyu- hat ganz abweichende Bedeutung, cf. Geldner, *Ved.Stud.* 3,96."—Since the words are the same, the original signification must be the same, and the different moral and sentimental value is the effect of different history. A similar case is OI. "dā́sa, barbarian" as opp. to ārya, but OP. dāha, Aw. dåha, adj. dåhīnām dahyūnām, is the ethnic of a certain Aryan nation, the Dahae. The words are the same, their application differs (see 'Dāha' under 'Anērān-Tūrān').

Hertel translates *RV.* VII,5-6: "Du hast die dásyu aus ihrer Wohnstatt vertrieben, indem Du den ārya 'breites Licht erzeugst' " (?) and annotates: "dásyu = dahyu = Völker, bezw. Länder des Persischen Reichs." This would imply a date after 550 B.C. and the song is certainly much older. To *RV.* V,4, description of a fight with people of different cult, he remarks, p.143: "Die Gegner sind Mazdayasnier," which would put the verses in the 5th century B.C.—before which time the Iranians were devayasnians like the Indians. When using the term "Old Iranian" instead, the interpretation may be right. Not even songs as old as the Rgveda reflect conditions of the "Aryan Epoch": if indeed they

[5] Nyberg, 91, translates dahyu by "Kreis," dahyupati by "Kreishauptmann," in order to make the conditions appear small and primitive. But "Kreise," too, are only administrative parts of a province, a state. *Y.*46,1 alone disproves the idea: Zoroaster does not flee from one Kreis in another one of the same province. And dahyupati did not rise from "Kreishauptmann" to "sovereign" while dahyu made the contrary movement.

describe battles with Iranians, these would be encounters in East Iran after the immigration of the Iranians, after 900 B.C. At that time there were cultic differences between Indo-Aryans and Iranians, which had —in spite of identical religion and nationality—as disconnecting an effect as political systems in our time, and as color among anthropologic marks. Hertel emphasizes that the Vedic singers call people that worship gods, hostile to their own, "rakṣ́as, yātu.dhāna and druḥ (collect.)," and that the Iranians use their corresponding words in the same way: the rejection of the national gods characterizes the enemy. Only, since both had inherited this usage from their common past, it cannot be used for dating purposes. Though difficult to prove, it is possible that some songs of the Rgveda speak of wars against Iranians, cf. vrkazbarna : vrkadvaras under 'Māda-Pārsa.' The opposition of dásyu and ā́rya in *RV*. VII,5-6, which has no meaning in Iranian, but only in Indian, looks indeed like the opposition of Iranians and Indo-Aryans.

A trace of the origin of the Median title dahyupatiš can be observed in Assyrian texts. They render Ir. vispatiš by (ideogr.) EN.ER. ER, i.e. Ass. ālum, Bab. bītum, stands for Ir. vis; EN is "patiš, lord." In the Assyrian annals, EN.ER is the title of the chiefs of villages and towns with their districts, Ir. gēθā. Quite a number of these EN.ER are surely in fact zantupatiš, e.g. Artasiri and Šēpašarri of Šurgadia, i.e. *fšurgadi-~ Pasargadai, as chiefs of a tribe, zantu. In the Šamaš omina of Esarhaddon,[6] omen 2, Kaštariti-Xšaθrita—a Deiocid as the *Beh.* inscription proves—the EN.ER of KārKaššī, a strong fortress at the place of later Agbatana,[7] and certainly a zantupatiš, offers an alliance against the Assyrians to Wametiaršu = *vahmayat.rša, EN.ER of the Medes, i.e. of the dahyu Māda. In omen 5 and 8 the coalition is joined by the Saparda, of the Isfahan region, although the Assyrians try to prevent its expansion by diplomacy. In omen 1 and 6 Kaštariti leads not only his own, but also the armies of the Medes, i.e. of Wametiaršu, the Mannaeans of Ādharbāijān, and the Cimmerians, new immigrants. In 6, 11 and 15 they besiege and take with artillery Assyrian fortresses in regions which thereafter became Media; in 16 they attack the frontier fortresses against Man, Ādharbāijān.—The Assyrians use uniformly EN.ER properly "vis-

[6] J. A. Knudtzon, *Gebete an d. Sonnengott,* 1893.

[7] or Kišēsim, pictured in Assyr. sculptures, cf. *Arch.Hist.Iran* p.14.

patiš," for the chief of a vis, a zantu or a dahyu. Māda is a dahyu, and "EN.ER of the Māda" is in fact "dahyupatiš." The Assyrians either ignore the facts, or did not concede to the Medes a higher title. The royal title was given to them only by the Neo-Babylonians.[8]

Zoroaster replaces, in *Y.*31,16, the element -pati in those titles by the abstr. noun χšaθram of the dmāna, šoiθra and dahyu, and in st. 18, which is consciously formed after passages like *Yt.*10,2, vis is added, making that triad into the usual tetrad. In a similar way, in *Y.*48,10, he speaks, in plural, of the chiefs of the dahyu in abstract form as of the "χšaθra dahyūnām, governments of the provinces." Duchesne, §162, discusses the relation of the IE. compounds formed with the root-noun *pot, to the younger OI. and OIr. formations with -pati, and comes to the conclusion that Zoroaster's dang patiš is artificially developed from older *dąspat.—The Gathic fem. dmānapaθnī is preserved in *Frhg.Ēv.*—Therefore, a sentence like "Die im Mihr yasht zahlreichen Bildungen mit -pati fehlen in den Gatha" (Nyberg, 81) even when right, would not establish any local or temporal distinction, and not at all that the Gathic dialect was in this point the more archaic. A similar error was the attributing of a higher antiquity to the decomposed Gath. Mazdå Ahura than to OP. Auramazdā, which—with one exception—is always written as a compound. The observation would only draw the gatha closer to the inscriptions which equally ignore the compounds with -pati. In *Yt.*10, as recognized by Meillet, the language is more archaic, and the reason is that the social conditions were more archaic than at the time of the gatha and the inscriptions. In the very late *Y.*2,16, once a Gath. *šoiθrapati is decomposed into šoiθrahē pati.

The four-step structure did not exist as long as the words appear in the Awesta. Where the fourfold formula retains its genuine old meaning, the passages are older than the organization of the empire under Darius. If they appear in late places, like the wergild tariff of *Yt.*10, the surgeon's tariff of *Vid.*7, some fragment of high antiquity has been preserved.

The chieftainship over the fifth and highest unit is expressed in the yashts by upamam χšaθram vispānām dahyūnām, abstr. pro concr. like Aram. and Arab. šolṭān, sulṭān, and in *Yt.*10,145 by the Median title

[8] In 640 Assurbanipal gives Cyrus I the title "šarru, king of Parsua," as king of Anšan, a constituent part of the Elamite empire; similarly some Iranian chiefs of Saparda, El. Simaš, Isfahan region, are called šarru.

vispānām dahyūnām dahyupatiš. The historical reason for the different type of formation is obvious: there was no traditional term, like *χšaθrapatiš,[9] for this highest rank, because the unit did not exist before. When the course of history produced it, an expression had to be found, and it was derived from the previously highest rank, by expanding it. dahyupatiš retains its original sovereign signification through all times. It is not attested, so far, in OP. inscriptions, but in Paikuli it reappears, l.31: āryān χšatr masišt vχatāvi u dēhpati. In the *Dēnkart,* Luhrāsp is dahyupat as liege-lord over Nebuchadnezzar; in *Art.Vir.Nām.* dhyuptyh stands in parallel with p'tχš'lyh and as late an author as Biruni describes dahūfadhiyya by a definition of the Arab concept of the caliphate. The word was therefore unfit to serve, during the Achaemenian period, as official title of the χšayant of one dahyu only. These received the title "χšaθrapāvan, satrap," lit. caretaker of the country, with the rank of a χšāyaθya, a condition which explains the great-royal title χšāyaθya χšāyaθyānām.

The fem. of the ground unit, "nmānapaθnī > bānbišn, lady, Madame," was the title of the queens at the Sasanian period and probably before. In the writings of Mani—who follows the Arsacid style in that respect—visbeδ < vispatiš is no longer anything civil, but a divine attribute, and his pentad, created by adding pāhragbaδ "protector of the frontiers, margrave" to the tetrad, is a purely religious concept to which social institutions no longer correspond.

This vertical political structure is intersected by a horizontal one, Gath. hvētuš, aryamā and vāstrya.fšuyans, with varieties of denomination, and not counting the slaves.

The fully free or noble men, born members of the tribe with all privileges, are called "āzāta, OP. āδāta, Lat. agnatus," those with notorious degree of relationship, expressing the "agnatic" structure of the society. Hēsychios' words: *ἀζάτη ἐλευθερία παρὰ Πέρσαις,* correspond to the equation "āzātā—*ἐλεύθεροι*—liberi."[10] The signification of āzāta

[9] Gath. patiš χšaθrahya in *Y.*30,10, it is true, looks like and is a decomposition of *χšaθrapatiš, but it signifies "landlord, *οἰκοδεσπότης,*" not "lord of the empire" as one translates, see under 'Hospitium.'

[10] *Mir.Man.* II,32,18: 'č 'vy ny'g 'y.m'n "z'dyy, Henning: "durch jenen Ahn unserer Freiheit"; I prefer "ancestor from whom is (inherited) our nobility."

is perfectly defined by the Roman *XII tabulae:* "Si adgnatus nec escit gentiles familiam habento."

The normal Aw. designation for this social class is hvētu, which etymologically belongs to *sva- "suus," OI. svadhā́ = ἔθος "peculiar ethics," Goth. "sidus, Sitte, ethics," ἔτης "friend," ἑταῖρος, Lat. sodalis. It has more claim than aryaman to be translated by "sodalis" (see below). The Greeks translate it by συγγενής, cognate. The demonstrable degree of relationship inherent to the word does not reach beyond the sphere of the vis. Highly significant is that a "specific vice" is attributed to them in *Y.*33,4: "taromati, over-estimating themselves," in *Y.*32,3 "parimati, conceit, hybris," Arab. kibar and 'aṣabiyya, see under 'Ārmatiš.'

It would be wrong to put hvētu and the analogous terms in parallel to the vertical structure, they belong to the horizontal. A derivation of hvētu is "hvētuvadaθa, marriage inside the vis," especially between half brothers and sisters, not "eine streng auf den Adel beschränkte Ehe" (Nyberg), equally and more common among priests. The nobility is called hvētu for being related to each other, the marriage, for being contracted between relatives. The Iranians, when immigrating, superposed themselves on an aboriginal population with matriarchal family. Their endogamy is not only foreign to all other, strictly exogamic nations of IE. language, but something prohibited: *αἷμα ἐμφύλιον,* whereas for instance among the Arabs marriage between first cousins is the rule. The originally patriarchal Iranian society suffered changes by intercourse with the originally matriarchal natives of the country. hvētuvadaθa is connected with the right of inheritance. With the Aryans, the sons of the man were the heirs; with the aborigines there was only inheritance through the sister. The father of her children did not enter the family of the woman—less so vice versa—but remained in the family of his sisters.[11] Brother-and-sister marriage results from reconciling the two opposed principles of inheritance: it enables the son to inherit from his father as son of the father's sister. But never do children of the same mother marry.

The Babylonians translate OP. āδāta—agnatus in *Beh.* §3 by mārbanū, a term that replaced since the Kossaean period the older equivalent "mār-awēlim, Aram. bar ʾᵉnāš, son of man" (*Dan.*7,13). The gen-

[11] Cf. JRCAS 1936, 654ff., and a more explicit treatment of the problem in a still unpublished ms.

eral term "man, Ir. nar" enters also for hvētu, OI. kṣatríya, more often than indicated in *Wb.*1048. The correspondence between Umbr. nerf and Lat. principes shows how old this usage is.

nar designates the group of men else called raθēštā or raθēštar,[12] "warrior on the chariot," an archaic word which occurs in the *Y.Haft.* perhaps because at its time, the Achaemenian period, the bīt-narkabti "chariot-fiefs" were in the hands of ḥigher, richer hvētu, kṣatríya. Above their general level rose in wealth and power the kavi, and when limited to them, hvētu assumes the connotation "peer, pair," συγγενὴς or ὁμότιμος in relation to the king. Mithra is more than once invoked as raθēštā. The exact correspondent to OI. kṣatríya, Ir. χšaθriya, occurs in the yashts only as epithet of Hōma, ApāmNapāt, and—spurious—of AhuraMazdāh; in the gathas only in the comp. ēša.χšaθriya, see under 'Hvarnah.' But the Zoroastrian notion of χšaθram as one of AhuraMazdāh's aspects means sometimes collectively "χšaθriya, nobility," especially when opposed to ārmati as peasantry.

> In spite of its rare appearance, χšaθriya had not become obsolete at an early time, for it continues in eastern titles like šēr, šār Bāmiyān etc. and in 'Irāq and Assyria as šahrīg,[13] Bar Bahlūl: "shahrīgh and shahrīghān, Pers. sg. and pl., are aborigines, bukhnē, the most noble and important people, the most esteemed among the owners of a place. They are the old nobility of high rank: original dwellers of the soil." And Mas'ūdī, *murūdj* II,240: "the ṭabaqa (stratum, rank) of the shahāridja is above the dahāqīn [pl. of dihqān]. They were constituted in the Sawād as ashrāf, nobility, by Ēridj." This remark comes through al-Djāḥiẓ from the Pahl. *gāhnāmak*. shahrīgh is not, as Nöldeke seems to have thought, a neologism, but descends from OIr. χšaθriya.[14]

12 Both forms are used side by side in the very archaic hymn to "Mithra the Warrior" in *Yt.*10.

13 Arab. shihriyya, sg.fem. "thoroughbred mare" is OMed. χšaθrī, cf. Hertel IIQF VII, 76 and 80.—At the two places where *Wb.* assumes the connotation "human female," Y.65,5 and *Vid.*18,32, it means certainly "mare," and therewith "aršan, stallion."

14 Bar Bahlūl, cf. G. Hoffmann, *Syr.Akt.* 239.—The old interpretation of SaintMartin, ἀδειγανες, var. δειγανες in Polybius 5,54 = dēhīgān, was right, against criticism raised. This class of officials in Seleucia was recruited from the same class as the chiefs of tassūdj in Sasanian times. At the Arab conquest we find many of them; tassūdj is a "quarter" of an āstān, subdivision of 'Irāq. Mas'ūdī l.c.: "the dahāqīn descend from the ten sons of Vēhkirt [Eugene] who himself was the first to bear the title: they are organized in five marātib,

The relationship inside the vis is expressed by the frequent word sar, which sometimes forms a pair with "hozantu, cognate," and "haχman, Lehnsgefolgschaft, duty of a vassal to follow his lord (in war)." *Y*.49,3: "yearning for the sar with Vahumano," see under 'Yā-ahī!' In *Y*.32,2 AhuraMazdāh is "saramno, living in sar with Vahumano," and "hušhaχa with Rtam," which is more than "well-befriended." sar means connubium, in *Y*.53,3 downright "marriage," and is best translated by "wedding." The prohibition of sar and haχman in *Y*.49,9 and 53 (see below), if the words have their intense meaning, would be a deeply interfering order, but one for which there is certain historical support.

Y.49,9: noit ršvačå saram didans drugvatā

"who as a right-speaking one refuses the sar with a drugvant."

Y.49,3: antar vispān drugvato haχman mruvē

"I interdict all haχman with the drugvant."

Such verses produced the passage in the Fravarāni *Y*.12,4 and 6: "I renounce, antar mruvē, every sar with the dēva and drugvant, even as Zoroaster renounced the sar with the dēva, dēvāiš saram vyamruvīta." It is a kind of divorce formula, like "vizayaθa magam tam, if you separate this marriage. . . ." Nyberg remarks to *Y*.31,21: "sar ist die Bezeichnung der Gatha für die unio mystica." Nietzsche once speaks of "unio mystica et physica," and these things lie close together. When discarding certain sides of medieval mysticism, one may see in sar, applied to the relation of AhuraMazdāh to his partial figures, or aspects, a unio mystica. Else, it is an anachronism to transfer to that old period and milieu medieval Ṣūfī concepts of the relation of man to god. And in any case, if sar could assume such a metaphoric connotation, it must first have had the corresponding social meaning.

In the relation between AhuraMazdāh and his partial figures Zoroaster sanctifies human relations, social and of kinship. In doing so, he

degrees, which go differently dressed." Titles and designations of rank are difficult to separate. Theophylact Simoc. 1,9,6 says of the kardarigān: "it is a title, for the Persians love to call themselves by their title only." So it was to the present day. But the Arabs speak of dahāqīn because the chiefs of the tassūdj belonged to this class of nobility. Firdausi describes the dihgān as the people who transmitted the epics: the minstrels had always sung them at their courts, and for their benefit the old myth was transformed into a poem of courtly knights during the Arsacid period. The form is regular: MP. dēhīgān > Ar. dihqān, like rōzīg > rizq, garāmīg > djarmaq, hrōmīgān > rūmaqān; the meaning: "gentry, provincial nobility." Not OIr. *dahyauka, short form of a comp. with dahyu, but a MP. formation of dēh + īk, formed after the model of šahrīg.

transfers something that belonged to Mithra to his AhuraMazdāh. One aspect of his god of many faces, χšaθram, symbolizes the knighthood—as such he is later Shahrēvar; ārmatiš is the peasantry; and the bonds of kinship and society, the rvatiš and miθrā, upon which this society rests, are reflected in the relations between those aspects.

Membership of the tribe, zantu, is expressed, in Gath. and Aw., by huzantu. Its hu- is *sṃ-, not *su- Gr. ὑ-, as in huyāγna = +hoyaχna, "from the same liver, consanguine," hence "hozantu, of the same zantu, descent, συγγενής," a born member of the tribe, the fully entitled civis of the civitas, hozanθwa.[15] The three gatha passages in which the word occurs become at once full of meaning. *Y*.49,5 promises ambrosial food to those who live in sar with Vahumano and are hozantu of Ārmatiš. The notion "belonging to the family of Ārmatiš" corresponds to Mani's term "nāf" for his community. *Y*.43,3: θwāvans hozantuš spanto, Bartholomae: "zuverlässig, wie Du, wissend" is "congenial to Thy Highness, holy"; and *Y*.46,5 (see under 'Hospitium' and 'Mithra'): "Who as χšayant, satrap, or hozantu, civis, welcomes the āyantam, newcomer," according to 46,1 Zoroaster as refugee.

In opposition to the born members, hvētu, the aryaman belong to the tribe without being agnates. Ved. aryaman is "socius, fellow"; NP. ērman is "guest"; Sarm. Leimanos, Osset. limän "friend, socius." There is no reason to deviate, in Iranian, from this everywhere attested meaning, e.g. Bartholomae: "Sodalen, Genosse and zwar priesterlicher Angehöriger des ersten oder Priesterstandes; über die Bedeutung ist den gathischen Texten nichts zu entnehmen." Nyberg: "Priesterstand, und dieser als kollektive Gottheit." Andreas-Wackernagel on the contrary: "stammesverwandt," which would be hvētu. Only Hertel has the right word "Schutzgenossen." The aryaman are the Gr. métoikoi, metics,

[15] I write ho- only as distinction, without prejudice to the color of the vowel. For huyaγna see Krause, KZ,56,302; yākar, "liver" in the chapter on the microcosm of the *Gr.Bdh.*—For hu- cf. Bonfante in Rev. Belge de Phil. et d'Hist. XVIII,1939, 389f., on Hitt. sa-, not *sm-, Hitt. sawetes/z = Gr. ὀϝετής, and ὀγάστωρ, ὀπάτριος, with psilotic ὀ inst. of ὁ for ὁμο-. Previous interpretations were: Bartholomae *Wb.* "zu √ 2zan-, γιγνώσκω, rechtes inne-werden, gute Kunde haben von"; absol. "der die gute Kunde in Glaubenssachen hat." Andreas (Krause): "dem guten Stamm zugehörig"; (Lommel) to *Y*.46,5, also 43,8: "huzəntu, aus edlem Stamm"; but *Y*.48,9: "hoząθwa, var. huząθwa, Geschlechtsgenossenschaft, with ho < *sṃ-." Lommel annotates to *Y*.43: "die Sippen-[rather: Stammes-]gemeinschaft von st.3 soll in st.5 zu engerer Familiengemeinschaft, sar, werden." Nyberg follows Andreas-Krause, "rvatoiš huzantuš, ein guter Sohn der Rvatī," an alleged syn. of Ārmatī.

Rom. clientes, all who partake of the rights of the tribe into which they are admitted without being born to it.

The old oath by which an aryaman was admitted into the vis is preserved in the so-called "Fravarāni," where it is interpreted anew as the vow with which a neophyte embraces the Zoroastrian religion. But it is so little transformed that it remains unfit for a credo, and that the original is easily abstracted from it. Lommel's remarks on *Y*.46,6 are right in spite of wrong translation: "Die Aufnahme eines Bekehrten [in reality of a xénos] soll—scheint's—in den Rechtsformen der Aufnahme eines Schutzgenossen vollzogen werden" (cf. under 'Hospitium'). Like the hvētu, the clients do not belong to one of the four degrees nmāna etc., but intersect them.

Wherever, with people of IE. or Sem. language, the patriarchal clan, limited by agnatism, is the original social and juridical unit, we find similar conditions. With the Arabs, the 'ashīra represents the vis, under a mukhtār, the vispati; several 'ashā'ir form the ṭā'ifa under a shaikh, the zantupati; the agnatic members of the tribe are ḥurr = āzāta, and are called nafar = nar; also walad bait = vāspuhr. The old expression for foreign members of the clan is maulā = aryaman: they are metics which exist in every tribe. Ibn Khaldūn, *Prolég*. 1,284, quotes a ḥadīth relating to the maulā notion in connection with the case of the Barmacids, clients of the 'Abbasids: "Le client d'une famille est un membre de cette famille qu'il soit client par affranchissement, ou par adoption, ou par un engagement solennel; ce droit lui appartient."[16]

aryaman in itself designates nothing priestly, but it includes the magi and priests as the most important metoikoi of the vis and the zantu. In later times, the simple maguš goes out of use and mōbaδ < *magupati replaces it, i.e. the qāḍī; at the same time mōbaδān mōbaδ replaces *magupati, which is no new formation of MP. The Elam. cuneiform tablets of Persepolis teach that the magi, like the Muhammedan qāḍī, had the juridical and financial administration in their hands. If the word magu—save the hapax magu.tbiš which at any rate proves the existence—is missing in the Awesta, it is not because the magi were unknown, but because they are mentioned under their specific titles. Disregarding inferior degrees, these are karpan, tkēša, āθravan, ēθrya

[16] Cf. Goldziher, *Muhamm.Stud*. 1,104ff., on the maulā notion which replaces relationship by birth.

and ēθrapati. Vištāspa, who founded fire-temples, has his ēθrapati, fire-priest, in the person of Manθravāka; Zoroaster's bandva, as an ahura, one who has the right of judicature, has his tkēša "judge" about him. Those are magi. Krsāspa had a brother Rvāχšaya, who was also tkēša and moreover dātarāza, judge and legislator (see under 'Welcome'). All these were and always remained magi: judges, administrators of finance, priests. In all their functions the Greeks call them magoi, as superficially as Europeans call all Muhammedan preachers, judges and scholars "Mulla."

In the *Vidēvdād,* Aryaman appears as god and healer, not because the aryaman were physicians and medicine one of the accomplishments of the priestly class, but because priests and physicians—many of them foreigners—were clients. Thus the misconception of the aryaman entails that of the magi.

Herodotus I,101 calls the magi a "tribe, genos," in a passage inserted into the Deiokes legend, which begins and ends with ἔστι δὲ Μήδων τοσάδε γένεα. Apparently this phrase belonged to his source, perhaps Hecataeus. Comparison with I,125, on the "tribes of the Persians" and an analysis of the names—see under 'Māda-Pārsa'—reveals that both paragraphs are not Herodotus' own research, but reports of different origin, with even dialectic differences. Herodotus grasped the real Iranian tribal constitution no more than any other Greek, and his authority is not enough to accept the magi as a "tribe."

Nyberg, who does accept this, says, 336: "Über die Magier sind schon Ströme von Tinte vergossen . . . , ihr Problem kann wirklich etwas klarer dargestellt werden, als bisher. Jede Behandlung muss von der deutlichen Tatsache ausgehen, dass die Magier ein Glied der *Standesorganisation*"—hence no tribe—"des medischen Reichs ausmachten: die Priester*kaste*." As a clear fact it would be no problem, and every investigation not starting from aryaman only increases the "stream of ink." The phrase on p.374, "die eigentliche Priester*kaste* des medischen Reichs bildete einen *Stamm* oder Priester*staat* in Raga," is not a "wirklich klarere Darstellung," but the perfect picture of prevailing confusion: whether they were a tribe, class or state is the problem; "castes" developed only in India, not in Iran.

The magi as phenomenon resemble the Levites. IV *Mos.* I,48, II,32 (cf. 26): "Thou shalt not count the tribe Levi," and thus one shall not count the magi among the Iranian tribes. IV *Mos.* 25ff.: "The Levites dwell in 48 cities," and thus the magi dwell in all cities and countries of Iran. IV *Mos.* 26: "For to them no heritage was given among the children of Israel," and thus the magi did not own Ragā θrizantuš zāraθustrīš, the capital of three zantu, génea, which belonged to Zoroaster.

But without being a "tribe" in the genetic meaning, the magi were regarded as a "tribe" in the political meaning. In a society founded upon clans and tribes and becoming more complex in course of time, fictitious tribes originate. While the genuine tribes own their land, these have "no heritage," but are dispersed over the entire state. The abstract dēnā of Zoroaster, the religion, is a similar case: politically it is regarded as a vrzanam, community = township (see below).

In *Y.Haft.* 40,3-4 haχman replaces aryanam, a correct usage, for it does not signify "Zusammenschluss, Priesterkollegium," but "Gefolgschaft, followership" of clients, metics. √hak- is Lat. sequi, hence "suit." Pahl. transl. regularly "hambrātīh, brothership, comradeship." As a verb √ hak- is used in two closely related meanings: "to follow = obey" and "to belong = be owned," cf. Germ. hörig, gehören, gehorchen. The whole *Yt.*17 is full of the picture of Rtiš who "hačati, follows, belongs" to those she blesses "in long, voluntary marriage, sar." In Y.32,1 she is called hvō.awi.šak. *Wb.* translates "sich gerne zuwendend, gern bereitstehend," but it is "hvā-, αὐτο plus awi.šak = Gr. ἐφέπεσθαι, *αὐτο + ἐπισπομένη, in voluntary service," cf. hvā.išta under 'Hvarnah.' The term haχman describes several social relations of similar kind: that of the "clients, socii" to the tribe; that of the "hostes, guests of the tribe" to the hospes; probably also that of the half-free peasant and shepherd, vāstrya.fšuyant, to the full freeman.

Therewith it comes near to the notions bondage, "Hörigkeit," and "villainage, Leibeigenschaft"; it is the term for half-freedom or half-bondage, missing in modern languages; cf. armatišhak, rta.hak, rtišhak, Mithroaxes, where hak- has the meaning of Akk. awēl or arad, Arab. 'abd before divine names, type 'Abdallāh, Allāh's slave. haχman can also mean the military service of the auxiliarii, thus clearly in *Yt.*13,30, where the Fravarti who are coming (in 49) from their vis, visaδa, to the hamaspāθmēdaya, the muster of the army, are called "hušhaχmāno, the best auxiliaries." Xenophon calls such auxiliaries, namely the followers of the high nobility, συνεπισπόμενοι, which would be *hamawi.šak; they resemble the Arab "muṭawwi'a, volunteers."

Sometimes √rap- and rafnah are used as syn. of √hak-, haχman, e.g. *Y.Haft.*40,3: ahma.rafnah beside adyūš and haχman, "loyal to our service."[17] Hertel, IIQF VII,116, asked "besondere militärische Truppe?". √rap- is the stem more common to OP., "raftan, to follow," later for √šyū- "to go," when this became "to become."[18]

In view of the multitude of terms, there were surely several degrees of freedom, as in Babylonia, but they cannot be defined.

The slaves, OP. bandaka and marīka, Aw. vēsa, and the female slaves, ǰahīkā, play no role in the gatha; that they existed is obvious.

The terms for the peasantry are "vāstrya, man of the pasture," especially of large cattle; fšuyant, originally breeder of sheep and goats, resembling Lat. barbicarius > berger. The compound vāstrya.fšuyant is "cattle-breeder." The words are old and have developed to "owner of pastures" and "peasant, farmer" with the change of cultural conditions, as the notions civis, gens shifted in Roman history. Zoroaster's role as patron, mantuš, of the peasantry—a subject treated under 'Ārmatiš'—is reflected in his being figured as the first vāstrya.fšūyant, a concept attested by the Platonist Hermodoros (in Diogenes Laert., *Prooem.*2) who speaks of Astrampsychos, recognized by Markwart as OP. *vāstrya.fšu.ka. Under the Sasanians, the peasantry, like all classes, had an official chief, the vāsrōšānsālār.[19] In later legend he became a dishonest vezier Rāstraviš, i.e. vāstriyōš, of Vištāsp or of Bahrām Gōr, e.g. in the Siyāsatnāmah of Niẓām al-mulk and in 'Aufī's Djawāmi'.

In the gathas, the cow-breeders are called gōdāyah, to √dā(y), θάομαι, meaning "alere, then colere," whence NP. Kurd. "dā, dāya, wet-nurse," hence like Am. "cow-nurse." In *Y.*29,2, gōdāyo θwaχšo, with θwaχš-, MP. tuχšīdan, NP. zaḥmat kašīdan, hence the "hard-working cowboys." The expression is abstract, "labor" for "laborer." This is the base for Gath. vidans θwaχšahā gavoi in *Y.*33,3, with vi.dans

[17] Andreas, NGGW 1931, III,310, on rafəδra: "Wenn zweisilbig, rafθra, wenn dreisilbig, raftura"; right, but not proved by El. pa.k.si.s for OP. *bāχθ^r^is beside pa.k.t^u^r.ri.s for Med. bāχtriš.

[18] Pahl. transl. almost always rām, as if this were rām < rafnah, like šām < χšafnyah, and not rām < rāman; cf. Bailey, in *Orient.Stud.Pavry* 21ff. on stems with change of p and m.

[19] The Mas'ūdī mss. have disfigured this title to rāst-rōšan, and a Persian friend of mine once asked me to explain it, saying "this is neither rāst (right) nor rōšan (clear)."

to √dāy-, not with a disjunctive vi- (Nyberg, 137: "zwei Parteien versorgen, Ordal-verbum der Gatha"), but with intensifying vi- "to nurse thoroughly," cf. the n.pr. vidat.gav- in the memorial list of *Yt.* 13,127, to which *Wb.* remarks "Anspielung of *Y.*51,5: gām vidat vāstryo?" And, referring to sheep instead of cows, Aw. vidat.fšū and fradat.fšū, names of the two kršvars, see under 'Kršvar.'

The peasantry lives in half-bondage, in Akk. terminology "ḫarrān šarri." Geiger had painted, in his *Ostiran. Kultur,* an idealistic-romantic picture of a "Schweizer Alm," and Nyberg keeps to it, p.276: "Die alte Hirtenideologie ist natürlich voll lebendig [at the time of the *Y.Haft.*]; sie ist als festes Grundelement im [post-Zoroastrian] Zoroastrismus enthalten." The truth came nearer to the magnificent Bakhtiyari-film "Grass."

A passage in the *Nirangistān,* ed. Sanjana, *Pref.*5, discussed by Bartholomae *Wb.* s.v. vi.mā(y)-, gives insight into the life of these poor people, of whom Zoroaster took charge. It is badly transmitted and can be understood only by comparing it with a passage in Djuwainī 1,22,14ff.,[20] who describes the "bīgār i nafsī, bounden service of peasants," as an institution of Djingiz Khan. The institution is much older; the "leiturgies" of the early Muhammedan epoch are the same thing. Sentences like "if the man is not at home, his wife goes out in person and does the work" conform literally to the *Nirang.* "when both take care of the farmyard, gēθā, each of them shall go out; (if) the wife (takes care of) the farm, the man shall go out" etc.[21] There one has a glimpse of the life of a boundsman.

MP. byk'l > bīgār, is known to me from one passage in the *Ayātḳ.Zām..:* "'p.š'n hlg v byk'l 'L prm'y, and do not allot to them (your subjects) hlg and bīgār." Bartholomae, *Mir. Mundrt.* I, 1916, 10-16, sub "ark=Arbeit," translated "Arbeit (d.i. Frone) ohne Grund," wrongly mending the text to "hlg

[20] Gibb Mem. XVI, to which my attention was drawn by Minorskiy's *Soyurghal* in BSOS IX,950.

[21] Hübschmann, *Arm.Gram.* 218: "Arm. pahak unim or tarapahak varem = ἀγγαρεύω." But pahak < pāθraka means "watch, watchman." H. says: "Ich kann die Bedeutungen nicht ausgleichen." Perhaps through šahr pādan, *Mir.Man.* II,15 (cf. *Altp.Inschr.* 315) which seems to mean not only "to do military service" but every public service, ḫarrān šarri. "bīgār, corvée" is syn. of ἀγγαρεύω, from Akk. agru, agarru "hired slave," agrūtu, agarrūtu n.abstr.; cf. Jensen's note in Horn, *Etym.* 254. This appears first in the NT., before, there is only ἄγγαρος, ἀγγαρήιον referring to the imperial post, from Akk. "egirtu, message," see under 'Post and Travels.'

by k'r," because he did not grasp the social meaning of hlg, and believed it to be an Iranian word. It is Akk. ilku, corvée, in *Beh.* allūka, Pap.El. 'lvk, Aram. hlk (Ezra), which passed from Aramaic into MP. as hlg, TPārs. χrg, and thence into Arab. as "kharādj taxes," see *Altp.Inschr.* sub "mandā." Beside hlg v byg'r the pair hlg v b'l often appears, with "bār = φόρος, Akk. biltu, tribute," to be distinguished from "bār, fruit, interest" usually spelled bl; e.g. *Dēnk.* M. 533,17: "hlg v b'l MN škvh'n BR' DBRVN.šn BR' 'ytvn BR' DBRVN.šn 'YK 'dryh v dhvptyh BR' L' k'hyt, taxes and tributes are to be taken off of the poor classes, but only so far to be taken off as not to impair the subjects and the government." The most common group is "hlg v rnǰ, corvée and toil," where hlg takes on the more general meaning "exertion."[22]

Bartholomae, *Wb.* s.v. pištra, says: "Stand oder Kaste; es giebt drei, nur in *Y.*19,17 vier Stände: āθravan 'Priester,' raθēštā 'Krieger,' vāstrya.fšuyant 'Bauern,' hūti 'Handwerker.' Im Gathischen z.T. abweichend: Aryaman oder viell. [means *Y.Haft.*] haχman für den Priester, χvaētu und nar für die Krieger, vāstriya.fšuyant oder koll. vrzana, vrzanya für den Bauernstand." Nyberg follows with vrzanam as "tiers état," aryaman as "priest," adding "im *Y.Haft.* scheint vrzana zunächst Kultverband zu sein," no reasons.—pištra is no more than "profession," Arab. aṣnāf al-nās, not "Kaste, caste." "Bauernschaft" was a wrong translation introduced by Pischel-Geldner, *Ved.Stud.* II,19. None of the Gath. terms enumerated means "priests," nor are they the "first class." The Gath. and Aw. terms are no opposed systems of three or four classes at all.

The error entails a wrong analysis of vrzana in *Wb.*1424f., in "a) 'Gemeinschaft,' b) politisch 'civitas,' bezw. Ap. 'Stadt,' c) im Gegensatz zu Adel und Priesterstand der 'Dritte Stand.' "—vrzanam is nowhere the term for a "class, état, Stand" as opposed to others; nowhere does it signify anything but "oppidum, civitas." The different vocalization

[22] It is tempting to connect with it the title IPahl. 'rkpty or hrkpty, IPārs. hlgvpt, Aram. 'rgbt', usually translated "lord of the 'arx,' castle," and to translate "chief collector of taxes." But in Palmyra the ἀργαπέτης is the commander of the horse and dromedary corps, cf. F. Cumont, *Fouilles de Dura* p.xli,n.5, and Dittenberger, *Syll., Or.inscr.* 645 with φρούραρχος = argapati.

in Gath., Aw. and OP. is for us without importance. Ved. vr̥jánam is "village, oppidum," cf. Hertel, IIQF, VII,101. In *RV*. the vr̥jána have a "rāj, king."

In the OP. inscriptions vrδana designates the capitals of the dahyu in the sense of Aw. zantu, hence civitas > città. Where tribes and their country do not bear the same name, the name of the vrδana serves for purposes of administration. For the capitals of the great dahyu, e.g. Agbatana and Persepolis, special terms are used, like "diδā, acropolis" or "viθ, residence of the king." Likewise, in the Awesta, the residence of Vištāspa is called vis of the Nōtarya, the city of Tōs.

In the gathas, the meaning is the same. In *Y*.33,5, Zoroaster "prays away," removes by his prayer the nazdištām druǰam, the disadvantage that Druχš is the closest neighbor, from the vrzanam, Pahl. transl. "hamsāyakīh, life under the same shade," clearly life in a "town" (see under 'Ārmatiš'). In *Y*.46,1 the vrzana is the place of the tribunal, hence a "m^e^dīnā, place of tribunal," ideogr. for MP. šahristān, "capital."[23] In *Y*.33,3 and 4, vrzana appears at the side of vidans θwaχšahā gavoi, hence is certainly *not* the peasantry. Nyberg's notion, 48, of a tribe of cattle-breeders "die offenbar sesshaft sind" contains for Īrān and Tūrān a contradiction in adjecto: they are nomads by definition, and must at least change between summer and winter pasture, garmsīr and sardsīr, qyšlaq and yailaq.

Like all analogous terms, vrzana can signify the place and collectively the men in it; for individuals the adj. vrzanya, "citizen" is used. There is a dark passage in *Y*.45,9:

> mazdå χšaθrā VRZNY'(v) or VRZYN'(v) dyāt ahuro pasūš
> vīrān ahmākān fradaθāi.

Bartholomae, following the former reading VRZY N'v translated "möge uns AM. durch seine Macht zur Wirksamkeit verhelfen, damit . . ." Benveniste: "varzi, loc.sg. d'un nom racine varz- 'activité, pratique," hence "puisse AM. par sa royauté nous mettre en activité." On the contrary Lommel: "vərəzənyå, -nyā, ob gen. sg. eines fem., oder instr. sg. eines adj. in -ya, eng zu χšaθrā gehörig: 'Herrschaft der Dorfge-

[23] The transl. "Bauernstand" misled Hübschmann, *Pers.Stud*. nº.199. vrzana becomes mod. barzan (Med.), in Tabari also varzēn < vrzanya, quarter of a town. Usual Pahl.transl. is vālun, vālunīh (Pers.) expl. by hamsāyakīh; possibly, through Armenian, origin of "baron, baronet" which the Lusignans transplanted to France.

meinde' oder 'auf die Gemeinde bezügliche Herrschaft,' wird ausgeübt von einem, der mit den ved. Wörtern vr̥janasya rājā ist, . . . Abwandlung uralter arischer Ausdrucksweise." Nyberg, 125: "Zarathustra bittet um vrzana-Macht zur Förderung unseres Viehs. . . ." AhuraMazdāh with instr. χšaθrā "in his quality of χšaθram" is so common an expression of Zoroaster that other interpretations are improbable. The bad transmission of the text does not permit a decision between varzi nå or vrzanyā. "help to activity" is not very convincing, and "give us vrzanyå" would only require an emendation of the case termination, meaning: "give us members of the vrzana, of our community."

In the "Gatha of the Flight," *Y*.46,1 (text under 'Hospitium') a badly preserved vrzanā həčā (vv.ll. hə čā, haēčā) stands in parallel with sāstāro dahyauš "the commanders of the province." Andreas-Lommel refrain from translating. Bartholomae puts down a special fem. form vrzanā. The long ā, however, is but the usual notation in Gath. compounds, cf. Duchesne, *Comp.av.* §17,d; the faulty separation of the compound caused the assimilation of the rel. yā, instead of yo. The stanza speaks of the tribunal which exiled the prophet from his hometown. The corrupt second element which begins with h and ends in -ā must express in relation to vrzana, the town, what the sāstāro are in relation to dahyu, the province. Two letters must be corrected. That can be nothing but hartar, nom. hartā, which appears in *Yt*.10,80 beside mēθanahya patiš and vrzanahya patiš, in the shape nišhartā adrujām, in form and sense a counterpart to sāstar. Mithra is—*Yt*.10,103—the hartar and awyaχštar of all gēθā, the goods and chattels of all the vis, the world, its "custodian and guardian," a metaphor which presupposes the existence of the corresponding post in the vrzanam, that is of the *vrzana.hartā. Ach. χšaθ^{r}a.pāvan is another perfect counterpart.[24] The court of the vrzanam—m^{e}dīnā—šahristān was under the authority of an ahura, lord justiciary, presided over by a tkēša, judge, and the jury consisted of "hvētu, free cives"; aryaman, clients; the sāstāro dahyauš, military commanders of the province; and the "vrzana.hartar, consul civitatis," seemingly a member ex officio.

24 In the Ka'ba inscr. the satrap are all chiefs of towns, a change Hübschmann noticed also in Armenian; satrap deteriorated into "mayor" when šāh replaced the title.

To this banishment from his home town, Zoroaster refers also in *Y*.49,7:

ko aryamā ko hvētuš dātāiš ahat
yo vrzanāi vahviyām dāt frasastim

"Who is the client, who the nobleman, who, through dāta, for the vrzanam will obtain the good proclamation?" (See under 'Hāugava.') The frasastiš by dāta, royal edicts, is an official proclamation by heralds; what Zoroaster hoped for is the rescission of the verdict of the court of his home town. If he was banished for the sake of his doctrine, the frasasti would be at the same time the official recognition of the doctrine. Thus, the dative vrzanāi can, in principle, mean two things: (1) simply "town," and then refer either to the home town, the proclamation being ordered "for the town," to take place where the verdict was passed; or for the town where the prophet had found asylum. (2) vrzanam can refer to the doctrine itself. The normal term would be "dēnā, religion" as community of the adherents, defined by Nyberg as "Kollektivausdruck für die Schauseelen der Anhänger." For the government, not interested in "Schauseelen," a group of cives would be a civitas, not in the topic sense, but a fictitious vrzanam, as the magi are a fictitious tribe, zantuš, without land.

Among the members of the court were the "sāstāro dahyauš." The plural shows that a province—which had only one χšayant, *εἷς κοίρανος ἔστω*—had many sāstāro, and *Yt*.10,14 shows that there were sāstāro in all provinces of ārya.šayanam. Sāstar, from √sanh-, OP. θah- "to command," means "commander," like amīr from amara. In *Yt*.10,4 they dress the ranks of the "īrå, columns, regiments"; in 10,109 the highest sāstar hāmaχšaθro to whom Mithra grants this χšaθram puruspāδam hvanisaχtam has absolute authority to punish, power over life and death, and his verdict is at once executed. In *Yt*.14,13, the male camel stands there, "vidiδīvå yaθa sāstā, looking up and down like a sāstar" in front of his troops, that means quite humorously "like a commanding general," while in *Yt*.14,47 Vrthragna "virāzati, dresses the ranks, antar rāštā rasmanā, of the two phalanges," like a virāz, virāja (*Yt*.14,37), a captain. An assertion "sāstar, only used for enemies of Zoroaster" (Nyberg, 91) sounds strange in view of such material.

The sāstāro are the military officers of the province, as the name says: one commands soldiers. sāstar has nowhere a relation to a special territory. Nyberg, 57: "Wir hören auch von Herrschern über grössere Gebiete [than the dahyu], die also höher stehen, als der dahyupati, der Landesherr. Diese höheren Gebieter führen den Namen sāstar," and p.304 "vielleicht eine ostiranische Entsprechung zu achaem. χšāyaθya χšāyaθyānām." The "greater areas" are the words šayana and šiti, abstr. nouns, "the dwelling, living" of man and animal in any optional region. Dahyupati is sovereign, nobody can be more than sovereign. The plurality of the sāstāro of the dahyu are subordinate to the dahyupati and to the one χšayant of every single dahyu. The gen.pl. sāsθrānām, OP. *θāsθʳānām, *θāsānām is the origin of Sāsān, personified as son of Humāy and her father Bahman-Ardašīr, grandson of Vištāspa. He is the ancestor of the Sāsānakān, and the name of the dynasty is the old title. The Arsacid Spāhpat of Khurāsān, too, bear a title as family name. sāstar was certainly not East Iranian.

This does away, at the same time, with all "devic" interpretations of the word, and it has no "Bedeutung" at all that "a sātar [only once gen.sg. sāθrasčit and twice gen.pl. sāθrām[25]] in der zoroastrischen Gemeinde [i.e. in bad verses of the Arsacid period] formelhaft den kavi, karpan, Zauberern und Hexen [one may add: female frogs] gleichgeordnet wird, mit denen Zarathustra zu kämpfen hatte." Bartholomae assumed that another word sāstar, belonging to sādra and κήδω, was responsible for this application, but the misunderstanding is foreshadowed by verses like Y.46,1 (for sāstar) and 48,10 (for karpan), and no more reason is needed. The Gothic "hundafaþs, centurion," correspondent to the prototype of all Iranian sāstāro, the *satapatiš, became Germ. Hundsfott, i.e. "scoundrel, rogue."

[25] See 'Memor. Doc.,' footnote 15.

VIII. HOSPITIUM

"Allāhumma, ana ḍaifuka wa nazīluka!"
—'Alī al-Harawī

Bartholomae analyzes the frequent χšaθram, to √χši-, mastership over, imperium, regnum as (1) "Herrschgewalt, nicht immer auseinanderzuhalten von (2) Herrschgebiet, dies besonders als Aufenthalt der Seligen, Götter; (3) personifiziert als Amrta Spanta." In OP. the meaning is everywhere clearly imperium, (1) as governed country, thus used for Iran, Babylon; (2) as government.

Another one is the concrete use of the abstract. In the Aw. title upamam χšaθram vispānām dahyūnām the abstr. χšaθram stands for χšayant, χšāyaθya; equally in the gathas, very clearly in *Y*.48,10: "dušχšaθrā (n.pl.) dahyūnām, the evil satraps of the provinces," and in *Y*.48,5; 49,11: huχšaθra—dušχšaθra. In *Yt*.10,109,111, χšaθram serves, with the adj. puruspāδa, hvanisaχta, especially for military command. As collective it can designate the class of the χšaθriya; this particularly where it is the amrta spanta, aspect of AhuraMazdāh, later called χšaθram varyam > Shahrēvar, and pictured as a warrior.

But even after this extension, there still remain passages where none of these significations fits. Bartholomae calls *Yt*.5,87 "undeutlich":

θwām čarātīš zizanātīš	women in childbirth
ǰaδiyānte huzāmiyam	shall ask Thee for easy birth,
θwām kanīno vaδre yōna	marriageable maidens
χšaθra hvāpå ǰaδiyānte	of noble kind shall ask Thee
tahmamča nmānapatim	for χšaθra and a valiant husband!

Wolff-Bartholomae: "Dich sollen heiratsfähige emsige Mädchen . . . um (gute?) Herrschaft bitten."

Lommel, after Wackernagel, KZ.46,267: "Mädchen mit unfruchtbarem Schoss," and "die schöne Arbeiten machen? um Besitztum," note: "wörtl. 'Herrschaft,' hier anscheinend im Sinn von Reichtum."

hv.apah and hv.āpah—the script is incapable of distinguishing the quantity of the vowel—can correspond to Lat. opus or aqua, and must be separated accordingly. Referring to maidens wanting to marry, it means certainly, like NP. čihr, gōhr, āb, the noble descent, beauty, not needlework. Their desire is, as in *Yt.*15,39 (see below), to have children from their husbands, and the easiest solution would be to read čiθram for χšaθram as in *Yt.*15,130.[1] Otherwise, χšaθra ought to mean here "house, household, being mistress of a house."

Furthermore, all passages with masa.χšaθra, magahya χšaθra, patiš χšaθrahya and the comp. manzā.χšaθra and χšaθrakrta are subject to doubts.

*Y.*33,5 (commentary under 'Post and Travels'):

yas.te vispā.mazištam	srōšam zuvayā avahānē
āpāno drga.žyātim	ā χšaθram vahoš manaho
rtāt ā rzuš paθo	yēšu mazdå ahuro šēti

"I who will call forth Thy most-high srōša at the relay, arriving at the everlasting χšaθram of Vahumano, at the straight roads where Ahura-Mazdāh dwells as Rtam."

"Empire" is possible, but does not fit into the vivid image of the journey through life and heaven; χšaθram evidently resumes "avahāna, relay-stage" and must be a synonym: "Inn to the Eternal Life" would fit into the image.

*Y.*44,9 (Gatha of the Questions):

kaθā moi yām	yōš dēnām dāne
yām hudānoš	patiš sahyāt χšaθrahya
ršvā χšaθrā	θwāvans āsištiš mazdā
hadmoi rtā	vahūča šyans manahā

"Shall the lord of the χšaθram, Thou, o Mazdāh as Vahumano and Rtam, who dwellest in the same house, deign to grant as promised the high χšaθrā to my religion, to me who wants to purify it as a well-knowing one?"

Lommel-Andreas: "Wird mir ein Herr der Herrschermacht (des Reichs) die Lehre verkünden, die ich in Lauterkeit weihen will, die (Lehre) der Verständigen, (nämlich) die Verheissungen auf die Reiche hoch da droben, einer wie Du, o Weiser, der

[1] See below. The same fault in hu.χšaθra, *Purs.* 10, Pahl. transl. "hūk, pig"; it is +hū.čiθra, belonging to the genus "pig," archet. hvštr, with š for č, wrongly transcribed by χš in Awestic script.

mit Wahrsein und dem Guten-Denken im gleichen Hause wohnt?" Note: "yauš dā 'in Lauterkeit weihen' ist ein Notbehelf; 'vollkommen machen' (Bartholomae und ähnlich Andreas) scheint mir nicht zutreffend zu sein."

ɣōž-dā, cf. "iūsiūrandum, oath of purgation," encompasses "to make whole, to heal, to hallow, also to repair, to purify." Without straining the meaning one could translate "to reform." The gramm. construction puts dēnā, the regens of the rel. clause, into this clause with case changed. The transition from third person into vocative is typical for many gathic verses.

The end is the easiest to understand: "Your Highness, who dwellest as Vahumano and Rtam in the same house." That is not a statement that the god shares a house with his inseparable aspects, but that those to whom it is promised, āsišti, shall dwell in the same house, hadmoi, with the trinity Mazdāh-Rtam-Vahumano. Similarly in *Y.*46,14 (under 'Myastra'): "Those whom Thou, Mazdāh, wilt receive [at the banquet] in the same house [with Thee], I shall call out with words of good-will, vahumanah."

For āsišti cf. *Y.*30,10 (text under 'Myastra'): "Then, her vault shall be shattered for the Druχš, but those that are deemed worthy because of (their) good renown, shall partake in the fair abodes, hušiti, of Vahumano, Ahura and Rtam." The promise of such a dwelling is a contract with the owner of the house, called "patiš χšaθrahya, landlord" in the preceding line—οἰκοδεσπότης of the NT.—for a share in the house in which His Highness, θwāvans, dwells himself. There is no reason to give ršva in "the promised ršvā χšaθrā," as *Wb.* does, any other than the usual meaning "high," Ved. ṛṣvá, Gr. ὀρθός. They may be high like the "New Jerusalem, celestial abode, the high-built city," —cf. "manyustāta, built into heaven"—or as a "feast, MGerm. hochgezīten," or because the "High one" grants them—cf. srōša called vispā.-mazišta as His servant.

The plural χšaθrā forbids to see in the sg. χšaθram the "kingdom of heaven." The image is that of an abode in paradise. At our place, 44,9—see under 'Welcome'—the verses are preceded by "Shall my soul be greeted with 'Be welcome'?", the welcome in paradise.

Y.32,12, text under 'Welcome!' cf. the similar stanza 32,15 under 'Kavi':

"Because by their [epic] songs they do harm to the really good conduct of men, AhuraMazdāh curses them who destroy the livelihood of the cattle-breeder, gāuš ǰyōtum, with acclamations." Then:

12: yāiš grahmā rtāt vartā	karpā χšaθramča išnām druǰam
13: yā χšaθrā grahmo hišast	āčistahya dmānē manaho[2]

"(AhuraMazdāh curses those) by whom the karpan as favorite and the χšaθram of those bent on druχš are preferred to Rtam, at which χšaθram the favorite has a seat in the house of the wholly-evil spirit," that means "at the board of Hell." "Realm of Hell" cannot be the meaning of χšaθram, because the term for the aspect of AhuraMazdāh cannot be used for its own hellish contrast. Before and after, the verses speak of the consumption of sacrificial meat: χšaθram is somehow associated with eating.

The thought of *Y*.32,13 is similarly expressed in Arab. verses of Sayyid al-Ḥumairī, time of al-Manṣūr, equally referring to a qāḍī: "he sits at the day of resurrection on the baḥbūḥat al-nār, the seat of honor in the fire of Hell." *Aghānī* 10,35 explain baḥbūḥa by "midst": "at the Day of Djabala, the people made them sit in their midst, the baḥbūḥa of their house."[3] This again agrees with *Yt*.13,100: Vištāspa, arm and succor of the religion of Zoroaster:

yo hīm stātām hitām hatīm	who made the imprisoned, fettered one
uzvažat hača hinuwyo	freed of her fetters
ni hīm dasta maδyoišaδam	sit down on the "middle-seat."

To understand the metaphor fully, one must put in Zoroaster for the religion: it means the reception of the prophet as refugee. maδyoišad, middle-seat, equals NP. šāhnišīn "king's seat,"[4] name of the carpet spread at the narrow side of the reception room, opposite the entrance,

2 Cf. "grahma, favorite" under 'Bandva.' hišast according to Bartholomae *Ar.Forschg.* II,78; Andreas, NGGW, 1931, III,327: hišsat.

3 *Aghānī* VII,14. In epigraphy referring to the seat of honor in paradise, e.g. Aleppo, Sulṭāniyya, 602 H.; Shaizar, Baibars, 662 H.; Bistām, Oldjaitu, 708 H.; Isfahan, Dja'fariyya, 72x H. baḥbūḥa is derived from the exclamation of admiration, NP. baḥ baḥ!

4 Whence "šanāšīl, bay-window" of the upper stories in Baghdad.

on which honored guests sit, whereas inferior guests squat along the right and left wall of the room.

*Y.*51,16 (cf. commentary under 'Maga'):

tām kavā višta.aspo magahya χšaθrā nansat
vahoš padbiš manaho yām čistim rtā manta
spanto mazdå ahuro

"Her (acc.fem.), kavi Vištāspa has obtained by the χšaθra of the maga, on the paths of Vahumano, (her) the čistiš, whom the holy Ahura as Rtam has devised."

Čistiš is at the same time knowledge, insight, also religion, and the partial figure of AhuraMazdāh, into which she has changed from the original Ušå-Eos of *Yt.*16. From Eos she has inherited the "house" in which she assembles the souls in *Y.*30,9, see under 'Myastra.' maga is the "feast, hochgezīte," see under 'Maga,' and this χšaθra is either part of the feast or, as n.abstr., "to be guest, to be host" at the feast.

The last gathic passage is *Y.*49,10, text under 'Harvatāt-Amrtatāt':

yā ãrmatiš īžāča manzā.χšaθrā vazdahā ,avəmīrā'

"This, Thou, AhuraMazdāh, keepest in Thy house: the vahumano, the souls of the believers, and their prayer."

The place of keeping is the heavenly garo.dmāna, the "storehouse," see under 'Hvarnah.' The line 49,10 has no verb; the enumeration goes on; the words that follow are attached, as nominatives, to "namah, prostration, prayer," the first pair is "obedience and zeal," the last is "drink-of-health and food-of-immortality." Between these, manzā.-χšaθrā[5] cannot mean "Grossherrscher" or "grosse Herrschaft ausübend," as a vocative, but only something stored cool like the souls and the heavenly food. The verses that follow continue the thought: the impious receive in hell hellish food.

Two yasht passages make it even more obvious that this χšaθra cannot be the word "χšaθra, domination."

*Yt.*5,130:[6]

[5] Bartholomae attached manzā to OI. mahā; Duchesne calls it the regular compound form of mazant; but distinct from maz, it is always written with nasal, and I regard it as unexplained. Cf. *Y.*51,16 magahya χšaθra, *Y.*29,11 mazoi magayā, and the root √mang- under 'Maga'; also the Sasanian title maṣmoγān or masmoγān.

[6] I have collected previous translations in *Ušå-Eos,* Mélanges Cumont, 1936, pp.751ff.

yaθa azam ⁺huvāfrītā	Grant to me that I, much-beloved,
masā χšaθrā nivanāni	may win masā χšaθrā
⁺āš.pačanā stuvi.baχδrā	
frōθat.aspā ⁺hvanat.čaχrā	
χšvēwayat.āštrā aš.borvā	
niδāta.pitu hubōδī	
[upa] strmēšu vārama daδe	that I may bear, as by itself, on cushions . . .
⁺farnahvantam ⁺vispōǰyātim	fortunate, all-good-life-having
riθyantam ⁺čiθram zazāti	. . . . . ? offspring!

The text seems to be what Meillet called "refondu." To understand the badly preserved words, one must first grasp the general meaning. There is a certain resemblance with verses in the Homeric hymn to Demeter:

ὁ δ' ὄλβιος ὅν κε σὺ θυμῷ
πρόφρων τιμήσῃς τῷ δ' ἄφθονα πάντα πάρεστι . . . .
αὐτοὶ δ' εὐνομίῃσι πόλιν κατὰ καλλιγύναικα
κοιρανέουσ', ὄλβος δὲ πολὺς καὶ πλοῦτος ὀπηδεῖ.

Yet, *Yt.*5,130 is a woman's prayer. The words in g, upa.strmēšu and i, χšaθram zazāti are transparent: the first is no compound, χšaθram is a wrong rendering by Aw. χš of an archet. š for č: čiθram. varma? dade? cf. *Y.*10,14 under 'Hōma': "mā vārama čare, we do not want to reel without senses, without being aware of it," and *Yt.*17,2; 5,130: "vārma," as by itself, *ταὐτομάτου*, cf. *Altp.Inschr.* 347f.—"dade" is the same form as "čare," an unauthentic infinitive. The sentence means the same as *Yt.*5,87,d-e, see above. A man cannot wish to be "huvāfrīto, well-beloved," he is the lover, friyans—think of 'āshiq and ma'shūq—the maf'ūl must be fem. ⁺huvāfrītā, cf. Hutōsā's prayer in 14,35: friyā frītā.—*Wb.* attaches nivanāni to the second of its 4 √van-. The few passages that stand criticism can be associated under one van-, instead one and two.[7] riθyantam in i, is unintelligible to me, the usual adjective is rēvant; all these adj. should be acc. neutr. instead of masc.

The verses c-f illustrate what masā χšaθrā means. The last word,

[7] Cf. √^{3}van- "to desire, love" only Gath. vaunuš in *Y.*28,8 remains; √^{4}van- belongs to OP. van-, "to fill up, heap up."

"hubōδī, good-smelling" has in mind not flowers but the kitchen, and the seven other words describe different smelling dishes, the longest menu in the Awesta.

> aš.pačana: cf. NP. āšpaz "cook," properly "soup-cooking," Syr. 'špyzkn' "innkeeper"; the place name τρι[σ]βάζινα: Turšpēz > Turšīz; pačika "(brick- or potter's) kiln"; OI. āśa, "broth" in prātarāśa "breakfast"; NP. nāšta < *na.āšta, Gr. νηστίς "ieiunus"; MP. āš "grits, soup" in *Vid.*16,7, as translation of χšāuδrīnām yavānām "porridge of barley"; disposes of the belief that āš is a Turkish word. MP. āš is OP. *āšθʳa, Med. āštra in χšvēwayat.āštra, the verbal element of which belongs to Aw. χšviftavant in *Vid.*21,7 and N.P. šēᵇ/wīdan "to mix and knead wheat flour etc. in water etc." (not *Wb.*: "Reiche wo man die Peitsche schwingen lässt").
>
> aš.borva, "with much roast," cf. MP. pit ē bōr.—niδāta.pitu "with dishes set down," either on the carpet—the eating does not start before everything there is is set down—or "with preserved, pickled victuals," cf. Germ. "eingelegt, eingemacht."
>
> Only frōθat.aspa +hvanat.čaχra "with snorting horses, singing wheels" does not fit in. But, when the wheels of a car "sing," it soon will burn, while no harm is done when mills sing, cf. "suδuš 'corn-mill,' the noise of which deafens the devils," *Vid.* 3,32. Thus +hvanat.čaχra does not belong to the description of a chariot, but of a kitchen. Then—with the evident misinterpretation of the whole woman's prayer by the redactors—frōθat.aspa may be "refondu" and hide a similar word of different meaning: e.g. MP. frōšag, made of flour, butter and honey, Arm. hrušag, NP. Arab. frōšah, āfrōšah. The brother of the executed Māzyār b. Kāren orders an āfrōšah as his last meal; and ibn Ḥauqal extolls in many words the āfrōšah in his homeland, near Kōmis. aspa may replace afšah, a kind of burghul or polenta.

Surely, this χšaθra does not mean (Wolff-Bartholomae) "dass ich grosse Herrschaften," (Lommel) "Besitztum gewinne," referring to str.7: "wörtl. 'Herrschaft,' anscheinend im Sinn 'Reichtum.'" It means a kitchen, the "realm of the housewife."

*Yt.*17:

6: hubōδiš bōδati nmānam	good smells the house
yahya nmāne rtiš vahvī	of that one in which the good Rtiš
sūrā pāδā nidaθati	the strong one, puts her feet,
āgrmatī darγāi haχδrāi	the industrious one, for a long companionship.
7: tē naro χšaθrā +χšāyante	Those men are treated to a banquet
niδāta.pitu (hubōδī)[8] aš.borvā	with (pre?)served dishes, with much roast,
yahmiya strtasča gātuš	where there are beds with mattresses
anyåsča brχδå āvrtå	and other expensive furnitures,
yoi hačahi rtiš vahvi	with whom Thou, good Rtiš, associatest!

As a whole, these stanzas recall the Demeter hymn, 488:

αἶψα δὲ οἱ πέμπουσιν ἐφέστιον ἐν μέγα δῶμα
πλοῦτον ὃς ἀνθρώποις ἀφενὸς θνητοῖσι διδῶσιν.

The description goes on through several stanzas and is the best picture of a rich house of the Achaemenian period in the Awesta. Especially the beds, gātavo, are described:

hustrtā hu.upabustā hu.krtā barzišhavanto[9]
zaranya.paχšta.pāδåho

"beds, well made, well scented, well worked, with cushions, the legs inlaid with gold." Similarly ništarta.spaya niδāta.barziša in *Yt.*10,30. Athenaeus b.31[10] says, "according to Heraclides, the Persians invented the so-called bed-makers, that the 'strōsis' be proper and soft. Timagoras, the Cretan, or as Phanias says, the peripatetic Entimus of

[8] hubōδi is to be cancelled; the resemblance with *Yt.*5,130 misled several mss. to insert here those entire stanzas, spoiling the meter. brχδa, for household utensils and furniture, belongs to "brg-, rite, usus, fashion."

[9] The -šh- is a restitution, faulty but attested in the language, in analogy to an h after sandhi š, cf. under 'MādaPārsa.' In Tabari III,1421, subject: confiscation of the property of the qāḍī al-quḍāt Yaḥyā b. al Aktham, a word 'stw'nh appears, syn. of frš, hence apparently 'str'nh, formed from P. strta, as the first from stūna.

[10] Cf. *Pasargadae* in Klio 1907/08, VIII,49, and AMI VI,72.

Gortys, once traveled . . . to the great-king . . . Artaxerxes presented him with a tent . . . and a kline with legs of silver, ἀργυροπόδα, together with the bed-maker belonging to it, saying that the Greeks did not know how to make a bed."

There is a famous story in Tabari 1,1048, an authentic, contemporary record of Xusrau II in prison: "He was sitting on three namaṭ of dībāǰ i χusrawānī, royal brocades, woven with gold-threads, which were spread over a silk busāṭ, and was leaning against three wasā'id, woven with gold-threads; in his hand he held a perfectly round yellow quince. When he saw his visitor entering, he sat up and laid the quince on the place he had leant against, and it rolled from the highest of the three wasā'id—it was so round and the stuffed wisād so smooth—down on the uppermost of the three namaṭ, and from the namaṭ on the busāṭ, and neither did it come to rest on the busāṭ, but rolled on the floor, until at last it lay far off, covered with dust." busāṭ is a large carpet covering the floor, from basaṭa, to spread. Arab. namaṭ is loanword, through Aram. nmṭ', from Iran. namata, originally "strewing," later "felt," see under 'Kršvar.' Three namaṭ are laid one above the other to make a soft seat. wisād are cushions for head and arm, against which one leans, "anaklintēria," often in form of rolls, firmly stuffed. In *Yt.*15, fraspāt and upastarna appear together as here namaṭ and wisād. The correspondence upastarna: wisād is confirmed by NP. bistar, dial. gustar < *vistarna, "bed"; Arm. pastar < upastarna. In Esther 1,3 "white, green and blue 'hangings' [i.e. fraspāt], fastened with cords of fine linen and purple to silver rings and pillars of marble," and in *Ezek.*27,7, where colored "sails" are described, the Armenian translator uses "pastar" only because the LXX use Gr. στρώμνη; √str-, στρώννυμι and their derivatives mean making a bed, for which in Iran mattresses are characteristic. upa.starna are cushions, mattresses.

St.14, in the same context: "To them, the importer, ābrtar, brings gold and silver from far away lands into their nibrθa (trunk, closet, cf. anbār), and shining, ready-made garments. . . ." Evidently the poet thinks of Phoenician and Egyptian merchants.

Accepted translations of χšaθrā χšayante are: (Wolff-Bartholomae) "die Männer beherrschen die Reiche, in denen es viel zu kauen giebt, . . . wo man die Knute schwingt, . . ." (Lommel):

"gebieten in Herrschaften, wo Speise vorrätig ist" (Hertel): "herrschen durch eine Herrschaft, die mit vielen Speisen versehen ist." If χšayante belonged to √χši-, it ought to govern the genitive. It is not only improbable, but definitely wrong.

This χšaθra belongs to a root *χšan-, Gr. *ξένος*. Tedesco writes me, as confirmation: "χšayante, likewise, is at this place passive of the same root, to be read ⁺χšāyante, cf. zāyate to √zan-, and in analogy to it also in monosyllabic roots, cf. *RV*. tāyate to √tan-, tata-."

In the parable in *Matth.*22, the *γάμοι* of the king take place in the *νυμφών*, which is entirely filled by the many guests. Luther's "und die Tische wurden voll," fits the sense and is applicable to the gathic passages. In *Y*.51,16, Vištāspa obtains čisti "together with" or "through the magahya χšaθrā": that is no "Herrschaft über den Bund," no "Ekstase-Gymnastik" or "Ordalséance," but a banquet: Vištāspa, walking on the paths of Vahumano, takes a seat at the wedding table, or on the hustrta, rug-covered, floor of the harem, where the feast takes place. Contrasting with it, Grahma, in *Y*.32,13, takes a seat at the table in hell.

χšaθra, to √χšan-, is the hospitable reception. In the passages *Y*.32, 12-15, *Y*.51,16, and *Yt*.17,7 it is clearly the banquet itself; in *Y*.33,5, beside avahāna "relay-stage," and in *Y*.44,9 beside patiš χšaθrahya "landlord" and "hadmoi, in the same house," banquet is possible, but rather the place of the banquet, cenaculum, *ξενοδοχεῖον*.

This result is confirmed by χšaθra.krta in *Yt*.17,57-60, a song which one may call "The Lamentation of Rtiš" or "Pictures of Life in a Harem." The word appears there beside antara.arδam, "harem."

57: purviyām grzām grzēta	The good Rtiš, the high one,
rtiš vahvī yā brzatī	uttered her third lamentation
hača a.puθra.zanayāi ⟨jahīkayāi⟩	about the sterile wife,
⟨mā hē avi pāδam avahišta	⟨do not tread upon her threshold,
mā [hē] gāθum nipaδyahva⟩	do not lie down on her bed!⟩
kuθā ⟨hīš⟩ azam krnavāni	What shall I do about it,
asmānam avi frašusāni	shall I go away to heaven,
zām avi ni.rvisyāni	shall I turn my back upon the earth?

58:	bitiyām grzām grzēta	Rtiš, the good, the high one,
	rtiš vahvī yā brzatī	uttered her second lamentation,
	hača avahāi jahīkayāi	about that female slave
	yā avam puθram barati	who bears a son,
	anyahmāi aršānai varštam	one procreated by a strange man
	+paθaye upa.barati	and substitutes him to her master,
	kuθā azam krnavāni	What shall I do etc. etc.
	asmānam avi frašusāni	
	zām avi ni.rvisyāni	
59:	θritiyām grzām grzēta	The good Rtiš, the high one,
	rtiš vahvī yā brzatī	uttered her first lamentation
	imat mē stavištam šyōθnam	This did appear to me as the most
	martiyā vrzyanti sāsta	brutal thing that men do
	yat kanyo uzvāδayanti	when they take home a maiden in Nebenehe?
	⟨darγam⟩ aγruvo nijāmayanti	and do not consummate the marriage,
	kuθā azam krnavāni etc. etc.	What shall I do etc. etc.
60:	rti srīrē dāmidātē	O fair Rti, created by Dāmi,
	mā avi asmānam frašusa	do not go away to heaven,
	mā avi zām ni.rvisya	do not turn thy back upon the earth,
	iθa mē θwam hamčarahya	here take care for me
	antara.arδam nmānahya	of the harem of the house
	srīrahya χšaθra.krtahya	the fine one, built for the χšaθra!

hača with dative is as faulty an expression for "to lament about" as avahāi [sic edd., some mss. avahyāi] for the dat.fem. in 58,c. In 58,e anyahmāi is again dative and aršānai a bad analogic form instead of aršane, while varštam refers to the man —cf. *Yt.*15,39 "frazantīmča ho varzyāt"—and demands the abl. anyahmāt aršanāt and hača avahāt jahīkāt. In 57,f, the plur. hīš, instead of sg. hīm, relates to a.puθra.zanā; since the word spoils the meter, it has been interpolated along with the gloss 57,d-e. *Vid.*19,12 uses the formula increased by "hača avahyat drujat, as to this druχš." Hertel's interpretation "wie soll ich auf diese (pl.) einwirken?" rests upon the erroneous suppposition that hīš is genuine. The usual translation "hinab zur Erde" of "zām avi ni.rvisyāni" is impossible, for Rtiš's question "shall I go away to heaven?" shows clearly that the earth is the place where she is. √rvēs- means "to turn, turn back etc." Darmesteter translated a.fra.rvisyant in *Yt.*13,26 accurately by "the fravarti who never turn their back." Here, ni.rvisya means the same.

Rtiš is perplexed: "what shall I do?", about three cases. The first is the a.puθra.zanā, the childless wife. jahīkayāi "slave" must have been interpolated at an early time, for codd. as good as J10 and K12 emend, for this reason, a.puθra.zanā in "puθra.ǰanyā, murderess of her child." But the adding of ǰahīkā was entirely wrong: ill luck is only to have no children from a wife, so that the man must take a slave-girl; but a slave had not to be replaced for that reason. The modern translation "whore" of ǰahīkā is foolish: the fact that she is childless would be only an advantage; no nation wishes to have as many "sons of a whore" as possible.

The misunderstanding caused the gloss following in 57,d-e: the words mā avahišta, mā nipaδyahva, without correspondence in the other stanzas and obviously no words of Rtiš—who, in these verses, does not give, but asks advice—are an admonition, here out of place, not to go to a whore.[11]

A few verses on Rtiš went astray into *Yt.*18,3-4, viz. "fračarati/antara.arδam nmānahya/srīrahya χšaθrakrtahya," and "ēva.paδam nidaθati—antara.arδam nmānahya" etc., which are obviously modeled on 17,60 and 17,6: vahvī srīrå pāδā nidaθati. Wolff-Bartholomae translate: "éinen Fuss," Lommel "den einen Fuss setzt Rtiš nieder im innern etc." Hertel remarks, "the other foot," of which nothing more is said, "is in the heaven of light." The following verses say: "a thousand horses present themselves, . . . robust offspring; the whole Tištriya star, the whole wind created by Mazdāh, the whole Aryan glory grow excited. . . ." Duchesne explained nidaθati as middle-voice, ēva.paδam as

[11] In 57,d one can either eliminate avi (some mss. have ava) as odd and needless beside ava.hišta, or one can read +avi.padam as adverb and hišta without ava. padam, in *Wb.* 887, "Standort, Heimstätte," is rather "floor," in parallel with "gātu, bed"; cf. OP. adam patipadam akunavam adam.šim gāθavā avāstāyam in *Beh.* §14, with the same conjunction of pada and gātu in figurative meaning, cf. Gr. epípedon "on the soil, floor." Of the Akk. version only "ina ašrišu ultazziz" remains.

adv. "one-footed." Wolfgang Schultz, in *Orient.Stud.Pavry,* 409, connects it as "standing on one foot" with parijasat paritačat "she walked, ran around," used when the goddess grants a prayer; he supposes—without knowing that this is the exact sense of ni.rvisyāni—"to turn the back" as gesture of displeasure, and sees in these expressions an allusion to the very character of the goddess: Rtiš as dancer. But ēva.-arma, ēva.gava mean "having but one arm" not "using one only." I don't believe that ēvapaδam could be saved as the only good word in this degenerate sentence. It is difficult not to see in ēvapaδam a corrupt ⁺avipaδam = ἐπίπεδον, in view of OP. patipadam.

In the second lamentation, the jahīkā is in her right place: a slave-girl in the harem who brings, upa.barati, to her master[12] a subdititious child that is not his. She of course gains by becoming an umm walad. "subdititious" lies in the verb "upa.bar-."

*Vid.*15,20-42: "if a bitch anywhere brings forth young ones, the owner of the place, and in his absence a neighbor, is bound to feed her until the young ones can take care of themselves. 43: upača hē gātum barayan, and they shall put (or push) underneath her a bedding!" And the n.abstr. upabrti in *Nirang.*45: "in this case the bodily injury can neither be 'replaced, substituted' by fine or by corporal punishment," viz. after the wergildtariff.

The third lamentation has been interpreted in various ways, on insufficient reasons. One can discuss "men who bring home and rape virgins in 'Raubehe.' " That would aim at this obsolete form of marriage which was scarcely still existing at the time of the verses. The word sāsta in 59,d[13] may belong to √sand-, like Aw. sādaya, OP. θādaya "to appear as: this did appear to me."

> Against Hertel, uz.vāδaya cannot have the same meaning as the simplex "vāδayamna, bridegroom" (√vad-, to conduct, Germ. führen, zur Ehe führen) and as upa.vāδaya "to make conduct, Germ. (zur Ehe) führen lassen = geben." *Wb.*1344 says "entführen," which would be the term for "abduction,

[12] In 17,58f. the codd. have paθe (paθa) for paθaye, archet. *ptyy, Med. pataye, but pronounced, following oral tradition, like OP. *paθaye: paθiš with θ generalized from a cas. obl., as in the case of tu in gāθuš, χraθuš, *prθuš. The MP.NP. forms with θ < t, therefore, are Median.

[13] In no case is sāsta = sāstāro (Hertel), and hardly a nom.pl., adj. to martiyā, meaning "cruel" (*Wb.* 1573).

Raubehe"; at the time of these verses it is perhaps weakened to "Nebenehe."

Wb. takes ni.ǰāmaya as verb denom. "puerperam facere" with the alternative: caus. of ni- √²gam- [on p.502 there is no ²gam-] rejecting for reasons of semantics the combination with *RV.* x, 10,12 nigácchāt. Hertel, IIQF VII,61 maintains this equation: "ni+gam- 'niedergehen,' caus. zum niederlegen veranlassen, d.i. zu sich legen, nachdem sie lange ungeschwängert geblieben sind," both significations under the assumption—decisive for Hertel—that drγam is an integrant part of the sentence. But the text had only "kaniyo uzvāδayanti, aγruvo niǰāmayanti." In *Vid.*5,45 we find apuθrīm niǰasāt "if she 'goes down' in (=gets into the condition of) pregnancy." Verbs of motion with definitions of condition take, in general, the meaning "to get into, to be in a condition," e.g. *Yt.*10,95: "Mithra zam.fraθā awiyāti, goes wide-as-the-earth," i.e. is filling (with his light) the whole earth. Here, too, ni.ǰāmaya is causative of the same ni.ǰas- "he allows her to remain in the aγruvo condition, does not consummate the marriage." drγam is a gloss; thinking of *Y.*9,22-23:

> hōmo āzīzanātibiš daδāti χšēta.puθrim rtāva.frazantim
> hōmo tås.čit yå kanīno āhvare drγam aγruvo
> paθim rāδamča baχšati mošu ǰaδyamno huχratuš

"Hōma gives the women in labor (instr. inst. of dat.) magnificent children, pious offspring. Hōma allots to maidens who were a long time virgin, on their prayer, a husband and a guardian, a judicious one!" huχratuš, as nominative, would refer to Hōma himself; the acc. ⁺huχratum would be easier. Cf. Y.46,17 dahrā mantū "as learned guardian," misspelled in *Yt.* 15,39 to dahro danto, see below.

St.60 is introduced by the formula "Thus spoke AhuraMazdāh." Therefore Bartholomae translates "Hier ergeh dich im Innern meines [i.e. of the god!] schönen, für den Herrscher erbauten Hauses!" and Lommel: "verweile im Innern meines schönen, fürstlichen Hauses!" Hertel: "Da sagte der Herrscher Mazdāh . . . begieb dich hier mit mir zusammen hinein in das glänzende, von der Herrschaft gebaute

Haus, d.h. das Haus des Fürsten oder Königs." The introductory formula, worn out in the Awesta to the breaking point, is nowhere an integrant part of the stanzas. AhuraMazdāh is in no way connected with the "Lament of Rtiš." That she is called "dāmidāta" may be an old feature, overlooked by the redactors and not changed into "mazdādāta." It should not be necessary to say that the house is neither AhuraMazdāh's nor that of any prince, but that of the man who sings the song. √čar-, πέλομαι, never signifies "to walk about," but always the zealous activity of an "ancilla, ἀμφίπολος," OP. abičariš. That is why Rtiš has the epithet āgrmatī—Darius *Beh.* §8 āgrmā as word for the men who hamtaχšanta toiled with him—and hačate "follows, belongs to men in sar, marriage." The stanza says: "Don't go away, come into my harem, where none of the things you lament about ever happen!"

In *Yt.*18,3 the goddess goes and comes in the harem of the pretty house, fračarati antara.arδam nmānahya srīrahya. Long before, in a letter of franchise granted by Nebuchadnezzar I (1146-1123 B.C.) to RittiMarduk of Bīt Karziapku, the Cossaean goddess Šumalia is called (col.II,47): "the lady of the bright mountains, she who visits the houses, kābisat quppāti" (see under 'Architecture').

antara.arδam > *anḍarāl is the andarūn, the harem. An Iranian house has bērūn, i.e. serai, dār al-'āmma, and andarūn, or šapistān, harem, dār al-khāṣṣa. But already in the Hajjiābād inscription the Pārs. equivalent for Pahl. 'L LBR' ŠṬR' is byrvny; hence, Andreas' etymology "bē + rōn, Aussenseite" is right against an older one advanced by Nöldeke. The adjectives of direction formed with -rōn or with -vana are numerous and lead both in later language to -ōn, -ūn. Thus, the antonym to bērōn, *andarāl seems to be assimilated to them, by way of -ūl; an *andar.rōn is improbable.

From antara comes Soghd. 'ntr'yk, 'ntryk; in *Ka'ba* Pahl.l.27 drykn š'rr, Pārs.l.33 [']ndlyk'n srd'r, Gr. ΤΟΥ ΕΠΙ ΤΩΝ ΔΡΙΓΑΝΩΝ the grand-eunuch. In the opening sentence of the *Ayātk. Buzurgmihr* it is darīkpat ē šapistān, in *Šahr.Ēr.* s.v. Kōmiš and NahrTīrē mutilated [darīk]pat ē šapistān; darīkpat:andarīkpat as dar:andar, darūn:andarūn, darχvar:andarχvar.[14] Theophylakt III,18,12 says "δαρικβεδουμ (with Lat. ending) is the highest office at the Persian court, what the Romans call curopalates." Menander says παρευναστὴρ instead, i.e. cubicularius of the Caesars—εὐνοῦχος has the same meaning in Greek—and comes near to Arab. ḥādjib, properly "who keeps off the entry," chamberlain of the caliphs.

If the house with its harem is called χšaθrakrta, this can mean only "built for the χšaθram (neutr.)"[15] which takes place in the andarūn, as the γάμοι of *Matth.*22 in the νυμφών: "made for receiving guests, a banquet." For such a χšaθram in the antara.arδam of Persepolis Darius ordered, like a hero of the epics, a hundred lambs to be slaughtered, in celebration of the birth of his first grandchild, Artystone II.

Under the root χšan-, χšāya- one must also class the inf. χšanmanē in *Y*.29,9:

yā anēšam χšanmanē rādam
vāčam nrš asūrahya +yo +mā vasm̃i ēša.χšaθriyam

Bartholomae: "sich gedulden"; Benveniste: "moi, me contenter?"; Andreas, seemingly because of the acc. obj.: "Weh, dass ich hinnehmen muss." *Grdr.* §§68, 296,1 connects χšanmanē, from Ar. *kšan-, with OI. kṣamati. χšan-=ξένος is simpler, and the Pahl. transl. confirms it: ašādmānišnīh "life without peace" of the xenos.[16] The exact meaning of the verb depends on how one understands the construction: rādam, as in *Y*.9,23 (above) is a person, in the acc. of direction—cf. *Y*.43,12 rtam ǰaso fraχšnanē (below)—hence "to repair to R. for hospitium" or "take asylum with . . ." NP. bast giriftan.

There were temples with absolute right of asylum in various coun-

[14] Hübschmann, *Pers.Stud.* 60; the word is not derived from "dar, door, Porte." A similar formation is Arm. nerkhini, Meillet, Rev.Ét.Armen. II,1, p.5.

[15] Not "for the king." The old name of AltynKöprü, Syr. šahrqard, Arab. the same or šārqard, šāqird, is not OP. χšaθra.krta, as one reads occasionally. The *Chron. of Arbela* mentions Šahrāt, king (satrap) of Adiabene, i.e. χšāharāt, Skr. kśāharāta > khākharāta, gentilic of the "Western Kśatrapas," house of Nahapāna; the placename, hence, is *šahrāt.kirt (in which t disappears) "built by Šahrāt," Ptolemy's Ξατραχαρτα; important as a proof that the dynasty of Kirkūk, Adiabene were Sakā.

[16] mānišnīh, with y instead of ā, a short writing, cf. kārvān-, mānistān-mānišnīh (not mē°-) "life in the kārvān, army, and in the mānistān, house," Lat. "domi militiaeque," cf. *Altp. Inschr.* 311, s.v. spāθmēdaya, where vēšak- must be corrected in "viyān-mānišnīh, life in tents" (not "forests"), after Andreas, NGGW 1916, on viyāna and viδānmānān, cf. Henning, BSOS. IX, 1937, 89: wy'n m'n.

tries. Herodotus II,113, describes how the refugees were stigmatized, and thereby made property of the god, in the temple of Heracles at the Canobic Taricheia. Something similar must have existed in pre-Islamic Iran, for many great sanctuaries, especially the mashhads of the Imāms, and some small ones, are places of asylum to the present day, a thing unusual in the Arabic countries of Islam.

Hence the translation of *Y*.29,9 is: "I, to go in clientela with a rāda without means, having only the voice of an impotent nar, (=χšaθriya), I, who need a wealthy χšaθriya?"

With these words Zoroaster describes himself. In the foregoing st.8, the cow—not with change of person Vahumano[17]—laments to have found only a single protector, Zoroaster, ready to sing its ("our") praise, čarkrθra: that is the "Gatha of the Cow." In st.9 he is, as exul, asūra, *κύριος* over nothing, has neither means nor voice; therefore (Zoroaster, speaking through the "soul of the ox"): "When will come he, who will give him zastavant (almost:) 'palpable' help?" namely money. For iša.χšaθriya and zastavant, see under 'Hvarnah.'[18] The "voice" means the same as fra.mrūyat in *Y*.46,5 (see below): the fugitive or client cannot "speak" himself, but needs a hospes, rāda as "advocate" and guardian.

Gath. fraχšnan, too, belongs to √χšan-; it resembles *προξένεια*. *Wb.* attaches it, together with "fraχšni, fraχšnin, providus, careful" to √χšnā-, cf. *Grdr.* §86; Andreas, NGGW 1931, III,322, "zu *γνῶναι*?", hence Lommel: "um . . . kennen zu lernen." Benveniste has proved, *Inf.av.* 59, fraχšnanam in *Y*.43,14 to be the accusative, fraχsnanē in *Y*.29,11 and 43,12 the dative of the subst. fraχšnan. Only Andreas doubted the etymology; the translation resulting from it, "Unterweisung, instruction," has been generally accepted, unfit as it is, enhanced by Nyberg to "Erkenntnis."

Y.43,14:

yat nā friyāi — vidamno išvā dadīt
mabyo mazdā — tava rafno fraχšnanam

17 Usual interpretation because of "no . . . sāsnå, our . . . commandments": the "no" is objective "for us," not subjective.

18 iša.χšaθriya appears only here, and is perhaps simply "hospes," to be separated from "χšaθriya, warrior."

"As a man, recognizing the need,[19] shall give (or: do to) his friend, thus, o Mazdāh, give me [lit.: be to me from Thee] fidelity and hospitality!"

Y.29,11 (see under 'Maga'):

 āt mām rtā yūžam mazdā fraχšnanē
mazoi ⁺magayā patizāntā

"honor me [the soul of the ox] with hospitality [an invitation] at the great marriage-feast [*Matth.*: γάμοι] o Mazdāh, as Rtam!" Contin.: "we want to be of your domestics!, i.e. even though we are present as servants only!"

> Nyberg, 452, note to 157: "Nehmt mich gnädig auf zu gunsten des grossen maga, damit ich Erkenntnis erlange." Thus, the soul of the ox would talk like the Student to Mephistopheles: "Ich bitt' Euch, nehmt Euch meiner an! . . . Ich wünschte recht gelehrt zu werden, und möchte gern was auf der Erden und in dem Himmel ist erfassen!"

Y.43,12: "And when Thou saidst to me: 'rtam ǰaso fraχšnanē, thou shalt repair to Rtam (Right) for asylum!' Thou didst not order unobeyed [=I obeyed at once], 'uz.īradyāi[20] parā hyat moi āǰimāt srōšo, hurry, before my Srōša and Rtiš arrive!' "

> Lommel-Andreas: "Und als Du mir sagtest: komm, um das Wahrsein kennen zu lernen! da hast Du mir nichts geheissen was unbefolgt blieb, (nämlich) mich aufzumachen, bevor der Gehorsam zu mir kommen wird, der begleitet ist von der mit vielen Reichtümern versehenen Vergeltung usw." Should Truth have been unknown to Zoroaster, and should he have been obedient before Obedience came to him?

Whatever the exact role of Srōša and Rtiš was—the first is the "ear," the police, the second a Nike—the fugitive goes into the asylum inac-

[19] The usual translation "ein wissender" without object is empty, and "if he is able to" is worse. The sense demands "as a man gives who recognizes the need" or "one who sees the friend in need." Cf. the natural sentence "granting the help which a friend gives to the friend" in *Y*.46,3, not restricted by "if he is able to." išvan in *Y*.47,4 may mean "if one is indigent" or "if one needs him." *Wb.* puts it to √īs-; the Pahl.transl. is "χvāstar, beggar." I put it to √iš- "to want a thing," in *Yt*.15,33 with double acc. "to beg for (not "hören wollen," *Wb.*); cf. nā isamno, i.e. ἱκέτης mendiant" in *Y*.46,6.

[20] For "uzīradyāi, hurry!" see Benveniste *Inf.av.* 79.

cessible to them, takes refuge, bast, with Rtam itself. The great ṣūfī and traveler ʿAlī al-Harawī writes, as a stranger, gharīb, on his tomb at Aleppo, a° 602 H.:

اللهمّ أنى ضيفك ونزيلك وفى جوارك وفى حرمك وأنت أوّلى من اكرم الل — — —

"O Allāh, I am Thy guest and Thy protégé, and am in Thy court and Thy ḥaram, and Thou art the first to be hospitable to [him who takes refuge]." That means, he claims as ḍaif Allāh all the rights the Arab hospitium gives.[21]

In *Y*.29,9, rāda (*Wb.* "Fürsorger") is the patronus, the hospes as legal agent for the hostis, his advocate. Equally in *Y*.9,23, the paθiš, husband of the woman, is her advocate and guardian, rāda, cf. *Yt*.15,39, where the synonym "mantu, Vormund" is used. Therefore, the neutr. rādah in *Y*.46,13 is not "Bereitwilligkeit, sich bereitstellen in religiöser Hinsicht, nämlich das zu thun, was Mazdāh und der Prophet verlangen (*Wb.*)," but the patrocinium, the granting of hospitium, tending towards "liberalitas," hospitality, Ved. "rā́dhas, good action, charity." The Pahl. translation rād.dahišnīh is right: "granting of protection." Arab. "karama, to be hospitable" undergoes almost the same changes of signification.

Y.46,13:

yo spitāmam zaraθuštram rādahā
martēšu χšnāuš ho nā frasrūdyāi rθwo

"Who among men listens to me, the Spitāma Zoroaster, by granting hospitium, deserves well to be praised in song!"

Thus speaks the "errant minstrel." Cf. *Y*.51,12: "noit tā im χšnāuš vēhviyo, not listened to him (his supplication) the Vēhviya" (under 'Vēhviya').

Lommel-Andreas: "Wer unter den Menschen den Sp. Z. durch Bereitwilligkeit (Freigebigkeit) zufrieden stellt, der Mann ist würdig gerühmt zu werden!"

Nyberg, 238: "Vištāspa hat Zarathustra zufrieden gestellt,

21 ḍaifu l-ḥarami wa nazīluhu appears also in a genealogy which traces the family of the Ayyubids back to Adam, in the protocol of Ayyūb, Ms. Br.Mus. Rieu, Suppl. n°.557, al-fawāʾid al-djaliyya fī l-farāʾid al-nāṣiriyya, written by a son of malik al-nāṣir Dāʾūd b. ʿĪsā b. abī Bakr b. Ayyūb.

darum ist er wert gehört zu werden—der höchsten Einweihung teilhaftig." "Satisfying" is elsewhere a rather low predicate at an examination.

The signification "zufrieden stellen, to satisfy," which Bartholomae assigns to √χšnū- in *Wb.*558, is entirely wrong. Under aθā, *Wb.*66, he gives a different translation, not quoted under √χšnū-, of *Purs.*49: "yo noit naram rtāvnam hvāhva aθāhva ǰasantam χšnōšta vā χšnāvayate vā, wer einen auf seinen Hof ankommenden Flüchtling nicht bewirtet oder bewirten lässt." This is a perfectly right result reached the wrong way: it is not satisfaction of the stomach, but hospitium as "listening to the supplication of the fugitive." Cf. čiχšnūšo under 'Bandva' and 'Vēhviya.'

"To receive in hospitium, *ξένον τινὰ ὑποδέχεσθαι*" is expressed in *Y.*46,5 by ⁺ā ⁺dām drītā (see below). The praise in song is the poet's thanks. In the following words Zoroaster speaks entirely as beggar: Mazdå ahum dadāt, Mazdå gēθā fradāt! God give you life, God increase your family!

The original meaning of rāda has not entirely disappeared from Middle Persian, cf. *Mēn.Xr.*: "pa rāyēnītārīh ē kār u dātistān, to be legal agent in business and in court," and "patvand rāyēnītan, to become related by marriage," seen in its legal obligations. AhuraMazdāh is the "hamē.rāyēnītār, patron of the world."

In *Y.*33,4 the word mantuš is used for something much resembling the legal protection by the hospes, cf. under 'Ārmatiš.' Zoroaster removes by his prayer the "ačištam mantum, fact of having the worst mantuš," from the "gāuš vāstra, cow-pasture, i.e. peasantry," cf. "gāuš ǰyōtum, livelihood of the peasantry, the living on cattle breeding." To have the worst mantuš is the "shadowy side" of life as peasant. Bartholomae, *Wb.*282: "Das Rind, geschaffen dem Bauer und Viehzüchter zu dienen, hat deshalb keinen Anspruch auf Recht, sondern ist auf Wohlwollen angewiesen." And just because, as property of man, it is slave and without rights, the ox or cow is the symbol of the cultivator in Zoroaster's metaphoric idiom.

ačišta implies a contrast: in "removing by his prayer the evil mantuš,"

Zoroaster designates himself as the "good mantuš" of the bondsmen. Therefore, in *Y*.29,8, "the cow has found Zoroaster as the only one" who takes its side according to the divine order, and *Y*.29,9: "but he is poor and without 'voice,'" himself an exul, and hence cannot appear and speak as patronus. In *Y*.28,1, Zoroaster implores help

vahoš χratum manaho   yā χšnavišā gāušča ruvānam

"that I may listen to the will of Vahumano and to the soul of the ox" (which is cliens), that means, that I may give it patrocinium in accordance with the will of God.

In *Y*.46,16-17, rādah and mantu are combined, cf. under 'Poetry':

16: frašа.uštra   aθra tu ardrāiš idi
hōugava tāiš   yān usvahi uštā.stoi
yaθra rtā   hačate ārmatiš
yaθra vahoš   manaho ištā χšaθram
yaθra mazdå   vardmam šēti ahuro

"Hāugava Frašauštra, travel, thou, with the most ardent wishes, which we two cherish, thither where Obedience-to-law follows the Right, where Wordly-power is owned by Good-will, where AhuraMazdāh abides in abundance!"

> Lommel-Andreas: "O Fr. Nachkomme des Hugu, dorthin gehe mit den Einsichtigen?, von welchen wir beide wünschen, dass ihnen das erwünschte zuteil werde, (dorthin) wo von Wahrsein gefolgt ist die Fügsamkeit, wo die begehrten Reiche [L. reads χšaθrā, pl.] des Guten-Denkens sind, wo der Weise Herr in Freude wohnt."

"Both we" are Zoroaster and his wife, the Hāugavī, daughter of Frašauštra. uštā stoi!, the word translated by "wishes," is the exclamation itself: "it be according to wish!," a "please God, inshallāh!," a strong expression of hope, see under 'Fravarāni.'

St.17, text and explanation under 'Poetry,' runs: "Whither I shall sing verses, no bad-verses [=whither my best songs accompany you], Žāmāspa! Always I shall sing the praise of your protection, vahmān rādaho, you who know to distinguish dāθam and adāθam, dahrā mantū, as an erudite [doct] mantuš!"

dāθam adāθamča are opposed to afšman anafšman in the same

stanza, and are best referred to it, hence not "einsichtig und thöricht," nor "fromm und unfromm," but to √dāy- "colere" [cf. Tedesco, ZII,II, 47] "educated and uneducated," as neutr. "what is art and what is not," or like Arab.-Pers. "adabī bīadabī, urbanitas and inurbanitas, what is proper and what not." Referring to the following dahrā mantū, this quality would make Žāmāspa specially apt for his diplomatic mission. The three clauses with "where . . ." are imprecative, like Zoroaster's wishes: "where Right should dwell," where he hopes to find it. The place is obviously the highest court of appeal, the great-king himself. Cyrus is said to have constituted this court—first mentioned under Cambyses by Herodotus V,25 and III,31—which consisted of seven irremovable *βασιλήιοι δικασταί*. To this court the two Hāugava go as Zoroaster's fra.išta and +frasanhya, as mantū, an instr. of quality: because they are dahrā mantū, to achieve the rescission of his verdict.

dahra is "doctus,"[22] mantu the legal agent, the patron of the client (Zoroaster and the peasantry), or the hospes of the fugitive (Žāmāspa and Zoroaster), hence the guardian, OGerm. foramunt.[23] With this the word must be etymologically connected, and therewith with Lat. manus. Zoroaster calls Žāmāspa dahrā mantū because of his linguistic and juridical knowledge.

In *Yt.*15,39, a prayer of unmarried maidens to Vāyu, the same word is disfigured:

yat nmānapatim vindāma	that we may find a husband
yavano srāišta.krpa	a young, very-handsome one
yo nō hubrtām barat	who treats us well
yavata ǰava žīvāva	as long as we both live,
frazantīmča nō vrzyāt	and begets for us children,
dahro danto hizu.uχδo	as a learned guardian, an eloquent one.

hizu.uχδo makes sense only if it defines the husband as guardian who must "talk" for his wife, as huχratu defines rāda in *Y*.9,23. The poet aims at *Y*.46,17: the nmānapatiš is the guardian, paθiš and rāda of the wife, and one must read, as in 46,17, "dahrā mantū."

In the monolith inscription of ŠamšiAdad V, 825-810, third cam-

22 Cf. "hizvo danhahā, linguistic scholarship, philology" in *Ny.* 1,16 and *Yt.*13,18; later dastβar, dastūr < *danstvabara, from "danstva, dogma."

23 Germ. "munt," in family law, is the authority over the women.

paign, a Munsuartu of Araziaš appears, a name, the first element of which seems to be *manθva-; the place is Aw. rziša, Lištar in Luristān. In the Sasanian period, the mantu has developed into an official: "yātakgow, advocate," cf. the n.pr. Spandārmat-yātakgow, "having Ārmatiš as advocate" on a silver dish AMI IV, 1932, 159, and Sasanian bullae from Old Shīrāz with "artaχšatr-χvarrah dātware drigōšāne yātakgowe, judge, advocate of the poor, of Ardašīr-Xurrah"; one in my collection: "nvt'ltχštlkn dlvš'n y'tkgvy d'tvbly, advocate of the poor, judge of Nōδardašīrakān." Also *Gr.Bdh.*170: "yātakgowīh ē drigōšān, office of the advocate of the poor," in Bartholomae, *Mir.Mundrt.*II,22.

Thus we have traced in the Awesta a number of terms that belong to the IE. institution of hospitium, and have analogies in Gr. proxéneia and in Germanic law. In Old Roman law, clientes and hospitium govern the legal position of all who are not members of the body politic. Foreigners, whether envoys, merchants, exiles or other fugitives, are all hostes—etymologically = guest—and their sojourn in the country is made possible only by hospitium. They must have a "civis, Ir. hozantuš" member of the tribe, as hospes, who looks after their business and legal interests in the community, "kār u dātistān," and "speaks out for them," *Y.*46,5: fra hvētave mrūyāt, because as hostes they have no "voice" themselves, *Y.*29,9: vāčam nrš asūrahya.

The Roman hospitium is complemented by the notions "amicitiae and societates," relating to the law of nations, to which Iranian words like rvaθa, miθrā (plur.) and haχman correspond. The right of protection which the indigenous clients, Ir. aryaman, receive from their protector, Ir. rāda, is the clientela, the hospitium given by the hospes to foreigners. The functions are analogous, only different in their subjects. At a later period, the notions of patrocinium (Ir. rādah) and hospitium (Ir. √χšan-) coalesce. The scanty Iranian material does not allow the making of distinctions as exact as that.

rvaθa[24] corresponds to Rom. amicus. The "rvaθa, friendship, group of friends," often invoked in the *Ordeal-Yasht* 12 (see under 'Last Judgment'), are "cojurors, compurgators," which are called up, in many countries, in order to demonstrate the power of the partisans, the

[24] Nyberg: "in der Mithra-Gemeinde gleich Ordalgenosse, in der Gatha-Gemeinde aber Mysteriengenosse."

"friendship." The word belongs to √var- "to choose," original sense "love." The signification "friend" is outstanding in its negation, *Yt.* 14,38:

vispē trsantu a.rvaθa vispē trsantu dušmanyūš

"all non-rvaθa shall tremble, all enemies shall tremble!" dušmanyuš is "δυσμενής, NP. dušman, enemy"; the negation a.rvaθa is a full synonym; without negation it is εὐμενής, friend, NP. dōst. That is also valid for OP. rvaθa and ārvastam. rvaθa is amicus or socius as legal term when associated with hospitium and clientela. Wherever companions are called rvaθa, it is so because rvaθa means "friend"; the words do not lose their universal human signification when used as legal terms.

These researches throw new light on the gatha 46, of high importance for the life of Zoroaster.

Y.46,1:

kām namoi zām	kuθra namoi ayāni
pari hvētoš	aryamnasča dadāti
noit mā χšnāuš	+yo +vrzanah[art]ā
nēda dahyauš	yoi sāstāro drugvanto
kaθā θwā	mazdā χšnōšāi ahura

"To which country, to prostrate [=hide] myself, where to prostrate myself shall I go? They have cast me out from civitas and societas. The consul civitatis does not listen to me, nor do the drug-ish commanders of the province. How can I [then] listen to Thee, AhuraMazdāh?"

Lommel-Andreas: "In welches Land soll ich mich wenden? wohin soll ich mich wenden, soll ich gehen? Man trennt mich von Hausgenossen und Stammesfreund. Der Geschlechtsverband (=die Sippengemeinde), mit welchen . . . , ist mir nicht günstig, und nicht die, welche des Landes lügnerische Gebieter sind. Wie kann ich Dich, o Weiser, günstig stimmen, o Herr?" Note: "pari-dā etwas wie 'ausschliessen,' die Bedeutung 'trennen' steht nicht fest." Lommel believes that the sentences express "ein zeitweiliges Zerwürfnis mit den Sippengenossen."

Nyberg: "Mir zu Gefallen ist nicht das vərəzəna, dem ich folgen will(?), auch nicht die der Drug zugehörigen Fürsten des

Landes. Wie soll ich Dir zu Gefallen sein, o A.M.?" And 233: "Aus dem verzweifelten Klang merkt man sogleich, dass die Verhältnisse im Stamm sich zur Unhaltbarkeit zugespitzt haben. Alle Stände vereinigen sich gegen ihn, und die Fürsten des Landes sind ihm nicht gewogen. Offenbar hat der neue Kult im Stamme sehr bedeutend an Boden gewonnen, Flucht war das einzige was dem Propheten übrig blieb." But what he then does, he could comfortably have done at home: "seine einzige Hoffnung auf AhuraMazdāh setzend," the prophet begins his mission in his new, Mithra-worshipping parish (263): "indem er einfach [simply] an die Mithra-Religion anknüpft . . . keine Rede von Kampf . . . höchstens wird indirekt vor gewissen Seiten derselben gewarnt. Zarathustra betritt den Weg der *Religionspolitik*." This is awfully simple and simply awful.

Both translations sound as if the god showed his displeasure, disfavor by allowing those people to be disagreeable, ill-disposed towards the prophet.

namoi: Darmesteter accepted the variant namo "en prière" of K5. *Wb.:* "fliehen, eigentl. sich bücken." Andreas-Lommel: "entweder l.sg. subj.med. oder infinitiv." Benveniste, 56f.: "inf., ou dat. d'un nom-racine nam." The root, to which "namah, proskynesis" belongs has nowhere the signification "to flee," not even with the prev. fra-, but "to lie prostrate, lie low." *Yt.*19,34 says the same with other words: "Yama, expulsed from paradise, dāušmanahyāiča ho strto nidārat, hides prostrate in despair." The meaning is neither "flight," nor "turning in a different direction," but the attitude of prostration, like that of a hiding animal. pari-dā means solemnly "to consecrate, make 'sacer' to the gods"; with the abl. "away from hvētu and aryaman" it means "to cast out from" as a sacrilegus. The Pahl. transl. bē dāt, expl. bē kirt, "severed from, outcast" is right. √χšnū- does not signify "to favor" or "to please," but, as in OP., "to hear, to obey," cf. *Altp.Inschr.* s.v. For ⁺vrzana.hartar, see under 'Social Structure.'

For the historical interpretation see under 'Bandva.' Zoroaster, to whose defense at the "interrogation, χšnūt, hearing" no member of the court had listened, χšnaviš, was outcast by the verdict from hvētu and aryaman of his home town, Ragā. On his hidjra, he drives (Y.51,2) through the country of the Vēhviyo—who sends him off—to Vištāspa, who receives him. The train of thought of gatha 46,3 is: In st.2 Zoroaster complains about his poverty, as proscriptus. In 3, he hopes for the "dawn of day" and believes in his victory. St.4—see under 'Bandva': "Who deprives the drugvant [whose doing this exile is] of his rule and life, prepares as leader the path of the good Čistiš." Then st.5, soon to be discussed.

Further, st.6: "Who refuses the refugee that implores, isamno,[25] is a drugvant." St.7: "Who shall be given as protector, patronus, to my unworthy self?" St.8: "Thou, AhuraMazdāh, art the only ahura, lord justiciary." St.10: "Who is doing good to me, shall go to heaven!" In st.12 he expects to win over the Friyāna. St.13, see above: "Who listens to, receives Zoroaster, merits to be praised!" St.14: see under 'Yā-ahī!': Vištāspa has become Zoroaster's patronus. In the following verses the Hāugava brothers travel to the court to obtain the rescission of the verdict and the "frasastiš, proclamation" for the vrzana. Between these stanzas stands 5:

yo vā χšayans	+ā +dām drītā āyantam
rvatoiš vā	hozantuš miθroibyo vā
rāšnā ǰīvans	yo rtāva drugvantam
vičīro hans	tat fra hvētave mrūyāt
uzuθyoi im	mazdā χrūnyāt ahura

The text has ‚ādąs drītā', which Nyberg, 462, note to 234, emended in +ādandrīta, redupl. aor. of $\sqrt{}$²dar-, comparing OI. ādriyáte "to treat with respectful attention." Tedesco reads +ā +dām drītā, written with ligature of the prep. ā (*Wb.*303, with n°6 and 10), as in ‚ādąm', i.e. +ā +dām (nipāhe) in Y.49,10; similarly in 48,7 and more often. urvatoiš, (gen.)-abl. of rvati, in Gathic a hapax, is the same as Aw. rvati which *Wb.* translates by "foedus, fides." It is coupled by vā—vā with miθroibyo

25 Andreas, with Lommel: "isamno, medial; Bartholomae nimmt lediglich für diese Stelle passive Bedeutung an." Lommel: "Aber wer nicht mit diesem Wunsche (nämlich aufgenommen zu werden) zu diesem (dem einflussreichen Rechtgläubigen) kommt, der möge zu den Geschöpfen der Lüge zurückkehren!" Explanation: "Die Aufnahme eines Bekehrten soll—scheint's—in den Rechtsformen der Aufnahme eines Schutzgenossen vollzogen werden." The verses have neither orthodoxy, nor conversion, nor religion in mind, but solely the granting of hospitium. For isamno cf. prsamna in *Vid.* 3,29: "bāδa iδa hištate anyahya dvare srayano hvarantīš prsamnēšuča, verily, hereafter, you shall wait squatting at an other one's door among those who beg for food!", just like Arab. "sā'il, beggar" to "sa'ala, to ask."

(dat.)abl.pl., the "social bonds, societates," on which society rests (see under 'Mithra'). The two ablatives follow the verb and frame hozantuš, hence mean: "Who . . . receives, because as member of the tribe he is bound to do so by amicitiae and societates." rāšnā ǰīvans renders a similar thought: one who lives according to the mores that bind him to give protection. Cf. (under 'Kavi') *Y*.49,1: "he who, being my bandva, yet listened to the verdict! thereby failing in his duty"; and *Y*.51,12: The Vēhviya, being a kavi, yet refused hospitium, though peership obliged him to give it. All expressions are argumentative, not descriptive. The translation is:

"He who, be he satrap, receives the stranger (lit. him who arrives) according to the fides or, be he a member of the tribe, according to the societates, who lives as the moral obligations require, and who, (himself) an rtāvan, knows to distinguish a drugvant—that one shall, then, speak for him to his peers and protect him from sanguinary deeds, o AhuraMazdāh!"

Lommel-Andreas: "Oder wenn einer, der die Macht (das Vermögen dazu) hat, einen, der zu ihm kommt, aufnimmt, und bei sich behält auf Grund von Verträgen und Freundschaftsbündnissen, ein Mann aus edlem Stamme, der nach dem Recht lebt, wenn er ein Wahrhaftiger, der andre aber ein Lügner ist, und wenn er die Entscheidung darüber hat—so soll er es seinen Hausgenossen sagen, um ihm, o Weiser, gegen Gewaltthaten zu helfen, o Herr!" Note: "ādąs drītā āyantam, Andreas: wenn er aufnehmend einen zu (ihm) kommenden (bei sich) behielte." In this way, the noble man, in power, makes a treaty of friendship with the liar, has the decision, but is obliged to make the presence of the fugitive known, in order to protect him against violence, which only strict secrecy could achieve.

Bartholomae construed yo rtāvā drugvantam in parallel with yo χšayans āyantam, both governed by the verb as which he understood ‚ādąns drītā'. In this way, the χšayans hozantuš becomes the rtāvan, and the āyans, Zoroaster, becomes the drugvant. Even though—with Bartholomae's interpretation of ādans drītā—it would not be Zoroaster, but somebody unknown, this is impossible: "Wenn ein Kundiger einen festzuhalten vermag, nachdem er ihn dazu gebracht hat, von seinem Gelübde und seinen Bindungen weg (zu ihm) überzugehen" would be the conversion of a drugvant achieved by suborning to perjury and breach of faith, and the following stanza says: "For he is himself a drugvant, who favors a drugvant." Hence, one shall not convert a drugvant, nor—as it ought to be translated—"give asylum" to one. *Matth.*10,5-6: "Do not turn aside into a road of the heathens, do not enter a town of the Samaritans."

Bartholomae's construction isolates the words vičiro hans, which do not signify "die Entscheidung treffend," nor "wenn er dessen sicher ist": vi.čī- means to distinguish, *διαγνῶναι* of the judge or of the critic, for instance in the same gatha, st.15: "yat dāθān vičayaθa adāθānsča," and 17: "yo vičinōt dāθāmča adāθāmča." If the antonyms rtāvan and drugvant precede a vičiro, they can only be the object of distinction. The complex expression vičiro hans "being distinguisher" has, like the part. *vičinvans or like the noun-of-agent, the verbal power to govern the acc. obj. drugvantam, cf. OP. Ōramazdā.tē ǰantā biyā! Hence "who is distinguishing, (being himself) an rtāvan, a drugvant (acc.)," that is, who recognizes that not the convicted fugitive, but the judge who convicted, is the true drugvant.[26]

All translators construct in such a way that the first vā connects the stanza with the preceding one: "on the path . . . he leads, who . . . kills, or who. . . ." The contents of the stanzas are not closely enough related to permit that. Rather, yo vā χšayans belongs together with hozantuš, as if it was vā χšayans vā hozantuš, and the second vā is only omitted, because this pair intersects the other rvatoiš vā—miθroibyo vā. The same construction is found in *Beh.* §14: adam niyaθ^{r}ārayam[27] kārahya abičarīš gēθāmča mānyamča viθbišča, tyādiš . . . , with inversion: the gen.-abl. sg. kārahya is opposed to the instr.dat.pl. viθbišča. kārahya has no -ča, because this pair overlaps the other, gēθāmča mānyamča: "I placed again under the kāra their abičarīš, and their

[26] This power of distinction is expressed by Arab. fārūq "who knows to distinguish between truth and falsehood," surname of the caliph 'Umar, e.g. inscr. of Shaikh Djamāl, Aleppo, a^{o} 854 H.

[27] niyaθ^{r}āraya, in *Vid.* once nisrāraya, resembles *κλάω* and *κλῆρος*, *κληρουχεῖν*; "I gave them back their heritage."

gēθā and mānya under the viθ, of which Gōmāta . . . had deprived them."

Before it says: "who kills the drugvant, prepares the path of čistiš (religion)"; after: "who receives the fugitive." The same granting of protection is expressed, in 13, by "who listens, χšnāus < χšnaviš, to Zoroaster." The one who arrives, āyant, is Zoroaster, who asks in st.1: "kuθra ayāni, where shall I go?", the "poor" of st.2; the "imploring" of st.6; "my humble self" of st.7. The one who receives is the same who fulfils in st.3 the hope for the "dawn," gives protection in 7, shall go to heaven in 10, and who is Zoroaster's "friend for (at) the maga, and wants to be praised by him in song: He, kavi Vištāspa,yā-ahī!"

Vištāspa is the χšayant of the dahyu to which Zoroaster fled. Of course, χšayant, with a following verb, can mean "having the power to exercise" the activity of that verb. This would even make sense: powerful enough to receive Zoroaster, without being afraid of the lord justiciary who validated the verdict. But the explanation would impair the necessary parallelity of vā χšayans and vā hozantuš, which demands "satrap and civis." Vištāspa is the χšayant, χšāyaθya of the province, and the Hāugava are its cives. As hospites they must "speak" fra mrūyāt, for Zoroaster, who, as a fugitive, has no "voice," before their peers, hvētu, to protect him against attentates, χrūnyāt. Zoroaster is outlawed—pari dadāti—"vogelfrei," and threatened by murder.

The juridical terms which Zoroaster uses in this situation, rāzan, rvati, miθrā, also rtāvan, are the legal notions of bygone days upon which the pre-Zoroastrian society was built, descending from the ius talionis, the blood revenge. drugvant is the only Zoroastrian term in this gatha, replacing older miθradruχš. The god of social order was Mithra, therefore we shall meet these terms again in the Mithra yasht, from which their full understanding can be abstracted.

Zoroaster looks for asylum and finds it with Vištāspa, in Parthava. In the following verses the two Hāugava set out on their journey to the residence of the great-king, to obtain the revocation of his proscription.

IX. HOUSE HĀUGAVA

In *Y.*51,16 Zoroaster says that kavi Vištāspa has received him as fugitive, in 17 that Frašauštra, in 18 that Žāmāspa are his friends. These two are the Hāugava, the former the father of Zoroaster's wife, Hāugavī. The name is written hvōgva in the gathas, hvōva in *Yt.*13,118, a patron.adj. with vrddhi of hugu, hence hāugava, fem. hāugavī.

Members of this family, enumerated in the memorial list, are: Žāmāspa, a son Hanharvah, a grandson Varšna, and a Žāmāspa aparazāta "junior," another grandson or a great-grandson. Frašauštra, with two sons, Hušyōθna and Hvādēna, and the daughter Hāugavī. Another member is probably Avāra.uštriš with a son Vahunamah and a grandson Gēvaniš. In *frgm.Darmst.*7, varšnahe θwam ⁺hanharušoiš ǰāmāspanahe puθrahe puθram, it is not an anonymous son (*Wb.*1389) of Varšna, but himself who is invoked against an unknown evil called varšna: "of V. (gen.), thee (acc.), Hanharuš' (gen.), the Jāmāspian son's (gen.), son (acc.)," construed like the genealogy of Artaxerxes II in his Susa inscriptions, hanharuš.oiš, as there dārayavauš.ahya, with false gen. termination attached to the nominative.

The question in the "Gatha of the Cow," *Y.*29,9: "When will come he who will give him [Zoroaster] zastavat avo, practical help?" aims at Žāmāspa and Frašauštra, important for the chronological sequence of the gathas.

The Hāugava were hvētu and very wealthy, *Yt.*5,98: "for riches asked the Hāugava." In *Y.*51,18, Zoroaster himself calls Žāmāspa "ištoiš hvarnå, blessed with riches." The words show that Žāmāspa, not Frašauštra, was the chief of the house as the elder brother. In *Y.*49,7 Zoroaster asks "which hvētu will obtain the frasasti?" and expects it (st. 8 and 9) from Frašauštra as fra.išta and Žāmāspa as fšənghyo. In *Y.*46,16-17, after Zoroaster's marriage to the Hāugavī, the two brothers set out on their journey to obtain the frasasti. In *Y.*53, the "Wedding Gatha," Žāmāspa and Frašauštra are fathers and grandfathers of the young couples.

The name of the elder Hāugava is written in Gath. dəǰāmāspa, in Aw. ǰāmāspa. The same spelling is used once more in Gath. dəǰīt.arəta,

Aw. ǰiṯ.aṣ̌a, in a gloss *Vid.*5,4. dəǰ- is no syllable with a vowel, but one phoneme.

In Paikuli the spelling is Pahl. z'm[sp], Pārs. d'm[']sp.[1] In the Pārs. version of the Ka'ba inscr. the family name is spelled d'mspvhrykn. Therefore BPārs. (e.g. *Zarērn., Art.Vīr.Nām.*) d'm'sp—though d ≅ y and exceptionally = z—is better read "dāmāsp." The brother of Kavāt I, on his coins, writes z'm[sp or -'sp].—The Greek forms are Zamaspes, Zamasphes, e.g. in a versified inscription from Susa, time of Phraates III or IV. But Ctesias, who spoke Old Persian, calls the wife of Artaxerxes I, mother of Xerxes II, Damaspia; and Cosmas of Jerusalem (A.D. 743) has Ζάμης besides Δαμοίτης, both misspellings of +Ζαμασπης and +Δαμασπης, alleged sons or diadochs of Zoroaster, from a commentary to a poem of Gregor Nazianzen, about A.D. 360; the source must have been the Χρήσεις Ὑστάσπου, also known to Ammian Marc. at the same date, Greek paraphrase of an Ir. *Zāmāspnāmak.[2]

There were two dialectic forms, with z and d, opposed like Aw. zāmātar, NP. dāmād, OI. jā́mātar. The Gr. z, and so Syr. zāmāsp, express clearly this opposition, but are neutral for the problem raised by Arm. ǰamasp and Shahn. ǰāmāsp, since their z represents Ir. z, ž and ǰ. Inscriptional Pārs. z is only z; inscr. Pahl. z is z and ž.

> dəǰīt.arəta is to be classed under the type of compounds Duchesne §§206 and 207: part.perf. in -ta plus rta; +dəǰīta.rta. The vowel ə, introduced by Aw. script only in the middle of the 4th century A.D. and revealing that Āturpāt did no longer understand what the Arsacid double notation meant, must be eliminated: +dǰīta.rta. dǰīta is part.pref. of √*ǰyā-, attested in Gathic by n.abstr. fra.ǰyāti, *Wb.* "Verderben," Andreas "Bedrückung," in fact "the decreasing, impairing of. . . ." Thus the root has two different notations in Gathic, dəǰī- and ǰy-, and the problem is for the greater part a graphic one. The Awestic notation is likewise double.
>
> First: ǰ in *ǰyā-, only in ǰinati, *Frhg.Ēv.*15, "minuit, debilitat" = OI. "jinati, he ages"; in a.ǰyamna and a.fra.ǰyamna, part.pres.-med. with *a* priv., "not-decreasing." The simpl. ǰyamna appears

[1] Rawlinson's reading d'm- was right (against my z'm- in Paikuli). For the problems of rendering the palatals in MP. scripts see AMI VII, 57ff.

[2] See under 'Spitāma,' n.9.

in *Beh.* §30, in the date formula "θauravāharahya māhya ǰyamnam pati, Akk. on the 30th of Aiiaru," hence "when the θōravāra moon had decreased." Just as early Pārsīk borrowed its ideogr. BYRḪ (with prep. bi- "in the month") for "māh, month" from the Aram. date formula used since the Achaemenian period, or as late Pārsīk borrowed "bar māh" (with Med. bar < upari) from the Pahlavīk formula, thus OP. borrowed its date formula with ǰyamnam from the language of Median chancery. Inscriptional ǰyamna is not OP., but Median, like Aw. ǰyamna.

The rendering of OP. šyāta by El. sa.t.ta, *Xerx.Pers.daiv.,* in 478 B.C., and of *purušyātiš by Gr. parysatis, show that since 500 B.C. the y of šy was lost, probably without influencing the pronunciation of š. As to ǰy: Aw. huǰyāti, Gr. hygieia, and vispā.-huǰyāti, against *Beh.*§35 višpauzātiš, El. wi.s.p.o.ca.ti.s, name of a town in Parthava, in 520 B.C., foursyllabic as in *Yt.*5,130: +farnahvantam +vispōǰyātim (see under 'Hospitium'), show that already in 520 B.C. ǰy was pronounced ž, or even z. When OP. ǰyamnam was borrowed from Median chancery, the pronunciation was not what the signs indicate. Cuneif. ǰ[i] i y[a]- must imitate a Median spelling in script; Gath. dəǰ- renders the Aramaic symbols of the archetype, 1st century A.D., for a sound transmitted only by word of mouth.

The second Aw. spelling is √*zyā-, pres. zināt in *Y.*11,5, with double acc.; part.perf. act. zizyuša, without object, and comp. with fra- (as also fra.ǰyā-) in pass. frazyanta/e. To it belongs the pre-Zoroastrian term miθra.zyā, syn. of miθra.-druχš and miθra.gan. *Wb.*1770 gives √zyā- the signification "jem. um etw. benachteiligen." zināt corresponds (as does ǰinati) to OI. jinati. √zyā- and √ǰyā- are the same word in two modes of spelling. The pronunciation of zy- must have been z since the end of the 6th century B.C.

In OP. √dyā- corresponds; pres. dīna, part.perf. dīta ≅ Gath. dəǰīta-, Aw. ǰit(a), equally construed with double accusative. In *Beh.* §§12,13: "Gōmāta adīna, deminuit, impaired, deprived Cambyses of the χšaθram"; "nobody else dared χšaθram dītam čaχriya, to make him deprived, deminutum of the χšaθram"; "I, Darius, adīnam, deminui, deprived him of the χšaθram."

Finally *Beh.*§14: "abičarīš tyādiš gōmāta adīna, the vassals . . . of whom Gōmāta deminuit, had deprived them." The djīta.rto prta.tanuvo of the Gatha is Gōmāta, whom Darius makes dīta of his χšaθram, rulership and life. For the style cf. Y.46,4: "yas.tam χšaθrāt . . . moiθat ǰyātoš vā, who deprives (moiθat to √miθ-, Lat. mūtare) him of χšaθram and life," and Y.53,9: "ku rtāvā ahuro yo īš ǰyātoš hamiθyāt, where is the ahura to deprive them of life and liberty?"

The phonetic equation OI. jinati, Aw. zīnat, OP. dīna, and the relation of Gath. dəǰāmāspa, Aw. ǰāmāspa, OP. damaspia to OI. jā́matar, Aw. zāmātar, NP. dāmād, rule out an initial palatal in inscr. ǰyamnam as well as in Gath. dəǰīta.rta, dəǰāmāspa, Aw. ǰamaspa, ǰyamna. Not even the survival of Aw. ǰāmāspa in Arm. ǰamasp (as late as Sebeos), Shāhn. ǰāmāsp, can prove it. Inscr. j^i i y^a m^a n^a transliterates the Median spelling of a word which even at that antiquity was not pronounced ǰy-. Gath. dəǰ- represents the Arsacid notation, either *dš or *dz, preferably *dz. Aw. ǰ, ǰy is a simplified notation of this Gath. dəǰ- < *dz, as is e.g. Aw. bit(i)ya to Gath. da^i bi^o, OP. d^uvi^o. The Aw. spelling ǰ is enough to have caused the name to be pronounced ǰāmāspa since the 4th century A.D., against etymology. I choose the transcription žāmāspa and žītarta merely to indicate the problematic character: written dǰ or ǰ, yet correponding to OP. d, hence in essence a z (dialectically ž?), not a ǰ (dialectically ž?).

Markwart saw in such double notations "phonetische Glossen," as if the words were written in two dialects at the same time. Assuming *dz as Ars. notation of Gath. dəǰ-, this would mean: "written d-, spoken z-," and would cover also the case dəb-: "Pers. d, Med. b." But a modification is obviously necessary: dš, tš etc. is pahlavīk style, attested 70 years before the Awesta was first written in Aramaic script; and dəǰ- must be traced back to that first writing. But a "phonetic gloss"[2a] could only gloss the pronunciation of something written before, hence the theory implies some written Awesta before that first com-

[2a] Late Assyrian and NeoBabylonian scribes use "phonetic glosses" with rare ideograms, the ethod therefore can appear in Awestic.

plete writing under Volagases I, as Markwart assumed, for other, but erroneous reasons.

That the name Žāmāspa had an OP. correspondent in Dāmāspa is certain. Andreas' emendation +Yāmāspa cannot be maintained. If the Arsacid double notations were indeed "phonetic glosses," there would not only be two forms, but the OP. form with d would be the primary form, and the name of the vispatiš of the Hāugava would be Old Persian. That is probable, even if the premise of this deduction would be wrong; avāra.uštriš is also an OP. name. What matters historically is that the name of the Hāugava Žāmāspa is closely connected with the Achaemenid house.

While Žāma.aspa and Fraša.uštra were at the court of Vištāspa when he gave Zoroaster hospitium, there was a Prēxaspes i.e. Fraša.aspa, the cup-bearer, at the court of Cambyses, a Persian. Through him Cambyses had given the order, in 525 B.C., to have Smerdis secretly executed in prison. And when Cambyses, after the appearance of the Pseudo-Smerdis, asked him whether the order had been effected, he answered: "If +astyartes (astva. rta, not Astyages) will appear and the dead will rise, then you may expect to see Smerdis again!" The words are so utterly Iranian that no Greek could invent them and that Herodotus misunderstood his own story, as shown by the somewhat amazed gloss "the Median" to the name Astyages. The words show that Prēxaspes had heard of Zoroaster's doctrine of the last judgment and the appearance of the sōšyant Astvatrta at the end of the world; the tenor of the story is evidently: "If it is true, what some people now say that. . . ."

According to the rules of IE. onomastics, one must regard as brothers three men, contemporaries, that bear so closely related names as žāma.-aspa, fraša.uštra and fraša.aspa. Darius had a mace-bearer, vaδ^{r}abara, Aspačina = Aspathines, whom he honored exceptionally by having him depicted at Naqsh i Rustam. Aspathines had a son Prexaspes (II), hence was certainly a son of Prexaspes I. In the Arsacid and Sasanian periods all court offices were hereditary; here, the mace-bearer of Darius is the son of the cup-bearer of Cambyses. The *ḳitāb Baghdād,* fol.10r, tells in 204 H.: "The caliph, al-Ma'mūn, said to 'Abbās b. Musayyib b. Zubair, ṣāḥib al-shurṭa, who suffered from gout: You have grown old, the bearing of the lance comes hard to you! 'Abbās: Here is my son at my place, it was my office and my father's, and we are the people of the lance!"

Against *Beh.* §68, where Darius remembers his six companions, Herodotus tells a version in which Aspathines is one of the seven. He must have been close to them to be reckoned as one of them, for instance as a nephew of the two Hāugava. His father Frašāspa was the man who knew that the Pseudo-Smerdis was an impostor, and through him his brothers Žāmāspa and Frašauštra, and therewith the circle round Vištāspa, may have had the proof of the fact, all-important to them, who after the extinction of the elder line were the heirs claiming the succession. Brzyarštiš-Brδya had been one of their circle. Aspathines, though not one of the seven, belonged to the same group as Darius and his friends at the court of his father Vištāspa in Tōsa. One sees who were the initiated of whom Darius says in *Beh.* §§12-13: "The kāra was in fear of him, he might kill many who had known Smerdis before; for that reason he might kill them, that nobody may recognize that I am not Brδya, Cyrus' son." Having a brother who was Cambyses' cupbearer would explain why it was the Hāugava who went to the court to obtain the frasastiš for Zoroaster, and would at the same time explain Prēxaspes' answer to Cambyses.

Žāmāspa is a typical man's name; the gentilic in *Yt.*13,104 and *frgm. Darmst.* 7, is ǰāmāspāna. And, compared with Hutōsā, Humāyā, Puručistā etc., Damaspia is no personal name of a woman, but, like Hāugavī, Frānī, Θritī, Spitāmī the fem. of the gentilic *dāmāspiya. It designates the queen as "née Dāmāspī," of the house of Žāmāspa, just as Hāugavī designates the wife of Zoroaster as "of the house of the Hāugava" Frašauštra, brother of Žāmāspa. This old house—like that of the Vivāna-Vēfīkān—appears still at the time of Shāhpuhr I in *Ka'ba* l.31: "Narsahe ē vāspuhr ē dāmāspuhrīkān,"[3] a form of the name which is to žāmāspāna as gēwpuhr is to Vivāna.

Ctesias tells that after the death of Artaxerxes I, in 424 B.C., Xerxes II, son of Damaspia, succeeded as the entitled heir among the 17 sons. Other sons were: Sekydianos or Sogdianus (Manetho)—a name recall-

[3] nrsχy ZY BRBYT' ZY d'mspvχrykn, whereas the Pahl. vers. has nrysχv BRBYT' šhypvχrkn and Gr. ΝΑΡΣΑΙΟΥ ΤΟΥ ΕΓ ΒΑΣΙΛΕΩΝ ΣΑΒΟΥΡΓΑΝ. Evidently, šāhpuhrakān is a narrower, dāmāspuhrīkān the wider denomination, as, of old, ǰāmāspāna and hāugava.

ing Skythianos, the alleged predecessor of Mani and the OP. social term skauθiš—a son of the Babylonian Alogune. Ochos, satrap of Hyrcania, and Arsites, sons of the Babylonian Kosmartydene. Bagapaios, son of the Babylonian Andia (?), brother of Parysatis, the mother of Artaxerxes II and the younger Cyrus. Obviously, as Xerxes I, Xerxes II was heir-apparent because of the higher rank of his mother. After 45 days, he was murdered by Sekydianos; on the same day Damaspia died. Both were brought ἐς Πέρσας, to Persepolis, and buried there, at Naqsh i Rustam, in the tomb of Artaxerxes I, opposite the Ka'ba i Zardušt.

At the time of the memorial list, about 527 B.C., Žāmāspa had already a grandson Varšna and another, or a great-grandson, Žāmāspa II. Zoroaster's gatha 51, composed—not before 521—for the double wedding of a son and his only daughter from the Hāugavī, Puručistā, mentions Žāmāspa and Vištāspa as present. They are there because they give away a son (or grandson) and a daughter (or granddaughter) in marriage to the two children of Zoroaster (see under 'Maga'). Puručistā's bridegroom, not called by name, may well have been a grandson, or if Žāmāspa was born in 591, 22 years older than Zoroaster, a great-grandson of his.

In a hopeless attempt at disproving the identity of the historical and the Awestic Vištāspa, Nyberg says, 357: ". . . da muss man sich höchlichst darüber wundern, dass Darius, der in *Beh.* §68 seine Helfer aufzählt, so gänzlich den trefflichen Frašauštra und Jāmāspa vergessen hat, gar nicht zu reden von dem Propheten selber, aber diese ganze *Konstruktion ist so unsinnig wie nur etwas sein kann.*" I do not believe that the brothers deserve the trivial, trifling "trefflich," at any rate they helped Zoroaster, not Darius. And Zoroaster himself, who had recommended the murder, when discussing §68 with Darius, may have preferred, as a prophet, not to have this remembrance publicly perpetuated, for, as Nyberg says, 395: "Was sie in ihrem Innersten dachten, wissen wir nicht." Yet it seems that Darius did not at all forget the old gentleman Žāmāspa, whom he had known in Tōsa—nor his money.

Since Darius' first grandchild Artystone (II), a daughter's daughter, duχθ^{r}īš, was born in 506 B.C., his first grandson by a son, Artaxerxes I, was born after 506. Damaspia, if a daughter of Žāmāspa II and Puručistā, may have been born about the same time. But since Artaxerxes I and Damaspia died only in 424 B.C., Damaspia was rather a granddaughter of Žāmāspa II, in that case born about 488. Even then, Darius may have prearranged this marriage of his grandson still at his lifetime. He may have said to Žāmāspa II: "I remember well your ancestor and namesake, and have been told a granddaughter has been born to you; I beg you, to leave to me her affairs, because I wish my grandson and future successor to marry her!"

Since we "do not know what such great lords thought in their heart," it is good at least to read how men of their kind talked at a later period. Tabari III,1457f. tells for instance—Nyberg, 310, calls such an analogy an "Indizienbeweis": "al-Muntaṣir left, late in the evening, the reception hall of his drunk father al-Mutawakkil 'alā'llāh. When leaving, he took the hand of the majordomo Zurāfa (giraffe), saying: Come with me! Z.: O my lord, the Commander of the Faithful is not yet risen from the table! M.: Wine has overpowered the Commander of the Faithful, Bogha [commander of the Guard] and the guests will leave shortly. I want to beg you to leave to me the affairs of your children. Utamish [later vizier] has asked me to marry his son to your daughter, and your son to his daughter! Z.: We are your slaves, my lord, order us as you please!" Bunān, the singer, told: "Muntaṣir said to me: I just have married the son of Zurāfa to the daughter of Utamish, and the son of Utamish to the daughter of Zurāfa! I said: My lord, where are the 'nithār' (money etc., strewn over the guests), the nicest thing at a wedding? M.: Tomorrow morning, inshallāh, the night is almost past! Shortly after, one hears noise and cries, and Bogha, who had just killed al-Mutawakkil, enters. Muntaṣir asked: What means the noise? B.: Only good news, O Commander of the Faithful! M.: Woe betide you, what do you say? B.: Allah reward you amply for [form of announcing a death] our lord the commander of the faithful [al-Mutawakkil]; Allāh's slave [Muntaṣir as 'abd-allāh wa khalīfatuhu] has prayed, and He has heard his prayer!"

Frašauštra is called fšənghyo in *Y*.31,10; the acc. is spelled fšənghīm in *Y*.49,9; at both places the word is one syllable short. Bartholomae translated "förderlich," and, without giving an etymology of his own, called Darmesteter's a "Schaueretymologie," (*Wb*.1029). Andreas: "sehend, achtend auf," censured as "abenteuerlich" by Nyberg, 245f., who himself translates "der sich (durch Vohu Manah) binden lässt" without saying more about this Houdini act. H. W. Bailey, equally rejected by Nyberg, had considered in BSOS VII,275f., *fšahya, syn. of fšuyant "farmer." None of these proposals cures the metric deficiency.

Yt.31,9-10 (full text and commentary under 'ApāmNapāt'):

āt hi ayå fravarta	vāstriyam ahyai fšuyantam
ahuram rtāvanam	vahoš ‚fšənghīm' manaho
noit mazdā avāstriyo	dvansčina humrtoiš baχšta

"Suppose Thou wouldst let the ox have its own way, to leave either the vāstriya or him who is not a vāstriya, it would choose between the two for itself the vāstriya.fšuyant, as a good patron, a fš. of Vahumano. The non-farmer shall have no share whatever in the account [division of profit]!"

Zoroaster opposes often a notion and its negation, and where he uses the *a* priv., this implies, in contradistinction to the Awestic usage, always the opposition of good and bad. *Y*.49,4: "fšuyašū afšuyanto, the bad ones among the cattle-breeders"; *Y*.46,17: "afšmāni noit an.afšmām, verses, not non-verses," meaning really good ones. In his didactic style, 10b is the reason: "because he is a fš. of Vahumano, Good-Will," and fšənghyo cannot be a syn. of fšuyant, for that would be an explanation "by virtue of a virtue."

The second place is clear enough. *Y*.49 begins with the two stanzas about the bandva and his tkēša, see under 'Bandva.' In st.7 text under 'Social Structure,' Zoroaster asks: "which aryaman, which hvētu, will obtain, through dātā, the good frasasti for the vrzanam?" He expects it from the Hāugava. St.8 "give Frašauštra the most welcome wedding to Rtam . . . , for ever we want to be the fra.ištåho, envoys!" St.9, text under 'Yā-ahī!':

srōtu sāsnå	‚fšənghyo' suvē tašto

"He shall proclaim the orders, the fš., destined for my salvation, who as a duly-speaking one rejects all fellowship with the drugvant, . . . yā-ahī, triumph, Žāma.aspa!"

The drugvant, with whom Žāmāspa does not want to deal, is the bandva of st.1. The activity of the fšənghyo is to proclaim orders, decrees. The stanzas about the two brothers are built in strict parallelism:

fra.išta and fšənghyo are analogous notions, and the verses play upon the words frasasti, sāsna (both to √sanh-), fra.išta and fšənghya.

In *Y*.50,1 a similar pair of words is used; cf. 49,12 under 'Poetry':

kat moi ruvā   isē čahya avaho

"How little help has my soul got from any one, whom have I found as protector, θrātar, of my herd and myself, (as my) azdā zūtar, but Thee, AhuraMazdāh, Rtam and Vahumano!"

> Bartholomae: "Ob wohl meine Seele bei irgend jemand auf Hilfe zu rechnen hat?" Lommel: "Über was an Hilfe und von wem verfügt meine Seele?"

azdā zūtar (for zōtar < zavitar, to √zu-, zbā-) in parallel with θrātar must be understood as a poetical expression for the official "azdākara, herald" of the papyri. Xerxes writes: "patiyazbayam: dēvā mā yaδyēša!, I made proclaim: The dēvā shall not be worshipped!" patiy.azbayam is a Median term of administration, Aw. √zbā-, zbaya-, Akk. apteqira; pati seems to restrict the notion to "proclaiming a prohibition."

All these words are terms of official functions. Aw. fra.išta, is OP. *frēstaka, in Aram. 'frstky', LXX: *φαρεσθαχαῖοι, Ezra* 4,9: "R^{e}ḫūm, the b^{e} 'ēl-ṭ^{e} 'ēm, holder of a farmān,[4] Šimšai, the scribe, and their officers, the judges and envoys (frēstaka), the +ṭpsry', tablet-scribes[5] of the countries . . . write to Artaxerxes." To the same group of officials belong Akk. ^{lu}ip.ra.sa.ka.nu in the business documents of Murašū Sons (U.M. II,1, 189,16) and Aram. 'frsky', LXX: (α)φαρσαχαῖοι in *Ezra* 5,6 (and sim. 6,6): "Copy of the letter which . . . the governor of 'Abar nah^{e}rān (satrap of Syria) sent to Darius the king." Cf. Markwart *Gāth. ušt.* 4, on Med. *frasaxvan > frasaxv etc., with the significant quotation from the Lex. Rhet. Photios on the (*σαγγάδαι* and) *παρασάγγαι* which "may equally well designate the messenger as the mile-stone," the parasang.

"Φαρσαχαῖος (public) crier" is the word one needs in *Y*.49,9 and which fits in 31,10. fšənghyo which is one syllable short, must be

[4] "plenipotentiary," cf. *Altp.Inschr.* 318; Landsberger, AOF X, 1935, 140ff., in a text of Nimurta.Tukul.Assur, translates Ass. ṭēma šakānu by "zu befehlen haben"; but b^{e}'ēl ṭ^{e}'ēm is one who has a written order, a letter patent.

[5] +ṭifsar < Akk. dubsar; text: ṭrply'. I remember one ṭyrpt (?) in the acts of Mār Pethiōn, G. Hoffmann, *Syr.Akt.* which could be equally ṭfsar.

emended : pšnhy : prsnhy, ⁺frasanhya.[6] fra.išta and frasanhya, φαρεσθαχαῖοι and φαρσαχαῖοι are a common pair: rasūl and nabī, or ἀπόστολοι and προφῆται of the original Christian community in Jerusalem.[7] "frasanhyo frasastim frasanhati, the herald proclaims the frasasti."

There must have been several kinds of heralds. Governmental edicts, military orders, court sentences and many other things require publication, and frasasti, proclamation was the only means. typty, tpty in *Daniel* 3,2,12 and in *Pap.Strassb.* 27,9 is θēpati < *θahyapati, "maître de la proclamation" or chief-herald,[8] and OP. θahya is the simplex to Med. fra.sanhya. The officer is enumerated between judge and police, and the frasanhya seem to have been the special outcriers of the courts. In the Muhammedan time the army had spokesmen or commissioners of their own, the za'īm al-djuyūsh. Cf. *Beh.* §60: "yaδi imām handungām . . . kārahya θāhi—in the preceding § it is the imper. θādi—if you proclaim this edict to the army," or in wider sense "the free men"; also the unknown prototype of Aram. kārōzā[9] in *Daniel* 3,4.

What the frasanhya proclaims is the frasasti, proclamation. Bartholomae translated "Leumund." "leu" is OHG. hliu, Gr. κλέϝος, Ir. sravah, which expresses that notion in Iranian, with its derivatives, e.g. husravah, dušsravah, cf. Tištriya *Yt.*8,4:

"hačā brzyāt hāusravaham, from the high one (ApāmNapāt) is his fame!", or the curse of Hōma, *Y.*11,2:

uta būyå a.frazantiš uta dāušsravå hačimno

"childless thou shalt be and followed by shame!" Also vahāu sravahī in *Y.*30,10. √sanh- "pronuntiare," never takes this connotation, nor do the roots √vak- and √mru-.

> How big a mistake this translation was, becomes manifest by Nyberg's elaboration, 243, on *Y.*49,7: "Wer ist der aryaman, wer der χvaētu, nach den (göttlichen) Gesetzen, der dem vərəzəna guten Ruf geben kann?" Comm.: "Wo findet, so meint er,

6 Cf. *Yt.*14,28: hvāχštəm for ⁺huvaχštram, epithet of Vrthragna and n.pr. Kyaxares.

7 Cf. Ed. Meyer, *Christent.* 1,265.

8 With y < -ahya-, as in vyzdt(Pap.) < vahyazdāta, cf. under 'Memorial Document.'

9 Not Ir. χrōsa, Schaeder *Iran.Beitr.* 245. The second element -ōz, may contain -vāč, "vox"; kāra as first element? Gr. κῆρυξ is Homeric, too old to be a loan from Iranian.

seitdem die leitenden Männer meines eigenen Stammes vor ihrer Aufgabe [which?] versagt haben, der Priesterstand und der Adel, die das Ansehen des Hirtenstammes wieder aufrichten können?" Answer: "Frašauštra und Jāmāspa." Only the shepherd tribe themselves could achieve that, for every man is the cause of his own reputation, as one can read already in Homer, *Od.*1,329ff.:

ὃς μὲν ἀπηνὴς αὐτὸς ἔῃ . . . ἐφεψιόωνται ἅπαντες
ὃς δ' ἂν ἀμύμων αὐτὸς ἔῃ . . . πολλοὶ δέ μιν ἔσθλον ἔειπον.

One is socius and civis not by (divine) but by (civil) law, nor are there divine laws for the special case that leading men are found wanting, however frequent that may be. If ever the misguided idea had occurred to Zoroaster to mend the bad reputation of his enemies, he ought to have deleted the insult offered to the vaēpyo in *Y.*51,12, and the invitation to kill them, at the occasion, when (Nyberg, 247) "er selber seine Gesänge für den liturgischen Gebrauch seiner Gemeinde zusammenstellte und mit einer—natürlich nicht schriftlichen (sic)—Einleitung versah."

Thus Bartholomae failed to recognize this greatest event in Zoroaster's life, on which the introductory words put the highest emphasis: "AhuraMazdāh shall hear it as Vahumano, shall hear it as Rtam, hear it Thyself, o AhuraMazdāh! Who is the aryaman, who the hvētu, who through dātā will obtain for the vrzanam the good frasasti?"

The "good" frasasti—"bad" would be an interdict—is obtained by dātā, OP. "tyā manā dātā, my, the great-king's laws," "the inviolable dāt, law of the Medes and Persians" in Daniel, a term borrowed also by Akkadians and Elamites. What Zoroaster hopes so passionately to have "proclaimed" is the rescission of his banishment. "vrzanam, city," is either the town where the proclamation takes place, or his "religion" as fictitious "community." In both cases, the revocation of the verdict is the authorization for his teaching. We know from Daniel and Ezra that every religious community needed an official authorization, and Xerxes' "interdiction of the dēva cult" is the negative side of the frasasti for Zoroaster.

There is one other place where frasasti has its full meaning: *Yt.*10,60:

The cult of Mithra, long years prohibited (see under 'Mithra' and 'Dēva') obtained again the agreement of the government. The hideous verses were composed when the "proclamation, frasastiš" by Artaxerxes II belonged already to a not distant past, after 400 B.C., but before Alexander, before 330 B.C. Because the proclamation is a sanction, the true sense fades at late, empty and bad places.[10]

It is nowhere said whether the mission of the Hāugava was a success or not. In *Y*.46—separated from the time of *Y*.51 by Zoroaster's marriage to the Hāugavī, not necessarily a long interval—the brothers set forth on their journey. In 49 Zoroaster hopes that they will obtain the frasastiš, at a moment when he foresees already the end of Cambyses and, at the same time, hopes that this would entail the downfall of Gōmāta. If *Y*.46 is all of one piece and if no new gatha begins, e.g. in st.6, the attempt seems to have been made before Cyrus' death. *Yt*.9,26 implicates Hutōsā in it; that is not history, like the gathic passages, but might retain some truth: Atossa's influence upon her father Cyrus. If *Y*.49 is a unit, the frasasti was not yet granted at the end of Cambyses' reign. One must expect that it was not granted before the death of Cambyses, but only after the gatha *Y*.53,8-9, by Darius.

The sanction of Zoroastrism did not mean the eradication of the old cults. Zoroaster's doctrine did not live on as a separate religion, because fundamentally it was much too spiritualized ever to become a popular cult. It is the result of history, not of "mission," that parts of it survived at all. "Community" and "mission" are not, as a matter of course, notions complementary to religion. Zoroastrism has been introduced by a governmental act, the "frasastiš through dātā." The circle of Zoroaster, i.e. the clan of Vištāspa with his officials and clients—*Yt*.13 enumerates 240 names—came into power after the convulsion of the Gōmāta episode, and raised Zoroaster's ethical and political ideas, his monotheism and dualism, to the position which one can call a religion of the rulers. The two hundred years of peace of the empire are the reason that Zoroaster's thoughts, passing over into Judaism and thence into Christianity, acted upon human thought and thus on the course of universal history.

Not Zoroaster was "Religionspolitiker und Synkretist"—or everything

[10] For frasastayāi in the song of the caravan to Ušå, see under 'Post and Travels.' It is not "Rühmen, Ruf" (*Wb.* 1000).

would long since be forgotten—but the old cults, threatened by the turn history took, adapted themselves, by syncretism, to the new situation and thus became fit for reintroduction. Thenceforth, not before Artaxerxes II, Zoroaster's name is only the sign-board for the older religion which had absorbed a certain number of his thoughts. There has never been a "mission," and the profanum vulgus has never been Zoroastrian in the very meaning of the word.

X. HVARNAH

HVARNAH is a mythical notion common to all Iranians, and the Zamyasht 19 is in reality not a hymn to the Earth, but to the hvarnah. This is a fire, a flame, not generated by man with flint and steel or by rubbing wood. Other fire is called "bipiθwa, θripiθwa, twice-, thrice-fed," frapiθwa "well-fed," hamēšag.pihan "continuously fed." But the hvarnah is "ahvartam, MP. aχvarišnīk, not needing food," see the myth of the fight for this hvarnah under 'ApāmNapāt.' It dwells in the water of the ocean vurukrtam and is according to the Pahl. translation "agrift, unseizable." The conception is related to naphtha, the sources of which come from the depths of the ocean, and as such it belongs to ApāmNapāt. It is also related to the lightning, and as such it belongs to Vrthragna.

A problem of dialectology adheres to the word hvarnah, indicated by the two NP. forms χurrah and farr. The opinion, frequently uttered, that farnah belonged to western, hvarnah to eastern dialects, is not supported by observations.

> The change hv > f occurs first, at determined time and place, in the region of Kōmis and Gurgān, western Parthia, in the n.pr. vēfiya < *vēvahviya in Y.51,12, see under 'Vēhviya'; the time is the 1st century A.D. The next instance is, about A.D. 100, the name of the god ΦAPPO on the Kūshān coins in Bactria. At the modern phase of the language, f < hv appears only in the isolated, Median dialect of Sīvand near Persepolis. The MMed. of the Turfan documents, on the contrary, has vχ < vh < hv; the Zāzā and other Med.-Kurd. dialects have w < vh < hv. Consequently, if the Assyrians note p=f in Old Median and Old Parthian personal names, e.g. šitirparnu for *čiθrahvarnah (Parth.), the Neo-Babylonians equally p, e.g. dari.parnu for Med. *dārayat.hvarnah, the Greeks φ in -φέρνης, but Ctesias β, in -βέρνης,—that means chiefly in the group t.hv—one must understand this transcription as the nearest approximation these languages and scripts could reach to the real Median sound which seems already to have been vh.[1]

1 The sound is one of the type of labialized IE gutturals, or Engl. wh. E. A. Speiser, AASOR

OP. cuneiform writes $u+v^a$, because its character u is derived from Akk.-El. ḫu,[2] and because the script, which was not "invented" for the OP. dialect, offered no better means of expressing the sound of their dialect. Where divergently f is written instead of $u+v^a$, e.g. in the n.pr. $v^i i d^a f^a r^a n^a a$ = *vindat.hvarnah, the Median sound is thereby rendered—for the appearance of a name in OP. inscriptions does not make the name Old Persian—and probably also the Median spelling: the Medes probably used their f for the sound vh < hv of their dialect as nearest approximation offered by their script, which they too had not "invented," but, at the best, adapted.

In the dialects of the southeast, the problem is represented by the name Arachosia. Ved. sárasvatī, OP. harahvatī is properly the name of the river, mod. Hilmand. It appears also in a part of Media at that time occupied by Persians, as araquttu, in 728 B.C., in the annals of TiglathPilesar. The Elam. notation in the OP. inscriptions is har.ru.wa.ti.s or har.r.o.wa.ti.s, with m/wa for hva, as in waracmiia for OP. hvārazmiya etc. BPahl. raχvat seems to descend from the OP. form; NP.Arab. ruχaǰ, ruχχaǰ has uχ < aχv as in Persian dialects, but the East Ir. final palatal, as in Sogdian. The Akk. versions, on the other hand, write a.ru.ḫa.at.ti with Med. psilosis, the *Pap.El.* hrvχty, both after Med. *(h)aravhati with av > ō; also Gr. Ἀραχωσια comes from this form, with metathesis of a and ō for reasons of Greek euphony.

Beside "hētumant, rich in dikes," which lives in the mod. name Hilmand, the river had another surname "hvarnahvatī, rich in hvarnah." The same epithet is given to the lake Kansavya into which the river falls. Besides, at Alexander's time another of the rivers falling into this lake bore the name Φαρνακῶτις, i.e. hvarnahvatī, with Greek compensated aspira-

VIII,27f., n.50, cf. *Mesop.Origins* 92, quotes, from K.4675, the placename Hu.al.su.un.di (to be sought in Shahrzur) and compares it with parsindu in Assurnāṣirpal Annals a° 4 (Luckenbill I,455), situated in Zamua, i.e. Shahrzur. At first I believed this to be evidence for simultaneous rendering of Ir. hvar- by par- and hual-; but the year 4 of Assurnāṣirpal 880 B.C. is too early for an Iranian name to appear in that region.

[2] Therefore, aspiration is never written before u; opposite: i is never written after OP h^a, because this is derived from Akk.-El. hi. Equally: Ir. $č^a$ without added i can represent či, because $č^a$ < či < Akk.El.ṣi.

tion k:χ for *vharnavχatī, and with medial a + v > au > ō, and again metathesis of a and ō. The modern name is Harrut, but I regret not having ascertained the exact pronunciation and spelling. The annals of TiglathPileser I mention parnuatti < hvarnavhatī in Media 728 B.C.

In the "Song to the Sōšyant" (see under 'Last Judgment') the three saviours come, at the resurrection, from the Kansavya, i.e. the Hāmūn in Sīstān, from which rises the Kūh i Khwādja, old mount Ušidam. Nyberg says in his polemics against my opinion that Zoroaster sojourned on the hill in the lake, 304f.: "Der xvarnah Kult hat offenbar zwei Brennpunkte gehabt, einerseits voller Kontakt mit dem Vurukaša-Kreise"—i.e. vurukrtam, in fact the ocean—"andrerseits mit dem Bewässerungsgebiet des Hētumant verbunden, dem in ungewöhnlichem Masse xvarnah-Kraft eignete, ohne Zweifel deswegen, weil eine bedeutende Dynastie an seinen Ufern geherrscht hatte.[3] Die Lokalisierung der zoroastrischen Eschatologie daselbst ist nur ein Ausdruck des Strebens nach einer Zoroastrisierung des mächtigen xvarnah Kultes, der diesem Fluss und dem See zugehört. . . . Sie ist also sekundär und für die Geschichte der zoroastrischen Eschatologie fast ohne Interesse."

I cannot see how anything as completely unknown and unintelligible as "hvarnah power" could be "without doubt" the quality "in uncommon degree" of a river, because a dynasty as "unseizable" as the hvarnah itself had ruled at its banks. This elusive and illusive dynasty and its elliptic cult has left no trace in history and would have disappeared like circles in water. The "Song to the Sōšyant," "almost without interest for Zoroastrian eschatology" is, on the other hand, the only place where the Awesta touches this subject. Though not directly related to the hvarnah, it is interpolated in the parts of the Zam yasht that speak of hvarnah, seemingly because the detailed description of the "Sealand" on the Kansavya had also found a place in this yasht. The conception is abstracted from Gatha passages like Y.43,5;30,9, which the song elaborates, adding the placename. There is no reason to expect the return of a prophet from a precise spot, unless it be that he actually sojourned there. The Sealand, therefore, is the sole, primary and genuine place of this eschatology. If, then, the waters of this region are

[3] The source is *Wb.* 1730: "haētumant, die Beiwörter vielleicht darum, weil das kavische Königshaus von da stammt."

called hvarnahvant, it is not because a "dynasty" with a mighty hvarnah-cult dominated these waters which owned hvarnah power in uncommon degree, but because the "belief" was dominant that the "victorious, hvarnahvant saviour" would appear from there.

The notion "hvarnah" (see under 'Fravarti' and 'Tištriya') is difficult to define. The Pahl. translation of hvarnahvant, grouped with rēvant as surname of the river, is "l'y'wmnd GDH'wmnd," strikingly explained by "χvyšk'r v tvχš'k mynvg sgst'n, the dutiful and industrious genius (in or of) Sigistān." In Hellenistic style one would say "tyche of Sīstān."

Besides the mythical signification, the "victory-bringing hvarnah" must have one of daily use, evidenced by a few Gathic and Awestic expressions, like e.g. ištoiš hvarnå, which Zoroaster uses of Žāmāspa who helped him who was destitute as an exile.

F. Cumont, *Culte de Mithra* I, has dealt with the inscription from Mylasa, time of Artaxerxes II, CIGR. 2693b, dedicated to the τύχῃ ἐπιφανεῖ βασιλέως. Plutarch, *Alex.*30, makes Darius III speak of the τύχη Περσῶν which μακεδονίζει, has taken the side of the Greeks. Those are contemporary translations of the two notions kāvyam hvarno and āryānām hvarno which dominate *Yt.*19. ἐπιφανής, too, must translate an Iranian word derived from √sand- "to appear," for, like Vrthragna to whom the mythical notion belongs, the hvarnah assumes visible forms, becomes ἐπιφανής.

Aram. GDH serves as translation for τύχη and as ideogr. for hvarnah, because it was considered as a synonym as far back as the high Achaemenian period. Under the Seleucids one swears by the "tyche" of the king, a custom foreign to Greek, which must come from Iran. In the βασιλικὸν ὅρκος of the Iranian kings of Pontus, it is τύχην βασιλέως καὶ μῆνα Φαρνάκου. Among the divine honors bestowed upon Caesar, we find besides an image in the senate, and a gable of a temple, ἀετός, on his house, also "τὴν τύχην αὐτοῦ ὀμνύναι," Diod.49,6,1. In the martyrium of St. Pethion, G. Hoffmann, *Syr.Akt.*, the grand-mōbad swears "by the gaddā (i.e. hvarnah) of Hormizd and his crown!"

The Seleucids bear the predicates εὐσεβὴς εὐτυχὴς in their protocol, origin of Rom. pius felix fortunatus. With the Manichaeans, e.g. *Mir.*-

*Man.*ii,40,1 prvχ hvzdg nyvmvrv'h i.e. *εὐτυχὴς εὐγενὴς εὐοιωνιστός* (cf. humāyun) are the predicates of a prince of the church. In the protocol of Xusrau I, in Menander, *Exc.deLeg.*ii,3, we find: *ᾧ τὶνι θεοὶ μεγάλην τύχην* (Paik.: vχarrah) *καὶ μεγάλην βασίλειαν* (Paik.: χšaθr) *δεδώκασιν*. Also in Islam one uses the corresponding attributes.

Long before that time, the god *φάρρο* on the Kūshān coins since Kanishka holds as his emblem a bag of money in his hand: fortuna, in West and East Iran, meant money. Already in the Awesta, in many cases, hvarnah means "luck, tyche, fortune," going over into "riches." The antonym, too, duš.hvarnah, means—with the imprecative connotation of such terms—"he whose tyche may be bad," *δυστυχής*, as early as in *Yt.*10,108. The duš.hvarnah is "ašāta, a proscriptus," see under 'Mithra.' In groups of words like puru.hvarnah puru.gav puru.nar, together with išti puru.hvāθrā, the transition into "wealth" is completed; equally in *Yt.*18,1, where the "hvarnah of the Aryans" is called puru.vanθwam "consisting in many herds" and simultaneously puru.-ištam.

Out of regard to the myth of the fight for the hvarnah, puru.ištam is usually translated by "von vielen begehrt"—Duchesne §117: "désiré de beaucoup" or "beaucoup désiré"—attaching it to √iš-; only Lommel translates "besitzreich": like iša, aniša it belongs to √īs-, išta "to have power over possessions." The possession of cattle, men etc. is "hvarnah, wealth." išti, deriv. of išta, is "fortune, riches," Skr. translation lakṣmiḥ, Pahl. comment. χvāstak. Xvāstak serves also as translation of "šēta, possessions, money" in *Yt.*13,67:

yaθa nā taχmo raθēštā   hušhambartāt hača šētāt   patiγnīta

"as a swift warrior fights for his well-gathered (viz. in barns) property." It is the raθēštā who fights for his "hereditary" property, because he is the χvāstakdār, Armen. χostakdar "heir."

For ham.brta cf. *Vid.*3,27: ham.brθwa, f., with yavahya "harvest of grain"; ham.brti "gathering." *Yt.*6,1: "tat hvarno hambārayanti, a hundred thousand yazata (= elsewhere 99 999 fravarti) gather this hvarnah (water generated by light of the sun) and distribute it over the earth (as rain)." And *Yt.*10,52:

hām hīš čimāne[4] barahva	gather (the zōθra) as store,
ni hīš dasva gara.nmāne	lay it down in the store-house (of heaven)!

These verses prove that ham.bāraya, συμφορεύω, not ham + √²par-, is the stem of MP. hanbār, anbār; at the same time, that gara.nmāna means "store-house," not "house of praise" or "Haus der Glut," and that it belongs to √gar-, ἀγείρω, ἀγορά.[5]

In other passages, šēta, Pahl. transl. χvāstak, means simply "money," e.g. *Vid.*4,44: "When people are šēta.činah, claiming money, one shall collect money, ham iδa šētam hambārayān." In this way anbār becomes "capital" and sūt "interest."

Gold and silver were of old the scale of value, although the wealth of a χšaθriya was figured in men and cattle, horses and cows he owned, and although an old tariff for surgeons still demands payment in pecus, not in pecunia. During the second half of the 6th century B.C., dinars of Croesus were current, which may have been actually coined after the foreign model in Iran, whilst the proper Iranian coinage began only under the reign of Darius. The fact that the Awesta is silent about coined money—emphasized by W. Geiger, who in 1884 believed the whole Awesta to be prehistoric—says nothing: the oldest parts are slightly older, all the rest younger than the coinage.

NP. pūl "money" is Aw. prθa, to √par- "to equalize," cf. *Pahl.Vid.* 5,19 under 'Sea'; the MP. verb puhlistan, puhlēnītan means "to balance, compensate." MP. puhl is translation of Aw. api.pāramnāi "to balance," a.prti "compensation" etc. The redeeming of penalties by payments in kind, later in money, causes the change of meaning, but from which moment on the "payment" was made in coined money, is indiscernible.

MP. χvāstak is always wrongly explained as belonging to "χvāstan, want to have," money because everybody wants it. There was once a revolt in Teheran, and an unconcerned policeman answered to the question "what is going on?" laconically: "pūl mīχāhand! they want

[4] For čiman as noun see Benveniste, *Inf.Av.* 50.

[5] Andreas had used this root for explaining MP. +gērāk, which is but an erroneous reading of gyv'k, vy'k > ǰāh "place." "house of praise" (*Wb.*: nicht völlig sicher) connects gara- with abi.gar- "to praise," song of praise etc.

money." χvāstak is OP. *hvā.ista, Aw. hvō.ištēšva pasušva in *Nir.*58 "self(-acquired) possession and small-cattle (pecunia)."[6] hvō is the pron.refl. hvā, spelled with ō as in hvō.awišak, to be registered under Duchesne §205 instead of §47. Bartholomae assumed the same formation for θwā.išti "thine-property," which is not a true compound; on the other hand, the Manichaean term χvāštī, whether <*hvā.išti or *hvā.-aχštī, belongs to it.

In Gathic, too, hvarnah and išti have the same meaning. In Y.29,9, the "soul of the ox" complains at having found in Zoroaster—the only one who cares—only a nar asūra, ἄκυρος [here expressly called "Spitāma," to indicate that, though being a member of that rich family, as fugitive he is destitute], and what it needs is an iša.χšaθriya, a χšaθriya with wealth. The opposition to nar asūra seems to indicate that χšaθriya is used in its connotation nar = raθēštā, but it may belong to √χšan-, χšaθram "hospitium," whether iša.χšaθriya be a derivative of iša.-χšaθra, or a compound of iša + χšaθriya.[7] Zoroaster says, Y.46,2: "I know that I am powerless, an.iša," because, as an exile, kamnāfšva kamnāra, "accompanied by only a few herds and men," he is poor.

Y.46,3: "When will come he who makes rise the light of day? I trust Thou wilt for me perfect my work!" The soul of the ox says: "When will come he who will lend me [Zoroaster speaking] zastavat avo, a helping hand." Bartholomae refers for zastavant to Germ. "Hand und Fuss haben" i.e. to be practical. zastavant can be "handy, practical" or "open-handed." Zoroaster wants to have something "in hand," namely money. The Pahl. transl. understands the sentence rightly as referring to Zoroaster, not, as modern translations do, to the soul of the ox, and renders zastavat by "pa.tovān, cf. NP. tavāngar, rich." "To give a hand" is everywhere the figure for help, cf. *Mir.Man.*III,43,12, Narisaf hymn: " 'vmn hvfry'd' 'vm vχd dstd'r bv'h, help us and lead me by the hand!"

The fugitive Zoroaster finds the wealthy man in the Hāugava

[6] The distinction recalls Arab. tālid "slaves born in the house, cattle and inherited property" and ṭārif "newly acquired possessions." *Wb.* has erroneously +hvōišta "der höchste, erste"; not even Frhg.Ēv.4,2 "yōištō θwaχšitå hvōištō patišaθrå" seems to contain this word: θwaχšitå is 3,sg. opt.med. "the youngest shall work"; the rest is corrupt; patišaθrå is evidently the verb of this second clause.

[7] The Aw. spelling aēša rests only on 'Y, equally for i-. isə.χšaθra in *Yt.*1,13 is the same in abstr. form "fact of being master over property" or "a rich hospes," not "verlangend nach dem Himmelreich."

Žāmāspa; that is why he calls him in *Y*.15,18 "ištoiš hvarnå, fortunate (blessed) with riches." Both words have this material sense when single, and the more so when united. Zoroaster never uses the subst. hvarnah, the mythical notion of which belongs to the ahura Vrthragna and Mithra, any more than he uses miθradruχš and similar words; but he does not hesitate to use the trivial adj. "fortunate, rich." *Yt*.5,98 paraphrases the Zoroastrian expression: "ištim ǰaδyanta hōugavā, for riches asked the Hāugava," and the later legend retains the historical conception of the wealth of that family, scarcely without influence upon the marriage of Artaxerxes I and Damaspia, née Žāmāspī.

Nyberg (245), on the contrary, remarks to *Y*.51,18: "Ausserordentlich aufschlussreich ist der Ausdruck 'der Besitz als sein xvarna gewann, ištoiš xvarnå,' das letzte wort adj., 'xvarnah-besitzend, mit xvarnah versehen hinsichtlich išti'; išti, eigentlich 'Besitz,' steht hier prägnant für 'Besitz des Vohu manah.' Der höchste Ehrentitel der Zarathustra Gemeinde war es, Vohumanah empfangen zu haben; der Ehrentitel 'mit xvarnah versehen' wiederum war der höchste in der Mithra Gemeinde. Hier werden beide verkoppelt: wir können hier den Synkretismus zwischen Gatha-Religion und Mithra-Religion mit Händen greifen." When reading these sentences printed in spaced type nobody would surmise that the two honorific titles of the two communities and all the conclusions are nothing but a fantastic interpretation of the harmless hapax "ištoiš χvarnå, blessed with riches." The theory serves to support another one, of "Zoroaster's poverty," 194ff.: "Zarathustra ist nicht gerade ein besitzloser Proletarier"—a proles with the double gentilic spitāma hēčataspāna—"aber er gehört zu einer Gruppe bestimmten religiösen Charakters, gekennzeichnet dadurch, dass sie kein Eigentum im gleichen Sinne wie die übrigen Stammesmitglieder besass. Also nach allem zu urteilen, eine sakrale Armut."

While he thus makes Zoroaster Spitāma a darwīsh, Ctesias makes Spitakes Spitāma "satrap of the Derbissoi, the Darwīshs." darwēš comes from Aw. drigu, gen. drigoš; the MP. form is, according to the inscriptions, not daryōš, but drgvš, same as in Wais u Rāmīn: darγōš. Lommel translates drigu by "landflüchtig," one who flees into a foreign land, or MHG. ēlent (to "ausland"). Elend means poor, but poor does not mean elend, landflüchtig.

*Y.*10,13:

namo hōmāi yat krnōti	footfall to Hōma who makes
driγoš havat.maso mano	the poor one's spirit as high
yaθa rēvastamahyačit	as that of even the richest!

Or *Y.*57,10:

Srōšo	Srōša
yo driγošča drivayāsča	who puts together a house
amavat nmānam hamtašti	amavat for the poor man and
	woman, when the sun has set.

Lommel: "der den landflüchtigen ein mächtiges Haus hinstellt." Bartholomae has also the "mächtige Haus." In these verses, Srōšo, as home police, takes care of the night shelter of homeless people. amavat may mean "solid," better—with -vaṅt of tašbīh—"adequate, fit," at any rate "solid enough for the purpose," hence rather "modest" than "mächtig."

Nyberg continues: "In der Gatha (*Y.*44,18-19) erwartet Zarathustra als Lohn zehn tragende Stuten und ein Kamel. Man bemerke, dass es das Luxustier ist, nicht die Kuh wie in Indien . . . , während der Besitz des Stammes in Rindvieh bestand." What could a man who denies personal property for religious reasons do with such a stable that requires care and fodder? This price for one song still means 20 horses in the same year, enough for six cowboys, corresponding to work for a ranch of considerable value even today, much more than the 12,000 dirham which Vuzurgmihr got from Xusrau for his chess playing. Firdausi expected from Maḥmūd 100,000 gold dinars—much, but little in comparison with the noble prices the caliphs paid their poets per line. Such numbers reflect the permanent inflation of all money, and we do not know how many songs Zoroaster produced in a year. In Teheran lived a Qadjar prince, who composed panegyrics on all who arrived or departed, including myself, and lived upon this kind of royalty.

About the "Luxustier" there are many wrong notions. Bartholomae translated *Yt.*17,13: "Ihre Kamele [of the men whom Ardvī hačati] erregen Schrecken"; Lommel, doubtful: "bayanti, klärlich 'erregen Furcht'; ebenso in *Yt.*17,12 von den Pferden gesagt." The following verse has: "uštråho . . . uzayanto zmāt prtamnā vaδryavo"; Bartholomae: "Die Kamele die vom Boden sich (auf den Hinterbeinen) aufrichtend miteinander kämpfen, wenn sie brünstig sind"—that, indeed, would be a horrifying sight. Lommel: "ein Kampf zwischen Kamelshengsten oder ein Verhalten im Dienst des Menschen?" Bartholomae's words in brackets are contrary to the anatomy of camels. They raise themselves awkwardly to their four legs, and do not fight with their soft feet, but bite only; they lie, even in heat.[8] They look conceited and scornful, as the Arabs say, because to them alone the thousandth name of Allah is revealed, but maybe because their ambition to be a Luxustier is not satisfied. Their temperament is better than their looks. Once, in spring, when the whole valley was full of camel foals, I had a visit at Persepolis from a friend who did not quite dare, as he would have loved to do, to photograph the foals from nearby against the outspoken displeasure of their mothers. He left for Isfahan, and my Turkish chauffeur reported on the trip: "He is a good man!—Yes.—He is a pious man!—Yes.—He fears God.—Yes.—But I never before saw a man who fears a camel!"

Nyberg, 240, to *Y.*46,18-19: "Wer für den Sieg des Guten in dieser Welt wirkt, wird nach dem Erdendasein als Lohn alles das gewinnen, was die Ekstase zu bieten vermag, und ausserdem vollen Besitz der Seele des Stieres selber—wahrlich, eine strahlende Aussicht für einen Hirten!" I doubt it. The full ownership would, for all that, be shared by the souls of all the generations since Adam-Gayamart. The many shepherds I have seen were interested in milk, and would prefer two cows with calf in hand to the soul of the ox in the bush. Zoroaster thought the same, for in *Y.*46,19 he promises, besides the reward of future life, not at all the soul of the ox, but "on the spot a pair of cows with calf." If that was his "Missionspraxis," he or the one who financed him, Žāmāspa, must have had—as they probably had—thousands of cows and luxury camels. And when "his most ardent wishes" accompany Žāmāspa and Frašauštra on their journey to "where Rtam should rule and AhuraMazdāh should abide in abundance," whence he hopes to obtain the "frasastiš"—then he doctus mantuš represented at the same time considerable financial interests. For, the revocation of the banishment reinstates Zoroaster into his possessions, cf. *Beh.* §14. And

[8] Cf. Assyrian sculptures, e.g. AMI IX,41, p.206a.

the Spitāma owned large estates in Rhagiane. The wealthy people of that time had their money administered by non-Aryan suftidrnga, like Murašū Sons in Nippur, the greatest banking firm of the period, and that is why the family name of the Spitāma appears in their business papers.

Even as an exile, Zoroaster had enough money to pay his traveling, 500 miles, in a two-horse team, with attendants, from Ragā via Kōmiš to Tōsa, whether in a hired coach or his own. There was never a darwīsh who traveled with attendants in his own or a hired car.

XI. BANDVA AND GRAHMA

In the obscure background of Zoroaster's life—in the most passionate of his verses—two hostile figures appear whom he calls "my bandva and his tkēša" in *Y*.49,1-2, and "the kavi and the karpan grahma" in *Y*.32,12-14. No investigation has so far thrown the faintest light on these figures, and yet the tone of the stanzas, the allusions they contain to *Y*.46, "Gatha of the Flight," and the allusions to those stanzas in *Y*. 53,8-9, show from the beginning that they are the node of all threads of thought and that the poet speaks there of the decisive event of his life. Without solving this riddle one cannot attain an understanding of the gathas and of the life of Zoroaster.

Y.49:

1: āt ma yavā	bandvo pafrē mazišto
yo dušrθrīš	+čiχšnušo rtā mazdā
vahvī adā	gadi moi ā moi rapa
ahya vahū	ōšo vida manahā
2: āt ahya ma	bandvahya mānayati
tkēšo drugvå	dbitā rtāt rārišo
noit spantām dōršt	ahmai stoi ārmatim
nēda vahū	mazdā frašta manahā

Bartholomae: "Immer ist Bəndva für mich das grösste Hindernis, der ich die Verwahrlosten zufrieden stellen [note: zu Proselyten machen] will, . . . mit der guten Adā komm zu mir, sei mir eine feste Stütze! Ihm bereite, o V.M., den Untergang!—Dieses Bəndva Irrlehrer [*Wb*. Rabbi], der Druggenosse, steht mir schon seit langem im Weg, der von Aša abgefallene. Nicht sorgt er sich darum, die heilige Ārmatiš für sich zu haben, noch lässt er sich von Vohumanah beraten, o A.M.!"

Andreas-Lommel: "Und immer ist der ganz grosse Bondva verurteilt. Zu mir, der ich die übel Behüteten (?, die Unglücklichen?) durch Wahrsein zufrieden machen will, o Weiser, komm mit der guten Vergeltung. Seinen Tod bewirke durch das Gute-Denken!—Und mich erwartet dieses Bondva lügnerischer Misslehrer, der in zwiefacher Weise vom Wahrsein abgefallen ist: weder hält er daran fest, dass die kluge Fügsamkeit ihm (eigen) sei, noch hat er sich mit dem Guten-Denken beraten."

Hertel, *Beitr.*217: "der ich die schlecht-leuchtenden-Frauen (dušrθriš) durch das Licht-des-Heils zu erfreuen suchte," comment: "schlecht-leuchtend heisst 'die ein schlechtes Erkenntnis-Licht, daēnā, in sich tragen, also noch der daēvischen Lehre anhängen." He concludes: "Zarathustra suchte zunächst auf die Frauen einzuwirken, bei denen sein Bestreben, . . . Vieh-schlächtereien ein Ende zu bereiten, auf besseres Verständnis rechnen konnte."

Nyberg, 111: "Bəndva's Irrlehrer ist aufrührerisch gegen Aša und kümmert sich nicht darum, ob Ārmaiti ihm zugehören wird." 192: "Wichtiger ist [what precedes sounds 'unwichtig' indeed] dass bei Bəndva ein tkaēša lebt, der sich nicht darum bemüht, mit der wirksamen Ārmaiti Verbindung zu suchen, und sich nicht mit Vohumanah berät, d.h. sich über die ekstatischen Übungen und den normalen Verkehr des Stammes mit der Gottheit hinwegsetzt."

This is an amazing picture of a rabbi, an old renegade who delights bad women by the light-of-salvation, is too lazy to go to the maga for ecstatic exercises, spiritist séances or whatever the "normal intercourse" with the deity may mean, and waits inactively and is in the way.

The verses say in reality:

"And once, my brother-in-law will be forfeited to the law, the princeps, he who listened to (those that passed) the miscarried sentence. O Mazdāh, come as Rtam with Thy just punishment, be true to me! Find, as Vahumano, his death!"

"Then, my brother-in-law's drug-ish judge still remains, who in two ways injures Rtam: neither does he confirm 'Holy Ārmatiš, be mine!', nor does he judge by Vahumano."

Meillet considered the gathas to be among the most difficult products of IE. literature, and every word of the translation requires long study and commentary.

pafrē: *Wb.* "Perf. v. $\sqrt{}^{5}$par- 'obstare.'" Andreas-Lommel: "zu $\sqrt{}^{3}$par-." Bartholomae divided the root in $\sqrt{}^{1}$par-, represented by the part.pres. pāramna "Busse thuend" (better: atoning for); $\sqrt{}^{3}$par-, represented by pass. pryati, -te, only with "tanum," besides fra.prnōti in *Āfrīn.,* fra.pryati in *Vid.*5,9; the p.p.p. prta, used with čiθa = Gr. tísis, and āprti "making equal (balancing), atonement by corporal punishment"; further by Gath. prθa "atonement"; an.āprθa "unatonable"; prta.sara "having forfeited one's life (head)"; finally $\sqrt{}^{5}$par-. the alleged "obstare." "Je m'obstacle": the three $\sqrt{}$par- are one and the same word "to make even, par, to atone." To it belongs NP. pūl "money" as atonement for blood-guiltiness by disbursements in kind or money. The perf. pafrē, hence, means "he is forfeited to the law," just as prta.tanu in *Y.*53,9. The OIr. perfect has more than once the sense of the Lat. fut. exactum, Gr. fut.III, here made plain by yavā, according to *Wb.* "zu yav- 'Dauer,' dat. yavoi 'for ever'"; adv. instr. yavā "zu irgend einer Zeit = jemals, einmal." Only in *Y.*49,1 Bartholomae gives it the meaning "zu jeder Zeit, immer." yavā pafrē signifies "once (fut.) he will be forfeited to the law."

mazišto: Nyberg, 191: "Wahrscheinlich ein technischer Ausdruck." There are two old analogies. (1) In Behistūn the chiefs of the royal and of the rebellious troops are called maθišta, equivalent to the OP. military title frataraka in the *Pap.El.* These are commanders of a thousand, OP. *hazahrapati, a sort of magistri equitum or pagi. (2) In *Xerx.Pers.har.* maθišta, viz. of the sons of the king, means "princeps, heir, successor to the throne." The word goes on to be used as designation of rank. The Megistánes of the Arsacid period are a rank at the court, the table companions of the king. On the Papyrus 5 (Hansen) a mhstk'n mhstk' of Alexandreia is mentioned; al-Mundhir of Ḥīra received the honorific Rām-afzūd-Yazdegird and became mahist, Arab. a'ẓam.[1]

[1] For megistanes cf. Th. Mommsen, *Röm.Gesch.* v,343f. In Assyrian, "mār šarri rabū, the great king's-son" means successor to the throne. Cf. H. Winckler, *Altor.Forschg.* II,239f. on Hebr. "kabīr, princeps." The rank of the vazurkān, ideogr. RB', is rendered in Arabic by 'uẓamā'.

dušrθrīš: Andreas conjectured ⁺duš.rθīš "denen es schlecht geht"; Bartholomae: "Unsicher. Acc.pl.m. 'unter übler Obhut stehend, in religiösen Dingen verwahrlost'; Komp. v. duš + ⁺hrθrī, weil vor rθri duž- zu erwarten wäre; hrθrī = harθra, ungewöhnliche Bildung." In this way, it would mean in Zoroaster's didactic style: "the bandva listens to those who are under his evil charge" and would make sense. But the reasons for this change are untenable: Gathic has also rš.vačah against rž.uχδa, and dušiti—both with š—against Aw. dužita, Gr. δύσβατος. Such phonetic detail is not authentic. Bartholomae says "unusual formation," because -rθrī would be the fem. of a noun-of-agent. Therefore Hertel translates "Frauen." Duchesne places duš.rθrī behind niš.harθrī "surveillante," but translates, like *Wb.* "sous mauvaise garde," not "gardienne." One must class it with awi.miθri, Duchesne §25, with i-suffix. The following verses speak of things judicial and thereto dušrθri belongs, that means to √²ar- "adjudge," mostly with "rti, lot, destiny," also with zasta.išta = Ind. mudra, gestures of the lord justiciary, and with "savā, reward and punishment."[2] The acc.pl. dus.rθrīš signifies either "the miscarriage of justice" or "those who passed a miscarriage of justice."

⁺čiχšnūšo: participle of the desid. stem of χšnū- "to hear," written čiχšnūša, at the other places čiχšnūšo. Bartholomae took it (with -a) as 1.pers.sg.; Andreas, too, translated it as a first person, but remarks: "dieselbe form *Y*.45,9 čiχšnūšo (mit V für ') geschrieben," and to *Y*.45,9: "Form und Endung wie vīvarəšo in 45,8." Also like mimaγžo in 45,10. It is the same participle everywhere, for, against the previous translations, it refers to the preceding, not the following words, and there the 1st pers. is not possible. √χšnū- does not mean "zufrieden stellen" (see under 'Hospitium'), and čiχšnūšo not "zu Gefallen sein," but at all places "to listen, to lend one's ear to," in 49,1, thereby violating the obligation, founded on rtam, to give, as bandva, protection to Zoroaster. Likewise in the Yama myth, *Y*.32,19: "Who listened to men," breaking the food taboo, see

[2] To the same root: "arθa, plaintiff, or legal contest"; "arθra, trial, causa," and Gath. rθwa in *Y*.46,13.

under 'Yamā.' At the third place, end of the "Gatha of the Vision," 43,15: "never, noit poruš,[3] must one listen to the drugvant"; Bartholomae's "nicht soll man immer wieder, paruš, dem Druggenossen zu gefallen sein" is as wrong as Lommel's "nicht soll man den vielen Lügnern gefällig sein, denn diese bezeichnen alle Wahrhaftigen als böse!" In *Y*.45,8, finally, "winning over, āvivršo, with songs of praise" and "listening to him," without the connotation "to something forbidden."

vahvī adā: "the good, i.e. the just punishment, penalty," in parallel with frašta in 2,d; cf. OP. hufrastam aprsam "I have punished good i.e. justly."

ā moi rapa: √rap-, similar to √hak-, cf. under 'Social Structure,' expresses, like ahma.rafna in *Y.Haft*.40,3, the mutual allegiance between liege lord and vassals. The thought is that of l^emāh 'azabtāni in positive form.

ōšo vida: "find for him death!", to √vid-, vind-; as with Assurbanipal: "I, Ištar, mitūtu Aḫšeri eppuš, will achieve the death of A.," who then is murdered.

rtāt rārəšo: The archetype had no notation at all for the Aw. vowel ə. Bartholomae, *Grdr.* and *Wb.*, attached rārəšo as an a-participle of a redupl. intens.pres., and rārəšya as redupl. i̯a-pres. to a √rah-; no etymology, "abfallen, abtrünnig werden" probably because the verb is always connected with an ablative. Andreas read, in *Y*.32,11, rārušyon, and translated "die sich abwenden." The Pahl. transl. has always rēš-, hence regarded both forms as redupl. pres. of √riš-, against which there is no formal objection, but the ablative is disturbing.

The following word dōrəšt supplies a clue to the signification. *Wb.* and *Grdr.* regard this as an s-aor. of √dar- "to hold, have," with acc. and negation. "sich nicht sorgen um: non sacram curavit sibi esse armatim." Even less satisfying is the explanation of the identical word, written dārəšt in *Y*.43,13 "jem. (scil. AhuraMazdāh) verbinden, zwingen etw. zu thun." Pahl. transl. is nikēžītan "to give one's approval." One must compare *Y*.44,5: avāiš rvatāiš yā tū didržo (Pahl. transl. again

[3] Cf. noit dbitiyam, noit dvansčina under 'ApāmNapāt.'

nikēžītan), to √darz- "to fix, establish," and *Y*.19,13 "tkēšam ādranǰayati, he lays down the (third) tenet"; *Y*.48,7: didrγža (both in *Wb.* under √ drang-), finally Aw. handraχta, MP. andraχt "made fast, confirmed, sealed," with OP. handungā. Like Gath. daršat, OP. daršam, "firme, fortiter," this dōrəšt belongs to the s-aor. darž- of √darz-, OI. dr̥ṃhati "firmat." The sentence expressly states that the tkēša has not confirmed the formula of the Zoroastrian creed "Ārmatiš be mine!", as the following verses specify. The next stanza contains the whole Zoroastrian credo. The construction, with spantām ãrmatim in the acc., as in *Y*.29,7 āzutoiš manθram, shows that the short sentence is a quotation. Not having confirmed the tenet, the tkēša is no "renegade," and rārəšo cannot mean "abgefallen von," but means certainly more than "sich abwenden von." The real meaning must come close to žītarta in *Y*.53,9, "diminishing the rtam," for in the next stanza 49,3—see under 'Ārmatiš'—rtāt rarəšo is followed by the other formula of the Zoroastrian creed: "rtam sūdyai, rāšayahe druχš, rtam augendum, delendam esse druχš"—like rāšayahe drugvantam, savayo rtāvanam in *Y*.51,9—and what the tkēša does is just the contrary. Therefore, rārəšo must be attached to the root, put down in *Wb.* as √raš- "schädigen, damage, impair," of which only the just mentioned inf. rāšayahe and the noun rašah are safely attested.[4] The close semantic relation to √riš- "suffer injury" explains the Pahl. transl. rēš-. √raš- is the antonym of √sū-, and if this, according to Bailey's study, is a "miracle power producing prosperity," then raš-, is a "bad power producing injury," corresponding to Gath. √ǰyā-, whence žītarta (see under 'Hāugava'). Bartholomae refers for √raš-, against Kretschmer, to OI. rakṣas and Gr. *ἐρέχθω*, whereas Hertel *Beitr.* connects it with ranχšayanθya in *Yt*.10,27[5] "the countries offending against Mithra." In *Siegesf.* 143, to *RV*. IV,4, he emphasizes that Veda and Awesta both call the powers hostile to the own gods rakṣas etc.

[4] See the pres. rāšaya in *Y*.10,21 under 'Mithra,' in the gloss inserted into a magic charm for invulnerability, where Bartholomae remarks "one would expect short a": "though (the lance) hits the body, ātčit dim noit rāšayante, they do not wound him."

[5] The places *Yt*.10,78 and *Y*.12,4 are unreliable.

This remark is rather compelling to connect the words belonging to √raš- with ranχšayant and Ved. rakṣas. ranχšayant has the form of a verb.denom.; cf. Henning's attempt to elucidate √ra(n)ǰ—in ZII,IX,199.

mānaya: caus. of √man-, means, as in Old Persian, nothing but "to remain," viz. to be left over, to survive the bandva, whose death is hoped for or foreseen. pafrē "he is forfeited" and mānayati "he survives" are the logical opposites.

dbitā: means "twofold"—as in OP. dvitāparnam—not "long since," and is specified by the two lines with noit and nēda. frašta does not mean "sich beraten, take counsel, confer," but is the juridical term "to ask, inquire = to sentence," cf. under 'Last Judgment.'

Nobody translates bandva. Bartholomae saw a proper name in it; Andreas, as Geldner before him, an appellative "zu Aind. bandhu, Verband, Genossenschaft, Kultgemeinschaft." Lommel remarks: "Für das Verständnis kaum ein Gewinn. An die Sippengenossen, mit denen sich Zarathustra nach Y.46,1 zeitweilig in Zerwürfnis befand, kann nicht gedacht werden, ihnen hätte er nicht den Tod angewünscht." For no other reason than the sentimentality of a fanciful image he misses the point on which the whole understanding depends.—Under 'Kavi' we have touched the subject: bandva must be a term of relationship, because Zoroaster raises the special accusation against the ahura, lord justiciary, that he failed, though being his bandva, to protect him against the verdict of the hostile court, that means to have been disloyal to his duty as relative. ōšo vida "find death for him!" can be said only of a definite person. Geldner-Andreas' identification with OI. bandhu is incontestable, only the German translation is not exact. It is indeed a term of relationship, and corresponds to Gr. *πένθερος* as term for affinitas through women, a notion yet unknown to the original IE. language. The men in question are hvētu and kavi, between which connubium existed. bandva is a brother-by-marriage of Zoroaster, either through his mother or a sister, hence approximately what modern languages express by step-brother or brother-in-law.

Nyberg speaks frequently of "Bəndva and his tkēša," e.g. 243 "der die Mysterienfeier zerstört, *natürlich* durch einen neuen Kult," or 191: "tkaēša, *aller Wahrscheinlichkeit nach* der Ordalpriester in der Mithra-Gemeinde"; 65: *"in hohem Masse wahrscheinlich,* aber anfänglich war tkaēša ein ganz spezieller Ausdruck, √tkaēš- 'struere, bauen' [in reality: √čiš-, kēš- 'to teach'] in der Ordaltechnik speziell 'ein Ordal anordnen' etc." However: "Die Bedeutung 'Richter' ist übrigens im Jüngeren Awesta ausdrücklich bezeugt." Descartes: "All things merely probable are probably wrong." Younger Awesta is an obsolete term for the non-Gathic texts. "Judge" is the sole signification of tkēša everywhere: he is the qāḍī al-quḍāt, the mōbaδān mōbaδ.

Wb.: "tkēšá, Lehrer des Glaubens, Rabbi, im Gath. spez. Irr-, Afterlehrer," only on the strength of this passage, and against the right Pahl. transl. "dātwar, judge." Further: "tkéša in Y.49,3 'Lehre,' bes. auf religiösem Gebiet, im Gath. spez. von der Lehre des falschen Glaubens, Irr-, Afterlehre," again only on the strength of this passage against the right Pahl. transl. dātastān. All follow, without an afterthought. To his Gatha translation Bartholomae annotates: "tkaēša gehört also wie daēva u.a. zu den Schlag- und Kampfwörtern der zarathustrischen Zeit . . . , später hat sich diese Bedeutung verwischt," an unfounded bias obstructing the understanding of the entire Awesta.

The words vičīro ahuro in *Y*.29,4 show that the ahura, the lord justiciary in whose name justice was administered, is also the one who "decides," namely the king who δικάζει; however, "vi+či-, distinguere, διαγνῶναι" is the very activity of the judge, and the tkēša stands beside the ahura as later the vizier beside the sultan.

With the words of *Y*.49,2 and 32,2 "Ārmatiš, obedience to the law, be mine!" the neophyte confirms by oath his adherence in the Fravarāni, *Y*.12,1. The six crimes he forswears at that occasion—two against live, two against immobile possessions, two against body and life of the Mazdayasnians—are "Six" instead of our "Ten Commandments."[6] Therefore the candidate for confirmation is "ahura.tkēšo, one who observes the commandments of Ahura," formed after an older rta.tkēša "he who observes the commandments of rtam" in *Yt*.10,84. And purvya.-tkēša were the first that observed the commandments.

The *kitāb al-Aghāni* tells 18,78: "al-Ḥadjdjādj b. Yūsuf had the

[6] The commandments are in fact those of the pre-Zoroastrian period, see under 'Mithra,' and the observants would be properly speaking "rta.tkēša."

choice between a good Christian and a bad Muslim teacher for his young sons, and chose the Muslim saying: It is a repulsive thought to give my sons to somebody who would not initiate them into the 'law' and the 'doctrine' of Islam." That is what matters. tkēša is the sharīʿa, the "Ten Commandments" of Zoroaster. The Pahl. transl. explains its dātastān by pēšēmārīh, and pasēmārīh, vičīr u dātwarīh, all judicial terms.

Further on in *Y*.49,7-9, Zoroaster speaks of the frasastiš which he hopes to obtain through Žāmāspa and Frašauštra as his emissary and herald. The frasastiš is the revocation, by the court of appeal, of the dušrθrīš, the miscarriage of justice, which the court, arθra, of his home town had passed.

Y.46,1 (text under 'Hospitium'):

"To which country, to hide myself, where, to hide myself, shall I go? They have cast me out from hvētu and aryaman; the vrzanahartar does not listen to me, nor the drug-ish commanders of the province!"

These verses describe the court of the province: it is located in the vrzana, the capital; Aram.Arab. madīna "seat of the court" is the Pahl. ideogr. for šahristān, provincial capital. Ragā was the capital of that part of Media. The court consists of nobles and clients, that is here magi, of the consul civitatis, and of the military commanders of the province. They do not listen to Zoroaster's defense. But the verses do not mention the judge who passed this sentence, nor the justiciary who confirmed it to make it valid. The two are revealed only in *Y*.49. The sentence was outcasting from hvētu and aryaman, hence loss of all civil rights, proscription. We shall soon discover what the indictment was. A lord justiciary, ahura, is a man risen from the military nobility, raθēštā, satraps and kings. Therefore this ahura is called one of the "kavitāt" in *Y*.32,12-15 (see under 'Vēhviya'), he is kavi. His attribute mazišta, "the greatest" in *Y*.49,1, makes him an "ahura mazišta, successor to the throne." In *Y*.49, Zoroaster calls him "my bandva."

Zoroaster's style is never descriptive, always explanatory, argumentative: By listening to the wrong sentence, dušrθrīš of the court, the ahura himself becomes guilty, pafrē. As bandva he injures, in doing so, the rtam, which demands that he protect his relative; thus he becomes himself a "sacrilegus," like a next-of-kin murderer, and therefore Rtam must come as injured moral law, and Vahumano as Justitia to punish him. And even when vengeance would strike him, the mōbaδ remains who is doubly sacrilegious, because, himself a judge, he neither observes the law himself, nor judges conscientiously. Thereby he impairs rtam, becomes rtāt rārišo, i.e. žītarta, and has deserved death, for the commandment is: "rtam sūdyāi, Rtam must be increased!"

Therefore the "Gatha of the Flight," *Y*.46,4, says:

yas.tam χšaθrāt mazdā moiθāt ǰyātoš vā
ho tān frōgå paθmān hučistoiš čarat

"he who deprives him of his rule and life, prepares as leader the path of good-knowledge (čistiš = religion)."

For the style cf. *Y*.53,9: yo īš ǰyātoš hamiθyāt vaso.itoišča, and *Beh.* §13: hya avam . . . χšaθram dītam čaχriya. The drugvant to whom the words refer is the judge who passed the sentence. In the following stanza Zoroaster asks protection from "murderous deeds," because, as a proscript, he is threatened by murder.

Y.32 describes how at the same time his relatives and adherents are persecuted, st.11:

tē.čit mā mrndān ǰyōtum yoi drugvanto mazbiš čikoitrš
ahvīšča ahuvasča apayāti rēχnaho vēdam

Andreas: "Alle die zernichten das Leben, die bedacht sind, die Hausfrauen und Hausherren um den Besitz ihres Erbes zu bringen. . . ." Hertel, *Beitr.*253: ". . . die Fürstinnen und Fürsten an der Auffindung des Erbes zu hindern."

ǰyōtu is not *βίος* "life," but *βίοτος* "livelihood," which requires regular succession. vēda, to √vid-, vindātan, is the "falling-in," not the possessing or finding of the heritage. What is done is confiscation of the inherited estate of the lords and ladies. The maltreated and dispossessed ones are Zoroaster's relatives. The similar expression arǰīš narpīš in *Y*.53,9, refers to the "disinherited" nōtaryåho.—Proscriptions and confiscations were the method of Gōmāta; therefore Darius says in *Beh.* §14: "I restored to the nobility their vassals, and their clan and family possessions to the viθ, of which Gōmāta the magus had deprived them."

Y.32:

12:	ēbyo mazdå aka mrōt	yoi gāuš mrndan rvāχš.uχti ǰyōtum
	yāiš grahmā rtāt varta	karpā χšaθramča išnām druǰam
13:	yā χšaθrā grahmo hišast	ačištahya dmānē manaho
	ahoš mrχtāro ahya	yēča mazdā ǰigrzat kāmē
	θwahya manθrāno dūtam	yo īš pāt darsāt rtahya
14:	ahya grahmo āhoiθoi	ni kavayasčit χratūš dadat
	varčāhiča fradivā	

"AhuraMazdāh curses those who destroy the peasant's livelihood with acclamations, (those) by whom the karpan, as grahma, and the χšaθram (hospitable reception) of those bent on Druχš, are preferred to Rtam, at (the occasion of) which χšaθram the grahma has a seat in the house of the wholly-evil spirit—the corrupters of this (human) life, there, they will groan, to the pleasure (kāmē) of the dūtam, Thy poet's, who keeps them back from beholding Rtam. For his capture the grahma and the kavis have spent thought and energy for a long time. . . ."

The following stanza 15, "because of these their actions the karpatāt, priesthood, and the kavitāt, 'kavi-ship' are cursed etc." see under 'Kavi.' For the meaning of χšaθram "hospitality" see under 'Hospitium'; for rvāχš.uχti see 'Welcome.'

> The passage "kāmē . . . dūtam" is difficult. For dūta, see under 'Ārmatiš'; to kāmē cf. OP. yaθa mām kāma "as was my pleasure," later "kāmist, it pleases me," construed with accusative: dūtam, but "θwahya manθrāno," in apposition, stands in the genitive. āhoiθoi is noun, not inf., to √hī- "to put the horses to the chariot," by means of ropes, Germ. "siele," same root; *Ved.* "syáti, put the oxen to the plough"; *Y*.29,ii: "mā ēšmo . . . ā hišaya drščа tavišča, Hēšm . . . holds me (the soul of the ox) in fetters," and *Y*.46,6: "druǰo ho dāmān hēθahya gāt, he shall reach the prison of the Druχš," not (*Wb.*) hēθahya, acc.pl.n. "zum Verband gehörig."[7] āhoiθi is "capture, imprisonment."

In st.11 the enemies persecute Zoroaster's relatives, in 14 they scheme

[7] To √hī- belong: "hītā, biga"; avahāna < *ava.hayana (Tedesco); and perhaps Aw. "hētu, OI. setu, dam, dike, NP. band."

to capture himself, the manθran of AhuraMazdāh. In 14 they are called grahmo kavayasčit; in 13, a grahmo is the one who hišast; thereby the word is defined as designing an individual person, just as the words "ōšo vida" define bandva. In 15, the abstr. nouns karpatāt and kavitāt resume the two subjects grahmo and kavayo of 14. This connection of grahma and karpan suggests the same in 12,c: grahmā must determine karpā.

The Pahl. transl. is, as always, a word by word rendering, without construction:

yāiš	grahmā	rtāt	varta	karpā	χšaθramča	išnām	drujam
avēšān	grahmak	ač ahrākīh	dōšaktar	kē karp hēnd	u χvatādīh	χvāhēnd	pa drōžišn

By itself, one would probably interpret the Pahl. sentence as "by those who are karp, grahmak is more beloved than Rtam, and they want to rule by committing crimes," but that would not be a normal Pahl. expression of the idea, and it contradicts the Aw. text which has: "by them the karpan is preferred to Rtam, as is the χšaθram etc." Therefore, only the vocable grahmak or grāmak is of value.

> Withdrawing an older proposal, Bartholomae remarked in *ZAir Wb.* 221: "grəhma, with Ar. s (meaning: not to √van-)"; he took grəhmā in 12,c as n.pl. "G. and his adherents." Andreas-Wackernagel: "grəhmā, in 12 neutr. man-Stamm, 'Opferfrass'; grəhmo in 13, 14 < Ar. *grasma 'Opferfresser.'" Hertel, *Beitr.* 218, disproved this meaning. I should not assume two stems for a word which occurs only three times in such close connection in these stanzas: grahmo is nom.sg.masc. of an adj., and grahmā instr.sg. (of quality) "the karpā is preferred as grahmā."

The origin of the word remains unknown, but it survives. *Māh i Frav.* §1: "Why do men prefer the day Fravartīn of the month Harvatāt to all others?, pa mas u vēh u grāmīktar dārēnd." In *Xusr. Rēt.* §§82 and 91, grāmīkān is syn. of dōstān. grāmīk, dōst dāštan is the same idiom as the Pahl.transl. of Aw. "grahmā—varta" by "grāmak—dōšaktar." NP. girām, with derivatives,[8] means "carus, cherished, dear," hence "grahma = persona grata, favorite," a sense which fits Y.32 perfectly: the kavi and his favorite.[9]

[8] N.pr. girāmīk.kirt, son of Zarēr, in *Ayātk.Zar.* §79ff. is Girāmī of Firdausi (Daqīqī). NP. girām, girāmī, girāmišn, semantically influenced by Arab. kirām.

[9] After this was written, Henning corrected, in JRAS 1944, 139,n.2, the reading gr"g in

The plural "the kavis," again intentionally undefined, means the person of the bandva who is a kavi. He and his grahma scheme to throw Zoroaster into chains, as was done to Smerdis by Cambyses. St.15: "The priesthood, karpatāt, and the high nobility, kavitāt [grahma belongs to the first, bandva to the second] are sinners, . . . those whom they do not allow to be masters of their lives, shall ascend to heaven!", see under 'Kavi.' Once more, intentionally undefined, the two abstracts stand pro concreto—an idiom Zoroaster often uses. Here, in 32,14-15, grahma is connected with the bandva just as in *Y*.49,1-2 the tkēša with the bandva. And the persons, too, are the same, for, as *Y*.46,1 contains the sentence, excommunication from hvētu and aryaman, so this passage that speaks of the peasantry, contains the indictment which led to Zoroaster's condemnation: he strives for a liberation of the peasantry and is banished as a revolutionary and offender against religion. One cannot help thinking of Socrates.

In *Y*.46,4, Zoroaster openly invites to a murder, either of the brother-in-law who confirmed, or of the judge who pronounced the sentence. In *Y*.49,1, he foresees, in the near future, that fate will overtake the brother-in-law, and that his favorite will follow him. The third phase is the gatha *Y*.53,8-9:

8:	anāiš ā dužvaršnåho	dafšniyā hantu	
	zahiyāča vispåho	χrōsantām upa	
	huχšaθrāiš ǰanrām . . .	rāmāmča āiš	dadātu šyātibyo vižbyo
	īratu īš dvafšo ho	drzā mrθyāuš	mazišto mošuča astu
9:	dužvaršnāiš vēšo rāsti	toi narpīš arǰīš	
	ā išasā žīta.rto	prta.tanuvo	
	ku rtāvā ahuro	yo īš ǰyātoš	hamiθyāt vaso.itoišča
	tat mazdā tava χšaθram	yā ržǰiyoi	dāhi drigove vahyō

*Mir.Man.*III, a 13, to gr'mg, corresponding to Sogd. γrāme. The MMed. text is: "like nomads who with their tents, horses and gr'mg move from place to place"; the Sogd. text: "(nothing can help you), neither treasure, γzny, nor γr'm-, neither hostel, 'sp'nčh, nor palace nor a strong tower, etc." This is clearly "cherished, treasured valuables." In the footnote Henning applies his translation "possessions" to Aw. grahma; 32,12 "the karpan preferred money, possessions to Right," 32,13 "they shall get that wealth in hell," and 32,14 "even the kavis had an eye on his money," (which would be Zoroaster's money), mainly because "there is no reason to deviate from the Pahl. translation." Though agreeing with several points of his deduction, I cannot accept the authority of the Pahl. translation, nor his translation of the passages; nor his assuming two neutr. stems grahma and grahmah.

To st.8: hu.χšaθra, when connected with √χši- or opposed to duš.χšaθra or the notion of bad rule, means of course "who is a good ruler." In the epithet of the Amrta Spanta, hu- may mean "co(rulership), fellow(-rulers)." The more so here, where there is no talk of ruling and quality of rule, hu- seems to me to be *hm-, as in huzantu, huyaχna, "he with (his) hu.χšaθra, fellow-χšaθriya."

All mss. except K4 add to ǰanrām (janarām?) the syn. χrūn-rām.ča "murder and bloodshed"; the text cannot be safely restored. vižbyo is dat.pl., OI. viḍbhyás; in *Beh.* §14 we find OP. viθbiš, OI. viḍbhíṣ, the instr. which replaces the dative in OP.

dvafšah, in 44,14 dvafša, has neither etymology nor continuation; the Pahl. transl. did not understand the text: it uses frēft, hence thought of √dab- "deceive."

dafšnya: cf. *Y.*10,15: "yā manyate dāvayati, hā yā daftā apanasyati, she who thinks (I am the one) who deceives (outwits), shall (be she who) perish(es) deceived." This dafta is simple predicate; the Gath. form is an invitation or permission: "dafšniyā hantu, they shall be to-be-deceived-ones," i.e. deceit is permissible against these deceivers. Herodotus, III,65, makes the dying Cambyses say: "*εἴτε δόλῳ ἔχουσι αὐτὴν (τὴν ἡγεμονίην) κτησάμενοι δόλῳ ἀπαιρεθῆναι ὑπὸ ὑμεων*, if they have obtained the dominion by deceit, you shall take it from them by deceit," almost a translation of the Gathic words and entirely Persian in concept. Like the words about +Astyartes and the resurrection in the Prexaspes story, this must come from an excellent Persian source. īratu and astu refer both to the same subject, ho, and mazišto belongs to astu, "he (not: it) shall be," cf. Hertel, IIQF I,45 n.1.

To st.9: The parallelism of the two stanzas requires a close correspondence between dužvaršnåho dafšniyā hantu and dužvaršnāiš vēšo rāsti. The exact meaning of vēšo rāsti is here of no consequence: instead of √rāθ-, I prefer √rād- to connect rāsti with, "is prepared, destined for them"; vēšo, quite unknown, I assume, is a word for "death, annihilation." Tedesco explained to me the difficulties of the sentence "toi narpīš arǰīš ā išasā": "narpīš and arǰīš seem to be two acc.pl.; the verb ought to be contained in ā išasā." This might be √iš-, ēš- in the sense "to seek (a person's life)," cf. *Yt.*10,45: yim išanti miθra.drujo, "to waylay," also *Y.*32,12: "χšaθramča išnām drujam." √narp- is syn. of √zyā- "to diminish, impair." √arg- is "to be fair, have claim to," cf. *Altp.Inschr.* s.v. aržanam = Akk. simannu "convenance." arji perhaps "entitled (to inheritance), legitimate." Thus we arrive at the translation:

"Therefore, those whose acts are evil shall be allowed to be deceived. Deserted they shall all scream. With his fellow-χšaθriya he shall achieve murder and carnage among them and peace for the joyous clans. He shall bring down torture upon them and the fetters of death, and the greatest, at once, he will be!"

"To those who act with evil arbitrariness, death is destined(?). They who seek the life(?) of the deprived(?) legitimate ones(?), where is the ahura, faithful to Rtam, to deprive them of life and liberty? Mazdāh, Thine is the kingdom by which Thou wilt give to the right-living poor the Best!"

Nyberg calls these verses, 153, "an das Hochzeitsritual [*Y.*53,1-7, where in his opinion Puručistā pretends as goddess of fertility] angehängte derbe Flüche über die Druganhänger." Lommel, NGGW, 1935, 1,4,137: "Damit spricht Zarathustra . . . aus, dass er von guten Herrschern rücksichtsloses Durchgreifen erwartet." The two stanzas are attached in the Awesta to the "Wedding Gatha" for the only reason that both have the same rare and late meter, and because the meter dominates the arrangement. Nor are the verses an instruction for sergeants. They are a demand to kill the tkēša, mōbaδ of the bandva. Though Nyberg portrays Zoroaster as a ḥashshāsh, yet he was no grandmaster of the Assassins. His religion is, from the start, a political mission, but if he hopes for or recommends an assassination three times in his few songs, it is not each time different persons, but the same persons that shall be killed.

ahura, which refers to the mazišta, brother-in-law or step-brother of Zoroaster, in *Y.*49,1, has here, too, the meaning: somebody entitled to inflict imprisonment and even capital punishment, a power otherwise —e.g. in *Yt.*10,109—owned only by the sāstar hāmaχšaθra, the military commander-in-chief of the empire. At the same time it means "son of the king," a title expressed in *Yt.*14,59 by ahura.puθråho, in parallel with puθråho bēvarpatayo, and Zoroaster promises here to the ahura who will kill the tkēša and drugvant, the magus and impostor: mazišta mošuča astu!, the ahura mazišta, successor to the throne, at once he will be!

He brings šyāti—the OP. syn. of rāman—to the dispossessed clans. To do that is in pre-Zoroastrian polytheism the work of a god; Mithra, before all, is the rāma.šayana, also Tištriya. Darius' words in *NiR* a "hya imām šyātim adā" show the Zoroastrian concept of Ahura-Mazdāh as rāma.šayana. So does *Vid.*1 "azam daδām aso rāmaδātim noit kudāt.šātim" (see under 'Vidēvdād'). Since remotest antiquity, this quality has belonged to the ideal ruler who brings an "era of bliss." Cyrus says in his Ur inscription, as other Babylonian and Assyrian kings before him: "I made the people abide in peace" (see under 'Mithra'). The ahura who with his companions, the huχšaθra, shall cause the šyāti of the viθ, is such an expected ideal ruler. "For Thine is the χšaθram, the kingly power, to give the kingdom, āryānām χšaθram, to him who now is poor, narpiš, driguš, but soon will own the kingdom!"

The words are spoken in the circle round Vištāspa, and are addressed to the ahura, the sons of Vištāspa and their young friends. Zoroaster expects that one of them will kill the tkēša and grahma, mōbaδ and favorite of his brother-in-law whom fate had already overtaken.

According to the traditional date, Zoroaster was born in 569 B.C. The "Wedding-Gatha," *Y.*53,1-7, is some years younger than the Memorial List, of about 527, in which Puručistā is still a child, not yet 16 years old. *Yt.*53,8-9, too, is younger; it belongs therefore in the last years of Cambyses or the nine months of Gōmāta. The reasons for not mentioning names are obvious.

The bandva is Cambyses, his mōbaδ and favorite is Gōmāta, the magus.

When Cambyses confirmed Zoroaster's proscription, he was, according to *Y.*49,1, still successor, mazišta, and at the same time lord justiciary in the home country of Zoroaster, Ragā. In 539 B.C., the year of the conquest of Babylon, he was, quite young, "šar Bābili, king of Babylon," but only during that year, and no western records tell where he went. The assumption closest at hand is that he learned how to rule in Media, the largest and most important province of the empire, at Agbatana, the town to which he returned before his suicide. Ctesias says that he obtained this and other provinces when Cyrus settled the succession. Tabari has preserved the documents of an analogous settlement of the caliph al-Mutawakkil: the first successor, al-Muntaṣir, not yet adult, received the west and the center of the empire, the second, al-Mu'tazz, a small boy, Khurasan in the widest extent (so does Smerdis according to Ctesias). Thus, Ragā, as a Median zantu was under the jurisdiction of Cambyses as satrap of Media. Already at that time, he was entirely under the influence—čiχšnūšo—of his magus and qāḍī, tkēša, Gōmāta, who apparently taught him to rule. For this there are many later examples. Mutawakkil appointed the tutors and viziers of the princes, for al-Mu'tazz e.g. Aḥmad b. Isrā'īl. At the events that led to the murder of Mu'tazz, the commander of the Turkish guards, arrested this Aḥmad who played the sinister role of Gōmāta with Mu'tazz, and the young caliph said: "Give me Aḥmad back, he is my secretary and has educated me!" (Tabarī III,1707). It is likewise customary to appoint such a man regent during a ghaiba, an absence, just as Cambyses when leaving for Egypt made Gōmāta "coropastes" (Akk. qardupatu or NP. qahramān, Herodotus' *μελεδωνὸς τῶν οἰκίων*, majordomo), the dbitā drugvå, who deceived him too: "The deceivers shall be those to be deceived!"

The "Gatha of the Flight" was composed while Zoroaster lived in Vištāspa's hospitium, after the marriage to the Hāugavī, at the occasion of the journey of the two Hāugava to the court of appeal of the greatking, of Cyrus, while Cambyses was still heir apparent, hence a few years after 539, but before 529 B.C. The lord justiciary and the judge are not mentioned in these verses, but in st.4 it is said to be a meritorious deed to deprive the drugvant, evidently the judge, of his χšaθram, office, and life.

In *Y.*32,5 the same drugvant is χšayo, a word meaning any high position of power. The time is the reign of Cambyses, to whom the abstr. expression kavitāt alludes; Gōmāta, one of the karpatāt, of the magi, is his grahma, favorite.

In *Y.*49, the end of Cambyses is foreseen, the disappearance of Gōmāta expected as its sequel, and the prophet hopes to obtain the frasastiš and therewith the revocation of his banishment. This brings the verses near to the end of Cambyses' reign, to 523 B.C.

Y.53,8-9 is composed after the revenge of rtam and vahumano had struck Cambyses in his suicide—ōšo vida—as the oracle of Buto had announced, in the beginning of 522 B.C.

The §§11-14 of the Behistun inscription are Darius' answer to this gatha, written only two years after. The "viθbiš" to whom Darius restored their gēθā and māniyā, of which Gōmāta, the žītarta, had deprived them, *dīta krta, are the ahvīšča ahuvasča of Y.32,11, whom the drugvant, Cambyses, had robbed of their rēχnaho, and the very "šyātibyo vižbyo" of Y.53,8, šyāta, joyous, because they no longer needed to be "afraid he, Gōmāta, might kill many, daršam atarsa kāram vasai avājanyā, who had known Brδya-Brzyarštiš before, hyā parvam brδyam aδānā."

Zoroaster calls Cambyses his bandva, and bandva, like Gr. πένθερος, designates affinitas through women, mother or sister. Affinitas existed between the Spitāma and the older branch of the Achaemenid house since the marriage of the daughter of Astyages to Cyrus. According to Ctesias, Spitakes son of Spitāmas and this daughter, was a half-brother of Cambyses through their mother. bandva can express step-brothership, through the same mother, not through the father. But this relation is not true: Cambyses was not the son of Astyages' daughter, but of Kassandane. In reality, Spitakes and Cambyses both had in Atossa a half-sister, Spitakes through his mother, Cambyses through his father. Also this relationship through their sister would be expressed by bandva. Atossa, not born before 549 B.C., was not married before 533 to Cambyses, perhaps only in 529. The gatha 49 is later than 529. Bandva would equally cover the relation between Spitakes and Cambyses as husband of the sister.

Zarathuštra Spitāma uses for his relationship to Cambyses the term bandva which covers the relationship of Ctesias' Spitakes, son of Spitāma, to Cambyses, in every aspect. While the traditional date for Zoroaster's birth, 529 B.C. left enough space for his being either the Spitakes or the Spitamas of Ctesias, the word "bandva" decides that he is Spitakes, the grandson of Astyigas by his daughter, the mother of Atossa.

XII. MAGOPHONIA

"When Herod the king had heard these things, he was troubled."

In *Beh.* §13, Darius says that with his six companions he killed the magus Gōmāta and his principal adherents on the 10th of bāgayādiš, i.e. September 29, 522 B.C. That is his answer to *Y*.53,9: huχšaθrāiš ǰanrām χrūnrāmča dadātu! The place was Gōmāta's castle at Sikayahvatiš in Nisaya, Media, mod. Sikawand in Nisā, between Kirmānshāhān and Harsīn.

The Greek tradition goes back to three popular reports. Herodotus and Ctesias ignore the true name of Gōmāta; Ctesias calls him Spendadates. In Her. III,16—the source would be Dionysius of Milet according to Markwart, UGE. II,145—the magus has become a pair of brothers; the name of the really active one is there πατιζείθης, the name of the other, who is put in the foreground as a natural double of Smerdis, was —by chance and with no advantage to the story—also Smerdis. A third tradition, in Trogus, according to Nöldeke Herodotus' precursor Chares of Lampsacus, speaks also of a pair, but calls the one with his true name Cometes < Γωμήτης, the other "oropastes, coropastus." The endeavor of the popular tradition to make the imposture more conceivable by doubling the agents is evident.

The word πατιζείθης exists: Arm. payazat "heir" < OMed. *pāθyāzāti, deriv. of (hu)paθyāzāta in *Ōgmad.*, OP. *pašyāzāta "collateral heir." Πατιζείθης hence was not the brother of the Pseudo-Smerdis, but the title of the true Smerdis, confirming Ctesias' report on the settlement of Cyrus' succession.—The office of the magus is explained, more than once, in Herodotus, by τῶν οἰκίων μελεδωνός or ἐπίτροπος,[1] i.e. majordomo. This is what Trogus' coro-, oropastes must signify: a title, not a brother of the magus, probably to be linked with the OP. title rendered in Akk. by "qardupatu ša šarri," an officer only responsible to the king, not to a satrap.

Ctesias (Photius) transfers the name spantadāta > Isfandiyār from Darius to Gōmāta in saying "The Persians celebrate the festival of

[1] In VII,56 (Doriskos) Herodotus uses the expression ἐπιτροπεύσας to designate a vice-satrap, cf. βασιλεὺς: βασιλεύων, βασιλεύσας, viz. Megapanos of Babylonia. To cor[d]opa < s > ta cf. Aw. krθwa "who takes care," and NP. Arab. qahrumān "majordomo," similar to ustādār, pēškār.

magophonia, at which the magus Spendadates was killed," if this is not a fault of transmission for "was killed by Spendadates."

The day of the murder was the festival of Mithra in the middle of his month miθrakāna. It is necessary to emphasize that the murder happened at this festival, and that this was not constituted in commemoration of the murder. All Greeks describe it as the main popular festival. The king, else invisible like a god—*παντὶ ἀόρατος* (Aristotle)—had to show himself to the people. Ctesias frgm. 55M.: "*παρὰ δὲ Πέρσαις τῷ βασιλεῖ ἐφίεται μεθύσκεσθαι μιᾷ ἡμέρᾳ ἐν ᾗ θύουσι τῷ Μίθρῃ.*" "The day on which they sacrifice to Mithra" is a correct translation of "bāgayādiš," Mithra being the baga par excellence. According to Duris of Samos (in Athenaeus) the king not only got drunk on this day, but danced in public, which was considered good exercise: *τὴν ἐκ τῆς ἐργασίης ταύτης κίνησιν ἐμμελῆ τινα λαμβάνειν γυμνασίην τοῦ σώματος ῥώμης*. If Herodotus remarks that no magus was allowed to show himself, *φανῆναι ἐς τὸ φῶς*, on this day, all were to stay at home, this may be true without any relation to the "murder of the magus": I believe it is the 11th day after Nōrūz where, on the contrary, it would bring ill-luck to stay at home, and the *Māt. Sīrōz* calendar knows similar superstitions. Even Gōmāta could not break the old custom, but had to observe the pre-Zoroastrian festival and to show himself in public. Therefore, the seven conspirators chose that very day for killing him.

Markwart had recognized, as early as in his *Assyriaka,* 1892, p.653, and later in UGE.II, 132 and 135, that Herodotus' expression "magophonia" is an interpretation of OP. bāgayādiš, with mago- for bāga-, as often mega- for baga-. That Ctesias makes use of Herodotus' term indicates that the passage was part of his polemics against Herodotus, and his words "the day on which they sacrifice to Mithra" prove that he knew the true meaning.[2] Dinon tells, Artaxerxes Ochos, being told

[2] In JRAS 1944,134, Henning attacks that meaning of bāgayāδiš, (1) "only case of vrddhi in OP. month-names, not counting θāigrčiš (of uncertain etymology)": El. writes "so" for "θa," indicating the pronunciation "ōi"; vrddhi of θigr-, Aw. siγr-, NP. sīr "garlic," √cī- "legere, gather" exactly Germ. "Knoblauch-lese." El. transcription torwara demands also θōravāra hence θūra with vrddhi, and vāhara invers for -vāra < vahāra. Also mārkazaniš, not *mrka-; āδukaniš, all vrddhi. (2) A "form of √yaz-, corresponding to yādi, unknown," is OP. ā.yadana, Aw. *āyazana in Gr. *ἰασόνιον*; cf. OI. ati-, pra-yājá. (3) "Pre-Iran. *ātr.yāziya would appear in OP. as *āt(a)ryādiya." Since OP. has gāθu, χraθu, *prθu for Med. -tu, it had also θ^{r} for tr; hence āθ^{r}iyādiya is regular OP., with vriddhi, and -yādi-. (4) The opposition of "western and

that the Egyptians called him "ónos, ass," said: This ass shall eat your ox!, and ἔθυσε τὸν *Ἄπιν, slaughtered the Apis. Thus, φόνος enters for √yaδ-, θύειν, by a popular etymology. For the Greeks, bāgayādiš meant "slaughtering of the magi," but in the mouth of a Persian such a name for their highest festival would have been bitter sarcasm. Herodotus was too wise to say that the festival commemorated the murder of the magus, but only "the Persians call it magophonia," namely OP. bāgayādiš, while the other Iranians say miθrakāna. And even when he adds "after the murder, the mob assailed also the other magi"—Darius only: Gōmāta and his main adherents; and the notion that these were all magi is of course wrong—"if night had not fallen, they would have killed them all," the slaughter would still be limited—failing megaphone, telegraph and radio—to the small place of Sikayahvatiš.

There is no sense in doubting—Nyberg 376 (and 579)—Markwart's interpretation, and in trusting Herodotus—"si Herodoto fidem habemus, hätten die Perser noch zur Zeit Herodots zur Erinnerung (an das Blutbad) das Fest der Magophonie gefeiert," because Herodotus does not say so.[3]

After Cyrus' death, Cambyses had incarcerated and secretly executed the paθyāzāta Smerdis, and during his absence in Egypt he had conferred the lieutenancy to his favorite Gōmāta, as +cor[d]opates. This impostor succeeded in impersonating Smerdis, and in winning over so

eastern" use of baga for Mithra is a worn out pseudo-argument: Mithra was universal, and what we know is only a Median and Persian Mithra. If in a calendar, introduced by order of the Achaemenian government [the name younger or older Awestan is indifferent], not miθrakāna, but bagakāna > Sogd. baγakān [and in analogy the day name baγa, not miθra; > Xvār. biγ] appears, then, not the Median [Strabon's mithrákina] but the OP. form of the name was introduced, and the OP. name of the month was *bagakāna, with the festival of bāgayādiš.

[3] The Man. Sogd. word "mwγzt, killing of the Magians, not: feast devoted to remembrance of that act, ascribed to Alexander," a story the Manichaeans took over from Sasanian priests, can never prove, as Henning l.c. wishes to maintain, that the magi transferred Darius' act to Alexander. His words, 133: "(the Persians) instituted an annual feast to remind the Magians of their humiliation: it was called τὰ μαγοφονία, Her. III,79" are his, not Herodotus'. And Gilmore's remark to Ctesias §46: "agreement of Herodotus and Ctesias" is unwarranted, for we do not have Ctesias' full text, but two fragments which may well be polemic: the one mentions the name magophonía, the other says "ἐν ᾗ θύουσι τῷ Μίθρῃ." This is a correct translation of OP. bāgayādiš, not of Med. Miθrakāna. "Compromises" are always bad, and so the one Henning chooses: that the two festivals, bāgayada-Mihrgān = autumnal equinox, and magophonía = the 10th day of bāgayādi, coincided at the year of Gōmāta's death. The slip shows how impossible it is to avoid the right conclusion: the month was called miθrakāna and *bagakāna, because it was the month of the bāgayādiš festival.

great a following that Cambyses, in despair, committed suicide,[4] and that the impostor became, for nine months, actual ruler of the newly founded empire. The reaction was a conspiracy of the few who knew, and a group of seven young men of the high nobility destroyed the impostor, cleverly choosing the festival for their plan: dužvaršnåho dafšniyā hantu! Besides this cause célèbre of the world's history all those of criminal history fade away, and if ever it is justified to speak of a unique case, it is here. "Dass es sich im Falle des Gaumāta um einen wirklichen allgemeinen Aufruhr von ihrer (the magi's) Seite handelt" (Nyberg,356) is not "über allen Zweifel erhaben," but a misconstruction.

A general revolt of the magi would mean a general strike of the civil service, the activity of which can never have been interrupted. "Den Charakter dieses Aufstandes hat man meines Erachtens völlig missverstanden, als man darin einen Religionskampf sehen wollte: es ist die medische Herrschaft, die noch einmal ihr Haupt erhebt." Whoever is meant by "man" but similar opinions have repeatedly been uttered since Vivien de Saint Martin and Heeren; indeed, Herodotus makes the dying Cambyses say: *μὴ περιδεῖν τὴν ἡγεμονίην αὖτις ἐς Μήδους περιελθοῦσαν*. But Gōmāta just does not appear as what he was, a magus—that he was a Median is not at all proved—but as heir presumptive of the Persian Cyrus, he owes his success to the uprising of the Persians in Persis against Cambyses, marries, for legitimization's sake, Atossa, the heiress, without showing himself to her, and—since he kept himself invisible at Sikayahvatiš—would have known how to hide successfully his true aims to the very last. The second Pseudo-Smerdis, likewise, relied upon the Persians' hatred of Cambyses. Fravartiš, the Median pretender, actually tried "to bring the hegemony back to the Medes." The revolts in the East Iranian provinces were directed against the strict centralization of the Achaemenid empire, and were politically reactionary. The rebellions in Babylon were attempts to recuperate the lost independence. Nowhere does the hand of the magi show itself.

A "general revolt of the magi" would have been aimed at Cambyses, and would have been victorious with Gōmāta's accession; it would have been no concern of Darius, not an "Aufstand den er unterdrücken

[4] Herzfeld, "*Tod d. Kambyses*: hvāmršyuš amryata" in BULL. SOS VIII,1936, 589-97; add there, on p. 594f. the example v.Rawl.9,33: "iḫšuḫa mītūtu, his desire was suicide."

musste." With Gōmāta's triumph, the elder line of the Achaemenids had come to a premature end, and the claim to succession passed to Ršāma and his son Vištāspa, at that time in Parthava. Gōmāta must have reckoned with being murdered and must have seen danger from the circle round Vištāspa. But that it was precisely Darius who became the agent was an historical accident. Not the alleged "revolt of the magi" was the goal of the conspiracy, but the legitimate succession. This fight would be, on p.295, "religiös gesehen ein Kampf zwischen achaemenidischem Hofkult und Staatsreligion gegen den Medischen Kult der Magier," while, on p.375, it would be "a complete misunderstanding, darin einen Religionskampf zu sehen." "Welche religiösen Motive immer die Magier in diesem Streit erfüllten, jedenfalls gingen sie nicht um Zarathustras willen in ihn . . . ich leugne ganz bestimmt . . . dass der Zoroastrismus . . . daran Anteil hatte. . . . Der Zoroastrismus hat bei den Magiern keine Kreuzzugsstimmung ausgelöst. . . . Die Magier wurden die Priester der Achaemeniden. . . . Kambyses' Zug nach Aegypten gab. . . . Wind in die Segel, und 'so' kam es zu dem Aufstand. . . . Als der Kampf abgeblasen war . . . , als der Sturm sich gelegt hatte, gewannen die Magier 'natürlich' ihre Stellung . . . zurück." The whole fight—for this fight is a fight against windmills—the whole noise is for a false St. Bartholomew, the wrong interpretation of magophonia = bāgayādiš as "murder of the magi" instead of "sacrifice to Mithra." Darius killed the magus, but never fought the magi.

Occasionally an entirely opposite opinion has been advanced, namely identification of Gōmāta himself with Zoroaster. To this view Meillet was inclined when he said (*Trois Conf.*55) of Gōmāta: "un véritable sectateur de Zoroastre, ce que n'était pas Darius lui-même." Markwart, at various places, and Messina, *Ursprung der Magier* 90, speak similarly. One could support such a view by Herodotus III,67, where he attributes to Gōmāta a number of measures, intended to attract the lower classes to himself against the ruling ones. As Herodotus describes it, it would be a radical disorganization of the old social order. The restoration which Darius describes in *Beh.* §14 puts Herodotus' story in the right light. The situation reminds one of the restoration under Xusrau I after the communist episode of Mazdak. But one cannot avoid thinking that Herodotus might give, partly, a distorted picture of reforms actually due to Zoroaster.

On Darius' fight against the magi, Nyberg builds up, 362, his theory of Darius' religion. As captatio benevolentiae he concedes that Zoroaster's name need not to appear in royal inscriptions of a country uniformly Zoroastrian of old. This not being the case, Darius had every reason to make his Zoroastrism known to the world, the more so, "da er, wenn wir Hertel, Herzfeld u.a. glauben dürfen—fidem habemus—einen Kampf auf Leben und Tod mit Gōmāta für den Bestand der zoroastrischen Religion gewagt hatte." He calls it more than remarkable that Darius has no room for the Aməša Spənta and no word for the daēnā māzdayasniš. A definite indication of the daēnā would under no condition be permitted to be missing. Climax: all this would be an entirely inexplicable and unthinkable (!) attitude for a neophyte.

Zoroaster deserves reproach for having no room for the Amrta Spanta and the dēnā as much as Darius; only, the "Immortal-Holy ones" were brought into a system after his time, and the notion and term dēnā māzdayasniš is not older than Artaxerxes II. On the other hand, it is unjust to reprove Darius for his silence, and yet not to commend Xerxes for saying some words on aša [he writes rtam] or Artaxerxes for combining in his name two of the Amrta Spanta. I cannot speak for Hertel, but it is certainly not my way "to risk a fight to death for the existence" of a thing that did not exist before.—A country parson may demand of his candidate for confirmation to say a word about the religion, but who are we to dictate, 2,500 years after, to the ruler of the then known world, who himself legitimatized one of the many religions of his empire, to legitimatize himself by certificate of baptism and confirmation, or to tell the people something about Amrta Spanta unknown to them. He demands, like many much smaller people today, that one knows who he is. "I am the worshipper and agent of Ōramazdā, and Ōramazdā is the greatest of gods" is all he needs to tell the 127 nations of his kingdom.

XIII. HOUSE VĒHVIYA

"Thereafter, we need no other proof!"

*Y.*51,12, gāθā vahuχšaθrā:

noit tā im χšnāuš VYPYV kāvyano prta.zimo
zaraθuštram spitāmam yat ⁺ā ⁺him rurōst ašto
yat hoi im čaratasča ōdršča zoišnū vāzā

"Not listened to him, then, the Vēfiyo, the kāvian, in (month) prta.-zimo, to him, Zoroaster, the Spitāma, when he denied him hospitality, him and his attendants and the two-horse team that shivered with cold!" It goes on: That is a sin for which the soul of the sinner shall scream when the guilt will be proved at the Činvat bridge!

Because of the fundamental importance of this stanza for the life of Zoroaster, I had briefly indicated my interpretation of VYPYV as n.pr. vēfīk, in AMI.VIII, Nov.1936; with some commentary in *Old Iranian Peership*, BSOS.VIII,1937, p.938, and in *Altp.Inschr.* 1938, p.199,2. Nyberg's book is the result of lectures given in the spring of 1935, and appeared October 1937 in Swedish, and April 1938 in Schaeder's German translation. On p.403 he writes: "Die uns den vornehmen Adligen Zarathustra malen, wie er sich auf den Höhen der achaemenidischen Gesellschaft bewegt, . . . unter den Spitzen des Reichs, gehen weiter als es sich die Zoroastrier des Westens je haben träumen lassen." Note: "So z.B. Herzfeld, AMI.VIII, 76f. Das Bild ist durch eine Emendation der Gatha-stelle 51,12 gewonnen, die auch den abgehärtetsten sprachlos machen kann."

He operates several times with West and East Iranian dreams, and of hashīsh smokers to boot; I find it difficult enough to see the truth of what people say when awake. The remark about my painting is more than a year older than my alleged emendation, and refers in fact to AMI.II,1 (1930)—where Zoroaster moves on the heights of society; the footnote has been added belatedly with a wrong reference. So he proves the "callousness"; as to the "speechlessness" Herakleitos said: *βλᾶξ ἄνθρωπος ἐπὶ παντὶ λόγῳ ἐπτοῆσθαι φιλεῖ.* A new translation which Nyberg refrains from giving would have been more effective than a mere rejection, the passion of which is easy to understand: if this VYPYV is a Vēfī of Iranian history, his whole structure, already considerably shaken, tumbles down, "fällt unrettbar dahin." I, too, reject something, namely all translations so far made, the authority of which I am expected to respect, and I would reject them even if they were grammatically correct. It is time to speak bluntly and unadornedly.

Bartholomae: "Nicht hat ihn zufrieden gestellt der Buhlknabe des kavay- an der Pforte des Winters, den Zarathustra Spitāma, indem er es ihm verwehrte, bei ihm Unterkunft zu nehmen, und als sie zu ihm kamen, auch dessen vor Kälte zitternden Zugtieren." Note: "Eine sehr bemerkenswerte Strophe. Das Ereignis das sie verewigt ist: Zarathustra, mit seinem Gefährt vom Sturm überrascht, sucht auf dem Herrenhaus an der 'Pforte des Winters' (s. Anm.12) um Unterkunft nach; aber dessen zu Bəndva (s. Anm.11) haltender Besitzer—verächtlich wird er darum als sein 'Buhlknabe' bezeichnet—weist ihn zurück." Anm.11: "Bəndva?"—Anm.12: "Ortsname."

Bartholomae takes čaratasča as dual pres. for praeter. (subj.: vāzā "two-horse team"), audrš as gen.abl. "with cold," zoišnū as nom.acc. His explanation sounds of a miscarried carriage drive, and according to his translation, Zoroaster arrives before his horses. These, therefore, must have known their way, and we have the situation of Mas'ūdī's tale, in *murūdj* VII,320f., where a noble Quraishite, banished to 'Arafāt, denies having continued his orgies there, and the people of Mecca say to their Wali: "There is a decisive proof between us and him. Call for the donkeys of the jobbers and let them run to 'Arafāt; if they do not go straight for his house, as the libertines have accustomed them to do, you may accept his word! The Wali said: Therein is a proof indeed! and called for the donkeys. They were brought, set loose, and ran straightway to the plaintiff's house. The Wali was informed and exclaimed: Thereafter we need no other proof!"[1]

The bandva, in Y.49, has jurisdiction over Zoroaster's home-town. In Y.51, also in 46, the prophet is in flight, and comes further on to Vištāspa's place. No word indicates any relation between the "owner of the manor-house" and the bandva. He is abused only because he refused hospitality to the fugitive. *Matth.*25.43: ξένος ἤμην καὶ οὐ συνηγάγετέ με. Whereas it ought to be the other way, Bartholomae drags him in

[1] Mas'ūdī believes the offender to be unknown, but a comparison with the short novels, worthy of Boccaccio, in the *Aghānī* IV,64f. (of the Quraishite) and 76, shows that it was the singer Dallāl al-mukhannath.

as a support for his translation of VYPYV by "Buhlknabe." Thus the situation arises which Lommel and Nyberg develop: Zoroaster would have asked the Buhlknaben of his deadly enemy for night-shelter, and complained, "auf dem Höhepunkt seines Wirkens," "in feierlicherem und schwerer gewordenem Rhythmus," not to have been "zufrieden gestellt," satisfied by him.

Lommel: "Der Fürstenknecht Vaēpiyo (=der entartete Lüstling) der weites Land besitzt, erwies Zarathustra dadurch keinen Gefallen, dass er ihm verwehrte zu ihm zu kommen, als seine beiden Zugtiere zu ihm eilten und auch vor Kälte zitterten." Note: "vaēpyo: v(o)ipoyo, viell. Personenname (Andreas); doch ist Bartholomaes Anknüpfung an √vip- 'widernatürliche Unzucht treiben' wohl möglich: Zarathustra hat in verdammendem Zorn harte Worte gebraucht."

If Zoroaster was displeased by the refusal of the voipoyo to receive him, the opposite would have pleased him and he would better have curbed his indignation. "Satisfy" is utterly wrong; √χ̌šnū- means "to listen to," here to the entreaty of being received in hospitium.

KVYNV—cf. the spelling yəvīno—is kāvyano, normal patron. adj., the "kāvian." "Fürstenknecht" is an anachronistic blame: Darius calls his greatest grandees "manā bandakā"; the highest Arab and Kurdish grandees call themselves and their sons, in face of the caliphs and sultans, always "thy slaves." In NP. the word for "I" is "bandah, the slave." That is but an honor. One of my first slips in the East, near Mossul, was in asking a negro: Are you the servant of such and such? His offended answer was: No, his slave!

Andreas read ūδurš, judging from his translation "sie zitterten"; this plur. of a perfect would then be connected by -ča -ča with the dual of the present čaratas; zoišnū seems to be translated by "vor Kälte," hence instr.sg., which cannot be reconciled with the other occurrences of the word. The difficulty existing in Bartholomae's translation is not solved.

> The apodosis with yat—yat means: "when he (V.) refused hospitality to him (Z.), when (he refused it) to the accompanying-ones of his (or: to him and his) and to the shivering-with-cold two-horse team." I owe the explanation of the hidden difficulties again to Tedesco: Bartholomae, *Wb.*565 and 575,

emphasized the "auffällige Stellung des -ča -ča: man verlangte zaraθuštram . . . vāzāča yat čarato," an observation which in fact invalidates all previous translations. ašto is not inf., but acc. of a noun, with Benveniste. ahmi is loc., and one expects with rurōst ašto the acc. of the person, which one obtains by the slight emendation (Tedesco's) ⁺ā ⁺him, suggested by the following "hoi im": "when he refused him shelter." This acc. stands in parallel with the acc. dual vāzā, determined by ōdrš zoišnū, placed in front and connected by -ča -ča with čaratas. This, therefore, is not a verb, but an acc.pl., namely of the part. čarant, which has the obj. "im." In *Altp.Inschr.* 51f., I had explained OP. abičariš in *Beh.*§14 as acc.pl. "the attendants," to OI. abhicara, Gr. amphípolos. "im čarato," here, has the same meaning, Germ. "die ihn Begleitenden," his servants. The last verse has no verb of its own, and the repetition of yat indicates that yat rurōst is valid for the whole. The simplest translation of this yat would be "and likewise." Whether or not the gen. hoi "whose," is correct, is a question here negligible, because it would involve no change.

Instead of the owner of the manor-house "Winter's Gate," Lommel's translation has a great land-owner whose fortune "olet." But why, then, did the horses that have been running and ought to be all of a sweat, shiver "also" with cold, and who else shivered? In the whole of Iran and Turkistan, for at least half the year, it is so hot that the horses ought to be in sweat without running. Here, too, Zoroaster does not describe, but argues: the "Winter's Gate" is the reason why they shiver, hence no placename, but a season. The season is December-January.

It stands correctly in the genitive, like OP. χšapa "by night," θarda "in the year," māhya < māhahya "in the month." *Wb.* takes prto as loc.sg., instead of prtāu, written prtå in *Y.*51,13, of "prtu, passage, ford, bridge," only here "entrance, porta," to √⁴par-. ‚prtō zəmō' must be a compound, hence ⁺prta.zimo. The first element equals Aw. pəṣ̌a, i.e. prta, which enters in the compounds "prta.čanga, with claws out-spread," *Yt.*15,113 describing the dragon humayaka; and "prta.parna, with wings stretched out," *Yt.*14,35, describing the vāragan bird, both proved genuine by their sculptures (see under 'Sculpture'). *Wb.* compares it with OI. sphuṭa, "unfolded (leaves)." Thus the name resembles "porta hiemis" but means "where the winter unfolds itself," a name of the same type as Aw. "zimahe zarδaēm, the winter's heart" in *Vid.*1,3, and OP. "θauravahāra, where spring becomes θūra, powerful over the winter" or "garma.pada, heel, track of warmth."

Nyberg 244 and 154: "Der Auftakt zu *Y.*51 schildert den Höhepunkt von Zarathustras Wirken im Friyāna-Stamm . . . , der Rhythmus ist schwerer und feierlicher . . . , der Auftakt giebt eine Ordalszenerie . . . , es sieht so aus, als habe Zarathustra jetzt endlich die grosse Krise (yāh) erreicht, von der er so oft gesprochen hatte. In str.1-10 werden denn auch die eschatologischen Saiten kräftig angeschlagen." Since "strings are touched," "Auftakt" cannot mean "arsis" but only "overture": the curtain rises over an "ordeal scenery," the refusal of the VYPYV, which at the same time is the "acme of Zoroaster's work in the Friyāna tribe." "Heavier rhythm": the meter has two pada less than the gāθā ahunavatī. Zoroaster never "speaks of" the crisis "yāh," he shouts "yā-ahī! hurrah!" but only in the last act. No word hints at eschatology: the gatha is a thanksgiving to Vištāspa. And yet "Auftakt to *Y.*51" is no printer's error, for it goes on: "Der Prophet fragt: Wer ist Mysteriengenosse, wer hat die Ekstase im maga erlebt? Antwort: Nicht der unzüchtige kavi-Bube . . . solche fahren in die Hölle . . . seligeres Los ist den maga-Männern beschert: Das grosse Ereignis ist dies, dass Vištāspa jetzt die Ekstase erlebt hat und dadurch ein vollmündiges[2] Mitglied des maga geworden ist."

"maga" is the feast after the racing, the "hochgezīte"; "magavan, the guest at the feast," see under 'Maga.' Fellow of mysteries: "rvaθa, friend" means here, like amicus in Roman law, "hospes," who gives hospitium. Everything is more blissful, "seliger" than hell. There is no trace of ecstasy. Bandva is no name, but an appellative, p.119: "Er heisst mazišta . . . vielleicht war er ein kavi, und vielleicht war es sein unzüchtiger Bube (der 'kavische'), der *eines Abends* an der 'Pforte des Winters' dem Spitāma Zarathustra das Quartier verweigerte, obwohl seine beiden Pferde vor Kälte zitterten."

[2] One may be "volljährig" or "mündig," but "vollmündig" would rather mean "with a full mouth."

This gives the tale the finishing touch: "one evening" is not in the text, but is the thought simply crowding into one's mind when reading these translations: did Zoroaster, one evening, come with his team to the "unchaste knave" to pray with him—according to the famous words of the presumptions to the Corpus Juris, or, with Hertel "um den schlecht-leuchtenden durch das Licht-des-Heils zu erfreuen"? This again reminds one of an Arab veni-vidi-vici anecdote in the *ḳit. al-Aghānī* 17,189: "A courtier of al-Ma'mūn, during the Byzantine campaign, in a pitch black storm night, met with the greatest singer of her time, the beautiful Barmacid 'Arīb, on horseback, and asked her: Where do you come from in such a night?—From Muḥammad b. Ḥāmid (an officer, her lover).—But what have you been doing there? And she answers: 'Arīb comes from Muḥammad b. Ḥāmid, in such a night, run away from the caliph's camp, and now riding back, and, that being the situation, you ask her: what have you been doing there?, perchance praying twenty raq'a, reading a cḥapter of the Qur'ān, or giving a lesson in jurisprudence? Blockhead! Cavillati, confabulati, reconciliati sumus, lusimus, bibimus, cantavimus, coivimus, abivimus! —The hearer was put to blush."

Nyberg 297: "Die Anrufung der fravarti des Hvōgva hilft u.a. gegen ōifra 'schlechte Seher.' " Note: "So geschrieben für vifra 'kundig,' seinerseits gleich Ved. vipra 'inspirierter Sänger';[3] Bartholomaes schreckliche Erklärung *Wb.*357 ist mir unfassbar." This is: "pathicus, statt vifra, zu √vaēp-, vgl. vaēpya-." Nyberg does not seem to have come across Djuwainī's description of the shamans, *tār. Djihāngūshā* 1,43s, or that in Bar Hebraeus,[4] else he would be aware that, in describing Zoroaster as a shaman, he makes the prophet himself an effeminate pathicus, or as ethnologists call them, "hermaphrodite." Whether the invocation of a Hāugava against inspired singers—like Zoroaster—is effective—as the silly interpolation in the name list *Yt.*13,104 says—or not, is indifferent, but not this preposterous interpretation. The VYPYV plays a remarkable role in Zoroaster's life, and therefore, the "schreckliche" translation of this proper name was to me "unfassbar." The great family of the Vēfīkān can be traced through over 1,200 years of Iranian his-

[3] Cf. Andreas, NGGW, 1931,III,315.

[4] Markwart, *Südarmenien* 141f., in the history of the Armenian king Pap.

tory. For a while, they occupied the throne. The Behistūn inscription states that they were Persians.

MP. vēfīkān is the adj. vēfī, written VYPY with the adj. ending -k. The variants of vaēpyo in *Y*.51,12 give VYPY, read vēfiya, as spelling of the Arsacid archetype. The equation VYPY = VYPY requires no proof, but proves that Aw. vēpyo and MP. vēfīk are the same name. There is no "emendation." The question is only its etymology.

In the *Gr.Bdh.* 128,7 we find the gentilicium VYPK'N, vēfakān; the ending -akān beside -īkān, as in Paikuli s's'NK'N, sāsānakān, but Kaʿba s's'NYKN, sāsānīkān. The simplex is vēf, the adj. vēfīk. According to *Gr.Bdh.* 128 (and similarly Šahr.Ēr. § Kōmiš) Kōmiš-Dāmghān was one of the residences of the family (see below); else, they are the princes of Hyrcania-Gurgān which adjoins to the north. The best known members of the house are Gotarzes I, represented in 111 B.C. on the rock sculpture of Mithradates II at Bīstūn, bearing the title "satrap of satraps" and coining as "aršaka gutarza, king of Babylon" from 90 to 86 B.C. And ΓΟΤΑΡΣΗΣ ΓΕΟΠΟΘΡΟΣ who perpetuated his victory over the Arsacid Meherdates in A.D. 50 at the side of the sculpture of his predecessor, and calls himself "adopted son of Artaban" on rare coins.[5] There are reasons to believe that Gotarzes I was the adopted son of Mithradates the Great. In analogy of Ῥεομίθρης: rēwmihr, Γεόποθρος represents gēwpuhr, and the contemporary form Meherdates < miθradāta proves that -θr- was preserved in the family name only, whereas it had changed to -hr- in common language. The later form appears in the Kaʿba inscription of Shāhpuhr I, ab. A.D. 265,[6] *Pahl.* l.27: 'rtχštr vypṙẏdkn Pārs. l.33: 'rtχštr ZY vyplkn, ΑΡΤΑΣΑΡΟΥ ΓΥΙΦΕΡΙΓΑΝ all rendering Sasanian pronunciations, partly in historical spelling (v for g or b) of *gēpuhrīgān. An analogous formation with -puθra is dāmāspuhrīkān, d'mspχrykn in the Pārs. text l.31, of

[5] Cf. *Tor von Asien* pl. 21-22, and p.45; AMI IV, 58f.

[6] Pahl. reading from a photo reproduced in autotype only, Pārs. from a too small photograph, both insufficient for exactly establishing the spelling; Greek after an unchecked Latin transliteration. One expects Pahl. vyphrkn, Pārs. vyplkn; Gr. ΟΥΙΦΕΡΙΓΑΝ, perhaps ΓΗΦ °. Cf. Pahl. l.24: vysprkn, Pārs. 29 ult. vsplykn, Gr. ΓΟΥΑΣΠΕΡΙΓΑΝ, i.e. vēs- or vāspuhrīgān, and (joining) vyprd prdkn—vypry ZY? .pldk'n—ΟΥΙΦΕΡ.Τ? ΟΥ ΟΥΙΦΕΡΙΓΑΝ. —ΦΕΡΙΓΑΝ renders Ir. -puhrīgān.

the same inscription, as against Aw. ǰāmāspāna and OP. *dāmāspī, in Damaspia.

In the *Gr.Bdh.* 197, the name Vēv ē Gōtarzān is spelled VYV, written with two diacritical points above the first v, indicating the frequent pronunciation gēv; the *Ind.Bdh.* has at the corresponding place gīw in Aw. script. This vēv, gēv—later also bēv, bē—son of Gōtarz, is no historical figure, but merely the family name gēwpuhr personified, similar to Tōs ē Nōδarān and Nōδar.

In the Syr. *Acts of St. Thomas,* the Iranian heir to the throne is called wēžan (his wife manēžak), in the Greek version Οὐαζάνης, var.l. Ἰουζάνης i.e. +Γουζάνης, the same figure as Firdausī's Bēžan, husband of Manēža, with "ž/z an, génos" instead of "puθra, son." In Tabari and Hamza the same name appears with imāle as Ar. wāǰan < vēžan. This vēžan, too, is no real person, but the family name or the title of the heir apparent *vāspuhr ē vēžan; it is OMed. *VYV.ZN. Its OP. equivalent VYV.DN stands for OP. vivāna in the Aram. text of the Behistun inscription, *Pap.El.* Sachau pl.54,8. From this OP. form the others are distinguished by vrddhi of guna: vēva.δana etc. In OP. vivāna (Akk. ᵘwi.wa.na, El. wi.wa.na) the ā is the product of a contraction. The Aw. correspondent is vivaŋhana, patronym of Yama in *Yt.*13,130 and *Vid.*2, deriv. of vivahvant; in *Y.*9,5 vivahvato puθro "son of Vivahvant," Ved. vivasvant in *RV.* 10,14,5, cf. 8,5,1. The etymology of Gath. VYPYV, vēfiyo, hence, is not "vaēpiyo, pathicus," but the name of the god.

The MP. forms vēv and vēf both descend from *vēhviya, -iya adj. with vrddhi of *vivahva-, a plain dialectic difference: the much discussed change hv > f (see under 'Hvarnah') belongs to the home land of the family, Kōmiš-Gurgān, western Parthava. But the appearance of VYPYV in *Y.*51,12, does not fix the time of this change as that of the gatha, one cannot possibly assume that vēfiya was actually the Old Parthian form of the name in 530 B.C. The family was a Persian one and had come to Parthava at that very time. One must consequently assume that the notation VYPYV was chosen when the Awesta was first fixed in writing, for rendering *vēhviya or *vēvhiya of the oral tradition. This was done under Volagases I, A.D. 51-77. He also used for the first time Aramaic script—attested 70 years earlier on the Awramān parchment —on his coins, while under his predecessor on the throne, the gēwpuhr Gotarzes II, A.D.41-50, proper names appear for the first time on Arsacid coins. Gundofarr of Sigistān was their contemporary, the central figure of the Acts of St. Thomas; his name is old vindat.hvarnah, written guduvHara on his Indian coins. At that time, the name of the dynasty was pronounced vēfīkān, and nothing was closer at hand than to note VYPYV for oral vēhviyo. It is the time when the Hyrcanian Vēfīkān contended with the Atropatenian Arsacids for the throne of Iran. The scribes were on the side of the Atropatenians, and they may have chosen the writing in order to make the identity of the names—to them a matter of course—understood by everybody, because in these verses Zoroaster cursed the ancestor of their enemies.

Only a phonetic or graphic problem remains. In *Y*.51,12 Zoroaster uses the form VYPYV for the name of his contemporary and peer, whom he calls "the kāvian, kāvyano" as vispatiš of the house. At that place VYPYV must present the form generally used. But for the mythical eponym Zoroaster uses in *Y*.32,8 the form v(a)ivahušo, a nominative, to which in *Yt*.19,35 the abl. v(a)ivahušat is formed. v(a)ivahuša is derivative of *vivahuš, weak stem or nominative (Bartholomae: vocative) of *vivahvah. In the memorial document *Yt*.13,139, about 530-525 B.C., the OP. name visatarušī appears, fem. of the -ya adj. from the n.pr. masc. visataruš <*visatarvah. At the same time OP. forms haχāmanišiya from the nom. haχāmaniš, see under 'Nōtarya.' Those are simultaneous neologisms of the end of the 6th century, and only vivaŋhana in the Yama myth, *Yt*.13,130 and *Vid*. 2, is a traditional form. What we transliterate by -ŋh- is merely the Aw. notation of old -hv-, hence *vivahvana. This is the real and the oldest form of the family name, from which all others descend. OP. vivāna and Gath. VYPYV must belong to the same stem as this *vivahvana, hence to *vivahva(n).[7]

The *Pap.El.* presents the name, written in OP. (*Beh.*) vahyazdāta, by VYZDT, cf. VYGMT *vahya.gmata and the other examples

[7] (n) indicates difference of zero and normal grade only.

given under 'Mem.Doc.' These are cases of -ahya- > ē, and vivāna is the analogous case -ahva-> ā (for Aw. å): vivāna < *vivahvana.[8] Med. vivahvana, OP. vivāna and VYV.DN are no longer used in later phases; we find only vēžan < Med. *VYV.ZN, the compound gēwpuhr, and the simplex vēv (and gēv, bēv) or vēf (with adj. vēf^{i}/$_{a}$kān), the last corresponding to VYPYV in Y.51. All these forms descend from old vrddhi formations, and vrddhi was no longer active in MP. OP. vivāna < vivahvana and VYZDT < vahyazdāta show, about 520 B.C., the vanishing h in these phonetic groups. Therefore, VYV.DN, i.e. vēvaδana shows vēva <*vēvava <*vēvahva, but Gath. VYPYV, less than 20 years older, shows vēfiya < *vēhviya *vēvahviya, -iya adj. with vrddhi of *vivahva-.

The Vēfiya are the third known historical name in the gatha of Zoroaster: (1) Zoroaster's own family name Spitāma = Σπιτάμας, a Median house. (2) the name of his protector Vištāspa = Ὑστάσπης, a Persian with a Median name. (3) the Persian house of the Vēfīkān,= Γεόποθροι.

So far, this house has been known to us since the time of Darius, cf. AMI.IV, 58-64. One can hardly assume that the Median kings would have given fiefs in Parthava to Persian families, and obviously it was Cyrus who invested the Nōtarya with Tōsa, the Pātišhvāri with the country after which they were called, and the Vivāna with Kōmiš-Gurgān. The Vivāna of Behistun, in 522-21, only called by the family name, must be regarded as the vispatiš of the clan. The event told in the gatha happened in the year of the flight, shortly after 539 B.C. Thus, the two might be the same man, but rather father and son. The refusing attitude of the father is comprehensible: he was subordinate to Vištāspa as satrap of Parthava, but it is before Vištāspa had acted, and Ragā, where Cambyses had jurisdiction, was so much nearer than Tōsa. In the course of Cambyses' reign, the son may have joined the party of the Nōtarya.

Judging from their name, the Vēhviya regarded Yama as their heros eponymus. Among others they bore the peculiar title "nāfapatiš, paterfamilias" as lords of Dahistān, written NPPTY and N'HPTY in Paikuli.

[8] The opposite: OP. avāhana, instead of avāna < ava.hāna, and θauravāhara instead of θauravāra El. to.r.wa.r < *θauravahāra, both inverse historical writings.

Although they were Persians, their hereditary possessions were Gurgān and Dahistān, the former a part of Parthava. Conditions in the east and the west of the empire were similar; the vast domains of Medes and Persians e.g. in Asia Minor are known. As late an author as Tabari has preserved (1,685) the old tradition that Bištāsp, when constituting the "Seven Houses" with the title 'uẓamā', i.e. vāspuhr, kavi, had given Dahistān and Gurgān to the nāhabaδ, whom he mentions as the first of the seven; this means the time of Zoroaster and is historically correct. They owned also land in Arachosia, e.g. Darius' satrap Vivāna, to whom belonged the "rmatam Ršāda," a stud (see under 'Ārmatiš'), and the *Šahr.Ēr.* ascribe to them the foundation of Raχvat, capital of Arachosia-Harahvatiš.

Zoroaster speaks of the kāvyano Vēhviyo when fleeing from Ragā to the residence of Vištāspa, hence between Ragā and Tōsa. That is the situation of the district Kōmiš. *Gr.Bdh.* 128: "ātaχš ē frambar, its appearance, pētākīh, is unknown, for without needing food, aχvarišn, it burns always, in day time as smoke, by night as fire. . . . One writes: it is beside the palace of the Vēfakān. One writes: a fire of this type is in Kōmiš. Also: its name is ātaχš ē aχvarišnīk, fire not needing food, no need to breathe on it, it consumes fire-wood which one puts on it, if one does not, it burns equally well. One writes: the Frambar fire is even this fire."

Mas'ūdī IV,74: (cf. Markwart, UGE II,240f.): "In Kōmis there was a famous fire temple the founder of which is unknown, called χuriš; they say, Alexander, having conquered it, did not permit to destroy it and to extinguish the fire." The name frambar means pell-mell.[9] Ptolemy has Φ⟨α⟩ραμβαρα, his source being the Bematists of Alexander. The place is the oil-sources of Shāhkūh i bālā, less than 20 miles north-northeast of Dāmghān, capital of Kōmis, Hecatompylos of Alexander's time. Not far to the north is the natural marvel of the Tang i Shamshīrburr, "sword-cut cañon," which Diodorus 17,75 describes under the name Stiboites, Curtius 6,4,4 as Ziobetis, Ir. *stuvi.vatī; also Tagaí of Polybios

[9] *NiR.* §4: "yō[δantīm] būmim, El. p^{i}r.ra.m.pe.lam, i.e. OP. *framparam or *framfram; √fram- "excitari" (Bailey, BSOS VII,297) = √yuδ-; cf. "fra.frav-, to see-saw, rock," and excitari?. The type of the name is the same as that of the fire Bābā Gurgur, Sem. qrqr, cf. Gr. bárbaros, with onomatopoetic reduplication, IE. *g^{w}ṛretay.

10,29, Ṭāq of the Arabs.[10] The Greek knowledge goes back to the general staff of Alexander, who must have personally visited the oil springs, like those of Bābā Gurgur and Mandalī. In this region, Darius III was murdered.

The palace of the Vēfīkān, "the manor-house Winter's Gate," thus lay near north of Dāmghān through which passed the great highroad from Ragā to Tōsa. *Šahr.Ēr.* §18: "šahristān ē Kōmiš . . . māniš[n] ē pahlavīkān anōd būt, town Kōmiš: there was a residence of the Pahlavīkān," meaning the Vēfakān, cf. Moses of Chorene [in Hübschmann, *Arm.Gramm.* 63]: "These are the pahlavīk kings: Aršak . . . , Aršavir, who had three sons and one daughter: Artašeš, Karn, Suren and Košm [district Kōmiš, personified as daughter], hence the houses Karn Pahlav, Suren Pahlav and Aspahapet Pahlav." Similarly Tabari (Nöldeke, 437): "Kāren, Sūrēn and Sfandiyār Pahlavī," the last name faulty for Spāhbaδ. The group is frequent in the Sasanian inscriptions. In reality, Tōs belonged to the Spāhbaδ (see under 'Nōtarya') and Kōmiš to the Vēfīkān. The Armenian confounds them because at the time of the Arab conquest, the Kāren bore the title "spāhbaδ i Xurāsān, šāδ [< χšēta] of Padišχvārgar [Kōmiš] and Gēl Gēlān."

The great highroad from Ragā through Kōmiš to Tōsa, the Khurasan road of the Arab geographers, had been constructed during the Achaemenian period as a post-road, see under 'Post and Travels.' Banished from Ragā by the sentence confirmed by Cambyses, Zoroaster fled through Kōmiš, residence of the Vēhviya, to Tōsa where Vištāspa was satrap. That is the "rzūš paθo, the straight road" of the gathas on which he traveled in his vāzā, the two-horse coach. I have made the long 500 miles on horseback, and once drove from Ragā to Kōmis in the month of prta.zimo, through deep snow, shivering with cold.

In these verses, again, although the picture is full of life, the style of the poet is not descriptive, but causative. This affects even the use of the names (see under 'Poetry'). Where names of other great families appear, he calls himself not merely Zoroaster, but uses his family name. The obtrusive contrast of the family names Vēhviya and Spitāma in *Y.*51,12 means entirely true to his style: "a Vēhviya, a kavi like myself, has refused hospitium to me, a Spitāma!" That is the crime against Rtam, the mores.

[10] ZDMG (1926) v,279, *Reisebericht.* I never had an occasion to publish my photographs.

Nyberg loves comparisons, for instance 357, speaking of the identification of the two Vištāspa: "Wenn dies möglich ist, so kann man ebensowohl Karl XII von Schweden mit Karl II von Spanien oder Wilhelm von Hohenzollern mit Wilhelm von Oranien gleichsetzen!" The emperor William may have asked himself in 1918: "Will the lady of Orange, the queen, receive me, William of Hohenzollern?" Thus speaks Zoroaster, explaining, not describing. As a Spitāma he hopes to find refuge first with the kavi Vēhviya, then with the haχāmaniš kavi Vištāspa, himself a kavi, as the grandson of the last kāvian great-king of Media.

XIV. POST AND TRAVELS

> "Non quasi mansoria dilectio et dilectatio sed transitoria potius tanquam viae, tanquam vehiculorum."
> —S. Augustinus, *De Doctr. Christ.*

THE royal Achaemenian post had an old history, going back to high Babylonian antiquity; but its organization over the whole empire and for a long duration is due to Darius. Not only the Greeks, but also later Persians report it.[1]

The loanwords, Gr. ἄγγαρος "courier, letter-carrier" in Herodotus III,126, Xenophon *Cyrop.* VIII,6,17: ἀγγαρήιον "the post," Her. 8,98; ἄγγαρον πῦρ "fire signals," Aeschylus *Agam.* 273, have not yet been ascertained in Iranian; their origin is, with Landsberger, Akk. egirtu "letter, message."[2]

Aristotle, *de mundo*, Berl.Ak. f° 398, mentions the light-telegraph: specularii excubitores qui ignes edere praenuntios et tollere e speculis soliti sunt. Fire signals were used in Iran in pre-Median antiquity. Sargon, 8th Camp. (714 B.C.) ll.249ff., Thureau-Dangin: "pour faciliter leur observation de la province sur les pics des montagnes des tours, dīmātē, étaient construites et se dressaient . . . qidāt abri ša šēpē^{II} nakri ullu (s'agit-il de 'feux'?) . . . matin et soir ils regardaient, puis faisaient connaître. . . ." Luckenbill II,163: "To . . . the look-outs of the districts, towers were constructed on the summits of the mountains and set up to . . . the fire of brushwood, by which means they saw the approach (lit.: feet) of the enemy from a great distance, morning and night, and made it known to. . . ."

Ayātk.Zar. §3: "On the mountains and highest summits let them light fires, announce [azd kun, by azdākara, heralds] to the empire, announce by couriers, biyaspān: Except the magi attending the fires, no male between 10 and 80 shall stay at home!"

The towers called dīmātē in Assyrian are meant in the verses *Yt.*10,45, on Mithras lookout men, by the words:

vispāhu pati brzāhu	vispāhu viδayanāhu
on all mountains,	on all viδayana.

[1] E.g. ibn al-Balkhi, *Fārsn.*, p.56, under "Dārā i buzurg b. Bahman."
[2] Cf. "ἀγγαρία, bondage, corvée" under 'Social Structure.'

In 46, the lookout men are called spaš viδētar.[3] In *Yt.*10,7, Mithra is "prθu.viδayana, outlooking far and wide," i.e. over the whole earth, not "auf breiter Warte (*Wb*)." *Yt.*14,13: The he-camel stands "vidid(ī)vå, looking to and fro like a sāstar, commander."

These towers were erected along the roads, also above the entrance and at the corners of caravanserais, and serve for observation of traffic and military purposes. The Arabs call them mīl or burdǰ,[4] which belongs to viδayana as to type, to brzah as to etymology. Tabari, when speaking of Afshīn's campaign against Bābak, early 9th century A.D., describes flag- and fire-signals; the signal troops are called "kūhbāniyya, mountain-guards," the towers dayādiba, pl. of dīdbān <*dēta.pāna, Arm. det, to √dī- like vi.dayana. I have noted such watch-towers on my map in "Paikuli" along the old Turco-Persian boundary; another series can be seen between Teheran and Kum along the salt-desert.

Carrier-pigeon post, too, is said to be of Persian origin, but I know only of much later reports. Pigeon towers—for guano, not for post—characterize the landscape around Isfahan. A poem of Khadīdja, daughter of al-Ma'mūn (*Aghāni* 14,114) speaks of these burdj lil-ḥamām, and the 1001 Nights (ed. Cairo 3,101, night 698) tell of the cunning Dalīla: "Her husband had been barrādj (inspector of the pigeon-towers) with Hārūn al-Rashīd, with a salary of a thousand gold-pieces a month; he bred carrier-pigeons that fly with letters and messages, and each of these birds, when needed, was dearer to the caliph than one of his own sons." Dalīla gets the office as reward for her ingenious pranks. That is really true to life.—Ibn Shaddād, in ibn Shiḥna's "durr" p.75: "The Mongols under Hulagu had destroyed the citadel of Aleppo at the first conquest, Febr. 1260; after returning from Palestine, they found that a pigeon-tower had been built there, declared that to be a breach of treaty and under this pretext destroyed the citadel completely in February-March 1261."

Hecataeus and Herodotus describe the "Royal Road" from Sardis to Susa with its relay-stations, σταθμοί, avahāna; watches φυλακαί, pāθraka; bridges, prθu; and "gates," i.e. toll-bars. Under Alexander

[3] Wackernagel in *Stud.Ind.-Ir. Geiger:* viδayana to √dī, to see; Bailey, *Ir.Stud.* II, BSOS, VII, 75, assumes vrddhi: vāiδayana.

[4] Against S. Fraenkel, loanword from Gr. pýrgos, not Lat. burgus.

the section beyond Susa, the ἁμαξιτὴ ὁδὸς from there to Persepolis is mentioned. These causeways were surveyed and provided with milestones, parasangs. So was the Great Trunk-Road of India, mentioned by Megasthenes. Ctesias, in Diodor. 2,1,5, tells Semiramis had built such a highway from Babylon to Agbatana, κρήμνους κατα κόψασα κοίλους τόπους χώσασα, leveling the eminences and filling the depressions, "in order to leave an immortal monument, and it is called to the present time Σεμιράμιδος ὁδός," a designation in which Semiramis must be substituted for a Persian word similar to, or equivalent of, the name of the queen. Ctesias' words strikingly resemble *Isaiah* 40,3-4: "In the desert clear the way of YHWH, make straight a high road for your God in the 'arābᵇāh. Every valley shall be raised, and every mountain and hill made low; and the crooked shall become straight and the rough places a plain."[4a]

"King's road, girru šarri" is already an Assyrian term, e.g. in Sanherib's texts, and it lives on as appellative. Ammian Marc. 23,1: "At Carrhae the road to Persia branches in two viae regiae, laeva (via Nisibis) per Adiabenam (=Assyria proper) et Tigridem, dextera per Assyrios (=Sas. asūristān, Babylonia) et Euphratem." In the parable of the five gates, *Mir.Man.*II,14,22 (T.Pārs.) we read: "like a man who travels with many treasures on the king's road, pd r'h 'y bg rft." Henning translated "auf sicherem? Wege," but "bg, god" is here royal title, as in IPārsīk; on the contrary, "by" is the number 2 in by'sp'n, the epithet of Mani, usually translated "god's messenger."—On the pass of Ṭāq i Girrā, the "Zagros Gates," a point of the "Semiramis road," where Antiochus III, in 220 B.C. had crucified Molon, the dismembered body of St. Pethion was exhibited: "the crowd was so large because the 'road of the great-king' passed at the foot of the mountain: this road goes to the utmost confines of the kingdom." In A.D. 800, al-Asma'ī says of the great poet abu l-'Atāhiya: "His verses are like the 'king's road, sāḥat al-mulūk,' upon which fall jewels, gold, earth, potsherds and date-stones." And still today šāh rāh, rāh i šāh is the word for great highways.

A source contemporary with the Achaemenian period, the book of *Esther* 8,10 and 14, says: "So the posts that rode upon mules (and)

4a See Sidney Smith, *Isaiah* Ch.XL-LV, Schweich Lectures, Brit.Acad. 1940, p.65, with the remark "this must be the earliest known allusion to the Persian highroads in literature," and the definition of the locality: the Wadi 'Arabah east of the Jordan.

camels went out (Kg.James)"; (Luther:) "und die reitenden Boten auf Maultieren ritten aus," and "And he wrote in the king Ahasverus' name and . . . sent letters by post on horseback (and) riders on mules, camels (and) young dromedaries"; (Luther): "und er sandte die reitenden Boten auf jungen Maultieren." Cf. *Beh.* §70:

El.: me.ni ʳtip.pi.me am.min.ni ¹ta.i.i.o.s mar.ri.ta ha.ti.ma
OP.: pasāva ima dipi[š - - -]āma [-]āvata [ ] antar dahyā[vā]

"thereupon I sent out the documents to all countries."

The much discussed words in *Esther* 8,14 are: rōkᵉbē hā.räkäš hā.-ᵃḫašt ᵉrānīm bᵉnē hā.rᵉmākīm.

rōkᵉbē are the Akk. rakbu, RÁ.GAB "riding couriers"; cf. the unclear passage of the kudurru L.W.King n° VII, where a mār Ḫanbi receives from a courtier, rēš šarri, as payment for arable land:

6 rak.kab sīsē (horses), value of 300 shekel silver,
2 rak.kab imēr (donkeys), value of 50 shekel silver,

hence the first at 50 shekel, the second at 25 shekel each, while in the same list a fully harnessed chariot is worth 100, one amurrū-donkey 30, one ox 30 shekel. If rakkab sīsē were "saddle-horses," a "western saddle-donkey" would be cheaper than a "western donkey"; if rakkab were "saddle," a donkey's saddle would cost half as much as a horse's saddle, and almost as much as a donkey, and the list would have no instance for the value of a horse. On the other hand, 50 shekel for one saddle-horse would be in proportion to 100 for a chariot with its harness (not including the horses themselves).

To räkäš cf. the letter Harper n° 71, K.113, time of Assurbanipal, Delitzsch *Hwb.* s.v. RKS: sīsē rakkasute (adj.) mesai̯a (from Mesa in Man, mod. Ṭashtepe) ša kai̯amani̯a urakkasuni, of doubtful meaning, and Eg. "reksu, team."—The ᵃḫaštᵉrānīm, ḪŠTR'N, are Med. *χšaθrāna, syn. of χšaθrī, "thoroughbred mares"[5] and ramāk is "mule" as in NHebr., equus mulus, whose mother is a mare, not eq. hinnus, hinny.

Comparison of 10 and 14 shows that the first place is enlarged by an apposition, certainly a gloss, which begins with "bᵉnē . . . , the sons of. . . ." There is a proverb, widely known in the East, Arab.: "Ask a mule who is your father, and it will answer: my khāl, maternal uncle

[5] See de Goeje, in B.G.A. Gloss. s.v. shihriyya.

is a noble stallion!", or Turkish: "qatyra sormušlar babañ kimdir, anam at demiš, the mule was asked who is your father, it replied, my mother is a mare!" This idea is implied in the gloss, which must be "the sons of noble mares." That is the meaning of ḪŠTR'Nym, and one must reverse the order of the words: rōk^{e}bē hā.räkäš hā.r^{e}mākīm b^{e}nē hā.-^{a}hšatrānīm, riding couriers on räkäš mules, "the sons of noble mares." räkäš r^{e}mākīm and Ass. sīsē rakkasute may mean either saddle- or carriage-horses or mules.

That the royal post used two-horse teams is shown by the Med. word for coachman, postilion: biyaspān, MP. *dēspān in Arm. despan, Arab. dusfān, from OIr. *dvi.aspāna, lit. "two-horse-man." At first I believed it to mean "rider with a lead-horse." But Arm. despak, Talm. dyspq, is NP. du.aspah "two-horse team," of the "royal carriage, the golden, drawn by two mules," according to its etymology by a pair of horses. Arm. bastèrn, Lat. basterna, "sedan-chair carried by mules," is evidently a modern kajāwah, with one mule in front, one behind, for it is *dva.-astarana. Also the Roman post used pairs, M.Lat. reda < Celt. dériad = biga.

Zoroaster uses "raθya" for the road, *Y*.50,6-7: "AhuraMazdāh . . . will point out the rules, to be a raθya for my tongue." raθya > rāh is the track of the chariots in the circus, then a carossable road. As the passage in Isaiah shows, the conception of the rzūš paθo "the straight roads on which AhuraMazdāh dwells" in *Y*.35,6 and more often, is derived from the great highways. And it was on the longest and oldest highway of Asia, which was measured by Alexander's bematists, described by Isidorus of Charax for C. Caesar and by the Arab geographers as the "Great Khurāsān Road," that Zoroaster drove, as fugitive, from Ragā by way of Kōmiš to Tōsa, with a two-horse team, vāzā, *Y*.51,1: "when the Vēhviya denied him hospitality, him and his attendants, and the pair of horses, shivering with cold." The dual vāzā means a traveling coach, and the word implies that there were raθya, carossable highways, without which one could not drive in the mountainous country.[6]

The normal team of such a coach would be mules which, when

[6] According to a document quoted by B. Meissner and A. Ungnad, C.4564, "eriqqu qūtītu, Gutian waggons," heavy cars were used for transportation in high Media before the period of the Aryan immigration.

ambling steadily, cover the long distances in less time than horses do. Alone and for short distances a horse outdoes a carriage, but where there are roads, in the long run, the carriage is quicker. In 1924, when suddenly called to Teheran, from Shiraz, Fīrūz Mīrzā Farmāyān told me that his ancestor, Agha Muhammad Khan, in 1779, covered that distance of 600 miles in three days, and thereby won the throne.

Gr.Bdh. 210, description of the mythical Kang: "kē ač dar ō dar pat asp xxii rōč u pa vāhr[7] xv rōč šāyēt raftan, from gate to gate it is a travel of 22 days on horseback, of 15 days in a coach," hence three or two weeks. Driving was reckoned to be quicker by the half than riding.

In *Yt.*5,4 (= *Y.*65,4) the circumference of a sea is given as "čaθwarsatam ayar.barānām huvaspāi narē baramnē, 40 days' journey to ride for a well-mounted man," and the *Gr.Bdh.* reduces this distance to 1,900 farsangs, another number for infinite.

Another term of postal affairs is parvānag. *Maf. al-'Ulūm* 64: "al-furāniq are the carriers of the post-bags, for (Ar.) khādim is in Pers. parvānah." parvānak, therefore, is a deriv. of MMed. parvān, corresp. to MPars. pēš, "coram, in adspectura"; parvānak, or pēšēnīk, cf. pēšēnīkān sālār in *Ayātḳ.Zar.*, is "officer, servant in waiting." Qudāma, 184: "It falls to the duty of the ṣāḥib al-barīd, postmaster, to superintend the service of the farwānaqiyyīn, and he must control the aṣḥāb al-kharā'iṭ." kharīṭa is post-bag, then money-bag. Ibn Khurdādhbih, 153; in his description of the post, says, the furāniqīn are placed under the yanādira, chiefs of the stations. *Mir.Man.*ii,7,11: "Men need a parvānag and rāhnamūdār who shows them 'r'h v vdr, way and passage' (Aw. vitāra, NP. gudār) to salvation." Syr.: "parwānqā, courier, runner," Arab. barwānah, defined by Quatremère as "ministre" and "chambellan, ḥādjib"; cf. van Berchem, *Inscr.Arab. de Syrie* 88,1, where the ǰamdār Ḥusām al-dīn Ladjin is a barwānī: the ǰamdār were diplomatic couriers.

parvānak is not necessarily a person; it can be, like the simplex parvān, an object "in conspectu, a visa." Salemann, Mél.As. ix, 1886, read

[7] Text: "vāhr u pa," transposed; Tavadia, in Christensen *Kayanides* 84 proposed: "à cheval en 22 jours de printemps et en 15 jours (d'été)." The characters must be read v'hr, not vh'r, from Aw. vrta or varta, spelled vāša. NP. gardūn, MP. vardyōn, against NP. gird < Aw. *vrta, supports the reading varta, against Andreas' rule, NGGW 1931,iii,307: "lig. VHR, nie aus *art(h)."

parvānak in *Māt.Čatr.* where the Bombay edition presents "fravartak, letter." The Pers. glossaries give it the meaning "ḥukm, decree" or "farmān, rule, patent" of the government.[8] D. Hoshang Jamasp translated it by "pass, passport" in his glossary, and as such the obsolete word has been revived in the latest NP. to replace Ar. djawāz. *Pahl.Vid.* 1,2: "čē ač kišvar ō kišvar bē pa parvān ē yazdān NY'Š? raftan nē tovān, from Kišvar to Kišvar, except with a divine passport, visa, one cannot travel."

Apollonios of Tyana, middle of the 1st century A.D., traveling from Agbatana to India, says: "The guiding camel bore a golden tablet on the forehead, as a sign for all they met with, that the traveler was one of the king's friends and traveled with royal authorization." Twelve hundred years later, Marco Polo describes the Mongol "paizah,"[9] e.g. in China "silver tablets with: Our imperial order for post-horses, urgent"; under Ghazan Khan in Iran: "bronze tablets for persons traveling in official mission with post-horses." A few gold and silver paizah are preserved in the Hermitage.[10]

The usual word for traffic, traveling is "√čar-, versari, circulate," cf. under 'Hellenism,' the edict of the Byzantine autokrator in *Yt.*9,24: "not shall, henceforth, an āθravān (fire priest) travel, čarāt, in my country!"

*Y.*62,8: The Fire observes the hands of all "para.čarantām, passing travelers": "what present has the friend for his friend, the traveler, fra.-čarθwant, for him who sits quiet, armē.šaδē." The Pahl. transl. is armēšt, a word in which this armēžd and armēštā "still-standing" have coalesced. MP. armēšt means in general "sick, invalid," e.g. in *Pahl. Vid.*5,59; 7,19; their place is the armēštān gāh, *Pahl.Vid.*9,33, Aw. arimē gātu. This word does not contain the notion "isolation"—any more than does vitrta.tanu [*Wb.*: "wobei der Leib, die Person (an einen besonderen Ort) weggebracht, isoliert werden muss," rather "(leprosy) by which the body becomes mutilated"]. armē.šad, here, does not mean simply sitting quiet as opposed to traveling, but being

8 Syn. of the demin. parvānčah; the deriv. parvānači is "secretarius"—cf. Minorskiy, BSOS, IX,906: "registrar," and *Notices et Extraits* XIV,i,250,n.2. parvānag-burtār is an "animal which goes in front of the lion," metaphorically "pēšrau i laškar, dux exercitus."

9 Cf. Henry Yule's remarks in *Marco Polo* 1,351ff.

10 Smirnoff, *Argenterie Orientale,* pls. 93 and 94.

unable to move, invalid. The armēštān gāh is a "house of invalids," the bīmāristān of later times, "hospital," and Islam has taken over the institution at the very earliest period from Iran.

The comp. ā.čar- means "to alight, to put up (at a station)." *Yt.*10, 137: "Mithra āčarati, puts up at the farmyard of the pious," and *Vid.* 13,49: "If a couple want to put up, čara, in this house, they shall not forbid them, apa.rōδaya[11] to do so." About 1903, in a hotel in Patras, was written: "Messieurs les voyageurs sont priés de ne pas introduire ici des demoiselles avec lesquelles ils ne sont pas légitimément mariés, jusqu'à 11 heures, après quoi ils paieront le double."

From √čar-, finally, comes *vāičāra, vrddhi of *vičāra, MP. vāčār, NP. bāzār, "market, trade, 'Handel und Wandel.'" I formerly followed Bailey who combined Kurd. Bijār with *vičāra, but that placename is rather Aw. "vičarna, bifurcation" of a road.

aštah is, according to Benveniste, *Inf.av.* 39, "la halte, halting, resting place, shelter"; *Wb.* attaches it to √ans- "anlangen, arrival." It comes near to Arab. manzil from nazala and marḥala from raḥala, and means the mansiones or stathmoì along the post-roads, which Ctesias call "empória, caravanserais"; cf. the placename aštaχōst, 3 fars. from Marw, Yāqūt 1,277 and 293. One usually connects it with "ašta, ašti, messenger"; the god Naryasanha is ašto, Mercury, with AhuraMazdāh, also the saviour Astvatrta is so called, as Mani is "biyaspān, courier," but cf. under 'ApāmNapāt.'

In the Mongol period the term for the post-houses, which originated from the Iranian institution, is yam, yām, yamb, ǰam, ǰām, a word spread over the whole of Asia and Russia. I discovered it once in the inscription of the khān Ortmah in Baghdad, which is the only such building known to exist, under the Arab. form yam < OP. *yuman, gen. *yumnah (attested by the deriv. OP. yāumani) to √yū- "to put (the horses) to" and "to brace" (both: Germ. "anspannen"). Herodotus says καταλύσεις "place of unharnessing," Germ. "ausspann = halting place," while relais and relay are lit. "Anspann," cf. *Altp.Inschr.* 365 and *Arch.Reise* II,187ff. The postmaster is called, already at the end of the Sasanian period, yundār, Arab. pl. yanādira, [ينادرة] , in Ibn Khurdādhbih, 153, with wrong points, banādira, [بنادرة] , also several times in Tabari. It is the Old Turk. loanword yamtar.

11 Cf. čaratasča and rurōst ašto in Y.51,12 under 'Vēhviya.'

Qudāma, 241: "In Kaskar was a canal called ǰanb, and the track of the post-couriers to Maisān . . . was on the area of its southern bank"; later, when the baṭā'iḥ became swampy, the swamps on the side of the post-road, ṭarīq al-barīd, were called "ādjām al-barīd, post-swamps," the other side, in Nabataean, "agmē rabtā, i.e. al-ādjām al-kubrā', the great swamps."

The mamluks had a numerous corps of pages, called al-khāṣṣakiyya, from which came all their officials and even the sultans themselves. Whether khāṣṣah be genuinely Arabic or not, at any rate the Persian formation khāṣṣakī proves the institution to come from the Seldjuq court in Isfahan. Many of these pages were ǰamdār, or barwānī—like the above mentioned Ḥusām al-dīn—and served as diplomatic couriers. ǰamdār is the younger form of yundār and merges with ǰāmdār "cup-bearer" and ǰāmadār "keeper of the wardrobe."

*varta.yōna > gardūn, Benveniste J.As. 1936, 201, "attelage de char, place of harnessing of coaches," belongs to the same radical word. Henning, in *Mir.Man.*III, translates vrdyvn by "gefährt"; and in *Art.Vir. Nām.*XIV, where "dahyupat and heroes" appear in resplendent apparel BYN ZK y škvft lh v vltyvn P'N KBD ŠKVH (or ŠKN'?), it seems indeed to be a vehicle. But p.16,8, m'h vrdyvn means rather "orbit of the moon, meeting point of gods, 'mvrdn bg'nyg"; cf. Bartholomae, *Sas.Recht* v,31 (*Pahl.Riv.Dād.* 57,12): "čigōn biyaspānān āvarišn ō 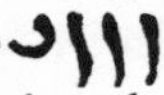[i.e. yvnb] yazdān.ič rasišn ō mān ē ātaχš ē varhrān, as the couriers hurry to the post-station, thus the gods arrive at the place of the Varhrān Fire." And Mani says, *Mir.Man.*II,19,12: "For your sakes I will wait above at the water-station, vrdyvn 'byn [= moon-station as navis vitalium aquarum], to send you help evermore!" Also 19,19: "Brighter than the light of the sun, the vrdyvn shines," that is one of the spheres. m'h vrdyvn is but a more figurative expression for normal m'h p'yg.

This yōna is the first element in the epithet of the fox, yōna.χvata, which describes its kennel, on account of which the Arabs call the fox "father of the little fort, abu ł-ḥuṣain." Aw. χvata, i.e. HVT, must be read "-hūt, who builds his yōna with skill"; cf. hvāyōnåho pantāno (below). gardūn, like the syn. s'panǰ, "inn" is the usual metaphor for "world." spanǰ, spinǰ, is the first element of Aw. spinǰaγrya and spinǰaruška. According to *Wb.* the first would be the "Name eines daēva, der vom Feuer vāzišta [Andreas: "superl. of vazraka 'great'"] bekämpft wird," on the strength of an irrelevant passage. The second would be "name of an unbeliever . . . ruška = Lat. luscus?, spinǰa perhaps tribal name?" Justi, *Namenbuch* 508: "spinǰaruška, enemy of post-houses, hostelries, a charitable state institution . . . spinǰaγriya, der mit Gebrüll (Lithuan. spengti, Gr. φθέγγω) gellende, Verkörperung des Donners." spinǰa > sipanǰ is hostelry, inn; aγrya (der. from aγrā "scab, mange") = NP. āir, ēr, is something like boils, pustules. The alleged dēva is called "boil-host" or "lousy fellow." I once had a shepherd bitch, whom I had called, because of her golden coat and her behavior like a diva, spinǰaruškā "Flohberger," per antiphrasim, as the beautiful wife of the caliph al-Mutawakkil was called "al-Qabīḥa."

There is a traveler's song in *Yt.*16,2-3:

us.hišta hača gāθva	rise from thy couch
frašusa hača dmānāt	go forth from thy house!
yazi ahi parva.nēmāt	If thou art (there), from the western half,
āt ahma avi nmāniyā	come to us, lady!
yazi [ahi] paska[.nēmāt]	If thou art (yonder), from the eastern half
āt ahma avi apaya	here come to us!
aθana aχštā būyān	May security be ours
yaθana būyāt - -	that we may find
hvāyōnåho pantāno	the highways having good hostelries
huvāpaθanå garayo	the mountains having good byways
huvātačinå arzurā	the forests having pretty brooks,
huprθviyå afš nāviyå	the ditches having good bridges,
ahmāi sōkāi frasastayāi	for our safety, our permission,
fravākāi uta framānyāi	our vocation and our craft!

Lommel translates the beginning: "Sie (Čisti-dēnā) verehrte Zarathustra, von seinem Sitz aufstehend, aus seinem Hause herausgehend" and remarks: "Zarathustras Gebet an die Einsicht in v.2 enthält in naiver Form wirkliche Weisheit, wie sie einen, bei Beschäftigung mit dem Awesta, für den Augenblick erquicken kann," a condemnation of the Awesta, smashing but mainly due to wrong interpretation. There is enough deep and true wisdom in it. As everywhere else, one must eliminate the stereotyped introductory words on AhuraMazdāh and Zoroaster; the "Lament of Rtiš" is a perfect analogy. The verses are naïve, and that alone would prove that they are not Zoroaster's, to whom it would have been an easy matter to make verses also in Awestic, though none are preserved. It is a pretty song, which the caravans sing before sunrise, the only good piece in the Dēn Yasht dedicated to Čistiš-dēnā, and it shows at once that these abstractions "Insight-Religion" are merely substituted to the old Ušå-Eos. The beginning of the song resembles *Od.*v,1:

> *'Ηὼς δ'ἐκ λεχέων παρ' ἀγαύου Τιθωνοῖο*
> *ὤρνυθ' ἵν' ἀθανατοῖσι φοὼς φέροι ἠδὲ βροτοῖσι*

Zoroaster uses another word for the post-house in *Y.*33,5:

> yas.tē vispā.mazištam srōšam zbayā avahānē
> āpāno drga.ǰyātim ā χšaθram vahoš manaho
> rtāt ā rzūš paθo yēšu mazdå ahuro šēti

"I who want to call forth Thy most-high Srōšo, at the stage, when arriving at the eternally-living hostelry of Vahumano, on the straight roads on which AhuraMazdāh is dwelling!"

Bartholomae: "Der ich Deinen Srōša als den allerhöchsten anrufen will bei der Vollendung usw." vispā.mazišta is a courtly word: Srōša is subaltern, but "most-high" as servant of the Most-high, see under 'Poetry.' The name means "hearing, ear" as title, i.e. police, Arab. shurṭa.[12] χšaθra may be the common word, the kingdom, empire, but that would stop and weaken the metaphor, while χšaθra = hostelry fits in perfectly, see under 'Hospitium.'

zbā- is "to cry out, call forth"; thus Pārva the sailor, in *Yt.*5,62, calls the same Ušå out of her house. Mithra's old companions, Srōš ē nēkōk and Rašn ē razišt, are on sentry duty at the heavenly stage; one must call Srōša to open the gate, for the yards of the stations are always closed because the horses are in them. I have done it many times, in 1905, when traveling čapar from Shiraz to Teheran, and, here below, had always to wait a long time.

Wb. puts Gath. avahāna "Abschluss, Vollendung im eschatologischen

12 Cf. *Yt.*10,26: "srōšya, those to be chastised"; *Yt.*10,109: "srōšyā, chastisement," ordered by the military commander in chief: "srōša.vrz-, constable, bailiff."

Sinne" to √hī- "anschirren"; but OP. avahana "Wohnplatz, Flecken" to √vah- "weilen," cf. Arm.Lw. avan < OP. *āvāhana." Andreas, NGGW 1916,1, p.5,n.: Die von mir herrührende Gleichung Arm. avan = Ap. *åvohonom, ZDMG.47, 1893, 702, hielt Hübschmann *Pers.Stud.* 170 und *Arm.Gram.,* für unsicher, "da h < ursprgl. s im Pers. zwischen Vokalen nicht schwindet." This whole equation falls with the etymology.[13] As early as 1885, G. Hoffmann[14] had explained Arab.-Syr. awānā as "post-stage," syn. of Arab. sikka. This is of course not a loanword from Gathic poems, but from OP. official language, an OP. *avāna. In the inscriptions, Zuzu-Succa in Armenia and Abirāduš in Asia Minor are called avahana; both must be sought along the Royal Road, hence the first probably in Van on the lake, the second not far from Sardis and Kyzikos (OP. χūž . . .). Gath. avahāna and OP. avahana are identical, the letter an inverse, historical spelling for spoken *avāna < *avahāna[<*ava.hayana, Tedesco], from ava + √hī-, "place of unharnessing, Germ. ausspannen, abseilen,"[15] cf. OP. Vivāna < *vivahvana. avahāna and yōna are synonyms, because the roots √yū- and √hī- have a similar meaning. Arab. Wāna < avāna is the name of a place well-known to me, south of Samarra opp. 'Ukbarā, on the road to Baghdad, cf. Yāqūt *mu'djam* 1,395 and *mušt.* 30. Another Awānā Nīqṭōr, mentioned by G. Hoffmann, *Syr.Akt.* was situated at the foot of the Νικατόριον ὄρος (Strabo), where the battle of Gaugamela took place, hence equally on the Royal Road. Cf. Bāna in Kurdistan. Elam. ʰuwanis seems to be a deriv. of the same avāna.

Nyberg translates Gath. avahāna also by "Losspannung," but explains: "Die 'Losspannung' kann . . . nicht sowohl ein eschatologisches Ereignis meinen, . . . sondern . . . es handelt sich offenbar um eine Befreiung der Seele vom Körper und ihre Flucht zu den himmlischen Wohnungen . . . , die Himmelfahrt der Seele in der *Ekstase.* Die 'graden Wege' sind ein für uns nicht deutlicher Ausdruck, zeigen aber Aša's nahe Verbindung mit dem Paradiese." On p.147 he counts it among the "Erscheinungen (phenomena), die mit Sicherheit auf ekstatische

13 Also the etymology of NP. "χānah, house" falls therewith.

14 In *Nachträge zu H. Kiepert's Begleitworten zur Karte der Ruinenfelder von Babylon,* ZGErdk.Berlin, XVIII,414.

15 aha, āha and ahā > ā corresponds to āva and avā > ā; āya and ayā > ā, against ava > ō, aya > ē. The change is pre-Iranian, cf. Bartholomae, *ZairWb.* 97,4, and works in Iranian.

Erscheinungen in der Gatha-Gemeinde hinweisen." The other "Erscheinung-appearance" of an ecstatic "Erscheinung-phenomenon" is the wrong translation of "hvafna, sleep" by "trance," see under 'Yamā.'

The verses of *Y*.33,5 are a metaphor: life as traveling, the cammin di nostra vita, or death as journey to heaven. Cf. *Y*.32,15: "they shall drive, bryāntē, lit. be driven (in a coach), to the house of Vahumano." The Qur'ān 39,73 says: "Those who believe in their Lord shall be driven in multitudes to paradise, and when they arrive there, the gates shall be opened and their keeper says: Hail! you were good, enter for evermore!" In heaven, the roads are straighter and plainer. Zoroaster's "straight road" is no less "clear" than Isaiah's "make straight a highway for our god!" There are so many mountains in Iran—2,244 according to *Yt*.19—that one imagined the transfigured world to be a perfect plain; Plutarch, *de Iside,* 47: *τῆς δὲ γῆς ἐπιπέδου καὶ ὁμαλῆς γενομένης*.

It is a similar metaphor, when Mani calls the spheres of the soul's journey vardyōn, and the thought continues. In the *Andarz,* Testament of Xusrau I:

> gētīh pa spinǰ dār u tan pat ast ('.ST.N < '.S'N.N)
> nēvkīh pa KRT' dār u bazak pa rōč spōž[16]
> mēnūk pa χvēš kunišn

Full of difficult readings and hardly correct, meaning: "Regard the world as a hostel, and the body as an inn, regard a good deed as a completed?, a sin as a delayed day's journey, the heaven as to be made your own! (your very goal)."

Similarly in *Dēnk*. M.478:

> χvatāyīh magavan? ē χvāstak, χvāstak magavan? ē tan,
> tan magavan? ē ravbān

where mgvn?, as in *Pahl. Texts* 131: tan pa magavandīh ē dēn dāštan, must mean something like "hostel, host": "to regard the body as the hostel, host of the soul," cf. under 'Maga.'

Islam has developed the poetical metaphor into a veritable doctrine, cf. the inscription of the Muẓaffarid Shāh Shudjā' at Persepolis, AMI

[16] Cf. Hübschmann, *Pers.Stud.* 73, Arm. spužel "to delay," spužumn "delay."

VIII,100f.: "This world is a house to pass through, not to stay in." Bazaroff says, with Turgenieff: "I have discovered here in my trunk an empty place and pad it now with hay as well as I can. Thus one must do with the trunk of life: pad it with everything that falls into one's hand, anything rather than leave an empty place therein!"

XV. POETRY

"καὶ σέ πολυμνήστη λευκώλενε πάρθενε Μοῦσα ἄντομαι
πέμπε παρ' Εὐσεβίης ἐλαοῦσ' εὐήνιον ἅρμα"

—Empedokles

ZOROASTER was a great poet. The gathas are poetry. Be there ever so much darkness in them, the train of thought clears up with the progress of study.

One perceives traces of IE. connections in metrics, archaic syntax, grammatical forms and vocabulary, standing formulas and metaphors. In some verses one can observe an imitation of the style of older passages in the Mithra yasht; *Y.*29, the "Cow gatha" is the transformation of an older poetical theme, the "Lament of the Cow," of which an example, incorporated in *Yt.*10, is preserved; the "Gatha of the Questions" is related to "Mithras Questions" in *Yt.*10. Other verses, alluding to Yama, son of Vivahvant, or to the "Twins, yamā, Sleep and Death," presuppose that the hearers were fully acquainted with those myths, which therefore were parts of an epopee, the primal form of which existed before the oldest preserved parts of the Awesta.

Those are features of old tradition, in sharp contrast with an entirely personal style, rooted in the philosophy of the poet. The main characteristic of his style is that he never describes, but always speaks didactically. This we can wholly recognize only through Duchesne's analysis of the "explaining" Gathic compounds, in contradistinction to the "descriptive" Awestic compounds. Zoroaster was also creative in language: many words were certainly never used before or after in the sense he gives them; he prefers certain forms, e.g. abstract for concrete ones, and has created some of them. Even a superficial comparison between the gatha and the Yasna haftahāti is enough to show that these qualities are personal, that all gathas bear the stamp of the same personality, for in the Yasna haftahāti—though composed in the same dialect—all these qualities are lacking. The gathas are no popular poetry, but one ruled by art, and are all of one and the same poet.

They themselves express this claim more than once. *Y.*50,6 begins: "The manθran who raises his voice, vāčam barati, befriended, rvaθa, with rtam, after prosternation, namahā, is Zoroaster!"

It has not been recognized that this is an isolated sentence and a self-introduction of the poet, certainly a conventional formula of this old poetry. H. H. Schaeder once called the introductory formula of the OP. inscriptions "I, NN, the king, pleno titulo" a "self-introduction of the kings." There it seems to me wrong to supplement an "ahmi, I am"; the formula rather means "In the king's name!" similar to a Muhammedan "Bismillāh!" But a connection exists between the two formulae, and the antique fashion is maintained throughout Iranian poetry, known to us mainly by imitations of Oriental poetry by our Romanticists. Ḥāfiẓ mentions his name regularly at the end of his verses.

manθra means a "thing thought out, poem," cf. Germ. denken—dichten. Sometimes it means "proverb," cf. under 'Harvatāt-Amrtatāt.' manθran is the poet, προφήτης in the sense "inspired singer,"[1] not of "prophet = rasūl." *Y.Haft.* 41,5 says: "θwoi stōtarasča manθranasča A.M. ōgmadēča, we are called Thy glorifiers and singers." Once, in *Y.*46,3 "θwa sanštrē vrnē ahura," Zoroaster calls himself "the chosen one," like Muḥammad al-muṣṭafā.

All poems were sung. The word for it is √vāk-, as in the n.pr. manθravāka. That is not the "Stimme in der Ritualliteratur"—what after all is a "voice in literature"?—but a singing voice, "voce." The MP. mahrnāmak is the index of a hymnbook. The Arabs render vāč-, used for the praying of Zoroastrian priests, by "zamzama, to murmur," but the old poets "vāčam baranti, i.e. vociferantur," sang loud like the "cock that raises his voice at the dawn, vāčim barati upa.ušanham," *Vid.*18,15; cf. *brza.vačiya > bulōč under 'Māda-Pārsa.' Occasionally, "brzam vāčam, high voice" means "shouting," e.g. in *Yt.*10,113; 17,61; antonym of namravak in *Frhg.Ēv.* 3, the low, polite talk.

By his self-introduction, Zoroaster describes himself expressly as the author, in the first place as author of gatha 50. But in most gathas, I believe in all of them, one finds quite distinct signs of his authorship—apart from the style. All counterarguments rest upon wrong translations—examples under *Y.*50,8—and on sophisms like the insignificant change between first and third person, which the poet uses as he likes, even in one and the same gatha. Meillet, l.c. 15, criticized adversely

[1] Aw. +vifra, written ōifra, in *Yt.*13,104, where the invocation of the name of the Hāugava is recommended against such "vifra and parikā," Peris, which shows that the interpolation was made at a period devoid of understanding.

the gatha which we number *Y*.50: "dénué de caractère, fait l'effet d'une oeuvre d'école"—the common brass plate in picture galleries. Such a stylistic censure I consider as not possible in principle, and I feel that *Y*.50, once it is entirely understood, will take its place among the best gathas, beside the psalm: "The heavens declare the glory of God!"

But the formula in 50,6 proves that with st.6 a new gatha begins, and that *Y*.50, therefore, actually consists of two. In *Y*.53, likewise, a new gatha begins with st.8. On the contrary, the end of *Y*.29 must not be separated, as Andreas considered. The tradition of the gathas is amazingly good, yet their arrangement is not absolutely correct. The reason is that they were collected and arranged not according to their historical sequence, but to their meter, a formal point of view, similar to the arrangement of the sūra of the qur'ān according to the number of their verses.

The attempt to restore their chronological order has never been made and would be still precocious. A few instances have been given here under 'Bandva.' But *Y*.50,6-11 is better fit than any other gatha to count as the first one. In that case, the self-introduction of the poet would stand—a fact at all events probable—at the top of all gathas, expressing the authorship.

Y.29,8:

ho no vašti čarkrθrā srāvayahe
yat hoi hūdmam dyāi vaχdrahya

"Zoroaster wants to sing our (the cow's) praise. Sweetness of tongue shall be given to him!"

srāvaya, caus. of √sru-, the verb for reciting verses, often with fra-, NP. surūdan, MHG. "singen und sagen,"[2] cf. *Mir.Man.* II,15,4 in the parable of the maiden in the fortress: "a man ky pd bvn 'y dyv'r nv'g 'y šyryn frsrvd, who at the foot of the wall sang a sweet song." čarkrθra "glory," to "čarkrmahi we praise, glorify," also "to quote, laudare."[3] In st.7-11 the speaker does not change, as is usually assumed; it is always Zoroaster speaking through the mouth of the "Soul of the Ox": "Nobody listens to Thy commandments; Zoroaster alone have we (the

[2] √sru- is insufficiently treated in *Wb*.1639-43. Wrong is: srōtu in *Y*.49,9; srāvī in *Y*.32,7,8; 33,7; 45,10; 53,1; asravātām in *Y*.30,3; asruždvam in *Y*.32,3; frasruta in *Y*.50,8.

[3] In *Altp.Inschr.* 197 is an erroneous remark on the wrong Pahl. transl. čārak kirtārīh.

cow, i.e. peasantry) found, visto, who, following the commandments given in our favor, has our interest at heart. He wants to sing our praise. Therefore you, A.M., must give him the gift of poetry. But he is a poor nar=χšaθriya only, and what we need is a rich one, iša.-χšaθriya. When shall come the one who gives him practical help, zastavat avo?" The last words aim at Žāmāspa. In these verses Zoroaster glories in his being a poet, like Mani in being a painter.

*Y.*50,8:

mat vå padāiš	yā frasruta ⁺īžayā
pari.ǰasāi	mazdå ustāna.zasto
āt vå rtā	ardrahyača namahā
āt vå vahoš	manaho hunartātā

"With dithyrambs recited with passion I want to circumambulate Thee, with hands outstretched, with the prosternation of one ardent (with joy) and with the skill (gift) of Vahumano!"

Zoroaster sings here like Hans Sachs in the Meistersinger or like R. M. Rilke "Ich kreise um Gott . . . und ich weiss noch nicht, bin ich ein Sturm oder ein grosser Gesang!" With padāiš I walk around Thee, my songs walk around Thee, stretch out their hands, prosternate themselves, are my sacrifices. "Und meine Lieder rinnen rauschend zurück in Ihn!"

Bartholomae: "Immer (wieder) will ich mit den Versen, die bekannt sind als die des frommen Eifers, vor Euch treten." Always again the same, known verses which he had not made himself. Lommel: "Mit Versen die erhört werden wegen (meines) Strebens"—reminds one of Faust "Wer immer strebend sich bemüht . . ." Nyberg, 162: "Mit Versen, welche von īžā (= ārmaiti, dem Stamm) gesungen werden, umgehe (= nahe ich mich) Euch . . . die Hände ausstreckend, . . . mit den Anbetung des brennenden Mannes . . . , mit guter Manneskraft." Interrupting an invocation of the god, a descriptive clause "welche gesungen werden" would be a footnote of the scenario or a sotto voce remark spoken to the audience, revealing at once that the poet was an actor posing as prophet.

pada, metrical foot, is the same term as in the Veda. Zoroaster speaks of something like hexameters and dithyrambs. frasruta does not mean "known" or "heard, granted"; to hear, grant, is √χšnu-, never √sru-, in Gathic as in OP. When the poet "circumambulates the god with these verses" he is the author, he cannot fool the god by presenting him what actually is the "tribe's." īžā—cf. under 'Harvatāt'—belongs to "āz, desire, passion"; frasruta īžayā means "recited con passione," just as the "prosternation of the ardent one" is one made con fuoco.

Lommel and Nyberg explain "pari.gam-, circumambulate" by "sich nahen, to approach," hence do not know the rite. Equally p.159, in *Y*.43: "Als das (Göttliche) mich umging (umschloss) mit Vohu Manah." It must be: "when the god in his quality (shape) of Vahumano circumambulated me." Lommel-Andreas, to *Y*.43,7: "pari.gam-: 'besuchen' ist abschwächende Ubersetzung für 'umschreiten.' Dies, sonst Huldigung gegenüber Höher stehenden, ist von Seiten des Gottes gegen den Propheten auffallend. Markwart und Hertel geben keine wirkliche Erklärung . . . etwa: jemanden (mit seinem Besuch) beehren." In mod. Persian every visit is a "bringing and carrying away of honor, tašrīf āwurdan and burdan," but such a phrase can of course be used only by the one honored, not even the Shah could say that in the first person, let alone one who prays to his god. Hertel understands the words perfectly; *Beitr,* 240 and IIQF VII,191, and refers for *Y*.51,20 to the Rgveda. In *Y*.43, the "Gatha of the Vision," AhuraMazdāh in his aspect as Vahumano circumambulates the prophet five times, asking and answering questions. This rite means a worshipping of Zoroaster by the god, and Markwart described Zoroaster there as Arhat, very much to the point and better than Nyberg's "pneumatischer Mensch."

In Buddhist India the rite is called pradakśina. The Sasanian fire temples were planned for the same ceremony of circumambulation of the fire as are the modern temples. Already the pre-Islamic Arabs circumambulated the cella of the Nabataean temples and the Ka'ba, calling it ṭawāf. *Aghāni,*19,142: "The poet 'Alī b. 'Abdallāh al-Dja'farī al-Ṭālibī told: Once a woman passed me at the ṭawāf of the Ka'ba, while I was just reciting to a friend my verses: 'I love the religion with eagerness, but I love the worldly pleasures not less. What am I to do with such a mind, can holy and worldly love be combined?' Just then, the woman turned to me and said: Let one of them go and keep the other, no matter which one!" In Shi'ite Iran and 'Irāq, the ṭawāf is part of the cult of the mashhads, the tombs of the Imāms, cf. *Arch.Reise* I,85, II,52 and *Arch.Hist.Ir.* 93.

ustāna.zasta: Ved. uttāná.hasta is used in a similar way; it is Διὶ χεῖρας ἀνασχών. The outstretched, open hands are of course the gesture of imploration. Duchesne, *Comp.av.* 221 says: "Est employé dans les gatha . . . avec une signification précise: la strophe 50,8 est un abrégé de liturgie: l'office rituel comporte geste, ustāna.zasta v.2; parole, ardrahya namahā v.3; pensée, vahoš manaho hunartātā v.4; cf. *Y*.28,1 ustāna.zasta désignant le seule acte matériel admis dans le culte Réformé [Meillet's term for the true Zoroastrism], résume, en quelque sorte, une doctrine à lui seule."

√nam-, MP. namāz, is "to bow, down to the soil," salutation to men of higher rank, as Herodotus describes, called proskýnesis by the Greeks. The MP. ideogram is SGDH = Arab. sadjada for the same posture in praying. Thus, namah is another gesture of praying, whilst hunartāt is every skill, art, here poetry. Even when these words do not represent "parole" and "pensée," Duchesne's description of the formula as "doctrine" and "office rituel" stands. ustāna.zasta is a Zoroastrian gesture of prayer; on the other hand, Ātar in *Y*.62,1, Mithra in *Vid*.3,1 are invoked "ēsma.zasta barsma.zasta gō.zasta hāvana.zasta, with fire-wood, barsman, milk and mortar in hand"; to Anāhitā one prays, in *Yt*.5,98 with barsman in hand, and, since the goddess herself holds in *Yt*.5,127 the libation cup, ⁺bātiyaka and barsman in her hand, probably with hydria or phiale for the zōθra.

hunartāt is not the "Manneskraft des brennenden Mannes," ambiguous, not to say equivocal, words, by which Nyberg crowns his translation, but means "skill, art," as it has always been translated. hūnara—see under 'Architecture,' is derived from √hū- "to produce skillfully"; the popular etymology "hu + nar, good man"—as in Goethe's poem—is wrong. AhuraMazdāh's activity when creating the world is called so; Darius calls his sportly skill, κατὰ τὸ σῶμα ἀρεταὶ, "hūnarā received from AhuraMazdāh" and Zoroaster his poetry "hūnartāt received from Vahumano."

The whole verse is very picturesque: Zoroaster executes the divine service according to his own rite by circumambulation, out-stretching of the arms and prostration, and his songs are his sacrifices, yasna, as he calls them in the first verse. In the same way he says in *Y*.51,22: "To whom, for my sake, A.M. through [the mouth of] Rtam has destined paradise as reward for their worship (sacrifice), those . . . I want to circumambulate with songs of praise!" (text under 'Maga,' commentary under 'Dēva'). The last words mean an adoration of his helpers.

In Y.46,16-17, text under 'Hospitium'—the situation is: The two Hāugava, Frašauštra and Zāmāspa, set forth on their journey to the place "where obedience to the law, ārmatiš, follows right, rtam, where power, χšaθra, is in the possession of the good-will, vahumano, and where AhuraMazdāh dwells in abundance (or "joy"), vardmąn."[4] Like the following sentences, this description of the purpose of the journey is a wish: where justice ought to be found, the highest court, the great-king himself. The purpose of the journey was to obtain the frasastiš, the revocation of Zoroaster's banishment. At their departure Zoroaster sings "in Zamaspem et Prexostrem legatos Agbatanam proficiscentes": "You, Frašauštra, go there, ardrāiš tāiš yān usvahi uštā.stoi!" "ardent, aglow" are here, once more, not the travelers, but Zoroaster's wishes, the word for which is "uštā.stoi, inshallāh!" "Both our, i.e. Zoroaster's and the Hāugavī's ardent wishes for your success accompany you, my father-in-law!"

St.17:

yaθra vå	afšmāni sanhāni
noit anafšmām	žāma.aspa hāugava
hadā vās.tā	vahmān srōša rādaho
yo vičinōt	dāθamča adāθamča
dahrā mantū	rtā mazdā ahura

"While I shall speak verses, real verses, o H. Žāmāspa; always I shall sing the praise of your protection, you who know to judge what is art and what is not, as a learned guardian! O AhuraMazdāh as Rtam!"

Lommel-Andreas: "(dort) wo ich eure Verdienste verkündigen will, nicht eure Schuld, o Yāmāspa, du Nachkomme des Hugu, (und eure) Gebete samt diesem eurem Gehorsam aus Bereitwilligkeit (dem verkünden), der den frommen und den nicht-frommen unterscheidet, (nämlich) der Weise Herr, durch

[4] Andreas: "vorδmon, loc.sg. eines man-Stammes, 'Freude,'" with reference to MP. "vār- < *vard- 'to rejoice.'"

seinen wunderkräftigen Berater, das Wahrsein!" Note: "a: 2 Silben fehlen; Henning ergänzt aθra vor yaθra. afšman 'Verdienst,' anafšman, das Gegenteil, so auch Kent, *Language* IV, 106f." I wonder whether somebody else can find rhyme and reason in this translation, according to which Zoroaster, by passing over the "guilt" in silence, would tell in Žāmāspa's favor a half-truth to his god, who through his adviser, Truth, knows better. Bartholomae translated: "wo ich eure Nachteile melden will, nicht eure Vorteile," the way Arab satirists used to threaten their victims with a satirical poem.

With srōša as noun, the construction, if possible at all, is very difficult. Tedesco saw the solution: srōša is s-aor. of √sru-, 1.p. aor.act., cf. *Grdr.* §373, and the med. srōšāni in §156, χšnaviša in §157. The first sentence means: "I must remain at home and can only express my wishes in poems." afšman or afsman is the "chain," the term for the verse consisting of pad. noit an.-afšmām, with double negation—stronger than the positive—"not non-verses" are really good ones. Cf. *Y.*46,8: "huǰyātoiš noit dužǰyātoiš, good-life, real good-life." In order to judge the verses one must be able to distingish between dāθam and adāθam. These words may refer to something that would make the Hāugava especially fit for his mission (see under 'Hospitium'), but the parallelism between the two pairs of words with negation is so obtrusive, that one must relate the neutr. dāθam to the "verses." Zoroaster calls Žāmāspa a "learned" man who knows what education or lack of education (or skill and lack of skill) really means, calls him a Dr. jur et phil.

As to etymology, Bartholomae, *Grdr.* §33 attached afšman to √pas-, *πήγνυμι*, Lat. pangere (versus).[5] The composing of poems is also called "to weave," and Gath. vafuš is "carmen," thus in *Y.*43,8 and 28,3: "yo vå . . . ufyāni . . . aparviyam, I want to make poems to Ahura-Mazdāh as never before!" as good as never verses have been "woven" to him. The same etymology is the best one advanced for Gr. hymnos. The word for "strophe" is "vača.tašti, i.e. voces + texere, like sermones

[5] The spelling with š in *Y.*46,17, with s in Awestic, makes no difference; the Pahl.transl. for both is the same, with right: patmān, not a "Verwechslung," *Wb.*104.

texere." Andreas' objection, in NGGW 1931, III,315, is difficult to understand: "Bartholomae's Kombination von ufyāni mit dem verbum des Webens wird dem Sinn nicht gerecht." The tertium is the artificial joining of the words, like threads in weaving a pattern. In just the same way "hazār.bāf, thousandfold-woven" is the term for artificial assemblage of bricks. Gath. afšman, too, means the "chain" (opp. weft) of the weaver's loom. The figurative expression has analogies in all languages. The Aramaeans "weave, zaqar" the speech, the Romans' speeches and letters. They use also "faber," as Germanic languages "to spin" and "to forge." Abu l-'Atāhiya, the poet, when asked whether he was really a potter, answered: "I am a rhyme-potter, my brother is a potter by trade."

Certain expressions of this poetical language, e.g. addresses, belong to a "courtly" style and are significant for the "Horatian" character of these carmina: instead of the direct pronouns derivatives in -vant are used.

Y.44,1: "θwāvans may tell it māvans" does not mean "one like you to one like me," but in Zoroaster's causative style: "although you are so great and I am so small, you will tell me because (I love you)." *Y*.44,9: "θwāvans ... hadmoi ... šyans," according to Lommel-Andreas "einer wie Du, o Weiser, der mit ... im gleichen Hause wohnt" means rather: "Your Highness who is dwelling in the same house." Or *Y*.43,3: "(ardro) θwāvans hozantuš spanto mazdā, of the same kind, essence, as Your Highness, holy!" The derivatives in -vant intend to avoid the vulgar "I" and "thou," as recognized already by Markwart, *Gāth.ušt.* p.63.

In *Ar.Forschg.* II,155, Bartholomae called māvant (1.p.sg.) and θwāvant (e.p.sg.) correctly "nur Umschreibungen für ich und du"; *Wb.* 1304: "yušmāvant, χšmāvant, 2.p.pl., nur im Sinn von 'Ihr' mit Beziehung auf die Götter gebraucht"; but erroneously *Ar.Forschg.* II,169: "gemeint ist: Du, der du am besten dazu imstande bist." The NP. grammarians call this -vand "i tašbīh (similarity) or i ziyādah (increase)." Here it is not similarity.

The 1.pers. māvant means "my unworthy self," thus in *Y*.46,7: "Who will be given as protector, pāyu, to one as humble as me?" Today one says "bandah, the slave" or "al-faqīr, the poor." For the 2nd pers. one says "ǰanāb i 'ālī, sarkār, haẓrat, high presence etc." MP. renders the 2.p.sg. by "to havand," 2.p.pl. by "šmāχ havand."[6] The word for the 3.pers., hvāvant, only in *Yt.*13,146, lives on in modern language. The passage is a late interpolation into the memorial document and speaks of the "manθra spanta, the revealed word," the lieutenant, ašta, of Ahura-Mazdāh, which Zoroaster has allotted to men as hvāvantam, Bartholomae "als einen wie er selber ist." It means "as master." The real meaning of the passage is expressed, in a slightly different idiom, in the Manichaean frgmt. D278 (*Mir.Man.* II,18, cf. *Altp. Inschr.* 212): "and they receive the nišān (a sealed manθra) from him and keep them with such reverence, as if one would regard as his master, χvd'y, something over which oneself is master, χvyš χvd'vd." hvāvant contains the notion χvadāvand, which itself is the same -vand derivative of χvadāy "autokrator."

In NP. the word appears as χvnd, χ'vnd, χv'nd [beside the comp. with ā- and the short-form χvn]. The *Burhān* explains χvāvand from its usage, not etymologically, as "ṣāḥib, master of the house." It is hvāvant, as courtly expression for "he" in the address. χvand < χvānd is the predicate of the Mamluk sultans of Egypt, and one usually follows Quatremère, *Hist.Sult.Maml.* I,67 and 96, in assuming that the word had been introduced only after Timur, in about A.D. 1400. The earlier use of χvandgār, as predicate of the Seljuks of Rūm, disproves that date; this word is not a short-form, but a syn. of χudāvandgār. The address "yā χvand!" is older. al-Ṣafadī, Ms.Berl. f° 170f., says in the biography of Yelbogha, founder of the mosque in Damascus which bears his name: The young Yelbogha said to the sultan Nāṣir Muḥammad [before 741 H.] when he mentioned 20,000 gold pieces: Sire, yā χvand, I have never seen so much money in one pile!, and the sultan sends him that much money with the baχšiš to be given to the carriers.

Yet earlier, the word appears in the biography of Shīrkūh, ibn Khallikān n° 297, p.121: The prince malik al-ashraf muẓaffar al-dīn Mūsā, son of nāṣir al-dīn Ibrāhīm of Ḥimṣ, explained to ibn Khallikān at Damascus, in 661 H., how he got his name: "My father received the news of my birth returning from the campaign in Anatolia, in ramaḍān

[6] This havand is Aw. "avant, tantus," used with correl. yavant or čivant, which Bartholomae considered as possible neologisms, whilst he remarks to the same, merely aspirated havant of *Vid.* and *Nir.* "eigtl. ihm ähnlich."

627 (July A.D. 1230) and said to al-ashraf Mūsā "Sire, yā χvand, you have one slave more!"; the sultan answered: "Call him after my name!" Therefore these Kurds, the Ayyubids, brought the word with them, which they certainly had learned at the Seljuk court. The meaning has not changed in the 1,700 years from Cyrus to Saladin.[6a]

There is also "servus," e.g. *Y*.32,1: "θwoi dutåho ahāma, we want to be Thy servants!" see under 'Ārmatiš.' And *Y*.29 ends, emphatically, with the words of the "soul of the ox": "Invite us to the wedding, ahāma rātoiš yušmāvatām!, we want to be among the servants of Your Highness!"

The opposition of greatness and own humbleness appears also in verses like *Y*.49,12:

kat toi rtā	zbayantāi avaho
zaraθuštrāi	kat toi vahū manahā
yo vå stōtāiš	mazdā frīnāi ahura
avat ǰāsans	yat vå ištå vahištam

"How little would it matter to Thee, as Rtam, to Thee as Vahumano, to help Zoroaster who is imploring Thee, me, who wants to please Thee with songs of praise, only asking for something that, as the best, is in Thy power!" That means, what is the best for me and an easy matter to you.

> Bartholomae: "Was für Hilfe hast Du, o Aša, was Du, o Vohu Manah, für mich, den Zarathustra, der ich rufe? der ich mit Preisliedern um Eure Gnade werbe, o M.A., nach dem verlangend, was in Eurem Besitz das beste ist?" Most exacting.
>
> Lommel: "Was hast Du durch das Wahrsein, was hast Du durch das Gute-Denken an Hilfe für den Zarathustra, der (Dich) anruft, der ich Euch, o Weiser Herr, durch Lobpreisungen erfreuen will, um das bittend, was nach (entsprechend) Eurem Wunsche das Beste ist (oder: was Eure begehrtesten Güter sind?)." Note: "Andreas betrachtete ištā als instr.sg., vgl. Ai. iṣṭa- n., 'Wunsch,' ebenso *Y*.46,16: wo das χšaθram entsprechend dem Wunsche—ištā—des VohuManah ist."

6a In mod. Persian the king is addressed with "qurbānat mīšavam," or simply "qurbān," may I be thy sacrifice, offering, exactly as in Kassite, fourteenth century B.C. "ikribu," and at the same time the scribe Marduk.muballiṭ calls himself "kiribtu ša ili u šarri, consecrated to the god and the king," viz. Assur.uballiṭ of Assur.

"kat toi" is NP. ba-tu či?, what does it matter to you?, or "what concern is it of yours?" The instrumentals are instr. of quality "you (in your quality) as Vahumano." avaho is governed by kat—cf. *Y*.50,1: kat moi under 'Hāugava'—this in the sense of "quantillum," but put behind zbayantāi, for which an avahe must be supplied from avaho. Cf. Qur'ān 19,21, legend of Miryam: "huwa 'alayya hayyinun, it is an easy matter for Him." Therefore, išta is the normal "have power over."

Bartholomae translated *Y*.46,5: "es wird ihm AhuraMazdāh das (zweite) Leben schenken"; Lommel: "und ihm wird der Weise Herr das Leben geben, er wird ihm durch Gutes-Denken Vieh und Leute fördern." Both fail to hit the character of the sentences: Zoroaster "weaves" into his verses the ancient beggar's cant: A.M. shall give him life! Mazdå dadāt!, = χudā bidihad! Allāh ya'tīk! God will give you! Mazdå ahum dadāt = Allāh yuṭawwil 'umrak!, God make your life—of course not the "second"—long!, Aw. drgaǰyāti and huǰyāti. A.M. as Vahumano shall increase his property and family! Mazdå gēθå fradāt! = Allāh yu'ammir baitak! The Sasanian epistolary guide, Nāmak nipišnīk, says dēržīvišnīh ē ǰān ut āpātīh ē hēr, or dēržīvišn u χvāstak, long life of soul and flourishing of possessions, long life and wealth! Spanish: salud y pesetas!

Andreas translates *Y*.32,9: "Mit diesen Worten, die der Ausdruck meiner Gesinnung sind, o Mazdā"—l'expression de mes sentiments—one cannot help going on "I have the honor to be yours truly," and the verse actually contains something of such polite phrases of an epistolary guide, highly developed in the Nām.Nip.—All these things come under the category of "narma.vak, MP. āpātgowišn, NP. narmgōy, cultivated, polite, courtly speech."

One can include *Y*.33,5 (see under 'Post and Travels'): "I, who wants to call forth your most-high Srōšo at the stage." Srōšo is subaltern, most-high only as servant of the Most-High. For exactly this reason, Xusrau I, the Theos, calls his ambassador θεῖος (Menander, *Exc. de Leg.* II,3). There is nothing "divine" about the ambassador himself. The same style is also Byzantine.

Among the ancient traditional patterns of this poetry are the metaphors taken from racing, often conforming to metaphors in the Veda and in Homer. On our understanding of them depends much besides the Iranian conception of the "aeons," discussed at the beginning under 'Chronology.'

The Husravah legend, *Yt.*5,50 (=19,77) speaks of a race-course:

yat vispānām yuχtānām	that of all teams
azam fratamam θanǰayā⟨ni⟩	I may drive the foremost
ana +tacartām[7] yām drgām	along the long race-course
nava.fraθwrsām razurām	the Nine-round-forest
yat mām mariyo +nrmano	when the slave N. competes
aspēšu +pati.prtati[8]	with me in the horse-racing!

rzurā > NP. lur; the place is to be looked for in Luristan, the region famous for the Nēsaian horses. Nine rounds are the maximum, as the tablets of Kikkuli of Mitanni describe it, see under 'Chronology': nāvartanē važ' anasai̯a. One circuit of the course is a rvēsa, etym. = Gr. ῥοικός and assuming all connotations of Gr. κύκλος, "round, course, cycle." *aspa.rvēsa > NP. asprēs "hippodrome." Another term is "θwarsah, section," whence on the one hand θwarsah as term for the nine millennia of the world's history, on the other the nine θwarsah of the "var i Yamkirt." pati.prtati is "compete, contest."

The MP. term for the paradisiac condition after the end of the world, "apatiyārakīh, being-no-longer-contested," and the old word frašam—always with ellipsis—"beyond (contest by evil)" are taken from the races: the ninth and last turn round the 'meta' is the image of the ninth and last millennium. When the victorious chariots go through the goal, all shout: Yā-ahī!, triumph! To Lat. meta Gr. "terma" corresponds, and "meta vitae, terme de la vie" is the universal metaphor.

From the time of Kikkuli and Husravah to the present day, the style of the yearly races for testing the Turcoman and Arab horses at GümüšTepe near Astarābād in Hyrcania has not changed. One races round the course three, five, seven, and nine times, nāvartanē, only one no longer drives chariots, but rides on horseback. The nine rounds measure together one double parasang or about seven miles. The course, of necessity, is an elongated ellipse, the spina of which measures about

7 Text: čartām, 1 syllable short; archet. ᴛš for tač-, erroneously transliterated by č-.

8 Text: yo, in *Yt.*19,77 yat and prtati: the lines are taken over—as all corresponding ones—from the epic, where they appeared in narrative form, and are deficiently adapted to the meter.

700 yards. One tačara, the length of one round, hence would be over 1,400 yards. *Frhg.Ēv.* 27a says: "biš ētavat hāθram yavat tačaram, two lengths of a hāθra equal one tačara," and the hāθra is determined as "M gām ē do pāy, 1,000 paces at 2 feet," which gives the hāθra exactly the normal length of the spina and the tačara the double of it.

The old myth of Yama's var describes the four sides of this castrum as 1 tačara long; this is actually the size of the qaṣr Balkuwārā in Samarra. *Vid.*2,25, there, writes "1 čartu.drājah," *Pahl.Vid.* "asprēs drahnād, one race-course long," with note: "=2 hāsr." The archetype must have had TŠRTV, with š for č and v in the joint of the compound, read ⁺tačarta.drājah. Tazar remains a placename; one of them, which the early Arabs mention near Dastagird Xusrau, is called hippódromos by the chroniclers of Herakleios.

Another word for race-courses is NP.-Arab. maidān, used, like tazar, as placename. Many towns had several maidān in front of their gates; Aleppo e.g. had four or five, and besides a quarter asprēs. Ibn Shaddād describes a column there, the meta of the antique hippodrome, the shape of which one can imagine from the remark that it had the power of healing urinal troubles. In Iran, the double posts of polo-gates are always phalloid, e.g. the oldest ones preserved on the largest and most beautiful maidān, the one in Isfahan. This maidān, at present the center of the town, was before the Arab conquest outside the south-gate of the old City of Gay, as the name of this gate, bāb asprēs shows.[9]

Thus, asprēs and maidān are synonyms, and both are Iranian words. OIr. maitāna appears as placename in the list of 45 Median chiefs in the Hamadan region who bring tribute to Sargon, when he added the region to his province Parsua, with the seat of administration in Ḫar-ḫār-Nihāwand; *Prism A*: ^{p}is.te.li.ku and ^{p}a.di[r?]ri.pa.ar.nu, bēl alāni^{pl} ša ^{mat}[m]a.i.ta.ni. maitāna is der. of mita, Lat. meta, $\sqrt{}$*mei-[10] and is identical with Ar. ma.i.te.ni in the letter of Saušššatar, founder of the kingdom of Mitanni, to his vassal, the king of Arrapḫa,[11] which is the oldest form of the name of the country, mi.ta.na of the Amarna letters, transformed to mitanni in Akkadian, probably from the Ar.

[9] abu Nu'aim, *akhbār Isbahān* 1,10,l.13: 'sfys inst. of 'sfrys.

[10] Cf. OP. mayūχa, > NP. mēχ, = Akk. zikkatu, and Lat. mūto, which explains the phalloid shape.

[11] E. A. Speiser, JAOS.49, 1929, 269ff., and e.g. Knudtzon, *Amarna* nº.86.

locative. The group of horse-breeding Aryans which segregated from the main body on the way from the Oxus and Iaxartes to Sárasvatī and founded a kingdom in Mesopotamia, called the vast plains—which they reached when leaving the Iranian mountains—"hippodrome," as the syn. asp tāz is used in NP. for an entirely plain country, zamīn i hamvār.

Not a few metaphors in the gatha refer to the races.

Y.50,6:

dātā χratoš hizuvo raθiyam stoi
mahya rāzān vahū sāhyāt manahā

"AhuraMazdāh, who as Vahumano has given me χratuš,[12] will (also) point out the rules that shall be a way for my tongue."

Previous translations differ only in the interpretation of rāzān and sāhyāt. Benveniste takes the verb as absolute, the infinitive phrase as contents of the "proclamation": "Que ses commandements soient la voie de ma langue!" Andreas-Lommel take rāza as object, "the direction," not to rāzar, -°zan, but like paθo sāh in *Y*.34,12; 43,3, or *Ved.* anu.śās: "Damit für meine Zunge eine Bahn sei." Nyberg needs "rāzan, Heilige Regeln" for his "Ordalterminologie."

The rules and the way are those of the "tongue," the language, not "holy," but philological. In *Y*.31,19 Zoroaster says:

rž.uχδāi vačahām χšayamno hizvo vaso

"having full mastery of my tongue as to correct speaking of words." "rš.uχta vaχš, correctly spoken word" in *Yt*.11,3, see under 'Yā-ahī!' "vaso χšayamna," with vaso lit. "as you like," cf. "vaso.χšaθra, absolute ruler"; OP. "manahā hvēpašyahya daršam χšayamna ahmi, over my will I am severely ruling." Full mastery of the language of poetry and its rules means professional study of language. "Way, method," the only thing worth while learning and the only thing a good teacher can give his pupil, is a figure for study the world over. Aw. raθya is—with Lommel—the carriage-way in contradistinction to paθo "foot-path," cf. OI. "rathya, street," MP. rēh, NP. rāh, der. of "raθa, carriage." It was first the race-track, then the highway.

The metaphor goes on in the next stanza, *Y*.50,7: "I will harness for

12 χratu unites power of understanding and volition.

You the speediest racers, the . . . , the broad ones, of Your praise, the strong ones; with them You shall reach the (winning) post, be ready to help me!"

Bartholomae: "Ich will Euch anschirren die raschen Renner, durch die Anregung Eures Preises, die breiten, die starken, o A.M., mit denen Ihr herankommen sollt. Zu meiner Hilfe macht Euch bereit!"

In *Wb.* 604 he remarks to "ǰaya, Anregung": "d.h. sobald der Preis der Götter angestimmt wird, schirrt sich ihr Wagen zur Herfahrt." Jayāiš is obscure, probably an attribute of the horses, similar to "višta(aspa), excited at the start." Lommel-Andreas: ". . . , die durch die Gewalt der Euch (gewidmeten) Anbetung breit(?) (und) durch Wahrsein und Gutes-Denken stark sind. . . ." In the supplement: "(das befremdliche 'breit') allenfalls zu stützen durch Sophokles, *Aias,* 1250: *πλατεῖς εὐρύνωτοι.*" A. v. Gutschmid, in his review of Nöldeke's Tabari translation, explained the surname of Shāhpuhr "dhū l-aktāf, shoulder-man" by *εὐρύνωτος, εὐρὺς ὤμοισιν,* which would be OIr. prθuvarah. Race-horses, too, are not flat-, but deep-chested, but the metaphor of the "song-horses," misinterpreted by Bartholomae, is in fact not driven to that point. Lommel takes mazdå rtā and vahū manahā, in which Bartholomae saw vocatives, as instrumentals, but they mean, as they stand in the verses, "(dedicated to) you Mazdāh as rtam and vahumano."

Nyberg: "Um Euren Siegespreis zu gewinnen, Mazdāh mit Aša, will ich Euch die nutzreichen, raschen, breiten, durch Vohumanah kräftigen Renner anspannen, auf dass Ihr mit ihnen hierher kommen möget; möget Ihr mir zu Hilfe kommen!" And: "Der eine Wendepunkt der Rennbahn ist der Himmel, wo die Götter wohnen, . . . die Hymnen (Pferde) laufen von der Erde zum Himmel, von wo sie als Preis die Götter herabholen, der in den Göttern selbst und ihrer Seligkeit besteht." According to 303, the "Ausgangspunkt, start" of the race course would be the "Urschöpfung," the "Endpunkt" the "grosse Ordal." This concept is derived from Bartholomae's translation, but with a mistake: Germ. "Preis" is (1) price, (2) prize, (3) praise; the Aw. word in the text is vahma, Lat. preces, song of praise, not Aw. mižda, Lat. praemium. The verses do not speak of a "Siegespreis." Moreover, the "Preis" is not won at the "turn" which Nyberg puts in heaven, but at the goal or post; a race course, as the names rvēsa and vartana say, is of necessity a closed curve, Herakleitos: *ξυνὸν γὰρ ἀρχὴ καὶ πέρας ἐπὶ κύκλου περιφερείας*. The tired horses do not draw the chariot back, be it loaded with all the bliss of the gods. Already Kikkuli describes, about 1380 B.C., how they were cared for by their grooms, moved, washed, rubbed and fed.

The song is the chariot in which AhuraMazdāh drives in the shape of his aspects, Zoroaster's verses are the racers. azāθā, too, must stay inside this figure: "With them you shall arrive at, reach. . . ." The god shall help the poet to win "im Kampf der Wagen und Gesänge" (Schiller).

Zoroaster's songs, the gatha, are carmina or rather "odes." Nyberg, 291: "Yasht-Dichtung ist im Kreise um Zarathustra nicht eigentlich zu Hause." In a circle around a poet, the center, the poet, makes the poems. This circle was not a school of hymnbook poets of the 17th century. "Yasht-dichtung" never existed in any circle. The Awestic yashts are not created as such, they became liturgical yashts step by step. If one dissolves, with the acid of criticism, the glue which the diaskeuasts have smeared over the yasht during a long period, the residue consists of fragments of poems and some prose pieces of various kinds, among them mythical, scientific, juridical, bucolic and martial ones, and a few larger parts of hymns to gods, as they may have been sung at many places in different ways. Sometimes, for instance in the Mithra, Tištriya and Vrthragna yashts, one can form an approximate picture of their original whole. But over against the songs of Zoroaster they are all naïve, like a folk song against a work of literature.

The poet was Zoroaster, and around him there were many inca able to do the same, and a few, able to distinguish dāθam and adāθam. The brighter Greeks, yet, called Herakleitos "dark, *σκοτεινός*." With him, Zoroaster has much in common—as to form also with Horace, and one cannot imagine any poems that would have a better claim to the motto: odi profanum vulgus et arceo. Therefore, although his doctrine was officially recognized as a "community, vrzanam," one can only speak of a "Zoroaster community" in the sense one says "Tolstoy, Goethe community." The high dignitaries, all belonging to the court and clan of Vištāspa as head of the younger branch of the Achaemenids, are enumerated in the memorial list of *Yt.*13, altogether 240 names.

Zoroaster calls himself "manθran, poet, inspired singer," and claims to own, beside "sweetness of tongue" just virtuosity and perfect mastership of language. But he does not call himself "prophet" in the sense of "rasūl Allāh," God's envoy.

The claim is justified. The gatha are works of a high art, full of archaic forms acquired by study, but in style and thought entirely individual. This is a quality one rarely finds in Eastern countries, where more artists sign their works than is usual in the Western world, and yet their works look non-individual. Some of the good fragments in the old yashts—the rest, even when not younger than the Achaemenian period, is not worth mentioning—are very typical and conventional, and would be anonymous even when the authors were known by name. But however high and studied the art of the Zoroastrian verses be, they are no longer "classical." Everywhere their art is on the verge of mere virtuosity. To use an archeological term: the gathas are "archaisant," not "archaic."

Some Awestic passages flaunt their "erudition" and "correct language," and though just these are post-Alexandrian, yet what they express is valid for the entire redaction of the Awesta.

*Yt.*3,18 and *Niy.*1,16: "hizvo danhahā manθrāča vačāča šyōθnāča zōθrābyasča rš.uχδēbyasča vāγžbyo."

Bartholomae's translation "mit Zungenfertigkeit . . . und mit richtigen Sprüchen" misses the meaning (cf. *Wb.*681 danhah, 746 √danh-, and 1815 hizu-). Hertel, who in *Beitr.* 28 says: "d.h. mit einem Lied in awestischer, nicht mittelpersischer Sprache," perfectly to the point, yet translates: "mit der Gelehrsamkeit der Zunge . . . und mit leuchtend gesprochenen Worten." rš, in rš.uχδa, means, as always, the "correctness" of speech, here the grammar; and "danhah, to √danh-, docere" is not rhetorical fluency of speech, but science of language, philology, such as the bilingual or trilingual Achaemenian scribes owned, whose serious philological studies enabled them to keep the inscriptions of Darius free from faults—while all others are faulty. *Yt*.3,18 means "with words correctly spoken," e.g. the instr. pl. vāγžbyo of vaχš, according to Bartholomae's phonetic law, in contrast to rš.uχδēbyo.

In *Yt*.5,17 and 104, and *Yt*.9,26; 19,13, the expression hizvo danhahā is also applied to the prayers of AhuraMazdāh and Zoroaster, who both therefore would have known Awestic, as the authors of these verses believed themselves to do. They claimed to be danha, doctores, but, as the examples prove, no longer spoke rš.uχδa, correctly. The false topic name 'airyanəm vaējo vahvyå dātiyayå' places these verses in the time of Vidēvdād I, the 2nd century B.C.

I once came, a little late, to a meeting of a literary society in Teheran. In a large reception room a poet stood on a pulpit, reciting verses in one and the same difficult meter with always the same rhyme. When he had at last finished, a second stood up and continued, and then a third. While I asked myself how such an improvisation and inspiration—eclipsing Firdausī's examination—was possible, the chairman rose and said: "And for our next meeting we prepare this meter and that rhyme!" Agha Furughi expressed more than once his opinion to me that there have been no more poets since Sa'dī and Ḥāfiẓ, which would give a period of almost 2,000 years, with one high point at the beginning and one at the end, and gaps in between.

The opinions about the two dialects, Gathic and Awestic, cannot be expressed in short sentences, and have shifted much since the study of the problem began. But in general it is still admitted today that the Gathic dialect is older than the Awestic which continued as lingua sacra. Unless one would assume that Gathic was an older phase of Awestic, this would mean a change of language and would involve problems of religious history which nobody has even tried to formulate. The assumption of a difference in age is justified only when speaking of the character of the dialects, in the sense in which e.g. the character of the Baltic languages is very archaic, that of German younger, of English still younger. But the conclusion that the Gathic songs were older than the Awestic hymns is totally erroneous. The phase of development, the linguistic character of a dialect does not allow a conclusion as to the date of poems composed in it. The gatha have found a place in young surroundings, the Yasna; the yasht, product of a redaction older than the yasna but younger than the gatha, also include old parts, and these, though in Awestic, not in Gathic, are pre-Zoroastrian, hence older than the gatha.

Meillet, *Trois Conf.* 41, says on the Irish epics: "Si l'on les rapproche des gâthâs . . . , on comprend d'où vient l'obscurité et pourquoi le vocabulaire y fait presque à chaque strophe quelque difficulté . . ." and p.42s, on the lyric verses of the Greek drama and those coming near to prose: "La différence profonde entre les deux parties est soulignée par le fait que les parties lyriques ont une couleur dialectale qui les sépare de la langue courante." By these analogies, Meillet described exactly the relation of the two Iranian dialects.

Treating both dialects as living ones, as is usually done, can be maintained only with strong qualifications. Zoroaster's virtuosity was so superior that he composed his songs in the learned language of an archaic, traditional poetry. Gathic, like Homeric, has never been the common language of any tribe or region. It is the language of poetry. The gatha are carmina, no people and no community. Not even Zoroaster's name belongs to the dialect of his verses.

I wonder whether the quotations from the epics, of the stratum preceding the Husravah legend, could be translated into Gathic, a problem connected with that of the Yasna haftahāti, which perhaps contains also a few epical fragments in Gathic. The Awestic quotations are hardly ever free of metrical and other deficiencies, which might be cured by such a "retranslation." That means it is not impossible that Gathic was the language of the original Epic, and that the fragments were transposed into Median when the quotations were inserted into the yashts.

In the following chapter we shall study some specific terms of this poetical language of Zoroaster, namely yā-ahī, maga, myastra and vahu āgmata, behind which one has looked for deep secrets, but which disclose themselves as the simplest notions and therefore make plain sense of a number of verses, incomprehensible before.

XVI. YĀ-AHĪ!

"Conquer, fortune of the Blues!"

In *Y.*49,9 and 46,14, also *Yt.*11,3, a word yā.ahī appears, the case of which cannot be determined; in *Y.*50,2, after parā, we find the abl. yå.åho; in *Yt.*13,41 and *Y.*36,2 (=58,7) the acc. yā.ahām. The stem is considered to be yāh, which *Wb.* assumes to be the first element of the adj. yās.krt (with compar. and superl.). This adjective appears only at very bad places of *Yt.*13 or worse ones, and may belong together with yaso.brta.—yā.ahī has no true etymological connection.

Bartholomae translates, in *Wb.* "Krise, Entscheidung, Wendepunkt, insbes. eschatologisch von dem entscheidenden 'Schlusswerk,' das den Sieg der ahurischen Welt vollenden wird." Nyberg, 227: "Der Ausdruck 'letzter Wendepunkt der Schöpfung' ist von der Rennbahn hergenommen . . . fällt also mit dem yāh zusammen, das Zarathustra demnächst erwartet. . . . Man pflegt, wohl etwas zu unbestimmt, dies Wort mit 'Krise' zu übersetzen. Wahrscheinlich war es ein gewöhnlicher Ordalbegriff, der seinerseits den entscheidenden Augenblick der Ordalhandlung ausdrückte." A term unknown, but congruent with a term of sport, can "with probability" only be another term of sport.

The word has been totally misunderstood: it is no noun of undeterminable case, but an exclamation, yā-ahī!, the inciting cry at the end-spurt of the races. When Kurds and Lurs yodel their yā-ahī-yā-ahī today, it carries for miles from mountain to mountain.

*Y.*46,14:

zaraθuštra kas.tē rtāvā rvaθo
mazoi magāi ko vā frasrudyāi vašti
āt ho kavā višta.aspo yā-ahī!

"Zoroaster! which faithful one is your friend for the great festival? Who wants to be praised in song? He: kavi Vištāspa, triumph!"

Bartholomae: "O Z.! Welcher Gläubige ist dein Freund für den grossen Bund? Oder wer will dass man von ihm höre? Das ist der k.V. bei dem Schlusswerk."

Lommel-Andreas: "O Z.! Wer ist dein dem Wahrsein ergebener Freund für die grosse (Gabe?) und wer wünscht gerühmt zu werden? Nun, das ist der Fürst V. bei der Entscheidung." Note: "yāhi: yōhi (Andreas)."

Nyberg: "Z., wer ist dir ein aša.gläubiger Mysteriengenosse für den grossen maga? Oder wer wünscht gehört zu werden? Er, der k.V. bei der Krise."

maga is the celebration of victory—see under 'Maga'; √sru-, "recite, praise in song" especially with fra-, as in frasrudyāi, cf. frasruta in *Y.* 50,6. Here and in the following stanza Zoroaster speaks entirely in the figurative language of old poetry, that drew its metaphors mainly from the race sport.

*Y.*49,9:

srōtu sāsnå — +frasanhyo suvē tašto
noit rš.vačå — saram didans drugvatā
yat dēnå — vahištē yujan miždē
rtā yuχtā — yā-ahī žāma.aspa

"He shall proclaim the orders, the herald destined for my salvation, who as a duly-speaking one rejects all fellowship with the drugvant,—when those who are harnessed to rtam shall harness the best prize of victory to the chariot of their faith! Triumph, Žāmāspa!"

Nyberg: "Möge derjenige, der sich (von Vohu Manah) binden lässt, der geschaffen ist heil zu verschaffen, diese vorschriften hören: der recht-redende kümmert sich nicht um Vereinigung mit dem Drug-Anhänger, wenn die mit Aša verbundenen ihre Schauseelen im besten Lohn bei der Krise vereinigen, o Žāmāspa!"

Bartholomae translated the last sentence: "wenn die mit A. verbundenen ihr Ich beim Schlusswerk des besten Lohns teilhaftig machen." Lommel: "wenn sie . . . bei der Entscheidung die geistigen Persönlichkeiten mit dem besten Lohn verbinden." Markwart protested in *Gāth.ušt.* against translating savah by "Nutzen, profit" instead of "Heil, welfare, salvation."

suvē tašto: √taš- is the word for AhuraMazdāh's purposeful creation; cf. *Y.*44,8: "for whom (else) hast Thou destined the cow?" under 'Ārmatiš.' The purpose is here suvē, dat. of "sū, welfare" produced by miraculous power. As term of handicraft √taš- means "to timber." suvē tašto means in Zoroaster's didactic style "because A.M. created, sent him for my salvation," exactly "a godsend."

rš.vačah: "proper, becoming talk." Žāmāspa talks, the verses do not speak of Zoroaster issuing orders. The "commandments," sāsnå, are those of the government, the frasastiš of the preceding stanza, proclaimed by the herald, frasanhya. noit didans: the negation reverses the sense of the verb: "not-wanting" means "rejecting," cf. *Y*.49,3. The "drugvant" is the bandva's tkēšo.

In the preceding stanza, Frašauštra is the fra.išta, envoy, and the question is "which hvētu will obtain the frasastiš for the vrzanam?" Here, the brother, Žāmāspa, is +frasanhya, herald; srōtu, to √sru- "to praise" replaces here √sanh- "to proclaim," viz. the sāsnå (to √sanh-), the order proclaimed by the frasanhya, see under 'Social Structure' and 'Hāugava.'

The play upon the words yuǰan and yuχtā shows that the original sense, the harnessing of the horses to the "yoke," was not lost; cf. *Y*.50,7, where Zoroaster harnesses his verses to the victorious chariot. The rtā yuχtā are the victors, because they are harnessed to rtam. The victor harnesses himself, i.e. his chariot, to the prize of victory, or drives home the prize tied to his chariot; cf. *Yt*.10,38, under 'Mithra': "the cow goes the way of captivity on the raθa of the thieves," tied to their off-driving chariot.

The verses address "those harnessed to rtam" who (lit.:) "harness their faiths (plur.) to the prize of victory." This moment comes when (yat, temp.) Frašauštra and Žāmāspa have obtained the frasastiš, and Žāmāspa announces it as frasanhya.

Y.50,2:

srōta gōšāiš vahištā	āvanēta sučā manahā
ā var nå vičiθahya	naram naram hvahyāi tanuvē
parā mazo yå-åho	ahmāi sazdyāi bōdanto pati

"Hear with your ears, see with your eyes, in Good-Will, come here to us, man by man for his own person, before the great triumph of the decision: it shall become true in our favor, (you) who (shall) perceive it!"

Bartholomae: "Höret mit den Ohren das Beste—sehet es euch an mit dem lichtesten Sinn—für die Entscheidung zwischen den beiden Glaubensbekenntnissen, Mann für Mann für seine Person vor dem grossen Schlusswerk darauf bedacht, dass er es zu unserem Gunsten vollende!"

Andreas: "Höret . . . , sehet . . . , die beiden Wahlmöglichkeiten, die zur Entscheidung stehen, indem ihr darauf achtet, dass jedermann für seine Person uns vor dem grossen Entscheidungskampfe gefalle!"

Nyberg: "Das grosse yāh in *Y.*30,2 ist das grosse Ordalurteil: Höret . . . sehet mit brennendem Sinn (manah) das Beste; kommt hierher zu uns zur Entscheidung, Mann für Mann [ein jeder] für seine Person, darauf bedacht, es für *uns* vor der grossen Krise (yāh) zu vollenden!"

These translations are at variance mainly in the conception of b: Bartholomae: ā varnå; Andreas: āvarnå; Nyberg: ā var nå (with cod. K5). A dual of device or decision is out of the question, Zoroaster does not invite votes against himself. The impers. "ā var nå, come here to us!" is the only possible reading; srōta and āvanēta are equally imperatives, sazdyāi and bodanto have imperative meaning. The instr. vahištā manahā (superl. of vahu manah) refers to the three imperatives. There is no other regens for the gen. vičiθahya but parā mazo yå.åho. vičiθa is "choice, decision," cf. *Y.*33,3 rš višyāta, *Y.*49,6 rš vičidyāi, and tat moi vičidyāi in *Y.*31,5 (Benveniste *Inf.av.* p.81).

sazdyāi: as in *Y.*51,6 "aθā no sazdyāi uštā, thus it shall become apparent for us, if He wills!" cf. under 'Fravarāni.' The verb √sand- means "to become ἐπιφανής, apparent, manifest, reality"; the subject "it" is the decision; the dat. ahmāi is "for us, in our favor." pati.bōdanto is participle, at the end of a stanza, as usual, vocative: "you (who are) perceiving ones, spectators"; √bōd-, "sentire," scil. perceiving (srōta, āvanēta) what shall "become manifest, sazdyāi." pati.bōdanto, hence, means "qui vivra verra," you shall witness the decision in our favor, you all shall live to see the yā-ahī, the triumph.

Of the three Awestic passages only the first, *Yt.*13,41, has some value:

dāθrīš ahmāi vahu hvarno	yo hīš aθā frayazate
kahmāičit yå.åhām ǰaso	kahmāičit anzahām biwivå

The sentence is part of the mythical description of the Fravarti who help in all fights and troubles: "who bring luck to him who implores them constantly, whenever it comes to a yā.ahī, whenever he is in trouble."

hvarnah = tyche, at the end of the 5th century = fortuna, also in the gatha. anzah = anger, anxiety, Germ. "Enge" and "Angst." biwivå, redupl.perf. of √bī- "to become frightened," NP. bīm; its etymological connection with OHG. bibēn > beben, bibbern, to quiver, is contested, but that is the meaning, here and elsewhere.

yā.ahī, again, is the triumphal shouting that accompanies the last spurt in racing. The "pire misère intellectuelle" of the redactors has disfigured also this passage by interpolating "like the orthodox Zoroaster, the iudex of the material world, the koryphè of the two-legged ones, baršnuš bipatištānayå," thereby making Zoroaster the one who lives in a continuous state of fright.

Yt.11,3: rš.uχδo vaχš yā.ahī vrθrajanstamo

The verses speak of the ahunavarya prayer as magic charm, and one must translate: "the correctly pronounced (ahunavarya) word is the most conquering yā-ahī!"

Y.36,2, repeated in *Y*.58,7: Ātarš shall come to meet the worshippers namištahya namahā nå mazištāi yåhām patijamyā, at their "footfallest"[1] footfall at the greatest of yā-ahī!

On a little church in front of the east gate of Ruṣāfa I once discovered an inscription: *νίκα ἡ τύχη 'Αλαμουνδάρου*, "Conquer fortune of al-Mundhir!"[2] In circuses one often finds: *νίκα ἑ τίχη τὸν Βενέτον*, Conquer, fortune of the Blues! There is also Lat. nika.[3] It is the usual cry of applause at the end spurt, the victory in the race. But one finds also *νικα ἡ τύχη τῶν* XP[*ριστιανῶν*], hence the figure under which Zoroaster speaks of his religion applied to the victory of Christianity. In Constantinople and in Syria the spectators—bōdanto pati—shouted níka, in Iran yā-ahī! The exclamation belongs to *ἰήιε Παιάν*, or *ἰήιος*,

1 Text: nąm-, equally worthless whether superl. of namra, nāman, or as I take it, of namah.
2 Cf. *Mshattā, Ḥira und Bādiya* in Jahrb.Preuss.Kunstslg. 1921, 115.
3 PPUAES III,A,3, to inscr. 256. A coincidence: Pers. nīkā for "bravo" is good Persian.

ἰάιος as call of the Apollon of Delphi, or to εὐοῖ. Lat. euhoe, Germ. eia, heia, juchhei etc., and is of IE. age.[4]

The antonym of yā.ahī!, equally old, is Gath. Aw. vayoi, vayū, āvoi, Lat. vae (victis), Got. wai, e.g. *Y*.53,7: "then, vayoi shall be your cry at the very end!" or *Y*.54,6: "to the vayū.brdbyo they serve hellish food," a typical example of Zoroaster's "causative compounds": they cry vayū because such food is served to them. And just as yā.ahī in *Y*.50,2 and in the yasht, vōya, āvōya are inflected like a noun in *Had.N*. and *Vid*. 18,9.

In Psalter, *Ps*.122, avoy is written with inverse d: 'vᴅy, cf. χvslvᴅy = χusrōy. This word occurs also in *Mir.Man*.II,24,11, where the meaning does not fit, and Henning tries "rette!"; it may be Aw. avahē, help!—In *Mir.Man*.II,39,20, Henning translates TPārs. v'y—which can scarcely be anything but vayoi—by "triumph(?)," that is the sense of yā.ahī. There, it might not be synonym, but antonym to "hail!"

When an exclamation "yā.ahī = hurrah!," of which we have discussed all instances, is translated by "crisis," strange concepts are bound to originate, and did so beyond expectation. Nyberg, 194: "Die Gatha 46 ist die Gatha der Grossen Krise," beside smaller nervous crises. 191: "Über die Bedeutung dieser Krise ist eine lange Diskussion geführt. . . ." Representative specimens of interpretations are: "akuter Konflikt zwischen den beiden arischen Hauptvölkern, Iraniern und Indern; oder inner-iranischer Konflikt; a) kulturell: Ackerbauern gegen Nomaden; b) sozial: Klassenkampf der Armen gegen die Herren; c) lokal: West Iran gegen Ost-Iran." p.196: "Halten wir fest: Ausgangspunkt des Streites ist: ein neuer Kult, kombiniertes Hauma- und Stier-Mysterium dringt in Zarathustras Stamm ein. Wer sich in der Nacht mit Hauma berauschte, konnte unmöglich am Tage danach arbeitsfähig sein." 288: "Zarathustras grosse geistige Krise wurde dadurch verursacht, dass der Hauma-Kult . . . sein Werk vernichtete . . . , den er selber in seiner Gemeinde einführte." 201: "Der Angriff des neuen Kultes ist eine le-

[4] Ir. bax bax, Arab. baḥ baḥ has the same sense, whence baḥbūḥa (see under 'Hospitium'). I heard also, in Persia, bah bah! which I regard as the otherwise obsolete pos. vahu, of the compar. bēh < vahya. At any rate it is the same as χvaš χvaš, e.g. in *Art.Vir.Nām*. 3,18. Zamakhsharī, *Lex.Ar.-Pers*. 84: "nīkā nīkā dar waqt i riḍā gūyand, aḥsant aḥsant!" On the so-called baχī-dirham baχ baχ is written like rāst on Sas. coins, or like babbanū, Akk. transl. of OP. naiba (nēv, nīkā) applied to Seleucid coins: "good, of full weight." Stickel, *Bleisiegel*, ZDMG 20 (1866), 346, quotes Fleischer, ZDMG 9, 612, Turk. *Qāmūs:* "everyone who sees these dirhams, because they are unalloyed and good, says: baḥ baḥ!"

bensgefährliche Bedrohung dessen, was der Herzpunkt in der Religion der Gatha-Gemeinde war: des maga-Mysteriums, der Ekstase." 202: "Der neue Kult ist nicht nur negativ schädlich, er enthält auch ein positives Übel, eine neue Mysterienfeier, welche die alte aufhebt. *Das ist die wirkliche Bedeutung der Krise"* (emphasis in the original).

The "real signification" of the "crisis" yā-ahī is "hurrah!" The word was mysterious, but has nothing to do with mysteries.

XVII. MAGA

"Von froeuden hochgezīten
muget ir nu wunder hoeren sagen."

MAGA was more mysterious even than yā-ahī! The accepted translation was "league, Bund," first advanced by Geldner and Justi, without etymology, merely on the strength of *Y*.54,7: "if you desert this maga." Bartholomae defined it (*Wb*.): "Bund, Geheimbund, spez. von der zarathutrischen Religionsgemeinschaft, ein term. techn., dessen eigentliche Bedeutung nicht zu entscheiden."

Messina, *Ursprung der Magier* and Markwart saw in it *Ved*. "magha, gift, present," and interpreted it as the "Zoroastrian religion"; similarly Andreas, as an abbreviation of "vahoš manaho maga, gift of Vahumano," NGGW 1931, III,323. In *Altp.Inschr*. 171, I described it in analogy to the figure of the racing for the victory of religion as a metaphoric expression, referring to something similar to the modern zōrkhānah, half Greek gymnasium, half takiya of dancing darwishes. Nyberg's explanation is, 201: "Das maga Mysterium, Herzpunkt in der Religion der Gatha Gemeinde" and "maga, to √mang-, mag- (1) primarily the 'Sangschar' der Ekstatiker, deren vornehmstes Mittel zur Erreichung der Ekstase der Gesang war; (2) secondarily: der Platz wo sie die Ekstase erreicht, der magisch geschützte Raum für Daemonenaustreibungen." Since demons used to be especially active during a prima nox, in *Y*.51,7 this consummation takes place on that protected area; finally, the "magisch geschützte Raum" alone remains. Darwish exercises are well known to me, with their long hours of "huwe, huwe, huwe," that have the same "virtus dormitiva" as "duce, duce, duce," "cuius est natura sensus assoupire" (Molière). None of these ways leads to cognition.

The rarely used word is not a common term—as e.g. dēnā is—for the religious group around Zoroaster, but its use is restricted to a certain metaphor: wherever the word appears, the verses speak of friends, guests or banquet, praising and singing. The term is solely a figurative one. It appears only six times, the derivative magavan twice. Of these eight instances three are in *Y*.51, two in 53, and there one must look for the solution.

In *Y.*51,7 the exact meaning of maga is plain. The train of thought begins in 51,5:

saχvāni vazamnābyo kanībyo mrōmi
χšmabyasča +vādayamnā manča ī dazdvam

"I will tell commandments for the bridal maidens and for you, bridegrooms, impress them on your memory (and grasp them in your hearts)!"

The many var.lect. of vādayamna lead to archet. v(')dymn, regular caus., lit. "those who lead to marriage" (Germ. "zur Ehe führen"), bridegrooms, as Geldner already foresaw. They must of necessity be mentioned, among other reasons because they are addressed in the vocative, whereas the brides, vazamnā, are spoken of only in 3rd person. Bartholomae's interpretation "mahnend" is as impossible as Nyberg's "(Priester) der mit seinen Kräften (=kraft seines Amtes) zur Ehe giebt." The "giving away in marriage" was done by the "þatiš," in whose "potestas" the girl was, the father who gives away a daughter, or the brother his sister, cf. *Y.*9,23 or upa.vāδaya in *Vid.* 14,15.

St.6 begins: "This is true, you men and women!" What follows is much disturbed by infiltration of glosses. If a charm against demons should be found in these verses, it would be no more significant for the religion of Zoroaster, than the bismillah, the Muslim is supposed to pronounce in the same situation, for the religion of Muhammad.

St.7:

ātča vo miždam ahat ahya magahya
yāvat āžuš zarzdišto bunoi haχtiyå
parā mrōčans ōrāča (rest corrupt, gap)
vizāyaθa magam tam
āt vo vayoi ahati apamam vačo

"Yours shall be the award from this maga, simulatque penis in infima parte femorum vehementissime ardet, prorsum retrorsumque movens— But if you desert this maga, yours shall be cries of woe at the very end!"

The Pahl. transl. had correctly understood the decisive sentence: kā +āzūk rawēt pa bun ē haχt ē zan ku.š hamāk pa tan andar.šavēt bē āyēt. . . . Also Kh. E. Punegar:[1] "and-also unto-

[1] *The Gathas, transl. and summar. by Khodabakhsh Edalji Punegar, B.A.,* Bombay, Taraporevala, in the "S. K. R. Cama Prize Essays."

> you there-shall-be a-reward of-this eminent-act (enterprise) [i.e. maga]. So-long-as the-most-heart-felt passion [i.e. āžuš] is-going off and down into-the-bottom of-the-sexual-organ [there the text becomes incomprehensible: whither reaches the spirit of the wicked . . .]." Nyberg gave already the Latin translation, only omitting parā mrōčans ōrāča, but without recognizing that he had, thereby, the solution of the problem of maga in his hand.

In this passage the meaning "marriage, wedding" of maga is unquestionable. With the prohibition of divorce in st.7, the "Wedding Gatha" ends, and with st.8—as in *Y*.50 with st.6, see under 'Poetry'—a new gatha begins.

Bartholomae remarks: "Die einzige Gatha, von der wir den äusseren Anlass zur Dichtung kennen: es war das Fest der Vermählung Jāmāspas mit Zarathustras jüngster Tochter Poručistā. Bei dem kirchlichen Akt, dem der Fürst Vištāspa, ferner Frašauštra und ein Sohn Zarathustras beiwohnten, wurden noch einige weitere Brautpaare zusammengesprochen." When reading these "Society News" of an old-fashioned provincial paper, one believes one hears the princely guests singing, in church, hymn n° 53, verse 7, which Bartholomae had failed to understand.

Nyberg sees, on the one hand, in vādayamna the priest celebrating the marriage ceremony, but says on the other hand, 27: "In *Y*.53 wird ein Versuch gemacht, eine spezifisch zoroastrische Fruchtbarkeitsgöttin einzuführen, nämlich Zarathustras Tochter Poručistā," against two old rivals, Ardvī and Rtiš; he believes the attempt "suffered shipwreck"—one of the many shipwrecks in the book—because Rtiš "was too deeply anchored," and allows finally the old Ardvī to come out as victress.—The Goddess of Fertility in modern literature is simply sickening.

The rule given about marrying off young girls is preserved in *Vid.* 14,15: "kanyām a.skandām an.upa.itām ⟨nrbyo rtāvabyo rtaya vahvya rune čiθim nisrinvyat dātar . . . kā yā kanyā? āt mrōt AhuraMazdā⟩ hvanha vā duγδa vā nāmani mat gōšāvarā pasča pančadasyam sarδam nrbyo rtāvabyo upa.vāδayanta," "they (scil. the patayo) shall give a healthy virginal maiden, whether her relation be (their) sister or daughter, equipped with earrings, after her fifteenth year, in marriage to orthodox men." This fragment of a civil law code is, in the Vidēvdād, worked into penalties for a blow by which an otter has lost its eyesight, besides many other disbursements in kind, all measured by ten thousands, which the whole Iranian empire at its apogee would never have been capable of delivering.

The "Wedding Gatha" is a few years younger than the memorial list where Puručistā is yet unmarried, but Zoroaster has already a little grandson, Rvatatnara aparazāta, and Žāmāspa has a namesake in a grandson or rather great-grandson, Žāmāspa aparazāta. According to Bartholomae's interpretation, universally accepted and I believe based on the so-called "tradition," Puručistā would have married the elder brother of her grandfather. It is customary to marry at sixty a girl of sixteen preferably, but those are wives of such and such a degree, and Zoroaster could never have given his daughter, and moreover have made a poem, for such a misalliance.

The verses address at least two bridal pairs. Zoroaster's son and daughter are both quite young and marry for the first time. The instruction—even without the "Einschärfer" (incalculator) whom Bartholomae saw in ⁺patyāstim, st.3—cannot be meant for people of sixty, but only of sixteen. If none but the children were mentioned, one ought to conclude that they married each other in hvētuvadaθa. But Vištāspa and Jāmāspa, of the generation of the fathers and grandfathers, can only be present, like Zoroaster himself, as giving away their own children or grandchildren. The children of Zoroaster, hence, did not marry each other.

Both son and daughter are called with double gentilic: zāraθustriš spitāma and spitāmī hēčataspānā. A passage in Mas'ūdī, *murūdj* VIII,60, elucidates what that means: "The insolence of the army of the Zandj was such that women of the house of Ḥasan, Ḥusain, 'Abbās, Hashimites and Quraish, of the most noble Arab houses—abnā al-nās—were sold at auction. The price of a girl was from two to three dirham, and the outcrier shouted: Such and such, daughter of such and such, of the house of such and such!" The double gentilicia of the gatha express that Zoroaster's children marry, as of equal birth, into the families Hāugava and Nōtarya (Haχāmanišiya). Puručistā, here expressly called "youngest" (daughter or child), was a daughter of Zoroaster's third wife, the Hāugavī; the reason for Žāmāspa's presence is that he was her great-uncle and vispatiš of the clan (not that he marries her).

As eligible husband for Puručistā in this circle, only Vištāspa's eldest son Pišišyōθna or Žāmāspa's grandson (or great-grandson) Žāmāspa II are in question. Not much speaks in favor of the first: Vištāspa may be present as giving away a granddaughter to Zoroaster's son (Hvarčiθra); no other reason, but the role, Pišišyōθna plays in the eschatological legend, which makes him the helper of the sōšyant—analogy to Vištāspa as protector of Zoroaster—but also the superior of Hvarčiθra. This feature reminds one of 'Alī, son-in-law of Muhammad, in shi'ite eschatology which borrowed many features from the Iranian: the son-in-law, deified against all historical deserts, is the ancestor of the Mahdī-sōšyant. Žāmāspa's grandson has much better claim: Artaxerxes I married Damaspia-Žāmāspī who may well be a granddaughter of Puručistā's marriage to Žāmāspa II, hence a great-granddaughter of Zoroaster and the Hāugavī (cf. under 'Hāugava').

For the other occurrences of maga and magavan, the signification "marriage," fitting in *Y*.51, is too narrow; it is not the act of marrying, but the ceremony of the "wedding," Germ. "Hochzeit" especially in the wider meaning of MHG. hochgezīte, OI. mahāvrata, festival, celebration.

In *Y*.29,11, end of the "Gatha of the Cow," the soul of the ox speaks, also in the name of the cow:

	āt mā(m) rtā
yūžam mazdā fraχšnanē	mazoi magāyā patizānta
ahura nū nō āvar	ahāma rātoiš yušmavatām

"You, Mazdāh, honor us by letting us be guests at the great celebration, come, we want to be of your Highness' servants!"[2]

The style is courtly, the soul of the ox speaks like a servant, only "nū nō āvar," an imperative, Arab. ta'āl!, come here, do it! seems to be intentionally unpolished. In Tabari III,1544, Bāikbāk, leader of the Turks of Samarra, says to the caliph al-Musta'īn in Baghdad: "If you really have pardoned us, then come and ride with us to Samarra, the Turks are waiting for you! The Ṭāhirid Muhammad b. 'Abdallah gives somebody a wink, and the man gives Bāikbāk a cuff on the mouth, saying: Is that the way to speak to the Commander of the Faith-

[2] fraχšnanē and patizānta see under 'Hospitium' and 'Myastra.'

ful? You are to ride with us! Musta'īn laughed and said: Those are a pack of barbarians, qaum min al-'udjm, they have no idea what one may say and what not" (dāθam and adāθam).

Y.46,14 (text under 'Yā-ahī!'): "Zoroaster, which faithful is your friend, rvaθo, for the mazoi magāi, the great festival, who wants to be praised in song? He, kavi Vištāspa, io triumphe!"

rvaθa is hospes as well as xenos; the dative of intention "for the festival" means "invited or inviting to" the celebration of victory, at which one eats, drinks and sings odes or panegyrics. rvaθa is here equal to magavan.

Y.51,11: "Who is the Spitāma Zoroaster's friend?" with rvaθa in the sense hospes; "ko vā vahoš manaho +āčisto magāi ršvo, which high one is ready for Vahumano's festival?"

ršva designates the high rank, OP. tunvant. Vahumano, as always, has the twofold meaning Good-Will as way of thinking and as aspect of AhuraMazdāh. āčista, if to čiθ-, is "persuaded," if to √čit-, "intent," cf. √ciš- "promise"; at any rate, it means accepting the invitation. Nietzsche: "Freund Zarathustra kam, der Gast der Gäste." The names of the "high ones" follow: not the kavi Vēhviyo who rejected Zoroaster, but kavi Vištāspa, the hvētu Hāugava, and others.

Y.51,16:

tām kavā višta.aspo	magahya χšaθrā nansat
vahoš padbiš manaho	yām čistim rtā manta
spanto mazdå ahuro	aθa nō sazdyāi uštā

"Kavi Vištāspa has obtained her by the banquet of (or: by being guest at) the festival on the paths of Vahumano, her, the čistiš, whom as rtam the holy AhuraMazdāh has devised. Thus it shall become apparent (reality) for us, as He wills!"

Čistiš is "cognition" and AhuraMazdāh's partial figure, devised by Zoroaster, and substituted, by him, to Ušå, the Dawn.[3] At the end of this gatha Zoroaster offers to these high ones his songs as sacrifice and circumambulates them in worship with his songs of praise.

"magavan" expresses "belonging to the maga."

[3] See χšaθra under 'Hospitium,' and cf. Y.32,9 "where Cištiš will be at home" under 'Myastra.' uštā = "if God wills" see under 'Fravarāni' and 'Yā-ahī!'

*Y.*51.15:

hyat miždam zaraθuštro magavabyo čoišt parā

"the award, Zoroaster has promised the magavan, celebrators."

*Y.*33,7:

yā srūyē paro magavano

"that it may be praised (extolled) also outside the magavan, the celebrators."

While in *Y.*51 maga has the narrower meaning "marriage," at all other places it is "wedding" in the wider meaning, like γάμος in the parable *Matth.* 22 (see under 'Hospitium'). It is a celebration, part of which was singing and music, as in Greece and Arabia. maga is far from being a technical term for Zoroaster's community, but solely a metaphor: just as racing serves as figure for his strife, so the celebration as figure for his success.

magavan appears in the Rgveda. In Hertel's translation, *Siegesf.* 142, RV. v,16,5 says: "Bei seinem Preise sind die Reichen in der Freundschaft des Agni."

Die "Reichen, maghávanaḥ," are the magavano. "In der Freundschaft sein"—opp. to Lat. essere in odio, to be hated—means "to be loved." The gathas use the same idiom: *Y.*43,10 "parštā ahma, to be in-the-question," i.e. such that are to be questioned, judged; or *Y.*32,8 "θwahmi vičiθoi ahmi, I am in-separation by you," i.e. you must separate me from, cf. Benveniste, *Inf.av.* 33. "Bei seinem Preise" corresponds to "yasnē pati" in the last stanza of *Y.*51,22:

yahya moi rtāt hača vahištam yasnē pati
vēdā mazdå ahuro yoi āharča hantiča
tām yazāi hvāiš nāmaniš pariča ǰasāi vantā

"To whom, for my sake, A.M. through [the mouth of] Rtam has destined paradise 'at' (as reward for) their yasna,—those who were and those who are—those I want to circumambulate with songs of praise!"[4]

Accordingly RV.v,16,3 means: "the maghávanaḥ are treated by Agni as friends (rvaθa=guests) when [occasion and reason] they praise him" [by yasna and vahma]. The conformity between the Vedic and

[4] The stanza is the origin of the "yahya hātām," see text under 'Dēva.'

the Gathic concept and wording proves that the whole notion comes down from high Aryan antiquity. Only traces survive in India and Iran. Those who participate in the maga, the magavan, are men who celebrate; songs are always mentioned in the neighborhood of maga. It is therefore possible that maga belongs to √mang-, as Nyberg assumed, only in a different sense.

√mang- appears only as mimaγžo in Y.45,10:

tam nō yasnāiš	ãrmatoiš mimaγžo
yo anmani	mazdå srāvī ahuro

These verses stand in parallel with Y.45,8:

tam nō stōtāiš	namaho āvivršo
āt hoi vahmān	dmānē garo nidāma

And 45,9:

tam nō vahū	mat manaho čiχšnūšo

(8:) "trying to win Him with hymns of prosternation, for Him we want to lay down our songs in the store-house (of heaven)," (9:) "trying to be obedient to Him together with Good-Will," (10:) "wishing to glorify Him with offerings of Ārmatiš, Obedience." Zoroaster's sacrifices are never sanguinary ones, but his songs. "Sacrifices of Ārmatiš" means "Obedience to the law, replacing sacrifices." Bartholomae *Wb.*: mimaγžo, desid.praes. "zu verherrlichen suchend, sva. feiern." In this way, maga, to √mang- "celebrate," is directly "celebration, festival," the main part of which was originally singing, song.

This touches the problem of mąza in Gath. mązā.χšaθrā Y.49,10 (and in mązā.rayi, Y.43,12). With its striking nasal ą, it might *not* be the "normal form of composition of mazant, great," an interpretation that rests on the assumption "χšaθra to √χši-, rule, empire," whereas it is "χšaθra to √χšan-, banquet, hospitality" (see under 'Hospitium'). As in Y.45,8 the vahma are laid down in the garo dmānē, so in Y.49,10 the mązā.χšaθrā are laid down[5] together with the "souls" of the faithful, their prayer, namah, and their obedience, ãrmatiš. It is tempting to attach +mangza (? with ą for ang) to √mang-. On the other hand, with manza = mazant, one may compare Skr. mahā.vrata.

In *ZAirWb.* 152, Bartholomae quoted, from F. W. K. Müller, the

[5] In parallel with "īžā, draught of health" and "nectar and ambrosia," see under 'Harvatāt.'

Turfan frgmt. (=*Mir.Man.* II,14,18): "pas dušmēnān [1]spaχr virāst srōd u nuvāg ē vas, thereupon a banquet was served up by the enemies, much music and song; the besieged looked at it covetously." Salemann *Manichaica* IV,45 took spaχr as "Täuschung, tricks" in the sense of "Gaukler, Akrobaten u.dgl" (jugglers, acrobats). The passage of *Ayātk. Zar.* §§41-42, quoted by him, does not at all support this interpretation (see under 'Industries'). Henning accepted it, *Mir.Man.* II. Whether Bartholomae's etymology "to us + pačati = Festmahl" is right or not,[6] the word must contain the idea of eating, for at nothing else would the besieged look "covetously."

The place decisive for the understanding of maga is st.7 of the "Wedding Gatha"; maga means just that: "wedding." In Zoroaster's style it means as much as and not more than γάμος in the parable of the wedding in *Matth.* 22. As metaphor for the acceptance of the religion, the wedding-feast with its celebrating guests is an analogy to the expression "sar, connubium, with Vahumano"; "vahoš manaho maga" would be exactly the same: to live in sar with Vahumano. In a broader sense maga is Gr. ἑορτή, and "maza maga" corresponds to Skr. "mahāvrata, the great festival, hochgezīte." Nietzsche: "Die Hochzeit kam für Licht und Finsternis."

[6] Not to be confounded with spēhr, spihr < spayaθra, but perhaps connected with a corrupt word, in incomprehensible context, in *Y.*51,6, transcribed by Bartholomae by ++hōiš piθa+, to be read hišpiθa, redupl. perf. of √ spiθ-.

XVIII. MYASTRA

"Nun feiern wir das Fest der Feste,
Freund Zarathustra kam der Gast der Gäste."

*Y.*46,14 (under 'Yā-ahī!') "Zoroaster, which faithful one is your friend for the great festival, who wants to be praised in song?" goes on:

yāns.tu mazdā	hadmoi minaš ahura
tān zubayā	vahoš uχdāiš manaho

"Those whom Thou, A.M. wilt gather(?) in the same house (with Thee), those I will announce with words of Good-Will!" The great triumph, yā-ahī!, is celebrated in AhuraMazdāh's house, and in continuation, the train of thought passes to the contrary, to hell, where the drugvant are "haθyā astayo, fit guests" for the table of Ahriman.

zbaya- (the meter requires zub/vaya-) means "to cry, call out," OP. patiyazbayam, done by a herald. Zoroaster will announce—not only "He, kavi Vištāspa!"—all the entering guests, rvaθa. The metaphor is full of court ceremonial. In *Vid.*19,30, also in *Art.Vir.Nām.*XI, it is Vahumano, Good-Will, himself who greets the souls with Welcome! as mihmāndār or andēmānkar. There is no difficulty, except the hapax "minaš," for which the context requires the meaning "to gather, receive hospitably" or the like.[1]

The idea of the same festival recurs in *Y.*30,9:

ātča toi vayam hyāma	yoi im frašam krnavan ahum
mazdåsča ahuråho	ā myastrā barana rtāča
yat haθrā manå bavat	yaθrā čistiš ahat mēθā—

"We want to be those who make this world beyond (contest), Mazdāh and you other ahura, and Rtam, grant hospitality, so that the souls may come together in the house where Čistiš will be!"

Bartholomae: "Und die möchten wir sein, die die Menschheit tauglich machen! Mazdāh und ihr andren Ahuras, heran

[1] Bartholomae, at first, in *Ar.Forschg.* II,170, defined minaš as "2.sg. pres.act. Ar. *minaχš-, cf. mēχtan." This √mič-, mēk-, cf. Hübschmann, *Pers.Stud.* 9, is represented by mēkant, *Y.Haft.*38,3, "the mingling (not, *Wb.*1104: hervorsickernd), gathering, forthflowing waters, in which is good swimming, good bathing." Later, *Wb.*1190, Bartholomae put minaš as nasal pres. to √myas-, a verb else only attested by the obscure həməmyāsaitē in Y.33,1, in *Pahl.Vid.* hām ya saitē, which refers to the hamēstagān gāh, the purgatory. In *Sas.Recht* III,33, he put hamēst (which can hardly be separated from +ham.myāsatē), as part.perf.pass. to "the verbal base in myastra." This he connected not with √myas-, but with √mid-, in Aw. hamid.pati. I conjecture that minaš belongs to this group.

(kommt)! Eure Bundesgenossenschaft gewährend, auf dass die Gedanken sich sammeln, wo die Einsicht noch schwankend ist!"

Andreas: "- - -, die dieses Leben zu einem herrlichen (oder: Wunder) gestalten. O A.M. und ihr andren Herren, und Du, Rt., gewährt euer Bündnis, damit sich die Gedanken auf einen Punkt richten, wo die Einsicht falsch ist!"

Nyberg, 144 (cf. 226, 228): "damit die manah (pl.) dort zusammenkommen, wo die Paargenossin (Doppelgängerin) Čisti ist." Thereupon follow reflections on the divine powers, simple or combined as plural, which dissolve themselves, totally or partially, in the highest god, moreover on doubles.

The frašam-making takes place after the great yā-ahī!, at the end of the ninth millennium. It is always again the same metaphor of the race course: the frašakrtiš, apatiyārakīh is the condition after the races, when the world, itself the struggle of good and evil, will be "beyond (struggle)." After the contest comes the feast with eating, drinking and singing. In *Y.*49,9 (under 'Yā-ahī!') it is the dēnā (pl.), the faiths of the faithful that carry home the victory harnessed to their chariots; in *Vid.* 19,30 they are called "ruvano, souls, lives"; here "manah, mentes." They gather at the festival at which AhuraMazdāh is present, in all his garments, especially as Rtam, granting societatem—"hospitality," not alliance, confederacy—myastra barana. Andreas read ⁺maistra; OP. would be *misθ^ra > misa; the meaning is "party, Gesellschaft."

The guests are here the manah, there the dēnā; host is here the one who is myastrā barana, in 46,15 he who minaš hadmoi, receives in his own house: the date, too, is the same: the 1.1.9000. The address cannot possibly have been lacking: "where Čistiš is mēθā[-]" corresponds here to "hadmoi with AhuraMazdāh." The word is one syllable short; the Pahl.transl. is "andar mēhan, at home."[2] Čistiš replaces Ušå-Eos with Zoroaster, and Eos' house Ušidam is known; Mithra, too, gets a mēθanam "apportioned" by AhuraMazdāh on the High Harā, see under 'Mithra.' The final -ā in Arsacid script is hardly distinguishable from -NY; the text which the Pahl. transl. used had MYTNY = mēθanē, andar

[2] Nyberg, 143: "maēθa, fehlgedeutet als "schwankend, wandelbar," heisst immer "paarweise verbunden," "maēθā, Paar."

mēhan, and "mēθanē" must be restored. In Odyssey xii,3, dancing took place in the house of Eos.

The verses describe the feast in heaven after the victory of Good over Evil, at the end of the world, and this metaphor is continued in the next stanza, *Y*.30,10:

adā zi ava drǔjo	bavati skando spayaθrahya
āt āsištā yōǰante	ā hušitoiš vahoš manaho
mazdå rtahyača	yoi ⁺zaznatē vahāu sravahi

"Then, collapse of the vault of the druχš will come to pass, but those will partake of the promise of the fair abode of Vahumano, Mazdāh and Rtam, who in (their) good reputation are deemed worthy (of it)."

Andreas: "Dann wird stattfinden jene Zertrümmerung des Glückes der Lüge, dann werden der Verheissung auf die gute Wohnung des Guten-Sinnes, des Weisen und des Rechts, diejenigen teilhaftig werden, die im Besitze des guten Rufes sind."

The two last lines speak once more of dwelling in heaven, the house of AhuraMazdāh. To dwell in the same house with him is promised to the pious.—Where āsišti appears for the second time, in *Y*.44,9, see under 'Hospitium,' it is equally associated with the ršvā χšaθrā, the "high halls" of paradise.

The pious are qualified by the rel. clause "yoi ⁺zaznatē vahāu sravahi, who are deemed worthy"; Pahl. transl. nāmakīh, for the loc. vahāu sravahi. This expression alludes to hāusravaha, the worldly, epical fame, and means the ethically good reputation. Andreas followed Bartholomae's explanation of zazanti (*Wb*. 1795 and *Grdr.*): "redupl. them. praes. of √haz-, sie halten fest, die sich guten Ruf erwerben." Except for zazvah and its superl. zazuštama, no form ascribed to √haz- is free from objections. The clause yoi zazanti/ē āsištā yōǰantē hušitoiš expresses a similar thought as fraχšnanē magāya patizānta in *Y*. 29,11, viz. to be deemed worthy to partake of the maga, or here of the hušiti. In the parable of the wedding, *Matth*. 22,8: "they which were bidden were not worthy." Cf. the noun patizanti and *Yt*.15,36 patizantā in the nmāna of Vištāspa, under 'Nōtarya.' Tedesco explained to me that in reading ⁺zaznate the form can be attached to √²zan-, *γιγνώσκω*.

The first sentence of the stanza must stay inside the same picture: while the pious move into heaven, something corresponding to heaven, but belonging to the Druχš collapses, her spayaθra. Though not recognized, this is a well known word: TPahl. 'spyhr, in BPārs. usually spelled sp'hl for spyhl, all = spēhr > NP. spihr "vault of heaven," see under 'Astronomy.' The "vault" of the Druχš is the same as her "hēθa, prison" in *Y*.46,6.

In *Y*.30,9, Mazdāh and his partial figures are "hosts" in the house of Čistiš. AhuraMazdāh minaš hadmoi, i.e. gives hospitality, is receiving the guests in his own house, and Vahumano is greeting them like a mihmāndār. The ēθrapatiš Manθravāka, son of Sāimužiš, bears in the Memorial Document *Yt*.13,105 the second title "hamidpati." He follows in the list upon the family of Vištāspa and the Hāugava, and precedes Rtastu, the son of Māδyomåha, cousin of Zoroaster, who in *Y*.51,19 is described as Spitāma, and in *Yt*.13 follows Zoroaster as the very first. Manθravāka, hence, was one of the very great ones among those around Vištāspa and Zoroaster. As ēθrapati > hērbaδ he was a magus, hence an aryaman, client of Vištāspa. The magi were judges, priests and financial officers. Vištāspa had his ēθrapatiš > hērbaδ just as Cambyses had his tkēša = mōbaδ in Gōmāta. The late legend transforms the client, nōtaryāno, into Mahrōk·ē Nōδarān, son of Nōδar. Together with Vištāspa and Māδyomåha he was drawn into the apocalyptic literature, cf. *Altp.Inschr.* 85,2; 135f., and as Mahrōk, son of Huvahm[3] he became one of the magi who came to Bethlehem. Finally, in the Kārnāmak, the wise Kēt (or Kēhan) ē Hindūkān, prophesies Ardašīr that only a descendant as well of Ardašīr as of this Mahrōk—there called "ē anōšakzātān"—could become monarch of Eran.

Bartholomae abandoned a former interpretation of hamidpati, the second title—*Grdr.* §§264, 268: "Herr des Brennholzes, OI. samít.pāṇi," whence Lommel's "Flammenherr"?—and advanced "Meister der (Gelehrten) Genossenschaft," where the scholars for once would be indispensable. hamid without object is no "society," but a social meeting; as chief of this activity the man is the mihmāndār, maître d'hôtel of

[3] Instead of "father of Vahmēdāta." There are no other names formed with vahma, except Ass. wamitiaršu < *vahmayat.ṛša-, the EN.ER, dahyupatiš of Media under Esarhaddon at the time of the foundation of the Median empire.

Vištāspa, a financial officer. As ēθ^{r}apati, considering his prominent place in the list, Manθravāka was surely the mutawalli of the waqf, the leading priest of the memorial fire founded by Vištāspa, and as hamidpati he was his mihmāndār. In both qualities he must have had business with Zoroaster ever since Vištāspa gave him hospitium.

Both myastra and hamid must be attached to a root √mid-.

A synonym of hamid.pati would be OP. *misθ^{r}a.pati. That is the origin of a name which has harassed me since my first journey through that region in 1906: Μασσαβατική, Μεσσαβάται, Arab. māsabadhān. The occasional Arab. spelling with māh- is merely an assimilation to the many names formed with Māh = Media. Μεσσαβάται, māsabadhān is not one of the frequent compounds with -pāta,[4] but one with -pati, scil. *mēsbaδ, māsbaδ < OP. *māisθ^{r}apati, vrddhi of *misθ^{r}apati.[5] The same office is called in MP. NP. χvānsālār "dapifer, High Steward." The n.pr. Μασαβάτης in Plutarch, *Artox.* 17 may be that title.

Therewith the name of Darius' general in *Beh.* §§29, 30, Vahumisa, *Pap.El.* VHVMYS, Gr. 'Ωμίσης, is explained: OP. *vahu.misa < *vahu.-misθ^{r}a. He "bewegt sich," it is true, "auf den Höhen der achaemenidischen Gesellschaft" (Nyberg, 403), but that is not the meaning of the name, but "(cui) Vahu(mano) societatem (praebet)," with the same abbreviation of vahumano to vahu as in the name of Darius.

As derivatives of √mid-, myastra, mistra, misa and hamid belong together with Aw. myazda, Ved. miyédham, MP. myazd "meal."[6] The Median form appears probably in the names Amístrēs and Amḗstris "he or she who keeps a good table." *kitāb al-Aghānī,* 14,113: "Shāriya (the singer, pupil of Ibrāhīm b. al-Mahdī) used to visit Hārūn b. Shu'aib al-'Akrī, whom she called 'my father.' He was the cleanest of Allah's creatures as to his table, mā'ida, and the most generous in all things,

[4] Atropates and the country Atropatene, *ātarpātakāna > āδarbāijān; also *Tab.Peut.* Thermantica, i.e. Ο⟨υ⟩ερπα⟨ν⟩τικα, *vrd(a)pātakāna > Gulpāigān, cf. vrdpt as name or title, and vrdptkn as patr. or nisba in the Ka'ba inscription.

[5] To "b" cf. miθrapāta, already in Herodotus, time of Cambyses, and in Xenophon, Μιθροβάτης; also 'Ορoντοβάτης, satrap of Karia in Arrian I,23, II,5,7, but on his coins 'Ροοντοπάτης, rvantapāta, important for the reality, contested by Andreas, of the OIr. anlaut rv-.

[6] In *Sūr Āfr.*: "mēh u vēh kē yazdān pat ēn myazd arzūk kirt, the good and great whom God has invited to this meal." The word goes on in NP. in the artificial forms miyāzd, mīzād, Genuine is mēz, syn. of χvān "table, meal," with deriv. "mēzbān, host," mēzbānī, syn. of mihmānī, hospitality," explained by ḍiyāfat; and many more. myazda > MP. myazd > NP. mēz shows zd > z, cf. H. W. Bailey, BSOS,VII, 85. √mid- may help to explain OP. "hamaspāθmēdaya, muster of the army," as foreseen by R. Roth, ZDMG, 1888, 706, cf. *Altp.Inschr.* s.v.

and had a house in Samarra, in which was a great garden." And ibn al-Athīr concludes his great Chronicle: "On the 12th of rabī' I, 628 (18. 1.1231) died at Aleppo my friend, abu l-Qāsim 'Abdalmadjīd al-'Adjamī. He and his family were the leading persons of the Sunnites of Aleppo. He was a man full of muruwwa, virtus, and loved to live well. Who had ever a meal with him, loved him. . . . Allah award him amply in His mercy!"

XIX. WELCOME

"Willst du in meinem Himmel mit mir leben,
So oft du kommst, er soll dir offen sein!"
—Schiller

*Y.*44,8: kā mo ruvā vahū rvāšat ⁺āgmatā

The stanza begins: "This I ask Thee, answer me truthfully!" and the short sentence is that question. At the first glance one recognizes: "Will my soul with vahu āgmata . . ."

In modern language the everyday greeting is χoš āmadī, and NP. χoš replaces old vahu. ā.gmata is NP. āmad, part.perf. of √gam- "to come," with prev. ā "to arrive." Obviously, vahu āgmata is "welcome, willkommen, bienvenu, benvenuto" and so in almost all languages. vahu-āgmata is a variant of vahya.gmata "welcome," as n.pr. in the memorial list, and Behāmaδ as name of one of the Three Magi.[1]

The pos. vahu disappears from the language, unless it survives in the exclamation baḥ baḥ! χvaš χvaš!, perhaps because the word was unusual in OP. In the salutation "drva, whole, healthy" takes its place. IPārs. and TPārs. have "drvɒst 'vr, lit. well-come," with 'vr (cf. nū nō āvar! in *Y.*29,11) as imperative of the threefold suppl. system part. 'mt, pres. 'y; as n.pr. drust.āmad. The farewell is correspondingly pa-drōδ! < druvat, Arm. drvat, < Aw. drvatāt, the abstr. noun instead of the superl. druyist in the welcome; Aram. bišlām = ἐν εἰρήνῃ, Lat. salus, salutare. Yāqūt 1,677,22 translates the archaic NP. hilēδ va-drōδ by ḥallūhā bi l-salām!

In *Vid.*19,31, Vahumano asks the souls that enter paradise: "kaθā iδa rtāvan no āgato?, how have you, faithful, arrived?" Wolff-Bartholomae's translation "Wie (ist's geschehen) aša.Gläubiger, (dass du) hergekommen (bist)?" makes of the "how do you do?" a "how did you do it?", an inconvenient expression of surprise instead of a welcome. The souls do not even reply as much as "vahu," but "go satisfied" by the hearty welcome straight to AhuraMazdāh's golden throne. *Ōgmadēča* 10 says: "yātakgowb bavāt pa ravān ē avē ē anōšakravbān vahman ē amuhraspand u handēmān ē ohrmizd bavāt, advocate (interceder) for the soul of the blessed ones will be Vahman, the amuhraspand, and he

[1] The spelling is one of the many unwieldy and cumbrous ones in the Awesta. The majority of codd. has urvāšaṭ āgəmaṭ tā, K5 better urvāšat āgəmaṭtā. Tedesco wrote to me: "The grammatical value can be as well nom.pl. as sg. or instr.sg. of a neutr.abstr."

will lead them to the presence of Ohrmizd." Vahumano acts as handēmānkarānsālār, exactly as Zoroaster in *Y*.46,14: "Those whom Thou A.M. wilt gather in the same house (with Thee), those I will announce with words of Vahumano!"

In *Art.Vir.Nām.* 10,2 the souls of the blessed "drvt pvrsynd v 'pryn 'ḤDVN.d, ask after Artavirāz's health, get a blessing" as answer, and then say the same words of greeting as Vahumano in *Vid*.19,31. In the next chapter, XI,8, Vahumano himself greets Artavirāz with "namāz o tu, artavirāz, drust-āmat, prosternation to you, welcome!" and again the words of *Vid*.19,31. He then leads him into AhuraMazdāh's presence, dēmān, who is surrounded by the amuhraspandān, archangels. Qur'ān, 39,73: "The gates of paradise shall be opened and their keeper [in *Art. Vir.Nām.* Srōš and Āδar] says: Hail, you were good, enter for evermore!" This is followed by "You shall see the angels circumambulating the Throne!" Thus Islam has adopted the Zoroastrian notion.

The more so it is this reception which Zoroaster himself has in mind in *Y*.44,8. The understanding of vahu āgmata decides at the same time the correct reading of the verb and the case of vahū āgmatā: rvāšat is right against rvāχšat of several codices: s-aor. of √rvāz-, "laetari, to rejoice at" with the cause in instr. Hence, āgmatā is instr., the exclamation itself, vahuāgmata! is inflected like yā-ahī!, āvōya![2] "kā" is the particle of interrogation. Thus the question is: "Will my soul rejoice at 'welcome!'?"

> Bartholomae: "Wie wird meine Seele des beglückenden Guts teilhaftig werden?" with āgmatā as 3.p.pret.med. and rvāχšat "acc. sg. n. of rvāχšant, adj. aus einer Basis, die mit urvād- und urvāz- verwandt ist," *Wb*.1542. Together with this rvāχšant, the support for other semantic definitions falls. Nyberg, 158, recognized rvā(χ)šat as verb, but attached it to √rvag-.

Other places where √rvāz- appears, speak equally of the admission into paradise, e.g. *Y*.50,5, where AhuraMazdāh is named in a, and b says

yat yušmākāi manθranāi vavrāzaθa

[2] In agreement with the inflection of short proverbs, cf. Y.29,7: tam āzutoiš (gen.) manθram gavoi, χšvidamča (acc.) huhuršēbyo, under 'Harvatāt'; and Y.49,2: dōršt: ahmāi stōi ārmatim! (acc.) under 'Bandva' and 'Ārmatiš.'

The verb is 2.p.perf. of √rvāz-. In d the god makes "zasta.ištā, a wink"; beckoning with the hand is a mudra, thus called in India, or something like pollice verso and recto in the Roman circus. This mudra of the judge is the permission to enter: from vavrāzaθa the thought leaps at once to paradise, and the perf. of rvāz- must have a more intense meaning than Bartholomae's "freundlich gesinnt sein," rather NP. qabūl kardan, "to agree, approve, sanction," Arab. taqabbal Allāhu minhu, or "riḍā, being well pleased": *εὐδόκησα* in *Matth.* 3,17.

Y.31,1, text under 'Ārmatiš': "If only the hvētu, vrzana, aryaman and the dēva (gods) would strive to obtain AhuraMazdāh's rvāzman, then He would say: We love your obedience, Ārmatiš, she be ours!" There the god accepts, with rvāzman, graciously, the offer of gods and men, just as Allāh 'accepts' men and their work. The words he speaks express this rvāzman, are his rvāχš.uχti, "word of greeting."

Y.30,1: "I will speak . . . of the rvāza, grace [if from god to men, if vice versa 'delight'] which he who takes it [my words] to heart, will perceive [darsata, "live to see, erleben"] together with the luminaries [of heaven in paradise]."

It is hard to believe, but this simplest of all questions ("Will my soul rejoice at welcome?") has been made by Nyberg the "cornerstone" of his "Theory of Ecstasy": "Wie wird meine Seele verzückt werden mit der Schar der guten Angelangten?", 159: "vohū āgmatā kann nichts andres bedeuten als 'der gute Angelangte,' in kollektiver Bedeutung 'die Schar der guten Angelangten,' die seligen Abgeschiedenen, die in VohuManah's Welt gelangt sind." 158: "Die guten Angelangten ist das Kollektiv der Toten des Stammes; also: Wie wird meine Seele eine solche ekstatische Vereinigung mit VahuManah gewinnen, dass das Ziel damit erreicht wird." At another place one learns that the "Ziel" is "not to forget a previous vision." "Verzückt werden, to be enraptured" is not a higher degree of "rvāz-, joy," but is extracted from rvāχšat to √rvag- "to wander": "Wandern bedeutet die Vereinigung mit VahuManah in der Ekstase: der Ekstatiker, nicht der Tote geht über die Činvat-Brücke." Ātarpāt, who knew the Awesta, for he wrote it, says in his *Andarz* 139: "Though he live a hundred years, at the end every man must go the way to the bridge."

√vrag- is only attested by rvāχšat, 3.pl. s-aor., in *Y*.34,13, to OI. vrajati "procedit." rvaṭ.čaya in *Yt*.13,11 (22 and 28) translated in *Wb.*, under wrong presumptions, by "wieder verbinden," is a causative, describing what the Fravarti do to the embryos, something like "make grow, develop." An interior -t.č- is always a wrong spelling for an unusual orthography of the archetype. If тš = č, the stem may be vrak-, to be connected with the hapax rvāχra in *Yt*.19,69, anton. of ōta "cold," hence "heat," as verb "to heat." Hertel, *Venus* 41, translates "bei den Auseinanderkochungen werde ich mit Glut erfüllen"; for "Auseinanderkochung" read "pregnancy." Perhaps the warmth of the body was conceived as an inner fire, causing and preserving life. If -т.š- stands for -χš-, rvaṭ.čaya would belong to √vrag-, "procedere," caus. "to bring into existence, make born." The text, in both cases, is a syllable short, and no decision can be reached.

In *Y*.46,10-11 and *Y*.51,13, the two places where Zoroaster speaks of the Činvat bridge—which leads to heaven over the chasm of the netherworld—he himself "leads all followers safely across into the 'Kingdom,'" whereas the sinners, arriving at the bridge "shiver with fright and become—[precipitated]—yavoi vispāi, for all eternity, guests in the house[3] of the Druχš." Nyberg defines, 185, činvato prtuš as "Übergang (aus dieser Welt in die andre) des (zu jener Welt) hinzielenden (Ekstatikers)," but 234: "Nicht *nur* der Weg des Toten, sondern der des Ekstatikers," and "Činvato prtuš ist also hier *in erster Linie* der Weg der Ekstase . . . , die Schlussworte 'für alle Zeit Gäste . . .' können jedoch darauf hindeuten, dass die Stelle von der endgiltigen Trennung vom Irdischen im Tode handelt." This backstepping recalls the poem of the child nearing the "Liar's bridge," the Činvat bridge in German folk-lore. The final sentence is in no way ambiguous: heaven and hell mean eternity. √cī- in činvat does *not* signify "hinzielen," but always —also in Vedic—"lēgere, pick out, select." What happens at the bridge is illustrated by some Turfan fragments: "ud dušqērdagān az dē[nvarān] vičārēd ušān ō χōy ārag ēstēnēnd" and "ud dēnvarān kē aǰ dašn ēstēnd," sinner and pious are "separated, vi.cārēd, √či-," the sinners are made to stand to the left, the pious to the right, or in the words of

[3] Dative, not loc., as in *Y*.46,14 (under 'Yā-ahī!'): "your friend for (= at) the festival," mazoi magāi, meaning "destined for, invited into the house."

Matth. 23,32: "καὶ ἀφορίσαι αὐτοὺς ἀπ' ἀλλήλων ὥσπερ ὁ ποιμὴν ἀφορίζει τὰ πρόβατα ἀπὸ τῶν ἐρίφων." No man ever came back from the bridge. It is Job's "path without return," leads to the "land without return" of the Babylonians.

But Zoroaster believed in the last judgment, and this notion and the mythical notion of the bridge are incompatible: if the judgment should take place before coming to the bridge, the apparatus would be of no use; if after, the fallen souls would be condemned without being judged. Therefore, in Zoroaster's mouth the ancient notion is merely a metaphor, no part of the creed.

rvāzišta and rvāza in *Y.Haft.* 36,2—see under 'Yā-ahī!'—have the same meaning as the verb rvāz- in *Y.*50,5 and 31,1, hence belong to it. Ātarš is invoked: "rvāzišto ho nå . . . patiǰamya ātar . . . rvāzištahya rvāzayā, as most gracious one come to meet us, o Fire, with most gracious greeting, to the great triumph, yā-ahī!" meaning: "it would be extremely gracious if. . . ."

"coming to meet" is a well known ceremony: pati.gam- is an istiqbāl (to qabala); not merely is the guest met at the door of the house, but one rides as far as a day's journey to meet him, with many attendants. The Pahl. transl. uses for rvāza, rvāzišta, the same expression as for rvāχš.uχti (word of greeting), spelled 'vlv'χ.MNY', i.e. urvāχ.saχvan "word of greeting," salutation,[4] perfectly right.

Bartholomae: "Als wonnigster komme du uns, o Feuer, mit der Wonne des Wonnigsten entgegen, zu der grössten der Entscheidungen." *Wb.*1545: "bezieht sich wohl auf den Metallstrom beim letzten Gerucht." Similarly s.v. initī: "Pein, in *Y.*30,11. Die worte beziehen sich auf das Wohlgefallen der Gerechten und die Pein der Gottlosen beim Durchschreiten des glühenden Metallstromes im letzten Gericht, wovon (*Ind.*)*Bdh.* 30,19 erzählt."[5] huvitīča initī in *Y.*30,11—see under 'Fravarāni'—do not aim at any ordeal, though the Pahl. transl. seems to think so, but are "paradise and hell," predetermined end of history. The *Ind.Bdh.* 30,19, after describing how, at the end of the world, the

[4] In *Nirang.* 84 corrupt 'vlv'χmmnynyt, either (u)rvāχ.gōyēt, or (u)rvāχ.mēnēt, the first to guftan, gōy-, the second to mēnītan, "speaking" or "thinking."

[5] Under ayah, *Wb.*159, to which he refers, he interprets in the same way the passages which speak of ascertaining guilt through ordeal. And under "ātar," *Wb.*316, even more material is implicated, wrongly.

metal in the mountains melts, says only: "all men pass through it for purification, the pious feel as if they walked through warm milk, but to the sinners it is really like molten metal." This description, written in the 10th century A.D., has been developed from Zoroaster's scanty allusions to the ordeal as means of ascertaining guilt at the last judgment, and out of the pre-Zoroastrian, mythical conception of the end of the world in fire. But even there no word speaks of "rapture" at the crossing of the metal stream. The idea is purely negative: the pious do not feel it as the impious do.

Nyberg 279: "Selber erfüllt von grösster Verzückung mögest du zu uns kommen zur Entscheidung(?) . . . zu uns (während wir) in der Verzückung des Verzücktesten . . . (sind) mögest Du zur grössten der Krisen (yāh) kommen!" and comments: "Schwerlich eine maga- oder Ordal-séance im Still der gathischen Zeit . . . der Ausdruck yāh [hurrah!] leitet die Gedanken der Gemeinde zu dem grossen Ordal hin, bei dem sie in der Verzückung um das Feuer die Verzückung der aša.Gläubigen bei der grössten der Krisen erleben." An ordeal is the drinking of sulphur water and the like, not the "Ewige Wonnebrand" of the Pater Ecstaticus in Faust.

To the "Wonne" in the footnotes of the *Wb.* he then adds an overdose of Hertel's "radiation-theory" and thus produces the perfect "theory of ecstasy," 201: "Der Herzpunkt in der Religion der Gatha-Gemeinde war das maga-Mysterium, die Ekstase." "Der maga [=wedding, see under 'Maga'] wird als göttliches Kraftzentrum aufgefasst." He describes also the methods and techniques of the ecstasies, abstracted from those harmless words, (245): "Jāmāspa u.a. haben sich für das Kraftzentrum [power-center, as if it was a central power-station] des maga entschieden"; 139: "Für eine Vision ist erforderlich, dass eine göttliche Strahlung mit einer menschlichen zusammentreffen." "Čisti, die Sehstrahlung, geht sowohl vom Menschen wie vom Göttlichen aus; diese beiden schneiden einander im maga." "iriχtam [=relictum, what is 'left' over], die Kraft, die für alle losgelassen ist, entlädt sich oder wird entladen, vgl. *Y.*48,7: Vohu Manah's Entladung durch Aša, also ein himmlischer Kraftausfluss. . . ." That sounds explosive—Schiller: Wehe, wenn sie losgelassen!—and what I have learnt, as student, of statics and physics is out of date in view of these metastatics of ecstatic kinetics.

In *Yt.*10,73, Mithra "raises his voice joyfully, rvāzamno abaroit vāčam," and then follow exactly the same words as in *Yt.*10,63, where he "wails" before AhuraMazdāh. The passage belongs to the mazdayasnian "rehabilitation" of the god, see 'Return of the Gods,' and is late, but important, because the phrase is the verbal expression of the gath. compound rvāχš.uχti.

*Y.*32,12:

yoi gāuš mrndan rvāχš.uχti ǰyōtum

"who destroy with rvāχš.uχti the livelihood of the peasants." ǰyōtum is not "life," Gr. bíos, but "livelihood," Gr. bíotos; killing the ox would not destroy its livelihood, hence gauš is not the ox, but in Zoroaster's figurative style the peasant. Cf. the Assyrian expression, Sargon, *8th Camp.* 1.275: "ebūra tuklat nišē.šu u ^{sam}pu.e napšat buli.šu, I destroyed the harvest, the support of its people, and the chaff, the life of its cattle."

Bartholomae: "Die das Leben des Rindes unter Freudengeschrei zu grunde richten," note: "Es handelt sich um mit Orgien verbundene Tötung des Rinds zu Opferzwecken." He thinks of *Y.*32,14 (text under 'Hōma') where Zoroaster makes the Hōma priests say: "The ox is to be killed, gauš ǰadyāi, that it may inflame to help him-before-whom-death-flees, durōša." i.e. Hōma, whose name Zoroaster does not let pass his lips. *Wb.*1549: "Hauma wird dazu veranlasst, indem man ihm vom Opfer einen Anteil zuweist," according to *Yt.*11,4 the jaw-bone.

In *Y.Haft.*38,5 is a highly archaic sentence which could be Vedic: "apāsča vå azīšča vå mātrāsča vå agnyå drigu.dāyaho vispā.pitiš āvōčama, we invoke you, waters, as the pregnant ones, the mother-cows, the not-to-be-slaughtered ones, the providers-of-the-poor, them that-water-all (-creatures)." The description of the cows as "agnyå, Ved. ághnyā, not-to-be-slaughtered" implies that steers were slaughtered and that the later Indian attitude did not yet prevail. The reason for Zoroaster's rejection of sanguinary sacrifices in general is not a peculiar bias against the cult of a certain god, but his general attitude towards "cult," and his standing up for the peasantry. There have never been anything like continuous hecatombs of horses and oxen. This wrong notion is only the result of the quotations from the epics in the yashts, where "a hundred [horses, a thousand oxen, ten thousand] sheep" are slaughtered every time. The deficient meter of the verses alone proves that the passages are retouched; if one eliminates the words between "a hundred" and "sheep," the meter is correct. Only hecatombs of sheep are historical: Darius ordered the slaughter of a hundred sheep for celebrating the birth of his first grandchild Artystone II, according to the Persepolis tablet, which books the expense. It means a big "banquet, misθʳa," and everything beyond that is unreal.

Bartholomae adds: "Die mit Tieropfern zu Ehren des Hauma verbundenen orgiastischen Feste . . . fanden jedenfalls, wie die Dionysien zur Nachtzeit statt." "Jedenfalls" means nothing but "probably," and the comparison with the Dionysia is the only support of this assumption, not only of their happening by night, but of their happening at all. But the idea has taken root. Nyberg 244: "Orgiastische Feste mit Stieropfern gehören in Zarathustras Predigten (?) unauflöslich mit Hauma-Orgien zusammen." Zoroaster always declaims, 286: "gegen die nächtlichen Orgien des Hauma-Kultes," and yet, no word about "nächtliche Orgien" appears. His proof for these nocturnal orgies is the magnificent verse *Y*.50,10: "The works, past and future, the sun's light and the dawn of day, whatever the eyesight perceives, praise Thee, AhuraMazdāh." "Diese inspirierte Huldigung an die Mächte des Tageslichts ist eine versteckte"—"bien caché," he says at another occasion—"Polemik gegen den Hauma-Kult, ein neues Beispiel für Zarathustras diskrete Art, empfindliche Punkte bei den neuen Freunden zu berühren." Obviously, the new friends did not take the hint, for the Hōma cult went on. Never have such conclusions been drawn from the psalm: "The heavens declare the glory of the Eternal."

Such is the background of the translations of rvāχš.uχti: Bartholomae's "Freudengeschrei," Andreas, gentler "unter Freudenrufen," Nyberg, "ekstatische Rufe." Against these Hertel's remark is aimed, *Venus* 77: "uχti, OI. ukti, immer nur 'Aussage' rvāχs.uχti kann also nur bedeuten durch die Aussage (Angabe) dass"—so far right, but not the anticlimax:—"die Aussage dass der Genuss von Rindfleisch rvāχš, Glut verleihe." gauš is not the beef consumed, but something that consumes its ǰyōtum itself. In the related case of compounds with -vāk,—e.g. krkavāka, he who says krka, "kikeriki," cock—the element before uχti is the "saying" itself, here *"grace, thanks"*: "Give thanks to the Lord, for His rvāzman, kindness, rvāza, grace, lasts eternally!" The "ecstatic cries" are the common "words of welcome and of thanks," for instance vahu āgmata, or alḥamdulillāh, in general "thank God" and applause.

The Činvat bridge contracts, in old belief, under the sinner, to the width of a knife blade. Therein it is like the "way of ecstasy," one falls down from both. We are all sinners.

A problem is, whereto the n.pr. "rvāχšaya" belongs. It is the name of the brother of Krsāspa, whose titles are in *Yt.*9,10 tkēša and dātarāza. He is killed by Hitāspa, of whom Krsāspa takes blood-revenge, kēnā, *Yt.*15,28. The two titles describe him as magus; how this is compatible with being the brother of Krsāspa, the two fragments of the myth do not allow us to perceive. When the "dāta" of a judge is "rāzan, law," he is what was called till recently "mudjtahid." I remember the answer of an octogenarian mudjtahid of Isfahan, whom I had asked long ago for a written fatwa, referring to a precedent a hundred years before: "Certainly I could give it to you, but the precedent was under Fatḥ 'Alī Shāh; today, I am not sure whether the people would obey such a fatwa by me!"—Nyberg 68: "Der Name deutet auf ekstatische Übungen hin," and 191: "tkēša 'Ordalmeister' "; 6: "dātarāza, einer dessen (Ordal)regel (AhuraMazdāh's) Gesetz ist." This would be an anachronism, since "rāzan" is the term of the polytheistic period, and Krsāspa and his brother belong to a phase of the myth where AhuraMazdāh may still have been called Varuna.

The two titles recall those of Manθravāka in *Yt.*13,105: ēθrapati and hamidpati, fire-priest and introducer of guests, mihmāndār, see under 'Myastra.' Bartholomae interpreted rvāχšaya as "der Freude bringende?"; Hertel assumes a causative stem. I prefer abbreviation of a compound, e.g. *rvāχšabara, cf. Ctesias *οἰβάρας* < *vahyabara, which he translates by agathángelos; cf. rvāχš.uχti "salutation." If the name be a "talking" one, it may mean "who welcomes," mihmāndār.

In *Kārn.Art.* (Nöld. p.51) Ardashīr gives the town he founded for joy at the rediscovery of the Shāhpuhr child, the name vl'š- or vlχš-šāhpuhr. The first element cannot be the Arsacid name valāš < vlgš, thus on the coins of Volagases I, the etymology of which is obscure. *Ka'ba inscr.* Pārs. l.31 has vrd'χšy for Pahl. vlgšy, Gr. ΟΥΑΛΑΣΣΟΥ, with inverse rd < l.- The name of the town may be rvā(χ)š: vrāš-šāhpuhr, "Welcome" or "Thanks-Shahpuhr."

XX. LAST JUDGMENT

"Dies irae dies illa
solvet seclum in favilla"

LAW was administered under the power of an "ahura, lord justiciary." He decides, δικάζει, by making the verdict of the court valid or not. The task of the court is διαγνῶναι, vi.čī-. It consisted of a jury of members of the vrzanam, presided by a judge, tkēšá—qāḍī, mōbaδ—who knew the "laws, tkḗša."

Many words for the procedure are derived from √ar-, "adjudge": "arθra, trial, causa, task" and "court"; "arθa, legal contest" and "plaintiff"; "duš.rθriš, miscarriage of justice." A remarkable shifting is to be seen in the notion of "passing a sentence," expressed by √prs-, fras- "to question, interrogare," cf. inquisition. OP.: "hufrastam aprsam, I have justly punished." The expression reveals that the inquiry, χšnūt, hearing, was the essential part of the procedure.[1] The notion "atonement, adjustment" is rendered by √par-, = Lat. par, see under 'Bandva,' with many derivatives.[2] The word for "pronouncing" a sentence, and likewise for the "deposition" of a witness is √sanh-, cf. *Y.*43,6: "Ārmatiš sanhati, pronounces the sentences, ratūš, of the undeceivable χratuš,

[1] Cf. OP. and Gath. prsāi (*Y.*44,12); fraša, prštā and frašta (*Y.*49,2). In view of the relation existing between Ir. dēnā and Akk. dīnu, Arab. dīn, the relation of Ir. √prs- and the following Akk. words ought to be studied: Old Akk. verb puruš, lipruš, noun pirištum etc, "establishing of facts and decision of the judge." Ass. "parāsu, to separate, cf. Ir. vi-či-," Aram. loanw. "faraša, to determine, explain," cf. Zimmern in ZDMG 74, 1920, 434.

[2] Wrong interpretation of the OIr. words affects also MIr.—*Mir.Man.*III,15: " 'vt m' prm'y'h ky 'ž tv 'frsgyft pdk'rnd byč 'vh z'n'h kv 'yvyž 'bǰyrvng my 'h'd ky 'mvχtg 'č kdg 'syyd byč rvč rvž 'mvχsyd, (Henning): und lass dir's nichts ausmachen, wenn sie von dir dauernd Trivialitäten erfragen(?), sondern wisse, dass es noch nie einen Schüler gegeben hat, der das Haus (des Lehrers gleich) als Gelehrter verlassen hat, vielmehr jeden Tag lernt er zu." Thus the words recall the quadrivium of a university. 'frsgyft is misinterpreted, following Andreas' αὐτός ἔφα (*Mir.Man.*II,321,4 and ZII,9,223) "Tpārs. 'prs'gyh, mit begriffsverneinendem apa, zu NP. räsā(y), "Verächtliches." 'frsgyft is used as adverb, α priv. + frsg, "unpunished," cf. "ayōš-tagīhā, without investigation"; Pārs. 'prs'gyh is n.abstr. or adverb; prm'y'h means, like OP. framāy-, "to allow," not "to command," and pdkr, as always, "to contend, contest," not "befragen, to query." In *Nir.*21, a passage likewise speaking of disobedient pupils, Aw. prnamnē and aprnamnē (with n supplied as in pr[na]mnē *Frhg.Ēv.*4,c) are equally rendered by "avē ē patkārēt." Finally: 'mvχs is "to learn, be educated, παιδεύεσθαι." Hence: "and do not allow them to remain unpunished when refractory, but understand that never was a pupil who left school his education finished, unless he had been educated day by day." This is no "dies diem docet," but ὁ μὴ δαρεὶς ἄνθρωπος οὐ παιδεύεται. The text goes on: "There are obedient and refractory, pšgvn'v, pupils; one must tolerate all of them in the same way, you must not become nhym'ng of one of them, but in hmvdyndyft (equanimity, justice, here opposed to nhym'ng) . . . to each who y'dyd the hand, . . ." the last words give the etymology of "dastyārak, pedagogue, lit. handholder," cf. Hübschmann *Arm.Gr.* 135.

mental power of the god," who, in *Y.*29,4 (see below) is the vičiro ahuro and ⁺sahvar.mārišto.

Legal procedure also includes oath and ordeal. Bartholomae defined "varah, oath, ordeal" as "eigentl. Beglaubigung, Erhärtung des Rechts, der Unschuld." √var- is "to choose," but in many Aw. passages it means "to swear." It furnishes also terms for professing, embracing a religion, with or without prev. fra-, cf. the relation of Gr. pístis, Lat. fides to the oath, and Arab. shāhid and shahīd, witness and martyr, shahāda "confession of faith," ashhadu'llāh, "God be my witness." Oath and ordeal come down from the IE. epoch and are often expressed by the same word in IE. languages, thus also in Iranian. The passage decisive for OP., *Beh.* §57, is mutilated: "a u r m z d - - - - - r t i y i y yaθa ima haθyam nē druχtam adam akunavam," evidently a current legal formula, I presume a verbal form of fra.var-, or denom. of fravarti: "Ōramazdā be my witness that this is the actual truth (what) I have done!" The modern word for swearing is "saugand χurdan, to drink sulphur water"—āpo sōkantavatī in *Vid.*4,54—to suffer the most common ordeal.

The oath, Aw. yōž(dā), Lat. iūsiūrandum, an oath of "purgation," is a curse upon one's self. Some peoples of antiquity, so the Elamites, called forth the ancestors, also the whole clan, as witnesses, "Eidesbrüder," and often the oath took place at the ancestors' tombs. These "seconds, compurgators," Teut. "der Umstand (those who stand around)" are not produced as witnesses of the alleged crime, but in order to manifest the number of the followership, the power of the "friendship."[2a] That is what "rvaθā, amicitiae" means in the "Rašnu" or "Ordeal-Yasht," 8: "the rvaθā . . . I call forth to the ordeal, varah-, here arranged!" Therefore, "fravarti," term for the "manes, OI. pitáraḥ, ancestors" may originally mean "compurgator, witness of the oath." The "amicitia" as "Umstand" is also the role of the Roman "vindex," to "vin-, clan" and "deico, dīco, to point out." Daily life, especially law, requires the confirmation by oath of many things. At the trial of Afshīn, in Samarra, Isḥāq b. Ibrāhīm, cousin of Ṭāhir I, says, when Afshīn ad-

2a The caliph al-Muhtadī, Tabari III,1791f., says "I take no oath except in presence of the Hāshimids [his clan], the qāḍī's . . . and the aṣḥāb al-marātib," i.e. "people of the steps" such as descendants of 'Uthmān, Umayyads and Ṭālibids.

mitted to have tolerated the address "god of gods": "Woe to you, Khaidar, how can you swear to us by Allāh, and how can we believe you and accept your oath, and treat you as a Muslim, if you are overweening like Pharao?" It is instructive to compare the attitude of modern law, which does not abandon the oath that has lost its old significance, but tries to maintain its holiness by fear of a penalty for perjury.

Between oath and ordeal there is only a difference in degree. In the severer form, the ordeal, "Gottesurteil," the knowing gods manifest, at once, guilt or innocence unknown to men.[3] The ordeal is the "testimony" of the gods, a deposition. The *Dēnkart* expresses this plainly in the chapter on the tradition of the Awesta: Ātarpāt ē Māhraspandān corroborated the accuracy of the Awesta-text, as he wrote it, by an ordeal: "pas ač bōχtan ē Ātarpāt pat gowišn ē passāχt, after A. had been acquitted by the 'gowišn, deposition' of the ordeal."[4] The *Art.Vir. Nām.* describes the form of this ordeal, I,16: "Ātarpāt ē Māhraspandān MNV P'N.Š P'N.S'χt ZY P'N.dyn krt rvy vt'χt MDM vl lyχt, who underwent an ordeal relative to the religion (Awesta) by molten brass poured on his breast."[5] See Bartholomae, *Z.Sas.Recht* II,9: "dem Beschuldigten 'geschmolzenes Erz auf die Brust giessen' wird *Dēnk.* M.644,18 als eine Methode des var-Vollziehens, var passāχtan, bezeichnet," and Salemann, *Grdr.*I,292, §87: passāχt, ordeal, to √sāz-, sāχt, caus. of √saz-. *Y.*32,7: "yā - - sanhatē - - hvēnā ayahā, which is 'spoken' (√sanh-, saχvan, deposition) by the red-hot brass," the same as "gowišn (= saχvan) of the ordeal."

The "Ordeal-Yasht" 8, a poor compilation of formulae, mostly picked up from other yashts, does not contribute more than the detail of the "rvaθa, amici-compurgators" to this picture. One can just recognize the traces of these immemorially old institutions in Iranian.

The Awesta does not describe an ordeal that actually took place; still less do the gatha contain any allusion to an ordeal to which Zoroaster

[3] *Zum ältesten Strafrecht der Kulturvölker,* Fragen gestellt von Th. Mommsen etc, 1905, and O. Schrader, *Sprachvergl. und Urgeschichte,* 3.ed. II,ii,408ff.

[4] Nyberg 418f.: "lit. nachdem A. 'auf die richtige Rede hin' erlöst worden war," freely translated "nachdem er glücklich die Ordalprobe 'für die Richtigkeit des religiösen Wortes' bestanden hatte." In translating "passāχt" by "right talk, rightness of religious word" he reveals that the word for "ordeal, passāχt" is unknown to him who developed a whole "Ordalterminologie."

[5] Not, as M. Haug translated "on whose breast, in the tale which is in the Dēnkart, melted brass was poured."

had been subjected. I believe Markwart introduced this error by an interpretation of *Dēnk.* VII,4,3 (vol.XIV,37 Sanjana). Not even this passage, based on material dating from the time of Xusrau I, says that Zoroaster had submitted to an ordeal, but only that "he had made 33 kinds." That means, the legal procedure, about A.D. 500, knew many kinds. But not even the number is real: all multiples of 11 are mystic. Instead of 3 × 11 one finds only three kinds in the whole literature. At the end of the 9th century A.D., Zātsparm paraphrased the *Dēnk.* passage: "The amuhraspand 'shows' three kinds of ordeals (1) by fire: i.e. āθrā of Y.31,3; (2) by red-hot iron, i.e. hvēnā ayahā of Y.32,7; Zoroaster walks three steps on it without burning his soles; (3) by molten brass, i.e. ayahā χšustā of Y.51,9, poured on the chest; Zoroaster seizes it with his hands and offers it back to the archangel," a story one could find in acts of Syrian martyrs. It does not report an event, but describes, figuratively, the introduction of the institution as such by Zoroaster. Of course, he was believed to have created, at the beginning, all judicial institutions existing at that time, and, of course, he had not introduced the ordeal which existed for many centuries before his time.

Oath of purification and its severer form, the ordeal, are constituent methods of judicial procedure, especially for ascertaining guilt during the inquiry. The ordeal is neither the eruption of a volcano, as one might think when reading "Ašas Reich kommt in der Sturmglut des Ordals," Nyberg 111, 126, 246, nor a Greek tragedy, "der Auftakt giebt eine Ordalszenerie," 154, 244, nor a masonic meeting "tkēša, Ordalpriester, zu struere, bauen maurern."[6] "Ordalgenosse, Ordalmeister, Ordalkollegium, Ordalséance, Ordalszenerie, Ordalurteil, Ordalregel, Ordalbegriff, Ordaltechnik, Ordalbutter, Ordalverbum" etc., all this "Ordalterminologie" are exciting, empty words. I once was the only foreign guest at a military dinner given by the commanding general in honor of the occupant of the Djamshīd throne, which passed in complete silence. When the kāmkārtar patiχšāy at last rose from the table, he turned to me and said, over the head of our host, perfectly to the point: I suppose that was the worst dinner you ever had in your life! And while I stuttered some answer, he called to the minister of the

[6] Germ. "mauern" is to make a "mauer, wall"; "maurern"? would be "do mason's work, be a mason."

court: Repeat it to him in French! That one could call an "ordeal-séance."

The same constituent methods of judicial procedure Zoroaster assumes also for the last judgment, and wherever he uses some of these terms in the gatha, the last judgment is the subject.

The gathas mention three kinds of ordeals:

*Y.*31,3:

yām då manyū ā*θ*rāča rtāča čoiš rānōbya χšnūtam ·

"the hearing, χšnūt, that Thou as (Spanta)manyuš ordainest by fire, and (which) as Rtam Thou hast constituted, čoiš[7] for the two parties, rānā."

*Y.*51,9:

yām χšnūtam rānōbya då	*θ*wā ā*θ*rā suχrā mazdā
ayahā χšustā abi	ahvāhū daχštam dāvoi
rāšayahē drugvantam	savayo rtāvanam

"The hearing which Thou, Mazdāh, ordainest for the two parties by Thy red fire, by molten metal, to impress into the minds the brand: the drugvant shall be destroyed, the rtāvan saved!"

*Y.*32,7:

ēšām ēnahām	nēčit vidvå ōǰoi hadrōyā
yā ǰōyā sanhate	yāiš srāvī hvēnā ayahā
yēšām tu ahura	riχtam mazdā vēdišto ahi

Wb. gives √χšnu- the meaning "zu Gefallen sein, please," and hence χšnūt, as a derivative, "Belohnung (reward) in gutem und bösem Sinne." Others tone it down to "Vergeltung, requital," merely masking the offence: the ordeal is neither reward nor punishment. √χšnu- means always "to hear," like NP. šunūdan, and "χšnūt, hearing." The procedure of inquiry is a trial by ordeal; both parties submit to it, receive "audience" at this "hearing." The tenet is: Nobody shall be sentenced unheard. rānā, used as dual only, are the "two parties," not "two hostile

[7] *Wb.*429 puts čoiš as pres. to √ ²kēš- "to teach," whereby the god would teach also his enemies. It puts čēšəmno in *Yt.*19,93 as part.fut. under √ kāy- "to atone." This passage I understand as "Vištāspa, the 'founder, organizer' of the armies of Rtam." Thus, both, čoiš and čēšamna, seem to belong to √ ¹kēš-, "to build, found, constitute."

parties," but a metaphor taken from the two litigants in court, for "pious and sinners," to be distinguished only by the ordeal.

> Y.32,7 contains three entirely obscure hapax: ōǰoi, hadrōyā and ǰōyā. For the first two lines one must compare 32,6: "ēnå yāiš srāvahyati, the misdeeds for which epics are sung to them" and 32,8: "ēšām ēnahām vivahušo srāvi yamasčit, among those villains (or: for such misdeeds) Yama V. of all is praised," see under 'Yama χšēta.' Therefore, "yāiš srāvi" refers to "misdeeds," "that are testified, made notorious—as ǰōyā?—by the hvēnā ayahā, ordeal." The knowing god is speaking, sanhatē, through the ordeal. Last line: "What they have left behind, riχta, Thou A.M. knowest best." riχta, to √rič-, rēk-, linquĕre, (hereditate re)lictum, "left" property—cf. rēχnah "heritage" in 32,11 under 'Maga'—is in general the balance of men's good and evil actions. The verses evidently oppose the testimony of the "most knowing god," yēšām tu riχtam vēdišto ahi, to the ignorance of men, ēšām ēnahąm nēčit vidvå, as the Pahl. transl. understands: "avēšān kēnīk nē.čič ākās, expl. čē čand nē dānēnd." Cf. Y.32,7: "he who knows shall not defend them," under 'Yama χšēta.' "nēčit vidvå" may mean "even though unknowingly." As far as the verses are intelligible, they forbid Bartholomae's translation: "keine von diesen Unthaten soll der Wissende verüben, im Verlangen nach der Erreichung des Gewinnes, der wie bekannt durch das lohende Metall kund wird, i.e. der Metallstrom beim Jüngsten Gericht," which sounds as if somebody might try to reach paradise by illicit means.

The three ordeals are: āθrā suχrā, by red fire; hvēnā ayahā, by red-hot brass; ayahā χšustā, by molten brass, certainly nothing to inspire rapture or ecstasy.

Y.31,19:

θwā āθrā suχrā mazdā   vahāu vidāta rānayå

"(when) through Thy red fire, M., the vahāu of the two parties will be established."

Y.47,6:

tā då spantā manyū mazdā ahura
āθrā vahāu vidātim rānōbya

"as Spanto manyuš, o. A.M., through fire, Thou ordainest the vahāu vidātim, establishing of guilt or innocence for both parties."

Bartholomae (*Wb.*) explained "vidāti" with loc.sg. "vahāu" as "Einweisung (installation) auf das Guthaben (in the sum due to him)—in gutem und üblem Sinne—wie es sich beim Abschluss der Buchungen, dāθra (closing of accounts) ergiebt."[8] He failed to see that the verses do not speak of passing sentence, but of collecting evidence. The primary meaning of vi-dā- is "to establish": √dā-=*τίθημι*, prev. vi-, Lat. dis-, imports "in detail"; the word comes near to "analyze, examine." It is the activity of the examining magistrate, inquiry, *διαγνῶναι* of the vi.čiro, and the Pahl. transl. "giving vičārišn" is right: ascertain guilt or innocence. Therefore, vahāu cannot be a loc. sg., but only a dual, corresponding to "rānā, the two parties," "savā, the two returns" (cf. hvafnā, the two sleeps), hence "vahāu, the two goods, their good and bad actions," the balance both parties "leave behind."

In *Y*.48, the train of thought is: St.1, when Rtam will have defeated druχš, the dēva and martiya, *θεοί τε βροτοί τε*, receive their "savā, two returns, good and evil." The victory of the good principle at the end of the "mixed world" is a fact, not conditional; to achieve it, all men must "choose rtam," vi.čiθa in *Y*.30,2, under 'Yā-ahī!' or swear to it, √var-. St.2: The human bearers, rtāvan and drugvant, replace the powers rtam and druχš: "Announce to me, A.M. who knowest what shall come: will the rtāvan defeat the drugvant *before* the atonement, prθā, which Thou hast planned?" The atonement, payment, takes place at the Last Judgment which is part of the primal plan of the god. St.2 ends:

hā zi ahoš vahvī vistā ākrtiš

"That is: the good ākrtiš of the world has taken place!" or imprecative:

[8] Bartholomae refers to the verb vidāya- in *Y*.43,12 and 34,12, to which *Wb*.722 attributes six meanings, a different one to each place. For the two places quoted "etwas verteilen an," the same error as in the translation of the noun.

"that would be the transfiguration, the end of the struggle of good and evil."

> Bartholomae: "Das wäre ja gewiss eine der Welt frommende Botschaft!" or alternatively: "das ist bekannt als." Lommel: "Denn das ist bekannt als die gute Gestaltung des Daseins," note: "Andreas: ākrtiš, cf. OI. ākrti, äussere Form, Gestalt." Why should Zoroaster ask, if it was "bekannt, a known fact"? vista cannot belong to $\sqrt{}$¹vid-, "to know." Nyberg attaches it to $\sqrt{}$²vid-, but his translation "befunden" means "judged, ascertained as," whereas $\sqrt{}$²vid- is "to find, obtain," pass. "to take place." $\sqrt{}$kar- with prev. ā is "to make into something." *Wb.* puts ā.krnam, with obj. nmānam, in *Vid.*22,1, under $\sqrt{}$kart-, "durch Schneiden gestalten," meaning "to shape into something." The words are synonymous. Here, the existing world is made into another one, hence "ā.krti = transfiguration." *krsti < kart- would have a bad connotation: to fake.

The question means: "Will the victory of the religion, of good over evil, become a reality while the world lasts, before its end?" The double signification of the "Coming of the Kingdom" is the same as in earliest Christianity.

The problem is inherent in every doctrine that teaches a final compensation in the hereafter. Nobody can teach: We live in the year 3030, after 5,970 years you will rise from your tombs to be judged! The founder of the religion believes that he brings the kingdom of heaven, not only an era.[9] The kingdom must come in the lifetime of the generation that hears the promise: "bōdanto pati! you shall live to see!" And it is significant that Zoroaster speaks only of "rtāvan" and does not distinguish, as Xerxes does soon after, between "šyāta in life, rtāvan in death." Only after the prophet's time the contradiction between a resurrection at the end of days and the passing into the beyond at death becomes apparent. Various solutions are tried; for instance in the late *Art.Vir.Nām*,xviii: The tortured soul of the sinner in hell says " 'MT III YVM V šp'n YḪVVN.t YMNNVN.yt 'YK, when only three days and nights have elapsed, IX M ŠNT bvndk YḪVVN.t 'P.m BR' L' ŠBKVN.d, the 9,000

[9] An anecdote, already belonging to history: I once brought a portrait of Riẓā Shāh Pahlavī to the emperor William, and said, answering a question of the emperor "He believes himself to have inaugurated an era!" The emperor said: "I did so once myself!"

years are completed, and yet they will not release me!" There, reward and punishment begin with death, and punishment even comes to an end with time, with the beginning of eternity.

The notion, Zoroaster expresses by "ākrtiš, transfiguration," is clearer in *Y*.30,9, see under 'Myastra':

ātča toi vayam hyāma yoi im frašam krnavān ahum

"and we will be those who make this world here frašam!" This is what a "sōšyant, saviour" does, and on this and a few similar passages rests the later doctrine of the sōšyant. Andreas translated "die dies Leben zu einem herrlichen (oder: Wunder) gestalten," NGGW, 1909. A whole literature grew up around this note.[10] I too allowed myself to be misled and corrected the error only in *Altp.Inschr.* s.v.: frašam means solely "beyond," always used with ellipsis, "beyond (the post, the target etc.)." fraša + √kar- is originally a term of racing; as such it formed frašakara, as epithet of Vrthragna in *Yt.*14,28 and as n.pr. in *Yt.*13,102. The moment of which Zoroaster speaks is the last day of history, when the world has finished its ninth round, when time stops and eternity begins. From the verbal idiom frašam krnavān in *Y*.30,9 the Aw. abstr. noun frašakrti has been derived in analogy to ākrti. frašakrti "the making-beyond" is no good model of a word and occurs only once in the Awesta, in a gloss interpolated at the end of the old verses *Yt.*13,57—see under 'Fravarti'—behind rvēsam: "yam frašakrtoit vahviyå." It is the "good" frašakrti, like the "good" ākrti, frasasti. Actually, MP. fraškirt has been coined after "frašam krnavān" and has been transposed into a learned Aw. frašakrti. Pahl. tāk fraškirt zamān means "ilā yaumi l-qiyāma, till resurrection day," syn. of apatiyārakīh "state of no-more-being-contested." It is the counterpart of the notion expressed in *Vid.*2,20 (see under 'Chronology'): "3,000 years spiritual existence and 3,000 years material existence without antagonism; then comes patiyārakīh, contest: 3,000 years from the beginning of human history to the coming of the religion, and another 3,000 years to the last judgment," after which apatiyārakīh reigns.

Zoroaster speaks many times, in singular and plural, of the sōšyant,

[10] Lommel, ZII, 1,30; H. Junker, in "Wörter u. Sachen," XII, 132f.; Duchesne, *Comp.Av.* §78: "frašam 'splendide,' établi par Andreas."

whereas notion and word do not appear—as even a glance at the arrangement of the places in *Wb.*1551 shows—in any old passage of the yashts.[11] It appears only in *Yt.*19,88ff., post-Zoroastrian verses describing their activity at the resurrection. St.92,a-c are the beginning of this song, 88,c-i its end. The same verses recur in *Yt.*19,11 and 13ff.

The formula by which the verses are inserted into the Hvarnah yasht at the mazdayasnian redaction, is: "We worship the hvarnah, which follows (belongs to) NN, in order that he may . . . ," i.e. "and which enables him to. . . ." In st.11 AhuraMazdāh who needs no "kāvian hvarnah" to create the living beings, is the N.N. To this the words "yat krnavān frašam ahum" are ungrammatically appended, which imitate Y.30,9, "that they (viz. the sōšyant who are dropped at this place) make the world frašam." In *Yt.*19,13ff. the verses are appended, likewise unbefittingly, to the Amrta Spanta. In 88f. the same introductory formula is used, with hvarnah, but the NN is not the god nor the immortal-holy ones, but

yat upa.hačāt sōšyantam	vrθrajanam
uta anyasčit haχayo	yat krnavāt frašam ahum

"the hvarnah that belongs to the varthragnian sōšyant and his other companions, that he (sg.) make the world frašam." He needs the hvarnah no more than AhuraMazdāh, and the non-Zoroastrian epithet "varthragnian," which brings the relationship of the hvarnah (not of the sōšyant) to the god Vrthragna into prominence, is added only to adapt the originally independent verses to the hvarnah yasht, to which they did not belong. In 88 and 91 the hvarnah-formula is twice interpolated, tearing the original asunder and forcing the insertion of a "yat" that spoils the meter. *Yt.*19,11 and 13 may be left alone as mere repetition, out of place, of the original in 88. The verses themselves are disfigured by a few additions, but have suffered neither changes nor omissions. The line "uta anyasčit haχayo" must be admitted, because the plural of the verb krnavān, grammatically faulty in 11a, is not introduced directly from Y.30,9 in *Yt.*19,11, but in the "Song to the Sōšyant" which was taken over as a whole, and became faulty only when the subject was changed from the plural to sg. AhuraMazdāh. Thus the original verses were:

11 About the insertion of their names in the memorial list of *Yt.*13 see that chapter.

Astvat.rto frahištātē	Astvatrta will set forth
hača apāt kansaviyāt	from the water Kansaviya
ašto mazdå ahurahya	the champion of AhuraMazdāh
uta anyasčit haχayo	and his other companions,
yat krnavān frašam ahum	that they make humanity frašam,
azaršyantam amaršyantam	not-aging, not-dying,
afriθyantam apūyantam	not-decaying, not-rotting,
yavējiyam yavēsūvam	ever-living, ever-flourishing.
yat ristā pati us.hištān	When the dead will rise up,
ǰasāt ǰīvayo amrχtiš	the reviver, the imperishable will come,
daδāti frašam vasnā ahum	he will make humanity frašam, please God!

Herodotus III,62, in the story of Cambyses and Prexaspes renders the thought of these verses by: *εἰ μὲν νῦν οἱ τεθνεῶτες ἀνιστᾶσι* [yat rista pati us.hištan], *προσδέκεό τοι καὶ* 'Αστυάγεα (read: *'Αστυάρτεα) ⟨*τὸν μῆδον*, faulty gloss of Herodotus⟩ *ἐπαναστήσεσθαι* [astvat.rto frahištātē]. The whole notion was too foreign for Herodotus to understand it rightly, a cogent proof that he did not invent the story, but heard it from the best source. The name astvat.rta [Median, OP. *astva.rta, +'Αστυάρτης] is derived from *Y*.43,16, end of Gāth.ušt.: astvat rtam hiyāt uštāna ōjahvat, and means Rtam in human shape. The Achaemenid name 'Οξυάρτης[12] i.e. vaχšyat.rta, OP. vaχšya.rta, name of the second sōšyant, attests that the tripling of the sōšyant was known in about 420 B.C., and Herodotus' words, about 440 B.C., project that conception back into Cambyses' time, 529-523 B.C. The time of the 'Song to the Sōšyant' is the middle or second half of the 5th century. At that time the n.abstr. "frašakrtiš, the making-beyond" was not yet in use.

In *Māh Frav.* and some other Sasanian works, the name uχšyat.rta is spelled χVRŠYTR, revealing how these eschatological speculations worked. The *Gr.Bdh.* 92f., speaking of the "var i avinast, the sinless lake" which—since avinast replaces anāhitā as epithet of Ardvī, e.g. *Gr.Bdh.*82—is another name for the "source of Ardvīsūrā, the immaculate," quotes a lost fragment of the Awesta "čgvn YMLLVN.t 'YK, as is

[12] Oxyartes, bei Athenaios XIII,89 nach Phylarchos, b.19, *Frgm.Hist.Gr.* 1,343, son of Darius II, brother of Artaxerxes II and the younger Cyrus. A brother was called Artostes, shortform of Gath. rtam.yahmāi.uštā.

written": χvlšyt ptlvkmtn 'dvpm [var.l. -pn, read -pmn] 'vyn'st vly ḤZYTVN.t' ZK [or ZY.š?] MY' plškrt' vyl'stn' l'd BYN 'pyst, Xvaršēt, the sun, pāθramēθana adaβyamna, saw the sinless lake and needed its water for preparing the transfiguration."[13] This is the rest of an old myth, of the same kind as that of a god of thunder setting the world ablaze by his lightning.

"adaβyamna, undeceivable" is a frequent epithet of Mithra, and once, in *Yt.*10,80, he is called "mēθanahya pātā, keeper of the farm-yard." The compound *pāθra.mēθana lives on in the n.pr. p'tmytn, on a Sasanian seal in the Calcutta Museum. Both are divine epithets, fitting Hvarχšēta as well as Mithra. In *Gr.Bdh.*197 and *Dāt.Dēn.*, Pišyōθna, son of Vištāspa (*Yt.*13) has the epithet pāθromēhan (corrupted into Či°-)[14] as immortal helper of the sōšyant. The *Dēnk.* IX,40 says: "Pāθromēhan, also called Pišyōθn," and the *Bahman Yt.* speaks of "Pāθromēhan, son of Vištāsp."

Hvarčiθra, son of Zoroaster (*Yt.*13), another helper of the sōšyant, is called in *Gr.Bdh.*235 "the artēštar, knight, spāhsālār, commander of the army of Pišyōθna, son of Vištāspa." The posthumous career of the historical Pišišyōθna, after eschatology had taken hold of him, is that he disappears behind his surname pāθra.mēθana, originally a surname of the gods Mithra and Hvarχšēta, while Hvarčiθra—i.e. XVRŠTR > XVRŠYTR, as if it be a comparative of XVRŠYT—takes the place of Hvar, the sun—like Sas. manuščiθra for manuš—and disappears behind the coalescent names of uχšyat.rta and hvar.χšēta. The actual process was that the legend substituted these human figures for gods of an older period, conferring upon them the divine epithets, and that these old epithets survive, clearly revealing a much older phase of thought, where gods like Mithra, Hvarχšēta, Anāhitā and Vrthragna took part in the final ἐκπύρωσις of the world.

The name of the lake Kansaviya, mod. Hāmūn, is derived from an unknown *kansu. From the Kansaviya rises mount Ušidam, as the meaning of the name, "house of dawn" shows, originally a mythical

[13] Messina, Orientalia I,2,15, misunderstood my old remark in AMI II,57 on this passage of the *Bdh.* that had escaped attention: "l'affermazione riguardante il sole (as sōšyant) si fonda sopra una etimologia del termine ušētar-χvaršētar etc." I never considered an etymological connection of χvaršētar and uχšyat.rta.

[14] Readings like čiθromēnōγ etc should be given up.

mountain imagined at the east point of the border of the Ocean, but at the time of the verses of *Yt.*19 already located at the hill in the lake, the modern Kōh i Xvāǰa, "mountain of the Lord," whose name was, in modern belief, Sarā i Ibrāhīm, i.e. a son of Ibrāhīm Zardušt. It is regarded as holy, and is the only mountain invoked as "yazata, adorandus" in many yashts. Moreover, in the same yasht 19, in st.66, verses are inserted which give a detailed description of the Sealand with the lake, the mountain in the lake, and the ten rivers which fall into the lake, the like of which is not given of any other country in the Awesta. A commentary of this description is the *Awdīhā ē Sigistān,* "Mirabilia of Sīstān."

The placenames in the epical fragments quoted in the great yashts are motivated by the action of the mythical heroes. The placenames in the description of the sunrise in *Yt.*10, equally, have a good historical and geographical reason. The description of the Sealand has no motive and no connection with other things, it is simply the description of a country as a Holy Land. The saviour, expected from there, is a reincarnation of Zoroaster, his son [Sarā i Ibrāhīm Zardušt, in *Māh Frav.* Zoroaster himself]. I do not believe that a prophet can be expected to return as saviour from any special place or country, unless he has been there.[15] Therein I see the reason for the peculiar holiness and, with it, the description of the country in the Awesta. Zoroaster actually sojourned there.

On the weird table mountain of basalt in the lake, one cannot "als Missionar wirken" (Nyberg), but only live as a hermit, perhaps with a few pupils. I stayed there twice, altogether four months. It is a place provoking visions like no other one. The Indian ascetics used to go "in the forest," the Arabian "into the desert," the Iranian "on the mountain," for instance Sāsān according to ibn al-Balkhī, *Fārsn.* 54,11; Vištāspa according to Baiḍawī, niẓām, a passage which comes from the Iran. *Žāmāspnāmāk and, by its Greek translation, the *Χρήσεις Ὑστάσπου*, is connected with the corresponding passage in Ammian Marc. (see AMI,VI,7). The Sealand, Zranka, belonged to the satrapy of Viš-

[15] The shiʿite Mahdī is expected in Samarra, an analogy familiar to me, as I lived in closest neighborhood of the "Ghaiba." This cellar, in which the Mahdī "disappeared," is actually part of the basement of the vast palace in which his father and grandfather lived in the ninth century.

tāspa, and under his protection Zoroaster sojourned there as a hermit.

He speaks of this hermit life in the 'Gatha of the Vision,' *Y*.43,15:

daχšat ušyāi   tušnāmatiš vahištā

"Thinking in silence has taught me to announce . . ."

Lommel's attempt to connect ušyāi with Skr. "ucyati, to like to do" (*Orient.Stud.Pavry,* 281ff.) is no improvement: one thinks in silence considering what one wants to say. As to the form cf. *Y*.32,4: +vašyantē dēvazuštā, text: vaχšənte. Mount Ušidam is the place of the Gatha of the vision. Zoroaster's sojourn on the mountain is the origin of the traditions told in the *Mirabilia,* also of the notes on Sēna Ahumstut "from Bust" in western Arachosia, and that Bust was founded when Vištāspa, at lake Frazdān (Zirih), created the religious law, in *Šahr.Ēr*. It is also the reason, long since forgotten, for the pilgrimages, attested since the fourth century A.D. and still performed today during the first fortnight after the Zoroastrian Naurōz, to the Kōh i Xvāǰa, the mountain of the Lord.

The gatha *Y*.48—with "ākrtiš"—speaks of the last judgment, not of an "Ordal das Zarathustras Religionsstreit entscheiden soll" (Nyberg, 227). I do not know whether Bartholomae was the first, or somebody before him, to ascribe to Zoroaster the Middle Iranian concept of the last judgment as a "destroying and purifying stream of fire" (see under 'Welcome'). The end of the world in fire, caused by lightning, is a thought of the oldest stratum of the myth; Zoroaster's concept, on the contrary, is the judgment, as all the verses here already quoted express, and very clearly the Gāthā uštavatī, 43,5-6 (see Markwart's translation):

5: dāmoiš rvēsē apamē
6: yahmi spantā   θwa manyū rvēsē ǰaso
mazdā χšaθrā   ahmi vahū manahā
yahya šyōθnāiš   gēθå rtā frādantē
ēbyo ratūš   sanhati ārmatiš
θwahya χratoš   yām nēčiš dābayati

After the last rvēsa, the last turn of the nine millennia, AhuraMazdāh appears as SpantoManyuš and in all his aspects, χšaθrā, vahū manahā; Ārmatiš pronounces the sentences of the undeceivable knowledge and will of the supreme judge.

For this last judgment the dead will rise, us.hištān, *Yt.*19,88; the verb, with us- and pati, used with the ablative, e.g. up from the sea, from the bed, means originally "from the graves" see under 'Vidēvdād.' The reward after death, for good and evil actions in life, is Zoroaster's fundamental thought, expressed in every single gatha, and equally in Darius' inscription *Beh.* §§73 and 76, and Xerxes' *daiva,* Persepolis. The entire dualistic concept of the world rests on this thought. Resurrection, being the necessary premise of the judgment, is the unavoidable consequence of reward, an integrant part of Zoroaster's doctrine. Prēxaspes speaks doubting—"if"—to Cambyses; but Darius and Xerxes believe in Zoroaster's doctrine of resurrection.

Nyberg says, 310: "Der Auferstehungsgedanke ist in den Gathas mit keinem Worte berührt; mehr, es fehlen alle Voraussetzungen, die Vereinigung der Seele in der Ekstase mit der himmlischen Welt hat die Todesvorstellung vollkommen überwogen." "Heavenly world" is a "Vorstellung-concept"; "ecstasy" is a mere "Vorstellung-imagination" of Nyberg; death is neither conception nor imagination, but a fact, the most stubborn, that nothing can "overweigh." "Wenn die Himmelsreise der Seele der alles beherrschende Gedanke gegenüber dem Tode ist—[it is not]—so giebt es keinen Boden für den Auferstehungsgedanken," a conclusion that would be wrong even if the premise were true. "Zoroaster borrowed from the tribe among which he founded his community, den auf die Erdbestattung begründeten fravaši Kult and den darin wurzelnden und ohne ihn nicht denkbaren (unthinkable) Auferstehungsglauben," which was however "nichtsdestoweniger natürlich eine kühne Neuschöpfung grossen Stils." Whence comes such knowledge, when no word as much as touches the subject, and why did Zoroaster do so, when there was no "Voraussetzung, premise" and no "Boden, premises" to build on? Zoroaster never mentions the Fravarti in the gathas; more than that, in his 'Creation Gatha' he describes AhuraMazdāh in their old cosmologic role, that means, he rejected the popular notion of these "manes."

In the whole Fravardīn Yasht, 13, see under 'Fravarti,' there is no hint of any transfigured life. On the contrary, the "tušnišad, those who sit, live in silence," continue to act on earth as dead ones. The same concept prevails in Greece and Italy, and since the Ir. fravarti are also female "valcyries," this is the primeval Indo-European concept of existence after death. Pre-Zoroastrian and Zoroastrian notion are totally different and clearly distinguished.

The cult of the fravarti, the OI. pitáraḥ, Greek "hḗroes," Roman "mānēs," depends in no way on the special and varying modes of disposing of the body, nor these different funerary customs on that cult. Whatever is done to the body, the "uštāna, life" which has left the "astvant body," does not die, but lives, somehow bound to the place where the material shape rests, with which it was endowed. Nor is there any connection between the funerary customs, whatever they were, and Zoroaster's idea of resurrection, which does *not* "root in the Fravarti cult, founded on and 'unthinkable' without interment." "Es ist keinen Augenblick daran zu denken"—one ought to have a minute of thought for everything—"dass der Zoroastrismus [means: after Zoroaster's death] eine solche Grabsitte übernommen hätte, die er zu allen Zeiten mit dem grössten Abscheu betrachtete," another revelation, since the yashts are just as silent as the gathas. A minute of thought and many things "unthinkable" become thinkable; but coexistence of transfigured life and life in silence is indeed unthinkable, as is a "borrowed thought, and yet a bold new creation in grand style." As remarked above, the word pati us.hištan presupposes "rising up from tombs."

Zoroaster's picture of the last judgment is that of a court, of a settling of accounts, hankrti. *Y.*31,14: "yaθa tå ahan hankrtå hiyāt, when it comes to settling accounts." The good and evil acts are put to account, their balance is the riχta, which is "left" behind.

*Y.*32,7:

yēšām tu ahura riχtam mazdā vēdišto ahi

"what they have left, Thou, A.M., knowest best!"

*Y.*44,2:

ho zi rtā spanto riχtam vispabyo
hāro manyū

"He, the holy one, . . . who regards in spirit what every one has left behind." Ahura means lord justiciary, mazdå "to bear in one's memory"; the verses paraphrase the name of the god as "the omniscient judge," not as "der Weise Herr."

Y.49,4:

yēšąm noit hvarštāiš vans dužvarštā

"whose good works do not make level the bad ones." Pahl. transl.: "ku.š kirpak vinās bē nē kanēt, whose good deeds do not make even their sins." Similarly *Y*.31,1: "with whom false and right həməmyāsaitē, is (equally?) mixed?", cf. *Art.Vir.Nām*.VI, chapter 'Hamēstakān': kē.šān kirpak u vinās rāst būt, those whose good and evil deeds are even.[16] All terms are clearly such of accounting and the beginning of the notion "zero." Bartholomae translated 49,44 "bei denen nicht die Gutthaten (sondern) die Übelthaten überwiegen," as sole instance of intrans. √¹van-, "superare"; it is OP. √van- "fill, heap up" said of "θikā, gravel, pebbles, calculi." Counting pebbles is the beginning of "calculare, calculate." Calculating and weighing are intimately connected. The picture of an account takes the form of a banking house in heaven in the later notion of the "ganǰ i hamīša sūδ, the treasure of eternal interest."

The origin of the whole conception is the old custom, inherited from Babylon, to keep written records of everything the king did and ordered; examples are found among the tablets from Persepolis. The word for these records is "hypomnḗmata, memorandum," in *Ezra* 6,2: dkrvn', NP. yād.dāšt. From these deeds the ephemerids were excerpted, the *βίβλια ὑπομνηματισμῶν*, spr dkrvny' in *Ezra* 4,15, spr hzkrnvt in *Esther* 6,1, explained in 2,33 by "spr dbry hymym, deeds of daily acts." Excerpts from longer periods were the *βασιλικαὶ διφθέραι*, deposited in the byt gzny', the "archives" (not "treasure-house"). The "garo dmāna, house of collecting" is the heavenly counterpart of these earthly archives.

Special merits to the king were recorded like his own actions, and the honorific (OP.) *ὀροσάγγαι*, Gr. *εὐεργέται* was conferred upon such men. Herodotus VIII,85: "Phylakos was recorded as Euergétēs of the king." Xerxes writes to Pausanias, Thukydides I,129,3: "Regarding the men from Byzantium whom you have saved for me beyond the sea, the *εὐεργεσία* lies booked for you in our house for ever!" And Darius speaks similarly in the Gadatas inscription (Dittenberger, *Syll.* n° 22).

Markwart tried an etymology of *ὀροσάγγαι* together with *παρα-*

[16] NP. ba zamīn rāst kart, e.g. Baiḍawī, *niẓām,* twice: Buχtnaṣṣar makes bait al-maqdis, Jerusalem, "even with the earth."

σάγγαι: oro- for vuru- "wide," -sangai to √sanh- "announce," unconvincing, because "euergétai" would be no translation of it. F. W. Thomas, *Sakastan*, JRAS.1906, was on the right track; the title must hide one of the words for "good works"; but vrzy.anhvā, *Wb.* "mit energischem Antrieb, Schaffensdrang" is a misleading translation; vrziyahvåho in the Hōma-verses *Y.*10,14 means "in full possession of one's senses" as opp. to "drunk." The Gr. translation is as precise as possible: *εὐ* < hu, *ἔργος* < vrzyah "work(ing)"; existing compounds with duš- can be paralleled by such with hu-, hence *hu.varzyah. There was a noun *srāvanha, deriv. of sravah, of which srāvanhyati is the denom. verb; similarly Aw. upōšanhva, deriv. of upa.ušah, MP. Pōšang. Hence, the deriv. *huvrzyanhva gives *ὀροσάγγαι*.

*Y.*29,4:

mazdå ⁺sahvar.māršto	yā zi vāvrzoi paričitit
dēvāišča martiyāišča	yāča varšate apičitit
ho vičiro ahuro	aθā ahat yača ho vasat

"Mazdāh is the best witness-rememberer of what is wrought in the past by gods and men and of what is wrought in future. He is the justiciary who judges, His will be done!"

What AhuraMazdāh remembers or calculates are the actions of men, recorded with attest in the archives. The wordly institution is transferred to heaven.

sahvār marišto is written in two words, so that the relative clauses "which have been" and "which will be wrought" refer to sahvār; this would be an acc.pl. with the meaning restricted to "actions, intentions." But Bartholomae's "Anschlag, Plan, eigtl. Ankündigung (eines Vorhabens)," Meillet's doubtful "indications?" ("Anschlag" would be "plot"), do not fit √sanh-, OP. θah-, pronuntiare, authoritative or solemn speaking. The Pahl. commentary says: "pa vinās u kirpak amār kunēt, he keeps account of sin and good deeds." The same words are used for the compound hātā.marāni in *Y.*32,6, all but a synonym, "meriti memor." sahvār must be freed of the relative clauses, therefore be read as compound, like hātā.marāni, cf. also našta.rāzišta in *Yt.*10, under 'Mithra.' It is a superl. of *sahvar.mar(ant). The relative clauses, then, relate to the participle: "the best rememberer or accountant of what has been done etc."

The Pahl. transl. of sahvar by sχvn is right. In *Y*.32,7 "sanhate, pronunciatur" is used for the "deposition, speaking" of the ordeal; equally *Dēnk̦*. uses "gowišn=sahvan" for the "speaking, testimony" of the ordeal. *Y*.31,5: "hyat rvatam čazdahvabyo," *Y*.44,5: "yå manōθrīš čazdahvantam arθahya," where rvata, OI. vratá—cf. Ir. rvāta, ῥητόν—is "sentence" in the juridical meaning; "arθa," here "daily task," but also juridical term. Pahl. transl. of čazdahvant is both times "amār vičārtar, who determines the number"; Geldner translated "berechnend," referring to *Ved.* kiyedhā́s. The "number" is obviously the "amount" of punishment. "amār vičārtar" combines the two words of 29,4, (sahvar)-mar(išto) and vičiro (ahuro). Therefore, "sahvar, spoken word" is the deposition of witnesses, the attestation of the action. "marant" means "mental arithmetic," a "marant" is a "hamāra.kara, accountant."

The idea of *Y*.29,4 resembles Thales'

σοφώτατον ὁ χρόνος . ἀνευρίσκει γὰρ πάντα,

which again returns in the zurvanistic saying in *Gr.Bdh.*

zamān adawakān adawaktar
zamān pursišnīkān pursišnīktar
Time is the most undeceivable of undeceivables,
Time is the greatest inquisitor of inquisitors.

Bartholomae was right in speaking of "heavenly book-keeping." Nyberg objects, 211: "Woher sollten die Rinderhirten der Steppe, die keine Ahnung von der Schrift hatten, . . . den Gedanken an himmlische Geschäftsbücher genommen haben?" The book-keeping cannot be denied; the "cowboys of the prairie" are a mere theory. The book-keeping is not absurd, but the cowboys are. The Iranian bureaucracy came from their Babylonian neighbors.

Zoroaster's thought of the judgment as account passed into the other religions. *Daniel* 12,1: "Thy people will be saved, all those who are written down in the book." Or *Daniel* 7,10, vision of the judgment of the four beasts: "The court set, the books were opened." The vision was conceived in Babylon under the Achaemenids, that is place and time where Zoroastrian thoughts went over into Judaism and thence into Christianity, and thus influenced universal history.

Enoch, 92-104, in the treatise on resurrection: "For the spirits that died in justice everything good . . . is written down as reward," and "The sinner may say [*Yt.*10,105: iθa manyatē duš.hvarnå]: Our sins will not be investigated and recorded [noit imat vispam dušvarštam miθro vēnati . . .]; and yet, the angels write down all your sins every day!"—Islam, too, borrowed the idea: "athābahu Allāhu wa-ḍā'afa lahu l-ḥasanāt wa-dja'ala dhukhrahu l-bāqiyyatu l-ṣāliḥāt, Allāh reward him and double him his charities and make him a treasure of good works!" And *Qur.* 9,5: "Allāhu khabīru bimā ya'malūna" is word by word "Mazdå sahvar.mārišto yā zi vāvrzoi."

XXI. YAMĀ

"Still it cried: sleep no more!
Glamis has murdered sleep
And therefore Cawdor shall sleep no more!"

*Y.*45,2: "The good one of the two manyū prviyā, primordial spirits, said to the bad one: Neither our manå, nor our sanhā, χratavo, varnā, uχδā, šyōθnā, dēnå, ruvāno join, hačantē."

"Spirits" is no accurate rendering of manyū: they are something spiritual, nothing concrete; they speak, but they are neither anthropomorphous, nor theomorphous. The best translation would be "the two forces" or "principles," Good and Evil.

Lommel: "Nicht unser beider Denken, . . . Reden, . . . Verstand (Wille?), . . . Wahlentscheidung, . . . Worte, noch Thaten, . . . geistige Natur, . . . Seelen gehen zusammen." The eight hardly definable notions cannot be really translated: complexes of phenomena are compressed in single words, and there are not two languages where these coincide, because the notions behind the words are no realities. One could say "thought, sayings, will, love, words, deeds, essence, soul." It is not yet a psychologic system like that which Mani developed from beginnings already foreshadowed in Darius' tomb inscription, cf. *Altp.Inschr.* 84ff. The eight words have the same purport as καρδίη, ψυχή, διάνοια in the Gospels. The definition of "ruvān, soul" in the *Gr.Bdh.* is elucidating: "Soul is what by the senses in the body sees, speaks, and perceives," or "the soul is the master over the body, like the chief of the family over his house, the horseman over his horse, it is the rāyēnītār, patron, of the body." It is the same with Gr. μένος, ψυχή, φρένες, Lat. mentēs, sententiae, animi or Hebr. rūᵃḫ = πνεῦμα, mēmrā = λόγος, khōkhmā = σοφία. The verses seek to convey: in all the faculties and motives of our spiritual life, we, Spantamanyuš and Ahramanyuš, Good and Evil, are incompatible, unreconcilable opposites.

The verses do not say that good and evil were "twins," not even in a figurative sense. The "Gatha of Good and Evil" is *Y.*30, and there the expression "the two principles" appears once more.

A chapter in *Dēnk.* IX (statement of contents of the VarstmansrNask, ch.7) has been interpreted as being a sort of exegesis to *Y.*30,3-5, cf.

Schaeder, *Beiträge* 288 and Benveniste, in Monde Or. 26,207ff. Translations and inferences therefrom are both erroneous. One must read (cf. *Altp.Inschr.* 130): "ač avēšān amuhraspand[ān] ān ē vattar dōšīt, lit. he [viz. the demon Araš of whom the paragraph speaks] chose the worse share than the Am.Sp." i.e. the share worse than that chosen by the Am.Sp., or better: "in opposition to the Am.Sp. the wholly-bad share," "pat.ān kā.š χšnāsakān dēvān āyazišnīh guft, in teaching: those who know shall worship the dēv!" and "bring offerings to the planetary gods!" These gods are not Xuršēd, Māh, Tīr etc., but astral gods imported from Babylon. Nothing can be gathered from this paragraph for the interpretation of *Y.*30.

*Y.*30,3:

āt tā manyū prviyē	yā yamā hvafnā asruvātām
manahiča vačahiča	šyōθnoi hi vahyo akamča
+ayås.ča hudåho	rš višyāta noit duždåho

"But those two primordial manyū that are praised in song as the 'sleep-twins' are Good and Evil, in thoughts, words and conduct. And between these two [Good and Evil] the good-minded have chosen right, the not-ill-minded."

Bartholomae: "Die beiden Geister zu Anfang, die sich durch ein Traumgesicht als Zwillinge offenbarten, (sind) das Bessere und das Böse in Gedanken, Worten und That." *Ar.Forschg.* II,120: "Dass die beiden Urgeister Zwillinge genannt werden, ist gewiss auffällig." In fact, it is only "the two sleeps" that are called so. At that time, he translated hu.afna asruvātām still by "sie (dual) schufen kunstreich."

Andreas, NGGW, 1909, 48: "Jene beiden . . . Geister, die die selbstherrlichen Zwillinge heissen," an interpretation that cannot be maintained.

One must not render the Iranian by the German (or English) comparative: "the better" would be "better than bad," the lesser evil, while it is a comp. abs. "the wholly good"; vahya comes near to Aristotle's *αὐτοαγαθόν*. "yā . . . asruvātām" is a relative clause, but does not signify "which . . . are called"; it is no parenthesis, and all the less signifies "as has been transmitted" (Nyberg, below); it says "who have been praised in song," in perf.pres. "who are praised in the epic," see under 'Poetry' and 'Yama χšēta.'

Bartholomae compared the dual "the two sleeps" with "savā, the two returns," viz. reward and punishment. Other analogies are "rānā, pious and sinners," "vahū, good and evil," see under 'Last Judgment'; also "dva narā" in *Vid.*2,41, a human pair, man and woman; "hvarθē" in *Yt.*19, eating and drinking. The dual means "sleep and its brother."[1]

The manifestations of spiritual life are usually combined in the stereotyped formula "manah, vačah, šyōθna," from which the three virtues originate: "humat, huχt, huvaršt, good thought, talk, conduct." This most natural idea is found all over the world, in Christianity and earlier, e.g. Democritus: *τὸ εὖ λογίζεσθαι, τὸ εὖ λέγειν, τὸ πράττειν ἃ δεῖ* or *γίνεται δὲ ἐκ τοῦ φρονεῖν τρία ταῦτα · βουλεύεσθαι καλῶς, λέγειν ἀναμαρτήτως καὶ πράττειν ἃ δεῖ.*

Xenophanes says merely "form and thought":

εἷς θεὸς ἔν τε θνητοῖσι καὶ ἀνθρώποισι μέγιστος
οὔτε δεμὰς θνητοῖσι ὅμοιος οὔτε νόημα

The triad always means the total of functions of the soul. Corpses that neither think, nor speak, nor act, are beyond good and evil. The eight manifestations of the soul in *Y.*45,2 have the same purport as this triad.

The mere mention of the dual-name is enough to remind the hearers of the myth which they knew as well as that of Yama Vivahvato puθro, "to whom epics are sung, srāvahyati," and of other heroes, not from lectures at a theological seminary, but from the old epic tales, "yāiš asrōždvam būmyå haftaθē, sung on this seventh of the earth," *Y.*32,3, in the whole of Ērānšahr. Cf. Xenophanes:

τοῦ κλέος Ἑλλάδα πᾶσαν ἐφίξεται οὐδ' ἀπολήξει

and Homer, e.g. *Il.* IX,264:

τοῦ δὴ νῦν γε μέγιστον ὑπουράνιον κλέος ἐστίν.

In these verses, Zoroaster gives the myth—which, as a thing known

[1] Cf. the very same idiom in Arabic: al-'Irāqain, al-Baṣratain etc; as early as in the inscr. of Imrulqais b. 'Amr, "the two Asad" mean "Asad and 'Anaza," see *Mshattā, Ḥīra and Bādiya* in Jahrb.Preuss. Kunstslg. 1921, 108f.

to everybody, he does not detail any further—a new ethical interpretation: "Your epics speak of the primordial twins sleep and his brother; I speak of the two principles Good and Evil." They are two different pairs.

*Y.*30,4:

ātča hyat tā ham manyū ǰasētām prviyam dazdē
gayamča aǰyātimča yaθa⟨ča⟩ ahat apaman ahuš
ačišto drugvatam āt rtāvanē vahištam mano

"When these two spirits [Good and Evil, which I have compared in st.3 with your twins, and defined in my gatha 45,2] came together, they first established life and death, how it shall be at the end: hell, for the drugvant, but paradise for the rtāvan."

That is the passage which Ed. Meyer, following Bartholomae's "they agreed" for ham.ǰasētām, believed to prove that Zoroaster himself knew already the "agreement" of 9,000 years between AhuraMazdāh and Ahramanyuš, of which Plutarch, de Iside, speaks. The number 9,000, though not uttered, may have been in Zoroaster's mind, but the form is not that of a treaty. The "ham.ǰasētām, coming together" is neither procreation nor a compromise, as Bartholomae interpreted the sentence in *Ar.Forschg.* II,122: "Lat. convenire, übereinkommen, weil sie schon beisammen waren." The words of the *Gr.Bdh.* "u.šān miyān tuhīkīh būt, hast kē vāy gōyēnd, between them was a void, others say the atmosphere" are wrong speculations of Sasanian theologians who thought of creation instead of history. "ahu" is the period of "patiyārak, contest." The address by the good principle is the challenge, the false twins were not together, but come together for battle, the *πατὴρ ἁπάντων*, cf. *Yt.* 14,47:

yat spāδā han.ǰasåntē raštam rasmā katarasčit.

Or OP.:

pasāva hamiθ^{r}iyā hangmatā paraitā hamaranam čartanē.

The law gayamča aǰyātimča, that all life must die, and the dwelling places for the dead, paradise and hell—called "huvitīča initī" at the end of the same gatha—are predetermined at the beginning of the "ahu, i.e. the human world." When the fight of history is over, the frašam, apatiyārakīh begins, the zrvan akarana, eternity after the end of time.

*Y.*30,5:

ayå manyuvå vartā	ya drugvå ačišta vrzyo
rtam manyuš spaništo	ya χrōždištān asāno vastē
yēča χšnōšan ahuram	haθyāiš šyōθnāiš fravrt mazdām

"Of these two manyū, the drugvå (manyuš) chose to work the wholly-bad, but (to work) the rtam the spaništo manyuš, who is clothed in the most-solid heavens, and all who, by conduct as it should be (ἂ δεῖ), are voluntarily obedient to AhuraMazdāh."

Gathas and OP. inscriptions use this type of inversion. In these verses the two principles make themselves the moving forces of the world's history. The realm of the one is heaven, of the other hell. The verses do not speak of creation, but of history.

Creation, cosmology is the subject of the "Gatha of the Vision," 43, and of the "Gatha of the Questions," 44. In 43, Zoroaster says, speaking as a poet, not a theologian, st.5:

spantam at θwa	mazdā manhi ahura
hyat θwa ahoš	zanθoi darsam prviyam
hyat då šyōθnā	miždavān yāča uχδā
akām akāi	vahviyām rtim vahvē
θwā hūnarā	dāmoiš rvēsē apamē

"As the holy one I knew Thee, A.M., when I beheld Thee at the procreation of life, as the primordial one, when Thou ordainedst the works and the words to be bearing return, the bad lot for the bad (deeds) and the good for the good, through Thy handy-work, at the last turning of the creation!"

The birth of life is not the law of dying, and paradise and hell for good and bad ones is merely the execution of the law of reward given by the god at the creation. There is no contradiction.

hūnara, to √hū-, whence "hūti, handicraft," is the handy-work, *δημιουργία,* AhuraMazdāh is the demiurge of the world. Hertel is mistaken in relating the last words to the last act of the creation "bei der letzten Wendung der Spendung," instead of the end of the world.

The sentence "as the holy one, spanta, I knew *Thee,* when *he* circumambulated me as Vahumano," many times repeated in this gatha, makes it perfectly certain that AhuraMazdāh himself is the Spanta who appears in the aspect of Vahumano. In *Y.*30,5, the manyuš spaništa is clothed in the most-solid heavens, asāno vastē, as is Mazdāh in *Yt.*13,3, vastē vahanam, and "those who are obedient to Mazdāh have chosen like Spanto manyuš" = Mazdāh. In 43,6, he appears as spanto manyuš and as Vahumano and in all his aspects simultaneously at the last judgment.[2]

Bartholomae wrote in *Wb.*1621: "Dass Geldner u.a. sich . . . wieder dazu verstehen konnten, spanta von KSl. svetu loszureissen, ist mir nicht begreiflich, . . . ohne die Pü. awzūnīk würde niemand auf den Gedanken kommen, spanta anders als mit 'heilig' widerzugeben." Lommel translates, almost thirty years later, "klug" und "der klügere"; Nyberg "wirksam." Hertel objected to "heilig" and contributed an interesting treatise on the origin of the German word, starting from Wulfila's Bible translation. H. W. Bailey established the etymology of the Iranian words derived from √sū- and their Slavic correspondents and other IE. words. Markwart said "heilig," especially insisting on the fact that "Nutzen" (profit) does not belong to Zoroaster's sphere of thought, and contributing the explanation of Skol. ἐξαμπαῖοι = ἱραὶ ὁδοί, äfsand = spanta. After all these investigations, one must go back to "holy." Starting from different notions, the semantic development of Ir. spanta, Lat. sanctus, "holy" and "heilig," has taken such a turn, that the notions coincide to a large extent. It is a delusion to believe that greater accuracy can be reached at all in worlds of ideas so far removed in space and time.

Thus, spanta manyuš is the Spiritus Sanctus, the Holy Ghost. On the other hand, akam mano—equally clear in other gathas—is Ahramanyuš. But nowhere is there a trace of a corresponding organization of evil in aspects of Ahramanyuš, as e.g. aka manah, ēšma, drug etc.

Vahumano, well translated in Greek by εὔνοια or εὐνομία, is Good-Will, as Markwart emphasizes, *Gāth.ušt.* 62, "keine Eigenschaft des Intellekts (Sinn), sondern des Willens." It is sometimes "conscience," always contrasted to "malevolence," an opposition meaning much more than that of truth and lie. Vahumano is the force by which Spantamanyuš effects Rtam in the "ahū, human life." This notion of Good-Will foreshadows already the Christian "Love."

[2] Cf. Y.31,3; 33,12; 43,1,2; 47,1,6; 51,7, with "Mazdāh as SpantaManyuš" in instr. of quality, mostly in connection with the last judgment.

If in *Y*.30,4 the two principles Good and Evil establish first of all life and death, and reward in heaven and hell at the end of the ahu, if in *Y*.30,5 they are the moving forces of history, and if in 43,5 the primordial AhuraMazdāh "procreates life" and "ordains the works to bring return," then the two primordial spirits, manyū prvyā of 45,2, compared in 30,3 with the "twins sleep," are none but AhuraMazdāh (in his quality as Spantamanyuš) and Ahramanyuš.

But here again no word says that AhuraMazdāh and Ahramanyuš were twins, descendants from the same parents. The verses contain not the slightest indication of Zurvanism. That is a doctrine attested first by Eudemus of Rhodus, Aristotle's pupil, who is quoted by Damascius, *de prim.princ.* 125 (ed. Kopp, 384): "The magi and the whole nation of the Aryans call—the ones 'tópos, space,' the others 'chrónos, time'—the homogeneous primordial being from which either a good god or an evil demon, or light and darkness, dissociated themselves."

Nyberg, 122, translates Y.30,3: "Jene beiden Ur-manyū, die Zwillinge Schlaf (und sein Bruder) waren, *wie überliefert worden ist,* das Bessere und das Schlechte," and infers from this translation: "Die Vorstellungen von den Zwillingen bilden also einen Bestandteil einer *traditionellen* Theologie, die es *vor* Zoroaster in der Gatha-Gemeinde gab. Die beiden manyū sind zwar von Anfang an Gegensätze, aber sie sind es nur in Gedanken, Worten und Thaten; mehr wird nicht gesagt." Nobody could say more than all. "Die Aufteilung in Gut und Böse beruht auf Wahl, nicht auf Erschaffung. Sogar die manyū (sind so) durch Wahl, nicht aus innerer Notwendigkeit," which reminds one of squabbles of Byzantine, Sunnite and Protestant sects, typical for religiously unproductive periods. "Die Gatha-Gemeinde [all in spaced print] hat eine gegensätzliche Perspektive ethischen Inhalts auf einem monistischen Hintergrund." This "traditional theology in the Gatha-community before Zoroaster" also "theology of the pre-Zoroastrian community," presupposes gathas before the gathas, and is the foundation of the "theology of the Gatha-community." The gathas are "carmina, odes," and all this results from the wrong translation of "yā asruvātām" by "as has been transmitted," instead of "that are praised in song."

A conception different from *Y*.30 seems first to appear in the very late, identical passages of *Yt*.11,12 and *Y*.57,17, where Srōšo is described like Argos in Hesiod's hymn:

yo noit pasčēta hušhvafa	who no more slept
yat manyū dāmān dāδitām	since the two spirits created the world,
yasča spanto yasča ahro	the Holy and the Bad one.

This is late enough to be Zurvanism. A few lines after, the dāta vidēva, Vidēvdād is mentioned: the preceding lines, too, must be dated in the time of the *Vidēvdād,* the Arsacid period. In Zoroaster's concept, the bad spirit is no creator, he merely "works the evil" in the existing creation. It is only 1,500 years later that e.g. al-Khwārizmī says: "ahraman khāliq al-sharr, Ahriman is the creator of Evil."

The Sasanian theologians were the first to advance the doubly false interpretation that the "two principles" were themselves the "twins," and that Zrvan, Time, was their father. Without seeing the first error, which makes every discussion useless, Nyberg declaims against the second, 104: "In den Gathas ist AhuraMazdāh unzweifelhaft der höchste Gott; eine Vorstellung, nach der er ein abgeleiteter Gott wäre, würde der gesamten gathischen Religion zuwider laufen. AhuraMazdāh, der *Vater der Zwillinge,* ist eine dem Zurvan des Westens parallele Erscheinung im Osten. Hieraus folgt ein sehr wichtiger Schluss: AhuraMazdāh steht jenseit von Gut und Böse. [Nietzsche: jedenfalls nicht jenseit von gut und schlecht!] Er hat die Schöpfer dieser Gegensätze hervorgebracht, aber nicht sie selbst. . . . Es kann keinem Zweifel unterliegen, dass in der Theologie der vorzarathustrischen Gemeinde AhuraMazdāh wesentlich [essentially] ein *deus otiosus* war."

Whether "derived in the west" or "parallel in the east," in no case is he the "father of the twins" with one of whom he is compared. Neither is he the "creator of the creator of evil." In *Y*.44,3, Zoroaster asks "Who is the procreator of Rtam?" but does not go on "Who is the procreator of Ako manyuš?" These verses do not describe an "unessential" interruption of the "otium," *Y*.44:

3:	kasnā zanθā	patā rtahya prvyo
	kasnā huvan	stāramča dāt adwānam
	ko yā mâ	uχšyati nrfsati θwat

4: kasnā drta zāmča ado nabåsča
avapastoiš ko āpo urvāråsča
ko vātāi dvan- mabyasča yōgat āsū
kasnā vahoš mazdā dāmiš manaho
5: ko huvapå rōčåsča dāt tamåsča
ko huvapå hvafnamča dāt zēmāča
ko yā ušå aram.piθwā χšapāča
yå manōθriš čazdahvantam arθahya

3: Who is the procreator of Rtam, the primordial father?
Who has created the sun and the course of the stars?
Who is it through whom the moon waxes and wanes?
4: Who supports the earth below and the heaven,
that it do not fall? who the waters and plants?
Who harnesses to wind and clouds their racers?
Who, Mazdāh, is the creator of Vahumano?
5: Which master created light and darkness?
Which master created sleep and wakefulness?
Who dawn, midday, and night?
the reminders of his task to the thoughtful?

The verses are like *Ps.* 33,6-7: "By the word of the Lord were the heavens made. He gathereth the waters of the sea as in a skin, [he layeth up the depth in store houses]." Or *Ps.* 19,1: "The heavens declare the glory of God, and the firmament sheweth his handy-work." St.4 transfers the cosmologic activity of the Fravarti, *Yt.*13,2-16, to Ahura-Mazdāh: the continuous movement of the Universe, without a minute of "otium."

From these verses Nyberg quotes only the line "Who created light and darkness, sleep and wakefulness?" in the erroneous belief that these were the "Sleep and its brother," and says: "Die Antwort ist ohne Zweifel AhuraMazdāh." This is aimed against Zurvan of the Sasanian theologians, for, sharing their assumption that twins must have a father, and doubly mistaken in the belief that sleep and wakefulness were sleep and its brother and these good and evil, he wants to lay them at AhuraMazdāh's door.

hvafno can no more be a son of AhuraMazdāh than hypnos, the master of all gods, a son of Zeus. As "primordial," the twins are a rare case of "lam yūlid." A recherche de la maternité would probably find clues leading to "nakta, nyx, night"; but neither Zurvan nor Ahura-Mazdāh was their father; they are "prvya," with no father at all: dinanzi a me non fur cose create!

What we know about the twins is: they belong to an immemorially old myth, bear the dual-name "the two sleeps," and Zoroaster says: "You have twins, so do I!" He uses the pair as a metaphor for his two principles. From the mistaken premise Nyberg draws the "justified conclusion": "Der Schlaf repraesentiert das Licht [= Tagesgott]. . . . Nicht die physiologische Erscheinung die wir Schlaf nennen ist gemeint, sondern—weil Schlafen und Wachen letztlich in uralten kultischen Verhältnissen [what about animals?] begründet sind, und weil der Kult des Tagesgottes mit Trance und hypnotischer Betäubung verbunden war—darum heisst der manyu des Tagesgottes xvafna 'Trance.' " There is still: "Der Umstand dass 'Schlaf' als Name des wirksamen [= spanta] manyu auftritt—122: Spanta manyu trägt den Namen xvafna 'Trance' —zeigt, dass der *trance-Zustand des Schamanen* gemeint ist, in dem sein Geist sich auf dem Fluge befindet. . . ." This sounds like a solution of one of the darkest sayings of Heraclitus: *οἱ καθεύδοντες ἐργάται καὶ συνεργοὶ τῶν ἐν τωι κόσμωι γινομένων.*

Raving madness, ecstasies, frenzy and the epileptic conditions, exhaustions, stupor, trance connected with them, have been expertly described by Iamblichus, "On Mysteries" and Cicero "On Divination." The *Gr.Bdh.*, too, speaks of trance, in the chapter on opposites, f°. 47f., where the words are arranged under two columns, evil and good. Under "evil" it gives "trance, būšasp < bušyanstā," under "good" it gives "sleep, χvāp < hvafna." Bušyanstā, with the epithet "zarinā, making decrepit," is a specially pernicious female demon; in *frgm. Westerg.* 10, she calls "hvafsata martiyākåho, hvafsata mrzu.ǰīyåho, hvafsata mrzu.ǰītayo, go asleep mortals, go asleep short-living ones, go asleep short-lived ones!" Bartholomae, KZ.29,547, explained bušyanstā as "condition of him who will become, i.e. will come to," euphemistically for unconscious trance, which was believed to be a temporary death. So, what Nyberg describes as the "Holy Ghost," is in Iranian belief the work of the most-unholy ghost.

Zoroaster quotes a name from an antique myth, well known to his hearers, but not mentioned in the yashts. This name is a dual of hvafna, hypnos, somnus. He compares this pair with his Good and Evil, the powers which determine first of all that all life must die, gayamča aǰyātimča. These words, hence, contain the tertium comparationis, which is neither trance nor wakefulness, but death.

Homer, *Il.* XIV,231, calls hypnos-hvafna *κασίγνητος θανατοῖο ἄναξ πάντων τε θεῶν πάντων τ᾽ἀνθρώπων*. Hesiod and Herakleitos, too, philosophize on the brothers Hypnos and Thanatos. More than "partir" the sleep is "mourir un peu," and death is the sleep from which no one awakes. Sleep generates new life, is the good death, belonging to light. Death is wholly darkness. Nyberg 231: "Für den aša-gläubigen Ekstatiker ist schon jetzt der Tod eine bedeutungslose Episode, und er wird es in noch höherem Masse in der verklärten Welt sein, wo alle Schranken des göttlichen Ewigkeitslebens gefallen sind" [sic].

This gallimathias can indeed "auch den abgehärtetsten sprachlos machen" (482).

μὴ δή μοι θανατόν γε παραύδα φαίδιμε Νύβεργ!

The thought of the twins, sleep and death, pervades all myths, legends and fairy tales of IE.-speaking peoples, and the myth to which Zoroaster alludes was certainly one of the primeval period. The whole conception derived from this verse, namely of a Gatha-community with traditional theology and contrary perspective of ethical contents on monistic background, of a deus otiosus, A.M., who, beyond good and evil, restricts himself in his otium cum indignitate to create the "effective spirit," called "sleep, trance" for working only with senses fuddled, and the bad spirit, bad without inner necessity, and who then leaves his creation—Zola: "jamais on n'abandonne une oeuvre!"—to these creatures, altogether a ghastly picture, and moreover the "much more highly insignificant episode of death in the limited life of eternity (or life in limited eternity?)," the whole Gatha-community, a kind of theological seminary, in the steppes of the Tūryan tribe of Friyāna, "stürzt rettungslos zusammen," as a construction "die so unsinnig ist wie nur etwas sein kann" (357).

XXII. YAMA XŠĒTA

"Ομηρος ἄξιος ἐκ τῶν ἀγώνων ἐκβάλλεσθαι καὶ ῥαπίζεσθαι"—Heraclitus

Y.32 is Zoroaster's song against the dēva and dēvayasna, the gods and heroes of a "heroogonia" or of an epopee, of which small fragments are preserved in the Awesta: *Yt*.5, Ardvīsūrā, *Yt*.9, Druvāspā, 13, Fravarti, 14, Vrthragna, 15, Vāyu, 17, Rti, and 19 Zam-Ārmatiš. Among them, *Yt*.13 stands by itself, while 5, 15, 17 and 19 conform wholly as to the three oldest cycles of Yama, Krsāspa, and the Kavi; of the fourth cycle, of Vištāspa, parts have been subsequently introduced, with variants, in *Yt*.5 (with more detail) and in 15, 17 and 19 (quite short).

The Median history of Herodotus, in which myth and truth are mixed, and a few legends told by Ctesias as if they were history, show how widely the old myth, including the kavi cycle, was spread among the people during the fifth century B.C. Xenophon's words, *Cyrop*.1,2, *ὁ Κῦρος λέγεται καὶ ᾄδεται ἔτι καὶ νῦν ὑπὸ τῶν βαρβάρων*, attest the Husravah legend at the end of the 5th century, and, in the middle of the fourth, Dinon apud Cicero quotes from it the tale of Cyrus' dream. Chares of Mytilene tells, at the end of the fourth century, the most explicit version of the legend of Vištāspa and Zarivariš. Some of Ctesias' tales show also how soon historical events of a near past were absorbed by the legend: the "mythic thinking" of the people worked quickly and constantly, using the old patterns over and over again.

There was no reason to have the fragments arranged in the yashts in any specific order. If *Yt*. 5, 9, 15, 17 and 19 have them in an identical sequence, this is because the tales had been subjected to a uniform redaction. If *Yt*.13 deviates in some points, it is because something belonging to the phase before that redaction has been preserved.

The feature most conspicuous to us, of that redaction, is the chronological arrangement of the stories, which is fitted into the old system of nine aeons. We can observe it best because it was maintained throughout the Arsacid period, which was especially fertile in transformations and alterations, and it survived unaltered in the Sasanian *χvatāynāmak* and Firdausi's Shāhnāmah. The redaction therefore consisted in collecting formerly isolated tales and welding them together into a great epopee. The fragments preserved in the Awesta are quotations from this epopee, the uniform redaction of which, hence, is older than the redaction of the yashts themselves, and must have taken place during an early phase of the Achaemenian period. We shall see that it was done after the time of the gathas. The younger legend of the Vištāspa cycle originated at that time, and, to be quoted in the yashts, must first have been added to the epopee. But the variants show that it was not subjected to so strict a redaction as the older parts. Before the time of Alexander it was admitted into the Awesta redaction made under the reign of Artaxerxes II. Thus the development of the epopee and of the Awesta took place in parallel to each other, and both unite materials that had existed for a long time. But the epic materials were the first to be collected: the "proto-Shāhnāmah" is older than the Awesta.

For the introductory stanzas 1-2 of *Y.*32 see under 'Ārmatiš.' St.3-7 speak in general of the gods and heroes. St.3:

āt yuš dēvā vispåho	akāt manaho stā čiθram
yasča vå maš yazatē	drujasča parimatoišča
šyōmām api dbitānā	yāiš asrōždvam būmyå haftaθē

"You, the gods all and who worship you, are the brood of the evil Spirit, the Druχš and Pride, and the deeds are double-sided for which you are praised in song on this seventh of the earth!"

The "seventh of the earth" is the middle kršvar,—see under 'Kršvar'—and the words say that the epics were sung over the whole of āryānām χšaθram. Cf. *Vid.*2,20: "Yamo χšēto sruto āryanē vējahē, Jamšēd, praised in song in Ērānvēj." "Pride," parimatiš, Gr. hybris, is the typical vice of the Iranian nobility, see under 'Ārmatiš.' "dbitāna, double-(sided, -faced)" is defined by the following stanza, st.4:

yāt yuš.tā framimiθa	yā martiyā ačištā danto
+vašyantē[1] dēvazuštā	vahoš siždyamnā manaho
mazdå ahurahya	χratoš nasyanto rtātča

"For you tell fables of wholly evil deeds so that men doing them are

[1] Text: vaχšənte, Bartholomae: subj. of √vak-; Duchesne: +vaχšantai, to √vaχš- "ils deviennent." The verb must be √vak-, beside framimiθa, asrōždvam etc, and rather +vašyantē than vaχšyantē.

called 'beloved-by-the-gods,' while they are a horror to Vahumano and sinners against AhuraMazdāh's will!"

"yāt, ex quo," only here, cannot be temporal "since" (*Wb.*), but only causal, or perhaps, referring to sravah (to be abstracted from asrōždvam) "in which songs," the causative connection of the stanza being already expressed by "tā—yā." This would give the meaning "For in your epics you invent tales of such a kind that. . . ." For dēvazušta, i.e. *ὅντιν' ἂν φιλῇ θεός*, see under 'Dēva.' St.5:

tā dabnōta martiyam   hujiyātoiš amrtātasča
hyat vå akā manahā   yān dēvān akasča manyuš
akā šyōθnam vačaha   yā fračinas drugvantam χšayo

"Thereby you cheated man out of his good-living and immortality etc." Instead of "thereby" perhaps better—like "yāt" in st.4—"in those (epics)." With these words the prophet alludes for the first time to the Yama myth: hujyāti describes the paradisiac life of the golden age, when men were still immortal. The rest, with "the evil Spirit contrives a drugvant to be ruling," seems to allude to AžiDahāka, who succeeded Yama, and at the same time to establish an analogy between AžiDahāka and Gōmāta (or Cambyses?). St.6:

poru ēnå an.āχštā yāiš   srāvahyati yazi tāiš aθā
hātā.marānē ahura   vahištā voista manahā

"Their many acts of violence and discord, for which epics are sung, Thou, Lord remembering-men's-merits, knowest as VahuMano!"

srāvahyati, as denom.pres. of *srāvanha, vrddhi deriv. of "sravah, fame," must be an expression more intense than the simple √sru-, "to praise in song," viz. "to sing epics." "hātā.marāni, meriti-memor," resembles sahvar.mārišta in Y.29,4. The Pahl. commentary to both words is the same: "he keeps account of sin and good deeds."

St.7: (text under 'Last Judgment'): "The testimony of the ordeal will reveal their true riχta, the value of what they leave behind, well known to Ahura."

The whole tenor of these verses is of the same spirit as Herakleitos' *οὔ τε γινώσκων θεοὺς οὐδ ἥρωας οἵτινές εἰσι.*

√sru-, sravah, Gr. *κλέϝος*, OHG. hliu, is by etymology and sense the word for the singing and reciting—NP. surūdan—of the epics. It appears in this gatha more frequently than anywhere else, clearly indicating its purport: the gatha is a declamation against the "heroes, helden lobebaeren" (=Ir. *sravahvant) of the "Proto-Shāhnāmah." *srāvanha is apparently the word for the epopee itself. Not to have grasped the meaning of √sru- is the reason all translations went astray.[2]

In st.8, Zoroaster chooses, for explaining his transvaluation of moral values, the individual case—to which he had already alluded in st.5:

ēsām ēnahām vivahušo srāvi yamasčit

"among these villains, Yamo Vivahušo of all is praised!"

Christ explains his doctrine in the Gospel of Matthew by saying: "Have you not read in the law . . . but I say unto you. . . ." Zoroaster's way is the same, only his audience is different, and therefore, instead of the Law and the Prophets, it is the epic from which he takes his example. If a very short quotation in a verse of Zoroaster was enough to remind his hearers of a myth, that shows that the epic not only existed, but was known by heart by almost every man. Like the quotations in *Yt.*13, Zoroaster's allusions do not conform with the uniform redaction of the epic reflected by the great yashts; they represent a phase older than the early Achaemenian redaction, and that phase—of separate epics—is older than the gathas.

The figure of Vivahvant-Vivasvant is common to Iranian and Indian myth, hence at least of Aryan antiquity. From the Veda we can infer that Vivasvant was, in the Aryan myth, a god of light, father of Ušå-Eos and of her brothers, the Aśvin twins. In Iran, his son is Yama, i.e. the twin; of the father—beside the patronym of the son—nothing is left but a short remark in Hōm-yasht *Y.*9,4, that he was the first to press Hōma, and therefore was rewarded by having a son like Yama χšēta.

Bartholomae, *Wb.*1452, qualifies as "mir höchst zweifelhaft" the usual

[2] √sru-, MP. srōd, "song," NP. surūdan "to sing," means MHG. singen und sagen. The translations, *Wb.* gives of srāvi in *Y.*32,7 and 8; 33,7; 45,10; 53,1; of srōtu in *Y.*49,9; of frasruta in *Y.*50,8, are all wrong. *Y.*50,8: padāiš yā frasruta īžayå, means "verses sung con passione"; the denom. srāvaya in ho no vašti čarkrθrā srāvayahe, means "he wants to sing our fame"; ēnå yāiš srāvahyati "the misdeeds for which epics are sung to him," not "by which he has succeeded [a wrong etymology of an.āχšta, i.e. "unpeaceable"] to get in ill-repute" (*Wb.*). Cf. Ass. wa.me.ti.ar.šu, king of Medes, presupposing an analogous verb.denom. vahmayat- (part.) from vahma "praise, prayer." *Y.*46,14: ko vā frasrūdyāi vašti, "who wants to be praised"; *Y.*46,34: "frasrūdyāi rθwo, who is worth to be praised?" *Vid.*2,20: "yamo χšēto sruto āryanē vēǰahē, Jamšīd, praised in song in Ērānvēž," etc.

combination of vivahvant and OI. vyúcchati, √[1]vah-. This root, also with vi-, appears in Iranian only as inch. pres. "usa," and only for the "flashing up" of Ušå. Zoroaster uses a neologism, vivahuša, for the traditional vivahvana, OP. vivāna (see under 'Vēhviya'), and for the vulgar language, the word seems to have been merely a name no longer conveying any meaning.

His epithet χšēta Yama shares with the sun, hvar, and with Apām-Napāt. The fem. χšoiθnī is the epithet of Ušå and Rtiš. H. Collitz, in *Orient.Stud.Pavry,* compared Yama χšēta with the Nordic Baldur, i.e. king, prince, and with sāturnus, old saeturnus, this to *sātus < *saetus as taciturnus to tacitus, and *saetus equal to Ved. kṣetaḥ "ruler" in *RV.* 9,97,3; kṣetavant in *RV.*6,2,1. Aw. χšēta survives in Soghd. iχšēδ, NP. šēδ, with Arab. imāla šāδ. It may have been by the influence of the epic that this title, like kay < kavi, never quite disappeared though its sense was lost.

In *Yt.*13 and *Vid.*2-3, Yama is the first man and king, ruler of the primeval golden age. The fact that Zoroaster chose just him as example proves that to him, too, Yama was still the first, whereas in the uniform redaction of the great yashts the strangers Hōšyanha and taxmo Rupiš precede him. In the original myth, the whole earth was Yama's kingdom, but this earth was limited by the horizon of Ērānvēž, the old home of the Aryans, it was not yet Ērānšahr. There, men lived in eternal spring, eternal youth and immortal.

A first man and king of the old myth is something quite different from the incorporeal, theological figure of the first man "Urmensch," gayamart, which was created in connection with eschatologic speculations. The "Urmensch" is more than once subject of Nyberg's discussions, e.g. 388: "Unser Awesta giebt . . . keine Vorstellung davon, welch zentrale Gestalt der Urmensch im iranischen Glauben war"; 84: "Eine Urmenschgestalt wird im Mithrayasht nicht sichtbar . . ."; 300: "Die Urmenschgestalten dürften in der Gatha-Gemeinde nicht stark entwickelt gewesen sein; dort interessierte man sich mehr für den Urstier und die Urkuh"; 96: "Die Grosskönige haben keinen Anlass gefunden, Zarathustra besondere Aufmerksamkeit zu schenken. . . . Es besteht aller Grund zu glauben, [the quoted passages cannot be that reason] dass sie interessiert zuhörten, wenn Magier ihnen vom Urmenschen erzählten." He says himself "what they thought in their innermost, we do not know," but an analogy might help: *Kit. al-Aghānī,* 6,8: " 'Ubaida b. Hilāl used to call, when people gathered round him: Some of you come forth! Thus, two young fellows of the army stepped forth and he asked: What do you like better, something from the Qur'ān or poems? They said: The Qur'ān, wallāh, we know as well as you, recite us poems! 'U.: You rascals, now I know, you prefer poems to the Qur'ān! And then he treated them with poems till they were full. They did not part sooner." Likewise, Darius may have said to the magi: "Zoroaster—I know him better than you rascals, tell me something of the first man!" But, from talks I had at Takht i Djamshīd, on "Yama's throne," with successors of Yama and Darius about their predecessors, I got the impression that the first-man was Hecuba to them.

The text of *Y.*32,8 is:

ēšām ēnahām	vivahušo srāvi yamasčit
yo martiyān čiχšnūšo[3]	ahmākān gāuš bagā hvaramno
ēšām +čitā ahmi	θwahmi mazdå vičiθoi api

"Of these villains Yama Vivahuša of all is praised, who hearkened to the mortals (still) immortal, by eating beef. From them, at the revenge, I want to be separated by Thee!"

The second line, a fragment of the myth itself, will be discussed later.

Bartholomae translated the beginning: "Zu diesen Frevlern gehört wie bekannt, auch Yima der Sohn des Vivahvant." The Aghāni tell a nice anecdote of abū l-'Atāhiya, where he says: "All men make verses, they just are not aware of it!" Andreas: "Als einer dieser Frevler wurde zumal bekannt, Yama der Sohn des Vivahvant." Nyberg: "Als solcher Sünden schuldig ist Vivahvant's Sohn genannt worden."

In the last translation, "guilty of such sin" brings in a new thread of thought, whilst Zoroaster declaims already in five full stanzas against the same villains. Andreas' "zumal" is right: it puts an accent on the greatest hero as greatest "ēnah, ὑβρίζοντα."[4] But in the epic Yama was exalted, srāvahyati, not as criminal, but as the first of heroes, radiant, with eyes like the sun, who surpassed the gods, and the poets,

[3] Tedesco: "perhaps better verb.finit. +ciχšnūšat."

[4] Cf. dršta.ēnah in *Y.*34,4 "causing severe pain," NP. durušt < MP. društ, OP. *društa, not (*Wb.*) "sichtbare Gewaltthat ausübend."

with human understanding, felt only sympathy when he finally sinned and lost immortality. If this "Urmenschgestalt der Mithra-Gemeinde" had been generally rated—"wie bekannt"—as criminal, or had been enumerated—"genannt"—among a list of such, there was no need for Zoroaster to get excited. Just the contrary is the case, and his words purport: "You glorify Yama, and yet your greatest hero is the greatest villain."

In 32,c one used to read "ēšām.čit ā"; the emendation "ēšām čitā" is Andreas'. Justi translated "in deiner Entscheidung, vičiθoi, bin ich," meaning "es steht bei Dir, in Thy discretion." H. Collitz, l.c. 91, "hierüber will ich Dir die Entscheidung anheimstellen," with api as postpos. to vičiθoi. "vičiθoi ahmi" is not "anheimstellen," the prophet would not dare but to "leave everything to his god's discretion." Bartholomae, *Wb.*: "ab his sum in tua separatione postea," improved by Benveniste, *Inf.av.* 33, who compares Lat. "essere in odio," hence "(loin) d'eux je suis désormais dans ta séparation," i.e. "je serai . . . par toi séparé d'eux." It is imprecative: "I want to be separated by Thee." Andreas: "bei deren Bestrafung (čitā—τίσις) bin ich alsdann unter Deinen Auserwählten"; vičitoi to √či- "auserwählt" is wrong. The same thought is expressed in *Mir.Man.* II,24 by "and do not count us together with the višōbagān, rebels." The sentence means: "When the revenge of the last judgment overtakes the sinners, do not let me suffer with them!"

Abandoning the special example, Zoroaster continues in st.9: "duš.sastiš sravå mrndat, telling of ill(-fame) spoils fame!"

duš.sasti, *Wb.* "üble Lehre, evil doctrine." There is nothing doctrinal e.g. in θāti dārayavauš χšāyaθya. sasti, to √sanh, OP. θah-, is simply "pronunciatio, proclamatio," usually a solemn speaking, but even that not always. *Y.*62.7: to all those for whom he has cooked dinner and breakfast, Ātar—the Fire—addresses the "sasti, call," viz. "Come and get it!" The similar word duš.sravah, δυσκλεϝής, means "ill-famed"; and *Gr.Bdh.* 47f., chapter on opposites, says: "deceit and lies, antonyms of rāstīh-sravbīh, saying-truth." But in Zoroaster's idiom "duš-" is syn. of "miθah, wrong," and has a moral quality; duš.sasti

> is close to "miθa.vačah, saying the wrong thing." *Y.*45,1: "noit dbitiyam duš.sastiš ahum mrndat, not shall, a second time, (= never again) saying-things-immoral corrupt the human-world!" The evil (duš-), the telling of which destroys fame (sravå), is "duš.sravah, shame." One may consider whether sravå means here straightway "the epopee." At any rate, *κλέϝος* is "epic fame," and the sentence says: "The Iranian epics glorify what is shame, tell ignominies!"

This criticism of the *θεοὶ καὶ ἥρωες οἵτινές εἰσι* is revolutionary and would hurt still today. The whole gatha makes manifest how unpopular Zoroaster's ideas were, just as unpopular as Heraclitus' "Homer deserves a thrashing!" And he knew it, for st.9 ends with the words:

tā uχδā manyoš mahya   mazdå rtāiča yušmabya grzē,

"these words are of my thinking, I lament them for you, Mazdāh and Rtam!"

In st.5, the words dabnōta martiyam hujiyātoiš amrtātasča allude to the Yama myth, by describing life in the golden age. The very verses of the epics are preserved in quotations in *Yt.*19,32 and 5,26. The first place has the introductory formula in the 3rd pers.: "yo uzbarat hača dēvēbyo," the second in the 1st pers.: "yaθa azam uzbarāni hača dēvēbyo." The verses on the races of Husravah, *Yt.*19,77 and 5,50, show the same difference, which is a clear evidence of 'quotation' from the epic, and it is not permissible to restore the meter, because it was of necessity wrong in the yasht. In the epic the beginning may have been: "Yamo vivahvato puθro uzbarat hača dēvēbyo." *Yt.*19,32:

uwē ištišča sōkāča   uwē fšōnīča vanθwāča
uwē θranfšča frasastīča   uwē hvarθē ajiyamnē
amaršantā pasū.vīrā   +ahōšamnē[5] āpaurvarē

There are three dvandva connected with ča—ča, and three with epithets in form of participles. The first three are: riches and prosperity, cattle-breeding and herds, satiation and "proclamation." All—except the last—have an archaic air, and, not necessarily so, but the symmetry of the composition makes the authenticity of frasasti probable. This

[5] Text: ahaōšəmnə, perhaps +a.hušyamnē.

would be possible, if the word meant a kind of professional licence, as in the "Song of the Caravan," *Yt.*16,2-3, see under 'Post and Travels.' The three duals with participles are: "the two foods, i.e. eating and drinking, never decreasing," never becoming scanty; "cattle and men not dying"; "water and plants, i.e. the fields, never dry." Altogether this is "hu̯iyāti, good-living," or "vispā.hu̯yāti" (see under 'Harvatāt'), and in all this Yama "uzbarat hača dēvēbyo, surpasses the gods."

Lommel translates these words "brachte er von den Teufeln weg nach oben"; Hertel, *Siegesf.* 43: "welcher den dēva raubte, wörtl. von den dēva heraufbrachte; die Heimat der dēva liegt *unter* dem Erdboden." hu̯yāti, one of the things the beggar wishes his benefactor—see under 'Poetry'—was never in hell. Not even this absurd conclusion could induce the translators to doubt the supposition, the equation "dēva = devil." dēva is divi, the divine ones.

uz.barati is a clear expression: uz—hača means "up from the point where the measuring starts," "higher than" in direction or degree, syn. of pari and upari; OIr. uz—hača is MP. ač—apar, NP. az—bar. *Purs.* 37,f.: "yo upari hūnaram mano barat, lit. who carries his will beyond his skill"—i.e. attempts a thing beyond his capacity, overrates himself; Pahl. transl. "kē . . . apar ač hūnar mēnišn barēt, expl. χvēštan pat.ān hūnar mēnēt kē.š nēst, who fancies himself to be so skillful as he is not." upari barati is ὑπερφέρειν; uz.barati hača, in 19,32, is Lat. efferre, excellere: "he surpasses the gods in wealth etc."

The verses describe Yama before his fall, *Yt.*19,33: "parā an.ādruχtoit, before his not-temptation," with the inimitable negation "before he wasn't tempted." Hertel, *Siegesf.* 43,9: "vor der Aufhebung der nicht-Vernichtung!" The following words explain it: "parā ahmāt yat him ayam drōgam vāčam ahaθyam činmanē pati.barata, before he admitted drōga, the voice that-speaks-forbidden-things in his appetites," and 19,34: "Then, after having admitted the voice etc., the hvarnah parted from him."

haθya is Gr. ἃ δεῖ, "as it should be"; the anton. a.haθya is "forbidden." Thus opposed, the words correspond to Arab. halāl and ḥaram, and "a.haθya" means "taboo." Wolff-Bartholomae:

"Aber als er anfing, sich in Gedanken mit ihm, dem lügnerischen, unwahren Wort zu beschäftigen." "drōga" is not "mendacious" and "vāč" is "voice," not "word"; "sich beschäftigen," even if "be preoccupied with," misses the point.—Of the following words, avēno hvarno fraišto yimo, Benveniste says "défie l'analyse." I take "avēno hvarno," whatever fraišto means, as part.abs. "with the hvarnah no longer visible." Lommel goes on translating "wurde er wegen seiner üblen Gesinnung gestürzt und verbarg sich überall auf der Erde." After having brought up from hell—Lommel's translation—all good things of life, Yama would suffer the blackest ingratitude for his pain by such a revolution in paradise.

*Yt.*19,34 (see under 'Hōma') says only:

brāsat—yamo ašāto	Yama roams about peaceless (= outlawed)—
dāušmanahyāiča ho strto	prostrate in misery
niδārat—upari zām	he hides—over the earth.

The verses are deranged by interpolations, but could be restored by inserting χšēto, as opp. to ašāto, and changing the sequence of the words. dāušmanahya is Ved. daurmanasya, formed like hāumanahya.[6]

In *Y.*32,8b, the verse we have left to be studied, Zoroaster reveals what *Yt.*19 (and 5), the Hōm yasht, and *Vid.*2-3, pass over in silence: through whose "voice" the temptator speaks, and what was the "taboo":

yo martiyān čiχšnūšo ahmākān gauš baga hvaramno

Bartholomae: "der um die Menschen zufrieden zu stellen, den unsrigen die Fleischstücke zu essen gab; nach uralter Sage der Fürst, der seine Unterthanen durch Fleischspeise unsterblich gemacht hat." "Fleischstücke" would be an unnecessary "rationing" in a country where "the two foods were ajyamna, not diminishing" however much they ate. The food of immortality was vegetarian, see under 'Harvatāt.' The paraphrase is totally wrong. Since Yama's time men are mortal, so,

[6] *Wb.*1634.—Cf. dāušdātahya in *Ōgm.*56, *Wb.*: "wegen Mangel an Einsicht," Duchesne "par ignorance." It is rather deriv. from "dāta, fixed date" and means—similar to amanimna—"unexpectedly," scil. as bad surprise (death comes), Germ. 'zur Unzeit,' untimely, opp. to Gr. εὐκαίρως, and equal to Ass. ina ūm lā šēmtu.

a priori, he cannot have made them immortal, but only the contrary, as Zoroaster says "have cheated man out of his good-living and immortality."

> čiχšnūšo—or here, with Tedesco ⁺ciχšnūšat—desid. of √χšnu- "to hear," means "hearken, listen to," with the connotation "to something forbidden," see *Y*.49,1: yo dušrθriš čiχšnūšo under 'Bandva.' The acc. martiyān—ahmākān belongs to this verb, not to hvaramno, which in no case means "give food to." Translating "baga" by "Fleischstücke" means confounding portion and ration: it is not the portion the butcher cuts out as a beefsteak, but the share God allots to men. gauš baga is syn. of Akk. pitipabagu < OP. *piθwabaγa, Gr. deriv. *ποτίβαζις*, a diet, habit of life, see under 'Harvatāt.'

The only improvement in Andreas' translation "der den zu uns gehörigen Menschen zu gefallen suchte, indem er Stücke vom Rind ass" is that martiyān ahmākān are objects of čiχšnūšo. Nyberg's "der um den Menschen zu gefallen, die Unsren Stücke vom Rind zu essen lehrte" is a step back: teaching to eat pieces could only mean "not the whole ox." Andreas had already rejected the causative interpretation of hvaramna, however near at hand. It is everywhere the task of the "first one"—Arab. al-awā'il—to teach all imaginable things, and in the late legend of Yama, e.g. in Tha'ālibī, Yama-Djamshīd teaches the fabrication of weapons, saddles, bridles, other tools and implements, spinning and weaving of silk, linen and cotton, the whole national economy, quarrying and masoning of stones, making chalk and cement, architecture, hydraulic wheels and mills, bridge-building, mining, perfumery, pharmaceutics, medicine, ship-building and pearl-fishery. He is a university without theological, philological and juridical faculty, with enough work for the 716½ years of his rule. But "Stücke vom Rind essen" is not among these subjects; on the contrary, according to the legend even under his successor Dahāk men did not yet eat meat. Under Dahāk only, Iblīs-Ahriman had the bright idea of offering himself as chef and giving him the habit of an exclusive meat-diet, in order to make him bloodthirsty. Iblīs starts, to Dahāk's delight, with partridges—toujours perdrix—goes over to lamb, then to mutton, and finally to nothing but beef: "the stomach is a cursed Satan!"

The three translations quoted are worse than wrong. ahmākān qualifies martiyān, the men in Yama's paradise, who lived 3,000-2,000 years before Zoroaster. Yama could not "satisfy" his men by giving something to eat to Zoroaster's "Unsrigen, ours." Neither can ahmākān have the meaning of "*ahmavant, (mortals) like ourselves," for man lost his immortality only by Yama's fall. So says Zoroaster in *Y*.32,5: dabnōta amrtāta, and *Yt*.19,32: amaršantā pasū.vīrā. There is no problem: ahmākəng is a clerical error for amahrkəng, i.e. "amhrkān, immortals": "Yama who listened to the (still) immortal mortals and ate beef."

This was the taboo. *Gen*.3,17 says: "Thou hast hearkened, čiχšnūšo, to the voice, vāčam ahaθyam, of thy wife, and hast eaten, hvaramno, of the tree!" In both cases, immortality was bound to the interdiction of a special food, here beef, there an apple. *Gen*.1,29 permits the eating of "every herb bearing seed, to you it shall be for meat!" The yahwistic version, *Gen*.1,9 and 2,17, permits eating from every tree, "but of the tree of the knowledge of good and evil, thou shalt not eat of it: for in the day that thou eatest thereof thou shalt surely die!"

The seducer is, in the Biblical story, the serpent, which first seduces Eve, to whose voice Adam listens. In *Yt*.19,33, drōga is the seducer, and in *Y*.32,8 Yama listens to the voice of the martiyān who—seduced by drōga—claim meat. This feature was transformed, in the late legend, into Iblīs as chef of Dahāk. There is a story in *Num*.11,4, where "the mob fell a lusting, who shall give us flesh to eat?", and whereas Moses says "sooner kill me!" Yama gives way to public opinion and trespasses the taboo. Thereupon, the hvarnah, his "Fortuna" parts from him, and men, created immortal, lose their immortality, *Y*.32,5.

In contrast to this mythic concept, Zoroaster makes the law "gayam ajyātimča" be established at the very beginning.—To consider eating and dying as complementary is common in the East. *Nām.Nip*. §80, says in a letter of condolence: "There is no remedy against death and dying for the food-eating humanity." And Shā'ūl b. Salmān of Hillah, my manager in Samarra, who had the whole wisdom of Solomon tanumanθra, in his body, used to say: "We all die from eating."

For his sin, Yama is expelled from paradise and hides as an outlaw without peace. The fact that he was being killed (sawed in two) by Aži-Dahāka could be combined with this motif, though the fragments of text preserved do not show how. But the motif is unreconcilable with the other one, of which large parts have survived, that the paradisiac life ended with winter and flood and extinction of two-thirds of all life. This is announced to Yama with the instruction how to save himself and the remaining third, *Vid*.2,22, cf. 2,23 under 'Ardvī': avi ahum astvantam aγam zimo ǰanhantu! Bartholomae (cf. *ZAirWb*. 98): "Upon the evil humanity the winters shall come!" Justi, on the contrary, "upon humanity the bad winters." The Pahl. transl. has indeed, like Justi, "apar ō aχv ē astowand ān ē vattar zamistān rasēt," and aγavant is adj. to "winter" in *Vid*.7,27. Language and grammar are too inferior to decide whether the announcement implies "punishment for their guilt" or not.

Against this winter, Yama builds his "var" in *Vid*.2,30. AhuraMazdāh prescribes: "make the var one tačara long on all four sides; the fratamam dahyāuš, front part of the dēh, village, make nine, the middle six, the back part three prθwo, alleys?"—a text grammatically deficient; on the first nine prθwo a thousand men and women shall dwell, on the second 600, on the third 300. The sum—1,900—means "infinite."

In *Vid*.2,28, Yama is ordered to bring into this var the biggest and handsomest of all men and women, of all animals, the highest and most fragrant of all plants, the best tasting viands: "tē krnava miθwarē aǰyamnam ā ahmāt yat aite naro varəfšva ahān."

> Bartholomae regarded this varəfšva as a loc.pl. of var, confused with the verbal varfšva of st.10, and so arrived at the startling translation: "die lass sich paaren ohne Unterlass, solange Männer in den varšva sind." But there is only one var, and, of necessity, the sentence speaks of both sexes and moreover of humans and animals. The adv. aǰyamna is not "incessantly," but "not-diminishing"—see under 'Hāugava'—in the sense "that their number may not decrease," and "naro varəfšva," corrupted as it is, hides probably the dvandva narā-pasū with vā—vā, meaning "not to let the number of men and animals become less than when they entered."

Excluded from entering the var are people with infirmities and sicknesses, a list of ten words, related to those excluded from sacrificing in

*Yt.*5,92-93, but composed in such poor language that only a few can be determined with some certitude.

In the epic of Gilgamesh, the building of the ark is thus described: "Timber a house, build a boat! Equally long shall be its breadth and length! From the plan? 120 cubits were - - - Its walls, —— 120 cubits the —— of its roof. I covered? it sixfold, divided it at the outside? sevenfold, inside? I divided it ninefold." One cannot fail to see a connection, perhaps a closer one than the mutilated text allows to see. The comparison shows also that the measurements are part of the original story. They are given in archaic "lengths of a race-course," +(ta)čarta.drāǰah, Pahl. transl. asprēs-drahnād (see under 'Poetry'). The length of an old race-course must have been one-ninth of a double parasang or almost four-fifths of a mile.

St.31: "Thereupon Yama thought: by what means shall I build the var, as AhuraMazdāh has commanded?" and the god says: "Handsome Yama, anhå zmo pāšnabyo vispara zastābyo viχaδa (mānayan ahe yaθa nū martiyāka χšivisti zmē višāvayante)," "stamp the clay with the heels, knead it with the hands," Pahl. transl.: "ēn zamīk pašnak bē uspurr u pa dast bē afχāst (humānākīh ō čigōn nūn martom šusr zamīk bē šāvēnēnd)." The gloss says: "just as, still today, men stamp liquid and earth," which is still true at our time. The gloss is old, for the Pahl. translation takes it as a part of the text and paraphrases "liquid-earth they make go asunder." "hušk u χvēt, dry and wet" is a standing idiom, e.g. *Ayātk.Zar.* 2,14; and in a cosmologic fragment *Mir. Man.* "'v hvšk v χvyd v'ryst, it rained on dry and wet." The Aw. formula is interpolated in *Yt.*19,58:

uwayam hamrēθwayāni vispā tršūča χšuδrāča

Wb. takes the impossible χšivisti as a loc. χšusti, and zmē as loc.sg. "syntaktisch nicht in Ordnung." The language is indeed Middle Persian, with incorrectly reconstructed endings.

What the verses describe is the fabrication of sun-dried bricks, adobe. In *Vid.*8,10, the pair zmoištve vā zarštve appears, i.e. sun-dried and burnt brick (see under 'Industries'). OP. išti > NP. χišt is the only genuine, old form; zmoištve is not an Awestic, but an artificial pseudo-Aw. compound of MP. zam u hišt, clay and brick. +χšusti zmē, likewise, is an attempt at rendering an old dvandva "liquid and clay." The verb for making adobe is "ažāni, to batter" in *Dar.chart.Sus.,* and višāvaya in *Vid.*2,31. "bē-šāvēn-, to make go asunder" of the Pahl. translation, is a mechanical transcription: vi.šāvayo is not caus. of √šyu- "to go," but, like "awišhūta < *awi.šūta, pressing (of grapes)" in *Y.*11,3, caus. of √hū- "stamp, press." The activity is the same when making sun-dried bricks or wine: treading with the feet. The sandhi-form of the word proves the pre-Iranian age of the technique. However badly the verses are transmitted, but χšusti zmē višāvayante is a formula inherited from Aryan antiquity. In their homeland the Aryans lived in adobe houses and drank wine.

St.32: "Thereupon Yama did, as AhuraMazdāh had commanded, he trod the clay with his feet, he kneaded it with his hands (the gloss, too, repeated)." St.33: "Thereupon Yama built the var, as commanded, one stadium long on all its four sides etc."

The fact that sun-dried brick is the building material precludes the translation "Höhle, cave" of var, advanced by Lommel. The purport of the story is: Yama must learn how to build, for before the threat of winters men had no need of houses in the paradisiac country. The god first describes the square plan, and on Yama's question "which material?" he teaches him to make sun-dried bricks. Then Yama builds the large castrum, four-fifths of a mile square, the plan of which one can understand with the plan of the qaṣr Balkuwārā at Samarra, exactly as large as that, at hand.

There is a very obscure point in *Vid.*2,6: Yama receives from the god two tools: "⟨yat he⟩ zayā ⟨frabaram azam yo ahuro mazdå⟩ suwrām zaranēnīm, aštrāmča zaranya.pēsīm, Pahl.transl. z'y sūrākawmand ut aštrič zarrēn.p(ē)sīt."

In the original myth it was not AhuraMazdāh who told the story. Eliminating these mazdayasnian additions, we have a genuine metrical fragment. Bartholomae translated "zwei Geräte (Hoheitszeichen), einen goldenen Pfeil und eine goldgeschmückte Peitsche"; Darmesteter: "seal and dagger"; Lommel: "Ring? und Treibstachel." Certainly both are insignia, but primarily practical tools.

aštrā, *RV.* vi,53,9 áṣṭrā, cf. aštra.had in *Yt.*10,112, to √az-, Lat. "agere, to drive," is a stick with (iron) point for goading cattle, originally the oxen at the plough. Whence "to kick against the prick, Germ. wider den Stachel löcken"; Engl. goad to Teut. *gazdo, Lat. hasta, Nord. geisl. When used for horses, it becomes a whip, OHG. geisala. As insignia it corresponds to the shepherd's staff and bishop's crosier, the skēptron, scepter of the king or military commander.

√had- in the comp. aspa.had and vīra.had in *Ōgmad.* 78, descriptive adjectives of a snake, aži, which "attacks, bites, stings" men and horses; cf. the figurative zarizafar, the arrow "with golden mouth" in *Yt.*10.129. The verb appears in *Yt.*14,56, a song of Iranian soldiers, mocking the Vyamburadīva soldiers, "haδåho saδan noit haδan, it looks as if they would punch (or just their lances), they do not punch." In *RV.* 6,53,9 paśusā́dhani is the epithet of áṣṭrā, "the goad for stinging, goading or punching cattle."[7] "To punch" is used in an old translation of *Ezekiel* 34,21 for Lat. impingebatis, from pungere, pungent, "because you punch (Kg.James 'push') all the weak with your horns." Thus aštra.had and paśusā́dhani are exactly Amer. "cowpuncher." An old explanation of this word says: "at the end of each stick is a sharp iron spike with which they punch the beasts and force them into the cars."

*Vid.*2,10 (repeated in 13 and 18) shows the use of the aštrā. When the earth had become too small for the increasing humanity,

ho imām zām awišvat / suwraya zaranēnya /
Pahl: ḤN ZNH zamīk MDM.spt / P'N svl'k.'wmnd ZHB'.yn' /
avi dim sifat aštraya
'P.Š BR' ZK svpt P'N 'štr

The end is clear: "Yama stroke the earth with the stick." The verb sēf-, sif- is used in a soldier's charm, *Yt.*14,35 and 44-45[8] "strike the body with

[7] Jarl Charpentier, in *Orient.Stud.Pavry* 81ff.: OI. pūṣan, Aw. fšū.šan, a bucolic deity of cattle-breeders, Aw. vāstrya.fšuyans, is equipped with the ā́ṣṭrā, the epithet of which, paśusā́dhani, of course, means "providing cattle." The epithet of the attribute has nothing to do with the etymology of the name pūṣan, which may belong to Ved. √han- "obtaining, acquiring possession of," syn. of √īš-, ēš-, in Aw. isant, išti, awištar etc [but cf. Aw. √han-, OI. sánati]. The stick is for goading, not for "providing" cattle, paśu.sā́dhani contains √sad-, Ir. had-, like aštra.had.

[8] In the first charm, separated in the yasht, carrying a wing (feather) or bone of the vārangan bird as amulet, or hammering oneself with it, makes invulnerable. In the second charm, which must be united with it because else the indispensable name of the bird would be lacking, four wings are held up against the four directions. In the third charm, two such wings shall fly? (ā-, vi-, fra.dwažan), two shall "rub, sweep" perhaps "be shaken" (ā-, vi-, fra.marzan). The translation "to fly" of mrz- in *Wb.* is unfounded, cf. Hertel, IIQF VII,182.

that wing!"; the noun sēpa in *Vid.*8,87-90 is "forge," where metals are "hammered," see under 'Industries.' There the Pahl.transl. writes spt, here svpt, apparently thinking of "sunb-, suft, to pierce." For the verb awi.švat in the first part of the sentence, Bartholomae noted an otherwise unknown "šav-, šva-, ritzen, to scratch." Darmesteter linked it to √hu-, "to press (grapes, hōma)": "he stamped the earth with the seal." Lommel: "er trieb sie an mit dem Ring," to √hū-, erroneously "antreiben," in fact "produce with skill." All translators derived the meaning of the verb from the unproved sense they gave the noun suwrā. The right explanation is that of Dastūr Peshotan Sanjana, in cod. DPS of the *Pahl.Vid.*: "MDM.spt, better švt or rft, for Aw. awi.švat." It is nothing but awi-šavat, to √šyū-, šav-, "to go." Yama walks over the earth, in the four directions, with the stick, and makes the earth widen. The suwrā, which misled the translators, has no reason there, and since the verse is metrically deficient, the words have been inserted after the model of *Vid.*2,10, and must be eliminated. The text was a good verse:

ho imām zām awi šavat avi dim sifat aštraya.

suwrā: Justi translated "plough"; Bartholomae "arrow," on account of the assonance of Shighnī "surb, arrow," cf. *ZAirWb.* 233. Darmesteter "seal," adducing a passage in *Ind.Bdh.,* where Yama, by virtue of these insignia, is absolute ruler, and one in the Shāhnāmah, where Farīdūn invests Ērič with "sword and seal, ring and crown," and thereby with the suzerainty over his elder brothers. Neriosengh's "ring" could only mean "seal-ring," but that form is too young for the age of the myth. The seal of Solomon, too, was no "ring." The Pahl. transl. renders suwrā by "svl'k.'wmnd, provided with a hole, tube."[9] This is glossed by "mtr'k dstk," the first word of which is obscure, the second is "handle"; the words mean scarcely "seal," rather "lock and key."

*Vid.*2,30 (as order), and 38 (as execution) show the use of the suwrā:

awiča tē varfšva	and (imperative) . . .
suwraya zaranēnya	with the golden suwra
apica tam varam marza	and this var (acc.) (imperative)
dvaram rōčanam hvarōχšnam	its door, vent-hole, window
antara.nēmāt - - -	from inside. . . !

[9] See the description of the mythical water-works, with pipes, under 'ApāmNapāt.'

awi varfšva must contain the verb of the first sentence, an imperative, in parallel with marza of the second sentence. The Pahl.transl. misunderstood varfšva as "var.mānišnān rāδ, for the dwellers of the var," must therefore supply a verb "(apar)kun," and by retaining the instr. suwraya makes the sentence an anakolouthon. The object of marza (Pahl. "māl, to mālīdan, to rub, wipe," not "contrive," *Wb.*) is "this varam," detailed as dvaram, rōčanam and hvārōχšnam; the first is "door," the second "window" in the old sense of "opening in the roof," the third a real window for light, not "self-shining." "This" shows that "var" was mentioned in the first passage, in the corrupt varfšva. "antara.nēmāt, from inside": whatever was done, it was done from the inside, and Yama must first "go into the var." Therefore the first line was: "awiča +tum +varam +šava, and thou go into the var," in 38: awiča ho +varam +savat; nothing but a misreading of m for p (f).

"marza" must mean "shut!"; "and shut the var, the door, the vent-hole, the window!" The Akk. legend of UtNapištim says literally the same: after the ark was filled and the announced weather signs had come, "he entered the boat and shut its door," and when the flood at last receded, "I opened the vent-hole, nappāšu, the daylight fell upon my nose!"

This is a cogent proof for the emendation awi šavat in *Vid.*2,10, and for eliminating, there, suwraya zaranēnya. It is only 2,30 where one can see what purpose the suwrā serves: a tool to shut the door from inside. Old doors and windows had bolts at the inside; a Germ. term for them is "vor-reiber," "reiben, to rub = mrz, mālīdan," which may well describe the shutting and opening of the bolt.[10] Somewhat later, there was a contrivance to open and shut the bolts also from outside through a keyhole with a key. The words sur'k.'wmnd and mtr'k dstk may have this meaning. Such a key is the attribute, the sungod Šamaš holds in hand in old Akkadian glyptics, when appearing over mountains, having opened the gates of heaven. The key as attribute may originally have belonged to Hvar χšēta and have been inherited by Yama χšēta.

The ark of UtNapištim, a boat on high seas—see under 'Navigation'—had a captain, and his description throws some light on suwrā. "To

[10] Cf. Lat. clavis, Ital. chiave, and chiavare = mālīdan; and similar Arab figurative idioms: wulūdj al-mirwad fi l-mukḥula, pin of the kohl-box, *Aghāni* 14,45, tale of 'Umar and al-Mughīra.

the piḫu of the boat, the awēl malāḫi, I handed over the ēkallu and its stores, bušē." The awēl malāḫi is the Arab. "ra'īs al-mallāḥīn" or "ṣāḥib al-matā' al-maḥmūl fī l-safīna, overseer, supercargo, of the merchandise transported in the ship." The same words gloss also Arab. is/š-tiyām, a loanword from Aramaic.[11] S. Fraenkel, *Aram.Fremdwörter* 294, quotes an explanation of Aram. ištiyāmā: "an epítropos in whose hand are the *key* and *seal,* overseer of . . . the magazins of an (other) owner." The supercargo keeps his stores under lock and key, just as Yama locks the anbārs of the var, in which the animals and stores are kept. "(h)anbāštan, to put into the anbār" is written with the ideogram ḪTYMVN, to seal, and signifies also "to seal." Locking and sealing are always combined: as early as the stone age, seals are impressed on jar stoppers. Once, when I had obtained from Aḥmad Shāh permission to make a catalogue of the bronze treasure of Baznagird, which was kept in the throne room at Teheran, the first attempt failed, because the cupboards were locked and sealed, and the officers in charge no longer alive. The next day, representatives of seven ministries were appointed, the seals were broken, and when I had finished, the cupboards were locked and sealed again.

Thus, seal, lock and key are closely connected. Yet one feature restricts the meaning of suwrā in the *Vidēvdād* to "key": a seal is never impressed on the inside, and the shutting is done antara.nēmāt. If suwrā is a true Iranian word, I see no other word to connect it with, but MP.NP. "suftan, sunb-, to pierce, perforate." In the *Vidēvdād* it is once written sufrā. The Pahl. translator of *Vid.*2,10 must have thought so when writing svft for Aw. sifat, with regard to the preceding suwraya. To the same root belongs the Arab. loanword suftadj, suftah < OP. *suf-taka—cf. Aw. suftidrngā under 'Mithra'—which means "bill of exchange, money-order" sent by post and certainly sealed, probably sent in padlocked mail bags.

The close similarities between the var of Yama and the ark of Ut-Napištim are worth noticing, the more so as it is natural for the ark to have but one door and one vent-hole, while a building one tačara

[11] ra'īs al-mallāḥīn—the Sumerian word is still alive—is magister nautarum, cf. de Goeje, BGA IV, *Gloss.* 271; two recent articles by 'Abdalqādir al-Maghrabī and Salīm al-Djundī, in Rev. de l'Acad. de Damas, 17, 1942, mai-juin and sept.-oct., adduce a passage of abū l-'Alā al-Ma'arrī, *kit. 'abth al-walīd*: "The navigators in the sea of Hidjāz call the ra'īs al-markab, captain, al-ištiyām; a big fish bears the same name."

long on each side, like the var, ought to have, in the style of the Iranian legend, "a thousand doors, ten thousand windows." A feature proper to the ark seems to have been retained without change by the Iranian myth. With all its divergencies, the myth of the var belongs to the motif of the ark of Noah. The Iranian legend, somehow, combined the flood with the expulsion from paradise. The fact that it mixes different motifs proves that it is not independent, but had admitted elements from abroad, long before Zoroaster's time. Another Babylonian motif is, for instance, the seven walls of Kanhā, built with the seven metals that are attributes of the Babylonian planetary deities. As early an author as Herodotus transferred this legend to the town Agbatana. This contact with Babylon had been taking place since the ninth century, when the Iranians first appeared in West Iran, and before the foundation of the Median empire—that is at a period when both Parsua-Persians and Māda-Medes had been subjected to the Assyrians, whose province Parsua extended over Kirmānshāhān, Nihāwand and Hamadān.

XXIII. ĀRMATIŠ

"Dilexi iustitiam, odi iniquitatem,
propterea morior in exilio"
—Gregor VII

Zoroaster, who cursed other gods, has blessed Ārmatiš. In the gathas she bears often, in the yashts always, the epithet "spantā, the holy," hence her MP. name Sfandārmaδ. She is the goddess of earth, zam; ārmatiš is an epithet, of Aryan age, for it is Ved. arámatiḥ in the *RV*. In the archaic verses of *Y.Haft.* 38—see under 'Dēva': "This earth here —together with the wives—who bears us—who are Thy wives, Ahura!" the earth is the barθrī, that is the primeval IE. notion of the "mother Earth," surviving e.g. in TPārs. "zamīg kē harv čīz barēt." In the Greek world the name δαμματρι, Dēmēter, maintains the old notion; in Thrace her name was Semélē. The Scolotian Scyths, Herodotus IV,23, called Zeus παπαῖος and the earth 'απι, "father and mother"; in Phrygian the opposition of "ζεμέλως = terrestres," to "δέως = caelestes,"[1] in Thracian the n.pr. Zámolxis and Diaîxis (Aisch.), "qui regnat in terra" and "in coelo," express the same idea. Also in the Iranian world, Varuna-AhuraMazdāh and Zam-Ārmatiš must once have been a couple, but Zoroaster's god had neither wife nor children.

The chthonic signification belonged to the goddess since the same high antiquity. In Greece it is attested by a remark of Plutarch: "τοὺς νεκροὺς 'Αθηναῖοι Δημητρίους ὠνόμαζον παλαιόν, the dead were called by the Athenians of old 'those belonging to Demeter.'" Such a notion must have existed in Iranian, for a form of the name identical with OP. *santā ārmati passed into Armenian as "sandarmet," with the meaning "netherworld,"[2] whereas "spandarmet," derived from the Median form, means there "Bacchus." With the Greeks, Demeter and Dionysus are closely connected.

1 Cf. Jokl, in Reall. Vorgesch. s.v. Phrygia, p.151.

2 In Babylonia, the gods of the earth, ilāni erṣeti are the same as the gods of the netherworld, ilāni ereš.kigal; their king Nergal is "šar erṣeti" or "lugal usipara." In the Samarra-tablet, Thureau-Dangin, RAAO IX,1921, he is called "šar ḫawīlim^{ki}," which is Hebr. ḫawīlā, LXX 'Ευιλάτ, in *Gen.*2,10: "from Eden goes out a stream . . . and divides . . . in four branches; the name of the first is Pishon, the one who flows round the whole Ḫawīlā." Here, ḫawīlā, like Akk. ḫawīlum, means "the earth, erṣetum." But a gloss says "and there is the gold," like *Job* 37,22 "from midnight comes the gold." The midnight point of the horizon is mount Arallu, "mountain of gold," gold is the "product of the netherworld, nabnīt aralli." The midnight point is the gate of hell. And the gloss takes ḫawīlā in this meaning, just as the Samarra tablet in calling Nergal "king of Ḫawīlum."

In *Yt.*13,29, the fravarti, the "manes" of the dead, are called "tušnišad, sitting in silence," not as posture, squatting, but as abiding, living in silence. The association of silence and death shows itself also in the name of the Roman festival in commemoration of the dead, the silicernium: the rest is silence. The form of the word is archaic: tušnišad, not *tušnišhad—cf. armēšad in *Y.*62,8 against arime.had in *Yt.*13,73—and it was created at a time when the dead were still buried in the earth: the tušnišad live in the hadiš of the dead, the netherworld, ārmatiš.

In the gatha of the vision, *Y.*43,15, Zoroaster condenses the visions he saw into the words: "daχšat ušyāi tušnāmatiš vahištā, thinking-in-silence has taught me to announce . . ." see under 'Harvatāt.' vahištā has been regarded as object of ušyāi "to announce the best," or as attribute of tušnāmatiš, in the vocative "o best one!" and the whole expression has been interpreted as an allusion to ārmatiš as chthonic goddess. This is not necessary, but in both cases possible: tušnāmatiš as silent meditation can mean ārmatiš, patience, keeping still. In *Yt.*13, 139 tušnāmatiš, thinking in silence, appears, strikingly, as the name of a woman.

It is as goddess of agriculture, Agricultura, that Zoroaster introduced the mother earth, with other dēvas that had "chosen" AhuraMazdāh, into the more than τετραπρόσωπος nature of his god. These aspects embody on the one hand the forms of human society, thus ārmatiš the peasantry, on the other hand that which the good principle has laid into the souls of these human groups, their specific virtues. This usage, in the case of ārmatiš, seems not to be an innovation due to Zoroaster, but an older thought modified.

The passage most important for the understanding of the Zoroastrian Ārmatiš are the first two stanzas of *Y.*32:[3]

1:	ahyača hvētuš yāsat	ahya vrzanam mat aryamnā
	ahya dēvā mahmi mnoi	ahurahya rvāzmā mazdå
	θwoi dūtåho ahāma	tān dārayò yoi vå dbišanti
2:	ēbyo mazdå ahuro	sāramano vahū manahā

[3] Other stanzas of *Y.*32 see under 'Yama χšēta.'

χšaθrāt hača patimrōt rtā hušhaχā huvanvatā
spantām vå ārmatim vahvīm vrmadi hā no ahat

"Would that the hvētu, the vrzanam with the aryaman, and the gods, dēva, would endeavor to obtain AhuraMazdāh's grace, willing?: Thy servants we want to be who hold back those who are Your enemies!—then AhuraMazdāh, wedded to Vahumano, would reply through the mouth of Xšaθram, he the companion of the sunny Rtam: We love your ārmatiš, she be Ours!"

Thus the god receives Ārmatiš in "sar," into the group of his aspects: Vahumano, Xšaθram and Rtam. In *Y*.31,21, in a similar way, Harvatāt-Amrtatāt are received in "sar" like Rtam, Xšaθram and Vahumano.

Gods and men endeavor to obtain AhuraMazdāh's rvāzman by readiness to obey, for which NP. has the picturesque word "kamarbandī, having their belts tightened." ārmatiš is a passive attitude: "patience, keeping still." For the definition of rvāzman see under 'Welcome.' But instead of the normal formula "dēvā martiyāča, gods and men," a triad of men, hvētu, vrzanam and aryaman is here opposed to the gods, a peculiar qualification which must have a good reason.

mahmi mnoi: *Wb.*: "man-, n., Mass, Art und Weise"; "mahmi, to 'ma, mine,' together: in dem Masse wie ich sie gebe." The words are corrupt: the older Mss. have mahmi manoi, -noit, -nō, but the larger number have mahi manoi. Andreas emended "homoi monoi, in demselben Sinn." The Pahl.transl. explains: "ku mān mēnišnīh ētōn frārōn čigōn Zartušt, that we, as to our willingness, be as excellent as Zoroaster," hence saw in mnoi the √man-, and read perhaps "hama, same" as Andreas emended. The root man- is beyond question, because direct oration, characteristic for it, follows; cf. OP. "yadi avaθa manyāhi, if you think, want this" or Aw. "uti avaθa manhāno" in *Yt.*19,49, ApāmNapāt hymn. The form was a participle or verbal adjective, most probably manimna; cf. *manhamna and the denom. manahyamna; prev. ham- is possible, cf. MP. "homānāk, just as, like." But the whole situation is imaginary, not real; the answer is conditional.

Gods and men offer their service as dūta, Pahl.transl.: tu davāk bavēm, avēšān apāč dārēm ku šmāχ bēšēnēnd. "θwa dūtåho ahāma" can only be a variant of "ahāma rātoiš yušmāvatām, we want to be of your Highness' servants," *Y.*29,11, a meaning supported by the parallel in *Y.*49,7: "yavoi vispāi fra.ištåho ahāma."

dūta appears once more in *Y.*32,13: "kāmē dūtam yo īš pāt darsāt rtahya, as pleases the dūta who keeps them back from beholding rtam." In both cases the activity of the dūta is to keep hostile people back, not that of a "messenger" who brings something. In the Veda, Agni is devā́nām dūtá, usually translated "messenger of the gods," but Hertel remarks, *Siegesf.*: "wird nirgends von einem deva zum andren oder gar . . . von einem deva auf die Erde gesandt, um den Menschen eine 'Weisung' zu überbringen." In *Y.*32,1, the Pahl.transl. davāk is explained by "rāyēnītār, who puts in order," in 13 by "pēšopāy, forerunner." Such runners, on horse or on foot, hold back the crowd, like the modern farrāsh, who were originally cubicularii, but already at the Ṣafawid period forerunners and executors of punishment, equipped with hatchet and stick, like the Roman fascigeri. farrāsh is only the generic name of the class of servants to which also janitors belong, darbān, *πυλωροί*, cf. Arab. "ḥādjib, huissier, and chamberlain," from "ḥadjaba, to keep back." Still in 1905, in Isfahan, one used to go or drive out with such forerunners or foreriders.

Wb. connects dūta with a verb "dav-, to distance, remove," whence "dūra, far," but the two verbal forms it attributes to it, *Yt.*1,29 and *Vid.* 5,24, do not belong. dūta may be related to MP. "dūtak, familia" as possessions or servants.

AhuraMazdāh answers "through (the mouth of) Xšaθram," because this is his social-political aspect. The words "we have chosen your obedience" express his rvāzman, and are, with "She be ours!" part of the true Zoroastrian creed, as in Y.49,2: "spantām ahmāi stoi ārmatim," followed in st.3 by "rtam sūdyāi, rāšayahe druχš," articles of the faith. *Y.*12 quotes the formula in the mazdayasnian profession. The god returns the declaration of his adherents by his own, because it is a relation of fealty, a miθra, and this is uwayå, binding both parties.

The late Fravarāni, *Y.*12, joins to the ārmatiš formula an oath in which six crimes, theft and robbing of live property, damage to and unlawful use of immobile property, bodily injury and homicide are sworn off. This observing of the simple "six commandments" is a kind of exegesis of the formula "Ārmatiš be mine!" As ethic norm of actions, she is obedience to the law, tkēša, morals itself. Society is founded on feudal relations, and obedience to law is at the same time fealty. Lommel spoils his translation "Fügsamkeit" by adding "kluge" (for spanta), for that gives a bad connotation in German: "acquiesce even without approving."

In the *Kārn.Art.* 12,14 one reads: "Artaχšēr pa vēhīh u dēndōstīh ut ēkānakīh u framānburtārīh ē avēšān apēgumān būt, A. convinced himself of the sincerity of their vēhīh-vahumano, their dēndōstīh-dēnā, their ēkānakīh, being adyūš, and their framānburtārīh = ārmatiš." This is exactly "we want to be your dūta!—I love your Ārmatiš!" and shows the old idea still alive.

In *Y*.32,3 the thought leaps from ārmatiš to its opposite parimatiš (text under 'Yama χšēta'): "You gods all and who worships you, are the brood of Akam mano, the Druχš, and parimatiš, and your deeds for which they glorify you on this seventh of the earth, are dbitāna, dubious."

parimatiš, hybris, is the specific vice of the Iranian nobility, the hvētu, chastised at the example of Yama. Heraclitus: *ὕβριν χρὴ σβεννύναι μᾶλλον ἢ πυραίην*. The "motif of hybris" goes right through the whole epic. Yama, Sām, kavi Usan, Herodotus' Deiokes, all catch hybris. In history, Cambyses goes insane. The medieval *Heraclias* says of Xusrau Parwēz: "er nam sich an er waere got." An Arabic ḥadīth[4] says: "These are they who go to hell without hearing: . . . the Arabs because of their racial fanaticism, 'aṣabiyya, the Persian noblemen because of their arrogance, kibar, and the scholars because of their jaundice."

To the hvētu, vrzanam and aryaman, *Y*.33,4 adds as fourth group the "gāuš vāstra, peasantry"; the same four are also mentioned in the preceding st.33,3. Instead of parimatiš the similar notion taromatiš appears in these verses: "Zoroaster 'prays away,' removes by his song, disobedience, asruštīm, and evil-mind, akam mano, from four groups: taromatim from the hvētu, nazdištām drujam from the vrzanam, ⁺nidanto from the aryaman, and ačištam mantum from the gāuš vāstra."

The context is: to whatever station in life a man may belong, he shall

[4] After Ṣiddīqī, in Goldziher, *Muhamm.Stud.* II,108f.

love the faithful and hate the disbelievers. Or, adherence to the religion shall replace membership of the tribe. Islam proceeded similarly. Until 1914, an Oriental, asked for his nationality, would answer "muslim," an answer entirely right, because religion, not race, rules the actions, and what he who asks wants to know of a man is how he will act under certain circumstances.

Evil mind and disobedience are qualities of men, and it is unimportant that vrzana and gāuš vāstra are topical, hvētu and aryaman social terms. Such terms are always exchangeable. Neither must we expect in these odes a systematic terminology, nor see in such terms a social system distinct from others, for instance that of the *Y.Haft.* or the yashts. The terminology is rich and nowhere complete, but the choice is full of meaning. The four groups, without being all, represent the totality.

For the moment it is enough to ascertain that the group gāuš vāstra, i.e. "cattle-pasture," figurative for neat-herds and shepherds, are lacking in *Y.*32,1-2, where the peasantry should be represented first of all, since ārmatiš is the theme.

The specific aka manah of the four groups belong to two categories: they are either the "vices of their virtues" which Ahramanyuš has implanted in them, or his "gifts" for which they suffer innocently.

*Y.*45,11 elucidates tar̥omati: "Who, therefore, in future, will depise, taro mansta, the dēvā and martiyā, gods and men that despise Him [AhuraMazdāh, mentioned just before], instead of, anyān ahmāt yo, respecting Him,—the holy dēnā of the sōšyans, the dampatiš, will be his friend, brother and father!"

"taro-man, pensée hors (de la règle)," is not a quality bad in itself, but good or bad according to the right or wrong object. The wrong taromati of the hvētu is directed against other countrymen, aryaman, vrzanya and vāstriya. In the legend of Sām, the *Gr.Bdh.* 197f., says: "He was immortal until he tarmēnīt dēn ē māzdēsnān, despised the mazdayasnian religion," whereafter the arrow, shot by a Hiyōn, puts him asleep, see under 'Ardvīsūrā.' *Y.*45 is an early gatha, in which Zoroaster still fights the polytheism, and the "Imitation of Zoroaster" means, like his own exile, to leave friends and family. The dēnā of the sōšyans, religion of the saviour, takes the place of the social relations renounced; the followers enter in "sar"—reciprocal relationship of the hvētu—with him. Therefore, the sōšyans is called, just here, dampatiš, paterfamilias. One may take dēnā collectively as religion, or individually as the organ that senses religion, καρδίη; at any rate, the sōšyans is Zoroaster himself. Cf. *Matth.* 19,29: "And everyone that hath forsaken houses, or brethren, or sisters, or father, or mother, or wife, or children, or lands, for my name's sake . . ." and 12,50: "Whosoever shall do the will of my Father which is in heaven, the same is my brother, and sister, and mother." And the Qur'ān, 9,23-24 says: "If you love your father and children, your brothers and wives, your relatives, the property you have acquired, the business the ruin of which you fear, the houses that please you—more than Allāh and his envoy and the holy war, then expect that Allāh will visit you."

The specific "shady side" of life in a vrzanam, MP. "hamsāyakīh, life under the same shade," is the nazdišta druχš, druχš being one's close neighbor. Cf. *Y.*50,3: "yām nazdištām gēθām drugvå baχšati, the man who by the power of Rtiš will make prosper the farmyard, [be it] one neighboring [one] that is the lot of a drugvant."[5] The expression nazdištā druχš, characteristic for Zoroaster's diction, reveals at once what vrzana is: oppidum and civitas. In town, the neighborhood, the narrow dwelling among disbelievers is the rule. But this is no vice, but an Ahrimanic evil from which the vrzanya, citizens, suffer.

,nadənto', +nidanto, the detriment of the aryaman is less clear. Bartholomae took it as belonging to a base *nad-, Lästerer Meillet "qui l'outragent." It belongs apparently to √nid-, nēd-, Gr. ὄνειδος, OHG. nīt > Germ. Neid; also to "niδā.snaθiš, defying, challenging the arms." It may be the defiant, provocative attitude, or the envy, jealousy of the aryaman, or envy directed against them; probably the first: see "noit aram," here below.

The ačišto mantuš of the peasants is not a vice, but a suffering; the "worst patron" means their being deprived of rights. They have no freedom to move, vaso.yāti, vaso.šiti, they are serfs bound to their fields and pastures. The Fravarāni comprises them under "gauš," live property. *Y.*29,3 speaks of their lot: "nobody knows how the lofty, ršvåho, deal with the lowly, adrān," that is they are at their mercy.

5 A complicated case of putting words governing a relative clause, into this clause.

Or *Y*.51,14: "the karpāno, priests, act noit aram, disregarding the rvāθā dātobyasča, lawful customs established for the vāstra, pasturage-peasantry.[6] Because it is property and slave, gauš,[7] the ox is in Zoroaster's figurative speech the symbol of the peasant: ačišta mantu describes his living at the mercy of the hvētu. In the whole gatha *Y*.29, Zoroaster, himself an exile without means and protection, is the mantuš of peasantry. In *Y*.32,15, he says, referring to the special case of those persecuted as his own adherents: "For this suffering of theirs, those whom they (the hvētu) do not permit to be masters of their own life, shall drive to the house of Vahumano." They are restricted in their ǰyātuš, livelihood, like the *ανὴρ ἄκληρος ᾧ μὴ βίοτος πολὺς εἴη* in the Odyssey. But they abiyābryāntē, are driven to heaven in a carriage like a high lord: *μακάριοι οἱ δεδιωγμένοι ἕνεκεν δικαιοσύνης ὅτι αὐτῶν ἐστι ἡ βασιλεία τῶν οὐρανῶν.*

Gatha of the Questions, *Y*.44,6:

yā fravaχšyā	yazi tā aθā haθyā
rtam šyōθnāiš	dbanzati ārmatiš
+tēbyo χšaθram	vahū činas manahā
kēbyo azīm	rānyaskrtīm gām tašo

Bartholomae changed another translation in *Ar.Forschg.* (1886) in 1905 to: "Ob denn das auch wirklich so ist was ich verkünden will? Wird Aša mit seinem Thun (dereinst) Hilfe leisten? Wird von Dir her Vahumanah das Reich zuerkennen? Für wen (sonst) hast Du das glückbringende trächtige Rind geschaffen?"

Lommel: ". . . was ich verkünden will, ob das auch wirklich so ist? Giebt die Fügsamkeit dem Wahrsein durch Thaten Unterstützung? Hast Du für diese (Thaten) durch Gutes-Den-

[6] rvāθā, Pahl.transl. dōstīh, and dātā correspond to rvati and miθrā in *Y*.46,5, and are the "amicitiae et societates," foundation of "mores" = rāzan, see under 'Hospitium' and 'Mithra.'

[7] Since the application of the words bull, steer, ox, cow, neat cattle differs in old and modern languages, OIr. gav- cow, is difficult to translate. It is as well the generic term—even far beyond the bovine race—as that of the female. *Y*.29 is the "Gatha of the Cow," the speaker is "gāuš urvā," st.5: "mā urvā gāušča azyā, my soul and that of the pregnant cow," hence "soul of the ox." azī qualifies the female not so much as "being with calf" but as "grown up." Without azī and without being opposed to a male, gav- is ambiguous, in a degree which "cow" cannot equal.

ken die Herrschaft verheissen? Für wen hast Du die glückbringende Kuh geschaffen?"

Hertel, *Beitr.,* 1929: "Ob das auch alles so wahr ist was ich zu verkünden gedenke? Stärkt die Siedlung (ā̃rmati) durch Werke das Licht-des-Heils? Hat sie die Herrschaft Dir zuerkannt durch den lichten-Gedanken? Wer sind die Leute, für die Du die fruchtbare Kuh hast gebildet, die die Erquickung uns spendet?"

A complete translation is yet far away, but there is enough to show that this illogical picture of perplexity and helplessness is wrong. haθya, part.fut. "what will be," also "what should be," without moral quality, means the coming true, realization. The first question does not express a doubt in the truth of his own teaching, but: "Will you, god, make come true what I shall say?", viz. what you have inspired me to say. And then follow, in form of questions, but as certain as the glorifications of the Gospels, his annunciations.

The verb of the first is obscure: dbanzati. Bartholomae's first translation "wird Ārmati sich erwerben?" rested on a comparison with *Y*.46,15: "durch solches Tun erwerbt ihr euch. . . ." In *Wb.* he assumed "unterstützen," without any other support. √dbanz-, Aw. banz-, is some judiciary activity of AhuraMazdāh's aspects at the last judgment; also of the dogs at the Činvat-bridge, who, in *RV.* x,14,10, watch or waylay? the dead, as animals of the ruler of the netherworld. The activity seems to be connected with the "investigation" of the acts of men. As long as the verb is not determined, one cannot say whether rtam or ārmatiš is the subject. But ārmatiš is apparently the subject of činas in the following verse.

Of this second annunciation the end is clear: rānyaskrti[8] is a word of old poetry, originally associated with food, which later took the acceptation "paradisiac," Arm. erani = μακάριος. Bartholomae's "für wen (sonst)?" is necessary; otherwise the cow would appear like a bos ex machina, and the questions would be disconnected flashes of thought. If the two verses were syntactically connected, the interrogative kēbyo would change

[8] Cf. Bartholomae, *Ar.Forschg.* II,62; Benveniste, JAS. 1934, 184; Hertel, *Beitr.* 102.

into the relative. Bartholomae and Hertel follow a text-critical pattern, unfit for Awestic text research, in reading "tabyo, to Thee," thinking of AhuraMazdāh, although Bartholomae read originally "tēbyo, to them" with some Mss. "To thee" would make Ārmatiš judge over the god: "will Ārmatiš (a partial figure of the god) through Vahumano (a second figure) confer —or not—upon the god the third figure, χšaθram," a question without sense, still more, when translating ārmatiš by Fügsamkeit: "will passivity by acts support truth?" tabyo/tēbyo and kēbyo is so conspicuous for ears and eyes—cf. anāiš ā—avāiš in *Y.*32,15—that, whatever be the textual tradition, one must read tēbyo. But it is not the "ta, referring back" to "for these (acts)" but the one referring to direct oration that follows: "those, to whom . . . for whom else?"

χšaθram in 44,6 is not the "empire of heaven," but the abstract expression of ownership of cattle, the free command over the livelihood of the peasantry, which, in *Y.*32,15, priests and noblemen will not permit the followers of Zoroaster to enjoy. The same idea is expressed in *Y.*51,6: "Shall the peasant who [because he] is rtāvan in his doings, obtain the ownership of the cow through Rtam [according to the law]?" and in *Y.*31,9: "If the cow had the choice to belong either to the vāstriya or to him who is no cattle-breeder, it would choose the vāstriya because he is rtāvan." And the conclusion: "Therefore the nonfarmer shall have no share of the accounting!" in 31,10, see under 'ApāmNapāt.' There is no less certainty in these questions than in *μακάριοι οἱ πραεῖς ὅτι αὐτοὶ κληρονομήσουσιν τὴν γῆν*!

The verses speak of an agrarian reform for which Zoroaster stands, and which the former owners, priests and nobles oppose. That is the indictment for which he was sentenced to proscription, see under 'Bandva.' However, Zoroaster did not want to dissolve society, he did not come to *καταλύσειν τὸν νόμον*, but to replace serfdom by the voluntary, sworn-to obedience of the vassal.

*Y.*30,5: The good in the world's history is wrought by all

yēča χšnōšan ahuram   haθyāiš šyōθnāiš fravrt mazdām
"that obey AhuraMazdāh voluntarily by the right conduct."

Bartholomae, *Ar.Forschg.* II,123: "die durch rechtschaffenes Tun es dem Gotte Mazdāh gern recht machen."[9] *Wb.*: "fraorət, lies fravrt, adv. 'gern,' zu √var- [to choose, love], eigtl. 'mit Vorzug.'" fravrt, always connected with √χšnu- "hear, obey" and √hak-, "follow, obey," is more than "gern," viz. "by their own choice, free will." It corresponds to MP. kāmakawmand, opp. akāmakawmand, e.g. *Art.Vir.Nām.* I,38-39. With √χšnu- it is the word for "free obedience." haθya is ἃ δεῖ.

"Wedding Gatha," *Y.*53,2:

ātča hoi sčantu manahā	uχδāiš šyōθnāišča
χšnuvam mazdå vahmāi ā	fravrt yasnansča

Vištāspa, the two Hāugava, the son and the daughter of Zoroaster, "shall voluntarily follow [sčantu to √hak-] AhuraMazdāh's obedience and worship."

A similar idiom is already used in the *Mithra Yt.*10,9: yatārā

vā dim prvā frayazāti	Which of the two (warring)
fravrt fraχšni avi mano	countries is the first, voluntarily,
zrazdātoit (ahvayāt hača)	with regard to the future, faithfully,

(by their own initiative) to sacrifice to Mithra, those Mithra will help.

Zoroaster fights against what is called in *Exod.* 22 ʿNH, or in Islam "maẓālim," injustice, despoiling of right, a thing apparently adherent to the shepherd's life—not at all an "ideal" one—in the East through all its thousands of years. Islam created against it the "dīwān al-maẓālim, the court of appeal" under the personal presidency of the sovereign. The last origin of the institution seems to be Cyrus' highest court of the *βασιλήιοι δικασταί*, Herodotus V,25 and III,31. The rulers who took care of it are always specially praised, e.g. the caliph al-Muhtadī in ibn Khaldūn, Tabari and ibn al-Tiqtaqa. Ibn al-Athīr says, in the necrologue of Nūr al-dīn, this remarkable ascetic on the throne: "He built everywhere in his countries dār al-ʿadl, a house of justice, in which he used to give audience together with his qāḍī al-Shahrazūrī, administering

[9] "Es einem recht machen" means "do a thing as another wants it done"; "es einem nicht recht machen können" means "being unable to do a thing as the other wants it." Even "es gern recht machen" expresses that it is the will of the other, and that the agent is indifferent.

justice to the oppressed—be it a Jew, against the oppressor—be it his own son or first amīr." And just so Darius begins his testament entirely in the spirit of Zoroaster: "I love what is right, I hate what is wrong! It is not my pleasure that the lowly suffer injustice for the sake of the lofty!"

*Y.*33,5 speaks of the specific vices or detriments of the various classes; *Y.Haft.* 40,3, one could say, of their specific virtues: "Give that the nā(=hvētuš) rtāvan be rtačanah, eager to fight, that the vāstriya, peasants, be adyūš, vassals, for long (=continuous, hereditary) zealous, bəzvate?[10] vassalry, haχman, both in-fealty-towards-us, ahma.rafnah!" These verses are post-Zoroastrian.

Zoroaster uses gauš and vāstra, alone or together, as metaphoric expression for peasants; in the same way, ārmatiš is on the one hand their transcendent personification in the multiple nature of his god, on the other hand their specific virtue, their patience, obedience to law, founded on or being the foundation of Rtam, the social order. In *Y.* 33,4 the antonym to ārmati is "asruštī, disobedience," as aka manah to vahu manah. In Zoroaster's phraseology, therefore, this specific ārmati of the peasants is the virtue, *ἀρετή*, itself: the patient resignation to the order, Rtam, to God's will, or with Darius' words in *NiR* A,57: "hyā ōramazdāha framānā hō.tē gastā mā θandaya! what Ōramazdā has allotted to you, shall not seem hellish to you!"

That is the reason, why, in the passage *Y.*31,11, from which we started, where AhuraMazdāh "chooses" Ārmatiš, just the peasants which she personifies are not mentioned, and why, there, in the normal formula dēvā martiyāča, the three classes hvētu, vrzana and aryaman replace martiyā. Zoroaster voices a hope: "Would that the gods and [among men] the noblemen, the townsmen and the clients endeavored to obtain AhuraMazdāh's grace, willing?: Thy servants we want to be . . . , then AhuraMazdāh would reply: I accept your ārmatiš, your obedience which is like that of the peasants!" But this is only a hope, and the gods and those men do not do it in their parimatiš, hybris. Therefore the thought goes on: at all times you have been like that, all the heroes of your history, whom you glorify as "beloved by the

[10] to √ dbanz-, banz-?, see above *Y.*44,6.

gods," Yama first of all, have been nothing but ēnah, ὑβρίζοντες. But AhuraMazdāh, who knows their riχta, loves only obedience, ārmatiš, the virtue of the despised peasants: μακάριοι οἱ πραεῖς!

That is the new ethical and social idea of Zoroaster, *Y*.44,9: "moi yām yōš dēnām dānē, I who want to purify, reform the religion!", his transvaluation of values. Nyberg, 202: "Es findet sich keine Spur von einem Reformator bei Zarathustra, er behauptet leidenschaftlich das Bestehende." And while describing his Zoroaster without agrarian interests, but preaching "sermons" against other sects and composing an "oral preface" to the second edition of his "hymns" collected for the liturgical use of his parish, he goes on: "Das Bild eines fortschrittlichen Landpfarrers mit Interesse für agrarische Reformen, das die Forschung des 19. Jahrhunderts von ihm zu entwerfen pflegte, ist sicher sehr bezeichnend für das, was diese Zeit als zu einem richtigen Religionsstifter gehörig ansah"—the picture of a drunk shaman drawn in the early 20th is not even that—"es ist unter geschichtlichem [and every other] Gesichtspunkt von Anfang bis zu Ende verkehrt."

It may be a consequence of Zoroaster's new interpretation of the goddess of Earth as aspect of AhuraMazdāh that the Awesta retained so little of her pre-Zoroastrian cult and character. The gods banished by Zoroaster brought a good deal of their old hymns with them when they returned into the Mazdayasnian religion. But there is no Ārmatiš-yasht. *Yt*.19, the Zam-yasht, is very long, but, excepting karda 1, it is dedicated to the Hvarnah, not to Ārmatiš, in spite of its name "Zam," and this first chapter is no more than a list of names of mountains, a choice from 2,244, an orographic catalogue void of religious contents. In the epics a few features of the myth of the goddess are preserved, e.g. her flight before the dragon AžiDahāka. All the rest is lost, and even her name Ārmatiš remains obscure, the often discussed problem of its etymology unsolved.

In the *RV.*, cf. Hertel, *Beitr.* chapt.11, arámatiḥ is enumerated between ṛtá, dyā́us, námas (prosternation), and Indra, mitrá, varuṇa, bhaga and others, but, as Hertel says, the Indian tradition was no longer sure about the meaning of *RV.* arámatiḥ.[11] Hertel calls the etymology, given on

[11] Just as the Pārs. tradition had forgotten what Aw. ārmati meant. The Eur. dictionaries follow the etymology accepted by the *Petersb. Wörterbuch,* on the strength of a commentary

the authority of Sāyaṇa in the *PW*. "unsinnig," and whatever one thinks of his own, that one is wrong, and the true etymology remains to be found.

One can imagine that the notions earth as agriculture and obedience, patience as special virtue of the agriculturists became connected. But if one word could designate these two notions, then its etymological meaning must express the tertium comparationis, and its sphere would be "labor, field-labor."[12] Bartholomae regarded ãrmati as compound "aram + mati, to think according [to rules]," and therefore makes his article in *Wb.* begin with ãrmati as opp. to taro.mati. Why this "thinking" became the name of the earth remains a riddle. Duchesne, on the contrary, states, §113: "taromati, 'acte de penser de travers,' ne prouve rien pour l'étymologie de l'indo-ir. ārmati; il prouve seulement que le mot a été compris depuis la rédaction des gâthâs jusqu'à celle des Purs. comme comp. d'arəm et de mati." Even these last words concede too much.

Zoroaster uses an entirely personal phraseology when teaching in *Y*.45,11, to despise, taro-man, those who despise AhuraMazdāh, instead of respecting him, aram.man-. This intentional playing upon words is an example of his hūnartāt, virtuosity, his mastership of the language, hizvo χšayamno vaso. Meillet says, *Trois Conf.* 61: "taromati 'pensée hors (de la règle)' est fait pour s'opposer à ārmati . . . , [il y a] un artifice théologique dans la forme de ces oppositions." When used in the sense "obedience," the name of the goddess of Earth, ārmati, is interpreted as if it meant *aram.mati, "pensée selon (la règle)." Therefore, this cannot be its meaning; the artificial play forbids an assumption of etymologic connection.

With equal or better right one could state: In *Y*.43,15 Zoroaster alludes to ārmatiš vahištā by the words tušnāmatiš vahištā. Compounds with locative as first element are an archaic type, in this very case confirmed by the use as n.pr.—Tušnāmatiš and ārmatiš are opposed like tušnišad and armēšad (Fravarti, *Yt*.13,29 and 73) "living in silence"

of Sāyaṇa on *RV*.VIII,31,12. While he equates arámatiḥ in *RV*.VII,36,8 etc with "pṛthivī, earth," in VIII,31 in the sequence "mountains, rivers, pūṣán (Aw. fšūšan) wealth, bhaga, urúr ádhvā (the broad path)," he considers it as attrib. adj. to stōtṛjanaḥ—omitted, but to be supplied—"people who praise pūṣán, = alam.mati."

[12] Cf. Fr. labour, Engl. labor (with child) or travail, against Fr. travail; the earth as barθrī; also Germ. arbeit, Slav. răbōtă "corvée."

and "living in quiet," words, the pre-Iranian age of which is documented by the sandhi-form and by the correspondence with Gr. σιγῇ and ἠρέμᾳ ἔχειν, keeping silence, and keeping still, be patient. This is another play upon words, but no etymology.

Evidently, the word was so old and so isolated that, in Zoroaster's time as already in Vedic times, it had no longer any purport. The spelling ārmati is strictly carried through, but ārmati—which does not result from arámatiḥ—always counts for four syllables. Markwart, *Gāth.ušt.* 60f., tried to explain the trisyllabic spelling as abstracted from the pronunciation sfandārmaδ at the time when the Awestic script was invented. If the oral tradition was arámati, this would be impossible, for Ātarpāt could introduce a new spelling only when rectifying the meter. The pronunciation must have been ārmati, counting for four syllables, before the invention of the Aw. script.

A similar though simpler case is dēnā: bisyllabic spelling is strictly carried through, but the word always counts for three syllables. In this case the pronunciation dēnā is attested as early as 520 B.C., for the tablet *Susa* 20 has the Elam. loanword ta.t.te.ni.m, i.e. *dāt.dēnām,[13] instead of OP. "framātar, law-giver" and *NiR* A,57 has te.ni.m for OP. framānā, Akk. uṭa'ama. El. tē.ni.m renders dēnām, not *dayanam. With a trisyllabic dēnā and a four-syllabic ārmati Zoroaster uses—right or wrong—forms no longer living at his time.

There was an OP. rmatam, with which ārmatiš can be connected. rmatam, as form, corresponds to Lat. armentum, ārmatiš to Lat. sēmentis. It appears in the Elam. version of *Beh.* §47. The OP. text runs: "ršāda nāmā diδā[14] harahvatiyā avaparā atiyāiš, to a castrum named Ršāda in Arachosia, there he marched." After harahvatiyā the El. version adds: "[1]rmatam wiwanana, an rmatam of Vivāna." The placename Ršāda < *rša.hada, to √had-, means "stud," i.e. an area where horses were bred. The situation must be that of Aspacora (*Tab.Peut.*), mod. Asfuzār, "horse-pasture" in Arachosia. Thus the rmatam of Vivāna, a plantation, urvarā, with castrum in this horse-pasture country, was a ranch.

[13] Possibly OP. *dāta.dēni-, abstr., unless the El. ending -im will become otherwise explained.

[14] diδā > diz is (enclosure) wall; OP. paridaiδa > Gr. parádeisos, the garden, characterized by its enclosure. The El. version has the loanword ʰalwarris, an OP. noun in -iš, < OP. *ārvariš (undetermined quantity, also color of the vowels), probably deriv. of OP. urvarā "plantation."

The etymologic connection of urvarā and *ἄρουρα* has been proposed, but rejected on the ground that √ar- "to plough" is not attested in the Aryan branch of IE. Arguments from absence are never strong, especially because old local names may contain roots otherwise obsolete. Lat. armentum are the animals of agriculture, large cattle, oxen and horses, compatible with OP. "rmatam, ranch." And ārmatiš, as abstract, is to rmatam, as Lat. sēmentis to armentum. One day the etymology of ārmati will be found. Until then, one had better not introduce a different spelling.

XXIV. HARVATĀT-AMRTATĀT

LIKE Ārmatiš, the pair harvatāt-amrtatāt has been admitted by Zoroaster into his concept of AhuraMazdāh.

harvatāt, n.abstr. of harva, whole, is ὁλότης, "wholeness, physical integrity," then "health," but also "abundance," and Plutarch renders the personification, much to the point, by "Ploutos," son of Demeter-Ārmatiš. amrtatāt, n.abstr. of *amrta, Ved. amṛta, ἄμβροτος,[1] is "immortality," personified "ambrosia." The dvandva was at first harvatātā-amrtatātā, the second dual especially liable to haplologic shortening: amrtātā. Yet in most cases harvatāt keeps the first place, showing that the dvandva is older than the shortening, which is common already in the gatha. Then, harvatātā became harvātā, and the movement ended in NP. Arab. Harūδ u Marūδ.

The essence of the two powers is clearly expressed in *Yt.*19.96:

vanāt harvāsča amrtāsča	Harvāt-Amrtāt will conquer
uwā šuδamča tršnamča	both, famine and drought.

Benveniste describes the dvandva as "projection mythique" of āpā-urvarē, water-plants, which itself means the grain of the irrigated fields,[2] and is the prototype, extremely old, of quite a group of dvandvas, all variations of "liquid and solid." In harvatāt all saps of plants and animals are embodied, and, to apply amrtatāt to the vegetable kingdom, involves a deep insight: the up-rooted animal has paid the price of a determined, short life for its freedom of movement.

Y.31,21:

mazdå dadāt ahuro	harva[tā]to amrtātasča
būroiš ā rtahyača	hvāpaθyāt χ̌šaθrahya saro
vahoš vazdvar manaho	yo hoi manyū šyōθnāišča rvaθo

"AhuraMazdāh by his perfect union with Harvatāt-Amrtatāt, Rta and Xšaθra, may give the draught of Vahumano to him who is his friend in mind and acts."

"sar," in the social sense "connubium," is here as elsewhere the word for the union of the partial figures, or aspects, of the god. One cannot fail to feel another opposition besides "liquid and solid": harvatāt

1 Cf. +am(h)rka < ahmāka in Y.32,8 under 'Yama Xšēta.'

2 Benveniste, BSOS VIII,405. Ved. and Aw. urvarā = cultivated soil.

belongs to this life, to time, amrtatāt to the hereafter, to eternity. The god is wedded to the pair in his double quality of χšaθram, "lord of time," and of rtam, the "eternal." harvatāt means "blessed life on earth," amrtatāt the "eternal life."

*Y.*51,7:

dādi moi yo gām tašo	āpasča urvarāsča
amartātā harvātā	spaništā manyū mazdā
tavīšī utiyūtī	manahā vahū sānhē

"Give me, Thou who hast created the cow, the waters and plants, immortality and health as Spanto Manyuš, o Mazdāh, force and longevity as Vahumano, in Thy commandment!"

I leave utiyuti for better definition. amrtātā harvātā are eternal life and blessed life here, Arab. al-dunyā wa l-ākhira. The dying caliph al-Muntaṣir says to his mother: "I have forfeited al-dunyā wa l-ākhira!", Tabari III,1495. Since the wishes are for this and the other world,[2a] sānhē cannot mean "bei dem Richterspruch = last judgment" (Bartholomae), but must be the same as sāsnayā in the next verses, *Y.*29,7:

tam āzutoiš ahuro	manθram tašat rtā hazōšo
mazdå gāvoi χšvidamča	+huhuršēbyo spanto sāsnayā

The dvandva χšvidā-āzutī, "aliments liquides et solides" (Benveniste), is one of the variations of āpā-urvarē and appears in *Yt.*16,8 in parallel with harvatāt-amrtatāt. hazōšo: cf. *Y.*33,2: "who does harm, aka, to the drugvant, is quite to the taste, zōšāi, of AhuraMazdāh." +huhuršēbyo, reading corrected by Tedesco, ZII, II,1923, 43f., is regular desid. of √hvar-, "to eat, drink."

Meillet, *Trois Conf.,* translated: "La formule de graisse, A.M. saint l'a construite d'accord avec Aša, pour le boeuf, et aussi le lait pour ceux qui veulent le consommer, par son enseignement." Andreas, NGGW 1931, III,322, attributed the fact that χšvidam (acc.) is not, as usual, in the same case as āzutoiš (gen.) to "Laxheit der Konstruktion, viell. χšviδōm as gen.pl." The construction is right: in *Y.*49,2, the subject of the quotation "ahmāi stoi ārmatim!" stands in the acc., because it is governed by "dōršt": "He professes: ārmatim (acc.) be mine!" The

[2a] Cf. "rayo rtiš, award of riches, and life in paradise" in *Y.*43,1, under 'Fravarti.'

words "āzutim gāvoi, χšvidam huhuršēbyo" are the quotation, and the gen. āzutoiš is governed by manθra, MP. mansr, usually "dictum, poem," but here, with only one verse, "proverb."

Manθra as "adage" occurs once more in the frgm. *Nirang*.2: "apastāk čigōn dāt: maγno manθro," with Pahl. transl. "framān, rule (for measuring)." *Wb.* links maγno to "maγna, naked" as "bloss = bare, pure," and compares OI. nagná and Gr. gymnós. Then, it can be "+naγno manθro, the proverb of the bread" (about daily bread or salt and bread), whether maγno be correct or to be corrected in +naγno > NP. nān, nūn. This would be the only instance of the word for "bread" in the Awesta, a warning not to infer from such absence that a thing was unknown, as in the case of "salt."

"The adage (of the) 'āzuṭim for the cow, milk for the thirsty,' Ahura-Mazdāh, like-minded with Rtam, has coined it, the holy one, by His command." It goes on: "Whom doest Thou have among men, who would attend to us two [bull and cow]? I have found only one who follows Thy commandment in our favor: Zoroaster!" The Pahl. translation adds: "ān mizd ē ač mansr pētāk, that reward [viz. which the ox receives from men for its labor] which the adage makes clear." Zoroaster says: The obvious wisdom of the proverb ought to be the divine rule for the attitude of the peasant towards the cattle, or in his figurative style, of the ruling towards the peasants.

Nyberg, 197, explains āzutoiš manθram differently: "Das Gotteswort von der Begiessung, āzuti, für den Stier geschaffen. Begiessung sollen die Kühe vom Menschen dafür erhalten, dass sie ihm die Milch liefern," and concludes from this wrong translation: "In *Y*.29,7 bedeutet āzuti die Begiessung des Weideplatzes mit Kuhurin zum Gedeihen der Weide." In *Vid*.13,28 this same āzuti is called "the proper diet of the dog," but letting that pass along with the other anomaly that grass would grow—to prevent a middle-sized herd of 5,000 head on about a hundred square miles[3] from doing the sprinkling themselves would require an army of cowboys.

[3] The Assyrian annals often give the numbers of cattle carried away, e.g. Sanherib, *prism* 1,46ff.: 7,200 horses, 11,072 donkeys, 4,233 camels, 200,100 (v.l. 80,100) cows, 800,600 (v.l. 800,100) sheep." On the Nēsaean pasture Alexander saw still 60,000 of the original 160,000 horses. *Genesis* 31—much older—regrettably does not give the numbers of Jacob's cattle.

The care of the cattle—cf. the Gath. term gōdāyah, lit. cow-nurse, for cowboy, under 'Social Structure'—is also the theme of *Y*.48,5:

"Good-rulers (perhaps better 'economists'), not bad-rulers shall govern us with the works of the good Čistiš, o Ārmatiš!"

yōždå martiyāi api.zanθam vahištā
gāvoi vrzyātām tām no hvarθāi fšuyo

Bartholomae translated at first, *Ar.Forschg.* II,167: "Heilschaff dem Menschen (und) Nachkommenschaft!" with api.zanθam as compound; but *Wb.*85: "Vollbringe für den Menschen die künftige-Geburt, für das Rind die Landwirtschaft, lass es feist werden zu unserer Nahrung!", a twisted translation, made with regard to the two places, 5,21 and 10,18, where the verse is quoted in the *Vidēvdād,* the worst authority for gatha-interpretation. Lommel paraphrases only: "die für den Menschen die künftige-Geburt (in Lauterkeit) vorbereiter, für die Kuh die Werkthätigkeit, um sie für uns zur Nahrung zu pflegen." One wonders. Nyberg enhances Bartholomae's "künftige-Geburt" to "Wiedergeburt," analyzes, on the strength of this hypothetical hapax, Zoroaster's notions about "birth and rebirth," otherwise unattested, and finally pronounces: "Das ideale Hirtenleben in einem von allen hemmenden Schranken befreiten stamm wird hier als das grosse Endziel hingestellt."

Wb. posits a verb *fšav- only for this fšuyo in *Y*.48,4, "weil das Gath. keine o-nominative von ant-Stämmen kennt," giving it the arbitrary signification "fett machen." Since the logical consequence would be that cattle grow fat from labor, to assume that the poet or a copyist allowed an o-nom. to creep in would be the "interpretatio facilior." The eschatologic interpretation —a tendency that impairs Bartholomae's work only too often— is prevented by the second part of the verse: in "life in purity," according to *Māh Frav.,* one did eat no beef, or as Theopomp says, nothing at all. Also, while the ox is allowed to be slaughtered, ǰadyāi, the cow is "agnya, not-to-be-slaughtered," and the verses have milk and cheese in mind. In *Vid.*5,21, api.zanθam is correctly written as compound, following a text a thousand years older than our Mss. It means "progeny, offspring."[4] The

[4] In *ZAirWb.* 179 Bartholomae cites from the *Ganǰ i Šāh.* (Pahl. Texts 1,45) a word in Aw. script which he takes as dat.pl. of pati.čant-: "which man is pati.čanbyo? Who after his father

meter, 5 + 6 between 4 + 7 syllables, is not of necessity faulty. Hertel, *Beitr.* 67f., takes vahištā as instr., attribute to ārmatiš of the preceding verse. I prefer vocative at the end of the sentence. He takes vrzyātām as 3.sg. imper.med. "für das Rind arbeite der Viehzüchter, fšuyo, damit es uns ernähre." The second tām, left unexplained by Hertel, looks like a dittography, and Tedesco told me that, to compensate it, one may read ⁺hvarθāya for hvarθāi, as in *Y.*34,11; hence:

48,5: gāvoi vrzyātām no ⁺hvarθāya fšuyo

"Make healthy, to men, their offspring, o best one! For the cattle, that it may nourish ourselves, the farmer shall work!"

Čistiš is here, and in the entire *Dēn-Yasht* 16, Zoroaster's substitute for Ušå, the goddess of dawn and of labor; she is also midwife and physician.[5] The simple train of thought is: good government, healthy children, ample food, all this Ārmatiš gives as Agricultura, embodied in AhuraMazdāh.

Not Aw. "χšvid, milk," but OP. *χšifta, to OP. √χšip-, Aw. χšviw-[6] lives on in the West Ir. dialects. The verb describes the rotating and shaking movement which separates cream and whey. The OP. noun exists in Ctesias' (Photius) *σιπταχορα*, in a recently discovered text of Psellius[7] *ζητακωρα*, Pliny "psitthacora." Ctesias translates it by *γλυκύ, ἡδύ*; the variants give ⁺*ξιπταχωρα* as form used by himself, OP. *χšiftahvara NP. šiftaχur, "sweets," as Tychsen recognized 150 years ago.[8] The usual Aw. word for milk is payah, to √pi-, Pahl.transl. pēm < pēman. An article of food as important as "māst, Turk. yoghurt, Arab. laban, curdled milk" cannot be missing in the Awesta: it is χšudra, adj. χšāudri,

"ō škanb ē mātar šavēt, NP. pas uftād," which can hardly mean anything but "posthumous." The explanation is based on the phonetic similarity of OIr. čanb- and MIr. škanb, and the inverse correspondence of OIr. šk: MIr. č. It is written with the č which takes the place of z—without exception—in MP. fračant < frazanti, "progeny," e.g. inscr. Fīrūzābād, l.5: mtrnrshy v.š frčndyn, "Mihrnarseh and his progeny," also in the Pahl. Psalter. pati.čant- seems to be MP. pati.zant, comparable to fra.zanti and api.zanθa.

5 Cf. *Ušå-Eos* in *Mélanges Cumont,* Ann. Inst. phil.-hist. orient. IV, 1936, 731ff.

6 Cf. Hübschmann, *Pers.Stud.* 82.

7 *Indika,* C. Müller, frgm. 19.—Maas, in Z.f.vergl. Sprachf. XXXII,303ff.; E. H. Johnson, JRAS, 1942, 29ff. and 249: *Ctesias on Indian Manna.* Psellius, though writing two hundred years after Photius, yet seems to have used Ctesias directly.

8 In Heeren's *Ideen,* ed. 1824, II,384.

also payah χšāudri; the translation "wine, beer, alcoholic" is totally wrong. *Vid.* 16,17: "two portions of tāyurinām (yavanām), one of χšāudrinām shall be dispensed to the menstruating," certainly not "beer"; Pahl.transl. is "tēr nān (LḤM'), cheese bread" and "švsr āš," āš < OP. āšθʳa, is porridge, hence "barley in māst."[9] χšudra therefore is a deriv. of χšvid, probably both to √χšōd- "to foam." Aw. tāyuri or tūri, MP. tēr, NP. panīr, cf. Gr. τυρὸς and βούτυρος, is "cheese."

The crux is āzuti, coupled with χšvid in the dvandva. It is Ved. āhuti, to √zu-, whence such words of high Aryan antiquity as "zōtar, libans; zōθra, libation." Ved. āhuti is said to be an offering of preserved, i.e. melted butter, buttered again, and would be Aw. rōγna, MP.NP. rōγan, a thick, oily preserve, well known all over the East. Study of the Aw. passages does not confirm this signification in Iranian, and in Vedic, too, āhuti must not mean oil because oil is used as āhuti.

In the poor *Yt.*12,3 āzutim urvarānām appears beside rōγnya varah, ordeal-butter, and avi prnām viγžārayantīm. This is the only place where āχutī is qualified by a material, "of grains," in the Awesta. *Wb.* translates "Schmalz der Pflanzen," unknown to me, perhaps meant for "vegetable oil." The *Gr.Bdh.* enumerates "sesame, two kinds of hemp, šāhdang and dušdang, and olives" as oil-producing plants. To prnā, Bartholomae remarked "zu der überfliessenden Hohlhand, prnā to Lat. palma." prnā never appears without the epithet; it is the fem. of the adj. prna, hence "full, overflowing," scil. jug or flat bowl for libations, hydria or phiale.

*Had.N.*2,13 (repeated in *Ōgmad.*):

hvarθānām hē baratām zaramayahya rōγnahya

Duchesne: "Qu'en fait d'aliments on lui [Vahumano, rising from his golden bed for breakfast] apporte du beurre printanier, that is the food of the blissful heroes after death!" In 2,36, the damned sinners get "višaya and višgantaya, poison and of-poison-smelling food." "zahr, poison" is the antonym of "anōšak, ambrosia" in the chapter on opposites in the *Gr.Bdh.*47f. The preceding paragraph says: "the fravarti give the souls of the immortals, anōšravān, food of immortality, anōš χvarišn, such as is made in spring." And afterwards: "with water, wine, milk and honey." Milk and honey symbolize sweetness; the most

[9] On alcoholic drinks see under 'Hōma' and 'Industries.'

common word for "sweet" is šīrēn, lit. "of milk," used as transl. of χšvid. In *Vid*.13, "šīrēn u čarp, sweets and oil, fat" translates "χšvidā āzutī," but the commentary says "naγn u spētvāk," i.e. bread and ispīdbā, the latter being something made of curdled milk, māst.

Ir. āzuti cannot be rōγan, for this is never given to cows, as in *Y*. 28,7, nor to dogs, as in *Vid*.13,28:

paro χšvisča āzutišča	Here, with milk and āzuti, along
gauš mat baratu hvarθānām	with meat it shall be brought, as fodder,
sunahya ⟨ēva⟩ hē dāθya.piθwam	that is the proper meal of the dog!

āzuti functions in this dog's diet beside milk and flesh; besides, it is given to cattle. Actually, no fodder at all is given to cattle, either in summer or in winter. The caretaking consists in driving them to the right places where they find their grazing themselves. But the all-important question is watering, for water is rare, and not at all accessible at all pastures, it must be pumped or by other means conducted to the watering troughs. Hence, āzuti is a word not qualified by any material at all, it is merely the providing of drink; as "libation" it is drink-offering to the gods, else it is watering cattle and dogs: thus āzuti is the "mizd" for χšvid.

This research has revealed, at the same time, that there was a notion of "immortal food" strictly vegetarian. Meat diet is expressed by "pitu, etym. = fat," thus in the dog's ration. "PTBG, i.e. pitubaga, meat-ration," cf. Akk. pitipabagu or pitpibagu[10] < Ir. *piθvabaγa, in *Daniel* I, is the term for the provisioning of the sōmatophýlakes which receive rations instead of pay. Daniel and his companions become vegetarians to avoid eating meat not kosher. Dinon explains *ποτιβαζις* < *pāitubāǰiš as "bread, cypress-wreath and wine," quite unlike the food of the heroes after death. TPārs. pid u may nē χvarēm, ač zan dūr pahrēzēm (Bailey, BSOS VII,753) is avoiding of meat and wine as abstinence. In the legend of Ažidahāk, meat diet makes bloodthirsty. *Māh Frav*. §40: At the end

[10] Clearly showing the aspirated pronunciation of BGDKPT in Akkadian of the Achaemenian period.

of the world humanity will be immortal and not aging, and will need no more food. 41: Who has touched meat, will be resurrected only after 50 days, the others after 15. Meat diet takes the acceptation of food in general, for instance in the comp. "bipiθwa, θripiθwa, receiving two, three meals, fra.piθwa, well-fed, MP. hamēšag.pihan, continuously fed" all said of fire, opposite of ahvarta hvarnah, the hvarnah that burns "needing no food."

In *Y*.49,5 (borrowed in *Vid*.9,53) we find īžā āzutī instead of χšvidā āzuti: "īžāča āzutīča will be his who unites his faith with Vahumano—all of them in Thy kingdom, o AhuraMazdāh!" In st.11 follows the opposite: "but whose faith is evil, will be received . . . (in hell) with evil food, akāiš hvarθāiš."[11] Being interchangeable with χšvid, īžā must be a synonym, and at the same time a heavenly food, as antonym to hellish food.

Y.49,10:

tatča mazdā	θwahmiyā dām nipåhē
mano vahu	runasča rtāvnām
namasča yā	ārmatiš īžāča
manzā.χšaθrā	vazdahā ‚avəmīrā‘

"This, o Mazdāh, keep safely in Thy house, the Good-Will, the souls of the blessed, and (their) prosternations—obedience. . . ."

nipåhē: in *Y*.28,11 the god ni.pā-, "takes charge of" what man "deposits, ni.dā-." Upon the acc. objects of b-c three nom.dual follow without further verb, connected by the rel. yā: the enumeration goes on, but is no longer grammatically governed by nipåhē.[12] ārmatiš follows upon namasča as in *RV*. arámatiḥ upon námas. īžāča stands between it and manzā.χšaθrā which is "banquet" (see under 'Hospitium'). The following vazdahā ‚avəmīrā‘, soon to be discussed, belongs to the same sphere. īžā, here in st.10 as well as in 5, means a heavenly food.[13] The dual may mean "the two īžā," viz. īžā āzutī, which is a variant of χšvidā āzutī, itself analogous to āpā-urvarē and harvatāt-amrta-

[11] Also in *Y*.31,20 and 53,6 used for "hellish food."

[12] "yā (those things) which (are)," if referring to the foregoing = "also"; if to the following = "like."

[13] *Wb*. īžā "Streben, endeavor, zeal, to √āz-; in *Y*.49,10 "Glaubenseifer." *Wb*. does not separate the words.

tāt. In *Y*.34,11 this last pair is called "hvarθāi, the two foods." īžā designates a concrete, nothing abstract, it must be a sap or draught.[14]

vazdahā ‚avəmīrā': Bartholomae linked the hapax vazdah to vazdvar, *Y*.31,21 (see above), and translated "beständig, stable" and "stability." Against this, Andreas-Wackernagel, NGGW 1911, 32, called Geldner's connecting of vazdah with Ved. vedhás "evident": "*RV*.x,86,10 vedhā́ ṛtásya : Aw. rtavazdah, 'Αρταουάσδης, viell. zu √vad- 'führen,' also vazdvar in Y. 31, 21 'Führerschaft.' " Hertel, IIQF VII, 150f., modified this to "Führungsfähigkeit," something like "ability to command one's body, coordination." The n.pr. krsavazdah, which means neither (Bartholomae) "magere, d.i. geringe Ausdauer besitzend," nor "meager leadership," does not fit; therefore it is probably not √vad- "führen." From the Aw. passages one can only infer: (1) as tanuvo vazdvar, bodily v., it stands in parallel with drvatātam "integrity of the body," *Yt*.14,29; (2) it is a "gift of the waters" Y.68,11; (3) an "award" the believers obtain in paradise, *Vid*.9,44. Benveniste objected to "vazdvah, beständig": "alors que seul est établi un neutre vazdah 'santé,' " but his reasons are unknown to me.

A misinterpreted passage in *Yt*.8,43 (text under 'Tištriya') is conclusive: "Satavēsa washes off all illnesses, all važdriš uχšyati,[15] i.e. makes grow all medicinal herbs, heals all creatures."

"Vazdah" must be a healing potion, *nectar,* and ‚avəmīrā' can be nothing but "ambrosia,"[16] OI. amṛta, the food of immortality. In *Art.*

[14] This Gath. īžā is attested only as nom.dual; the script of the archetype could not indicate the quantity of init. i. Cf. *Ilias* v,340-2: "the divine blood of the goddess, *ichor,* such as flows in the blessed gods.

For they eat not grain, they drink not sparkling wine;
That is why they are bloodless and are exempt from death."

G.M. Bolling, in *Language* 21,2, 1945, 49ff., regards the last two verses as an Orphic notion, close to Epimenides, introduced into the *Ilias* in the 6th-5th centuries. He connects ἴχωρ, the sap of gods instead of blood of humans, with Skr. īhate, Hom. ἰχανάω "yearns," Aw. āzi "Begierde, Gier," and Aesch. ἴχαρ "vehement desire."

[15] *K15* važdriš, *J10* vazdarš; Bartholomae failed to recognize važdriš by misinterpreting uχšyati.

[16] In B.B.VIII,226, Bartholomae, reading avəm īrā, advanced the emendation "anəmīvā, free of illness," cf. *Wb*.141, Aw. amayavā and OI. ámīva "suffering, ailment." The word begins with *a* priv. and has four syllables: v and n are interchangeable; mīr can be √mr-, mrya.

Vir.Nām.x, the souls of the deceased say to Artavirāz as welcome in paradise: " 'nvš 'šTHn, drink immortality, that you may see here rāmišn, peace eternally." vazdahā-avəmīrā are nectar and ambrosia, the food at the manzā. χšaθrā, the banquet of the souls in the house of Ahura-Mazdāh. The dvandva is closely related to harvatāt-amrtatāt.

One may apply to it all the investigations made on Gr. nectar and ambrosia. These, too, are very old words, meaning "not-being-dead" and "not-dying," but, in course of time, interpreted as different foods and drinks. There was certainly a connection between the Greek and the Iranian notion, as old as the motif of the Yama myth, with its taboo on meat.

A peculiar heavenly food appears also in the Mithra Yasht. In 10,135, see under 'Mithra,' the four white horses of the god are called immortal and manyušhvarθa. This is Ar. *maniu.suartha, and means neither (Darmesteter, Nyberg) "den Luftraum zur Nahrung habend"—that would be "consuming parasangs, Kilometerfresser" or "living on air," nor (*Wb.*) "Nahrung des Geistes bildend"—that would be the device on the old Berlin Library "nutrimentum spiritus," but "feeding heavenly food," in *Y*.56,2 "being heavenly food." It is the reason why the horses are immortal, anōša. The notion is pre-Iranian, and as early as in the Aryan period manyu, manyava must have been a synonym of dēva, heavenly. From the beginning it implies the opposition of the MP. transcendent mēnōk to the earthly gētīk.

In *Y*.32, hujyāti replaces harvatāt in the dvandva. St.5: "Thereby you have cheated man out of hujyāti and amrtāt, good-living and immortality." hujyāti, etym. close to Gr. hygiéia, means, like εὐβίοτος, Lat. vīta < *vīvīta, life on earth, without the faintest eschatological afterthought (*Wb.*: "insbesondere im Jenseit"): the beggar wishes it his benefactor. It is opposed to life in the hereafter, amrtatāt, as OP. šyāta in this world to rtāvan. In *Vid*.3,3 it summarizes the preceding words "fat cattle, fat pasture, fat dogs, fat women, fat children, fat (= well-nourished) fires." The strange sequence is first outdoor, then indoor. To be fat is the visible sign of a successful life. There can be nothing more

The Pahl. transl.—useless for the rest—frōt.murt bavēt, had evidently a compound with mīr which it regarded as mrya > mīr. Perhaps an + ā.mrya-?

earthly than hujyāti. Epicharmos says: ἀνδρὶ δ' ὑγιαίνειν ἄριστόν ἐστι, and Simonides: "First good thing for man is health."

In the Yama-myth, *Yt.*5,26, the hero surpasses the gods "in riches and prosperity, breeds of cattle and herds, satiation and 'proclamation,'" the two foods never decreasing, cattle and men not-dying, waters and plants never dry. Altogether this is ⁺vispā.hujyātiš. Vispām.hujyātim in *Yt.*5,130, is a compound, wrongly inflected, one syllable too long, and can be restored from *Beh.* §35, OP. višpauzātiš, El. wi.s.p.o.ca.ti.s,[17] i.e. vispā.hužyāti, contracted and tetrasyllabic. The place, which I believed (in AMI VII,31) to be Hecatompylos-Dāmghān, is called so because it offers everything for good living; it lay in Parθava towards Vrkāna. The OP. name would give NP. *b/gusfōzāδ, or—as spantadāta > isfandiyār—*busfōzār. Today, I regard it as Sabzawār. This is not—as Aspacora > Asfuzār in Arachosia—an OP. *aspačāra, but *vispōzār, with dropping of init. vi- and assimilation to sabzah "vegetables."

The same explanation holds good for the n.pr. Hyspaosínes, son of Sagdodonacus, founder of Spasinou Charax, i.e. Muḥammira on the Shaṭṭ al-'Arab, Pliny *N.H.*VI,138f., from Juba, who is also the source of Pseudo-Lucian, *Macrobii* 16: "Hyspasínes, king of Charax and the regions on the Red Sea (=Persian Gulf), died of sickness at the age of 85." A clay tablet from Babylon, Landsberger in Z. Ass. N.F. VII,1933, 298, records a decree of the administrator and the collegium of Esagila, determining salaries for astronomers, dated 24.III.185, reign of Hyspaosines. 185 Sel. is 128/7 B.C.[18] Hence, the king is exactly contemporary with the founder of the Sakā dynasty of Kirkūk, just after 129 B.C. The name of the father sounds Babylonian: H. Winckler saw in it a Babylonian divine name plus -nādin.aḫḫē, and Αδαδναδινάχης of Tello-Lagash has been identified with him. In spite of it, Hyspaosínes might be a Saka: another Iranian name of this dynasty is Tiraios, Aram. Tīrē, short form of *tigrāhana, Tigranes "archer,"[19] to whom the *Šahr.Ēr.* ascribe the foundation of Nahr Tīrak in Khūzistān. An older Hyspaosines, a Bactrian, son of Mithróaxos < *miθrahaxš, appears in 180 B.C. in an inscription from Delos.

17 With Parthian(?) metathesis of the palatal: š and z for s and ž; a good example for OP. ž, not ǰ. OP. šyāti, pronunciation šāti, against *žyāti, pron. zāti.

18 There was a coin of Hyspaosines in the Berlin Cabinet with the date HΠP = 125/4 B.C.

19 See Andreas, NGGW. 1931, III,317.

The Palmyrenian inscriptions spell the placename 'SPSN'. Andreas (Lommel, in ZII,4,302) explained Hyspaosines as *vispōnčono; Markwart, *Südarmenien* 408,n.2 as Aw. uspansnu. It contains vispā, hu, and, instead of žyāta, the part.pres. žīvan or žīyan, contracted žīn, formation like vispā.tarvan, hence: *vispā.hu.žīn, vispaužīn, meaning **παν-εύβιος* or almost Polybios. In Spasinou Charax and 'spsn', the init. vi- is dropped as in Sabzawār.

Among the five cities founded according to the *Šahr.Ēr.* §§19-20 by Xusrau I, there is, beside Andēv.Xusrau, the new town of Ctesiphon, and beside Gēhān.farraχv.kirt.Xusrau (cf. AMI.IX,149) the name VSPŠ'TχVSLVB, visp.šāt.χusrau, not an entirely satisfying reading: it should be, with insignificant change, vispōžāt.χusrau. These names belong to the ostentatious official names, as used by Assyrians, Sasanians and Arabs, in OP. so far only documented by the name of the gate of Persepolis dvarθiš visa.dahyuš (= through which people of all provinces pass), and of the palace of Artaxerxes II at Susa, ǰ[i]ivd[i]iy prdydam, formed with MP. pardēδ, paradise, and ǰīva-, to √ǰyā in hu.-ǰyāti. Modern names like bāγ i Firdaus, Hašt bihišt, eight paradises, express a similar thought. vispē.ārya.rzurā, "pan-Aryan forest," name of a race-course, represents this class in the Awesta.

The name of Ctesias' river that carries manna is in the Photius text: *ἰνδιστὶ* "Υπαρχος, in the new Psellius text *Σπάβαρος*, in Pliny, NH. 37, 39. Hypobarus, in Nonnus Hysporus. Ctesias' translation is *φέρων πάντα τὰ ἀγαθά*, i.e. vispā.hu.bara; Ctesias himself wrote *"Υσπωβάρας. Another gloss of his is *οἴβαρας* = *ἀγαθάγγελος*, hence *vahyabara, stem-word of *vāhyabari > MP. vāvar. The river is called so, because it carries the manna, a tree raisin, *σιπτα-* or *ξιπταχορα, γλυκύ, ἡδύ*, which drops into it as tears, *δάκρυα*. All the names are correct, only they are not *ἰνδιστί*: Ctesias spoke Persian well, but not Indian, and his Indika are Persian tales about India, that means the Indian provinces of the Persian empire.

Dēnk. VII,4,66: Zoroaster and Vištāspa meet in 's p '/h[u]/n[v]/n l ē vištāsp. Xusrau I, in his testament, *Pahl.Texts* 1,55, orders his exposure at the same place. This is not, as Salemann believed, Isfahān (*Mél.As.* 1886, IX,247), but "the city of Kisrā, in which the īwān is built and where are the tombs of Salmān i Fārsī and of Hudhaifa," Ya'qūbī, *tanbīh* 30. Together with Ctesiphon proper it formed the old town of al-Madā'in.[20] The fact that Yāqūt quotes the authority of a mōbaδ Yazdegird i Māhbundāδ, and the many varieties of the name, show that it was no longer a living name at the Muhammedan epoch, but taken from Pahl. books. "aspān, horses" does not belong to the elements entering in the formation of such "display-names," and since the Pahl. characters can equally well be read 'sp.hv.vr, it is evidently vispa.hu.bara, the same as Ctesias' Hyspobaras, "bringing all that is good." Again, the init. vi- is dropped and replaced by a prothetic vowel before sp-.

Andreas, in Lentz, l.c. 302, speaks about the "gelegentliche Abfall des vi-," but gives only the doubtful examples šigarf < *višgarf and χun < vohuni,[21] to which one can add vi.fšānaya > afšāndan. But though the fall of vi- cannot be proved as a normal change of sound, it is yet possible in "allegro forms" of long, artificial names of places and persons, which are abbreviations, not changes of sound.

20 al-Khaṭīb al Baghdādī, Balādhurī and the mōbadh Yazdegird (279-89 H) in Yāqūt spell 'sfnbr; Ḥamza 'sf'br; Yāqūt, Mārī Sulaimān, and 1001 Nights 'sfnyr.

21 Ar. *u̯ahu̯an and u̯ahun, TPārs. gōkhan.

XXV. DĒVA

"Und dein nicht zu achten, wie ich!"
—Prometheus.

Nothing has been a greater obstruction to understanding the Awesta than the wrong, preconceived notion of the word *dēva.*

From the correspondence of Ved. dēva, Lat. dēus etc. and of Ved. dyóḥ, Aw. dyōš, Gr. Zeus etc., one has long since concluded that the concept of the "heavenly ones" in opposition to the "earthly" homines, and "mortal" mortales is Indo-European in general. Long since, too, the analogies have been pointed out that exist between what Caesar says about the Germanic gods (*Bell.Gall.*vi,21) sol, vulcanus, luna; Herodotus about the Iranian *οὐρανός, ἥλιος, σελήνη, γῆ, πῦρ, ὕδωρ, ἄνεμοι*; and what more recent authorities say about the Borussian sol, luna, stellae, tonitura and terra. To these must be added, not less old, the dawn, the lightning and others. Those are the "heavenly ones, dēva, dii" grouped around the "father Heaven" and the "mother Earth."

Herodotus sees with Greek eyes. Where he relates history, he depends more than we knew until recently on older logographs, first and foremost Hecataeus, and he gathered his knowledge of the Iranian religion in border provinces and from hearsay. His remarks about the temples and altars, Zeus in heaven, Uraníē-Mylitta, the feminine Mithra—none of it correct—prove that it was beyond his power to distinguish between the Zoroastrism as revealed in the gathas and the popular religion of his epoch. He wrote about 440 B.C.; about 400 B.C. the period of gathic Zoroastrism had already passed. The religion was in transformation. So far as such developments are conscious at all, they are not displayed, in most cases what grows is unknown to the contemporaries, and what has become is only perceivable to the later observer.

In *Yt.*10,145—under 'Mithra'—a hymn begins with the invocation of miθrā-ahurā, in dvandva form, and of stars, moon and sun; in the Veda, the invocation of mitrā́-váruṇā is frequent; and in the political treaties of the Mitanni Aryans, likewise, the gods of the oaths are invoked in form of two dvandvas, the first being mitrā-varunā. The reason the names appear as dvandva is obviously that they were frequently invoked together, and we may infer that the introductory formula of *Yt.*10,145 was a fixed type already used at the Aryan period. Herodotus may have had knowledge of such a formula, and may have derived his enumeration of Iranian gods from it, but hardly without combining therewith the notion of the early Ionic philosophers, as e.g. ὁ μὲν Ἐπίχαρμος τοὺς θεοὺς εἶναι λέγει ἀνέμους ὕδωρ γῆν ἥλιον πῦρ ἀστέρας.

One must not call this "primitive worship of the elements": in the middle of the fifth century B.C. nothing can any longer be "primitive" in Iran; that is a function of the state of civilization, and only "decadence" is possible.[1] One sees merely that the worship of the primeval dēva went on.

Bartholomae, *Wb.*667: "daēva, im Gath. Bezeichnung der vor Zarathustra in Iran geltenden Religion," entirely right, and implying that, before accepting the doctrine of Zoroaster, the Iranians were *dēva-yasna* exactly as the Indo-Aryans. Wrong is: "Im Gath. gehört der Begriff daēva in die gleiche Gruppe wie usig, kavi, karpan." To usig and karpan he remarks, *Wb.*406 and 454, with identical words: "Bezeichnung gewisser, der zarathustrischen Religion feindlicher Lehrer und Priester." They were not called so because they were hostile, but had these names long before Zoroaster came. *Wb.*813 he describes tkaēša and usig as "zu den Schlag- und Kampfwörtern der zarathustrischen Zeit gehörig." There he goes definitely astray, and to go farther on this way, and to translate, in the gatha, dēva by "demon, idol = Götze, devil = Teufel" is utterly absurd, cf. Hertel's justified remarks in the introduction to his translation of *Y.*32 in *Beitr.*251. It was equally absurd, even when still believing in the post-Zoroastrian date of the yashts, the so-called "Younger Awesta," to give the word the exclusive signification "götze, idol"; for the possibility always existed that the yashts contained old pieces in which dēva can only mean "god." The deteriorated, untranslatable signification which one can only render by MP. dēv, is limited to the cases collected in *Wb.* (669, under II,b) as "namentlich bezeichnet." With exception of the equally late passages in *Yt.*8 and 18, they all come from the *Vidēvdād,* a product of the Arsacid period, and even there the dēva Indra, Nāhaθya and Sarva of *Vid.*19,43 (the last two also in 10,9) are to be excluded. *Dēva signifies nothing but "heavenly ones, gods."* The passages where this sense is really lost are worthless and could be entirely deleted.

1 Used in its vulgar sense, "primitive" in comparison with our own time, would be irrelevant and misleading.

The oldest Aryan gods attested by documents are the gods of the oaths of the Mitanni people, the two dvandva Mitrā-Varunā and Indrā-Nāsatyā, well known from the Indian pantheon, while the Iranians have lost the second pair—see under 'Mithra.' In the "list of gods," III. *Rawl.* 69, K.4343 n.5, furthermore ᵈAssara ᵈMazaš appears, i.e. Ar. *asura maδdhas;[2] the same list contains also Mi.it.ra. The Assyrian scholars of the Assurbanipal library do not quote their sources, but the pre-Iranian form proves that similar invocations of gods in Mitanni treaties were the source. The worshippers of the god with the pre-Median name cannot have been Medes or magi, as Nyberg assumes: already in 1913, H. Winckler wrote in MVAG 18,4, 76: "Die Gottheiten der Meder konnten nicht in einer solchen Liste Aufnahme gefunden haben."

Nyberg, 339: "Das *Vidēvdād hat* die dēva Indra und Nāhaθya, mitanni Indra Nāsatyas"; the magi had "ursprünglich dasselbe altarische Pantheon wie die Arier von Mitanni," and 364: "die Religion der Meder war mit der der Mitanni wesentlich identisch." Identity does not suffer restrictions, and the *Vidēvdād* does not "have" the dēva, it mentions them only. The context is in 10,9: "Recite three times *Y.* 27,14, 33,11, 35,5, 53,9 and thereto I assault the dēva Indra . . . the Sarva . . . , the (sg.) Nāhaθya!" §10,10 adds Tauri and Zarik (unknown). Then, "recite four times *Y.*27,13, 34,15, 54,1 and thereto I assault ēšma . . . , akataš . . . , the Varunian dēvā, and vātiya!" This stuff merely shows that its authors had not the faintest idea of what the gatha 53,9 and other passages say.

*Vid.*19,43: "Ahriman does not know which way to talk, not know which way to think: Zoroaster is born, what can one do about it?", words said in an assembly of the dēvs on the "wooded peak, arzurahya pati kamrδam."[3] Are present: Indra, Sarva, the (sg.) Nāhaθya, Tarvi, Zarik, Ēšma, Akataš, the Winter, Maršavan, Būti, Driwi, Kasviš, Patiša. Maršavan is the winter month Aram. markheshwan and Aw. mahrkūša of *frgm.Westrg.* 8 (see under 'Vidēvdād'). The last names are diseases known from *Yt.*5,92 and *Vid.*2. The assembly resolves to

[2] Erroneous opinions about the rendering of this Aryan name in Assyrian were advanced by Hertel, IIQF.VI, and similar ones in 1932 by Olmstead in *Orient.Stud.Pavry, AhuraMazdāh in Assyrian.*

[3] kamrδam is exactly Germ. "Koppe," as the summit of the "Riesengebirge" is called.

meet again and meanwhile has a recess in hell. They do not even dance, like the witches on the Hexentanzplatz in the Harz. One can learn nothing about Iranian religion from this witches' sabbath.

Sarva and Nāhaθya appear—as do the names hinduš and harahvatiš—under Iranian not Indian form. But in the Veda, nāsatyā and dasrā, "undeceivable" and "miracle-working," is a dual epithet of the two Aśvin, sons of Vivasvant (= Ir. Yama), and the nāsatyā of the Mitanni Aryans are of course a pair; as names of each one of the twins the words are used only considerably later. The form of the *Vidēvdād,* on the contrary, is no dual, hence cannot come down from high antiquity, and only from India, not from Mitanni. The acquaintance with the Indian dēva can at the most go back to the Achaemenian period, when three Indian satrapies belonged to the empire. Soldiers' songs, like that of the dēva-worshipping Vyamburadīva people—see under 'Kršvar'—may have been the intermediary. The Mitanni episode came to an end three hundred years before the first Mede appeared on Median soil. What there was of somatic descendants of those Aryan "marianni" had long since disappeared in the polyphylic mass of the Mesopotamian population. They were lost as their language, and their religion—the Aryan religion of the 15th-14th centuries—could not be resurgent in Media.

The foundation of the religion of all Aryan tribes, at the time of their immigration in Iran, is one and the same, and developments lasting 500 years separated it from the point at which the Indo-Aryans and the Mitanni-people had branched off. That is the situation as to descent.

It is a normal historical process for one or another god of a polytheistic pantheon to obtain greater importance in certain regions. During migrations, foreign gods, too, may be admitted. But Herodotus' description fits entirely the Median religion which is not at all unknown.

The different songs to Mithra—see under 'Mithra'—collected in the Mihr Yasht, belong to the Median epoch, have the Median empire as their horizon, and show Mithra as one of the great Median gods. The bagastāna mountain, with the monument of Darius, was a Median sanctuary of the baga Mithra, a mithraeum. There, holy white horses from the near Nisaya stood saddled for the god to ride. In this case we can trace the sanctuary back to older periods. Ctesias attributes the monument to Semiramis. The first Muslims called the mountain "Tooth of *Sumaira*," after a lady in Muhammad's surroundings with a prominent tooth. The joke was suggested by the original name of the rock and its shape. Both are described in Sargon's "eighth campaign": *"Simirria,* ubān šadē, a 'finger-tip mountain,' sojourn of bēlit ilē, the Lady of the Gods, the top of which supports the heaven, the root of which reaches the center of the netherworld." The goddess is the Cossaean "bēlit šadē ellūti, āšibat rēšēti, lady of the snowy mountains, dwelling on the summits," *Šumalia* or *Šimalia.*

The worship of AhuraMazdāh, in itself a matter of course, is proved by the pre-Zoroastrian Median dvandva miθrā-ahurā and by names like Mašdaka of Andirpatianu = mod. Darwaδ, of Aradpati, of Awakki = mod. Āwah, all true Medes, mentioned in Sargon's list of Median chiefs in prism A and the account of the eighth campaign. Mašdaka is the short form of a compound name with Mazdāh, like Mazdayasna, name of the father of a man in the memorial document of *Yt.*13. There was, before Zoroaster, in Iran, as these Median names prove, in Media as well as in Pārsa (see below), a cult of Varuna, in which—a frequent phenomenon in religion and legend—the appellative designation AhuraMazdāh, "the omniscient judge," had replaced the proper name Varuna-Uranos. The Ass. transcript ^{d}Assara ^{d}Mazaš shows that the appellative itself goes farther back to the Aryan epoch.

The Awesta can scarcely have preserved much of the cult of this pre-Zoroastrian AhuraMazdāh, but some fragments exist. *Yt.*13:

viδāraya-	[the fravarti support]
2: avam asmānam yo usča	the heaven there which on high,
rōχšnam fradrsro imām zām	radiant, visible far away,
ača pariča bavāva	covers the earth here on all sides,
mānayan ahē yaθa viš	as if it were a palace
yo hištati manyustāto	which rises built-into-the-air,
handraχto dūrē.karano	solid, with far-away-confines,
ayaho krpa hvēnahya	looking like hvēno brass,
ročahino avi θrišva	shining forth over the thirds?,

3: yim mazdå vastē vanhānam	which Mazdāh put on as his raiment,
star.pēšaham manyutāštam	adorned with stars, timbered in heaven,
yahmai noit čahmai nēmānām	of the halves of which beginning
karanā pari.vēnoiθē	and end are never seen!

"Wearing the heaven as raiment" means being the heaven; Mazdāh is Varuna, a notion which Zoroaster sanctioned in saying, *Y*.30,5: "the most-holy manyu (mazdāh) who is clothed in the most-solid heavens" (see under 'Yamā'). Another trace of Varuna-Mazdāh is the description of Ātarš, the Fire, as "puθra ahurahya mazdå, son of A.M." in the myth of his fight for the hvarnah in the ocean, *Yt*.19, and similarly in *Y*.59 and 62, see under 'ApāmNapāt.'

An equally old song is preserved in *Y.Haft*.38, the original metric form of which still shines through at various places:

> St.1: "imām āt zām ganābiš haθrā yazāmade yā nå barati yāsča toi ganå ahura mazdā rtāt hača, [we bring offerings to] this earth here together with the women [that] bears us [and who are] Thy Wives, AhuraMazdāh [as Rtam]!"

"yā nå barati" means the IE. earth as barθrī, mother and support. The "as Rtam" added to AhuraMazdāh is meaningless, the usual Zoroastrian adaptation of the older prayer.

> St.3: "āpo . . . yazāmade mēkantīšča hambavantīšča fravazåho ahurānīš ahurahya huvāpåho huprθwāsča hvāγžaθāsča husnāθrāsča ubōbyo ahūbya čagmā, the waters . . . the mingling, uniting, forth-flowing ones, the ahura-wives of the ahura, the fair-faced ones, good for fording, good for swimming, good for bathing, a gift for both worlds!"
>
> St.5: "āpasča vå azīšča vå mātråsča vå agriyå drigu.dāyaho vispā.pitīš āvōčama!, the waters as the pregnant, the mother cows, the not-to-be-killed ones, the providers-of-the-poor, they who water all (creatures), we invoke!"

It is no mere chance that the style of these verses is that of the Veda. The notion of earth and waters as the wives of heaven, and fire as their son, is infinitely more archaic than Zoroaster's AhuraMazdāh, who, as a manyu, has neither wives nor sons: lam yalad wa-lam yūlid! The *Y.Haft.* has preserved, in these verses, a prayer to the pre-Zoroastrian Ahura-Varuna.

The two great Median fires, at Čēčist in Āδarbāijān and at Agbatana, belonged to Vrthragna. They are the origin of the later concept and name of the royal vahrām-fires, see under 'Chronology.' The fire of Shēz was called āδar gušnasp, "of the stallion," that of Agbatana āδar kavātakān, "of the colt," stallion and colt being—like the nar rēvant, man of 30, and the youth of 15 years—incarnations of Vrthragna, known from his yasht. He is the third of the great Median gods.

Berossus (in Agathias) calls him the Iranian Heracles, and his special worship in Media and Armenia—countries united at an early epoch—as Vahagn višapaqaǰ, Hēraklēs drakontopníktēs, of Agathangelos, may have a peculiar reason: the same dragon killer is represented in western Asia Minor by Ἡρακλεϝής, in Etruria by Fercle, Osk. and Lat. Hercle (voc. of Ἥρακλος). As AhuraMazdāh replaces the n.pr. Varuna, so the epithet vrθragna replaces the n.pr. Indra. No satisfying etymology has been advanced for either the Greek name or the Aryan epithet—to which also the adj. vāraγnahya (gen. of *vāragan) belongs —and both may reflect, assimilated to Greek and to Aryan, the same name of an Anatolic god.[4]

An inscription, discovered in 1822 by R. Ker Porter and better copied by H. Rawlinson (JRGS x,100), in the caves of Karaftō in the Zagros, finally surveyed by Sir Aurel Stein in *Old Routes of Western Asia,* 1940, figs. 98-99, p.337f., says, according to M. N. Todd's interpretation:

Ἡρακλῆς ἐντάθε κατοικεῖ μηθὲν εἰσέλθοι κακόν.

"Heracles abides here, nothing evil may enter!"[5]

The editors put the inscription, for its paleography, "about 300 B.C.," perhaps slightly too old in comparison with the Greek dedicatory inscriptions from Persepolis. These, too, display already the syncretistic

[4] Since they correspond in the first two syllables, I feel that ἥρακλος, ἡρακλεϝής and vāra.gna- must belong together; vrthra.gna would be a secondary synonym of the supposed meaning of vāra.gna-. Cf. OI. gandarváḥ and Gr. kéntauros, not descending from an IE. prototype but both reflecting the same non-IE. name, see under 'Sculpture.'

[5] This formula was first recognized in Rawlinson's copy by A. Wilhelm; in Arch.f.Religionswiss. XVII,8 O. Weinreich discussed the religious-historical meaning.

designation of the Iranian gods by Greek names: Zeus Mégistos for AhuraMazdāh, Apollon and Helios for Mithra, Artemis and Queen Athena for Anāhitā "bānōk nām, whose name is lady." On Iranian soil, the Heracles inscription of Karaftō purports a hellenized sanctuary of Vrthragna.

One attribute of Mithra, and yet more of Vrthragna, is hvarnah, Tyche. It is an error to say that it "appears im ganzen westlichen Iran in der besonderen Form farnah" (Nyberg,342). Word and notion "hvarnah" belong equally to all Iranian dialects, and farnah is not the peculiar western form, see under 'Hvarnah.' In the worship of Vrthragna and his attribute the Medes differ no more from other Iranians than in any other cultic things.

Herodotus reports that no sacrifice or prayer could take place without the presence of magi. If the magi—as Nyberg says—had had a religion differing from that of the Medes, they would have celebrated, every day, a cult that was not their own. "Der Zurvanismus war die Religion der Magier vor Ankunft des Zoroastrismus," which "ohne Schatten eines Beweises" he fancies to have happened "spätestens in Zusammenhang mit der Reichsgründung der Achaemeniden." While the Median religion through all this time was "wesentlich mitannisch" (396), "ist von da an die Religion der Magier wesentlich zoroastrisch, Die Magier waren in tieferem Sinne keine Zoroastrier." Then, not their depth, but their surface would be their "essence." Whatever the spiritual movements were that passed behind the form of religion approved by the state, and whatever the theories were that the magi projected into it in the course of centuries—the class in whose hands always lay the administration of the empire must have professed under Median rule the Median, under Achaemenian rule the Achaemenian religion, and so on.

Old Iranian, perhaps pre-Iranian and certainly pre-Zoroastrian, notions can be discerned in some of the mythic fragments dispersed through various yashts. In *Yt.*5,26 (in first pers.) and 19,32 (second pers.)—text under 'Yama χšēta'—Yama prays "that I may surpass the gods in riches and welfare!" Another meaning but "gods" is impossible in this old myth. Equally in the next case.

In the complex formula of the Hōšyanha myth, as we have it, "māzanian dēvā and varun-ian drugvant," dēva gets a pejorative connotation by being coupled with the Zoroastrian term drugvant; it did not have it before. By adding drugvant, the original formula was adapted to Mazdaïsm, only after Zoroaster's time when Hōšyanha was put at the head of the Iranian epopee. *Yt.*5,22 is the original, all other occurrences are quotations of it, see under 'Vidēvdād: Varuna.'

Alone, not as pair, varunya dēva and māzanya devā appear only at very inferior places, and merely the words "Grant me that I may slay two thirds of the māzanian and varunian gods . . ." can be considered as genuine. One can ponder much about this formula, for the Hōšyanha myth is unknown, perhaps a hyperbolic expression for "two thirds of the Māzanians and Varunians (who worship foreign) gods," or a promethean motif of hybris, or, better: in this non-Iranian myth, which originally belonged to Sakā or Scolotian Scyths, a god fought hostile gods. In later allusions to the legend, the varunya dēva are described as giants, see under 'Vidēvdād.' And Hellanicus says, in a scholion to Hesiod's *Theogonia,* v.139: "there are three kinds of cyclopes, first the builders of the walls of Mycenae, second the Homeric savages, and third the gods themselves, *αὐτοὶ οἱ θεοί.*" In *Theog.* 502 the cyclopes are called *Οὐρανίδαι.* From the same source the words of Aristeides Rhetor[6] seem to come: Three kinds of Cyclopes: (1) those in the Odyssey, (2) the *χειρογάστορες*=wall-builders; (3) *τοὺς καλουμένους οὐρανίους.* The varunya dēva imagined as giants and the *θεοὶ οὐράνιοι* or *οὐρανίδαι* as cyclopes are the same notion: not more than a vague reminiscence of them remained in Greece and in Iran. Somehow they were connected in pre-Aryan antiquity.

In *Yt.*19, the prayer—the shape in which all epic fragments appear in the yasht—has the formula

yat χšayata pati būmīm haftaθiyām   dēvānām martiyānāmča

applied in st.26 to the paraδāto Hōšyanho, in 28 to taχmo Rupiš, in 31, to Yamo χšēto, hence to the three first men and kings, who originally belonged to separate cycles, but are at that place already brought into the system which the Shāhnāmah still retains. The prayer is: "that I

[6] Aristides, ed. Dindorf III,408.

may rule on this (septempartite) earth, over heavenly ones and mortals, θεῶν τε βροτῶν τε or ἀνδρῶν τε θεῶν τε."

In *Yt.*5 the form is

upamam χšaθram vispānām dahyūnām	the sovereign rule over all
dēvānām martiyānāmča	provinces, over heavenly ones, and mortals.

applied in 21 to Hōšyanha, in 25 to Yama, and moreover to the younger figures kavi Usan and kavi Husravah, hence to two representatives of the Median kavi dynasty, which is joined in that system, conform to history, by the cycle of Vištāspa, protector of Zoroaster.

*Yt.*5 mentions several figures of this cycle. The prayer of Vištāspa, the nōtarya himself, has become: "victory over the dēvayasna, dēva-worshipping Prtana and Arǰataspa"; that of the very hero of this cycle, his brother Zarivariš-Zarēr is: "victory over the dēva-worshippers Humayaka and Arǰataspa"; and the man, client, of the nōtarya, Visatarus̆, a Persian, prays for "victory over the dēvayasna" in general. Of these figures, Zarivariš and Visatarus̆, who appear in the memorial document, are historical, the others mythical.

It does not matter, for our conclusions, whether the variants of the formula are due to retouching done in Median or in Achaemenian times. haftaθya implies the notion of the seven kršvar, with Iran as center, which is attested in the gathas, in still older parts of *Yt.*10, hence in the sixth century B.C. and may be still older. upamam χšaθram vispānām dahyūnām—see under 'Mithra' and 'Social Structure'—is a term impossible before the Median period: it has been transferred from the kavi who bore this title to the kings of the older phase of the epics. But dēvānām martiyānāmča is a pre-Iranian, and beyond it, a pre-Aryan formula.

The appearance of Zoroaster was epoch-making also for the epic: before him, the great Iranian heroes pray for ruling over dēva and mortals, and the word dēva has not the slightest bad taste or odor. They do not want to catch Dīvs in bottles, like the fisherman in 1001 Nights, but the gods shall serve them. The idea is old-mythical, pre-Zoroastrian. But after Zoroaster, the adversaries of the heroes are "dēva-worshippers," what the heroes themselves are no longer, and that is something odious and to be wiped out. The picture has completely changed.

The epics reflect lucidly that it was Zoroaster who gave to the word dēva a changed moral value: what had been good is henceforth bad. Therewith the descent of the word dēva begins in Iranian. A similar transvaluation came to pass in Greece at the same time, Xenophanes:

> πάντα θεοῖς ἀνέθηκαν Ὅμηρος θ' Ἡσίοδός τε
> ὅσσα παῤ ἀνθρώποισιν ὀνείδεα καὶ ψόγος ἐστίν.

or:

> ὡς πλεῖστ(α) ἐφθέγξαντο θεῶν ἀθεμίστια ἔργα.

Nyberg, 193: "In dem Augenblick, da die [pre-Zoroastrian] Ahura-Religion bei den Iraniern die herrschende wurde, war der Übergang der daēva-Gottheiten zu daemonischen Wesen gegeben," but on p.374: "verschwinden die daēva-Götter des altmedischen Pantheon . . . in der grossen Zahl der Daemonen" as a consequence of the infiltration of post-Zoroastrian Zoroastrism from Ragā into Media, which took place about the time of the foundation of the Achaemenid empire. The same event happened at two different times.

Zoroaster did not "invent" AhuraMazdāh, the god existed, but a special "Ahura-Religion" is disproved by the sole dvandva miθrā-ahurā. The "transition" was not impersonally "given," but Zoroaster gave the impulse which led to the complete degeneration of the word dēva in Iranian. This is an inner-Iranian development, neither connected with the pre-Iranian distinction between dēva and ahura, heavenly ones and lords, nor with the developments in India, where the deva remained and the pre-Indian asura came into disrepute. Indra, Varuṇa and the Āditya are asura in India, and their decline begins with the time of the tenth book of the Rgveda and the Atharvaveda, and ends in making them enemies of the deva. It was an error, emanating from Martin Haug and almost generally accepted, to consider this coincidental and not simultaneous contrariness of movements as something causally connected, and as an "Indo-Iranian schism."

Zoroaster offers to the whole world including the gods—not the devils—the "choice" of accepting his monotheism. It is he himself who decides which dēva choose right, by admitting some of them into the many-sided figure of his AhuraMazdāh. This only god is a multiplicity, a precursor of the Christian Trinity. From the time of the Yasna Haftahāti onwards, these partial figures are called "amrta spanta, immortal-holy ones," and since spanta, to √su-, is a power producing welfare, probably in the sense of powers, δυνάμεις. They are often mentioned beside AhuraMazdāh, where human qualities are attributed to him: he hears, talks, acts through them. They are also meant by the plural Mazdå ahuråho in *Y.*31,4 and 30,9.

To put an abstract conception between god and men is something resembling—probably caused by similar reflections—the mēmrā-λόγος-sermo and rūªḫ-spiritus in the OT. Apart from the case where they are directly invoked, the names of the partial figures or aspects appear in the instrumental, which is usually interpreted as comitative, even as substitute for the nominative. This interpretation not only encumbers the translations of the Gathic verses to a degree that to understand them one must skip the "comitatives," but it makes nowhere real sense and makes many verses incomprehensible. The god sees, hears and acts "through," not "with" these figures, the case is always just as instrumental, as e.g. in *Y.*32,2 where he speaks "χšaθrāt hača, by (the mouth of) χšaθram," cf. rtāt hača in the Ahunavarya. The only right translation is "in the quality of, as." Markwart, *Gāth.ušt.,* used this in the passage "als er (the spanta) mich umschritt mit (oder 'als') Gute-Gesinnung"; on p.66 he called the case "Instrumental der Eigenschaft," evidently so in the Ahunavarya. In *Y.*43,6 any other translation is impossible, the comitative "with" results in a complete misunderstanding: "at which turn, rvēsa, [the last one, of the judgment] Thou wilt come as spantā manyū, vahū manahā (ārmatiš, χratuš)," i.e. in all your aspects simultaneously and moreover *as*—not *with*—yourself as spantā manyū. In *Y.*47,6, too—see under 'Last Judgment'—AhuraMazdāh appears "as Spantamanyuš."

The idea is Zoroaster's and continues in Christianity. Dante, *Inf.* III,4ff.:

Giustizia mosse il mio alto fattore,
fecemi la divina Potestate,
la somma Sapienzia e il primo Amore.

One easily recognizes Mazdāh's χratuš, spanto manyuš and vahumano.

Which partial figures are named at the different places in this "instrumental of quality" depends on the context: rta for things judicial, ārmati for social, agricultural, χšaθra for political, vahumanah for moral subjects. Invocation of more than one means emphasis, thus in *Y.*49,7, when talking of the decision of the court of appeal, most momentous for Zoroaster's life: "AhuraMazdāh shall hear as Vahumano, shall hear as Rtam, hear it yourself, AhuraMazdāh!" Whether the partial figures are invoked alone or together with the god, whether they act alone or with him—also where he himself is not called, in all cases the *monotheos* is meant in his aspects.

These aspects result from the transformation of a polytheistic pantheon into a monotheistic conception, and are Zoroaster's most original and most personal thought. To call them "Götter und Götterreihen" is the way Muhammad thought of the Christian Trinity and the mushtarikīn. In doing so one cuts off the thread leading from this multiplicity to the Trinity, and therewith the possibility of comprehending, historically, the idea of the Spiritus Sanctus.

The great gods of the polytheistic pantheon that Zoroaster excludes by "choosing the evil," became "evil gods."

*Y.*30,5: "those who by conduct as it should be are voluntarily obedient to AhuraMazdāh, have chosen, varta, to work the Rtam, rtam vrzya like the most-holy spirit." And *Y.*30,3: "the hudåho noit duždåho chose right rš višyāta between the two (good and evil)," see under 'Yamā.'

*Y.*30.6:

ayå noit rš višyāta	dēvāčana yat īs adbōma
prsamnān upājasat	yāt vrnata ačištam mano
āt ēšmam handvaranta	yā bānayan ahum mrtāno

"Between these two (good and evil) the gods, too, did not choose right, since the deceiver came upon them when interrogated, so that they chose for themselves the wholly evil spirit; then they all ran to ēšmo, through which they corrupt the life for men!"

The "evil gods" stand outside of Zoroaster's dualism of good and evil; they do not belong to his system and exist only because they existed before. It is significant for the period that Zoroaster condemns them, but does not deny their existence. The Akk. version of *Xerx. Pers. daiv.* correctly renders the peculiar notion by "limnū^{pl}, the evil ones (gods)," a translation very Babylonian in omitting ilāni, because "evil" is no attribute applicable to a Babylonian god; they distinguish between good and bad demons, and their ilu limnū, Sum. dingir.ḫul is a demon of the dead from the netherworld. Hesychios has preserved the gloss:

Δέυας · τοὺς κακοὺς θεούς, μάγοι, cf. Lagarde, *Abhdlg.* 148, entirely apart from the *δαίμονες* *Ὦμανος*—Vahumano and *Ἀρειμάνιος*.

ēšma, Gr. *οἶμα,* Lat. īra, is, in Zoroaster's phraseology not "der Name eines dēva" (*Wb.*) but a moral idea, like good and evil. drugvadbiš ēšmam in *Y.*29,2 is not "ēšma together with the drugvant," but—instr. of quality—"ēšma as (collective of) the drugvant," and is the same as aka manyuš and the druχš. In as late a book as the *Vidēvdād,* where Ahriman has become the dēvan dēv, ēšma is personified as hēšm dēv, the Asmodaeus of the book of Tobit.[7]

In the late passages where "the dēvā" appear in plural, the notion is undefined; where they are "called by name," they are bad passions, sicknesses, great cold, and occasionally the above-mentioned Indian gods are added to them. But nowhere does the name of one of the ancient gods appear among them. That cannot be, because the old dēva did *not* "disappear in the great number of demons," but had again become the "great gods." Those which Zoroaster made to choose evil, ceded their title to the later dēvs. The place of the dēvs is hell; that dēva meant "heavenly" was no longer understood. In Zoroaster's doctrine the "evil gods" do not act at all as aspects of the Evil Spirit. They are a dynasty dethroned, but soon restored. Only after their restoration, after the word dēva had been separated from its old bearers, and after these gods had come back under another generic name, the further degeneration of the word to "demon, devil" could set in.

Who worships Mazdāh—as Darius and Xerxes say of themselves, mazdām yazatē—is an adherent of Zoroaster; who worships the dēva, dēvān yazatē—the divine enemies of his god—is his enemy. That is the origin of the later terms mazdayasna and dēvayasna both of which imply, as mutual negation, their antonym ex definitione, and which, like rtāvan and drugvant, are meaningless without the Zoroastrian dualism of Good and Evil. *Vid.*18 forms even the negation a.dēvayasna, meaning mazdayasna.

That gods were worshipped before Zoroaster is a matter of course, and "worshipper of gods" cannot have furnished the name for the

[7] In the late tale of Zoroaster's temptation Ahriman says: "Zoroaster, you are Purušaspa's son, from (your) birth zāviši," whatever the corrupt zāviši means, but if Ahriman prefers with these words a claim to worship, he seems to identify himself collectively with the dēvā worshipped by Zoroaster's ancestors.

adherents of the pre-Zoroastrian religion. The adherence of a peculiar group to the pre-Zoroastrian AhuraMazdāh would hardly have been expressed by mazdayasna, rather by mazdaka. Mašdaku appears several times in the Assyrian annals as n.pr. of Medes, and Mazdayasna in the memorial document of *Yt.*13, likewise as a proper name. If in that list an adult with patronym is enumerated, but not his father, the father belongs of necessity to the generation that preceded the "coming of the religion," and this Mazdayasna was no Zoroastrian. But as designation of religious groups of adherents and adversaries of his religion both words can have been used only after Zoroaster. As an appellative, mazdayasna is not attested earlier than dēvayasna; both appear just before the syncretistic redaction of the Awesta under Artaxerxes II, see under 'Fravarāni.' Therefore, the terms imply a date: where they are not used, one is close to Zoroaster's own time.

It cannot be otherwise, Zoroaster must talk in terms of generally accepted meaning when speaking to people whom he wants to convince. He does so, e.g. in *Y.*46,5 using the antique moral notions rāzan, rvati and miθrā, see under 'Mithra.' The term dēva, too, can have in the gathas no other meaning than in the old epic passages in the yashts: heavenly ones, gods. Zoroaster is still declaiming against them. "devil" or "Götze" (Andreas-Lommel) is just as impossible as "daemonische Wesen" (Nyberg). The example of *Y.*32,4—text under 'Yama χšēta'—makes that very clear: "For you tell fables of wholly evil deeds for which men doing them are called dēva.zuštā . . . , while they sin against AhuraMazdāh's will. . . ."

Although their acts are sins against Rtam, the heroes of the epics are glorified—of course not as "minions of the devil"—but as dēva.zuštā, OI. deva.juṣta, ὄντιν' ἂν φιλῇ θεός, "beloved by the gods." The word has not the slightest tinge of depreciation.

Likewise, in the myth of Yama—see under 'Yama χšēta'—the hero does not want to surpass the devils, but the gods. Nyberg writes: "Die daēva-Götter, in der Regel lauter heroische Götter, waren in diesem Kreise von unkriegerischen Hirten [at another place: gewaltige Krieger] abgestossen worden oder hatten jedenfalls allen Boden unter den Füssen verloren." So the gods float in air, as do the following contradictory definitions: 193: "Man braucht *nicht über die iranische Welt hinauszugehen,* um die daēva zu identificieren," and 365: "Gilt es den

Ursprung des Ausdrucks zu bestimmen, so muss man zunächst bedenken, dass hier *nichtiranische Götter* gemeint sind." No wonder that he never calls their names.

Dēva are all those whose names Zoroaster strictly avoids calling by name—as strictly as do the inscriptions of Darius and Xerxes—namely Mithra, Vrthragna, Anāhitā and all great rivals of his one Ahura-Mazdāh. Nyberg regards them as members of the pantheon of the "Zoroastrian Urgemeinde," probably "admitted by Zoroaster himself," but another reason than the prophets' absolute silence cannot be adduced.

An Arab ḥadīth tells:[8] "Two men asked 'Ā'isha, the Mother of the Faithful, who it was that had been with Muhammad at a certain occasion and she replied: Two, the other was NN! Afterwards, one of the interviewers said to the other: How strange, who, then, was the other one? and got the answer: Don't you know, Ali of course; if she speaks of somebody without a name, it is always Ali." Such silence is hatred and contempt. J. Lévy says in his article on the Xerxes inscription, Rev. Hist. 85, 1939: "Taire le nom d'un ennemi mépris est un fait bien connu dans l'antiquité sémitique," quoting *Isa.* VII,5 and 9, on Pekah of Israel and Nebukadnezar on Nekao, the "rebel satrap." In a book of modern explorations in Armenia, one of the partners describes the other as "whose near-sighted eyes had the effect of a magnifying lens at short distance," but does not reveal his well-known name. That is the curse of the effaced memory: Heine's "Nicht gedacht soll seiner werden!" So hates Zoroaster.

*Y.*32 is his promethean "song against the Dēva." It begins: "If gods and men would place themselves at AhuraMazdāh's command!" They do not; so he goes on, st.3: "You dēva all and who worship you, are the brood of akam mano, of the druχš and of parimatiš!" Yet severer he says in *Y.*34,5: "parā . . . vispāiš vavaχmā dēvāišča harfstrāiš martiyāiščā, we have severed ourselves from [=abjure] all vipers whether gods or men!" That is Zoroaster's "nāismi dēvo, I challenge the gods!" and is the origin of the condemnation of the gods in the younger fravarāni: "just as Zoroaster severed himself from the gods!"

[8] ZDMG, 38, pp.388-92.

dēva appears at many places, and nowhere is the signification otherwise. One place is difficult, *Y*.49, which begins with the stanzas on bandva and his tkēša; st.4: "Who by bad-will increase ēšma and rāma with their tongues, as false shepherds among shepherds, whose good deeds do not annul the bad deeds,

toi dēvān dān   yā drugvato dēnā!

Andreas-Lommel: "die schaffen (erzeugen) Teufel durch die Lehre (entsprechend dem Gesetz) des Lügners," which would make come true Luther's "und wenn die Welt voll Teufel wär!" —Bartholomae: "in der daēva Haus mit ihnen! (ins Haus) für die daēnā der drugvant!"

Bartholomae's interpretation of the elliptical construction is supported by the analogous end of the following stanza: "mit denen—in Dein Reich!" But the case of dān, loc.sg. of dam according to *Wb.* and *Grdr.* §§303, 403, is undefinable; dēvān cannot enter for the gen.pl., and yā drugvato dēnā is doubtful as to its construction. Both translations are unsatisfactory. The purport must be: "To hell with them!"

One point seems to be sure, this gatha verse is the origin of Xerxes' dēvadānam in *Pers.daiv.*37. My attempt in *Altp.Inschr.*131 to explain it as a contemptuous expression alluding to "house of gods," something like "den of the dēvs"—MP. says "nišēm ē uzdēsčārīh, nest of idol-worship"—has found unexpected approval.[9] The transmission of the text of 49,4 is hardly accurate; one solution would be to restore a compound of dēvān + dān, perhaps with a verse of 5 + 6 instead of 4 + 7 syllables. The last words are probably a vocative: "you soul of a sinner!"

The first change in the Zoroastrian terms can be noticed in the Yasna haftahāti, which, though written in the dialect of the gathas, is post-Zoroastrian, and remarkably poor of contents. There, for the first time, a "community" appears with priests called āθravan, and the beginning of a theology that makes a system of the aspects of Ahura-Mazdāh as Amrta Spanta; Zoroaster himself is invoked. According to Nyberg, for the first time in the history of Zoroastrism, a word cor-

[9] dāna, second element of compounds, IE. *dhāna, Gr. thḗke; cf. Aw. uz.dāna, MP. astodān, "container," in Arab. bait, house, corresponds.

responding to our god, entirely absent from the gathas, would appear there, namely "yazata, anbetungswert, to be worshipped, adorable."

In Mithra's Questions, *Yt.*10,108, we read

ko huyašti ko dužyašti	who believes me to be one to be worshipped
mām zi manyatē yazatam	with bad, who with good offerings?

and in the ApāmNapāt hymn, *Yt.*19,52:

yo upa.āpo yazato	the yazata dwelling in the water,
srut.gōšatamo yazamno	the best-hearing when offerings are made to him!

Both passages—see under 'Mithra' and 'ApāmNapāt'—are pre-Zoroastrian. The Yasna haftahāti is post-Zoroastrian. The assertion falls with the wrong assumption that the *Y.haft.*, composed in Gathic, ought therefore to be older than the yashts, composed in Awestic. The word yazata, a regular verbal adj. of √yaz-, of course, existed in the old language.

Zoroaster had three words at his disposal, all exactly corresponding to our god: "ahura, lord, dēva, heavenly, and baga, he who allots fate." The last one, baga is, in Iran and India, the epithet of Mithra and of Māh (*Yt.*7,5). Mithra's great festival was the bāgayādiš in his month miθrakāna, a place of his was Bagastāna, in *Yt.*10,141 he is called "bagānām aš.χraθwastamo"; in the "Questions" he asks "kahmāi . . . azam baχšāni χšayamno?" Baga is O.Sl. bog, hence a pre-Aryan word, and cannot have remained unknown to Zoroaster, but its connection with Mithra[10] may have caused his dislike. He uses ahura for his god, when speaking of his aspects also in the plural; dēva for the old gods of polytheism which he condemns. There is no occasion for a third word, for he never speaks of other gods or groups of gods.

Since he fights the dēva and their worshippers, the official recogni-

10 Henning, JRAS 1944, 134f.: "The assumption that baga had the value of another name for Mithra is unsupported by any evidence as far as western Iran is concerned; in a limited sense it can be admitted only for Sogdiana and Khwarezm in late Achaemenian times." Note: "At the time of the introduction of the 'Young Awestan' calendar in those provinces." There is no distinction between an eastern and a western Mithra. Soghd. baγakān: Mihrmāh, and Xvār. biγ: Mihr.rōz are instances of the normal use of baga for Mithra, see *Yt.*10,10 and 141 under 'Mithra,' and the song "kahmāi . . . azam baχšāni χšayamno," Mithra's Questions.

tion of his doctrine made this word unfit to be used for gods that are to be worshipped. It is the most natural thing that those allowed to be worshipped were henceforth called "yazata, adorandi, to-be-worshipped-ones," with the attribute that existed before. Thus yazata became the new generic name under which the old prohibited dēva came back into the post-Zoroastrian religion. Like the terms mazdayasna and dēvayasna, yazata implies a date: where it is missing, as in the OP. inscriptions, one is still close to Zoroaster's own time.

Y.49,3 is the genuine creed of Zoroaster, from which the fravarāni of *Y*.12 issued—see under 'Fravarāni.' The paraphrase shows the transformation of the thoughts which came to pass since the time of the gathas. The interval cannot have been a short one, Awestic had meanwhile become a dead language.

In this younger fravarāni, we find the terms mazdayasno, zāraθuštriš, vidēvo, ahuratkēšo, or four sides of the same idea: worshipper of Mazdāh, Zoroastrian, adversary of the dēva, follower of AhuraMazdāh's commandments. *Y*.12,4: "vi mruvē saram = interdico connubium, I renounce the community with the dēva, the bad, aγa, those without-Vahumano, a.vahu, without-Rtam, an.rta, that work evil, aka.då . . . , the wholly-drug-ish, drōǰišta, wholly-stinking, pōšišta, gods, dēva!" These gods are still those that have rejected AhuraMazdāh, but they are already gods of the past, the notion is dimmed. vi.mruvē, like antar.-mruvē in *Y*.49,3, is "interdico," equivalent to parā-vavaχmā in *Y*.34,5. The adj. aγa alludes to akāt manaho čiθram in *Y*.32,3.

Because they did not choose Vahumano, they are called a.vahu, i.e. a.vahumanah, with the same shortening as in dāraya.vahu for +dāraya.-vahumanah. Likewise an.rta, because they are without rtam. Together with Gath. žīta.rta, this an.rta proves that those who confess said rta, not aša. aka.då—syn. of duždå and opp. to hu.då in *Y*.30,3—means the "Kraft—die stets das Böse will."

drōǰišta: *Wb.*: "superl. zu drug-, (adj., als comp.-ende) und drauga, adj., in *Yt*.19,33." This adj. drauga does not exist; Benveniste, *Inf.av.* 51: "Dans l'Avesta comme en V.-P. drōga est seulement substantif, Skr. drogha, m." *Yt*.19,33, see under 'Yama χšēta': "parā ahmāt yat him ayam drōgam vāčam ahaθyam činmanē pati.barata, before he admitted drōga, the voice talking-(things)-forbidden, into his desires." It is not necessary to eliminate, with Benveniste, the apposition vāčam ahaθyam. This sentence is preceded by parā an.ādruχtoit, Pahl.transl. a.drōžišnīh, Bartholomae: "vor dem dass er log." Yama's fall is caused by trespassing a taboo of food, and is no more a "lie" than Adam and Eve's fall, when they allowed themselves to be tempted.

Beh. §54: drōga.di[š hamiθ^ri]yā akunoš tya imē kāram adružyaša, must be translated: "Drōga made them disloyal, by making those [the false pretenders] seduce [lit. make drug-ish] the army." OP. adružyaša is denominative and corresponds to the Aw. n.abstr. ādruχti. parā an.ādruχtoit means "before his ⟨not⟩ being tempted." OP. drōga, m. [OP. notation for ō is ^{a}u], Aw. drōga in *Vid.*, and Gath. drug- f., are identical. And drōǰišta is the superl. to the pos. Aw. drōǰina [in drōǰina.brta *Purs.*22], OP. drōǰana, drōžana.[11] The superl. drōǰišta corresponds to the OP. pos. martiyā drōžanā. Zoroaster calls the same notion drugvant, but it is OP. drōžana, not drugvant, that survives as drōžan in MP.[12]

On p.273 Nyberg speaks about drōǰišta, but not on p.361, where he asserts: "keine Stelle [of the OP. inscriptions] reicht aus um zu beweisen, dass drauga, drauǰana altzoroastrische, dem Osten gehörige Begriffe waren." Furthermore "Umsetzung in andre Dialekte kommt nicht vor" and "Wer wie die Perser yaδ- statt yaz- sagte ist kein Zoroastrier."

In *Masālik al-abṣār,* 262, the poet al-Manbidjī tells of a night he spent in the monastery of Dair al-Bāghūth, and of a monk there who spoke excellent Arabic, but had a lisp and pronounced s like θ. When the monk asked the poet the following morning for a few verses as remembrance, al-Manbidjī made a poem rhyming in -ūθ, -īθ, suggested by the name bāγūθ and the lisping of the monk, it begins:

[11] The Aw. archetype did not note any short vowel after palatal; Awestic script notes usually ə, which Bartholomae replaced by i. This may well have been the pronunciation since the 6th century B.C. OP. has one sign č^a = či, derived from Sem. ṣi; it writes a s p č^a n, Gr. Aspathínes, hence č^a without i pronounced či. The descent of the two signs ǰ^a and ǰ^i is not yet clear to me.

[12] e.g. *Art.Vir.Nām.* V: "gās ē rāstān u gās ē drōžanān, the place of the just and the wicked."

yā ṭība lailati dairi mar bāγūθ

and ends:

walaqad salaktu ma' al-naṣāra kull mā
salakūhu ghaira l-qaula bil-taθlīθ!

Could a Persian with a lisp not be a Zoroastrian? A prohibition issued today to the effect that the old Persians, as Zoroastrians, were not allowed to pray in their own dialect, has no binding power.

In *Y*.43,8 Zoroaster says, in his vision, as first word to AhuraMazdāh "a true hater I will be of the drugvant," of the gods and men who chose the Drug; and Darius says at the beginning of his tomb-inscription "of the martiya drōžana I am a hater." drugvant = drōžana, with their antonym rtāvan, have no sense and are impossible unless they refer to the dualism of good and evil in Zoroaster's moral doctrine. Before him there were only miθradruχš—see under 'Mithra.' Without Zoroaster, there can be no drōžana, and this word alone proves that the Achaemenids were Zoroastrians, just as it is proved by their sole worship of Ōramazdā, their belief in the dualism of good and evil, the resurrection and the reward at the last judgment. drōǰišta, the superl. of drōžana, is used in the Fravarāni: the fravarāni is late, and OP. drōžana is much older than this creed.

pōšišta is chosen for the rhyme, counterpart to OP. gasta. The home of Ahramanyuš, ahrāi vari of the Ōgmadēča, is called dužganti in the *Had.N.*, Aw. ganti "stench," adj. OP. gasta. Later, Ahramanyuš is written with the logogram anrā^{k}.mēnū^{k}, which Nyberg interpreted as "gannāk-mēnūk, stinking spirit." But he says 36: "Wenn die Altp. Inschriften gasta, eigentlich 'übelriechend,' für das Böse verwenden . . . , so befinden wir uns ausserhalb des Bereiches des Zoroastrismus." This judgment would eliminate simultaneously the Haδōχt Nask. "Gewiss ist auch im Awesta das Böse übelriechend, aber dafür wird ein ganz andres Wort gebraucht." This word, not mentioned, is pōšišta, the rhyme word of drōǰišta. The criterion, to distinguish religions from the different odor of their unholiness, is new. Only, they do not differ: Aw. duž.ganti and OP. gasta are both gand-, hydric sulphide, so permanent that we connect the imagination of the devil with smell of brimstone to the present day.

Y.12,6: "As Zoroaster renounced the community with the gods, dēvāiš saram vyamruvīta, thus I renounce, as Mazdayasnian and Zoroastrian, the community with the gods, dēva." One cannot say more clearly that renouncing the devayasnian polytheism means embracing mazdayasnian monotheism.

St.7: "I choose like the waters and plants, āpā-urvarē, the cow that-gives-what-is-good, gauš hu.då, like AhuraMazdāh, yo gām dadā, yo naram rtāvanam dadā etc."

The sunnite term "as AhuraMazdāh chose" indicates, again, the late time of the composition. To this peculiar concept, evidently, the Muhammedan orthodox doctrine is related. The caliph al-Mutawakkil says in his proclamation, directed against the ahl al-dhimma, with a point against the mu'tazila, Tabari III,1380: "Allāh, the blessed, the exalted, in His majesty without limits and His power over anything He wills, *has chosen* Islam for Himself, and approved it, favored His angels therewith, sent His envoys with it, helped His saints with it etc." And III,1392: "the religion which Allāh has chosen for the muslims." The doctrine involves the other one of the Qur'ān not being created, but eternally existent as a quality of Allāh, a doctrine not unconnected with St. John's ἐν ἀρχῇ ἦν ὁ λόγος, sermo, or mēmrā as mediator and hypostasis. Not long before, the caliph al-Ma'mūm wrote in a letter to Isḥāq b. Ibrāhīm, the confidant of al-Mu'taṣim, in Ṭaifūrī's *ḳitāb Baghdād,* fol. 130r:

"Apart from Allāh, all and everything is a work of His creation and a product of which He is the author. Although the Qur'ān expresses and explains it, precluding any doubt, one has compared with it what the Christians assert about Jesus, the son of Miryam: He is not created, since he is the Word of God. But Allāh says: Verily, We have set it as an Arabic Qur'ān (43,2), what clearly means nothing but: We have created, etc."

Thus, three religions have been under the strange spell of the same thought, and passionate about it. But hardly has a truer remark ever been made about this and similar disputes, than that by the great poet abu l-'Atāhiya, *Kit. al-Aghāni* 3,129: "Shu'aib, the friend of abū Du'ād, qāḍi al-quḍāt of al-Mu'taṣim, told: I said to abū l-'Atāhiya: Do you believe the Qur'ān to be created or not created? He said: Whom do you mean, Allāh or somebody else? And I talked and talked to him and polemized against him, and he always replied with the same question. Finally I said: What is the matter with you, don't you want to answer? and he said: I have answered, but you are an ass!"

The formula "AhuraMazdāh yo gām dadā yo naram rtāvanam dadā, who has created the cow, the orthodox man etc." is modeled after *Y*.44,3 and 51,7 (see under 'Harvatāt'). AhuraMazdāh has also created the non-orthodox; the verse means He created man and gave him the possibility of becoming rtāvan. The expression is clumsy and late, unless rtāvan be an added gloss. In Zoroaster's verses on the creation, *Y*.44, under 'Yama,' in every stanza, between the creation of earthly things, the questions are inserted: "Who is the creator of Rtam, who of Vahumano?" The prayer of Darius, in all his great inscription and repeated by Xerxes and Artaxerxes I, but no more by Artaxerxes II, says: "baga vazraka ōramazdā hya imām būmīm adā, hya avam asmānam adā, hya martiyam adā, hya šyātim adā martiyahya," hence, speaks of earth, heaven, men and the n.abstr. šyātiš. As Zoroaster inserts rtam and vahumano between the worldly objects, thus Darius puts in šyātiš, the Fravarāni rtāvan. But Darius' prayer expresses the deficient thought of the fravarāni in clear words: "who created šyātiš for men," in order to become šyāta. Xerxes *daiv*. ll.47f. says: "šyāta ahani žīva, mrta rtāvā ahani, šyāta I want to be in life, in death rtāvā." The El. version transcribes the untranslatable term by sa.t.ta = šāta. The wish is the same as Zoroaster's dadi moi amrtātā harvātā in *Y*.51,7, "blessed life here and eternal life." OP. šyātiš, Lat. quiēs, peace, and šyāta "peaceful"—like Aw. noit kudāt-šāti, "else-without-peace" in *Vid*.1—describe the blissful condition, happiness resulting from a religious life. The opposite is Aw. pati.rtayē, being-contested, opposed, MP. patiyārakīh, opposition of the patiyārak, fiend. MP. apatiyārakīh is the negative expression of OP. šyātiš, "being-uncontested, in peace," Aw. a.pati.rta neg. expression of šyāta. The oriental notion of bliss is rather primitive: quietism, kēf, freedom from activity. šyāta, harvatāt, is the earthly correspondent, gētīk, of the mēnōk, heavenly rtāvan, amrtatāt. The two words are complementary like Gr. *ὄλβιος* and *μακάριος*. By creating rtam, vahumano, šyātiš and rtāvan, AhuraMazdāh has made it possible for men to reach this bliss.

The ApāmNapāt hymn in *Yt*.19,52, see under 'ApāmNapāt,' reveals an entirely different and much older concept of creation and no trace of the Zoroastrian notions: "the yazata, dwelling in the waters, the χšaθriya = raθēštar, with the speedy horses, the male, ApāmNapāt, created the men, nar."

Xerxes' prayer and promise, "šyāta in life, rtāvā in death," contains the notion of reward in this and future life for the acts of men. This idea is not only foreign to, but impossible in pre-Zoroastrian polytheism which knew only of a "life in silence, tušnišad." The idea of religion as the relation of the individual man to the universal god was not yet born.[13] Wherever AhuraMazdāh is invoked as sole creator, as he who determined (*Y*.43,5) the return for good and bad acts, as in the true Fravarāni *Y*.49,3 and in Darius' prayer, we are facing Zoroaster's doctrine.

Nyberg calls (349) Darius' prayer "frei von religiösem Pathos" while it is "frei von religiösen Phrasen," and "eine Formel medischen Ursprungs," reason: the OP. word for "great" vazraka, is a Median loanword; baga is common to both dialects. vazraka was borrowed in the protocol formula "χšāyaθya vazraka," and if the Persians pronounced "great" in "great-king" with a z, they did not pronounce it with δ in "great god." This and similar ubiquitous arguments are utterly futile.

The three OIr. words for "god," ahura, dēva and baga, are all attested in OP. dialect. The inscriptions agree with the gathas in using ōra < ahura only in the name of the god. The dēva in Xerxes' inscription are the "evil gods," Akk. limnū, whose cult the king prohibits, again conform to the gathic style. Everywhere else, OP. uses baga.

Except in the Median formula "baga vazraka, a great god (is Ōramazdā)," OP. baga always implies the notion of non-Iranian gods beside the Iranian ahura and dēva.[14] This is plainly expressed in "uta anyāha bagāha tyē hanti, and the other (or alien) gods that are" beside Ōramazdā, the "god of the Aryans"; likewise in "hadā visēbiš bagēbiš, Ōramazdā along with all gods." Zoroaster, whose gathas only speak of the struggle of his AhuraMazdāh with the Iranian dēva, never has the gods of Elam, Babylon and other foreign countries in mind; the great-kings always, for they write in three languages and rule over many

[13] Cf. the remarks on Ed. Meyer, *Christent.* II,17, at the end of chapt. 'Chronology.'

[14] For the various formulae with baga see *Altp.Inschr.* s.v., and cf. *Yt.*7,5; 10,141; Y.10,10, 70,1.

non-Aryan nations with "other gods." Since nobody can be ahura beside "the lord justiciary who judges, vičiro ahuro" (*Y*.29,4), the "just lord justiciary, spanta ahura rtāvan" (*Y*.46,9), and since the dēva are banished, baga alone is left for a wider application. As in the gathas, yazata is not yet used.

anya, = alius, alienus in OP., can have the acceptation "hostile," in analogy to alien and enemy; for Awestic cf. *Yt*.10,28: "upā anyå sčindayati, he destroys the enemies" and anya.tkēša, anya.varna, heterodox, heretic. The anyāha bagāha are "alii dii" or "dii alieni." Nyberg, 354: "Sind also diese Götter Jahwe, Marduk u.a. gemeint? Gewiss nicht. . . . Wer damit gemeint ist, wird deutlich mit dem Ausdruck viθa baga 'Clan-Götter' bezeichnet. Es sind die Gottheiten der Ahnen und Eponymen des Hauses etc. Wie hienieden der Grosskönig sich über seinen Hofstaat erhebt, so erhebt sich in der himmlischen Welt AhuraMazdāh über einen Hofstaat der himmlischen Vertreter der verschiedenen Geschlechter. . . . Bezeichnend, dass Darius den Ausdruck 'der grosste der baga' nur da gebraucht, wo er sich an seine Landsleute wendet, die Arier der Persis." Also 375: "Kein prophetischer Geist hat (der Religion der Achaemeniden) ihr Gepräge gegeben, sie ist geschaffen von Grosskönigen für Grosskönige, und AhuraMazdāh erhebt sich in einsamer Majestät über einem Hofstaat von Clan-göttern, deren Namen man nicht einmal zu nennen für nötig hält."

Weissbach, in his edition, had never trusted Westergaard's reading "viθa baga?", and I had reported in AMI VI,1933,74, two years before Nyberg's lecture, that the reading is an error, thrice repeated, for the usual formula "hadā visēbiš bagēbiš, along with all gods." The lonely majesty, the households, and with them the unimaginable consequences of this accumulation in heaven could have been avoided. But the assertion that maθišta bagānām was used only where the king speaks to his countrymen does not depend on this false reading; 350: "Der Tonfall wird immer intimer . . . wenn er zu seinem eigenen Stammland, der Persis, spricht: . . . nebst den Clan-göttern, viθa baga."

maθišta bagānām appears on the gold-tablets from Agbatana (Media) and Persepolis; in *Pers.d;* in *Pers.g* (only Akk. text) as ša rabū ina muḫḫi ilāni; and in *Xerx. Van* (Armenia). The gold-tablets lay invisible in air-tight stone-boxes under the foundations; the visible inscription in Van was no more legible to the Armenians there, just as incomprehensible as the Akkadian inscription in Persepolis to the countrymen in Persis. On the other hand, the text of the gold-tablets indicates the four extreme points of the empire; *Pers.g* says "who granted to Darius the rule over this wide earth on which are many countries" and hence many gods, whereupon a short list of lands follows; and the very fact that two of the three inscriptions, *Pers.e-g,* all on the same panel, are written in foreign languages, evokes at once the idea of foreign nations and their gods. The "more intimate modulation" is an acoustic delusion, and the formula maθišta bagānām appears only where foreign nations are mentioned.

This is even more evident in the formula "Ōramazdā uta anyāha bagāha tyē hanti" in *Beh.* §§62-63, where the Elamite text, both times, inserts "Oramasta, the god of the Aryans, and the other gods that are," namely of the non-Aryans like the Elamites. P. de Vaux remarked in *Rev. Bibl.* 1937,12, that the similar addition made by the Babylonian scribes in the Akk. version of the gold-tablets to OP. "mām Ōramazdā pātu, viz. itti ilāni, A.M. may protect me with the gods" can only mean: "Marduk the god of Babylon—with whom Nyberg dispenses lightly by 'Gewiss nicht!'—must have his political share."

In the postscript to the Behistūn inscription, to be dated in 515 B.C., two pairs of short paragraphs are appended to the reports on the campaign against the European Sakā and on the suppression of an Elamite rebellion, §72:

a[vaiy . huvaž]iya [----------] utā[š]ām . auramazdā.
[avaiy . sa]kā . u]tā . naiy . auramazdā[

[naiy . ayadiya] . a[uramazdām .]ayadaiy . vašnā . aurama[zdāha .
[šām . aya]di[ya . a]ura[mazdām . a]yadaiy . vašnā . auramaz[dāha .

yaθa .] mā[m . kāma . āha . ava]θādiš . akunavam . §73: hya .
yaθa . m]ām . avaθādi]š . akunavam . §76: [hya]

auramazdām . ya[dātaiy .] ya[vā . taumā . a]hatiy . utā .
auramazdām . yadātaiy [. yavā . tau]m[ā . ahatiy . u]tā .

ǰīvahyā . [utā . mrtah]yā[---
ǰīvahyā . utā . [mrtahyā .---

"the Huvažiya and Sakā . . . by them Ōramazdā was not worshipped, I worshipped Ōramazdā. By Ōramazdā's will, as was my pleasure, so

I did to them. Who worships Ōramazdā as long as he has power [=lives], [of him, gen.] alive and [dead. . . ."

That the European Scyths and the Elamites did not worship Ōramazdā is a matter of course, and is not the reason for Darius' campaign against the former or for suppressing the revolt of the latter. The paragraphs say that the successes teach a moral: the king's victories over those aliens are due to the fact that his god is superior to the alien gods, that Ōramazdā is maθišta over the anyāha bagāha tyē hanti.

The unpublished gold tablet of Ršāma has: "ōramazdā baga vazraka hya maθišta bagānām mām χšāyaθyam akunoš, O.M. the great god who is the greatest of gods made me king." Since Ršāma lived to see the accession of his grandson Darius, the inscription must not have been written before his son Vištāspa received Zoroaster in hospitium, and does not prove the worship of the pre-Zoroastrian AhuraMazdāh. Yet it is possible that Ōramazdā was the highest god in the pre-Zoroastrian pantheon of the Pārsa.

Nyberg 373: "Damit bin ich vorbereitet, mein Schlussurteil über die Religion der Achaemeniden abzugeben." It begins "Sie ist von Zarathustras Werk und dem besonderen Glauben seiner Gemeinde nicht berührt," and ends "Was (von Hanfrausch unterstützte) ekstatische Übungen [translation of "the best conduct of life"] anlangt, so war dafür in dieser Religion ohne Zweifel wenig Raum, und die Hochspannung und der Flug der Seele, die der Mensch nun einmal ungern entbehren mag, wurden in einem ehrlichen Weinrausch gesucht." To the "Hanf- und Weinrausch" some remarks are to be made under 'Hōma.' The reflection on "der Mensch nun einmal = such is life," finds an answer in an anecdote, *Aghāni* 21,167: "al-Muntaṣir, about 12 years old, had not said a thing, but had cast glances at his little brother al-Mu'tazz, and their father, al-Mutawakkil, who had observed him said: Muḥammad, you have revealed a secret which one must keep veiled!" One can easily be deceived about one's own preparation, but the deception about the final judgment is the more unforgivable if the quoted one is presented as wisdom's last word: that is not our task.

One must see the whole problem of dēva clearly to understand the inscription Xerxes *Pers.daiv.*, cf. *Altp.Inschr.* n° 14.—While much has been criticized, the great mistake I made in AMI VIII, 1936, 64f., has not been observed: I inferred a date "before Salamis" from the mention of two groups of Ionians, "those in the sea = the true Ionians of the west coast of Asia Minor" and "those beyond the sea = Yōnā takabarā," Macedonians of *Dar.Beh.*

The fact that the inscriptions of Darius and of Xerxes are at variance in their designations of the Ionians is the most important difference in their lists of satrapies.

Beh., in 520 B.C., has two satrapies: "tyē drayahya, those in the sea" and "yōnā." That is the original condition: the first are Cyprus and Cilicia, the second the Ionians of the mainland of Asia Minor. *Dar. Pers.e* says the same more explicitly: "yōnā tyē drayahya uta tyē huškahya, the Ionians of the sea and those of the continent." *Dar.Sus.e,* older than *NiR.,* but closer to it than the first two, has: "i̯awana ša ina A[AB.BA u ša i]na nibirtim[15] nār marratum ašbū', the Ionians who dwell in the sea and those at the coast of the ocean." *NiR.* has only yōnā, suggesting the Ionians of the two satrapies. It must be said that the Persians do not distinguish between Greek tribes, they are all yōnā.

Xerx.daiv. says, ll.23f.: "yōnā tya drayahya dārayanti uta tyē paradarya dārayanti, i.e. Ionii quod maris occupant et qui ultramare occupant," language and grammar so bad, that one needs the clear Akk. version: "i̯awanna ša ina ^{nar}marrat ašbū u ša aḫu ullū ša ^{nar}marrat ašbū, the Ionians who dwell in the sea and who dwell beyond the sea." This official term clearly excludes the yōnā tyē huškahya, the real Ionians of the mainland of Asia Minor. The "Ionians in the sea" are, as everywhere, the Cypriotes, the "Ionians beyond the sea" are such Greeks, yōnā takabarā, as were still under Persian sway, beyond the Bosporus. In agreement therewith their northern neighbors, the Skudra, are still mentioned in the list and represented in the tribute processions of Persepolis. Pausanias in Byzantium, to whom Xerxes wrote the letter of thanks, making him an orosángēs (see under 'Last Judgment') was on the Persian side till 472 B.C. But Ionia was lost after Plataeae and Mykale, Sept. 479 B.C. The inscription must be dated after 479 and before 572, and since it uses still the style of Xerxes' first period, "speaks Xerxes the king" (not "the great-king") very close after 479, about

[15] Cf. "town Ṣirqu nibirtum ša nāri (purāti), on the bank of the Euphrates," and "luddu (Lydia) nagū ša nibirti tāmtim, on the coast of the sea." nibirtum is not "ša ebir tāmtim, beyond the sea," but translates "tyē huškahya," cf. H. Winckler, *Altor.Forschg.* 1,513.

478/77 B.C. The loss of Ionia is silently admitted. This silence, too, reveals hatred, besides humiliation. One would expect that those who criticized my interpretation would first have checked the date, but it has not been done.

§4, a: yaθā tya adam χ̌šāyaθya abavam
ultu muḫ̮ḫi ša anāku šarru atūru

b: asti antar ētā dahyāva - - - ayuda
ibaš ina matātē annēti - - - ikkiru

pasāva - - - ava dahyāvam adam ažanam
arki - - - matātē šin anāku adūka

uta.šim gāθavā nišādayam
u ina qaqqari ultēšibšunūtu

c: uta antar ēta dahyāva āha yadātya parvam dēvā ayadya
u ina matātē annēti ibaš ašar maḫru ana limnū^{pl} isinnu eppušu

pasāva - - - adam avam dēvadānam viyakanam
arki - - - anāku bīt limnū annūtu attabal

uta patiyazbayam dēvā mā yadyēša
u apteqirrama isinnu ana limnū la teppuša'

d: yadāyā parvam dēvā ayadya
ašar maḫru isinnu ana limnū epšu

avadā adam ōramazdām ayadē rtāča brazmani
ina libbi anāku ahurmazda' isinnu etēpuš artāša birazamanni
El. ^{i}rta.aci p^{i}r.racmanniia

Although the scribes no longer master the grammar, the composition of the text, in its strict parallelism of members, is perfectly clear. The method of the Akk. translation is just as mechanical as that of the Pahl. translations of the Awesta: they keep so close to the OP. text as to renounce their own style, and to become misleading, if one would try to interpret it as real Akkadian.

The first sentence (a) gives the date of the event: "just after my accession to the throne," which is six years back. The fourth sentence (d) gives the result: Ōramazdā is installed at the former places of dēvayasnian cult. The second sentence (b) says objectively: revolts broke out in some of the above-mentioned provinces, they were suppressed, order was restored. The third sentence (c) gives the reason: they were the provinces where of old the cult of the dēva prevailed; their temples were destroyed; the cult was prohibited.

The little grammatical faults—only the inscriptions of Darius are free of them—do not obscure the purport. ava dahyāvam, in (b), ungrammatical, El. transcription taii̯awa (plur.) right, Akk. translation matātē^{pl}, right, is just as pluralistic as the corresponding expression at the parallel places; dēvadānam, too, is a collective singular, meaning a plural. If the provinces and temples meant only one each, this ought to be expressed by "ēva, among them was one."

yadātya in (c), which I regarded as equivalent of yadāyā "where" in *Altp.Inschr.,* since the Akk. version uses the same "ašar," is "yadā, where" with enkl. causal tya, and has causative sense: "it was there where = because there"; the clause not only gives the reason, as I had assumed, but has also causal form. The prohibition in (c) are state-proceedings, publicly proclaimed; patiyazbayam is a Median term, and the following words are an imperative, as in the Akk. version, the proclamation itself in direct oration after √zbā-. The translation is:

"When I became king, there were among the above-mentioned provinces such that revolted;
"thereupon, these province(s) I subdued and restored order in them;
"and it was among these provinces, because there the dēvā had been worshipped before;
"thereupon I razed this dēvadānam (coll.sg.) to the ground and issued the prohibition: The dēvā shall not be worshipped!
"Where before the dēvā had been worshipped, there I worshipped Ōramazdā as Rtam, at (with, by) the brazman!"

The change of reign furnishes the occasion for the revolts; these affect more than one province, the names of which Xerxes intentionally passes over in silence, and which we must determine in order to understand the historical event. The reason of the revolt is that the cult of the dēva still prevailed in those provinces, and after their suppression, in the course of which places of that cult were destroyed, the cult is prohibited by a royal dāta proclaimed by heralds. The former cults are replaced by that of Ōramazdā, and were so still in 478/77 or later. This is not an isolated happening, but a political decision, general and valid for all future. Those are the conditions an historical interpretation must fulfill. For me the case is obvious.

Nyberg: "Aus diesem Text hat Herzfeld einen religionsgeschichtlichen Roman gemacht." I. Lévy, l.c.: "Il n'est pas excessif de qualifier de simple roman cette singulière reconstitution." These words are meant to be a blame, but only show that the authors are no historians. Historical analysis, the criticism of what we must recognize as facts, is very much a detective's work, and historical synthesis differs only in degree from the work of a novelist.

Nyberg goes on: "Die nüchternen Thatsachen sind diese." On these, again, J. Lévy remarks: "Pour ce qui est des mesures prises contre la réligion égyptienne, H. Hartmann (pupil of H. H. Schaeder, translator of Nyberg) et Nyberg ne les connaissent manifestement que de seconde main. . . . N. confesse qu'il s'est inspiré du récit de Hall, *Cambr.Anc. Hist.*III,314.—Il ne pouvait plus mal choisir—[*Y*.30,6: noit rš višyāta dēvačana]—son informateur: car Hall s'est contenté de copier, en forçant le trait, le récit un peu trop *romancé* que jadis Maspéro (*Hist.anc. de l'Or.class.*) donna des évènements qui, d'après la Stèle du Satrape, se seraient passés dans la vallée du Nil sous Xerxès." This stela is today regarded as "une forgerie sacerdotale; la donation de Habas, dont le règne ephémère est postérieur d'un siècle et demi à la fin du règne de Darius, est fictive; la spoliation du temple par Xerxès est une imposture. . . . Dans les inscriptions Xerxès s'appelle 'fils de Râ, seigneur exécutant les rites'—ce qui indique un souverain dévot et fidèle à la politique de Darius." Nyberg 347 calls Xerxes "den Exponenten eines Umschwunges in der Religionspolitik der Achaemeniden" who "in Verfolgung des gegenüber Babylon begründeten Systems, Athen in Flammen aufgehen liess."

On Babylon: "Les thèses de Hartmann et de Nyberg, sur ce point encore, s'appuient sur une doctrine capricieuse et surannée. . . . Sa (Hartmann's) construction est sans consistance et il est surprenant qu'il se soit trouvé un assyriologue [in *Sb.Berl.Ak.d.W.* 1938, 18] pour l'approuver. Le tableau fort arbitraire que Nyberg présente des actes plus ou moins sacrilèges de Xerxes n'a de toute manière qu'un rapport lointain avec les faits énumérés dans l'inscription de Persépolis."

Thus, the things are neither "sober," nor "facts," and not "important to retain." Considerably sobered one better forget them all, save the unforgettable sentence on p.366: "Die Frage ist jetzt, (a) waren die daēva in der Xerxes Inschrift schlecht weil sie nicht-arische Götter waren, oder, (b) waren die nicht-arischen Götter schlecht, weil sie daēva waren?," a talmudic dilemma which, against all expectation, Nyberg decides, in 1935, in favor of (b), adding: "Hier finde ich [personal] endlich eine zoroastrische Spur in der Religion der Achaemeniden"; shortly after he finds a second trace.

I. Lévy tried to explain the inscription in a different way, namely as dealing with the burning, by Xerxes, of the acropolis of Athens. For that purpose he must first of all devaluate the contradictory date implied by "just after my accession," but that is no "erreur initiale" of mine which everybody followed but what the words say. Neither is any other condition fulfilled: Athens was no province, no dēva were worshipped there whose worship caused a revolt—against Xerxes in free Athens, the Greek cults were never forbidden by a proclamation of Persian law, and were never replaced by the cult of Ōramazdā. Xerxes was "un souverain fidèle à la politique tolérante de Darius." Finally, the date of the inscription, after Mykale, rules the idea out. "I restored order, utašim gāθavā nišādayam, lit. I put them in their proper place"—while the loss of Ionia is silently admitted—does not refer to Athens. Those who composed the text would not have dared to hint even at the catastrophe of the Greek campaign.

I have quoted Lévy's criticism because it reveals how "unprepared" Nyberg-Hartmann were, not because it was right. Athens, Babylon, Egypt and any other foreign country is from the beginning ruled out by the real counter-argument against all such attempts: the *dēva.* The authors of all these romances do not know who the "heavenly ones" were. They had existed for 2,500 years at Xerxes' time; over them Hōšyanha and his successors had prayed to become masters; against them Zoroaster declaimed and composed his gatha *Y.*32; the fravarāni swears them off; their dynasty went on flourishing in India, where

"Mahadeo der Herr der Erde" descends "dass er unsresgleichen werde" (Goethe), and whose place was later occupied in Iran by figures as sinister as Asmodaeus. Zoroaster's words "You dēvā all and who worships you," and Xerxes' "It was among those provinces, because the dēvā had been worshipped there before" aim at the same dēvā and dēvayasna. "On n'a dû procéder ainsi que contre un ennemi particulièrement exécré, contre des dieux voués à une inimitié capitale." The gatha *Y*.43,8: "haθyadvēšo drugvatē hiyām!," the inscription *Dar. NiR.b*: "martiyam drōžanam nē dōstā ahmi!" and the *credo* "nāismi dēvo!" are unanimous. Dès lors, le problème est résolu: the mere term dēva precludes all interpretations of the provinces as non-Iranian ones. The cults prohibited, the temples destroyed, the places where Ōramazdā was installed were the former temples of Vrthragna in Čēčista and Agbatana, of Mithra in Rēvand near Tōs, of Anāhitā in Susa, and others of their rank. Whether a non-Iranian temple at some place for some reason had been more or less destroyed or not, was never the subject of any Achaemenian inscription.

Xerxes' words "where before the dēvā had been worshipped, dēvā ayadya, there I worshipped Ōramazdā, mazdām ayadē," and "the dēvā shall not be worshipped, mā yadyēša," show how the terms mazdayasna, dēvayasna and yazata come into being: as an effect only of the religious struggle of which Xerxes speaks. And nothing could be more exclusively Zoroastrian than his word "Ōramazdām ayadē rtāča, I worshipped Ōramazdā as Rtam." This one can call a personal idiom of Zoroaster. There is scarcely one gatha without it, and the *Y.Haft.* 38,1 makes the pre-Zoroastrian prayer to Ahura-Varuna a Zoroastrian one by adding "rtāt hačā, as Rtam" to "Thy wives, o AhuraMazdā."

It was not difficult to see, "du premier jour, combien il est frappant que Xerxès ne nomme pas les provinces révoltées: l'anonymat est rigoureux," because it is the Iranian mother-countries, Māda, Pārsa and Hūža, that revolted, where the dēva cult indeed had not been extinguished. It is not only not necessary, but not permissible "über die iranische Welt hinauszugehen, um die daēva zu identifizieren." And there is no need to waste words over their being the old "divi" that have chosen akam mano, and have become *κακοὶ θεοί*, all the dangerous rivals of the ēvχvatāy AhuraMazdāh. It was simple to write my romance, therefore it was the better one.

XXVI. RETURN OF THE GODS

WHEREAS Zoroaster in the gathas, Darius and Xerxes in their inscriptions never mention the name of a god other than AhuraMazdāh, in the inscriptions of Artaxerxes II, of a sudden, Mithra and Anāhitā appear on the same plane with him. Language and script are entirely decadent. Berossus said, at a place where he spoke about the Iranian gods in general, among them Heracles-Vrthragna (Clemens Alex. *Protreptio* c.5, from *Chaldaika* b.III): "After many years had passed, the Persians started worshipping images of gods in human shape, (an innovation) introduced by Artaxerxes, son of Darius, son of Ochos, ὃς πρῶτος τῆς Ἀφροδίτης Ταναΐδος τὸ ἄγαλμα ἀναστήσας ἐν Βαβυλῶνι καὶ Σούσοις καὶ Ἐκβατάνοις [καὶ] Πέρσαις καὶ Βάκτροις καὶ Δαμάσκῳ καὶ Σάρδεσιν ὑπέδειξε σέβειν." G. Hoffmann, *Syr.Akt.* 137, Exc. "Nanai," was the first to interpret the record accurately by inserting the indispensable [καὶ] before Πέρσαις, which is Persepolis, "es handelt sich um die Einführung von Bildern in den viel älteren Kult und Aufstellung der Idole in den Tempeln aller Provinzialhauptstädte." In the inscription of Mylasa, the *τύχη ἐπιφανής*, the "varthragnian hvarnah, victory-bringing fortuna" of Artaxerxes is invoked.

Berossus' remark as to the statues is only a striking detail of much wider reaching measures. Just as the silence of Darius and Xerxes, thus the mention of the names Mithra and Anāhitā in Artaxerxes' inscriptions indicates a general religious attitude: he was the "exponent" of the change. At his time, the whole old pantheon had come back. Many passages of the yashts, first of all the Mithra and Tištriya yashts, reveal this process unmistakably.

*Yt.*10,1: "āt yat miθram yim vurugavyūtim fradaδām azam . . . āt dim [in *Yt.*8,50: avam stāram yim tištriyam] daδām avåntam yasnyata avåntam vahmyata [and in 8,50: avåntam χšnōθwata avåntam frasastata] yaθā mām.čit yim ahuram mazdām, when I created Mithra, I . . . , I created him [or: the Tištriya star] with equal claim to sacrifices, praise [Tištriya: obedience, public proclamation] as Me myself, the AhuraMazdāh!"

This sentence might be that of a royal edict: "as equally honorable peer of My Majesty," but Mithra was already Varuna's peer, before the latter changed his name to AhuraMazdāh. avånt is a late contracted form of "avavant, tantus," not "ā + √bā-, strahlen" (*Wb.*). Bartholomae explained yasnayata, vahmyata, χšnōθwata, frasastata as instr. of the respective abstr. nouns in -tāt; if so, words like "adoranditas" are awful products of a dead language, like medieval Lat. "spectabilitas" and worse. The author says "I created him like me," but did not want to say that AhuraMazdāh created himself, but the others "as adorable as I am myself." One must not try to improve grammar and language of such passages: they were that bad. According to the polytheistic notion the gods were not "created by Mazdāh"; mazdadāta is only the password by which they return into the mazdayasnian religion.

*Yt.*10,50: "Mithra, to whom AhuraMazdāh allotted a palace, mēθanam fraθwrsat, on the encircling, radiant Harā brzatī"; the house was Mithra's property, neither a fief, nor rented. By such empty phrases, of which there are many, the mazdayasnian redactors sanction anew the old cults. With this question a long theological dissertation deals, of which several repetitions have found a place in the Mithra and Tištriya yashts.

In *Yt.*10,31, this dissertation follows upon the old song "tuvam ako vahištasča," and upon "Mithra as builder of the nmāna brzi.mita." In *Yt.*10,54-60, it stands alone in a patchwork of small fragments, alone also in st.74. In st.53, Mithra, ustāna.zasta, in the Zoroastrian attitude of prayer, utters in the presence of AhuraMazdāh, as "lament," the identical words which he recites in 73 "with resounding voice in merry mood."

In *Yt.*8,11, this dissertation is placed before the myth of Tištriya's fight with Apavrta, and the words, separately inserted between the three phases of that fight and repeated in 15, 17 and 19, belong to it: "This one, viz. Tištriya, vyāχmanyati, talks in the assembly, this one parsanyati, asks questions!", ending: "nūram ahmi yasnyasča vahmyasča, now I have (again) claim to yasna and vahma!" vyāχman is the prehistoric democratic assembly, the "boulè" of the Greeks, "thing" of the Germanic peoples; vyāχmanya is a late verb.denom. "to talk in parliament, as a demagogue"; parsanya, another denominative which appears nowhere else, is "to interpellate." Between the verses of the old myth, these words have the effect of a slap in the face. In *Yt.*8,23-25, they are repeated, unbearably, between the first lost round and the second victorious one of Tištriya's fight, and in 8,50, near the end of the yasht, intermingled with an extremely old prescription about sacrifices.

The text of this dissertation is: "noit mā nūram [thus in *Yt.*8,3; in 10,54: āt mā noit] martiyāka ōχtanāmana yasna yazayante yaθa anye yazatåho ōχtanāmana yasna yazinti; yadi zi mā martiyāka ōχtanāmana yasna yazayanta yaθa anye yazatåho ōχtanāmana yasna yazinti . . . , not worship me *now* men by yasna with-mention-of-my-name as other yazata are worshipped by yasna with-mention-of-their-names; if men would worship me by yasna with-mention-of-my-name, as other yazata are worshipped by yasna with-mention-of-their-name, then. . . ." Thereupon follows in *Yt.*8,11 (Tištriya) and in 10,55 and 74 (Mithra): "fra nrwyo rtāwyo θwarštahe zrūno āyu šušyūyām, then I should come to the orthodox men at the exact point of time, hvahe gayahe hvanvato amrtahe upa θwarštahe ǰaγmiyām, then I, of my own sunny, immortal life [phrase of different origin[1]] would be punctual to the minute." Tištriya adds in 8,11: "ēvam vā avi χšapānām dvē vā pančasatam vā, for one night, or for two, or be it fifty!", he evidently is bargaining. And, in the Mithra yasht, to ease the god's mind: "ōχtanāmana θwā yasna raθwiya vāča yazate bara.zōθro rtāvā, by yasna with-mention-of-thy-name the orthodox worships thee at the hours of prayer with voice [song] and zōθra, libations, ōχtanāmana θwā yasna raθwiya vāča sūra miθra yazāi zōθrābyo, by yasna with-mention-of-thy-name I will worship thee, strong Mithra, at the hours of prayer with voice and libations!"

The words upa θwarštahe ǰaγmiyām in *Yt.*10,56 etc., and yavat ēša āfš byāriχti upa.θwaršti frabavāt in *Vid.*14,13 (see under 'Apām-Napāt') explain each other mutually: "the water shall be ample for two irrigations at the precise (measured) time (interval)," because these have their fixed hours, day and night. θwaršta contains the notion of the measured, returning period: hour. I am not sure what should be its right grammatical form. raθwiya, from "ratu, interval, space of time" contains the notion of "prescribed regularity."

In *Yt.*8,24, Tištriya promises, after the tirade of 23: "avi mām avi.-bawriyām, I will offer to me dasanām aspānām ōǰo, the power of ten horses!" and likewise "the power of ten camels, oxen, mountains(!)

[1] Zoroaster uses huvanvant in Y.32,2 as attribute of rtam, it might originally belong to Hvar χšēta and Yama χšēta.

and canals, uštrānām, gavām, garīnām, apām nāvyānām." Instead of garīnām one must read "χarānām, donkeys" following a translation in the *Gr.Bdh.,* and for "mām, to me" evidently "tān, to the men who worship me with mention-of-my-name I will present. . . ." The redactor feels stimulated, by these words, to make AhuraMazdāh call in st.25: "I, I the AhuraMazdāh, worship Tištriya by yasna with-mention-of-his-name, I will give him the power of ten horses, camels etc.," whereas the return present ought to surpass the gift.

In *Yt.*8,50, Tištriya has claim to the frasasti, the governmental proclamation, and in the Mithra yasht the dissertation ends in 10,60: "We worship Mithra, whose is the good frasasti," the public proclamation. So, this proclamation is the aim of the dissertation.

One can trace the origin of the peculiar term "ōχtanāman, with-mention-of-name," opp. to "anonymous."

*Y.haft.*38,4: "uti yā vå vahvīš ahuro mazdå nāman daδāt vahudå yat vå daδāt tāiš vå yazāmade, thus, with the names that AhuraMazdāh, the giver of all that is good, gave you, when he created you, with those we want to worship you!"

Many feminine names precede this sentence, among them the earth, waters, Rtiš and Parandī, the ārmatayo (plural!) and a number of abstractions, all called "wives of AhuraMazdāh." However obscure the collection of just these names, one sees the "names given by AhuraMazdāh at the creation" indicate that they must be taken not in their vulgar, but in a special, perhaps symbolic value: it is Zoroaster who made his AhuraMazdāh grant those names. That is a thought of the Yasna haftahāti.

In the gatha 51,22 we find:

yahya moi rtāt hača	vahištam yasnē pati
vēdā mazdå ahuro	yoi āharča hantiča
tām yazāi hvāiš nāmaniš	pariča ǰasāi vantā

Not till comparing it with the often used yahya-hātām formula of *Y.haft.*41,7,[2] which is derived from it, does this dark stanza become intelligible:

2 Edition and translations give this text in Y.27,15 and refer to it in Y.41,7; but 41,7 is the original place to which the others should refer.

yahya hātām	ãt yasnē pati vahyo
mazdå ahuro	vēdā rtāt hača
yåhāmča tānsča	tåsča yazamade

"To whom [masc., gen. because of √vēd-] of those that are, then, for the sake of (their) worship, AhuraMazdāh has destined paradise [vahyo, comp. abs. = vahištam] through [the mouth of] Rtam—and to whom [fem.]—those [m. and fem.] we worship!"

Y.51,22 is accordingly: "To whom, for my sake, AhuraMazdāh through Rtam has destined paradise as reward for their worship, those who were and those who are, those I want to worship in their (own) name and to circumambulate with songs of praise!"

moi, dat. of purpose, here translated "for my sake" is not an expletive, but an idiom resembling "for my name's sake" in the sayings of Christ. Alongside an accusative and genitive object, it means approximately that the god "destines" promises on the plea of Zoroaster. The stanza is the conclusion of the gatha in which Zoroaster tells that the Vēhviya refused to receive him, that Vištāspa gave him hospitium, and that the two Hāugava and Maδyomåha helped him. The whole gatha is a thanksgiving. "Those who were and those who are" hence are his helpers. In the same way, Darius concludes his great Behistūn inscription in §§68-69 "these are the men who at that time . . . cooperated as my helpers," and "You who will be king in future, do honor to the issue of these men!" Zoroaster adores his helpers with songs "in their own name," his "sacrifices," and with circumambulation—ṭawāf, cf. *Y*.51,8—and promises them paradise. Darius rewards them and imposes upon his successors the responsibility to reward their issue. Shāhpuhr I, in the Ka'ba inscription, institutes masses to be celebrated for "those who were under Pāpak, who were under Ardashīr, who are under Shāhpuhr" and the same is the purport of the great list of names in *Yt*.13.

Duchesne, §274, uses ōχtanāman as an example for his thesis: "Si un composé de caractère liturgique . . . apparaît dans un yasht, c'est dans un passage non-métrique." This must be combined with Christensen's constatation: "Les yashts originaux n'étaient guère destinés, à l'origine, à servir de textes liturgiques." It follows, on the one hand, that the metrical passages are non-liturgical, on the other, that the time of poetry had passed, that the language was dead when ōχtanāman was formed. The term means the opposite of "anonymous." But how could a god not be called by his name in a prayer, or how could he need the "good frasastiš," how could his "being worthy of the frasastiš" be the condition to be called by name? It is the same frasastiš that Zoroaster hopes to obtain in *Y*.49,7, the proclamation of a dāta, a royal edict, by heralds, frasahya, as in the book of Esther: "and this order of the king may resound all over the empire!" The author of the frasastiš, hence, is not AhuraMazdāh, but the king, namely Artaxerxes II. Because he had given the frasastiš for the cult of Mithra and Tištriya, those who pray dare again to call them ōχtanāman, under their own names. The interval more than once designated in the Tištriya yasht by "nūram, now, today" is that between the interdiction by Xerxes and the sanction by Artaxerxes II. It seems that Xerxes, going far beyond Darius, had prohibited not only the cult, but the liturgical "call" of the zōtar, the mu'adhdhin, if not the invocation in prayer itself.

It is not significant that the late *Yt*.21 says "I want to worship ōχtanāman the star Vanant" (Wega), nor that in *Yt*.22,27 a long enumeration ends with "and the (=every) ōχtanāman yazata." But it is noteworthy that in *Y*.1,3 and 2,3 Mithra, in *Y*.3,20 Srōša, in 3,21 Hōma are called ōχtanāman yazata. yazata is "who *must* be worshipped," ōχtanāman yazata is "whom it is *permitted* to worship under his own name." The term is never applied to Ārmatiš or Rtiš, who were never banished. The dissertation has not been interpolated in the Anāhit-Yasht, but we know, through Berossus, that she too was a goddess "whom it is permitted to invoke by name."

The st.51-54 of the Tištriya yasht explain how foolish it would have been not to grant to the god the frasastiš, of which he was worthy (according to st.50): "Tištriya is the adversary of the parīkā dužyāryā yām martiyākā avi dužvačåho huyāryām ōjatē, of the bad-fairy 'bad-year' whom vulgar (Middle Persian) speaking people call 'good-year.' " The euphemistic huyāryā and the classification as parīkā are not older than the time when the stanza was composed; from the analogies in the *Vidēvdād* this date was about the beginning of our era.

St.52: "yazi azam noit daδyām - - - avam stāram yim tištriyam avåntam yasnyata etc. etc. 54: hamahya zi mē iδa ayān hamahya vā χšapo - - dužyāryā vispahya ahoš - - paroit pariθnam[8] ahvām ava.hišiδyāt,

[8] Cf. El. p[1]rram.pelam < OP. *framfram, meaning tohuwabohu, under 'Vēhviya.'

if I had not made the star Tištriya my equal for 'adoranditas' etc. etc. (to enable him to fight 'bad-year,' §51 repeats in extenso) then, now, nūram, here, every day and every night, dužyāram would ruin the human world all upside-down!"

This is an argument for the reintroduction of the cult of Tištriya, of a political and opportunistic kind. For the reintroduction of Mithra, *Yt*.10,92 (first part repeated in *Y*.57,24) gives a religious reasoning: "This (Zoroastrian) religion was professed by the orthodox Ahura-Mazdāh, by Vahumano, Rtam vahištam, Xšaθram varyam, Spantā ārmatiš, Harvātā-Amrtātā, by the Amrta Spanta [the figures just mentioned], according to the rite of the church, brǰå dēnayāi [wrong case]; Mazdāh conferred upon Mithra the judicature over the earth, gēθā (plur.), fra hē mazdå - - - ratuθwam barat gēθānām [just as he confers in the inscriptions the kingship upon the kings, χšaθram fra.barati], who sees in him (Mithra) the ratu and ahu, judge and justiciary [OP. framātāram] and the healer [or: reformator, yōždātāram] of the creatures." Mithra's "conversion" to the right religion is nowhere expressly stated, and the last part of the sentence sounds as if there were doubts whether the old god of revenge had indeed become judge and justiciary in the organization of heaven. In Zoroaster's concept this could only be AhuraMazdāh himself.

Yt.10,103: "AhuraMazdāh nominated Mithra as hartar and awya-χštar, keeper and guardian of his creation," because he never sleeps. Likewise, his bailiff Srōšo receives the post of dēna.diš "instructor of religion," and in *Y*.57,23 it is his doctrine that all others accept: he is the chastiser. Hōma takes care of the libations. Thus, the kingdom of heaven becomes a state in heaven, after the state on earth had developed a church. The theology is as poor as the language. It is pathetic to see how these theological poetasters figured out the "sanction" of Mithra. *Yt*.10,106 describes the "Revenger" as entirely harmless and orthodox: "no earthly man . . . thinks so well, talks so well, behaves so well."

But however piteous all this may be, it reveals the historical process in absolute chronology. How the cults banished by Zoroaster were reintroduced into the Mazdaism of the last Achaemenian phase is perfectly obvious. After their great time in the Median empire, Mithra and Tištriya—and with them other gods—had been interdicted at the beginning of the Achaemenian period. People did not dare pray to them in their name. Then, after their alleged conversion to Zoroastrism, or out of fear of war and famine, they were again sanctioned by Artaxerxes II and admitted into the mazdayasnian Olymp like the Amrta Spanta, with fixed and limited function: Mithra's province is judging and watching, in the way Astyages and Croesus received a province from Cyrus. The reintroduction was not a caprice of Artaxerxes, but the sanction of a condition that existed already before 400 B.C. Verses like those on "Mithra's Passion" are composed between Artaxerxes II and Alexander, or even later.

One sees also that it was Zoroaster's doctrine that caused the cults to be temporarily suspended. E.g. *Yt.*10,119: "You, o Spitāma, shall worship Mithra, tell the pupils about him!" Poor prophet in the posthumous role as schoolteacher: that was just what he did not want to teach. The order or admonition of the god, or better of the redactor, is the form under which things that do not belong to it were introduced into Zoroastrism. If the genuine doctrine, let alone Zoroaster himself—as Nyberg believes—had accepted Mithra, there was no need for a reminder.

The dēva-inscription of Xerxes is the most important document for the religious history among the OP. inscriptions so far known. After Darius had granted, about 520 B.C., the frasastiš to the pure Zoroastrism which he himself professes in Behistūn and in his tomb inscription, Xerxes, having suppressed the revolts that broke out at his accession in consequence of this innovation, interdicted, not later than 480 B.C., the cult of the old gods entirely, destroying the temples and even prohibiting prayer. But already Artaxerxes II, who invokes in his inscriptions Mithra and Anāhitā ōχtanāman besides AhuraMazdāh, who, according to Berossus, ordered to put up statues of Anāhitā in the temples of all provincial capitals, and of whose "victory-bringing hvarnah" the Mylasa inscription talks—thereby has revoked the prohibition of Xerxes, and sanctioned by his frasastiš, given about 400 B.C., the return of the old dēva, henceforth called yazata.

Those are the three documentary dates we have so far concerning the real history of Zoroastrism. They agree with the traditional date that places Zoroaster between 570 and 500 B.C., and with the date of the pre-Zoroastrian parts of the Mihr-Yasht which can be determined between 612 and 550 (see under 'Mithra').

There is much more to be seen. One needs only to think of any line of a Greek author of that period and to confront it with the poorness of mind which the passion of Mithra displays, to understand that the conquest of Iran by Hellenism was unavoidable and imminent.